T0227340

Mastering Cloud Computing

Mastering Cloud Computing
Foundations and Applications Programming

Rajkumar Buyya
The University of Melbourne and Manjrasoft Pty Ltd, Australia

Christian Vecchiola
The University of Melbourne and IBM Research, Australia

S. Thamarai Selvi
Madras Institute of Technology, Anna University, Chennai, India

AMSTERDAM • BOSTON • HEIDELBERG • LONDON
NEW YORK • OXFORD • PARIS • SAN DIEGO
SAN FRANCISCO • SINGAPORE • SYDNEY • TOKYO
Morgan Kaufmann is an imprint of Elsevier

Acquiring Editor: *Todd Green*
Editorial Project Manager: *Lindsay Lawrence*
Project Manager: *Punithavathy Govindaradjane*
Designer: *Matthew Limbert*

Morgan Kaufmann is an imprint of Elsevier
225 Wyman Street, Waltham, MA 02451, USA

Library of Congress Cataloging-in-Publication Data
Application submitted

British Library Cataloguing-in-Publication Data
A catalogue record for this book is available from the British Library

ISBN: 978-0-12-411454-8

Printed and bound by CPI Group (UK) Ltd, Croydon, CR0 4YY

For information on all MK publications visit our website at www.mkp.com

Contents

PART 2   CLOUD APPLICATION PROGRAMMING AND THE ANEKA PLATFORM

PART 3   INDUSTRIAL PLATFORMS AND NEW DEVELOPMENTS

Acknowledgments

First and foremost, we are grateful to all researchers and industrial developers worldwide for their contributions to various concepts and technologies discussed in this book. Our special thanks to all the members and consultants of Manjrasoft, the Cloud Computing and Distributed Systems (CLOUDS) Lab of the University of Melbourne, and Melbourne Ventures, who contributed to the development of the Aneka Cloud Application Platform, the preparation of associated application demonstrators and documents, and/or the commercialization of the Aneka technology. They include Chu Xingchen, Srikumar Venugopal, Krishna Nadiminti, Christian Vecchiola, Dileban Karunamoorthy, Chao Jin, Rodrigo Calheiros, Michael Mattess, Jessie Wei, Enayat Masoumi, Ivan Mellado, Richard Day, Wolfgang Gentzsch, Laurence Liew, David Sinclair, Suraj Pandey, Abhi Shekar, Dexter Duncan, Murali Sathya, Karthik Sukumar, Ravi Kumar Challa, and Sita Venkatraman.

We thank the Australian Research Council (ARC) and the Department of Innovation, Industry, Science, and Research (DIISR) for supporting our research and commercialization endeavors.

We thank all of our colleagues at the University of Melbourne, especially Professors Rao Kotagiri, Iven Mareels, and Glyn Davis, for their mentorship and positive support for our research and our efforts to impart the knowledge we have gained.

We thank all colleagues and users of the Aneka technology for their direct and indirect contributions to application case studies reported in the book. Our special thanks to Raghavendra Kune from ADRIN/ISRO for his enthusiastic efforts in creating a satellite image-processing application using Aneka and publishing articles in this area. We thank Srinivasa Iyengar from MSRIT for creating data-mining applications using Aneka and demonstrating the power of Aneka to academics from the early days of cloud computing.

We thank the members of the CLOUDS Lab for proofreading one or more chapters. They include Rodrigo Calheiros, Nikolay Grozev, Amir Vahid, Anton Beloglazov, Adel Toosi, Deepak Poola, Mohammed AlRokayan, Atefeh Khosravi, Sareh Piraghaj, and Yaser Mansouri.

We thank our family members, including Smrithi Buyya, Soumya Buyya, and Radha Buyya, for their love and understanding during the preparation of the book.

We sincerely thank external reviewers commissioned by the publisher for their critical comments and suggestions on enhancing the presentation and organization of many chapters at a finer level. This has greatly helped us improve the quality of the book.

Finally, we would like to thank the staff at Elsevier Inc for their enthusiastic support and guidance during the preparation of the book. In particular, we thank Todd Green for inspiring us to take up this project and for setting the process of publication in motion. The Elsevier staff were wonderful to work with!

Professor Rajkumar Buyya
The University of Melbourne and Manjrasoft Pty Ltd, Australia
Dr. Christian Vecchiola
The University of Melbourne and IBM Research, Australia
Professor S. Thamarai Selvi
Madras Institute of Technology, Anna University, Chennai, India

Preface

The growing popularity of the Internet and the Web, along with the availability of powerful handheld computing, mobile, and sensing devices, are changing the way we interact, manage our lives, conduct business, and access or deliver services. The lowering costs of computation and communication are driving the focus from personal to datacenter-centric computing. Although parallel and distributed computing has been around for several years, its new forms, multicore and cloud computing, have brought about a sweeping change in the industry. These trends are pushing the industry focus from developing applications for PCs to cloud datacenters that enable millions of users to use software simultaneously.

Computing is being transformed to a model consisting of commoditized services delivered in a manner similar to utilities such as water, electricity, gas, and telephony. As a result, information technology (IT) services are billed and delivered as "computing utilities" over shared delivery networks, akin to water, electricity, gas, and telephony services delivery. In such a model, users access services based on their requirements, regardless of where those services are hosted. Several computing paradigms have promised to deliver this utility computing vision. Cloud computing is the most recent emerging paradigm promising to turn the vision of "computing utilities" into a reality.

Cloud computing has become one of the buzzwords in the IT industry. Several IT vendors are promising to offer storage, computation, and application hosting services and to provide coverage on several continents, offering service-level agreements-backed performance and uptime promises for their services. They offer subscription-based access to infrastructure, platforms, and applications that are popularly termed Infrastructure-as-a-Service (IaaS), Platform-as-a-Service (PaaS), and Software-as-a-Service (SaaS). These emerging services have reduced the cost of computation and application hosting by several orders of magnitude, but there is significant complexity involved in the development and delivery of applications and their services in a seamless, scalable, and reliable manner.

There are several cloud technologies and platforms on the market—to mention a few: Google AppEngine, Microsoft Azure, and Manjrasoft Aneka. Google AppEngine provides an extensible runtime environment for Web-based applications that leverage the huge Google IT infrastructure. Microsoft Azure provides a wide array of Windows-based services for developing and deploying Windows applications on the cloud. Manjrasoft Aneka provides a flexible model for creating cloud applications and deploying them on a wide variety of infrastructures, including public clouds such as Amazon EC2.

With this sweeping shift from developing applications on PCs to datacenters, there is a huge demand for manpower with new skill sets in cloud computing. Universities play an important role in this regard by training the next generation of IT professionals and equipping them with the necessary tools and knowledge to tackle these challenges. These institutions need to be able to set up a cloud computing environment for teaching and learning with minimal investment. One of the attractive cloud application platforms that meet this need is Manjrasoft's Aneka, which (1) enables the construction of a private/enterprise cloud by harnessing the existing network of computers

(LAN-connected PCs), (2) provides a software development kit (SDK) that supports application programming interfaces (APIs) for multiple programming models such as Thread, Task, and MapReduce, and (3) supports, in a seamless manner, the deployment and execution of applications on diverse infrastructures such as multicore servers, private clouds, and public clouds.

Currently, expert developers are required to create cloud applications and services. Cloud researchers, practitioners, and vendors alike are working to ensure that potential users are educated about the benefits of cloud computing and the best way to harness its full potential. However, because it's a new and popular paradigm, the very definition of cloud computing depends on which computing expert is asked. So, although the realization of true utility computing appears closer than ever, its acceptance is currently restricted to cloud experts due to the perceived complexities of interacting with cloud computing providers. This book aims to change the game by simplifying and imparting cloud computing foundations, technologies, and programming skills to readers so that even average programmers and software engineers are able to develop cloud applications easily.

The book at a glance

This book introduces the fundamental principles of cloud computing and its related paradigms. It discusses the concepts of virtualization technologies along with the architectural models of cloud computing. It presents prominent cloud computing technologies that are available in the marketplace, including the Aneka Cloud Application Platform. The book contains chapters dedicated to discussion of concurrent, high-throughput, and data-intensive computing paradigms and their use in programming cloud applications. Various application case studies from domains such as science, engineering, gaming, and social networking are introduced, along with their architecture and how they leverage various cloud technologies. These case studies allow the reader to understand the mechanisms needed to harness cloud computing in their own respective endeavors. Finally, the book details many open research problems and opportunities that have arisen from the rapid uptake of cloud computing. We hope that this motivates the reader to address these in their own future research and development. The book also comes with an associated Website (hosted at www.buyya.com/MasteringClouds) that contains pointers to advanced online resources.

The book contains 11 chapters, which are organized into three major parts:

Part 1: Foundations
  Chapter 1—Introduction
  Chapter 2—Principles of Parallel and Distributed Computing
  Chapter 3—Virtualization
  Chapter 4—Cloud Computing Architecture
Part 2: Cloud Application Programming and the Aneka Platform
  Chapter 5—Aneka: Cloud Application Platform
  Chapter 6—Concurrent Computing: Thread Programming
  Chapter 7—High-Throughput Computing: Task Programming
  Chapter 8—Data-Intensive Computing: MapReduce Programming

Part 3: Industrial Platforms and New Developments
    Chapter 9—Cloud Platforms in Industry
    Chapter 10—Cloud Applications
    Chapter 11—Advanced Topics in Cloud Computing

The book serves as a perfect guide to the world of cloud computing. Starting with the fundamentals, the book drives students and professionals through the practical use of these concepts via hands-on sessions on how to develop cloud applications, using Aneka as a reference platform. Part 3 goes beyond the reference platform and introduces other industrial technologies and solutions (Amazon Web Services, Google AppEngine, and Microsoft Azure) and real applications, identifies emerging trends, and offers future directions for cloud computing.

Benefits and readership

Given the rapid emergence of cloud computing as a mainstream computing paradigm, it is essential to have both a solid understanding of the core concepts characterizing the phenomenon and a practical grasp of how to design and implement cloud computing applications and systems. This set of skills is already fundamental today for software architects, engineers, and developers because many applications are being moved to the cloud. It will become even more important in the future, when this technology matures further. This book provides an ideal blend of background information, theory, and practical cloud computing development techniques, expressed in a language that is accessible to a wide range of readers: from graduate-level students to practitioners, developers, and engineers who want to, or need to, design and implement cloud computing solutions. Moreover, more advanced topics presented at the end of the manuscript make the book an interesting read for researchers in the field of cloud computing who want an overview of the next challenges in cloud computing that will arise in coming years.

This book is a timely contribution to the cloud computing field, which is gaining considerable commercial interest and momentum. The book is targeted at graduate students and IT professionals such as system architects, practitioners, software engineers, and application programmers. As cloud computing is recognized as one of the top five emerging technologies that will have a major impact on the quality of science and society over the next 20 years, the knowledge conveyed through this book will help position our readers at the forefront of the field.

Directions for adoption: theory, labs, and projects

Given the importance of the cloud computing paradigm and its rapid uptake in industry, universities and educational institutions need to upgrade their curriculum by introducing one or more subjects in the area of cloud computing and related topics, such as parallel computing and distributed systems. We recommend that they offer at least one subject on cloud computing as part of their undergraduate and postgraduate degree programs, such as B.E./B.Tech./BSc in computer science and related areas and Masters, including the Master of Computer Applications (MCA). We believe that this book will serve as an excellent textbook for such subjects. If the students have already had exposure to the concepts of parallel and distributed computing, Chapter 2 can be skipped.

For those aiming to make their curriculum rich with cloud computing, we recommend offering two courses: "Introduction to Cloud Computing" and "Advanced Cloud Computing," in two different semesters. This book has sufficient content to cater to both of them. The first subject can be based on Chapters 1−6 and the second one based on Chapters 7−11.

In addition to theory, we strongly recommend the introduction of a laboratory subject that offers hands-on experience. The lab exercises and assignments can focus on creating high-performance cloud applications and assignments on a range of topics, including parallel execution of mathematical functions, sorting of large data in parallel, image processing, and data mining. Using cloud software systems such as Aneka, institutions can easily set up a private/enterprise cloud computing facility by utilizing existing LAN-connected PCs running Windows. Students can use this facility to learn about various cloud application programming models and interfaces discussed in Chapter 6 (Thread Programming), Chapter 7 (Task Programming), and Chapter 8 (MapReduce Programming). Students need to learn various programming examples discussed in these chapters and execute them on an Aneka-based cloud facility. We encourage students to take up some of the programming exercises noted in the "Review Questions" sections of these chapters as lab assignments and develop their own solutions.

Students can also carry out their final-year projects focused on developing cloud applications to solve real-world problems. For example, students can work with academics, researchers, and experts from other science and engineering disciplines, such as life and medical sciences or civil and mechanical engineering, and develop suitable applications that can harness the power of cloud computing. For inspiration, please read various application case studies presented in Chapter 10.

Supplemental materials

Supplemental materials for instructors or students can be downloaded from Elsevier: http://store.elsevier.com/product.jsp?isbn=9780124114548

Foundations

Introduction

Computing is being transformed into a model consisting of services that are commoditized and delivered in a manner similar to utilities such as water, electricity, gas, and telephony. In such a model, users access services based on their requirements, regardless of where the services are hosted. Several computing paradigms, such as grid computing, have promised to deliver this utility computing vision. *Cloud computing* is the most recent emerging paradigm promising to turn the vision of "computing utilities" into a reality.

Cloud computing is a technological advancement that focuses on the way we design computing systems, develop applications, and leverage existing services for building software. It is based on the concept of *dynamic provisioning*, which is applied not only to services but also to compute capability, storage, networking, and information technology (IT) infrastructure in general. Resources are made available through the Internet and offered on a *pay-per-use* basis from cloud computing vendors. Today, anyone with a credit card can subscribe to cloud services and deploy and configure servers for an application in hours, growing and shrinking the infrastructure serving its application according to the demand, and paying only for the time these resources have been used.

This chapter provides a brief overview of the cloud computing phenomenon by presenting its vision, discussing its core features, and tracking the technological developments that have made it possible. The chapter also introduces some key cloud computing technologies as well as some insights into development of cloud computing environments.

1.1 Cloud computing at a glance

In 1969, Leonard Kleinrock, one of the chief scientists of the original Advanced Research Projects Agency Network (ARPANET), which seeded the Internet, said:

> As of now, computer networks are still in their infancy, but as they grow up and become sophisticated, we will probably see the spread of 'computer utilities' which, like present electric and telephone utilities, will service individual homes and offices across the country.

This vision of computing utilities based on a service-provisioning model anticipated the massive transformation of the entire computing industry in the 21st century, whereby computing services will be readily available on demand, just as other utility services such as water, electricity, telephone, and gas are available in today's society. Similarly, users (consumers) need to pay providers only when they access the computing services. In addition, consumers no longer need to invest heavily or encounter difficulties in building and maintaining complex IT infrastructure.

In such a model, users access services based on their requirements without regard to where the services are hosted. This model has been referred to as *utility computing* or, recently (since 2007), as *cloud computing*. The latter term often denotes the infrastructure as a "cloud" from which businesses and users can access applications as services from anywhere in the world and on demand. Hence, cloud computing can be classified as a new paradigm for the dynamic provisioning of computing services supported by state-of-the-art data centers employing virtualization technologies for consolidation and effective utilization of resources.

Cloud computing allows renting infrastructure, runtime environments, and services on a pay-per-use basis. This principle finds several practical applications and then gives different images of cloud computing to different people. Chief information and technology officers of large enterprises see opportunities for scaling their infrastructure on demand and sizing it according to their business needs. End users leveraging cloud computing services can access their documents and data anytime, anywhere, and from any device connected to the Internet. Many other points of view exist.[1] One of the most diffuse views of cloud computing can be summarized as follows:

> *I don't care where my servers are, who manages them, where my documents are stored, or where my applications are hosted. I just want them always available and access them from any device connected through Internet. And I am willing to pay for this service for as a long as I need it.*

The concept expressed above has strong similarities to the way we use other services, such as water and electricity. In other words, cloud computing turns IT services into *utilities*. Such a delivery model is made possible by the effective composition of several technologies, which have reached the appropriate maturity level. *Web 2.0* technologies play a central role in making cloud computing an attractive opportunity for building computing systems. They have transformed the Internet into a rich application and service delivery platform, mature enough to serve complex needs. *Service orientation* allows cloud computing to deliver its capabilities with familiar abstractions, while *virtualization* confers on cloud computing the necessary degree of customization, control, and flexibility for building production and enterprise systems.

Besides being an extremely flexible environment for building new systems and applications, cloud computing also provides an opportunity for integrating additional capacity or new features into existing systems. The use of dynamically provisioned IT resources constitutes a more attractive opportunity than buying additional infrastructure and software, the sizing of which can be difficult to estimate and the needs of which are limited in time. This is one of the most important advantages of cloud computing, which has made it a popular phenomenon. With the wide deployment of cloud computing systems, the foundation technologies and systems enabling them are becoming consolidated and standardized. This is a fundamental step in the realization of the long-term vision

---

[1]An interesting perspective on the way cloud computing evokes different things to different people can be found in a series of interviews made by Rob Boothby, vice president and platform evangelist of Joyent, at the Web 2.0 Expo in May 2007. Chief executive officers (CEOs), chief technology officers (CTOs), founders of IT companies, and IT analysts were interviewed, and all of them gave their personal perception of the phenomenon, which at that time was starting to spread. The video of the interview can be found on YouTube at the following link: www.youtube.com/watch?v=6PNuQHUiV3Q.

for cloud computing, which provides an open environment where computing, storage, and other services are traded as computing utilities.

1.1.1 The vision of cloud computing

Cloud computing allows anyone with a credit card to provision virtual hardware, runtime environments, and services. These are used for as long as needed, with no up-front commitments required. The entire stack of a computing system is transformed into a collection of utilities, which can be provisioned and composed together to deploy systems in hours rather than days and with virtually no maintenance costs. This opportunity, initially met with skepticism, has now become a practice across several application domains and business sectors (see Figure 1.1). The demand has fast-tracked technical development and enriched the set of services offered, which have also become more sophisticated and cheaper.

Despite its evolution, the use of cloud computing is often limited to a single service at a time or, more commonly, a set of related services offered by the same vendor. Previously, the lack of effective standardization efforts made it difficult to move hosted services from one vendor to another. The long-term vision of cloud computing is that IT services are traded as utilities in an open market, without technological and legal barriers. In this cloud marketplace, cloud service providers and consumers, trading cloud services as utilities, play a central role.

Many of the technological elements contributing to this vision already exist. Different stakeholders leverage clouds for a variety of services. The need for ubiquitous storage and compute power on demand is the most common reason to consider cloud computing. A scalable runtime for applications is an attractive option for application and system developers that do not have infrastructure or cannot afford any further expansion of existing infrastructure. The capability for Web-based access to documents and their processing using sophisticated applications is one of the appealing factors for end users.

In all these cases, the discovery of such services is mostly done by human intervention: a person (or a team of people) looks over the Internet to identify offerings that meet his or her needs. We imagine that in the near future it will be possible to find the solution that matches our needs by simply entering our request in a global digital market that trades cloud computing services. The existence of such a market will enable the automation of the discovery process and its integration into existing software systems, thus allowing users to transparently leverage cloud resources in their applications and systems. The existence of a global platform for trading cloud services will also help service providers become more visible and therefore potentially increase their revenue. A global cloud market also reduces the barriers between service consumers and providers: it is no longer necessary to belong to only one of these two categories. For example, a cloud provider might become a consumer of a competitor service in order to fulfill its own promises to customers.

These are all possibilities that are introduced with the establishment of a global cloud computing marketplace and by defining effective standards for the unified representation of cloud services as well as the interaction among different cloud technologies. A considerable shift toward cloud computing has already been registered, and its rapid adoption facilitates its consolidation. Moreover, by concentrating the core capabilities of cloud computing into large datacenters, it is possible to reduce or remove the need for any technical infrastructure on the service consumer side. This approach provides opportunities for optimizing datacenter facilities and fully utilizing their

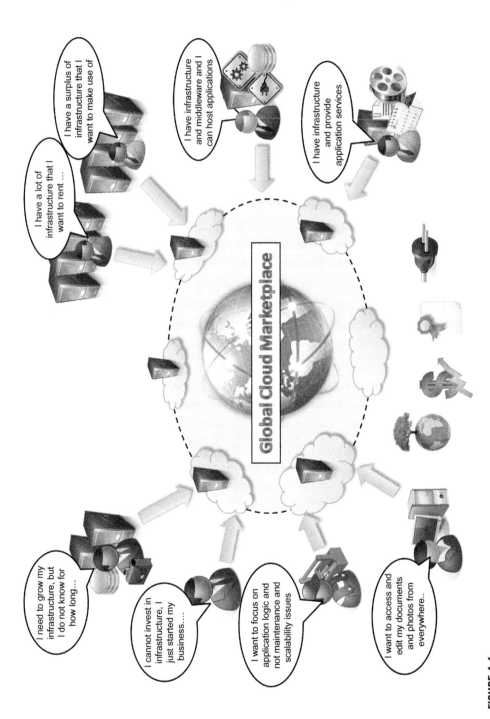

FIGURE 1.1

Cloud computing vision.

capabilities to serve multiple users. This consolidation model will reduce the waste of energy and carbon emissions, thus contributing to a greener IT on one end and increasing revenue on the other end.

1.1.2 Defining a cloud

Cloud computing has become a popular buzzword; it has been widely used to refer to different technologies, services, and concepts. It is often associated with virtualized infrastructure or hardware on demand, utility computing, IT outsourcing, platform and software as a service, and many other things that now are the focus of the IT industry. Figure 1.2 depicts the plethora of different notions included in current definitions of cloud computing.

The term *cloud* has historically been used in the telecommunications industry as an abstraction of the network in system diagrams. It then became the symbol of the most popular computer network: the Internet. This meaning also applies to *cloud computing*, which refers to an Internet-centric way of

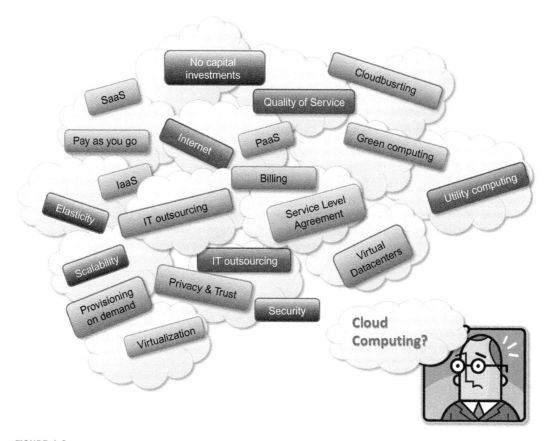

FIGURE 1.2

Cloud computing technologies, concepts, and ideas.

computing. The Internet plays a fundamental role in cloud computing, since it represents either the medium or the platform through which many cloud computing services are delivered and made accessible. This aspect is also reflected in the definition given by Armbrust et al. [28]:

> *Cloud computing refers to both the applications delivered as services over the Internet and the hardware and system software in the datacenters that provide those services.*

This definition describes cloud computing as a phenomenon touching on the entire stack: from the underlying hardware to the high-level software services and applications. It introduces the concept of *everything as a service*, mostly referred as *XaaS*,[2] where the different components of a system—IT infrastructure, development platforms, databases, and so on—can be delivered, measured, and consequently priced as a service. This new approach significantly influences not only the way that we build software but also the way we deploy it, make it accessible, and design our IT infrastructure, and even the way companies allocate the costs for IT needs. The approach fostered by cloud computing is global: it covers both the needs of a single user hosting documents in the cloud and the ones of a CIO deciding to deploy part of or the entire corporate IT infrastructure in the public cloud. This notion of multiple parties using a shared cloud computing environment is highlighted in a definition proposed by the U.S. National Institute of Standards and Technology (NIST):

> *Cloud computing is a model for enabling ubiquitous, convenient, on-demand network access to a shared pool of configurable computing resources (e.g., networks, servers, storage, applications, and services) that can be rapidly provisioned and released with minimal management effort or service provider interaction.*

Another important aspect of cloud computing is its utility-oriented approach. More than any other trend in distributed computing, cloud computing focuses on delivering services with a given pricing model, in most cases a "pay-per-use" strategy. It makes it possible to access online storage, rent virtual hardware, or use development platforms and pay only for their effective usage, with no or minimal up-front costs. All these operations can be performed and billed simply by entering the credit card details and accessing the exposed services through a Web browser. This helps us provide a different and more practical characterization of cloud computing. According to Reese [29], we can define three criteria to discriminate whether a service is delivered in the cloud computing style:

- The service is accessible via a Web browser (nonproprietary) or a Web services application programming interface (API).
- Zero capital expenditure is necessary to get started.
- You pay only for what you use as you use it.

Even though many cloud computing services are freely available for single users, enterprise-class services are delivered according a specific pricing scheme. In this case users subscribe to the service and establish with the service provider a service-level agreement (SLA) defining the

---

[2]*XaaS* is an acronym standing for *X-as-a-Service*, where the *X* letter can be replaced by one of a number of things: *S* for *software*, *P* for *platform*, *I* for *infrastructure*, *H* for *hardware*, *D* for *database*, and so on.

quality-of-service parameters under which the service is delivered. The utility-oriented nature of cloud computing is clearly expressed by Buyya et al. [30]:

> *A cloud is a type of parallel and distributed system consisting of a collection of interconnected and virtualized computers that are dynamically provisioned and presented as one or more unified computing resources based on service-level agreements established through negotiation between the service provider and consumers.*

1.1.3 A closer look

Cloud computing is helping enterprises, governments, public and private institutions, and research organizations shape more effective and demand-driven computing systems. Access to, as well as integration of, cloud computing resources and systems is now as easy as performing a credit card transaction over the Internet. Practical examples of such systems exist across all market segments:

- *Large enterprises can offload some of their activities to cloud-based systems.* Recently, the *New York Times* has converted its digital library of past editions into a Web-friendly format. This required a considerable amount of computing power for a short period of time. By renting Amazon EC2 and S3 Cloud resources, the *Times* performed this task in 36 hours and relinquished these resources, with no additional costs.
- *Small enterprises and start-ups can afford to translate their ideas into business results more quickly, without excessive up-front costs.* Animoto is a company that creates videos out of images, music, and video fragments submitted by users. The process involves a considerable amount of storage and backend processing required for producing the video, which is finally made available to the user. Animoto does not own a single server and bases its computing infrastructure entirely on Amazon Web Services, which are sized on demand according to the overall workload to be processed. Such workload can vary a lot and require instant scalability.[3] Up-front investment is clearly not an effective solution for many companies, and cloud computing systems become an appropriate alternative.
- *System developers can concentrate on the business logic rather than dealing with the complexity of infrastructure management and scalability.* Little Fluffy Toys is a company in London that has developed a widget providing users with information about nearby bicycle rental services. The company has managed to back the widget's computing needs on Google AppEngine and be on the market in only one week.
- *End users can have their documents accessible from everywhere and any device.* Apple iCloud is a service that allows users to have their documents stored in the Cloud and access them from any device users connect to it. This makes it possible to take a picture while traveling with a smartphone, go back home and edit the same picture on your laptop, and have it show as updated on your tablet computer. This process is completely transparent to the user, who does not have to set up cables and connect these devices with each other.

How is all of this made possible? The same concept of IT services on demand—whether computing power, storage, or runtime environments for applications—on a pay-as-you-go basis

---

[3]It has been reported that Animoto, in one single week, scaled from 70 to 8,500 servers because of user demand.

accommodates these four different scenarios. Cloud computing does not only contribute with the opportunity of easily accessing IT services on demand, it also introduces a new way of thinking about IT services and resources: as utilities. A bird's-eye view of a cloud computing environment is shown in Figure 1.3.

The three major models for deploying and accessing cloud computing environments are public clouds, private/enterprise clouds, and hybrid clouds (see Figure 1.4). *Public clouds* are the most common deployment models in which necessary IT infrastructure (e.g., virtualized datacenters) is established by a third-party service provider that makes it available to any consumer on a subscription basis. Such clouds are appealing to users because they allow users to quickly leverage compute, storage, and application services. In this environment, users' data and applications are deployed on cloud datacenters on the vendor's premises.

Large organizations that own massive computing infrastructures can still benefit from cloud computing by replicating the cloud IT service delivery model in-house. This idea has given birth to the concept of *private clouds* as opposed to public clouds. In 2010, for example, the U.S. federal government, one of the world's largest consumers of IT spending (around $76 billion on more than

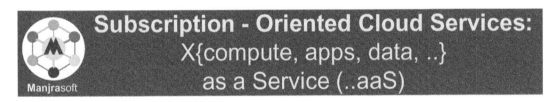

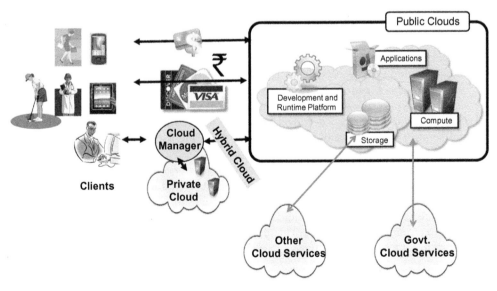

FIGURE 1.3

A bird's-eye view of cloud computing.

Cloud Deployment Models

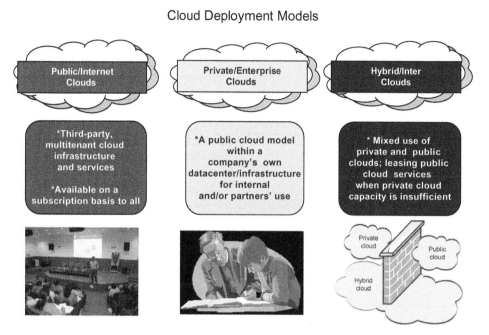

FIGURE 1.4

Major deployment models for cloud computing.

10,000 systems) started a cloud computing initiative aimed at providing government agencies with a more efficient use of their computing facilities. The use of cloud-based in-house solutions is also driven by the need to keep confidential information within an organization's premises. Institutions such as governments and banks that have high security, privacy, and regulatory concerns prefer to build and use their own private or enterprise clouds.

Whenever private cloud resources are unable to meet users' quality-of-service requirements, hybrid computing systems, partially composed of public cloud resources and privately owned infrastructures, are created to serve the organization's needs. These are often referred as *hybrid clouds*, which are becoming a common way for many stakeholders to start exploring the possibilities offered by cloud computing.

1.1.4 The cloud computing reference model

A fundamental characteristic of cloud computing is the capability to deliver, on demand, a variety of IT services that are quite diverse from each other. This variety creates different perceptions of what cloud computing is among users. Despite this lack of uniformity, it is possible to classify cloud computing services offerings into three major categories: *Infrastructure-as-a-Service (IaaS)*, *Platform-as-a-Service (PaaS)*, and *Software-as-a-Service (SaaS)*. These categories are related to each other as described in Figure 1.5, which provides an organic view of cloud computing. We refer to this diagram as the *Cloud Computing Reference Model*, and we will use it throughout the

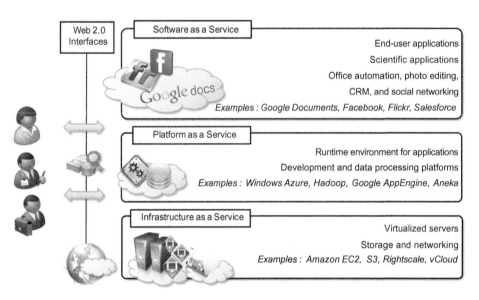

FIGURE 1.5

The Cloud Computing Reference Model.

book to explain the technologies and introduce the relevant research on this phenomenon. The model organizes the wide range of cloud computing services into a layered view that walks the computing stack from bottom to top.

At the base of the stack, *Infrastructure-as-a-Service* solutions deliver infrastructure on demand in the form of virtual *hardware*, *storage*, and *networking*. Virtual hardware is utilized to provide compute on demand in the form of virtual machine instances. These are created at users' request on the provider's infrastructure, and users are given tools and interfaces to configure the software stack installed in the virtual machine. The pricing model is usually defined in terms of dollars per hour, where the hourly cost is influenced by the characteristics of the virtual hardware. Virtual storage is delivered in the form of raw disk space or object store. The former complements a virtual hardware offering that requires persistent storage. The latter is a more high-level abstraction for storing entities rather than files. Virtual networking identifies the collection of services that manage the networking among virtual instances and their connectivity to the Internet or private networks.

Platform-as-a-Service solutions are the next step in the stack. They deliver scalable and elastic runtime environments on demand and host the execution of applications. These services are backed by a core middleware platform that is responsible for creating the abstract environment where applications are deployed and executed. It is the responsibility of the service provider to provide scalability and to manage fault tolerance, while users are requested to focus on the logic of the application developed by leveraging the provider's APIs and libraries. This approach increases the level of abstraction at which cloud computing is leveraged but also constrains the user in a more controlled environment.

At the top of the stack, *Software-as-a-Service* solutions provide applications and services on demand. Most of the common functionalities of desktop applications—such as office automation, document management, photo editing, and customer relationship management (CRM) software—are replicated on the provider's infrastructure and made more scalable and accessible through a browser on demand. These applications are shared across multiple users whose interaction is isolated from the other users. The SaaS layer is also the area of social networking Websites, which leverage cloud-based infrastructures to sustain the load generated by their popularity.

Each layer provides a different service to users. IaaS solutions are sought by users who want to leverage cloud computing from building dynamically scalable computing systems requiring a specific software stack. IaaS services are therefore used to develop scalable Websites or for background processing. PaaS solutions provide scalable programming platforms for developing applications and are more appropriate when new systems have to be developed. SaaS solutions target mostly end users who want to benefit from the elastic scalability of the cloud without doing any software development, installation, configuration, and maintenance. This solution is appropriate when there are existing SaaS services that fit users needs (such as email, document management, CRM, etc.) and a minimum level of customization is needed.

1.1.5 Characteristics and benefits

Cloud computing has some interesting characteristics that bring benefits to both cloud service consumers (CSCs) and cloud service providers (CSPs). These characteristics are:

- No up-front commitments
- On-demand access
- Nice pricing
- Simplified application acceleration and scalability
- Efficient resource allocation
- Energy efficiency
- Seamless creation and use of third-party services

The most evident benefit from the use of cloud computing systems and technologies is the increased economical return due to the reduced maintenance costs and *operational costs* related to IT software and infrastructure. This is mainly because IT assets, namely software and infrastructure, are turned into *utility costs*, which are paid for as long as they are used, not paid for up front. Capital costs are costs associated with assets that need to be paid in advance to start a business activity. Before cloud computing, IT infrastructure and software generated capital costs, since they were paid up front so that business start-ups could afford a computing infrastructure, enabling the business activities of the organization. The revenue of the business is then utilized to compensate over time for these costs. Organizations always minimize capital costs, since they are often associated with depreciable values. This is the case of hardware: a server bought today for $1,000 will have a market value less than its original price when it is eventually replaced by new hardware. To make profit, organizations have to compensate for this depreciation created by time, thus reducing the net gain obtained from revenue. Minimizing capital costs, then, is fundamental. Cloud computing transforms IT infrastructure and software into utilities, thus significantly contributing to increasing a company's net gain. Moreover, cloud computing also provides an opportunity for small organizations and start-ups: these do not need large investments to start their business, but they can comfortably grow with it. Finally, maintenance costs are significantly reduced: by renting the infrastructure and the application services, organizations are no longer responsible for their mainte-nance. This task is the responsibility of the cloud service provider, who, thanks to economies of scale, can bear the maintenance costs.

Increased agility in defining and structuring software systems is another significant benefit of cloud computing. Since organizations rent IT services, they can more dynamically and flexibly com-pose their software systems, without being constrained by capital costs for IT assets. There is a reduced need for capacity planning, since cloud computing allows organizations to react to unplanned surges in demand quite rapidly. For example, organizations can add more servers to pro-cess workload spikes and dismiss them when they are no longer needed. Ease of scalability is another advantage. By leveraging the potentially huge capacity of cloud computing, organizations can extend their IT capability more easily. Scalability can be leveraged across the entire computing stack. Infrastructure providers offer simple methods to provision customized hardware and integrate it into existing systems. Platform-as-a-Service providers offer runtime environment and programming mod-els that are designed to scale applications. Software-as-a-Service offerings can be elastically sized on demand without requiring users to provision hardware or to program application for scalability.

End users can benefit from cloud computing by having their data and the capability of operating on it always available, from anywhere, at any time, and through multiple devices. Information and services stored in the cloud are exposed to users by Web-based interfaces that make them accessi-ble from portable devices as well as desktops at home. Since the processing capabilities (that is, office automation features, photo editing, information management, and so on) also reside in the cloud, end users can perform the same tasks that previously were carried out through considerable software investments. The cost for such opportunities is generally very limited, since the cloud ser-vice provider shares its costs across all the tenants that he is servicing. Multitenancy allows for bet-ter utilization of the shared infrastructure that is kept operational and fully active. The concentration of IT infrastructure and services into large datacenters also provides opportunity for considerable optimization in terms of resource allocation and energy efficiency, which eventually can lead to a less impacting approach on the environment.

Finally, service orientation and on-demand access create new opportunities for composing sys-tems and applications with a flexibility not possible before cloud computing. New service offerings can be created by aggregating together existing services and concentrating on added value. Since it is possible to provision on demand any component of the computing stack, it is easier to turn ideas into products with limited costs and by concentrating technical efforts on what matters: the added value.

1.1.6 Challenges ahead

As any new technology develops and becomes popular, new issues have to be faced. Cloud com-puting is not an exception. New, interesting problems and challenges are regularly being posed to the cloud community, including IT practitioners, managers, governments, and regulators.

Besides the practical aspects, which are related to configuration, networking, and sizing of cloud computing systems, a new set of challenges concerning the dynamic provisioning of cloud comput-ing services and resources arises. For example, in the Infrastructure-as-a-Service domain, how many resources need to be provisioned, and for how long should they be used, in order to maxi-mize the benefit? Technical challenges also arise for cloud service providers for the management of large computing infrastructures and the use of virtualization technologies on top of them. In addition, issues and challenges concerning the integration of real and virtual infrastructure need to be taken into account from different perspectives, such as security and legislation.

Security in terms of confidentiality, secrecy, and protection of data in a cloud environment is another important challenge. Organizations do not own the infrastructure they use to process data and store information. This condition poses challenges for confidential data, which organizations cannot afford to reveal. Therefore, assurance on the confidentiality of data and compliance to security standards, which give a minimum guarantee on the treatment of information on cloud computing systems, are sought. The problem is not as evident as it seems: even though cryptography can help secure the transit of data from the private premises to the cloud infrastructure, in order to be processed the information needs to be decrypted in memory. This is the weak point of the chain: since virtualization allows capturing almost transparently the memory pages of an instance, these data could easily be obtained by a malicious provider.

Legal issues may also arise. These are specifically tied to the ubiquitous nature of cloud computing, which spreads computing infrastructure across diverse geographical locations. Different legislation about privacy in different countries may potentially create disputes as to the rights that third parties (including government agencies) have to your data. U.S. legislation is known to give extreme powers to government agencies to acquire confidential data when there is the suspicion of operations leading to a threat to national security. European countries are more restrictive and protect the right of privacy. An interesting scenario comes up when a U.S. organization uses cloud services that store their data in Europe. In this case, should this organization be suspected by the government, it would become difficult or even impossible for the U.S. government to take control of the data stored in a cloud datacenter located in Europe.

1.2 **Historical developments**

The idea of renting computing services by leveraging large distributed computing facilities has been around for long time. It dates back to the days of the mainframes in the early 1950s. From there on, technology has evolved and been refined. This process has created a series of favorable conditions for the realization of cloud computing.

Figure 1.6 provides an overview of the evolution of the distributed computing technologies that have influenced cloud computing. In tracking the historical evolution, we briefly review five core technologies that played an important role in the realization of cloud computing. These technologies are distributed systems, virtualization, Web 2.0, service orientation, and utility computing.

1.2.1 **Distributed systems**

Clouds are essentially large distributed computing facilities that make available their services to third parties on demand. As a reference, we consider the characterization of a distributed system proposed by Tanenbaum et al. [1]:

A distributed system is a collection of independent computers that appears to its users as a single coherent system.

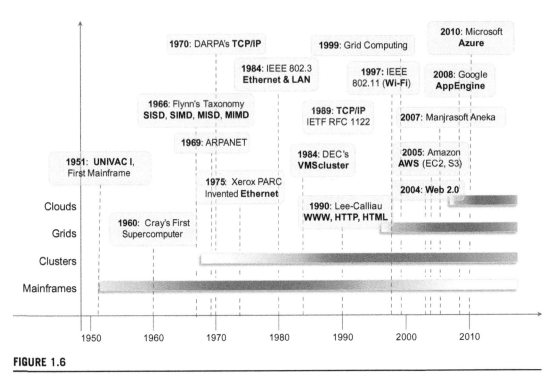

FIGURE 1.6

The evolution of distributed computing technologies, 1950s–2010s.

This is a general definition that includes a variety of computer systems, but it evidences two very important elements characterizing a distributed system: the fact that it is composed of multiple independent components and that these components are perceived as a single entity by users. This is particularly true in the case of cloud computing, in which clouds hide the complex architecture they rely on and provide a single interface to users. The primary purpose of distributed systems is to share resources and utilize them better. This is true in the case of cloud computing, where this concept is taken to the extreme and resources (infrastructure, runtime environments, and services) are rented to users. In fact, one of the driving factors of cloud computing has been the availability of the large computing facilities of IT giants (Amazon, Google) that found that offering their computing capabilities as a service provided opportunities to better utilize their infrastructure. Distributed systems often exhibit other properties such as *heterogeneity*, *openness*, *scalability*, *transparency*, *concurrency*, *continuous availability*, and *independent failures*. To some extent these also characterize clouds, especially in the context of scalability, concurrency, and continuous availability.

Three major milestones have led to cloud computing: mainframe computing, cluster computing, and grid computing.

- *Mainframes*. These were the first examples of large computational facilities leveraging multiple processing units. Mainframes were powerful, highly reliable computers specialized for large data movement and massive input/output (I/O) operations. They were mostly used by large organizations for bulk data processing tasks such as online transactions, enterprise resource planning, and other operations involving the processing of significant amounts of data. Even though mainframes cannot be considered distributed systems, they offered large computational power by using multiple processors, which were presented as a single entity to users. One of the most attractive features of mainframes was the ability to be highly reliable computers that were "always on" and capable of tolerating failures transparently. No system shutdown was required to replace failed components, and the system could work without interruption. Batch processing was the main application of mainframes. Now their popularity and deployments have reduced, but evolved versions of such systems are still in use for transaction processing (such as online banking, airline ticket booking, supermarket and telcos, and government services).

- *Clusters.* Cluster computing [3][4] started as a low-cost alternative to the use of mainframes and supercomputers. The technology advancement that created faster and more powerful mainframes and supercomputers eventually generated an increased availability of cheap commodity machines as a side effect. These machines could then be connected by a high-bandwidth network and controlled by specific software tools that manage them as a single system. Starting in the 1980s, clusters become the standard technology for parallel and high-performance computing. Built by commodity machines, they were cheaper than mainframes and made high-performance computing available to a large number of groups, including universities and small research labs. Cluster technology contributed considerably to the evolution of tools and frameworks for distributed computing, including Condor [5], Parallel Virtual Machine (PVM) [6], and Message Passing Interface (MPI) [7].[4] One of the attractive features of clusters was that the computational power of commodity machines could be leveraged to solve problems that were previously manageable only on expensive supercomputers. Moreover, clusters could be easily extended if more computational power was required.

- *Grids.* Grid computing [8] appeared in the early 1990s as an evolution of cluster computing. In an analogy to the power grid, grid computing proposed a new approach to access large computational power, huge storage facilities, and a variety of services. Users can "consume" resources in the same way as they use other utilities such as power, gas, and water. Grids initially developed as aggregations of geographically dispersed clusters by means of Internet connections. These clusters belonged to different organizations, and arrangements were made among them to share the computational power. Different from a "large cluster," a computing grid was a dynamic aggregation of heterogeneous computing nodes, and its scale was nationwide or even worldwide. Several developments made possible the diffusion of computing grids: (a) clusters became quite common resources; (b) they were often underutilized; (c) new problems were requiring computational power that went beyond the capability of single clusters; and (d) the improvements in networking and the diffusion of the Internet made possible long-distance, high-bandwidth connectivity. All these elements led to the development of grids, which now serve a multitude of users across the world.

---

[4]*MPI* is a specification for an API that allows many computers to communicate with one another. It defines a language-independent protocol that supports point-to-point and collective communication. *MPI* has been designed for high performance, scalability, and portability. At present, it is one of the dominant paradigms for developing parallel applications.

Cloud computing is often considered the successor of grid computing. In reality, it embodies aspects of all these three major technologies. Computing clouds are deployed in large datacenters hosted by a single organization that provides services to others. Clouds are characterized by the fact of having virtually infinite capacity, being tolerant to failures, and being always on, as in the case of mainframes. In many cases, the computing nodes that form the infrastructure of computing clouds are commodity machines, as in the case of clusters. The services made available by a cloud vendor are consumed on a pay-per-use basis, and clouds fully implement the utility vision introduced by grid computing.

1.2.2 Virtualization

Virtualization is another core technology for cloud computing. It encompasses a collection of solutions allowing the abstraction of some of the fundamental elements for computing, such as hardware, runtime environments, storage, and networking. Virtualization has been around for more than 40 years, but its application has always been limited by technologies that did not allow an efficient use of virtualization solutions. Today these limitations have been substantially overcome, and virtualization has become a fundamental element of cloud computing. This is particularly true for solutions that provide IT infrastructure on demand. Virtualization confers that degree of customization and control that makes cloud computing appealing for users and, at the same time, sustainable for cloud services providers.

Virtualization is essentially a technology that allows creation of different computing environments. These environments are called *virtual* because they simulate the interface that is expected by a guest. The most common example of virtualization is *hardware virtualization*. This technology allows simulating the hardware interface expected by an operating system. Hardware virtualization allows the coexistence of different software stacks on top of the same hardware. These stacks are contained inside *virtual machine instances*, which operate in complete isolation from each other. High-performance servers can host several virtual machine instances, thus creating the opportunity to have a customized software stack on demand. This is the base technology that enables cloud computing solutions to deliver virtual servers on demand, such as Amazon EC2, RightScale, VMware vCloud, and others. Together with hardware virtualization, *storage* and *network virtualization* complete the range of technologies for the emulation of IT infrastructure.

Virtualization technologies are also used to replicate runtime environments for programs. Applications in the case of *process virtual machines* (which include the foundation of technologies such as Java or .NET), instead of being executed by the operating system, are run by a specific program called a *virtual machine*. This technique allows isolating the execution of applications and providing a finer control on the resource they access. Process virtual machines offer a higher level of abstraction with respect to hardware virtualization, since the guest is only constituted by an application rather than a complete software stack. This approach is used in cloud computing to provide a platform for scaling applications on demand, such as Google AppEngine and Windows Azure.

Having isolated and customizable environments with minor impact on performance is what makes virtualization a attractive technology. Cloud computing is realized through platforms that leverage the basic concepts described above and provides on demand virtualization services to a multitude of users across the globe.

1.2.3 **Web 2.0**

The Web is the primary interface through which cloud computing delivers its services. At present, the Web encompasses a set of technologies and services that facilitate interactive information sharing, collaboration, user-centered design, and application composition. This evolution has transformed the Web into a rich platform for application development and is known as *Web 2.0*. This term captures a new way in which developers architect applications and deliver services through the Internet and provides new experience for users of these applications and services.

Web 2.0 brings *interactivity* and *flexibility* into Web pages, providing enhanced user experience by gaining Web-based access to all the functions that are normally found in desktop applications. These capabilities are obtained by integrating a collection of standards and technologies such as *XML, Asynchronous JavaScript and XML (AJAX), Web Services*, and others. These technologies allow us to build applications leveraging the contribution of users, who now become providers of content. Furthermore, the capillary diffusion of the Internet opens new opportunities and markets for the Web, the services of which can now be accessed from a variety of devices: mobile phones, car dashboards, TV sets, and others. These new scenarios require an increased dynamism for applications, which is another key element of this technology. Web 2.0 applications are extremely dynamic: they improve continuously, and new updates and features are integrated at a constant rate by following the usage trend of the community. There is no need to deploy new software releases on the installed base at the client side. Users can take advantage of the new software features simply by interacting with cloud applications. Lightweight deployment and programming models are very important for effective support of such dynamism. Loose coupling is another fundamental property. New applications can be "synthesized" simply by composing existing services and integrating them, thus providing added value. This way it becomes easier to follow the interests of users. Finally, Web 2.0 applications aim to leverage the "long tail" of Internet users by making themselves available to everyone in terms of either media accessibility or affordability.

Examples of Web 2.0 applications are *Google Documents, Google Maps, Flickr, Facebook, Twitter, YouTube, de.li.cious, Blogger*, and *Wikipedia*. In particular, social networking Websites take the biggest advantage of Web 2.0. The level of interaction in Websites such as Facebook or Flickr would not have been possible without the support of AJAX, Really Simple Syndication (RSS), and other tools that make the user experience incredibly interactive. Moreover, community Websites harness the collective intelligence of the community, which provides content to the applications themselves: Flickr provides advanced services for storing digital pictures and videos, Facebook is a social networking site that leverages user activity to provide content, and Blogger, like any other blogging site, provides an online diary that is fed by users.

This idea of the Web as a transport that enables and enhances interaction was introduced in 1999 by Darcy DiNucci[5] and started to become fully realized in 2004. Today it is a mature platform for supporting the needs of cloud computing, which strongly leverages Web 2.0. Applications

---

[5]In a column for *Design & New Media* magazine, Darci DiNucci describes the Web as follows: "The Web we know now, which loads into a browser window in essentially static screenfulls, is only an embryo of the Web to come. The first glimmerings of Web 2.0 are beginning to appear, and we are just starting to see how that embryo might develop. The Web will be understood not as screenfulls of text and graphics but as a transport mechanism, the ether through which interactivity happens. It will [...] appear on your computer screen, [...] on your TV set [...], your car dashboard [...], your cell phone [...], hand-held game machines [...], maybe even your microwave oven."

and frameworks for delivering *rich Internet applications (RIAs)* are fundamental for making cloud services accessible to the wider public. From a social perspective, Web 2.0 applications definitely contributed to making people more accustomed to the use of the Internet in their everyday lives and opened the path to the acceptance of cloud computing as a paradigm, whereby even the IT infrastructure is offered through a Web interface.

1.2.4 Service-oriented computing

Service orientation is the core reference model for cloud computing systems. This approach adopts the concept of services as the main building blocks of application and system development. *Service-oriented computing (SOC)* supports the development of rapid, low-cost, flexible, interoperable, and evolvable applications and systems [19].

A *service* is an abstraction representing a self-describing and platform-agnostic component that can perform any function—anything from a simple function to a complex business process. Virtually any piece of code that performs a task can be turned into a service and expose its functionalities through a network-accessible protocol. A service is supposed to be *loosely coupled, reusable, programming language independent*, and *location transparent*. Loose coupling allows services to serve different scenarios more easily and makes them reusable. Independence from a specific platform increases services accessibility. Thus, a wider range of clients, which can look up services in global registries and consume them in a location-transparent manner, can be served. Services are composed and aggregated into a *service-oriented architecture (SOA)* [27], which is a logical way of organizing software systems to provide end users or other entities distributed over the network with services through published and discoverable interfaces.

Service-oriented computing introduces and diffuses two important concepts, which are also fundamental to cloud computing: *quality of service (QoS)* and *Software-as-a-Service (SaaS)*.

- Quality of service (QoS) identifies a set of functional and nonfunctional attributes that can be used to evaluate the behavior of a service from different perspectives. These could be performance metrics such as response time, or security attributes, transactional integrity, reliability, scalability, and availability. QoS requirements are established between the client and the provider via an SLA that identifies the minimum values (or an acceptable range) for the QoS attributes that need to be satisfied upon the service call.
- The concept of Software-as-a-Service introduces a new delivery model for applications. The term has been inherited from the world of application service providers (ASPs), which deliver software services-based solutions across the wide area network from a central datacenter and make them available on a subscription or rental basis. The ASP is responsible for maintaining the infrastructure and making available the application, and the client is freed from maintenance costs and difficult upgrades. This software delivery model is possible because economies of scale are reached by means of multitenancy. The SaaS approach reaches its full development with service-oriented computing (SOC), where loosely coupled software components can be exposed and priced singularly, rather than entire applications. This allows the delivery of complex business processes and transactions as a service while allowing applications to be composed on the fly and services to be reused from everywhere and by anybody.

One of the most popular expressions of service orientation is represented by Web Services (WS) [21]. These introduce the concepts of SOC into the World Wide Web, by making it consumable by applications and not only humans. Web services are software components that expose functionalities accessible using a method invocation pattern that goes over the HyperText Transfer Protocol (HTTP). The interface of a Web service can be programmatically inferred by metadata expressed through the *Web Service Description Language (WSDL)* [22]; this is an XML language that defines the characteristics of the service and all the methods, together with parameters, descriptions, and return type, exposed by the service. The interaction with Web services happens through *Simple Object Access Protocol (SOAP)* [23]. This is an XML language that defines how to invoke a Web service method and collect the result. Using SOAP and WSDL over HTTP, Web services become platform independent and accessible to the World Wide Web. The standards and specifications concerning Web services are controlled by the World Wide Web Consortium (W3C). Among the most popular architectures for developing Web services we can note ASP.NET [24] and Axis [25].

The development of systems in terms of distributed services that can be composed together is the major contribution given by SOC to the realization of cloud computing. Web services technologies have provided the right tools to make such composition straightforward and easily integrated with the mainstream World Wide Web (WWW) environment.

1.2.5 Utility-oriented computing

Utility computing is a vision of computing that defines a service-provisioning model for compute services in which resources such as storage, compute power, applications, and infrastructure are packaged and offered on a pay-per-use basis. The idea of providing computing as a *utility* like natural gas, water, power, and telephone connection has a long history but has become a reality today with the advent of cloud computing. Among the earliest forerunners of this vision we can include the American scientist John McCarthy, who, in a speech for the Massachusetts Institute of Technology (MIT) centennial in 1961, observed:

> If computers of the kind I have advocated become the computers of the future, then computing
> may someday be organized as a public utility, just as the telephone system is a public utility ...
> The computer utility could become the basis of a new and important industry.

The first traces of this service-provisioning model can be found in the mainframe era. IBM and other mainframe providers offered mainframe power to organizations such as banks and government agencies throughout their datacenters. The business model introduced with utility computing brought new requirements and led to improvements in mainframe technology: additional features such as operating systems, process control, and user-metering facilities. The idea of computing as utility remained and extended from the business domain to academia with the advent of cluster computing. Not only businesses but also research institutes became acquainted with the idea of leveraging an external IT infrastructure on demand. Computational science, which was one of the major driving factors for building computing clusters, still required huge compute power for addressing "Grand Challenge" problems, and not all the institutions were able to satisfy their computing needs internally. Access to external clusters still remained a common practice. The capillary diffusion of the Internet and the Web provided the technological means to realize utility computing on a worldwide scale and through simple interfaces. As already discussed, computing grids provided a planet-scale distributed computing infrastructure that was accessible on demand. Computing grids brought the concept of utility computing to a new level: market orientation [15]. With utility computing accessible on a wider scale, it is easier to provide a trading infrastructure where grid products—storage, computation, and services—are bid for or sold. Moreover, e-commerce technologies [25] provided the infrastructure support for utility computing. In the late 1990s a significant interest in buying any kind of good online spread to the wider public: food, clothes, multimedia products, and online services such as storage space and Web hosting. After the *dot-com bubble*[6] burst, this interest reduced in size, but the phenomenon made the public keener to buy online services. As a result, infrastructures for online payment using credit cards become easily accessible and well proven.

From an application and system development perspective, service-oriented computing and *service-oriented architectures (SOAs)* introduced the idea of leveraging external services for performing a specific task within a software system. Applications were not only distributed, they started to be composed as a mesh of services provided by different entities. These services, accessible through the Internet, were made available by charging according to usage. SOC broadened the concept of what could have been accessed as a utility in a computer system: not only compute power and storage but also services and application components could be utilized and integrated on demand. Together with this trend, QoS became an important topic to investigate.

All these factors contributed to the development of the concept of utility computing and offered important steps in the realization of cloud computing, in which the vision of computing utilities comes to its full expression.

1.3 Building cloud computing environments

The creation of cloud computing environments encompasses both the development of applications and systems that leverage cloud computing solutions and the creation of frameworks, platforms, and infrastructures delivering cloud computing services.

1.3.1 Application development

Applications that leverage cloud computing benefit from its capability to dynamically scale on demand. One class of applications that takes the biggest advantage of this feature is that of *Web applications*. Their performance is mostly influenced by the workload generated by varying user demands. With the diffusion of Web 2.0 technologies, the Web has become a platform for developing rich and complex applications, including *enterprise applications* that now leverage the Internet as the preferred channel for service delivery and user interaction. These applications are

---

[6]The dot-com bubble was a phenomenon that started in the second half of the 1990s and reached its apex in 2000. During this period a large number of companies that based their business on online services and e-commerce started and quickly expanded without later being able to sustain their growth. As a result they suddenly went bankrupt, partly because their revenues were not enough to cover their expenses and partly because they never reached the required number of customers to sustain their enlarged business.

characterized by complex processes that are triggered by the interaction with users and develop through the interaction between several tiers behind the Web front end. These are the applications that are mostly sensible to inappropriate sizing of infrastructure and service deployment or variability in workload.

Another class of applications that can potentially gain considerable advantage by leveraging cloud computing is represented by *resource-intensive applications*. These can be either data-intensive or compute-intensive applications. In both cases, considerable amounts of resources are required to complete execution in a reasonable timeframe. It is worth noticing that these large amounts of resources are not needed constantly or for a long duration. For example, *scientific applications* can require huge computing capacity to perform large-scale experiments once in a while, so it is not feasible to buy the infrastructure supporting them. In this case, cloud computing can be the solution. Resource-intensive applications are not interactive and they are mostly characterized by batch processing.

Cloud computing provides a solution for on-demand and dynamic scaling across the entire stack of computing. This is achieved by (a) providing methods for renting compute power, storage, and networking; (b) offering runtime environments designed for scalability and dynamic sizing; and (c) providing application services that mimic the behavior of desktop applications but that are completely hosted and managed on the provider side. All these capabilities leverage service orientation, which allows a simple and seamless integration into existing systems. Developers access such services via simple Web interfaces, often implemented through representational state transfer (REST) Web services. These have become well-known abstractions, making the development and management of cloud applications and systems practical and straightforward.

1.3.2 Infrastructure and system development

Distributed computing, virtualization, service orientation, and Web 2.0 form the core technologies enabling the provisioning of cloud services from anywhere on the globe. Developing applications and systems that leverage the cloud requires knowledge across all these technologies. Moreover, new challenges need to be addressed from design and development standpoints.

Distributed computing is a foundational model for cloud computing because cloud systems are distributed systems. Besides administrative tasks mostly connected to the accessibility of resources in the cloud, the extreme dynamism of cloud systems—where new nodes and services are provisioned on demand—constitutes the major challenge for engineers and developers. This characteristic is pretty peculiar to cloud computing solutions and is mostly addressed at the middleware layer of computing system. Infrastructure-as-a-Service solutions provide the capabilities to add and remove resources, but it is up to those who deploy systems on this scalable infrastructure to make use of such opportunities with wisdom and effectiveness. Platform-as-a-Service solutions embed into their core offering algorithms and rules that control the provisioning process and the lease of resources. These can be either completely transparent to developers or subject to fine control. Integration between cloud resources and existing system deployment is another element of concern.

Web 2.0 technologies constitute the interface through which cloud computing services are delivered, managed, and provisioned. Besides the interaction with rich interfaces through the Web browser, Web services have become the primary access point to cloud computing systems from a programmatic standpoint. Therefore, service orientation is the underlying paradigm that defines the architecture of a cloud computing system. Cloud computing is often summarized with the acronym *XaaS—Everything-as-a-Service*—that clearly underlines the central role of service orientation. Despite the absence of a unique standard for accessing the resources serviced by different cloud providers, the commonality of technology smoothes the learning curve and simplifies the integration of cloud computing into existing systems.

Virtualization is another element that plays a fundamental role in cloud computing. This technology is a core feature of the infrastructure used by cloud providers. As discussed before, the virtualization concept is more than 40 years old, but cloud computing introduces new challenges, especially in the management of virtual environments, whether they are abstractions of virtual hardware or a runtime environment. Developers of cloud applications need to be aware of the limitations of the selected virtualization technology and the implications on the volatility of some components of their systems.

These are all considerations that influence the way we program applications and systems based on cloud computing technologies. Cloud computing essentially provides mechanisms to address surges in demand by replicating the required components of computing systems under stress (i.e., heavily loaded). Dynamism, scale, and volatility of such components are the main elements that should guide the design of such systems.

1.3.3 Computing platforms and technologies

Development of a cloud computing application happens by leveraging platforms and frameworks that provide different types of services, from the bare-metal infrastructure to customizable applications serving specific purposes.

1.3.3.1 Amazon web services (AWS)

AWS offers comprehensive cloud IaaS services ranging from virtual compute, storage, and networking to complete computing stacks. AWS is mostly known for its compute and storage-on-demand services, namely *Elastic Compute Cloud (EC2)* and *Simple Storage Service (S3)*. EC2 provides users with customizable virtual hardware that can be used as the base infrastructure for deploying computing systems on the cloud. It is possible to choose from a large variety of virtual hardware configurations, including GPU and cluster instances. EC2 instances are deployed either by using the AWS console, which is a comprehensive Web portal for accessing AWS services, or by using the Web services API available for several programming languages. EC2 also provides the capability to save a specific running instance as an image, thus allowing users to create their own templates for deploying systems. These templates are stored into S3 that delivers persistent storage on demand. S3 is organized into buckets; these are containers of objects that are stored in binary form and can be enriched with attributes. Users can store objects of any size, from simple files to entire disk images, and have them accessible from everywhere.

Besides EC2 and S3, a wide range of services can be leveraged to build virtual computing systems, including networking support, caching systems, DNS, database (relational and not) support, and others.

1.3.3.2 Google AppEngine

Google AppEngine is a scalable runtime environment mostly devoted to executing Web applications. These take advantage of the large computing infrastructure of Google to dynamically scale as the demand varies over time. AppEngine provides both a secure execution environment and a collection of services that simplify the development of scalable and high-performance Web applications. These services include in-memory caching, scalable data store, job queues, messaging, and cron tasks. Developers can build and test applications on their own machines using the AppEngine software development kit (SDK), which replicates the production runtime environment and helps test and profile applications. Once development is complete, developers can easily migrate their application to AppEngine, set quotas to contain the costs generated, and make the application available to the world. The languages currently supported are Python, Java, and Go.

1.3.3.3 Microsoft Azure

Microsoft Azure is a cloud operating system and a platform for developing applications in the cloud. It provides a scalable runtime environment for Web applications and distributed applications in general. Applications in Azure are organized around the concept of roles, which identify a distribution unit for applications and embody the application's logic. Currently, there are three types of role: *Web role*, *worker role*, and *virtual machine role*. The Web role is designed to host a Web application, the worker role is a more generic container of applications and can be used to perform workload processing, and the virtual machine role provides a virtual environment in which the computing stack can be fully customized, including the operating systems. Besides roles, Azure provides a set of additional services that complement application execution, such as support for storage (relational data and blobs), networking, caching, content delivery, and others.

1.3.3.4 Hadoop

Apache Hadoop is an open-source framework that is suited for processing large data sets on commodity hardware. Hadoop is an implementation of MapReduce, an application programming model developed by Google, which provides two fundamental operations for data processing: *map* and *reduce*. The former transforms and synthesizes the input data provided by the user; the latter aggregates the output obtained by the map operations. Hadoop provides the runtime environment, and developers need only provide the input data and specify the map and reduce functions that need to be executed. Yahoo!, the sponsor of the Apache Hadoop project, has put considerable effort into transforming the project into an enterprise-ready cloud computing platform for data processing. Hadoop is an integral part of the Yahoo! cloud infrastructure and supports several business processes of the company. Currently, Yahoo! manages the largest Hadoop cluster in the world, which is also available to academic institutions.

1.3.3.5 Force.com and Salesforce.com

Force.com is a cloud computing platform for developing social enterprise applications. The platform is the basis for *SalesForce.com*, a Software-as-a-Service solution for customer relationship management. Force.com allows developers to create applications by composing ready-to-use blocks; a complete set of components supporting all the activities of an enterprise are available. It is also possible to develop your own components or integrate those available in *AppExchange* into your applications. The platform provides complete support for developing applications, from the design of the data layout to the definition of business rules and workflows and the definition of the user interface. The Force.com platform is completely hosted on the cloud and provides complete access to its functionalities and those implemented in the hosted applications through Web services technologies.

1.3.3.6 Manjrasoft Aneka

Manjrasoft Aneka [165] is a cloud application platform for rapid creation of scalable applications and their deployment on various types of clouds in a seamless and elastic manner. It supports a collection of programming abstractions for developing applications and a distributed runtime environment that can be deployed on heterogeneous hardware (clusters, networked desktop computers, and cloud resources). Developers can choose different abstractions to design their application: *tasks*, *distributed threads*, and *map-reduce*. These applications are then executed on the distributed service-oriented runtime environment, which can dynamically integrate additional resource on demand. The service-oriented architecture of the runtime has a great degree of flexibility and simplifies the integration of new features, such as abstraction of a new programming model and associated execution management environment. Services manage most of the activities happening at runtime: scheduling, execution, accounting, billing, storage, and quality of service.

These platforms are key examples of technologies available for cloud computing. They mostly fall into the three major market segments identified in the reference model: *Infrastructure-as-a-Service*, *Platform-as-a-Service*, and *Software-as-a-Service*. In this book, we use Aneka as a reference platform for discussing practical implementations of distributed applications. We present different ways in which clouds can be leveraged by applications built using the various programming models and abstractions provided by Aneka.

SUMMARY

In this chapter, we discussed the vision and opportunities of cloud computing along with its characteristics and challenges. The cloud computing paradigm emerged as a result of the maturity and convergence of several of its supporting models and technologies, namely distributed computing, virtualization, Web 2.0, service orientation, and utility computing.

There is no single view on the cloud phenomenon. Throughout the book, we explore different definitions, interpretations, and implementations of this idea. The only element that is shared among all the different views of cloud computing is that cloud systems support dynamic provisioning of IT services (whether they are virtual infrastructure, runtime environments, or application services) and adopts a utility-based cost model to price these services. This concept is applied across the entire computing stack and enables the dynamic provisioning of IT infrastructure and runtime environments in the form of cloud-hosted platforms for the development of scalable applications and their services. This vision is what inspires the *Cloud Computing Reference Model*. This model identifies three major market segments (and service offerings) for cloud computing: *Infrastructure-as-a-Service (IaaS)*, *Platform-as-a-Service (PaaS)*, and *Software-as-a-Service (SaaS)*. These segments directly map the broad classifications of the different type of services offered by cloud computing.

The long-term vision of cloud computing is to fully realize the utility model that drives its service offering. It is envisioned that new technological developments and the increased familiarity with cloud computing delivery models will lead to the establishment of a global market for trading computing utilities. This area of study is called *market-oriented cloud computing*, where the term *market-oriented* further stresses the fact that cloud computing services are traded as utilities. The realization of this vision is still far from reality, but cloud computing has already brought economic, environmental, and technological benefits. By turning IT assets into utilities, it allows organizations to reduce operational costs and increase revenues. This and other advantages also have downsides that are diverse in nature. Security and legislation are two of the challenging aspects of cloud computing that are beyond the technical sphere.

From the perspective of software design and development, new challenges arise in engineering computing systems. Cloud computing offers a rich mixture of different technologies, and harnessing them is a challenging engineering task. Cloud computing introduces both new opportunities and new techniques and strategies for architecting software applications and systems. Some of the key elements that have to be taken into account are virtualization, scalability, dynamic provisioning, big datasets, and cost models. To provide a practical grasp of such concepts, we will use Aneka as a reference platform for illustrating cloud systems and application programming environments.

Review questions

1. What is the innovative characteristic of cloud computing?
2. Which are the technologies on which cloud computing relies?
3. Provide a brief characterization of a distributed system.
4. Define cloud computing and identify its core features.
5. What are the major distributed computing technologies that led to cloud computing?
6. What is virtualization?
7. What is the major revolution introduced by Web 2.0?
8. Give some examples of Web 2.0 applications.
9. Describe the main characteristics of a service orientation.
10. What is utility computing?
11. Describe the vision introduced by cloud computing.
12. Briefly summarize the Cloud Computing Reference Model.
13. What is the major advantage of cloud computing?
14. Briefly summarize the challenges still open in cloud computing.
15. How is cloud development different from traditional software development?

Principles of Parallel and Distributed Computing

Cloud computing is a new technological trend that supports better utilization of IT infrastructures, services, and applications. It adopts a service delivery model based on a pay-per-use approach, in which users do not own infrastructure, platform, or applications but use them for the time they need them. These IT assets are owned and maintained by service providers who make them accessible through the Internet.

This chapter presents the fundamental principles of parallel and distributed computing and discusses models and conceptual frameworks that serve as foundations for building cloud computing systems and applications.

2.1 Eras of computing

The two fundamental and dominant models of computing are *sequential* and *parallel*. The sequential computing era began in the 1940s; the parallel (and distributed) computing era followed it within a decade (see Figure 2.1). The four key elements of computing developed during these eras are *architectures, compilers, applications*, and *problem-solving environments*.

The computing era started with a development in hardware architectures, which actually enabled the creation of system software—particularly in the area of compilers and operating systems—which support the management of such systems and the development of applications. The development of applications and systems are the major element of interest to us, and it comes to consolidation when problem-solving environments were designed and introduced to facilitate and empower engineers. This is when the paradigm characterizing the computing achieved maturity and became mainstream. Moreover, every aspect of this era underwent a three-phase process: *research and development (R&D), commercialization*, and *commoditization*.

2.2 Parallel vs. distributed computing

The terms *parallel computing* and *distributed computing* are often used interchangeably, even though they mean slightly different things. The term *parallel* implies a tightly coupled system, whereas *distributed* refers to a wider class of system, including those that are tightly coupled.

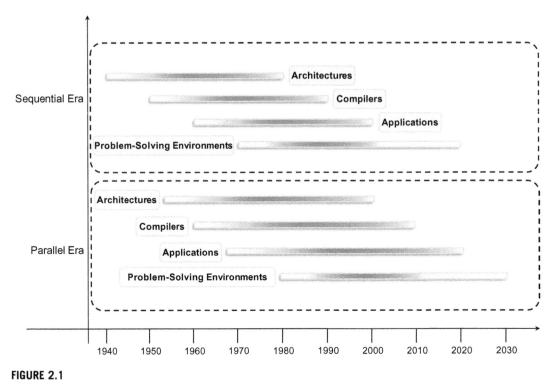

FIGURE 2.1

Eras of computing, 1940s–2030s.

More precisely, the term *parallel computing* refers to a model in which the computation is divided among several processors sharing the same memory. The architecture of a parallel computing system is often characterized by the homogeneity of components: each processor is of the same type and it has the same capability as the others. The shared memory has a single address space, which is accessible to all the processors. Parallel programs are then broken down into several units of execution that can be allocated to different processors and can communicate with each other by means of the shared memory. Originally we considered parallel systems only those architectures that featured multiple processors sharing the same physical memory and that were considered a single computer. Over time, these restrictions have been relaxed, and parallel systems now include all architectures that are based on the concept of shared memory, whether this is physically present or created with the support of libraries, specific hardware, and a highly efficient networking infrastructure. For example, a cluster of which the nodes are connected through an *InfiniBand* network and configured with a distributed shared memory system can be considered a parallel system.

The term *distributed computing* encompasses any architecture or system that allows the computation to be broken down into units and executed concurrently on different computing elements, whether these are processors on different nodes, processors on the same computer, or cores within the same processor. Therefore, distributed computing includes a wider range of systems and applications than parallel computing and is often considered a more general term. Even though it is not a rule, the term *distributed* often implies that the locations of the computing elements are not the same and such elements might be heterogeneous in terms of hardware and software features. Classic examples of distributed computing systems are computing grids or Internet computing systems, which combine together the biggest variety of architectures, systems, and applications in the world.

2.3 **Elements of parallel computing**

It is now clear that silicon-based processor chips are reaching their physical limits. Processing speed is constrained by the speed of light, and the density of transistors packaged in a processor is constrained by thermodynamic limitations. A viable solution to overcome this limitation is to connect multiple processors working in coordination with each other to solve "Grand Challenge" problems. The first steps in this direction led to the development of parallel computing, which encompasses techniques, architectures, and systems for performing multiple activities in parallel. As we already discussed, the term *parallel computing* has blurred its edges with the term *distributed computing* and is often used in place of the latter term. In this section, we refer to its proper characterization, which involves the introduction of parallelism within a single computer by coordinating the activity of multiple processors together.

2.3.1 **What is parallel processing?**

Processing of multiple tasks simultaneously on multiple processors is called *parallel processing*. The parallel program consists of multiple active processes (tasks) simultaneously solving a given problem. A given task is divided into multiple subtasks using a divide-and-conquer technique, and each subtask is processed on a different central processing unit (CPU). Programming on a multiprocessor system using the divide-and-conquer technique is called *parallel programming*.

Many applications today require more computing power than a traditional sequential computer can offer. Parallel processing provides a cost-effective solution to this problem by increasing the number of CPUs in a computer and by adding an efficient communication system between them. The workload can then be shared between different processors. This setup results in higher computing power and performance than a single-processor system offers.

The development of parallel processing is being influenced by many factors. The prominent among them include the following:

- Computational requirements are ever increasing in the areas of both scientific and business computing. The technical computing problems, which require high-speed computational power, are related to life sciences, aerospace, geographical information systems, mechanical design and analysis, and the like.
- Sequential architectures are reaching physical limitations as they are constrained by the speed of light and thermodynamics laws. The speed at which sequential CPUs can operate is reaching saturation point (no more vertical growth), and hence an alternative way to get high computational speed is to connect multiple CPUs (opportunity for horizontal growth).

- Hardware improvements in pipelining, superscalar, and the like are nonscalable and require sophisticated compiler technology. Developing such compiler technology is a difficult task.
- Vector processing works well for certain kinds of problems. It is suitable mostly for scientific problems (involving lots of matrix operations) and graphical processing. It is not useful for other areas, such as databases.
- The technology of parallel processing is mature and can be exploited commercially; there is already significant R&D work on development tools and environments.
- Significant development in networking technology is paving the way for heterogeneous computing.

2.3.2 Hardware architectures for parallel processing

The core elements of parallel processing are CPUs. Based on the number of instruction and data streams that can be processed simultaneously, computing systems are classified into the following four categories:

- Single-instruction, single-data (SISD) systems
- Single-instruction, multiple-data (SIMD) systems
- Multiple-instruction, single-data (MISD) systems
- Multiple-instruction, multiple-data (MIMD) systems

2.3.2.1 Single-instruction, single-data (SISD) systems

An SISD computing system is a uniprocessor machine capable of executing a single instruction, which operates on a single data stream (see Figure 2.2). In SISD, machine instructions are processed sequentially; hence computers adopting this model are popularly called *sequential computers*. Most conventional computers are built using the SISD model. All the instructions and data to be processed have to be stored in primary memory. The speed of the processing element in the SISD model is limited by the rate at which the computer can transfer information internally. Dominant representative SISD systems are IBM PC, Macintosh, and workstations.

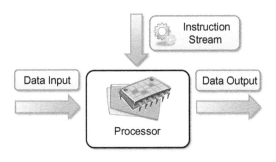

FIGURE 2.2

Single-instruction, single-data (SISD) architecture.

2.3.2.2 Single-instruction, multiple-data (SIMD) systems

An SIMD computing system is a multiprocessor machine capable of executing the same instruction on all the CPUs but operating on different data streams (see Figure 2.3). Machines based on an SIMD model are well suited to scientific computing since they involve lots of vector and matrix operations. For instance, statements such as

$$Ci = Ai * Bi$$

can be passed to all the processing elements (PEs); organized data elements of vectors A and B can be divided into multiple sets (N-sets for N PE systems); and each PE can process one data set. Dominant representative SIMD systems are Cray's vector processing machine and Thinking Machines' cm*.

2.3.2.3 Multiple-instruction, single-data (MISD) systems

An MISD computing system is a multiprocessor machine capable of executing different instructions on different PEs but all of them operating on the same data set (see Figure 2.4). For instance, statements such as

$$y = \sin(x) + \cos(x) + \tan(x)$$

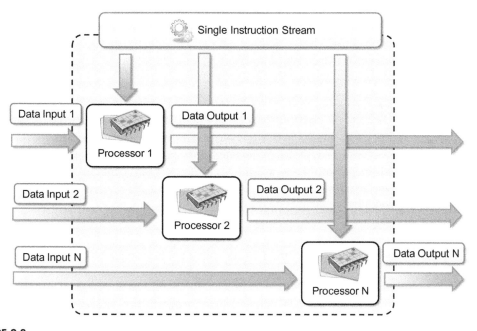

FIGURE 2.3

Single-instruction, multiple-data (SIMD) architecture.

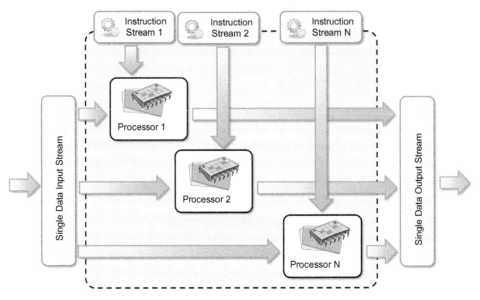

FIGURE 2.4

Multiple-instruction, single-data (MISD) architecture.

perform different operations on the same data set. Machines built using the MISD model are not useful in most of the applications; a few machines are built, but none of them are available commercially. They became more of an intellectual exercise than a practical configuration.

2.3.2.4 Multiple-instruction, multiple-data (MIMD) systems

An MIMD computing system is a multiprocessor machine capable of executing multiple instructions on multiple data sets (see Figure 2.5). Each PE in the MIMD model has separate instruction and data streams; hence machines built using this model are well suited to any kind of application. Unlike SIMD and MISD machines, PEs in MIMD machines work asynchronously.

MIMD machines are broadly categorized into shared-memory MIMD and distributed-memory MIMD based on the way PEs are coupled to the main memory.

Shared memory MIMD machines

In the *shared memory MIMD model*, all the PEs are connected to a single global memory and they all have access to it (see Figure 2.6). Systems based on this model are also called *tightly coupled multiprocessor systems*. The communication between PEs in this model takes place through the shared memory; modification of the data stored in the global memory by one PE is visible to all other PEs. Dominant representative shared memory MIMD systems are Silicon Graphics machines and Sun/IBM's SMP (Symmetric Multi-Processing).

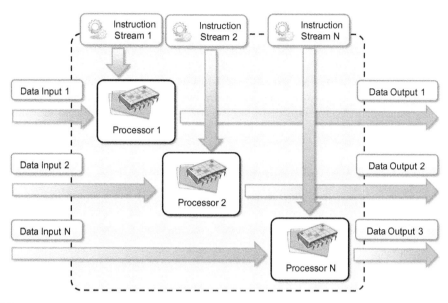

FIGURE 2.5

Multiple-instructions, multiple-data (MIMD) architecture.

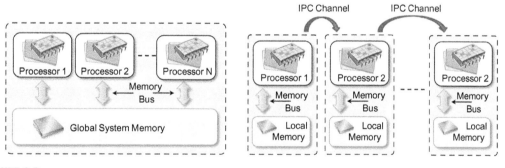

FIGURE 2.6

Shared (left) and distributed (right) memory MIMD architecture.

Distributed memory MIMD machines

In the *distributed memory MIMD model*, all PEs have a local memory. Systems based on this model are also called *loosely coupled multiprocessor systems*. The communication between PEs in this model takes place through the interconnection network (the interprocess communication channel, or IPC). The network connecting PEs can be configured to tree, mesh, cube, and so on. Each PE operates asynchronously, and if communication/synchronization among tasks is necessary, they can do so by exchanging messages between them.

The shared-memory MIMD architecture is easier to program but is less tolerant to failures and harder to extend with respect to the distributed memory MIMD model. Failures in a shared-memory MIMD affect the entire system, whereas this is not the case of the distributed model, in which each of the PEs can be easily isolated. Moreover, shared memory MIMD architectures are less likely to scale because the addition of more PEs leads to memory contention. This is a situation that does not happen in the case of distributed memory, in which each PE has its own memory. As a result, distributed memory MIMD architectures are most popular today.

2.3.3 Approaches to parallel programming

A sequential program is one that runs on a single processor and has a single line of control. To make many processors collectively work on a single program, the program must be divided into smaller independent chunks so that each processor can work on separate chunks of the problem. The program decomposed in this way is a parallel program.

A wide variety of parallel programming approaches are available. The most prominent among them are the following:

- Data parallelism
- Process parallelism
- Farmer-and-worker model

These three models are all suitable for task-level parallelism. In the case of data parallelism, the divide-and-conquer technique is used to split data into multiple sets, and each data set is processed on different PEs using the same instruction. This approach is highly suitable to processing on machines based on the SIMD model. In the case of process parallelism, a given operation has multiple (but distinct) activities that can be processed on multiple processors. In the case of the farmer-and-worker model, a job distribution approach is used: one processor is configured as master and all other remaining PEs are designated as slaves; the master assigns jobs to slave PEs and, on completion, they inform the master, which in turn collects results. These approaches can be utilized in different levels of parallelism.

2.3.4 Levels of parallelism

Levels of parallelism are decided based on the lumps of code (grain size) that can be a potential candidate for parallelism. Table 2.1 lists categories of code granularity for parallelism. All these approaches have a common goal: to boost processor efficiency by hiding latency. To conceal latency, there must be another thread ready to run whenever a lengthy operation occurs. The idea is to execute concurrently two or more single-threaded applications, such as compiling, text formatting, database searching, and device simulation.

As shown in the table and depicted in Figure 2.7, parallelism within an application can be detected at several levels:

- Large grain (or task level)
- Medium grain (or control level)

Table 2.1 Levels of Parallelism

Grain Size	Code Item	Parallelized By
Large	Separate and heavyweight process	Programmer
Medium	Function or procedure	Programmer
Fine	Loop or instruction block	Parallelizing compiler
Very fine	Instruction	Processor

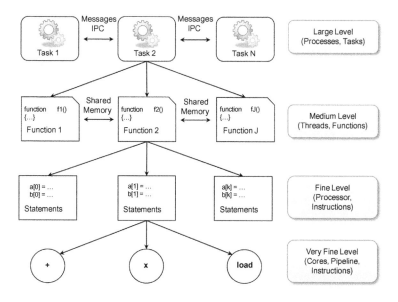

FIGURE 2.7

Levels of parallelism in an application.

- Fine grain (data level)
- Very fine grain (multiple-instruction issue)

In this book, we consider parallelism and distribution at the top two levels, which involve the distribution of the computation among multiple threads or processes.

2.3.5 **Laws of caution**

Now that we have introduced some general aspects of parallel computing in terms of architectures and models, we can make some considerations that have been drawn from experience designing and implementing such systems. These considerations are guidelines that can help us understand how much benefit an application or a software system can gain from parallelism. In particular, what we need to keep in mind is that parallelism is used to perform multiple activities together so that the system can increase its throughput or its speed. But the relations that control the increment of speed are not linear. For example, for a given n processors, the user expects speed to be increased by n times. This is an ideal situation, but it rarely happens because of the communication overhead.

Here are two important guidelines to take into account:

- Speed of computation is proportional to the square root of system cost; they never increase linearly. Therefore, the faster a system becomes, the more expensive it is to increase its speed (Figure 2.8).
- Speed by a parallel computer increases as the logarithm of the number of processors (i.e., $y = k*log(N)$). This concept is shown in Figure 2.9.

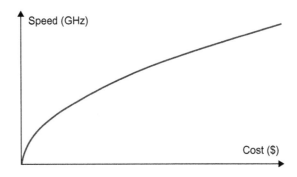

FIGURE 2.8

Cost versus speed.

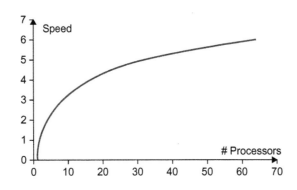

FIGURE 2.9

Number processors versus speed.

The very fast development in parallel processing and related areas has blurred conceptual boundaries, causing a lot of terminological confusion. Even well-defined distinctions such as shared memory and distributed memory are merging due to new advances in technology. There are no strict delimiters for contributors to the area of parallel processing. Hence, computer architects, OS designers, language designers, and computer network designers all have a role to play.

2.4 Elements of distributed computing

In the previous section, we discussed techniques and architectures that allow introduction of parallelism within a single machine or system and how parallelism operates at different levels of the computing stack. In this section, we extend these concepts and explore how multiple activities can be performed by leveraging systems composed of multiple heterogeneous machines and systems. We discuss what is generally referred to as *distributed computing* and more precisely introduce the most common guidelines and patterns for implementing distributed computing systems from the perspective of the software designer.

2.4.1 General concepts and definitions

Distributed computing studies the models, architectures, and algorithms used for building and managing distributed systems. As a general definition of the term *distributed system*, we use the one proposed by Tanenbaum et. al [1]:

> A distributed system is a collection of independent computers that appears to its users as a single coherent system.

This definition is general enough to include various types of distributed computing systems that are especially focused on unified usage and aggregation of distributed resources. In this chapter, we focus on the architectural models that are used to harness independent computers and present them as a whole coherent system. Communication is another fundamental aspect of distributed computing. Since distributed systems are composed of more than one computer that collaborate together, it is necessary to provide some sort of data and information exchange between them, which generally occurs through the network (Coulouris et al. [2]):

> A distributed system is one in which components located at networked computers communicate and coordinate their actions only by passing messages.

As specified in this definition, the components of a distributed system communicate with some sort of *message passing*. This is a term that encompasses several communication models.

2.4.2 Components of a distributed system

A distributed system is the result of the interaction of several components that traverse the entire computing stack from hardware to software. It emerges from the collaboration of several elements that—by working together—give users the illusion of a single coherent system. Figure 2.10 provides an overview of the different layers that are involved in providing the services of a distributed system.

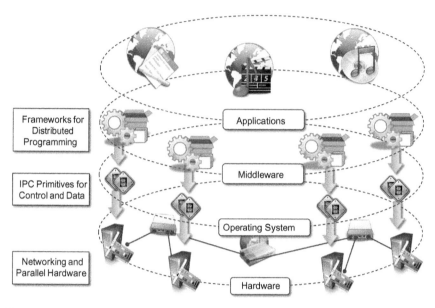

FIGURE 2.10

A layered view of a distributed system.

At the very bottom layer, computer and network hardware constitute the physical infrastructure; these components are directly managed by the operating system, which provides the basic services for interprocess communication (IPC), process scheduling and management, and resource management in terms of file system and local devices. Taken together these two layers become the platform on top of which specialized software is deployed to turn a set of networked computers into a distributed system.

The use of well-known standards at the operating system level and even more at the hardware and network levels allows easy harnessing of heterogeneous components and their organization into a coherent and uniform system. For example, network connectivity between different devices is controlled by standards, which allow them to interact seamlessly. At the operating system level, IPC services are implemented on top of standardized communication protocols such Transmission Control Protocol/Internet Protocol (TCP/IP), User Datagram Protocol (UDP) or others.

The middleware layer leverages such services to build a uniform environment for the development and deployment of distributed applications. This layer supports the programming paradigms for distributed systems, which we will discuss in Chapters 5–7 of this book. By relying on the services offered by the operating system, the middleware develops its own protocols, data formats, and programming language or frameworks for the development of distributed applications. All of them constitute a uniform interface to distributed application developers that is completely independent from the underlying operating system and hides all the heterogeneities of the bottom layers.

The top of the distributed system stack is represented by the applications and services designed and developed to use the middleware. These can serve several purposes and often expose their

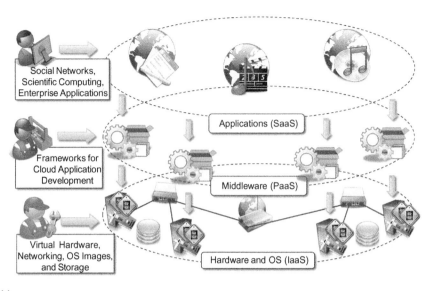

FIGURE 2.11

A cloud computing distributed system.

features in the form of graphical user interfaces (GUIs) accessible locally or through the Internet via a Web browser. For example, in the case of a cloud computing system, the use of Web technologies is strongly preferred, not only to interface distributed applications with the end user but also to provide platform services aimed at building distributed systems. A very good example is constituted by Infrastructure-as-a-Service (IaaS) providers such as Amazon Web Services (AWS), which provide facilities for creating virtual machines, organizing them together into a cluster, and deploying applications and systems on top. Figure 2.11 shows an example of how the general reference architecture of a distributed system is contextualized in the case of a cloud computing system.

Note that hardware and operating system layers make up the bare-bone infrastructure of one or more datacenters, where racks of servers are deployed and connected together through high-speed connectivity. This infrastructure is managed by the operating system, which provides the basic capability of machine and network management. The core logic is then implemented in the middleware that manages the virtualization layer, which is deployed on the physical infrastructure in order to maximize its utilization and provide a customizable runtime environment for applications. The middleware provides different facilities to application developers according to the type of services sold to customers. These facilities, offered through Web 2.0-compliant interfaces, range from virtual infrastructure building and deployment to application development and runtime environments.

2.4.3 Architectural styles for distributed computing

Although a distributed system comprises the interaction of several layers, the middleware layer is the one that enables distributed computing, because it provides a coherent and uniform runtime environment for applications. There are many different ways to organize the components that, taken together, constitute such an environment. The interactions among these components and their responsibilities give structure to the middleware and characterize its type or, in other words, define its architecture. Architectural styles [104] aid in understanding and classifying the organization of software systems in general and distributed computing in particular.

> *Architectural styles are mainly used to determine the vocabulary of components and connectors that are used as instances of the style together with a set of constraints on how they can be combined [105].*

Design patterns [106] help in creating a common knowledge within the community of software engineers and developers as to how to structure the relations of components within an application and understand the internal organization of software applications. Architectural styles do the same for the overall architecture of software systems. In this section, we introduce the most relevant architectural styles for distributed computing and focus on the components and connectors that make each style peculiar. Architectural styles for distributed systems are helpful in understanding the different roles of components in the system and how they are distributed across multiple machines. We organize the architectural styles into two major classes:

- Software architectural styles
- System architectural styles

The first class relates to the logical organization of the software; the second class includes all those styles that describe the physical organization of distributed software systems in terms of their major components.

2.4.3.1 Component and connectors

Before we discuss the architectural styles in detail, it is important to build an appropriate vocabulary on the subject. Therefore, we clarify what we intend for *components* and *connectors*, since these are the basic building blocks with which architectural styles are defined. A *component* represents a unit of software that encapsulates a function or a feature of the system. Examples of components can be programs, objects, processes, pipes, and filters. A *connector* is a communication mechanism that allows cooperation and coordination among components. Differently from components, connectors are not encapsulated in a single entity, but they are implemented in a distributed manner over many system components.

2.4.3.2 Software architectural styles

Software architectural styles are based on the logical arrangement of software components. They are helpful because they provide an intuitive view of the whole system, despite its physical deployment. They also identify the main abstractions that are used to shape the components of the system and the expected interaction patterns between them. According to Garlan and Shaw [105], architectural styles are classified as shown in Table 2.2.

These models constitute the foundations on top of which distributed systems are designed from a logical point of view, and they are discussed in the following sections.

Data centered architectures

These architectures identify the data as the fundamental element of the software system, and access to shared data is the core characteristic of the data-centered architectures. Therefore, especially

Table 2.2 Software Architectural Styles	
Category	**Most Common Architectural Styles**
Data-centered	Repository
	Blackboard
Data flow	Pipe and filter
	Batch sequential
Virtual machine	Rule-based system
	Interpreter
Call and return	Main program and subroutine call/top-down systems
	Object-oriented systems
	Layered systems
Independent components	Communicating processes
	Event systems

within the context of distributed and parallel computing systems, integrity of data is the overall goal for such systems.

The *repository* architectural style is the most relevant reference model in this category. It is characterized by two main components: the central data structure, which represents the current state of the system, and a collection of independent components, which operate on the central data. The ways in which the independent components interact with the central data structure can be very heterogeneous. In particular, repository-based architectures differentiate and specialize further into subcategories according to the choice of control discipline to apply for the shared data structure. Of particular interest are *databases* and *blackboard systems*. In the former group the dynamic of the system is controlled by the independent components, which, by issuing an operation on the central repository, trigger the selection of specific processes that operate on data. In blackboard systems, the central data structure is the main trigger for selecting the processes to execute.

The *blackboard* architectural style is characterized by three main components:

- *Knowledge sources.* These are the entities that update the knowledge base that is maintained in the blackboard.
- *Blackboard.* This represents the data structure that is shared among the knowledge sources and stores the knowledge base of the application.
- *Control.* The control is the collection of triggers and procedures that govern the interaction with the blackboard and update the status of the knowledge base.

Within this reference scenario, knowledge sources, which represent the intelligent agents sharing the blackboard, react opportunistically to changes in the knowledge base, almost in the same way that a group of specialists brainstorm in a room in front of a blackboard. Blackboard models have become popular and widely used for artificial intelligent applications in which the blackboard maintains the knowledge about a domain in the form of assertions and rules, which are entered by domain experts. These operate through a control shell that controls the problem-solving activity of the system. Particular and successful applications of this model can be found in the domains of speech recognition and signal processing.

Data-flow architectures

In the case of *data-flow* architectures, it is the availability of data that controls the computation. With respect to the data-centered styles, in which the access to data is the core feature, data-flow styles explicitly incorporate the pattern of *data flow*, since their design is determined by an orderly motion of data from component to component, which is the form of communication between them. Styles within this category differ in one of the following ways: how the control is exerted, the degree of concurrency among components, and the topology that describes the flow of data.

Batch Sequential Style. The batch sequential style is characterized by an ordered sequence of separate programs executing one after the other. These programs are chained together by providing as input for the next program the output generated by the last program after its completion, which is most likely in the form of a file. This design was very popular in the mainframe era of computing and still finds applications today. For example, many distributed applications for scientific computing are defined by jobs expressed as sequences of programs that, for example, pre-filter, analyze, and post-process data. It is very common to compose these phases using the batch-sequential style.

Pipe-and-Filter Style. The *pipe-and-filter style* is a variation of the previous style for expressing the activity of a software system as sequence of data transformations. Each component of the processing chain is called a *filter,* and the connection between one filter and the next is represented by a data stream. With respect to the batch sequential style, data is processed incrementally and each filter processes the data as soon as it is available on the input stream. As soon as one filter produces a consumable amount of data, the next filter can start its processing. Filters generally do not have state, know the identity of neither the previous nor the next filter, and they are connected with in-memory data structures such as first-in/first-out (FIFO) buffers or other structures. This particular sequencing is called *pipelining* and introduces concurrency in the execution of the filters. A classic example of this architecture is the microprocessor pipeline, whereby multiple instructions are executed at the same time by completing a different phase of each of them. We can identify the phases of the instructions as the filters, whereas the data streams are represented by the registries that are shared within the processors. Another example are the Unix shell pipes (i.e., *cat <file-name>| grep<pattern>| wc −l*), where the filters are the single shell programs composed together and the connections are their input and output streams that are chained together. Applications of this architecture can also be found in the compiler design (e.g., the lex/yacc model is based on a pipe of the following phases: *scanning | parsing | semantic analysis | code generation*), image and signal processing, and voice and video streaming.

Data-flow architectures are optimal when the system to be designed embodies a multistage process, which can be clearly identified into a collection of separate components that need to be orchestrated together. Within this reference scenario, components have well-defined interfaces exposing input and output ports, and the connectors are represented by the datastreams between these ports. The main differences between the two subcategories are reported in Table 2.3.

Virtual machine architectures

The virtual machine class of architectural styles is characterized by the presence of an abstract execution environment (generally referred as a *virtual machine*) that simulates features that are not available in the hardware or software. Applications and systems are implemented on top of this layer and become portable over different hardware and software environments as long as there is

Table 2.3 Comparison Between Batch Sequential and Pipe-and-Filter Styles

Batch Sequential	Pipe-and-Filter
Coarse grained	Fine grained
High latency	Reduced latency due to the incremental processing of input
External access to input	Localized input
No concurrency	Concurrency possible
Noninteractive	Interactivity awkward but possible

an implementation of the virtual machine they interface with. The general interaction flow for systems implementing this pattern is the following: the program (or the application) defines its operations and state in an abstract format, which is interpreted by the virtual machine engine. The interpretation of a program constitutes its execution. It is quite common in this scenario that the engine maintains an internal representation of the program state. Very popular examples within this category are rule-based systems, interpreters, and command-language processors.

Rule-Based Style. This architecture is characterized by representing the abstract execution environment as an *inference engine*. Programs are expressed in the form of rules or predicates that hold true. The input data for applications is generally represented by a set of assertions or facts that the inference engine uses to activate rules or to apply predicates, thus transforming data. The output can either be the product of the rule activation or a set of assertions that holds true for the given input data. The set of rules or predicates identifies the knowledge base that can be queried to infer properties about the system. This approach is quite peculiar, since it allows expressing a system or a domain in terms of its behavior rather than in terms of the components. Rule-based systems are very popular in the field of artificial intelligence. Practical applications can be found in the field of process control, where rule-based systems are used to monitor the status of physical devices by being fed from the sensory data collected and processed by PLCs[1] and by activating alarms when specific conditions on the sensory data apply. Another interesting use of rule-based systems can be found in the networking domain: *network intrusion detection systems (NIDS)* often rely on a set of rules to identify abnormal behaviors connected to possible intrusions in computing systems.

Interpreter Style. The core feature of the interpreter style is the presence of an engine that is used to interpret a pseudo-program expressed in a format acceptable for the interpreter. The interpretation of the pseudo-program constitutes the execution of the program itself. Systems modeled according to this style exhibit four main components: the interpretation engine that executes the core activity of this style, an internal memory that contains the pseudo-code to be interpreted, a representation of the current state of the engine, and a representation of the current state of the program being executed. This model is quite useful in designing virtual machines for high-level programming (Java, C#) and scripting languages (Awk, PERL, and so on). Within this scenario, the

---

[1]A *programmable logic controller* (PLC) is a digital computer that is used for automation or electromechanical processes. Differently from general-purpose computers, PLCs are designed to manage multiple input lines and produce several outputs. In particular, their physical design makes them robust to more extreme environmental conditions or shocks, thus making them fit for use in factory environments. PLCs are an example of a hard real-time system because they are expected to produce the output within a given time interval since the reception of the input.

virtual machine closes the gap between the end-user abstractions and the software/hardware environment in which such abstractions are executed.

Virtual machine architectural styles are characterized by an indirection layer between applications and the hosting environment. This design has the major advantage of decoupling applications from the underlying hardware and software environment, but at the same time it introduces some disadvantages, such as a slowdown in performance. Other issues might be related to the fact that, by providing a virtual execution environment, specific features of the underlying system might not be accessible.

Call & return architectures

This category identifies all systems that are organised into components mostly connected together by method calls. The activity of systems modeled in this way is characterized by a chain of method calls whose overall execution and composition identify the execution of one or more operations. The internal organization of components and their connections may vary. Nonetheless, it is possible to identify three major subcategories, which differentiate by the way the system is structured and how methods are invoked: top-down style, object-oriented style, and layered style.

Top-Down Style. This architectural style is quite representative of systems developed with imperative programming, which leads to a divide-and-conquer approach to problem resolution. Systems developed according to this style are composed of one large main program that accomplishes its tasks by invoking subprograms or procedures. The components in this style are procedures and subprograms, and connections are method calls or invocation. The calling program passes information with parameters and receives data from return values or parameters. Method calls can also extend beyond the boundary of a single process by leveraging techniques for remote method invocation, such as remote procedure call (RPC) and all its descendants. The overall structure of the program execution at any point in time is characterized by a tree, the root of which constitutes the main function of the principal program. This architectural style is quite intuitive from a design point of view but hard to maintain and manage in large systems.

Object-Oriented Style. This architectural style encompasses a wide range of systems that have been designed and implemented by leveraging the abstractions of object-oriented programming (OOP). Systems are specified in terms of classes and implemented in terms of objects. Classes define the type of components by specifying the data that represent their state and the operations that can be done over these data. One of the main advantages over the top-down style is that there is a coupling between data and operations used to manipulate them. Object instances become responsible for hiding their internal state representation and for protecting its integrity while providing operations to other components. This leads to a better decomposition process and more manageable systems. Disadvantages of this style are mainly two: each object needs to know the identity of an object if it wants to invoke operations on it, and shared objects need to be carefully designed in order to ensure the consistency of their state.

Layered Style. The layered system style allows the design and implementation of software systems in terms of layers, which provide a different level of abstraction of the system. Each layer generally operates with at most two layers: the one that provides a lower abstraction level and the one that provides a higher abstraction layer. Specific protocols and interfaces define how adjacent layers interact. It is possible to model such systems as a stack of layers, one for each level of abstraction. Therefore, the components are the layers and the connectors are the interfaces and protocols used between adjacent layers. A user or client generally interacts with the layer at the highest abstraction, which, in order to carry its activity, interacts and uses the services of the lower layer. This process is repeated (if necessary) until the lowest layer is reached. It is also possible to have the opposite behavior: events and callbacks from the lower layers can trigger the activity of the higher layer and propagate information up through the stack. The advantages of the layered style are that, as happens for the object-oriented style, it supports a modular design of systems and allows us to decompose the system according to different levels of abstractions by encapsulating together all the operations that belong to a specific level. Layers can be replaced as long as they are compliant with the expected protocols and interfaces, thus making the system flexible. The main disadvantage is constituted by the lack of extensibility, since it is not possible to add layers without changing the protocols and the interfaces between layers.[2] This also makes it complex to add operations. Examples of layered architectures are the modern operating system kernels and the International Standards Organization/Open Systems Interconnection (ISO/OSI) or the TCP/IP stack.

Architectural styles based on independent components

This class of architectural style models systems in terms of independent components that have their own life cycles, which interact with each other to perform their activities. There are two major categories within this class—communicating processes and event systems—which differentiate in the way the interaction among components is managed.

Communicating Processes. In this architectural style, components are represented by independent processes that leverage IPC facilities for coordination management. This is an abstraction that is quite suitable to modeling distributed systems that, being distributed over a network of computing nodes, are necessarily composed of several concurrent processes. Each of the processes provides other processes with services and can leverage the services exposed by the other processes. The conceptual organization of these processes and the way in which the communication happens vary according to the specific model used, either peer-to-peer or client/server.[3] Connectors are identified by IPC facilities used by these processes to communicate.

Event Systems. In this architectural style, the components of the system are loosely coupled and connected. In addition to exposing operations for data and state manipulation, each component also publishes (or announces) a collection of events with which other components can register. In general, other components provide a callback that will be executed when the event is activated. During the activity of a component, a specific runtime condition can activate one of the exposed events, thus triggering the execution of the callbacks registered with it. Event activation may be accompanied by contextual information that can be used in the callback to handle the event. This information can be passed as an argument to the callback or by using some shared repository between components. Event-based systems have become quite popular, and support for their implementation is provided either at the API level or the programming language level.[4] The main

---

[2]The only option given is to partition a layer into sublayers so that the external interfaces remain the same, but the internal architecture can be reorganized into different layers that can define different abstraction levels. From the point of view of the adjacent layer, the new reorganized layer still appears as a single block.

[3]The terms *client/server* and *peer-to-peer* will be further discussed in the next section.

[4]The *Observer* pattern [106] is a fundamental element of software designs, whereas programming languages such as C#, VB.NET, and other languages implemented for the *Common Language Infrastructure* [53] expose the *event* language constructs to model implicit invocation patterns.

advantage of such an architectural style is that it fosters the development of open systems: new modules can be added and easily integrated into the system as long as they have compliant interfaces for registering to the events. This architectural style solves some of the limitations observed for the top-down and object-oriented styles. First, the invocation pattern is implicit, and the connection between the caller and the callee is not hard-coded; this gives a lot of flexibility since addition or removal of a handler to events can be done without changes in the source code of applications. Second, the event source does not need to know the identity of the event handler in order to invoke the callback. The disadvantage of such a style is that it relinquishes control over system computation. When a component triggers an event, it does not know how many event handlers will be invoked and whether there are any registered handlers. This information is available only at runtime and, from a static design point of view, becomes more complex to identify the connections among components and to reason about the correctness of the interactions.

In this section, we reviewed the most popular software architectural styles that can be utilized as a reference for modeling the logical arrangement of components in a system. They are a subset of all the architectural styles; other styles can be found in [105].

2.4.3.3 System architectural styles

System architectural styles cover the physical organization of components and processes over a distributed infrastructure. They provide a set of reference models for the deployment of such systems and help engineers not only have a common vocabulary in describing the physical layout of systems but also quickly identify the major advantages and drawbacks of a given deployment and whether it is applicable for a specific class of applications. In this section, we introduce two fundamental reference styles: *client/server* and *peer-to-peer*.

Client/server

This architecture is very popular in distributed computing and is suitable for a wide variety of applications. As depicted in Figure 2.12, the client/server model features two major components: a *server* and a *client*. These two components interact with each other through a network connection using a given protocol. The communication is unidirectional: The client issues a request to the server, and after processing the request the server returns a response. There could be multiple client components issuing requests to a server that is passively waiting for them. Hence, the important operations in the client-server paradigm are *request*, *accept* (client side), and *listen* and *response* (server side).

The client/server model is suitable in many-to-one scenarios, where the information and the services of interest can be centralized and accessed through a single access point: the server. In general, multiple clients are interested in such services and the server must be appropriately designed to efficiently serve requests coming from different clients. This consideration has implications on both client design and server design. For the client design, we identify two major models:

- *Thin-client model.* In this model, the load of data processing and transformation is put on the server side, and the client has a light implementation that is mostly concerned with retrieving and returning the data it is being asked for, with no considerable further processing.

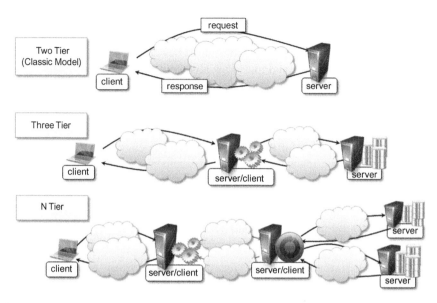

FIGURE 2.12

Client/server architectural styles.

- *Fat-client model.* In this model, the client component is also responsible for processing and transforming the data before returning it to the user, whereas the server features a relatively light implementation that is mostly concerned with the management of access to the data.

The three major components in the client-server model: presentation, application logic, and data storage. In the thin-client model, the client embodies only the presentation component, while the server absorbs the other two. In the fat-client model, the client encapsulates presentation and most of the application logic, and the server is principally responsible for the data storage and maintenance.

Presentation, application logic, and data maintenance can be seen as conceptual layers, which are more appropriately called *tiers*. The mapping between the conceptual layers and their physical implementation in modules and components allows differentiating among several types of architectures, which go under the name of *multitiered architectures.* Two major classes exist:

- *Two-tier architecture.* This architecture partitions the systems into two tiers, which are located one in the client component and the other on the server. The client is responsible for the presentation tier by providing a user interface; the server concentrates the application logic and the data store into a single tier. The server component is generally deployed on a powerful machine that is capable of processing user requests, accessing data, and executing the application logic to provide a client with a response. This architecture is suitable for systems of limited size and suffers from scalability issues. In particular, as the number of users increases the performance of the server might dramatically decrease. Another limitation is caused by the dimension of the data to maintain, manage, and access, which might be prohibitive for a single computation node or too large for serving the clients with satisfactory performance.

- *Three-tier architecture/N-tier architecture.* The three-tier architecture separates the presentation of data, the application logic, and the data storage into three tiers. This architecture is generalized into an *N*-tier model in case it is necessary to further divide the stages composing the application logic and storage tiers. This model is generally more scalable than the two-tier one because it is possible to distribute the tiers into several computing nodes, thus isolating the performance bottlenecks. At the same time, these systems are also more complex to understand and manage. A classic example of three-tier architecture is constituted by a medium-size Web application that relies on a relational database management system for storing its data. In this scenario, the client component is represented by a Web browser that embodies the presentation tier, whereas the application server encapsulates the business logic tier, and a database server machine (possibly replicated for high availability) maintains the data storage. Application servers that rely on third-party (or external) services to satisfy client requests are examples of *N*-tiered architectures.

The client/server architecture has been the dominant reference model for designing and deploying distributed systems, and several applications to this model can be found. The most relevant is perhaps the Web in its original conception. Nowadays, the client/server model is an important building block of more complex systems, which implement some of their features by identifying a server and a client process interacting through the network. This model is generally suitable in the case of a many-to-one scenario, where the interaction is unidirectional and started by the clients and suffers from scalability issues, and therefore it is not appropriate in very large systems.

Peer-to-peer

The peer-to-peer model, depicted in Figure 2.13, introduces a symmetric architecture in which all the components, called *peers*, play the same role and incorporate both client and server capabilities of the client/server model. More precisely, each peer acts as a *server* when it processes requests from other peers and as a *client* when it issues requests to other peers. With respect to the client/ server model that partitions the responsibilities of the IPC between server and clients, the peer-to-peer model attributes the same responsibilities to each component. Therefore, this model is quite suitable for highly decentralized architecture, which can scale better along the dimension of the number of peers. The disadvantage of this approach is that the management of the implementation of algorithms is more complex than in the client/server model.

The most relevant example of peer-to-peer systems [87] is constituted by file-sharing applications such as *Gnutella*, *BitTorrent*, and *Kazaa*. Despite the differences among these networks in coordinating nodes and sharing information on the files and their locations, all of them provide a user client that is at the same time a server providing files to other peers and a client downloading files from other peers. To address an incredibly large number of peers, different architectures have been designed that divert slightly from the peer-to-peer model. For example, in *Kazaa* not all the peers have the same role, and some of them are used to group the accessibility information of a group of peers. Another interesting example of peer-to-peer architecture is represented by the Skype network.

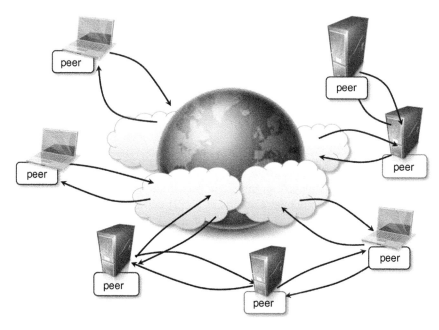

FIGURE 2.13

Peer-to-peer architectural style.

The system architectural styles presented in this section constitute a reference model that is further enhanced or diversified according to the specific needs of the application to be designed and implemented. For example, the client/server architecture, which originally included only two types of components, has been further extended and enriched by developing multitier architectures as the complexity of systems increased. Currently, this model is still the predominant reference architecture for distributed systems and applications. The *server* and *client* abstraction can be used in some cases to model the macro scale or the micro scale of the systems. For peer-to-peer systems, pure implementations are very hard to find and, as discussed for the case of *Kazaa*, evolutions of the model, which introduced some kind of hierarchy among the nodes, are common.

2.4.4 Models for interprocess communication

Distributed systems are composed of a collection of concurrent processes interacting with each other by means of a network connection. Therefore, IPC is a fundamental aspect of distributed systems design and implementation. IPC is used to either exchange data and information or coordinate the activity of processes. IPC is what ties together the different components of a distributed system, thus making them act as a single system. There are several different models in which processes can interact with each other; these map to different abstractions for IPC. Among the most relevant that we can mention are shared memory, remote procedure call (RPC), and message passing. At a lower level, IPC is realized through the fundamental tools of network programming. Sockets are the most popular IPC primitive for implementing communication channels between distributed processes.

They facilitate interaction patterns that, at the lower level, mimic the client/server abstraction and are based on a request-reply communication model. Sockets provide the basic capability of transferring a sequence of bytes, which is converted at higher levels into a more meaningful representation (such as procedure parameters or return values or messages). Such a powerful abstraction allows system engineers to concentrate on the logic-coordinating distributed components and the information they exchange rather than the networking details. These two elements identify the model for IPC. In this section, we introduce the most important reference model for architecting the communication among processes.

2.4.4.1 Message-based communication

The abstraction of *message* has played an important role in the evolution of the models and technologies enabling distributed computing. Couloris et al. [2] define a distributed system as "one in which components located at networked computers communicate and coordinate their actions only by passing messages." The term *message*, in this case, identifies any discrete amount of information that is passed from one entity to another. It encompasses any form of data representation that is limited in size and time, whereas this is an invocation to a remote procedure or a serialized object instance or a generic message. Therefore, the term *message-based communication model* can be used to refer to any model for IPC discussed in this section, which does not necessarily rely on the abstraction of data streaming.

Several distributed programming paradigms eventually use message-based communication despite the abstractions that are presented to developers for programming the interaction of distributed components. Here are some of the most popular and important:

- *Message passing.* This paradigm introduces the concept of a message as the main abstraction of the model. The entities exchanging information explicitly encode in the form of a message the data to be exchanged. The structure and the content of a message vary according to the model. Examples of this model are the *Message-Passing Interface (MPI)* and *OpenMP*.
- *Remote procedure call (RPC).* This paradigm extends the concept of procedure call beyond the boundaries of a single process, thus triggering the execution of code in remote processes. In this case, underlying client/server architecture is implied. A remote process hosts a server component, thus allowing client processes to request the invocation of methods, and returns the result of the execution. Messages, automatically created by the RPC implementation, convey the information about the procedure to execute along with the required parameters and the return values. The use of messages within this context is also referred as *marshaling* of parameters and return values.
- *Distributed objects.* This is an implementation of the RPC model for the object-oriented paradigm and contextualizes this feature for the remote invocation of methods exposed by objects. Each process registers a set of interfaces that are accessible remotely. Client processes can request a pointer to these interfaces and invoke the methods available through them. The underlying runtime infrastructure is in charge of transforming the local method invocation into a request to a remote process and collecting the result of the execution. The communication between the caller and the remote process is made through messages. With respect to the RPC model that is stateless by design, distributed object models introduce the complexity of object state management and lifetime. The methods that are remotely executed operate within the context of an instance, which may be created for the sole execution of the method, exist for a limited interval of time, or are

independent from the existence of requests. Examples of distributed object infrastructures are *Common Object Request Broker Architecture (CORBA), Component Object Model (COM, DCOM,* and *COM+), Java Remote Method Invocation (RMI),* and *.NET Remoting.*

- *Distributed agents and active objects.* Programming paradigms based on agents and active objects involve by definition the presence of instances, whether they are agents of objects, despite the existence of requests. This means that objects have their own control thread, which allows them to carry out their activity. These models often make explicit use of messages to trigger the execution of methods, and a more complex semantics is attached to the messages.
- *Web services.* Web service technology provides an implementation of the RPC concept over HTTP, thus allowing the interaction of components that are developed with different technologies. A Web service is exposed as a remote object hosted on a Web server, and method invocations are transformed in HTTP requests, opportunely packaged using specific protocols such as *Simple Object Access Protocol (SOAP)* or *Representational State Transfer (REST).*

It is important to observe that the concept of a message is a fundamental abstraction of IPC, and it is used either explicitly or implicitly. Messages' principal use—in any of the cases discussed—is to define interaction protocols among distributed components for coordinating their activity and exchanging data.

2.4.4.2 Models for message-based communication

We have seen how message-based communication constitutes a fundamental block for several distributed programming paradigms. Another important aspect characterizing the interaction among distributed components is the way these messages are exchanged and among how many components. In several cases, we identified the client/server model as the underlying reference model for the interaction. This, in its strictest form, represents a point-to-point communication model allowing a many-to-one interaction pattern. Variations of the client/server model allow for different interaction patterns. In this section, we briefly discuss the most important and recurring ones.

Point-to-point message model

This model organizes the communication among single components. Each message is sent from one component to another, and there is a direct addressing to identify the message receiver. In a point-to-point communication model it is necessary to know the location of or how to address another component in the system. There is no central infrastructure that dispatches the messages, and the communication is initiated by the message sender. It is possible to identify two major subcategories: direct communication and queue-based communication. In the former, the message is sent directly to the receiver and processed at the time of reception. In the latter, the receiver maintains a message queue in which the messages received are placed for later processing. The point-to-point message model is useful for implementing systems that are mostly based on one-to-one or many-to-one communication.

Publish-and-subscribe message model

This model introduces a different strategy, one that is based on notification among components. There are two major roles: the *publisher* and the *subscriber.* The former provides facilities for the latter to register its interest in a specific topic or event. Specific conditions holding true on the publisher side can trigger the creation of messages that are attached to a specific event. A message will be available to all the subscribers that registered for the corresponding event. There are two major strategies for dispatching the event to the subscribers:

- *Push strategy*. In this case it is the responsibility of the publisher to notify all the subscribers—for example, with a method invocation.
- *Pull strategy*. In this case the publisher simply makes available the message for a specific event, and it is responsibility of the subscribers to check whether there are messages on the events that are registered.

The publish-and-subscribe model is very suitable for implementing systems based on the one-to-many communication model and simplifies the implementation of indirect communication patterns. It is, in fact, not necessary for the publisher to know the identity of the subscribers to make the communication happen.

Request-reply message model

The request-reply message model identifies all communication models in which, for each message sent by a process, there is a reply. This model is quite popular and provides a different classification that does not focus on the number of the components involved in the communication but rather on how the dynamic of the interaction evolves. Point-to-point message models are more likely to be based on a request-reply interaction, especially in the case of direct communication. Publish-and-subscribe models are less likely to be based on request-reply since they rely on notifications.

The models presented here constitute a reference for structuring the communication among components in a distributed system. It is very uncommon that one single mode satisfies all the communication needs within a system. More likely, a composition of modes or their conjunct use in order to design and implement different aspects is the common case.

2.5 Technologies for distributed computing

In this section, we introduce relevant technologies that provide concrete implementations of interaction models, which mostly rely on message-based communication. They are remote procedure call (RPC), distributed object frameworks, and service-oriented computing.

2.5.1 Remote procedure call

RPC is the fundamental abstraction enabling the execution of procedures on client's request. RPC allows extending the concept of a procedure call beyond the boundaries of a process and a single memory address space. The called procedure and calling procedure may be on the same system or they may be on different systems in a network. The concept of RPC has been discussed since 1976 and completely formalized by Nelson [111] and Birrell [112] in the early 1980s. From there on, it has not changed in its major components. Even though it is a quite old technology, RPC is still used today as a fundamental component for IPC in more complex systems.

Figure 2.14 illustrates the major components that enable an RPC system. The system is based on a client/server model. The server process maintains a registry of all the available procedures that

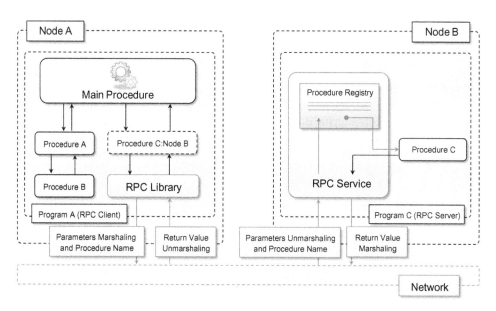

FIGURE 2.14

The RPC reference model.

can be remotely invoked and listens for requests from clients that specify which procedure to invoke, together with the values of the parameters required by the procedure. RPC maintains the synchronous pattern that is natural in IPC and function calls. Therefore, the calling process thread remains blocked until the procedure on the server process has completed its execution and the result (if any) is returned to the client.

An important aspect of RPC is *marshaling*, which identifies the process of converting parameter and return values into a form that is more suitable to be transported over a network through a sequence of bytes. The term *unmarshaling* refers to the opposite procedure. Marshaling and unmarshaling are performed by the RPC runtime infrastructure, and the client and server user code does not necessarily have to perform these tasks. The RPC runtime, on the other hand, is not only responsible for parameter packing and unpacking but also for handling the request-reply interaction that happens between the client and the server process in a completely transparent manner. Therefore, developing a system leveraging RPC for IPC consists of the following steps:

- Design and implementation of the server procedures that will be exposed for remote invocation.
- Registration of remote procedures with the RPC server on the node where they will be made available.
- Design and implementation of the client code that invokes the remote procedure(s).

Each RPC implementation generally provides client and server application programming interfaces (APIs) that facilitate the use of this simple and powerful abstraction. An important observation has to be made concerning the passing of parameters and return values. Since the server and the client processes are in two separate address spaces, the use of parameters passed by references or pointers is not suitable in this scenario, because once unmarshaled these will refer to a memory location that is not accessible from within the server process. Second, in user-defined parameters and return value types, it is necessary to ensure that the RPC runtime is able to marshal them. This is generally possible, especially when user-defined types are composed of simple types, for which marshaling is naturally provided.

RPC has been a dominant technology for IPC for quite a long time, and several programming languages and environments support this interaction pattern in the form of libraries and additional packages. For instance, RPyC is an RPC implementation for Python. There also exist platform-independent solutions such as XML-RPC and JSON-RPC, which provide RPC facilities over XML and JSON, respectively. Thrift [113] is the framework developed at Facebook for enabling a transparent cross-language RPC model. Currently, the term RPC implementations encompass a variety of solutions including frameworks such distributed object programming (CORBA, DCOM, Java RMI, and .NET Remoting) and Web services that evolved from the original RPC concept. We discuss the peculiarity of these approaches in the following sections.

2.5.2 Distributed object frameworks

Distributed object frameworks extend object-oriented programming systems by allowing objects to be distributed across a heterogeneous network and provide facilities so that they can coherently act as though they were in the same address space. Distributed object frameworks leverage the basic mechanism introduced with RPC and extend it to enable the remote invocation of object methods and to keep track of references to objects made available through a network connection.

With respect to the RPC model, the infrastructure manages instances that are exposed through well-known interfaces instead of procedures. Therefore, the common interaction pattern is the following:

1. The server process maintains a registry of active objects that are made available to other processes. According to the specific implementation, active objects can be published using interface definitions or class definitions.
2. The client process, by using a given addressing scheme, obtains a reference to the active remote object. This reference is represented by a pointer to an instance that is of a shared type of interface and class definition.
3. The client process invokes the methods on the active object by calling them through the reference previously obtained. Parameters and return values are marshaled as happens in the case of RPC.

Distributed object frameworks give the illusion of interaction with a local instance while invoking remote methods. This is done by a mechanism called a *proxy skeleton*. Figure 2.15 gives an overview of how this infrastructure works. Proxy and skeleton always constitute a pair: the server process maintains the skeleton component, which is in charge of executing the methods that are remotely invoked, while the client maintains the proxy component, allowing its hosting environment to remotely invoke methods through the proxy interface. The transparency of remote method invocation is achieved using one of the fundamental properties of object-oriented programming: inheritance and subclassing. Both the proxy and the active remote object expose the same interface, defining the set of methods that can be remotely called. On the client side, a runtime object subclassing the type published by the server is generated. This object translates the local method invocation into an RPC call

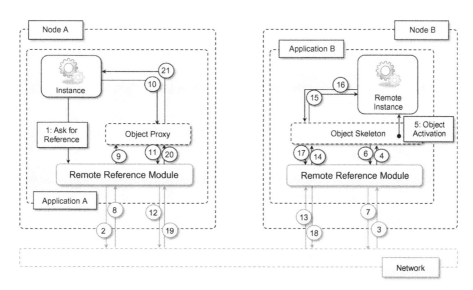

FIGURE 2.15

The distributed object programming model.

for the corresponding method on the remote active object. On the server side, whenever an RPC request is received, it is unpacked and the method call is dispatched to the skeleton that is paired with the client that issued the request. Once the method execution on the server is completed, the return values are packed and sent back to the client, and the local method call on the proxy returns.

Distributed object frameworks introduce objects as first-class entities for IPC. They are the principal gateway for invoking remote methods but can also be passed as parameters and return values. This poses an interesting problem, since object instances are complex instances that encapsulate a state and might be referenced by other components. Passing an object as a parameter or return value involves the duplication of the instance on the other execution context. This operation leads to two separate objects whose state evolves independently. The duplication becomes necessary since the instance needs to trespass the boundaries of the process. This is an important aspect to take into account in designing distributed object systems, because it might lead to inconsistencies. An alternative to this standard process, which is called *marshaling by value*, is *marshaling by reference*. In this second case the object instance is not duplicated and a proxy of it is created on the server side (for parameters) or the client side (for return values). Marshaling by reference is a more complex technique and generally puts more burden on the runtime infrastructure since remote references have to be tracked. Being more complex and resource demanding, marshaling by reference should be used only when duplication of parameters and return values lead to unexpected and inconsistent behavior of the system.

2.5.2.1 Object activation and lifetime

The management of distributed objects poses additional challenges with respect to the simple invocation of a procedure on a remote node. Methods live within the context of an object instance, and they can alter the internal state of the object as a side effect of their execution. In particular, the lifetime of an object instance is a crucial element in distributed object-oriented systems. Within a single memory address space scenario, objects are explicitly created by the programmer, and their references are made available by passing them from one object instance to another. The memory allocated for them can be explicitly reclaimed by the programmer or automatically by the runtime system when there are no more references to that instance. A distributed scenario introduces additional issues that require a different management of the lifetime of objects exposed through remote interfaces.

The first element to be considered is the object's *activation*, which is the creation of a remote object. Various strategies can be used to manage object activation, from which we can distinguish two major classes: *server-based activation* and *client-based activation*. In server-based activation, the active object is created in the server process and registered as an instance that can be exposed beyond process boundaries. In this case, the active object has a life of its own and occasionally executes methods as a consequence of a remote method invocation. In client-based activation the active object does not originally exist on the server side; it is created when a request for method invocation comes from a client. This scenario is generally more appropriate when the active object is meant to be stateless and should exist for the sole purpose of invoking methods from remote clients. For example, if the remote object is simply a gateway to access and modify other components hosted within the server process, client-based activation is a more efficient pattern.

The second element to be considered is the lifetime of remote objects. In the case of server-based activation, the lifetime of an object is generally user-controlled, since the activation of the remote object is explicit and controlled by the user. In the case of client-based activation, the creation of the remote object is implicit, and therefore its lifetime is controlled by some policy of the runtime infrastructure. Different policies can be considered; the simplest one implies the creation of a new instance for each method invocation. This solution is quite demanding in terms of object instances and is generally integrated with some lease management strategy that allows objects to be reused for subsequent method invocations if they occur within a specified time interval (lease). Another policy might consider having only a single instance at a time, and the lifetime of the object is then controlled by the number and frequency of method calls. Different frameworks provide different levels of control of this aspect.

Object activation and lifetime management are features that are now supported to some extent in almost all the frameworks for distributed object programming, since they are essential to understanding the behavior of a distributed system. In particular, these two aspects are becoming fundamental in designing components that are accessible from other processes and that maintain states. Understanding how many objects representing the same component are created and for how long they last is essential in tracking inconsistencies due to erroneous updates to the instance internal data.

2.5.2.2 Examples of distributed object frameworks

The support for distributed object programming has evolved over time, and today it is a common feature of mainstream programming languages such as C# and Java, which provide these capabilities as part of the base class libraries. This level of integration is a sign of the maturity of this technology, which originally was designed as a separate component that could be used in several programming languages. In this section, we briefly review the most relevant approaches to and technologies for distributed object programming.

Common object request broker architecture (CORBA)

CORBA is a specification introduced by the Object Management Group (OMG) for providing cross-platform and cross-language interoperability among distributed components. The specification was originally designed to provide an interoperation standard that could be effectively used at the industrial level. The current release of the CORBA specification is version 3.0 and currently the technology is not very popular, mostly because the development phase is a considerably complex task and the interoperability among components developed in different languages has never reached the proposed level of transparency. A fundamental component in the CORBA architecture is the *Object Request Broker (ORB)*, which acts as a central object bus. A CORBA object registers with the ORB the interface it is exposing, and clients can obtain a reference to that interface and invoke methods on it. The ORB is responsible for returning the reference to the client and managing all the low-level operations required to perform the remote method invocation. To simplify cross-platform interoperability, interfaces are defined in *Interface Definition Language (IDL)*, which provides a platform-independent specification of a component. An IDL specification is then translated into a *stub-skeleton* pair by specific CORBA compilers that generate the required client (stub) and server (skeleton) components in a specific programming language. These templates are completed with an appropriate implementation in the selected programming language. This allows CORBA components to be used across different runtime environment by simply using the stub and the skeleton that match the development language used. A specification meant to be used at the industry level, CORBA provides interoperability among different implementations of its runtime. In particular, at the lowest-level ORB implementations communicate with each other using the *Internet Inter-ORB Protocol (IIOP)*, which standardizes the interactions of different ORB implementations. Moreover, CORBA provides an additional level of abstraction and separates the ORB, which mostly deals with the networking among nodes, from the *Portable Object Adapter (POA)*, which is the runtime environment in which the skeletons are hosted and managed. Again, the interface of these two layers is clearly defined, thus giving more freedom and allowing different implementations to work together seamlessly.

Distributed component object model (DCOM/COM+)

DCOM, later integrated and evolved into COM+, is the solution provided by Microsoft for distributed object programming before the introduction of .NET technology. DCOM introduces a set of features allowing the use of COM components beyond the process boundaries. A COM object identifies a component that encapsulates a set of coherent and related operations; it was designed to be easily plugged into another application to leverage the features exposed through its interface. To support interoperability, COM standardizes a binary format, thus allowing the use of COM objects across different programming languages. DCOM enables such capabilities in a distributed environment by adding the required IPC support. The architecture of DCOM is quite similar to CORBA but simpler, since it does not aim to foster the same level of interoperability; its implementation is monopolized by Microsoft, which provides a single runtime environment. A DCOM server object can expose several interfaces, each representing a different behavior of the object. To invoke the methods exposed by the interface, clients obtain a pointer to that interface and use it as though it were a pointer to an object in the client's address space. The DCOM runtime is responsible for performing all the operations required to create this illusion. This technology provides a reasonable level of interoperability among Microsoft-based environments, and there are third-party implementations that allow the use of DCOM, even in Unix-based environments. Currently, even if still used in industry, this technology is no longer popular and has been replaced by other approaches, such as .NET Remoting and Web Services.

Java remote method invocation (RMI)

Java RMI is a standard technology provided by Java for enabling RPC among distributed Java objects. RMI defines an infrastructure allowing the invocation of methods on objects that are located on different Java Virtual Machines (JVMs) residing either on the local node or on a remote one. As with CORBA, RMI is based on the *stub-skeleton* concept. Developers define an interface extending *java.rmi.Remote* that defines the contract for IPC. Java allows only publishing interfaces while it relies on actual types for the server and client part implementation. A class implementing the previous interface represents the *skeleton* component that will be made accessible beyond the JVM boundaries. The *stub* is generated from the skeleton class definition using the *rmic* command-line tool. Once the *stub-skeleton* pair is prepared, an instance of the skeleton is registered with the RMI registry that maps URIs, through which instances can be reached, to the corresponding objects. The RMI registry is a separate component that keeps track of all the instances that can be reached on a node. Clients contact the RMI registry and specify a URI, in the form *rmi://host:port/ serviceName*, to obtain a reference to the corresponding object. The RMI runtime will automatically retrieve the class information for the stub component paired with the skeleton mapped with the given URI and return an instance of it properly configured to interact with the remote object. In the client code, all the services provided by the skeleton are accessed by invoking the methods defined in the remote interface. RMI provides a quite transparent interaction pattern. Once the development and deployment phases are completed and a reference to a remote object is obtained, the client code interacts with it as though it were a local instance, and RMI performs all the required operations to enable the IPC. Moreover, RMI also allows customizing the security that has to be applied for remote objects. This is done by leveraging the standard Java security infrastructure, which allows specifying policies defining the permissions attributed to the JVM hosting the remote object.

.NET remoting

Remoting is the technology allowing for IPC among .NET applications. It provides developers with a uniform platform for accessing remote objects from within any application developed in any of the languages supported by .NET. With respect to other distributed object technologies, Remoting is a fully customizable architecture that allows developers to control the transport protocols used to exchange information between the proxy and the remote object, the serialization format used to encode data, the lifetime of remote objects, and the server management of remote objects. Despite its modular and fully customizable architecture, Remoting allows a transparent interaction pattern with objects residing on different application domains. An application domain represents an isolated execution environment that can be accessible only through Remoting channels. A single process can host multiple application domains and must have at least one.

Remoting allows objects located in different application domains to interact in a completely transparent manner, whether the two domains are in the same process, in the same machine, or on different nodes. The reference architecture is based on the classic client/server model whereby the application domain hosting the remote object is the server and the application domain accessing it is the client. Developers define a class that inherits by *MarshalByRefObject*, the base class that provides the built-in facilities to obtain a reference of an instance from another application domain. Instances of types that do not inherit from *MarshalByRefObject* are copied across application domain boundaries. There is no need to manually generate a stub for a type that needs to be exposed remotely. The Remoting infrastructure will automatically provide all the required information to generate a proxy on a client application domain. To make a component accessible through Remoting requires the component to be registered with the Remoting runtime and mapping it to a specific URI in the form *scheme://host:port/ServiceName,* where *scheme* is generally TCP or HTTP. It is possible to use different strategies to publish the remote component: Developers can provide an instance of the type developed or simply the type information. When only the type information is provided, the activation of the object is automatic and client-based, and developers can control the lifetime of the objects by overriding the default behavior of *MarshalByRefObject.* To interact with a remote object, client application domains have to query the remote infrastructure by providing a URI identifying the remote object and they will obtain a proxy to the remote object. From there on, the interaction with the remote object is completely transparent. As happens for Java RMI, Remoting allows customizing the security measures applied for the execution of code triggered by Remoting calls.

These are the most popular technologies for enabling distributed object programming. CORBA is an industrial-standard technology for developing distributed systems spanning different platforms and vendors. The technology has been designed to be interoperable among a variety of implementations and languages. Java RMI and .NET Remoting are built-in infrastructures for IPC, serving the purpose of creating distributed applications based on a single technology: Java and .NET, respectively. With respect to CORBA, they are less complex to use and deploy but are not natively interoperable. By relying on a unified platform, both Java and .NET Remoting are very straightforward and intuitive and provide a transparent interaction pattern that naturally fits in the structure of the supported languages. Although the two architectures are similar, they have some minor differences: Java relies on an external component called *RMI registry* to locate remote objects and allows only the publication of interfaces, whereas .NET Remoting does not use a registry and allows developers to expose class types as well. Both technologies have been extensively used to develop distributed applications.

2.5.3 Service-oriented computing

Service-oriented computing organizes distributed systems in terms of *services*, which represent the major abstraction for building systems. Service orientation expresses applications and software systems as aggregations of services that are coordinated within a *service-oriented architecture (SOA).* Even though there is no designed technology for the development of service-oriented software systems, Web services are the *de facto* approach for developing SOA. Web services, the fundamental component enabling cloud computing systems, leverage the Internet as the main interaction channel between users and the system.

2.5.3.1 What is a service?

A *service* encapsulates a software component that provides a set of coherent and related functionalities that can be reused and integrated into bigger and more complex applications. The term *service* is a general abstraction that encompasses several different implementations using different technologies and protocols. Don Box [107] identifies four major characteristics that identify a service:

- *Boundaries are explicit.* A service-oriented application is generally composed of services that are spread across different domains, trust authorities, and execution environments. Generally, crossing such boundaries is costly; therefore, service invocation is explicit by design and often leverages message passing. With respect to distributed object programming, whereby remote method invocation is transparent, in a service-oriented computing environment the interaction with a service is explicit and the interface of a service is kept minimal to foster its reuse and simplify the interaction.
- *Services are autonomous.* Services are components that exist to offer functionality and are aggregated and coordinated to build more complex system. They are not designed to be part of a specific system, but they can be integrated in several software systems, even at the same time. With respect to object orientation, which assumes that the deployment of applications is atomic, service orientation considers this case an exception rather than the rule and puts the focus on the design of the service as an autonomous component. The notion of autonomy also affects the way services handle failures. Services operate in an unknown environment and interact with third-party applications. Therefore, minimal assumptions can be made concerning such environments: applications may fail without notice, messages can be malformed, and clients can be unauthorized. Service-oriented design addresses these issues by using transactions, durable queues, redundant deployment and failover, and administratively managed trust relationships among different domains.
- *Services share schema and contracts, not class or interface definitions.* Services are not expressed in terms of classes or interfaces, as happens in object-oriented systems, but they define themselves in terms of schemas and contracts. A service advertises a contract describing the structure of messages it can send and/or receive and additional constraint—if any—on their ordering. Because they are not expressed in terms of types and classes, services are more easily consumable in wider and heterogeneous environments. At the same time, a service orientation requires that contracts and schema remain stable over time, since it would be possible to propagate changes to all its possible clients. To address this issue, contracts and schema are defined in a way that allows services to evolve without breaking already deployed code. Technologies such as XML and SOAP provide the appropriate tools to support such features rather than class definition or an interface declaration.
- *Services compatibility is determined based on policy.* Service orientation separates structural compatibility from semantic compatibility. Structural compatibility is based on contracts and schema and can be validated or enforced by machine-based techniques. Semantic compatibility is expressed in the form of policies that define the capabilities and requirements for a service. Policies are organized in terms of expressions that must hold true to enable the normal operation of a service.

Today services constitute the most popular abstraction for designing complex and interoperable systems. Distributed systems are meant to be heterogeneous, extensible, and dynamic. By abstracting away from a specific implementation technology and platform, they provide a more efficient way to achieve integration. Furthermore, being designed as autonomous components, they can be more easily reused and aggregated. These features are not carved from a smart system design and implementation—as happens in the case of distributed object programming—but instead are part of the service characterization.

2.5.3.2 Service-oriented architecture (SOA)

SOA [20] is an architectural style supporting service orientation.[5] It organizes a software system into a collection of interacting services. SOA encompasses a set of design principles that structure system development and provide means for integrating components into a coherent and decentralized system. SOA-based computing packages functionalities into a set of interoperable services, which can be integrated into different software systems belonging to separate business domains.

There are two major roles within SOA: the *service provider* and the *service consumer*. The service provider is the maintainer of the service and the organization that makes available one or more services for others to use. To advertise services, the provider can publish them in a registry, together with a service contract that specifies the nature of the service, how to use it, the requirements for the service, and the fees charged. The service consumer can locate the service metadata in the registry and develop the required client components to bind and use the service. Service providers and consumers can belong to different organization bodies or business domains. It is very common in SOA-based computing systems that components play the roles of both service provider and service consumer. Services might aggregate information and data retrieved from other services or create workflows of services to satisfy the request of a given service consumer. This practice is known as *service orchestration*, which more generally describes the automated arrangement, coordination, and management of complex computer systems, middleware, and services. Another important interaction pattern is *service choreography*, which is the coordinated interaction of services without a single point of control.

SOA provides a reference model for architecting several software systems, especially enterprise business applications and systems. In this context, interoperability, standards, and service contracts play a fundamental role. In particular, the following guiding principles [108], which characterize SOA platforms, are winning features within an enterprise context:

- *Standardized service contract*. Services adhere to a given communication agreement, which is specified through one or more service description documents.
- *Loose coupling*. Services are designed as self-contained components, maintain relationships that minimize dependencies on other services, and only require being aware of each other. Service contracts will enforce the required interaction among services. This simplifies the flexible aggregation of services and enables a more agile design strategy that supports the evolution of the enterprise business.
- *Abstraction*. A service is completely defined by service contracts and description documents. They hide their logic, which is encapsulated within their implementation. The use of service description documents and contracts removes the need to consider the technical implementation

---

[5]This definition is given by the Open Group (www.opengroup.org), which is a vendor- and technology-neutral consortium that includes over 300 member organizations. Its activities include management, innovation, research, standards, certification, and test development. The Open Group is most popular as a certifying body for the UNIX trademark, since it is also the creator of the official definition of a UNIX system. The documentation and the standards related to SOA can be found at the following address: www.opengroup.org/soa/soa/def.htm.

details and provides a more intuitive framework to define software systems within a business context.

- *Reusability.* Designed as components, services can be reused more effectively, thus reducing development time and the associated costs. Reusability allows for a more agile design and cost-effective system implementation and deployment. Therefore, it is possible to leverage third-party services to deliver required functionality by paying an appropriate fee rather developing the same capability in-house.
- *Autonomy.* Services have control over the logic they encapsulate and, from a service consumer point of view, there is no need to know about their implementation.
- *Lack of state.* By providing a stateless interaction pattern (at least in principle), services increase the chance of being reused and aggregated, especially in a scenario in which a single service is used by multiple consumers that belong to different administrative and business domains.
- *Discoverability.* Services are defined by description documents that constitute supplemental metadata through which they can be effectively discovered. Service discovery provides an effective means for utilizing third-party resources.
- *Composability.* Using services as building blocks, sophisticated and complex operations can be implemented. Service orchestration and choreography provide a solid support for composing services and achieving business goals.

Together with these principles, other resources guide the use of SOA for *enterprise application integration (EAI)*. The SOA manifesto[6] integrates the previously described principles with general considerations about the overall goals of a service-oriented approach to enterprise application software design and what is valued in SOA. Furthermore, modeling frameworks and methodologies, such as the *Service-Oriented Modeling Framework (SOMF)* [110] and reference architectures introduced by *the Organization for Advancement of Structured Information Standards (OASIS)* [110], provide means for effectively realizing service-oriented architectures.

SOA can be realized through several technologies. The first implementations of SOA have leveraged distributed object programming technologies such as CORBA and DCOM. In particular, CORBA has been a suitable platform for realizing SOA systems because it fosters interoperability among different implementations and has been designed as a specification supporting the development of industrial applications. Nowadays, SOA is mostly realized through Web services technology, which provides an interoperable platform for connecting systems and applications.

2.5.3.3 Web services

Web services [21] are the prominent technology for implementing SOA systems and applications. They leverage Internet technologies and standards for building distributed systems. Several aspects make Web services the technology of choice for SOA. First, they allow for interoperability across different platforms and programming languages. Second, they are based on well-known and vendor-independent standards such as HTTP, SOAP [23], XML, and WSDL [22]. Third, they provide an intuitive and simple way to connect heterogeneous software systems, enabling the quick

---

[6]The SOA manifesto is a document authored by 17 practitioners of SOA that defines guidelines and principles for designing and architecting software systems using a service orientation. The document is available online at: www.soa-manifesto.org.

composition of services in a distributed environment. Finally, they provide the features required by enterprise business applications to be used in an industrial environment. They define facilities for enabling service discovery, which allows system architects to more efficiently compose SOA applications, and service metering to assess whether a specific service complies with the contract between the service provider and the service consumer.

The concept behind a Web service is very simple. Using as a basis the object-oriented abstraction, a Web service exposes a set of operations that can be invoked by leveraging Internet-based protocols. Method operations support parameters and return values in the form of complex and simple types. The semantics for invoking Web service methods is expressed through interoperable standards such as XML and WSDL, which also provide a complete framework for expressing simple and complex types in a platform-independent manner. Web services are made accessible by being hosted in a Web server; therefore, HTTP is the most popular transport protocol used for interacting with Web services. Figure 2.16 describes the common-use case scenarios for Web services.

System architects develop a Web service with their technology of choice and deploy it in compatible Web or application servers. The service description document, expressed by means of Web Service Definition Language (WSDL), can be either uploaded to a global registry or attached as a metadata to the service itself. Service consumers can look up and discover services in global catalogs using Universal Description Discovery and Integration (UDDI) or, most likely, directly retrieve the service metadata by interrogating the Web service first. The Web service description document allows service consumers to automatically generate clients for the given service and embed them in their existing application. Web services are now extremely popular, so bindings

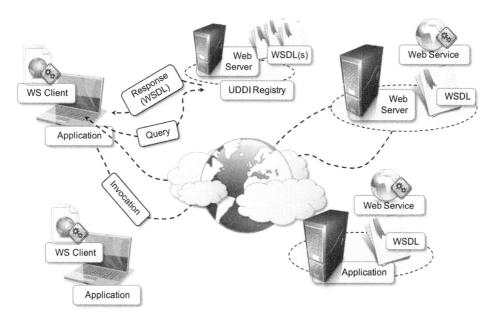

FIGURE 2.16

A Web services interaction reference scenario.

exist for any mainstream programming language in the form of libraries or development support tools. This makes the use of Web services seamless and straightforward with respect to technologies such as CORBA that require much more integration effort. Moreover, being interoperable, Web services constitute a better solution for SOA with respect to several distributed object frameworks, such as .NET Remoting, Java RMI, and DCOM/COM+ , which limit their applicability to a single platform or environment.

Besides the main function of enabling remote method invocation by using Web-based and interoperable standards, Web services encompass several technologies that put together and facilitate the integration of heterogeneous applications and enable service-oriented computing. Figure 2.17 shows the Web service technologies stack that lists all the components of the conceptual framework describing and enabling the Web services abstraction. These technologies cover all the aspects that allow Web services to operate in a distributed environment, from the specific requirements for the networking to the discovery of services. The backbone of all these technologies is XML, which is also one of the causes of Web services' popularity and ease of use. XML-based languages are used to manage the low-level interaction for Web service method calls (SOAP), for providing metadata about the services (WSDL), for discovery services (UDDI), and other core operations. In practice, the core components that enable Web services are SOAP and WSDL.

Simple Object Access Protocol (SOAP) [23], an XML-based language for exchanging structured information in a platform-independent manner, constitutes the protocol used for Web service method invocation. Within a distributed context leveraging the Internet, SOAP is considered an application layer protocol that leverages the transport level, most commonly HTTP, for IPC. SOAP structures the interaction in terms of messages that are XML documents mimicking the structure of a letter, with an envelope, a header, and a body. The envelope defines the boundaries of the SOAP message. The header is optional and contains relevant information on how to process the message. In addition, it contains information such as routing and delivery settings, authentication and authorization assertions, and transaction contexts. The body contains the actual message to be processed.

The main uses of SOAP messages are method invocation and result retrieval. Figure 2.18 shows an example of a SOAP message used to invoke a Web service method that retrieves the price of a

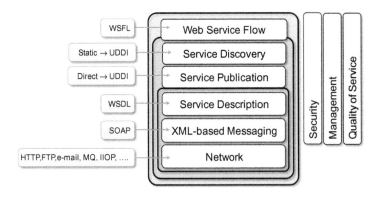

FIGURE 2.17

A Web services technologies stack.

```
POST /InStock HTTP/1.1
Host: www.stocks.com
Content-Type: application/soap+xml; charset=utf-8
Content-Length: <Size>

<?xml version="1.0">
```

```
<soap:Envelope xmlns:soap="http//www.w3.org/2001/12/soap-envelope"
  soap:encondingStyle="http//www.w3.org/2001/12/soap-encoding">

  <soap:Header></soap:Header>

  <soap:Body xmlns:m=http://www.stocks.org/stock>
   <m:GetStockPrice>
    <m:StockName>IBM<m:StockName>
   </m:GetStockPrice>
  </soap:Body>

</soap:Envelope>
```

Envelope

Header: Metadata & Assertions

Body: Method Call

```
POST /InStock HTTP/1.1
Host: www.stocks.com
Content-Type: application/soap+xml; charset=utf-8
Content-Length: <Size>

<?xml version="1.0">
```

```
<soap:Envelope xmlns:soap="http//www.w3.org/2001/12/soap-envelope"
  soap:encondingStyle="http//www.w3.org/2001/12/soap-encoding">

  <soap:Header></soap:Header>

  <soap:Body xmlns:m=http://www.stocks.org/stock>
   <m:GetStockPriceResponse>
    <m:Price>34.5<m:Price>
   </m:GetStockPriceResponse>
  </soap:Body>

</soap:Envelope>
```

Envelope

Header: Metadata & Assertions

Body: Execution Result

FIGURE 2.18

SOAP messages for Web service method invocation.

given stock and the corresponding reply. Despite the fact that XML documents are easy to produce and process in any platform or programming language, SOAP has often been considered quite inefficient because of the excessive use of markup that XML imposes for organizing the information into a well-formed document. Therefore, lightweight alternatives to the SOAP/XML pair have been proposed to support Web services. The most relevant alternative is *Representational State Transfer*

(REST), which provides a model for designing network-based software systems utilizing the client/ server model and leverages the facilities provided by HTTP for IPC without additional burden.

In a *RESTful* system, a client sends a request over HTTP using the standard HTTP methods (*PUT, GET, POST,* and *DELETE*), and the server issues a response that includes the representation of the resource. By relying on this minimal support, it is possible to provide whatever it needed to replace the basic and most important functionality provided by SOAP, which is method invocation. The GET, PUT, POST, and DELETE methods constitute a minimal set of operations for retrieving, adding, modifying, and deleting data. Together with an appropriate URI organization to identify resources, all the atomic operations required by a Web service are implemented. The content of data is still transmitted using XML as part of the HTTP content, but the additional markup required by SOAP is removed. For this reason, REST represents a lightweight alternative to SOAP, which works effectively in contexts where additional aspects beyond those manageable through HTTP are absent. One of them is security; *RESTful* Web services operate in an environment where no additional security beyond the one supported by HTTP is required. This is not a great limitation, and *RESTful* Web services are quite popular and used to deliver functionalities at enterprise scale: *Twitter, Yahoo!* (search APIs, maps, photos, etc), *Flickr,* and *Amazon.com* all leverage REST.

Web Service Description Language (WSDL) [22] is an XML-based language for the description of Web services. It is used to define the interface of a Web service in terms of methods to be called and types and structures of the required parameters and return values. In Figure 2.18 we notice that the SOAP messages for invoking the *GetStockPrice* method and receiving the result do not have any information about the type and structure of the parameters and the return values. This information is stored within the WSDL document attached to the Web service. Therefore, Web service consumer applications already know which types of parameters are required and how to interpret results. As an XML-based language, WSDL allows for the automatic generation of Web service clients that can be easily embedded into existing applications. Moreover, XML is a platform- and language-independent specification, so clients for web services can be generated for any language that is capable of interpreting XML data. This is a fundamental feature that enables Web service interoperability and one of the reasons that make such technology a solution of choice for SOA.

Besides those directly supporting Web services, other technologies that characterize Web 2.0 [27] provide and contribute to enrich and empower Web applications and then SOA-based systems. These fall under the names of *Asynchronous JavaScript and XML (AJAX), JavaScript Standard Object Notation (JSON),* and others. AJAX is a conceptual framework based on JavaScript and XML that enables asynchronous behavior in Web applications by leveraging the computing capabilities of modern Web browsers. This transforms simple Web pages in full-fledged applications, thus enriching the user experience. AJAX uses XML to exchange data with Web services and applications; an alternative to XML is JSON, which allows representing objects and collections of objects in a platform-independent manner. Often it is preferred to transmit data in a AJAX context because, compared to XML, it is a lighter notation and therefore allows transmitting the same amount of information in a more concise form.

2.5.3.4 Service orientation and cloud computing

Web services and Web 2.0-related technologies constitute a fundamental building block for cloud computing systems and applications. Web 2.0 applications are the front end of cloud computing systems, which deliver services either via Web service or provide a profitable interaction with

AJAX-based clients. Essentially, cloud computing fosters the vision of *Everything as a Service (XaaS)*: infrastructure, platform, services, and applications. The entire IT computing stack—from infrastructure to applications—can be composed by relying on cloud computing services. Within this context, SOA is a winning approach because it encompasses design principles to structure, compose, and deploy software systems in terms of services. Therefore, a service orientation constitutes a natural approach to shaping cloud computing systems because it provides a means to flexibly compose and integrate additional capabilities into existing software systems. Cloud computing is also used to elastically scale and empower existing software applications on demand. Service orientation fosters interoperability and leverages platform-independent technologies by definition. Within this context, it constitutes a natural solution for solving integration issues and favoring cloud computing adoption.

SUMMARY

In this chapter, we provided an introduction to parallel and distributed computing as a foundation for better understanding cloud computing. Parallel and distributed computing emerged as a solution for solving complex/"grand challenge" problems by first using multiple processing elements and then multiple computing nodes in a network. The transition from sequential to parallel and distributed processing offers high performance and reliability for applications. But it also introduces new challenges in terms of hardware architectures, technologies for interprocess communication, and algorithms and system design. We discussed the evolution of technologies supporting parallel processing and introduced the major reference models for designing and implementing distributed systems.

Parallel computing introduces models and architectures for performing multiple tasks within a single computing node or a set of tightly coupled nodes with homogeneous hardware. Parallelism is achieved by leveraging hardware capable of processing multiple instructions in parallel. Different architectures exploit parallelism to increase the performance of a computing system, depending on whether parallelism is realized on data, instructions, or both. The development of parallel applications often requires specific environments and compilers that provide transparent access to the advanced capabilities of the underlying architectures.

Unification of parallel and distributed computing allows one to harness a set of networked and heterogeneous computers and present them as a unified resource. Distributed systems constitute a large umbrella under which several different software systems are classified. Architectural styles help categorize and provide reference models for distributed systems. More precisely, software architectural styles define logical organizations of components and their roles, whereas system architectural styles are more concerned with the physical deployment of such systems. We have briefly reviewed the major reference software architectural styles and discussed the most important system architectural styles: the client/server and peer-to-peer models. These two styles are the fundamental deployment blocks of any distributed system. In particular, the client/server model is the foundation of the most popular interaction patterns among components within a distributed system.

Interprocess communication (IPC) is a fundamental element in distributed systems; it is the element that ties together separate processes and allows them to be seen as a whole. Message-based communication is the most relevant abstraction for IPC and forms the basis for several different techniques for IPC: remote procedure calls, distributed objects, and services. We reviewed the reference models that are used to organize the communication within the components of a distributed system and presented the major features of each of the abstractions.

Cloud computing leverages these models, abstractions, and technologies and provides a more efficient way to design and use distributed systems by making entire systems or components available on demand.

Review questions

1. What is the difference between parallel and distributed computing?
2. Identify the reasons that parallel processing constitutes an interesting option for computing.
3. What is an SIMD architecture?
4. List the major categories of parallel computing systems.
5. Describe the different levels of parallelism that can be obtained in a computing system.
6. What is a distributed system? What are the components that characterize it?
7. What is an architectural style, and what is its role in the context of a distributed system?
8. List the most important software architectural styles.
9. What are the fundamental system architectural styles?
10. What is the most relevant abstraction for interprocess communication in a distributed system?
11. Discuss the most important model for message-based communication.
12. Discuss RPC and how it enables interprocess communication.
13. What is the difference between distributed objects and RPC?
14. What are object activation and lifetime? How do they affect the consistency of state within a distributed system?
15. What are the most relevant technologies for distributed objects programming?
16. Discuss CORBA.
17. What is service-oriented computing?
18. What is market-oriented cloud computing?
19. What is SOA?
20. Discuss the most relevant technologies supporting service computing.

Virtualization

Virtualization technology is one of the fundamental components of cloud computing, especially in regard to infrastructure-based services. Virtualization allows the creation of a secure, customizable, and isolated execution environment for running applications, even if they are untrusted, without affecting other users' applications. The basis of this technology is the ability of a computer program—or a combination of software and hardware—to emulate an executing environment separate from the one that hosts such programs. For example, we can run Windows OS on top of a virtual machine, which itself is running on Linux OS. Virtualization provides a great opportunity to build elastically scalable systems that can provision additional capability with minimum costs. Therefore, virtualization is widely used to deliver customizable computing environments on demand.

This chapter discusses the fundamental concepts of virtualization, its evolution, and various models and technologies used in cloud computing environments.

3.1 Introduction

Virtualization is a large umbrella of technologies and concepts that are meant to provide an abstract environment—whether virtual hardware or an operating system—to run applications. The term *virtualization* is often synonymous with *hardware virtualization*, which plays a fundamental role in efficiently delivering *Infrastructure-as-a-Service* (IaaS) solutions for cloud computing. In fact, virtualization technologies have a long trail in the history of computer science and have been available in many flavors by providing virtual environments at the operating system level, the programming language level, and the application level. Moreover, virtualization technologies provide a virtual environment for not only executing applications but also for storage, memory, and networking.

Since its inception, virtualization has been sporadically explored and adopted, but in the last few years there has been a consistent and growing trend to leverage this technology. Virtualization technologies have gained renewed interested recently due to the confluence of several phenomena:

- *Increased performance and computing capacity.* Nowadays, the average end-user desktop PC is powerful enough to meet almost all the needs of everyday computing, with extra capacity that is rarely used. Almost all these PCs have resources enough to host a virtual machine manager and execute a virtual machine with by far acceptable performance. The same consideration applies to the high-end side of the PC market, where supercomputers can provide immense compute power that can accommodate the execution of hundreds or thousands of virtual machines.
- *Underutilized hardware and software resources.* Hardware and software underutilization is occurring due to (1) increased performance and computing capacity, and (2) the effect of

limited or sporadic use of resources. Computers today are so powerful that in most cases only a fraction of their capacity is used by an application or the system. Moreover, if we consider the IT infrastructure of an enterprise, many computers are only partially utilized whereas they could be used without interruption on a 24/7/365 basis. For example, desktop PCs mostly devoted to office automation tasks and used by administrative staff are only used during work hours, remaining completely unused overnight. Using these resources for other purposes after hours could improve the efficiency of the IT infrastructure. To transparently provide such a service, it would be necessary to deploy a completely separate environment, which can be achieved through virtualization.

- *Lack of space.* The continuous need for additional capacity, whether storage or compute power, makes data centers grow quickly. Companies such as Google and Microsoft expand their infrastructures by building data centers as large as football fields that are able to host thousands of nodes. Although this is viable for IT giants, in most cases enterprises cannot afford to build another data center to accommodate additional resource capacity. This condition, along with hardware underutilization, has led to the diffusion of a technique called *server consolidation*,[1] for which virtualization technologies are fundamental.

- *Greening initiatives.* Recently, companies are increasingly looking for ways to reduce the amount of energy they consume and to reduce their carbon footprint. Data centers are one of the major power consumers; they contribute consistently to the impact that a company has on the environment. Maintaining a data center operation not only involves keeping servers on, but a great deal of energy is also consumed in keeping them cool. Infrastructures for cooling have a significant impact on the carbon footprint of a data center. Hence, reducing the number of servers through server consolidation will definitely reduce the impact of cooling and power consumption of a data center. Virtualization technologies can provide an efficient way of consolidating servers.

- *Rise of administrative costs.* Power consumption and cooling costs have now become higher than the cost of IT equipment. Moreover, the increased demand for additional capacity, which translates into more servers in a data center, is also responsible for a significant increment in administrative costs. Computers—in particular, servers—do not operate all on their own, but they require care and feeding from system administrators. Common system administration tasks include hardware monitoring, defective hardware replacement, server setup and updates, server resources monitoring, and backups. These are labor-intensive operations, and the higher the number of servers that have to be managed, the higher the administrative costs. Virtualization can help reduce the number of required servers for a given workload, thus reducing the cost of the administrative personnel.

These can be considered the major causes for the diffusion of hardware virtualization solutions as well as the other kinds of virtualization. The first step toward consistent adoption of virtualization technologies was made with the wide spread of virtual machine-based programming languages: In 1995 Sun released Java, which soon became popular among developers. The ability to integrate small Java applications, called *applets*, made Java a very successful platform, and with the

---

[1]Server consolidation is a technique for aggregating multiple services and applications originally deployed on different servers on one physical server. Server consolidation allows us to reduce the power consumption of a data center and resolve hardware underutilization.

beginning of the new millennium Java played a significant role in the application server market segment, thus demonstrating that the existing technology was ready to support the execution of managed code for enterprise-class applications. In 2002 Microsoft released the first version of .NET Framework, which was Microsoft's alternative to the Java technology. Based on the same principles as Java, able to support multiple programming languages, and featuring complete integration with other Microsoft technologies, .NET Framework soon became the principal development platform for the Microsoft world and quickly became popular among developers. In 2006, two of the three "official languages" used for development at Google, Java and Python, were based on the virtual machine model. This trend of shifting toward virtualization from a programming language perspective demonstrated an important fact: The technology was ready to support virtualized solutions without a significant performance overhead. This paved the way to another and more radical form of virtualization that now has become a fundamental requisite for any data center management infrastructure.

3.2 Characteristics of virtualized environments

Virtualization is a broad concept that refers to the creation of a virtual version of something, whether hardware, a software environment, storage, or a network. In a virtualized environment there are three major components: *guest*, *host*, and *virtualization layer*. The *guest* represents the system component that interacts with the virtualization layer rather than with the host, as would normally happen. The *host* represents the original environment where the guest is supposed to be managed. The *virtualization layer* is responsible for recreating the same or a different environment where the guest will operate (see Figure 3.1).

Such a general abstraction finds different applications and then implementations of the virtualization technology. The most intuitive and popular is represented by *hardware virtualization*, which also constitutes the original realization of the virtualization concept.[2] In the case of hardware virtualization, the guest is represented by a system image comprising an operating system and installed applications. These are installed on top of virtual hardware that is controlled and managed by the virtualization layer, also called the *virtual machine manager*. The host is instead represented by the physical hardware, and in some cases the operating system, that defines the environment where the virtual machine manager is running. In the case of virtual storage, the guest might be client applications or users that interact with the virtual storage management software deployed on top of the real storage system. The case of virtual networking is also similar: The guest—applications and users—interacts with a virtual network, such as a *virtual private network (VPN)*, which is managed by specific software (VPN client) using the physical network available on the node. VPNs are useful for creating the illusion of being within a different physical network and thus accessing the resources in it, which would otherwise not be available.

---

[2]Virtualization is a technology that was initially developed during the mainframe era. The IBM CP/CMS mainframes were the first systems to introduce the concept of hardware virtualization and hypervisors. These systems, able to run multiple operating systems at the same time, provided a backward-compatible environment that allowed customers to run previous versions of their applications.

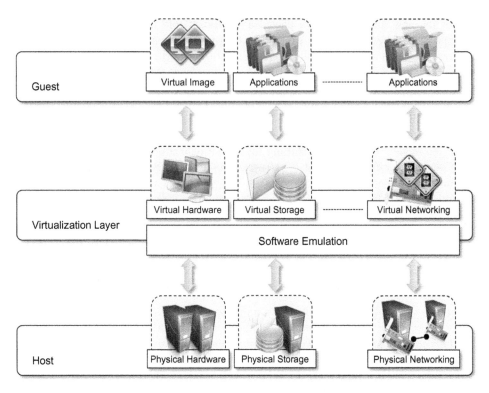

FIGURE 3.1

The virtualization reference model.

The main common characteristic of all these different implementations is the fact that the virtual environment is created by means of a *software program*. The ability to use software to emulate such a wide variety of environments creates a lot of opportunities, previously less attractive because of excessive overhead introduced by the virtualization layer. The technologies of today allow profitable use of virtualization and make it possible to fully exploit the advantages that come with it. Such advantages have always been characteristics of virtualized solutions.

3.2.1 Increased security

The ability to control the execution of a guest in a completely transparent manner opens new possibilities for delivering a secure, controlled execution environment. The virtual machine represents an emulated environment in which the guest is executed. All the operations of the guest are generally performed against the virtual machine, which then translates and applies them to the host. This level of indirection allows the virtual machine manager to *control* and *filter* the activity of the guest, thus preventing some harmful operations from being performed. Resources exposed by the host can then be hidden or simply protected from the guest. Moreover, sensitive

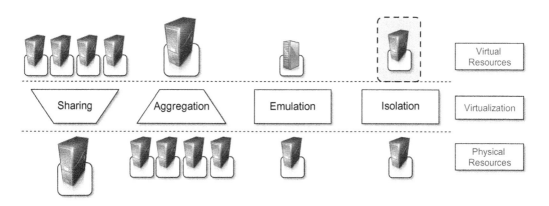

FIGURE 3.2

Functions enabled by managed execution.

information that is contained in the host can be naturally hidden without the need to install complex security policies. Increased security is a requirement when dealing with untrusted code. For example, applets downloaded from the Internet run in a sandboxed[3] version of the *Java Virtual Machine (JVM)*, which provides them with limited access to the hosting operating system resources. Both the JVM and the .NET runtime provide extensive security policies for customizing the execution environment of applications. Hardware virtualization solutions such as VMware Desktop, VirtualBox, and Parallels provide the ability to create a virtual computer with customized virtual hardware on top of which a new operating system can be installed. By default, the file system exposed by the virtual computer is completely separated from the one of the host machine. This becomes the perfect environment for running applications without affecting other users in the environment.

3.2.2 Managed execution

Virtualization of the execution environment not only allows increased security, but a wider range of features also can be implemented. In particular, *sharing*, *aggregation*, *emulation*, and *isolation* are the most relevant features (see Figure 3.2).

- *Sharing.* Virtualization allows the creation of a separate computing environments within the same host. In this way it is possible to fully exploit the capabilities of a powerful guest, which would otherwise be underutilized. As we will see in later chapters, sharing is a particularly important feature in virtualized data centers, where this basic feature is used to reduce the number of active servers and limit power consumption.

---

[3]The term sandbox identifies an isolated execution environment where instructions can be filtered and blocked before being translated and executed in the real execution environment. The expression sandboxed version of the Java Virtual Machine (JVM) refers to a particular configuration of the JVM where, by means of security policy, instructions that are considered potential harmful can be blocked.

- *Aggregation.* Not only is it possible to share physical resource among several guests, but virtualization also allows aggregation, which is the opposite process. A group of separate hosts can be tied together and represented to guests as a single virtual host. This function is naturally implemented in middleware for distributed computing, with a classical example represented by cluster management software, which harnesses the physical resources of a homogeneous group of machines and represents them as a single resource.
- *Emulation.* Guest programs are executed within an environment that is controlled by the virtualization layer, which ultimately is a program. This allows for controlling and tuning the environment that is exposed to guests. For instance, a completely different environment with respect to the host can be emulated, thus allowing the execution of guest programs requiring specific characteristics that are not present in the physical host. This feature becomes very useful for testing purposes, where a specific guest has to be validated against different platforms or architectures and the wide range of options is not easily accessible during development. Again, hardware virtualization solutions are able to provide virtual hardware and emulate a particular kind of device such as *Small Computer System Interface (SCSI)* devices for file I/O, without the hosting machine having such hardware installed. Old and legacy software that does not meet the requirements of current systems can be run on emulated hardware without any need to change the code. This is possible either by emulating the required hardware architecture or within a specific operating system sandbox, such as the MS-DOS mode in Windows 95/98. Another example of emulation is an arcade-game emulator that allows us to play arcade games on a normal personal computer.
- *Isolation.* Virtualization allows providing guests—whether they are operating systems, applications, or other entities—with a completely separate environment, in which they are executed. The guest program performs its activity by interacting with an abstraction layer, which provides access to the underlying resources. Isolation brings several benefits; for example, it allows multiple guests to run on the same host without interfering with each other. Second, it provides a separation between the host and the guest. The virtual machine can filter the activity of the guest and prevent harmful operations against the host.

Besides these characteristics, another important capability enabled by virtualization is *performance tuning*. This feature is a reality at present, given the considerable advances in hardware and software supporting virtualization. It becomes easier to control the performance of the guest by finely tuning the properties of the resources exposed through the virtual environment. This capability provides a means to effectively implement a quality-of-service (QoS) infrastructure that more easily fulfills the service-level agreement (SLA) established for the guest. For instance, software-implementing hardware virtualization solutions can expose to a guest operating system only a fraction of the memory of the host machine or set the maximum frequency of the processor of the virtual machine. Another advantage of managed execution is that sometimes it allows easy capturing of the state of the guest program, persisting it, and resuming its execution. This, for example, allows virtual machine managers such as Xen Hypervisor to stop the execution of a guest operating system, move its virtual image into another machine, and resume its execution in a completely transparent manner. This technique is called *virtual machine migration* and constitutes an important feature in virtualized data centers for optimizing their efficiency in serving application demands.

3.2.3 **Portability**

The concept of *portability* applies in different ways according to the specific type of virtualization considered. In the case of a hardware virtualization solution, the guest is packaged into a virtual image that, in most cases, can be safely moved and executed on top of different virtual machines. Except for the file size, this happens with the same simplicity with which we can display a picture image in different computers. Virtual images are generally proprietary formats that require a specific virtual machine manager to be executed. In the case of programming-level virtualization, as implemented by the JVM or the .NET runtime, the binary code representing application components (jars or assemblies) can be run without any recompilation on any implementation of the corresponding virtual machine. This makes the application development cycle more flexible and application deployment very straightforward: One version of the application, in most cases, is able to run on different platforms with no changes. Finally, portability allows having your own system always with you and ready to use as long as the required virtual machine manager is available. This requirement is, in general, less stringent than having all the applications and services you need available to you anywhere you go.

3.3 **Taxonomy of virtualization techniques**

Virtualization covers a wide range of emulation techniques that are applied to different areas of computing. A classification of these techniques helps us better understand their characteristics and use (see Figure 3.3).

The first classification discriminates against the service or entity that is being emulated. Virtualization is mainly used to emulate *execution environments*, *storage*, and *networks*. Among these categories, *execution virtualization* constitutes the oldest, most popular, and most developed area. Therefore, it deserves major investigation and a further categorization. In particular we can divide these execution virtualization techniques into two major categories by considering the type of host they require. *Process-level* techniques are implemented on top of an existing operating system, which has full control of the hardware. *System-level* techniques are implemented directly on hardware and do not require—or require a minimum of support from—an existing operating system. Within these two categories we can list various techniques that offer the guest a different type of virtual computation environment: bare hardware, operating system resources, low-level programming language, and application libraries.

3.3.1 **Execution virtualization**

Execution virtualization includes all techniques that aim to emulate an execution environment that is separate from the one hosting the virtualization layer. All these techniques concentrate their interest on providing support for the execution of programs, whether these are the operating system, a binary specification of a program compiled against an abstract machine model, or an application. Therefore, execution virtualization can be implemented directly on top of the hardware by the operating system, an application, or libraries dynamically or statically linked to an application image.

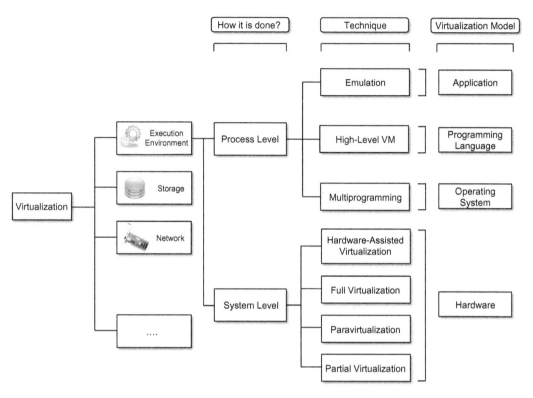

FIGURE 3.3

A taxonomy of virtualization techniques.

3.3.1.1 Machine reference model

Virtualizing an execution environment at different levels of the computing stack requires a reference model that defines the interfaces between the levels of abstractions, which hide implementation details. From this perspective, virtualization techniques actually replace one of the layers and intercept the calls that are directed toward it. Therefore, a clear separation between layers simplifies their implementation, which only requires the emulation of the interfaces and a proper interaction with the underlying layer.

Modern computing systems can be expressed in terms of the reference model described in Figure 3.4. At the bottom layer, the model for the hardware is expressed in terms of the *Instruction Set Architecture (ISA)*, which defines the instruction set for the processor, registers, memory, and interrupt management. ISA is the interface between hardware and software, and it is important to the operating system (OS) developer (*System ISA*) and developers of applications that directly manage the underlying hardware (*User ISA*). The *application binary interface (ABI)* separates the operating system layer from the applications and libraries, which are managed by the OS. ABI covers details such as low-level data types, alignment, and call conventions and defines a format for executable programs. System calls are defined at this level. This interface allows portability of applications and libraries across operating systems that

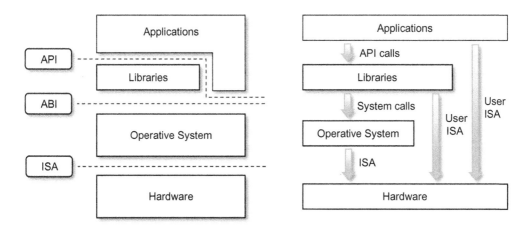

FIGURE 3.4

A machine reference model.

implement the same ABI. The highest level of abstraction is represented by the *application programming interface (API)*, which interfaces applications to libraries and/or the underlying operating system.

For any operation to be performed in the application level API, ABI and ISA are responsible for making it happen. The high-level abstraction is converted into machine-level instructions to perform the actual operations supported by the processor. The machine-level resources, such as processor registers and main memory capacities, are used to perform the operation at the hardware level of the central processing unit (CPU). This layered approach simplifies the development and implementation of computing systems and simplifies the implementation of multitasking and the coexistence of multiple executing environments. In fact, such a model not only requires limited knowledge of the entire computing stack, but it also provides ways to implement a minimal security model for managing and accessing shared resources.

For this purpose, the instruction set exposed by the hardware has been divided into different security classes that define who can operate with them. The first distinction can be made between *privileged* and *nonprivileged* instructions. Nonprivileged instructions are those instructions that can be used without interfering with other tasks because they do not access shared resources. This category contains, for example, all the floating, fixed-point, and arithmetic instructions. Privileged instructions are those that are executed under specific restrictions and are mostly used for sensitive operations, which expose (*behavior-sensitive*) or modify (*control-sensitive*) the privileged state. For instance, behavior-sensitive instructions are those that operate on the I/O, whereas control-sensitive instructions alter the state of the CPU registers. Some types of architecture feature more than one class of privileged instructions and implement a finer control of how these instructions can be accessed. For instance, a possible implementation features a hierarchy of privileges (see Figure 3.5) in the form of ring-based security: *Ring 0, Ring 1, Ring 2*, and *Ring 3*; Ring 0 is in the most privileged level and Ring 3 in the least privileged level. Ring 0 is used by the kernel of the OS, rings 1 and 2 are used by the OS-level services, and Ring 3 is used by the user. Recent systems support only two levels, with Ring 0 for supervisor mode and Ring 3 for user mode.

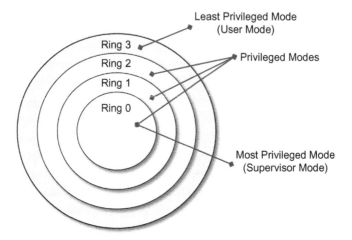

FIGURE 3.5

Security rings and privilege modes.

All the current systems support at least two different execution modes: *supervisor mode* and *user mode*. The first mode denotes an execution mode in which all the instructions (privileged and nonprivileged) can be executed without any restriction. This mode, also called *master mode* or *kernel mode*, is generally used by the operating system (or the hypervisor) to perform sensitive operations on hardware-level resources. In user mode, there are restrictions to control the machine-level resources. If code running in user mode invokes the privileged instructions, hardware interrupts occur and trap the potentially harmful execution of the instruction. Despite this, there might be some instructions that can be invoked as privileged instructions under some conditions and as nonprivileged instructions under other conditions.

The distinction between *user* and *supervisor* mode allows us to understand the role of the *hypervisor* and why it is called that. Conceptually, the hypervisor runs above the supervisor mode, and from here the prefix *hyper-* is used. In reality, hypervisors are run in supervisor mode, and the division between privileged and nonprivileged instructions has posed challenges in designing virtual machine managers. It is expected that all the sensitive instructions will be executed in privileged mode, which requires supervisor mode in order to avoid traps. Without this assumption it is impossible to fully emulate and manage the status of the CPU for guest operating systems. Unfortunately, this is not true for the original ISA, which allows 17 sensitive instructions to be called in user mode. This prevents multiple operating systems managed by a single hypervisor to be isolated from each other, since they are able to access the privileged state of the processor and change it.[4] More recent implementations of ISA (Intel VT and AMD Pacifica) have solved this problem by redesigning such instructions as privileged ones.

By keeping in mind this reference model, it is possible to explore and better understand the various techniques utilized to virtualize execution environments and their relationships to the other components of the system.

---

[4]It is expected that in a hypervisor-managed environment, all the guest operating system code will be run in user mode in order to prevent it from directly accessing the status of the CPU. If there are sensitive instructions that can be called in user mode (that is, implemented as nonprivileged instructions), it is no longer possible to completely isolate the guest OS.

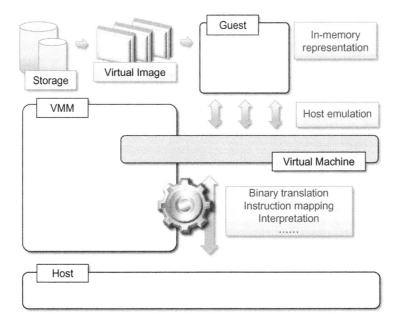

FIGURE 3.6

A hardware virtualization reference model.

3.3.1.2 Hardware-level virtualization

Hardware-level virtualization is a virtualization technique that provides an abstract execution environment in terms of computer hardware on top of which a guest operating system can be run. In this model, the guest is represented by the operating system, the host by the physical computer hardware, the virtual machine by its emulation, and the virtual machine manager by the hypervisor (see Figure 3.6). The hypervisor is generally a program or a combination of software and hardware that allows the abstraction of the underlying physical hardware.

Hardware-level virtualization is also called *system virtualization*, since it provides ISA to virtual machines, which is the representation of the hardware interface of a system. This is to differentiate it from *process virtual machines*, which expose ABI to virtual machines.

Hypervisors

A fundamental element of hardware virtualization is the hypervisor, or virtual machine manager (VMM). It recreates a hardware environment in which guest operating systems are installed. There are two major types of hypervisor: *Type I* and *Type II* (see Figure 3.7).

- *Type I* hypervisors run directly on top of the hardware. Therefore, they take the place of the operating systems and interact directly with the ISA interface exposed by the underlying hardware, and they emulate this interface in order to allow the management of guest operating systems. This type of hypervisor is also called a *native virtual machine* since it runs natively on hardware.

- *Type II* hypervisors require the support of an operating system to provide virtualization services. This means that they are programs managed by the operating system, which interact with it through the ABI and emulate the ISA of virtual hardware for guest operating systems. This type of hypervisor is also called a *hosted virtual machine* since it is hosted within an operating system.

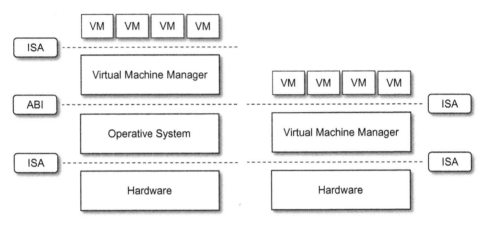

FIGURE 3.7

Hosted (left) and native (right) virtual machines. This figure provides a graphical representation of the two types of hypervisors.

Conceptually, a virtual machine manager is internally organized as described in Figure 3.8. Three main modules, *dispatcher*, *allocator*, and *interpreter*, coordinate their activity in order to emulate the underlying hardware. The dispatcher constitutes the entry point of the monitor and reroutes the instructions issued by the virtual machine instance to one of the two other modules. The allocator is responsible for deciding the system resources to be provided to the VM: whenever a virtual machine tries to execute an instruction that results in changing the machine resources associated with that VM, the allocator is invoked by the dispatcher. The interpreter module consists of interpreter routines. These are executed whenever a virtual machine executes a privileged instruction: a trap is triggered and the corresponding routine is executed.

The design and architecture of a virtual machine manager, together with the underlying hardware design of the host machine, determine the full realization of hardware virtualization, where a guest operating system can be transparently executed on top of a VMM as though it were run on the underlying hardware. The criteria that need to be met by a virtual machine manager to efficiently support virtualization were established by Goldberg and Popek in 1974 [23]. Three properties have to be satisfied:

- *Equivalence.* A guest running under the control of a virtual machine manager should exhibit the same behavior as when it is executed directly on the physical host.
- *Resource control.* The virtual machine manager should be in complete control of virtualized resources.

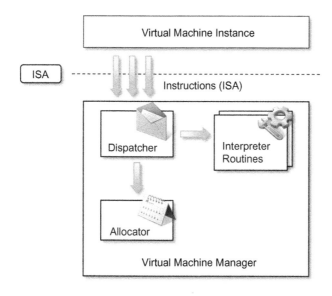

FIGURE 3.8

A hypervisor reference architecture.

- *Efficiency.* A statistically dominant fraction of the machine instructions should be executed without intervention from the virtual machine manager.

The major factor that determines whether these properties are satisfied is represented by the layout of the ISA of the host running a virtual machine manager. Popek and Goldberg provided a classification of the instruction set and proposed three theorems that define the properties that hardware instructions need to satisfy in order to efficiently support virtualization.

THEOREM 3.1

For any conventional third-generation computer, a VMM may be constructed if the set of sensitive instructions for that computer is a subset of the set of privileged instructions.

This theorem establishes that all the instructions that change the configuration of the system resources should generate a trap in user mode and be executed under the control of the virtual machine manager. This allows hypervisors to efficiently control only those instructions that would reveal the presence of an abstraction layer while executing all the rest of the instructions without considerable performance loss. The theorem always guarantees the resource control property when the hypervisor is in the most privileged mode (*Ring 0*). The nonprivileged instructions must be executed without the intervention of the hypervisor. The equivalence property also holds good since the output of the code is the same in both cases because the code is not changed.

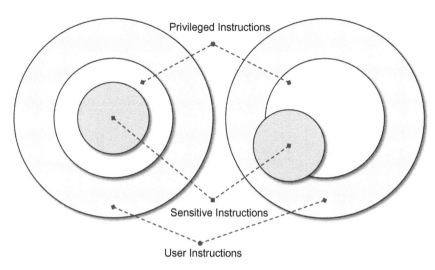

FIGURE 3.9

A virtualizable computer (left) and a nonvirtualizable computer (right).

THEOREM 3.2

A conventional third-generation computer is recursively virtualizable if:

- It is virtualizable and
- A VMM without any timing dependencies can be constructed for it.

Recursive virtualization is the ability to run a virtual machine manager on top of another virtual machine manager. This allows nesting hypervisors as long as the capacity of the underlying resources can accommodate that. Virtualizable hardware is a prerequisite to recursive virtualization.

THEOREM 3.3

A hybrid VMM may be constructed for any conventional third-generation machine in which the set of user-sensitive instructions is a subset of the set of privileged instructions.

There is another term, *hybrid virtual machine (HVM)*, which is less efficient than the virtual machine system. In the case of an HVM, more instructions are interpreted rather than being executed directly. All instructions in virtual supervisor mode are interpreted. Whenever there is an attempt to execute a behavior-sensitive or control-sensitive instruction, HVM controls the execution directly or gains the control via a trap. Here all sensitive instructions are caught by HVM that are simulated.

This reference model represents what we generally consider classic virtualization—that is, the ability to execute a guest operating system in complete isolation. To a greater extent, hardware-level virtualization includes several strategies that differentiate from each other in terms of which kind of support is expected from the underlying hardware, what is actually abstracted from the host, and whether the guest should be modified or not.

Hardware virtualization techniques

Hardware-assisted virtualization. This term refers to a scenario in which the hardware provides architectural support for building a virtual machine manager able to run a guest operating system in complete isolation. This technique was originally introduced in the IBM System/370. At present, examples of hardware-assisted virtualization are the extensions to the x86-64 bit architecture introduced with *Intel VT* (formerly known as *Vanderpool*) and *AMD V* (formerly known as *Pacifica*). These extensions, which differ between the two vendors, are meant to reduce the performance penalties experienced by emulating x86 hardware with hypervisors. Before the introduction of hardware-assisted virtualization, software emulation of x86 hardware was significantly costly from the performance point of view. The reason for this is that by design the x86 architecture did not meet the formal requirements introduced by Popek and Goldberg, and early products were using binary translation to trap some sensitive instructions and provide an emulated version. Products such as VMware Virtual Platform, introduced in 1999 by VMware, which pioneered the field of x86 virtualization, were based on this technique. After 2006, Intel and AMD introduced processor extensions, and a wide range of virtualization solutions took advantage of them: Kernel-based Virtual Machine (KVM), VirtualBox, Xen, VMware, Hyper-V, Sun xVM, Parallels, and others.

Full virtualization. *Full virtualization* refers to the ability to run a program, most likely an operating system, directly on top of a virtual machine and without any modification, as though it were run on the raw hardware. To make this possible, virtual machine managers are required to provide a complete emulation of the entire underlying hardware. The principal advantage of full virtualization is complete isolation, which leads to enhanced security, ease of emulation of different architectures, and coexistence of different systems on the same platform. Whereas it is a desired goal for many virtualization solutions, full virtualization poses important concerns related to performance and technical implementation. A key challenge is the interception of privileged instructions such as I/O instructions: Since they change the state of the resources exposed by the host, they have to be contained within the virtual machine manager. A simple solution to achieve full virtualization is to provide a virtual environment for all the instructions, thus posing some limits on performance. A successful and efficient implementation of full virtualization is obtained with a combination of hardware and software, not allowing potentially harmful instructions to be executed directly on the host. This is what is accomplished through hardware-assisted virtualization.

Paravirtualization. This is a not-transparent virtualization solution that allows implementing thin virtual machine managers. Paravirtualization techniques expose a software interface to the virtual machine that is slightly modified from the host and, as a consequence, guests need to be modified. The aim of paravirtualization is to provide the capability to demand the execution of performance-critical operations directly on the host, thus preventing performance losses that would otherwise be experienced in managed execution. This allows a simpler implementation of virtual machine managers that have to simply transfer the execution of these operations, which were hard to virtualize, directly to the host. To take advantage of such an opportunity, guest operating systems need to be modified and explicitly ported by remapping the performance-critical operations through the virtual machine software interface. This is possible when the source code of the operating system is available, and this is the reason that paravirtualization was mostly explored in the open-source and academic environment. Whereas this technique was initially applied in the IBM VM operating system families, the term *paravirtualization* was introduced in literature in the Denali project [24] at the University of Washington. This technique has been successfully used by Xen for providing virtualization solutions for Linux-based operating systems specifically ported to run on Xen hypervisors. Operating systems that cannot be ported can still take advantage of paravirtualization by using ad hoc device drivers that remap the execution of critical instructions to the paravirtualization APIs exposed by the hypervisor. Xen provides this solution for running Windows-based operating systems on x86 architectures. Other solutions using paravirtualization include VMWare, Parallels, and some solutions for embedded and real-time environments such as TRANGO, Wind River, and XtratuM.

Partial virtualization. Partial virtualization provides a partial emulation of the underlying hardware, thus not allowing the complete execution of the guest operating system in complete isolation. Partial virtualization allows many applications to run transparently, but not all the features of the operating system can be supported, as happens with full virtualization. An example of partial virtualization is address space virtualization used in time-sharing systems; this allows multiple applications and users to run concurrently in a separate memory space, but they still share the same hardware resources (disk, processor, and network). Historically, partial virtualization has been an important milestone for achieving full virtualization, and it was implemented on the experimental IBM M44/44X. Address space virtualization is a common feature of contemporary operating systems.

Operating system-level virtualization

Operating system-level virtualization offers the opportunity to create different and separated execution environments for applications that are managed concurrently. Differently from hardware virtualization, there is no virtual machine manager or hypervisor, and the virtualization is done within a single operating system, where the OS kernel allows for multiple isolated user space instances. The kernel is also responsible for sharing the system resources among instances and for limiting the impact of instances on each other. A user space instance in general contains a proper view of the file system, which is completely isolated, and separate IP addresses, software configurations, and access to devices. Operating systems supporting this type of virtualization are general-purpose, time-shared operating systems with the capability to provide stronger namespace and resource isolation.

This virtualization technique can be considered an evolution of the *chroot* mechanism in Unix systems. The *chroot* operation changes the file system root directory for a process and its children to a specific directory. As a result, the process and its children cannot have access to other portions of the file system than those accessible under the new root directory. Because Unix systems also expose devices as parts of the file system, by using this method it is possible to completely isolate a set of processes. Following the same principle, operating system-level virtualization aims to provide separated and multiple execution containers for running applications. Compared to hardware virtualization, this strategy imposes little or no overhead because applications directly use OS system calls and there is no need for emulation. There is no need to modify applications to run them, nor to modify any specific hardware, as in the case of hardware-assisted virtualization. On the other hand, operating system-level virtualization does not expose the same flexibility of hardware virtualization, since all the user space instances must share the same operating system.

This technique is an efficient solution for server consolidation scenarios in which multiple application servers share the same technology: operating system, application server framework, and other components. When different servers are aggregated into one physical server, each server is run in a different user space, completely isolated from the others.

Examples of operating system-level virtualizations are FreeBSD Jails, IBM Logical Partition (LPAR), SolarisZones and Containers, Parallels Virtuozzo Containers, OpenVZ, iCore Virtual Accounts, Free Virtual Private Server (FreeVPS), and others. The services offered by these technologies differ, and most of them are available on Unix-based systems. Some of them, such as Solaris and OpenVZ, allow for different versions of the same operating system to operate concurrently.

3.3.1.3 Programming language-level virtualization

Programming language-level virtualization is mostly used to achieve ease of deployment of applications, managed execution, and portability across different platforms and operating systems. It consists of a virtual machine executing the byte code of a program, which is the result of the compilation process. Compilers implemented and used this technology to produce a binary format representing the machine code for an abstract architecture. The characteristics of this architecture vary from implementation to implementation. Generally these virtual machines constitute a simplification of the underlying hardware instruction set and provide some high-level instructions that map some of the features of the languages compiled for them. At runtime, the byte code can be either interpreted or compiled on the fly—or *jitted*[5]—against the underlying hardware instruction set.

Programming language-level virtualization has a long trail in computer science history and originally was used in 1966 for the implementation of *Basic Combined Programming Language (BCPL)*, a language for writing compilers and one of the ancestors of the C programming language. Other important examples of the use of this technology have been the UCSD Pascal and Smalltalk. Virtual machine programming languages become popular again with Sun's introduction of the Java platform in 1996. Originally created as a platform for developing Internet applications, Java became one of the technologies of choice for enterprise applications, and a large community of developers formed around it. The Java virtual machine was originally designed for the execution of programs written in the Java language, but other languages such as Python, Pascal, Groovy, and Ruby were made available. The ability to support multiple programming languages has been one of the key elements of the *Common Language Infrastructure (CLI)*, which is the specification behind

---

[5]The term *jitted* is an improper use of the *just-in-time (JIT)* acronym as a verb, which has now become common. It refers to a specific execution strategy in which the byte code of a method is compiled against the underlying machine code upon method call—that is, *just in time*. Initial implementations of programming-level virtualization were based on interpretation, which led to considerable slowdowns during execution. The advantage of just-in-time compilation is that the machine code that has been compiled can be reused for executing future calls to the same methods. Virtual machines that implement JIT compilation generally have a method cache that stores the code generated for each method and simply look up this cache before triggering the compilation upon each method call.

.NET Framework. Currently, the Java platform and .NET Framework represent the most popular technologies for enterprise application development.

Both Java and the CLI are *stack-based* virtual machines: The reference model of the abstract architecture is based on an execution stack that is used to perform operations. The byte code generated by compilers for these architectures contains a set of instructions that load operands on the stack, perform some operations with them, and put the result on the stack. Additionally, specific instructions for invoking methods and managing objects and classes are included. Stack-based virtual machines possess the property of being easily interpreted and executed simply by lexical analysis and hence are easily portable over different architectures. An alternative solution is offered by *register-based* virtual machines, in which the reference model is based on registers. This kind of virtual machine is closer to the underlying architecture we use today. An example of a register-based virtual machine is Parrot, a programming-level virtual machine that was originally designed to support the execution of PERL and then generalized to host the execution of dynamic languages.

The main advantage of programming-level virtual machines, also called *process virtual machines*, is the ability to provide a uniform execution environment across different platforms. Programs compiled into byte code can be executed on any operating system and platform for which a virtual machine able to execute that code has been provided. From a development lifecycle point of view, this simplifies the development and deployment efforts since it is not necessary to provide different versions of the same code. The implementation of the virtual machine for different platforms is still a costly task, but it is done once and not for any application. Moreover, process virtual machines allow for more control over the execution of programs since they do not provide direct access to the memory. Security is another advantage of managed programming languages; by filtering the I/O operations, the process virtual machine can easily support sandboxing of applications. As an example, both Java and .NET provide an infrastructure for pluggable security policies and code access security frameworks. All these advantages come with a price: performance. Virtual machine programming languages generally expose an inferior performance compared to languages compiled against the real architecture. This performance difference is getting smaller, and the high compute power available on average processors makes it even less important.

Implementations of this model are also called *high-level virtual machines*, since high-level programming languages are compiled to a conceptual ISA, which is further interpreted or dynamically translated against the specific instruction of the hosting platform.

3.3.1.4 Application-level virtualization

Application-level virtualization is a technique allowing applications to be run in runtime environments that do not natively support all the features required by such applications. In this scenario, applications are not installed in the expected runtime environment but are run as though they were. In general, these techniques are mostly concerned with partial file systems, libraries, and operating system component emulation. Such emulation is performed by a thin layer—a program or an operating system component—that is in charge of executing the application. Emulation can also be used to execute program binaries compiled for different hardware architectures. In this case, one of the following strategies can be implemented:

- *Interpretation.* In this technique every source instruction is interpreted by an emulator for executing native ISA instructions, leading to poor performance. Interpretation has a minimal startup cost but a huge overhead, since each instruction is emulated.
- *Binary translation.* In this technique every source instruction is converted to native instructions with equivalent functions. After a block of instructions is translated, it is cached and reused. Binary translation has a large initial overhead cost, but over time it is subject to better performance, since previously translated instruction blocks are directly executed.

Emulation, as described, is different from hardware-level virtualization. The former simply allows the execution of a program compiled against a different hardware, whereas the latter emulates a complete hardware environment where an entire operating system can be installed.

Application virtualization is a good solution in the case of missing libraries in the host operating system; in this case a replacement library can be linked with the application, or library calls can be remapped to existing functions available in the host system. Another advantage is that in this case the virtual machine manager is much lighter since it provides a partial emulation of the runtime environment compared to hardware virtualization. Moreover, this technique allows incompatible applications to run together. Compared to programming-level virtualization, which works across all the applications developed for that virtual machine, application-level virtualization works for a specific environment: It supports all the applications that run on top of a specific environment.

One of the most popular solutions implementing application virtualization is *Wine*, which is a software application allowing Unix-like operating systems to execute programs written for the Microsoft Windows platform. Wine features a software application acting as a container for the guest application and a set of libraries, called *Winelib*, that developers can use to compile applications to be ported on Unix systems. Wine takes its inspiration from a similar product from Sun, *Windows Application Binary Interface (WABI)*, which implements the Win 16 API specifications on Solaris. A similar solution for the Mac OS X environment is CrossOver, which allows running Windows applications directly on the Mac OS X operating system. VMware ThinApp, another product in this area, allows capturing the setup of an installed application and packaging it into an executable image isolated from the hosting operating system.

3.3.2 Other types of virtualization

Other than execution virtualization, other types of virtualization provide an abstract environment to interact with. These mainly cover storage, networking, and client/server interaction.

3.3.2.1 Storage virtualization

Storage virtualization is a system administration practice that allows decoupling the physical organization of the hardware from its logical representation. Using this technique, users do not have to be worried about the specific location of their data, which can be identified using a logical path.

Storage virtualization allows us to harness a wide range of storage facilities and represent them under a single logical file system. There are different techniques for storage virtualization, one of the most popular being network-based virtualization by means of *storage area networks (SANs)*. SANs use a network-accessible device through a large bandwidth connection to provide storage facilities.

3.3.2.2 Network virtualization

Network virtualization combines hardware appliances and specific software for the creation and management of a virtual network. Network virtualization can aggregate different physical networks into a single logical network (*external* network virtualization) or provide network-like functionality to an operating system partition (*internal* network virtualization). The result of external network virtualization is generally a *virtual LAN (VLAN)*. A VLAN is an aggregation of hosts that communicate with each other as though they were located under the same broadcasting domain. Internal network virtualization is generally applied together with hardware and operating system-level virtualization, in which the guests obtain a virtual network interface to communicate with. There are several options for implementing internal network virtualization: The guest can share the same network interface of the host and use Network Address Translation (NAT) to access the network; the virtual machine manager can emulate, and install on the host, an additional network device, together with the driver; or the guest can have a private network only with the guest.

3.3.2.3 Desktop virtualization

Desktop virtualization abstracts the desktop environment available on a personal computer in order to provide access to it using a client/server approach. Desktop virtualization provides the same outcome of hardware virtualization but serves a different purpose. Similarly to hardware virtualization, desktop virtualization makes accessible a different system as though it were natively installed on the host, but this system is remotely stored on a different host and accessed through a network connection. Moreover, desktop virtualization addresses the problem of making the same desktop environment accessible from everywhere. Although the term *desktop virtualization* strictly refers to the ability to remotely access a desktop environment, generally the desktop environment is stored in a remote server or a data center that provides a high-availability infrastructure and ensures the accessibility and persistence of the data.

In this scenario, an infrastructure supporting hardware virtualization is fundamental to provide access to multiple desktop environments hosted on the same server; a specific desktop environment is stored in a virtual machine image that is loaded and started on demand when a client connects to the desktop environment. This is a typical cloud computing scenario in which the user leverages the virtual infrastructure for performing the daily tasks on his computer. The advantages of desktop virtualization are high availability, persistence, accessibility, and ease of management. As we will discuss in Section 4.5.4 of the next chapter, security issues can prevent the use of this technology. The basic services for remotely accessing a desktop environment are implemented in software components such as Windows Remote Services, VNC, and X Server. Infrastructures for desktop virtualization based on cloud computing solutions include Sun Virtual Desktop Infrastructure (VDI), Parallels Virtual Desktop Infrastructure (VDI), Citrix XenDesktop, and others.

3.3.2.4 Application server virtualization

Application server virtualization abstracts a collection of application servers that provide the same services as a single virtual application server by using load-balancing strategies and providing a high-availability infrastructure for the services hosted in the application server. This is a particular form of virtualization and serves the same purpose of storage virtualization: providing a better quality of service rather than emulating a different environment.

3.4 Virtualization and cloud computing

Virtualization plays an important role in cloud computing since it allows for the appropriate degree of customization, security, isolation, and manageability that are fundamental for delivering IT services on demand. Virtualization technologies are primarily used to offer configurable computing environments and storage. Network virtualization is less popular and, in most cases, is a complementary feature, which is naturally needed in build virtual computing systems.

Particularly important is the role of virtual computing environment and execution virtualization techniques. Among these, hardware and programming language virtualization are the techniques adopted in cloud computing systems. Hardware virtualization is an enabling factor for solutions in the Infrastructure-as-a-Service (IaaS) market segment, while programming language virtualization is a technology leveraged in Platform-as-a-Service (PaaS) offerings. In both cases, the capability of offering a customizable and sandboxed environment constituted an attractive business opportunity for companies featuring a large computing infrastructure that was able to sustain and process huge workloads. Moreover, virtualization also allows isolation and a finer control, thus simplifying the leasing of services and their accountability on the vendor side.

Besides being an enabler for computation on demand, virtualization also gives the opportunity to design more efficient computing systems by means of consolidation, which is performed transparently to cloud computing service users. Since virtualization allows us to create isolated and controllable environments, it is possible to serve these environments with the same resource without them interfering with each other. If the underlying resources are capable enough, there will be no evidence of such sharing. This opportunity is particularly attractive when resources are underutilized, because it allows reducing the number of active resources by aggregating virtual machines over a smaller number of resources that become fully utilized. This practice is also known as *server consolidation*, while the movement of virtual machine instances is called *virtual machine migration* (see Figure 3.10). Because virtual machine instances are controllable environments, consolidation can be applied with a minimum impact, either by temporarily stopping its execution and moving its data to the new resources or by performing a finer control and moving the instance while it is running. This second techniques is known as *live migration* and in general is more complex to implement but more efficient since there is no disruption of the activity of the virtual machine instance.[6]

---

[6]It is important to notice that cloud computing is strongly leveraged for the development of applications that need to scale on demand. In most cases, this is because applications have to process increased workloads or serve more requests, which makes them server applications. In this scenario, it is evident that live migration offers a better solution because it does not create any service interruption during consolidation.

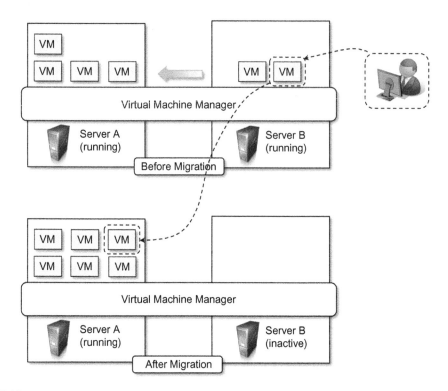

FIGURE 3.10

Live migration and server consolidation.

Server consolidation and virtual machine migration are principally used in the case of hardware virtualization, even though they are also technically possible in the case of programming language virtualization (see Figure 3.9).

Storage virtualization constitutes an interesting opportunity given by virtualization technologies, often complementary to the execution of virtualization. Even in this case, vendors backed by large computing infrastructures featuring huge storage facilities can harness these facilities into a virtual storage service, easily partitionable into slices. These slices can be dynamic and offered as a service. Again, opportunities to secure and protect the hosting infrastructure are available, as are methods for easy accountability of such services.

Finally, cloud computing revamps the concept of desktop virtualization, initially introduced in the mainframe era. The ability to recreate the entire computing stack—from infrastructure to application services—on demand opens the path to having a complete virtual computer hosted on the infrastructure of the provider and accessed by a thin client over a capable Internet connection.

3.5 Pros and cons of virtualization

Virtualization has now become extremely popular and widely used, especially in cloud computing. The primary reason for its wide success is the elimination of technology barriers that prevented virtualization from being an effective and viable solution in the past. The most relevant barrier has been performance. Today, the capillary diffusion of the Internet connection and the advancements in computing technology have made virtualization an interesting opportunity to deliver on-demand IT infrastructure and services. Despite its renewed popularity, this technology has benefits and also drawbacks.

3.5.1 Advantages of virtualization

Managed execution and isolation are perhaps the most important advantages of virtualization. In the case of techniques supporting the creation of virtualized execution environments, these two characteristics allow building secure and controllable computing environments. A virtual execution environment can be configured as a sandbox, thus preventing any harmful operation to cross the borders of the virtual host. Moreover, allocation of resources and their partitioning among different guests is simplified, being the virtual host controlled by a program. This enables fine-tuning of resources, which is very important in a server consolidation scenario and is also a requirement for effective quality of service.

Portability is another advantage of virtualization, especially for execution virtualization techniques. Virtual machine instances are normally represented by one or more files that can be easily transported with respect to physical systems. Moreover, they also tend to be self-contained since they do not have other dependencies besides the virtual machine manager for their use. Portability and self-containment simplify their administration. Java programs are "compiled once and run everywhere"; they only require that the Java virtual machine be installed on the host. The same applies to hardware-level virtualization. It is in fact possible to build our own operating environment within a virtual machine instance and bring it with us wherever we go, as though we had our own laptop. This concept is also an enabler for migration techniques in a server consolidation scenario.

Portability and self-containment also contribute to reducing the costs of maintenance, since the number of hosts is expected to be lower than the number of virtual machine instances. Since the guest program is executed in a virtual environment, there is very limited opportunity for the guest program to damage the underlying hardware. Moreover, it is expected that there will be fewer virtual machine managers with respect to the number of virtual machine instances managed.

Finally, by means of virtualization it is possible to achieve a more efficient use of resources. Multiple systems can securely coexist and share the resources of the underlying host, without interfering with each other. This is a prerequisite for server consolidation, which allows adjusting the number of active physical resources dynamically according to the current load of the system, thus creating the opportunity to save in terms of energy consumption and to be less impacting on the environment.

3.5.2 The other side of the coin: disadvantages

Virtualization also has downsides. The most evident is represented by a performance decrease of guest systems as a result of the intermediation performed by the virtualization layer. In addition, suboptimal use of the host because of the abstraction layer introduced by virtualization management software can lead to a very inefficient utilization of the host or a degraded user experience. Less evident, but perhaps more dangerous, are the implications for security, which are mostly due to the ability to emulate a different execution environment.

3.5.2.1 Performance degradation

Performance is definitely one of the major concerns in using virtualization technology. Since virtualization interposes an abstraction layer between the guest and the host, the guest can experience increased latencies.

For instance, in the case of hardware virtualization, where the intermediate emulates a bare machine on top of which an entire system can be installed, the causes of performance degradation can be traced back to the overhead introduced by the following activities:

- Maintaining the status of virtual processors
- Support of privileged instructions (trap and simulate privileged instructions)
- Support of paging within VM
- Console functions

Furthermore, when hardware virtualization is realized through a program that is installed or executed on top of the host operating systems, a major source of performance degradation is represented by the fact that the virtual machine manager is executed and scheduled together with other applications, thus sharing with them the resources of the host.

Similar consideration can be made in the case of virtualization technologies at higher levels, such as in the case of programming language virtual machines (Java, .NET, and others). Binary translation and interpretation can slow down the execution of managed applications. Moreover, because their execution is filtered by the runtime environment, access to memory and other physical resources can represent sources of performance degradation.

These concerns are becoming less and less important thanks to technology advancements and the ever-increasing computational power available today. For example, specific techniques for hardware virtualization such as *paravirtualization* can increase the performance of the guest program by offloading most of its execution to the host without any change. In programming-level virtual machines such as the JVM or .NET, compilation to native code is offered as an option when performance is a serious concern.

3.5.2.2 Inefficiency and degraded user experience

Virtualization can sometime lead to an inefficient use of the host. In particular, some of the specific features of the host cannot be exposed by the abstraction layer and then become inaccessible. In the case of hardware virtualization, this could happen for device drivers: The virtual machine can sometime simply provide a default graphic card that maps only a subset of the features available in the host. In the case of programming-level virtual machines, some of the features of the underlying operating systems may become inaccessible unless specific libraries are used. For example, in the first version of Java the support for graphic programming was very limited and the look and feel of applications was very poor compared to native applications. These issues have been resolved by providing a new framework called *Swing* for designing the user interface, and further improvements have been done by integrating support for the OpenGL libraries in the software development kit.

3.5.2.3 Security holes and new threats

Virtualization opens the door to a new and unexpected form of *phishing*.[7] The capability of emulating a host in a completely transparent manner led the way to malicious programs that are designed to extract sensitive information from the guest.

In the case of hardware virtualization, malicious programs can preload themselves before the operating system and act as a thin virtual machine manager toward it. The operating system is then controlled and can be manipulated to extract sensitive information of interest to third parties. Examples of these kinds of malware are BluePill and SubVirt. BluePill, malware targeting the AMD processor family, moves the execution of the installed OS within a virtual machine. The original version of SubVirt was developed as a prototype by Microsoft through collaboration with Michigan University. SubVirt infects the guest OS, and when the virtual machine is rebooted, it gains control of the host. The diffusion of such kinds of malware is facilitated by the fact that originally, hardware and CPUs were not manufactured with virtualization in mind. In particular, the existing instruction sets cannot be simply changed or updated to suit the needs of virtualization. Recently, both Intel and AMD have introduced hardware support for virtualization with Intel VT and AMD Pacifica, respectively.

The same considerations can be made for programming-level virtual machines: Modified versions of the runtime environment can access sensitive information or monitor the memory locations utilized by guest applications while these are executed. To make this possible, the original version of the runtime environment needs to be replaced by the modified one, which can generally happen if the malware is run within an administrative context or a security hole of the host operating system is exploited.

3.6 Technology examples

A wide range of virtualization technology is available especially for virtualizing computing environments. In this section, we discuss the most relevant technologies and approaches utilized in the field. Cloud-specific solutions are discussed in the next chapter.

---

[7]*Phishing* is a term that identifies a malicious practice aimed at capturing sensitive user information, such as usernames and passwords, by recreating an environment identical in functionalities and appearance to the one that manages this information. Phishing most commonly occurs on the Web, where the user is redirected to a malicious website that is a replica of the original and the purpose of which is to collect the information to impersonate the user on the original Website (e.g., a bank site) and access the user's confidential data.

3.6.1 Xen: paravirtualization

Xen is an open-source initiative implementing a virtualization platform based on paravirtualization. Initially developed by a group of researchers at the University of Cambridge in the United Kingdom, Xen now has a large open-source community backing it. Citrix also offers it as a commercial solution, XenSource. Xen-based technology is used for either desktop virtualization or server virtualization, and recently it has also been used to provide cloud computing solutions by means of Xen Cloud Platform (XCP). At the basis of all these solutions is the Xen Hypervisor, which constitutes the core technology of Xen. Recently Xen has been advanced to support full virtualization using hardware-assisted virtualization.

Xen is the most popular implementation of *paravirtualization*, which, in contrast with full virtualization, allows high-performance execution of guest operating systems. This is made possible by eliminating the performance loss while executing instructions that require special management. This is done by modifying portions of the guest operating systems run by Xen with reference to the execution of such instructions. Therefore it is not a transparent solution for implementing virtualization. This is particularly true for x86, which is the most popular architecture on commodity machines and servers.

Figure 3.11 describes the architecture of Xen and its mapping onto a classic x86 privilege model. A Xen-based system is managed by the *Xen hypervisor*, which runs in the highest privileged mode and controls the access of guest operating system to the underlying hardware. Guest

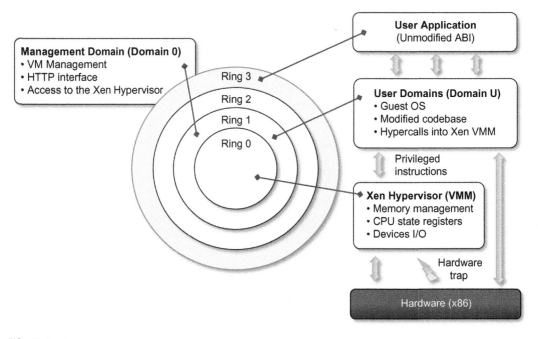

FIGURE 3.11

Xen architecture and guest OS management.

operating systems are executed within *domains*, which represent virtual machine instances. Moreover, specific control software, which has privileged access to the host and controls all the other guest operating systems, is executed in a special domain called *Domain 0*. This is the first one that is loaded once the virtual machine manager has completely booted, and it hosts a HyperText Transfer Protocol (HTTP) server that serves requests for virtual machine creation, configuration, and termination. This component constitutes the embryonic version of a distributed virtual machine manager, which is an essential component of cloud computing systems providing Infrastructure-as-a-Service (IaaS) solutions.

Many of the x86 implementations support four different security levels, called *rings*, where Ring 0 represent the level with the highest privileges and Ring 3 the level with the lowest ones. Almost all the most popular operating systems, except OS/2, utilize only two levels: Ring 0 for the kernel code, and Ring 3 for user application and nonprivileged OS code. This provides the opportunity for Xen to implement virtualization by executing the hypervisor in Ring 0, Domain 0, and all the other domains running guest operating systems—generally referred to as *Domain U*—in Ring 1, while the user applications are run in Ring 3. This allows Xen to maintain the ABI unchanged, thus allowing an easy switch to Xen-virtualized solutions from an application point of view. Because of the structure of the x86 instruction set, some instructions allow code executing in Ring 3 to jump into Ring 0 (kernel mode). Such operation is performed at the hardware level and therefore within a virtualized environment will result in a *trap* or *silent fault*, thus preventing the normal operations of the guest operating system, since this is now running in Ring 1. This condition is generally triggered by a subset of the system calls. To avoid this situation, operating systems need to be changed in their implementation, and the sensitive system calls need to be reimplemented with *hypercalls*, which are specific calls exposed by the virtual machine interface of Xen. With the use of hypercalls, the Xen hypervisor is able to catch the execution of all the sensitive instructions, manage them, and return the control to the guest operating system by means of a supplied handler.

Paravirtualization needs the operating system codebase to be modified, and hence not all operating systems can be used as guests in a Xen-based environment. More precisely, this condition holds in a scenario where it is not possible to leverage hardware-assisted virtualization, which allows running the hypervisor in Ring -1 and the guest operating system in Ring 0. Therefore, Xen exhibits some limitations in the case of legacy hardware and legacy operating systems. In fact, these cannot be modified to be run in Ring 1 safely since their codebase is not accessible and, at the same time, the underlying hardware does not provide any support to run the hypervisor in a more privileged mode than Ring 0. Open-source operating systems such as Linux can be easily modified, since their code is publicly available and Xen provides full support for their virtualization, whereas components of the Windows family are generally not supported by Xen unless hardware-assisted virtualization is available. It can be observed that the problem is now becoming less and less crucial since both new releases of operating systems are designed to be virtualization aware and the new hardware supports x86 virtualization.

3.6.2 VMware: full virtualization

VMware's technology is based on the concept of *full virtualization*, where the underlying hardware is replicated and made available to the guest operating system, which runs unaware of such abstraction layers and does not need to be modified. VMware implements full virtualization either in the desktop environment, by means of *Type II* hypervisors, or in the server environment, by means of *Type I* hypervisors. In both cases, full virtualization is made possible by means of *direct execution* (for nonsensitive instructions) and *binary translation* (for sensitive instructions), thus allowing the virtualization of architecture such as x86.

Besides these two core solutions, VMware provides additional tools and software that simplify the use of virtualization technology either in a desktop environment, with tools enhancing the integration of virtual guests with the host, or in a server environment, with solutions for building and managing virtual computing infrastructures.

3.6.2.1 Full virtualization and binary translation

VMware is well known for the capability to virtualize x86 architectures, which runs unmodified on top of their hypervisors. With the new generation of hardware architectures and the introduction of *hardware-assisted virtualization* (Intel VT-x and AMD V) in 2006, full virtualization is made possible with hardware support, but before that date, the use of *dynamic binary translation* was the only solution that allowed running x86 guest operating systems unmodified in a virtualized environment.

As discussed before, x86 architecture design does not satisfy the first theorem of virtualization, since the set of sensitive instructions is not a subset of the privileged instructions. This causes a different behavior when such instructions are not executed in Ring 0, which is the normal case in a virtualization scenario where the guest OS is run in Ring 1. Generally, a trap is generated and the way it is managed differentiates the solutions in which virtualization is implemented for x86 hardware. In the case of dynamic binary translation, the trap triggers the translation of the offending instructions into an equivalent set of instructions that achieves the same goal without generating exceptions. Moreover, to improve performance, the equivalent set of instruction is cached so that translation is no longer necessary for further occurrences of the same instructions. Figure 3.12 gives an idea of the process.

This approach has both advantages and disadvantages. The major advantage is that guests can run unmodified in a virtualized environment, which is a crucial feature for operating systems for which source code is not available. This is the case, for example, of operating systems in the Windows family. Binary translation is a more portable solution for full virtualization. On the other hand, translating instructions at runtime introduces an additional overhead that is not present in other approaches (paravirtualization or hardware-assisted virtualization). Even though such disadvantage exists, binary translation is applied to only a subset of the instruction set, whereas the others are managed through direct execution on the underlying hardware. This somehow reduces the impact on performance of binary translation.

CPU virtualization is only a component of a fully virtualized hardware environment. VMware achieves full virtualization by providing virtual representation of memory and I/O devices. Memory virtualization constitutes another challenge of virtualized environments and can deeply impact performance without the appropriate hardware support. The main reason is the presence of a *memory management unit (MMU)*, which needs to be emulated as part of the virtual hardware. Especially in the case of *hosted hypervisors* (Type II), where the virtual MMU and the host-OS MMU are traversed sequentially before getting to the physical memory page, the impact on performance can be significant. To avoid nested translation, the *translation look-aside buffer (TLB)* in the virtual MMU directly maps physical pages, and the performance slowdown only occurs in case of a TLB miss.

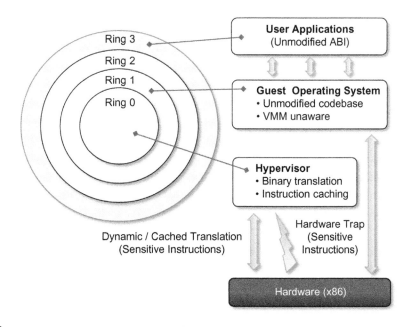

FIGURE 3.12

A full virtualization reference model.

Finally, VMware also provides full virtualization of I/O devices such as network controllers and other peripherals such as keyboard, mouse, disks, and universal serial bus (USB) controllers.

3.6.2.2 Virtualization solutions

VMware is a pioneer in virtualization technology and offers a collection of virtualization solutions covering the entire range of the market, from desktop computing to enterprise computing and infrastructure virtualization.

End-user (desktop) virtualization

VMware supports virtualization of operating system environments and single applications on end-user computers. The first option is the most popular and allows installing a different operating systems and applications in a completely isolated environment from the hosting operating system. Specific VMware software—*VMware Workstation*, for Windows operating systems, and *VMware Fusion*, for Mac OS X environments—is installed in the host operating system to create virtual machines and manage their execution. Besides the creation of an isolated computing environment, the two products allow a guest operating system to leverage the resources of the host machine (USB devices, folder sharing, and integration with the graphical user interface (GUI) of the host operating system). Figure 3.13 provides an overview of the architecture of these systems.

The virtualization environment is created by an application installed in guest operating systems, which provides those operating systems with full hardware virtualization of the underlying

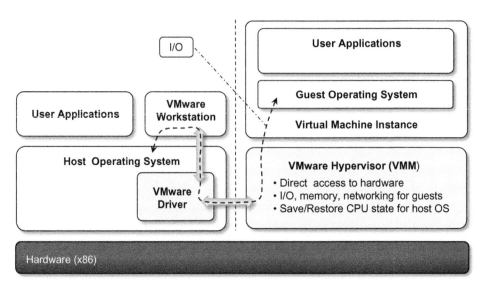

FIGURE 3.13

VMware workstation architecture.

hardware. This is done by installing a specific driver in the host operating system that provides two main services:

- It deploys a virtual machine manager that can run in privileged mode.
- It provides hooks for the VMware application to process specific I/O requests eventually by relaying such requests to the host operating system via system calls.

Using this architecture—also called *Hosted Virtual Machine Architecture*—it is possible to both isolate virtual machine instances within the memory space of a single application and provide reasonable performance, since the intervention of the VMware application is required only for instructions, such as device I/O, that require binary translation. Instructions that can be directly executed are managed by the virtual machine manager, which takes control of the CPU and the MMU and alternates its activity with the host OS. Virtual machine images are saved in a collection of files on the host file system, and both VMware Workstation and VMware Fusion allow creation of new images, pause their execution, create snapshots, and undo operations by rolling back to a previous state of the virtual machine.

Other solutions related to the virtualization of end-user computing environments include VMware Player, VMware ACE, and VMware ThinApp. VMware Player is a reduced version of VMware Workstation that allows creating and playing virtual machines in a Windows or Linux operating environment. VMware ACE, a similar product to VMware Workstation, creates policy-wrapped virtual machines for deploying secure corporate virtual environments on end-user computers. VMware ThinApp is a solution for application virtualization. It provides an isolated environment for applications in order to avoid conflicts due to versioning and incompatible applications. It detects all the changes to the operating environment made by the installation of a specific application and stores them together with the application binary into a package that can be run with VMware ThinApp.

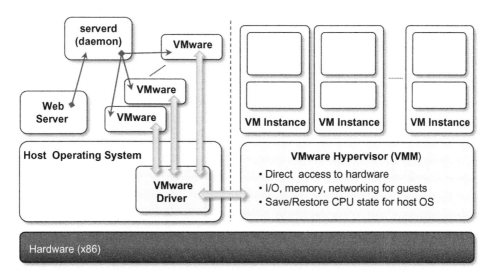

FIGURE 3.14

VMware GSX server architecture.

Server virtualization

VMware provided solutions for server virtualization with different approaches over time. Initial support for server virtualization was provided by VMware GSX server, which replicates the approach used for end-user computers and introduces remote management and scripting capabilities. The architecture of VMware GSX Server is depicted in Figure 3.14.

The architecture is mostly designed to serve the virtualization of Web servers. A daemon process, called *serverd*, controls and manages VMware application processes. These applications are then connected to the virtual machine instances by means of the VMware driver installed on the host operating system. Virtual machine instances are managed by the VMM as described previously. User requests for virtual machine management and provisioning are routed from the Web server through the VMM by means of *serverd*.

VMware ESX Server and its enhanced version, VMWare ESXi Server, are examples of the hypervisor-based approach. Both can be installed on bare metal servers and provide services for virtual machine management. The two solutions provide the same services but differ in the internal architecture, more specifically in the organization of the hypervisor kernel. VMware ESX embeds a modified version of a Linux operating system, which provides access through a service console to hypervisor. VMware ESXi implements a very thin OS layer and replaces the service console with interfaces and services for remote management, thus considerably reducing the hypervisor code size and memory footprint.

The architecture of VMware ESXi is displayed in Figure 3.15. The base of the infrastructure is the VMkernel, which is a thin Portable Operating System Interface (POSIX) compliant operating system that provides the minimal functionality for processes and thread management, file system, I/O stacks, and resource scheduling. The kernel is accessible through specific APIs called User world API. These

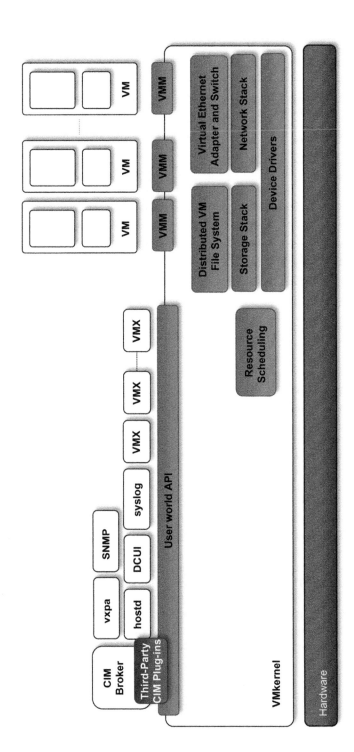

FIGURE 3.15

VMware ESXi server architecture.

APIs are utilized by all the agents that provide supporting activities for the management of virtual machines. Remote management of an ESXi server is provided by the CIM Broker, a system agent that acts as a gateway to the VMkernel for clients by using the *Common Information Model (CIM)*[8] protocol. The ESXi installation can also be managed locally by a *Direct Client User Interface (DCUI)*, which provides a BIOS-like interface for the management of local users.

Infrastructure virtualization and cloud computing solutions

VMware provides a set of products covering the entire stack of cloud computing, from infrastructure management to Software-as-a-Service solutions hosted in the cloud. Figure 3.16 gives an overview of the different solutions offered and how they relate to each other.

ESX and ESXi constitute the building blocks of the solution for virtual infrastructure management: A pool of virtualized servers is tied together and remotely managed as a whole by VMware vSphere. As a virtualization platform it provides a set of basic services besides virtual compute services: Virtual file system, virtual storage, and virtual network constitute the core of the infrastructure; application services, such as virtual machine migration, storage migration, data recovery, and

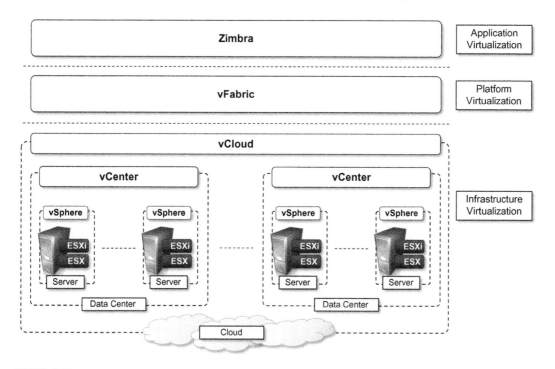

FIGURE 3.16

VMware Cloud Solution stack.

---

[8]Common Information Model (CIM) is a Distributed Management Task Force standard for defining management information for systems, applications, and services. See http://dmtf.org/standards/cim.

security zones, complete the services offered by vSphere. The management of the infrastructure is operated by VMware vCenter, which provides centralized administration and management of vSphere installations in a data center environment. A collection of virtualized data centers are turned into a Infrastructure-as-a-Service cloud by VMware vCloud, which allows service providers to make available to end users virtual computing environments on demand on a pay-per-use basis. A Web portal provides access to the provisioning services of vCloud, and end users can self-provision virtual machines by choosing from available templates and setting up virtual networks among virtual instances.

VMware also provides a solution for application development in the cloud with VMware vFabric, which is a set of components that facilitate the development of scalable Web applications on top of a virtualized infrastructure. vFabric is a collection of components for application monitoring, scalable data management, and scalable execution and provisioning of Java Web applications.

Finally, at the top of the cloud computing stack, VMware provides Zimbra, a solution for office automation, messaging, and collaboration that is completely hosted in the cloud and accessible from anywhere. This is an SaaS solution that integrates various features into a single software platform providing email and collaboration management.

3.6.2.3 Observations

Initially starting with a solution for fully virtualized x86 hardware, VMware has grown over time and now provides a complete offering for virtualizing hardware, infrastructure, applications, and services, thus covering every segment of the cloud computing market. Even though full x86 virtualization is the core technology of VMware, over time paravirtualization features have been integrated into some of the solutions offered by the vendor, especially after the introduction of hardware-assisted virtualization. For instance, the implementation of some device emulations and the VMware Tools suite that allows enhanced integration with the guest and the host operating environment. Also, VMware has strongly contributed to the development and standardization of a vendor-independent *Virtual Machine Interface (VMI)*, which allows for a general and host-agnostic approach to paravirtualization.

3.6.3 Microsoft Hyper-V

Hyper-V is an infrastructure virtualization solution developed by Microsoft for server virtualization. As the name recalls, it uses a hypervisor-based approach to hardware virtualization, which leverages several techniques to support a variety of guest operating systems. Hyper-V is currently shipped as a component of Windows Server 2008 R2 that installs the hypervisor as a role within the server.

3.6.3.1 Architecture

Hyper-V supports multiple and concurrent execution of guest operating systems by means of *partitions*. A partition is a completely isolated environment in which an operating system is installed and run.

Figure 3.17 provides an overview of the architecture of Hyper-V. Despite its straightforward installation as a component of the host operating system, Hyper-V takes control of the hardware, and the host operating system becomes a virtual machine instance with special privileges, called

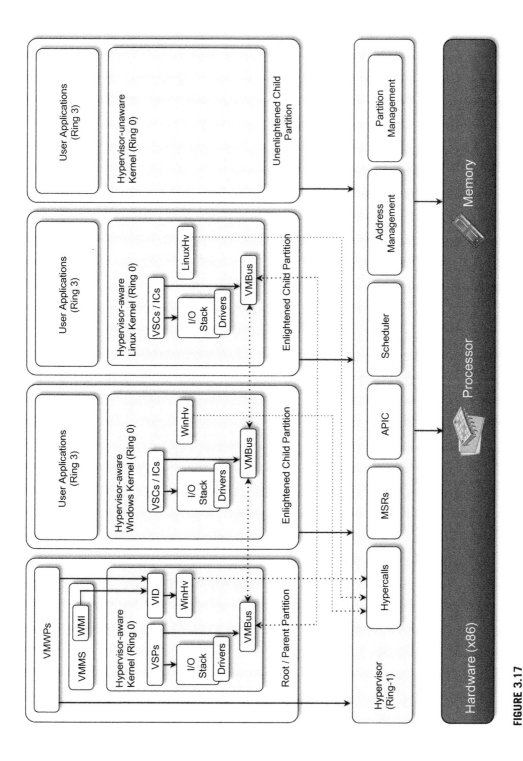

FIGURE 3.17

Microsoft Hyper-V architecture.

the *parent partition.* The parent partition (also called the *root partition*) is the only one that has direct access to the hardware. It runs the virtualization stack, hosts all the drivers required to configure guest operating systems, and creates *child partitions* through the hypervisor. Child partitions are used to host guest operating systems and do not have access to the underlying hardware, but their interaction with it is controlled by either the parent partition or the hypervisor itself.

Hypervisor

The hypervisor is the component that directly manages the underlying hardware (processors and memory). It is logically defined by the following components:

- *Hypercalls interface.* This is the entry point for all the partitions for the execution of sensitive instructions. This is an implementation of the paravirtualization approach already discussed with Xen. This interface is used by drivers in the partitioned operating system to contact the hypervisor using the standard Windows calling convention. The parent partition also uses this interface to create child partitions.
- *Memory service routines (MSRs).* These are the set of functionalities that control the memory and its access from partitions. By leveraging hardware-assisted virtualization, the hypervisor uses the *Input/Output Memory Management Unit (I/O MMU* or *IOMMU)* to fast-track access to devices from partitions by translating virtual memory addresses.
- *Advanced programmable interrupt controller (APIC).* This component represents the interrupt controller, which manages the signals coming from the underlying hardware when some event occurs (timer expired, I/O ready, exceptions and traps). Each virtual processor is equipped with a *synthetic interrupt controller (SynIC),* which constitutes an extension of the local APIC. The hypervisor is responsible of dispatching, when appropriate, the physical interrupts to the synthetic interrupt controllers.
- *Scheduler.* This component schedules the virtual processors to run on available physical processors. The scheduling is controlled by policies that are set by the parent partition.
- *Address manager.* This component is used to manage the virtual network addresses that are allocated to each guest operating system.
- *Partition manager.* This component is in charge of performing partition creation, finalization, destruction, enumeration, and configurations. Its services are available through the hypercalls interface API previously discussed.

The hypervisor runs in Ring -1 and therefore requires corresponding hardware technology that enables such a condition. By executing in this highly privileged mode, the hypervisor can support legacy operating systems that have been designed for x86 hardware. Operating systems of newer generations can take advantage of the new specific architecture of Hyper-V especially for the I/O operations performed by child partitions.

Enlightened I/O and synthetic devices

Enlightened I/O provides an optimized way to perform I/O operations, allowing guest operating systems to leverage an interpartition communication channel rather than traversing the hardware emulation stack provided by the hypervisor. This option is only available to guest operating systems that are hypervisor aware. Enlightened I/O leverages VMBus, an interpartition communication channel that is used to exchange data between partitions (child and parent) and is utilized mostly for the implementation of virtual device drivers for guest operating systems.

The architecture of Enlightened I/O is described in Figure 3.17. There are three fundamental components: *VMBus, Virtual Service Providers (VSPs)*, and *Virtual Service Clients (VSCs)*. VMBus implements the channel and defines the protocol for communication between partitions. VSPs are kernel-level drivers that are deployed in the parent partition and provide access to the corresponding hardware devices. These interact with VSCs, which represent the virtual device drivers (also called *synthetic drivers*) seen by the guest operating systems in the child partitions. Operating systems supported by Hyper-V utilize this preferred communication channel to perform I/O for storage, networking, graphics, and input subsystems. This also results in enhanced performance in child-to-child I/O as a result of virtual networks between guest operating systems. Legacy operating systems, which are not hypervisor aware, can still be run by Hyper-V but rely on device driver emulation, which is managed by the hypervisor and is less efficient.

Parent partition

The parent partition executes the host operating system and implements the virtualization stack that complements the activity of the hypervisor in running guest operating systems. This partition always hosts an instance of the Windows Server 2008 R2, which manages the virtualization stack made available to the child partitions. This partition is the only one that directly accesses device drivers and mediates the access to them by child partitions by hosting the VSPs.

The parent partition is also the one that manages the creation, execution, and destruction of child partitions. It does so by means of the *Virtualization Infrastructure Driver (VID)*, which controls access to the hypervisor and allows the management of virtual processors and memory. For each child partition created, a Virtual Machine Worker Process (VMWP) is instantiated in the parent partition, which manages the child partitions by interacting with the hypervisor through the VID. Virtual Machine Management services are also accessible remotely through a WMI[9] provider that allows remote hosts to access the VID.

Child partitions

Child partitions are used to execute guest operating systems. These are isolated environments that allow secure and controlled execution of guests. Two types of child partition exist, they differ on whether the guest operating system is supported by Hyper-V or not. These are called *Enlightened* and *Unenlightened* partitions, respectively. The first ones can benefit from Enlightened I/O; the other ones are executed by leveraging hardware emulation from the hypervisor.

3.6.3.2 Cloud computing and infrastructure management

Hyper-V constitutes the basic building block of Microsoft virtualization infrastructure. Other components contribute to creating a fully featured platform for server virtualization.

To increase the performance of virtualized environments, a new version of Windows Server 2008, called *Windows Server Core*, has been released. This is a specific version of the operating

---

[9]*WMI* stands for *Windows Management Instrumentation*. This is a specification used in the Windows environment to provide access to the underlying hardware. The specification is based on providers that give authorized clients access to a specific subsystem of the hardware.

system with a reduced set of features and a smaller footprint. In particular, Windows Server Core has been designed by removing those features, which are not required in a server environment, such as the GUI component and other bulky components such as the .NET Framework and all the applications developed on top of it (for example, PowerShell). This design decision has both advantages and disadvantages. On the plus side, it allows for reduced maintenance (i.e., fewer software patches), reduced attack surface, reduced management, and less disk space. On the negative side, the embedded features are reduced. Still, there is the opportunity to leverage all the "removed features" by means of remote management from a fully featured Windows installation. For instance, administrators can use the PowerShell to remotely manage the Windows Server Core installation through WMI.

Another component that provides advanced management of virtual machines is *System Center Virtual Machine Manager (SCVMM) 2008*. This is a component of the Microsoft System Center suite, which brings into the suite the virtual infrastructure management capabilities from an IT life-cycle point of view. Essentially, SCVMM complements the basic features offered by Hyper-V with management capabilities, including:

- Management portal for the creation and management of virtual instances
- Virtual to Virtual (V2V) and Physical to Virtual (P2V) conversions
- Delegated administration
- Library functionality and deep PowerShell integration
- Intelligent placement of virtual machines in the managed environment
- Host capacity management

SCVMM has also been designed to work with other virtualization platforms such as VMware vSphere (ESX servers) but benefits most from the virtual infrastructure management implemented with Hyper-V.

3.6.3.3 Observations

Compared with Xen and VMware, Hyper-V is a hybrid solution because it leverages both paravir-tualization techniques and full hardware virtualization.

The basic architecture of the hypervisor is based on paravirtualized architecture. The hypervisor exposes its services to the guest operating systems by means of hypercalls. Also, paravirtualized kernels can leverage VMBus for fast I/O operations. Moreover, partitions are conceptually similar to domains in Xen: The parent partition maps Domain 0, while child partitions map Domains U. The only difference is that the Xen hypervisor is installed on bare hardware and filters all the access to the underlying hardware, whereas Hyper-V is installed as a role in the existing operating system, and the way it interacts with partitions is quite similar to the strategy implemented by VMware, as we discussed.

The approach adopted by Hyper-V has both advantages and disadvantages. The advantages reside in a flexible virtualization platform supporting a wide range of guest operating systems. The disadvantages are represented by both hardware and software requirements. Hyper-V is compatible only with Windows Server 2008 and newer Windows Server platforms running on a x64 architecture. Moreover, it requires a 64-bit processor supporting hardware-assisted virtualization and data execution prevention. Finally, as noted above, Hyper-V is a role that can be installed on a existing operating system, while vSphere and Xen can be installed on the bare hardware.

SUMMARY

The term *virtualization* is a large umbrella under which a variety of technologies and concepts are classified. The common root of all the forms of virtualization is the ability to provide the illusion of a specific environment, whether a runtime environment, a storage facility, a network connection, or a remote desktop, by using some kind of emulation or abstraction layer. All these concepts play a fundamental role in building cloud computing infrastructure and services in which hardware, IT infrastructure, applications, and services are delivered on demand through the Internet or more generally via a network connection.

Review questions

1. What is virtualization and what are its benefits?
2. What are the characteristics of virtualized environments?
3. Discuss classification or taxonomy of virtualization at different levels.
4. Discuss the machine reference model of execution virtualization.
5. What are hardware virtualization techniques?
6. List and discuss different types of virtualization.
7. What are the benefits of virtualization in the context of cloud computing?
8. What are the disadvantages of virtualization?
9. What is Xen? Discuss its elements for virtualization.
10. Discuss the reference model of full virtualization.
11. Discuss the architecture of Hyper-V. Discuss its use in cloud computing.

Cloud Computing Architecture

The term *cloud computing* is a wide umbrella encompassing many different things; lately it has become a buzzword that is easily misused to revamp existing technologies and ideas for the public. What makes cloud computing so interesting to IT stakeholders and research practitioners? How does it introduce innovation into the field of distributed computing? This chapter addresses all these questions and characterizes the phenomenon. It provides a reference model that serves as a basis for discussion of cloud computing technologies.

4.1 Introduction

Utility-oriented data centers are the first outcome of cloud computing, and they serve as the infrastructure through which the services are implemented and delivered. Any cloud service, whether virtual hardware, development platform, or application software, relies on a distributed infrastructure owned by the provider or rented from a third party. As noted in the previous definition, the characterization of a cloud is quite general: It can be implemented using a datacenter, a collection of clusters, or a heterogeneous distributed system composed of desktop PCs, workstations, and servers. Commonly, clouds are built by relying on one or more datacenters. In most cases hardware resources are virtualized to provide isolation of workloads and to best exploit the infrastructure. According to the specific service delivered to the end user, different layers can be stacked on top of the virtual infrastructure: a virtual machine manager, a development platform, or a specific application middleware.

As noted in earlier chapters, the cloud computing paradigm emerged as a result of the convergence of various existing models, technologies, and concepts that changed the way we deliver and use IT services. A broad definition of the phenomenon could be as follows:

Cloud computing is a utility-oriented and Internet-centric way of delivering IT services on demand. These services cover the entire computing stack: from the hardware infrastructure packaged as a set of virtual machines to software services such as development platforms and distributed applications.

This definition captures the most important and fundamental aspects of cloud computing. We now discuss a reference model that aids in categorization of cloud technologies, applications, and services.

4.2 **The cloud reference model**

Cloud computing supports any IT service that can be consumed as a utility and delivered through a network, most likely the Internet. Such characterization includes quite different aspects: infrastructure, development platforms, application and services.

4.2.1 **Architecture**

It is possible to organize all the concrete realizations of cloud computing into a layered view covering the entire stack (see Figure 4.1), from hardware appliances to software systems. Cloud resources are harnessed to offer "computing horsepower" required for providing services. Often, this layer is implemented using a datacenter in which hundreds and thousands of nodes are stacked together. Cloud infrastructure can be heterogeneous in nature because a variety of resources, such as clusters and even networked PCs, can be used to build it. Moreover, database systems and other storage services can also be part of the infrastructure.

The physical infrastructure is managed by the core middleware, the objectives of which are to provide an appropriate runtime environment for applications and to best utilize resources. At the bottom of the stack, virtualization technologies are used to guarantee runtime environment customization, application isolation, sandboxing, and quality of service. Hardware virtualization is most commonly used at this level. Hypervisors manage the pool of resources and expose the distributed infrastructure as a collection of virtual machines. By using virtual machine technology it is possible to finely partition the hardware resources such as CPU and memory and to virtualize specific devices, thus meeting the requirements of users and applications. This solution is generally paired

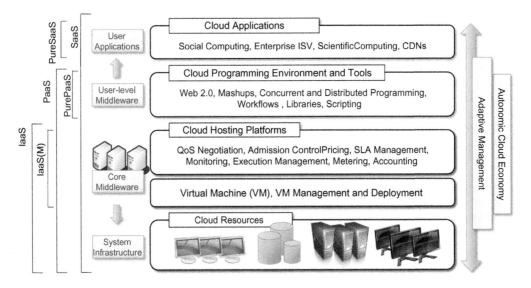

FIGURE 4.1

The cloud computing architecture.

with storage and network virtualization strategies, which allow the infrastructure to be completely virtualized and controlled. According to the specific service offered to end users, other virtualization techniques can be used; for example, programming-level virtualization helps in creating a portable runtime environment where applications can be run and controlled. This scenario generally implies that applications hosted in the cloud be developed with a specific technology or a programming language, such as Java, .NET, or Python. In this case, the user does not have to build its system from bare metal. Infrastructure management is the key function of core middleware, which supports capabilities such as negotiation of the quality of service, admission control, execution management and monitoring, accounting, and billing.

The combination of cloud hosting platforms and resources is generally classified as a *Infrastructure-as-a-Service (IaaS)* solution. We can organize the different examples of IaaS into two categories: Some of them provide both the management layer and the physical infrastructure; others provide only the management layer (*IaaS (M)*). In this second case, the management layer is often integrated with other IaaS solutions that provide physical infrastructure and adds value to them.

IaaS solutions are suitable for designing the system infrastructure but provide limited services to build applications. Such service is provided by cloud programming environments and tools, which form a new layer for offering users a development platform for applications. The range of tools include Web-based interfaces, command-line tools, and frameworks for concurrent and distributed programming. In this scenario, users develop their applications specifically for the cloud by using the API exposed at the user-level middleware. For this reason, this approach is also known as *Platform-as-a-Service (PaaS)* because the service offered to the user is a development platform rather than an infrastructure. PaaS solutions generally include the infrastructure as well, which is bundled as part of the service provided to users. In the case of *Pure PaaS*, only the user-level middleware is offered, and it has to be complemented with a virtual or physical infrastructure.

The top layer of the reference model depicted in Figure 4.1 contains services delivered at the application level. These are mostly referred to as *Software-as-a-Service (SaaS)*. In most cases these are Web-based applications that rely on the cloud to provide service to end users. The horsepower of the cloud provided by IaaS and PaaS solutions allows independent software vendors to deliver their application services over the Internet. Other applications belonging to this layer are those that strongly leverage the Internet for their core functionalities that rely on the cloud to sustain a larger number of users; this is the case of gaming portals and, in general, social networking websites.

As a vision, any service offered in the cloud computing style should be able to adaptively change and expose an autonomic behavior, in particular for its availability and performance. As a reference model, it is then expected to have an adaptive management layer in charge of elastically scaling on demand. SaaS implementations should feature such behavior automatically, whereas PaaS and IaaS generally provide this functionality as a part of the API exposed to users.

The reference model described in Figure 4.1 also introduces the concept of *everything as a Service (XaaS)*. This is one of the most important elements of cloud computing: Cloud services from different providers can be combined to provide a completely integrated solution covering all the computing stack of a system. IaaS providers can offer the bare metal in terms of virtual machines where PaaS solutions are deployed. When there is no need for a PaaS layer, it is possible to directly customize the virtual infrastructure with the software stack needed to run applications. This is the case of virtual Web farms: a distributed system composed of Web servers, database servers, and load balancers on top of which prepackaged software is installed to run Web applications. This possibility has made cloud computing an interesting option for reducing startups' capital investment in IT, allowing them to quickly commercialize their ideas and grow their infrastructure according to their revenues.

Table 4.1 summarizes the characteristics of the three major categories used to classify cloud computing solutions. In the following section, we briefly discuss these characteristics along with some references to practical implementations.

4.2.2 Infrastructure- and hardware-as-a-service

Infrastructure- and Hardware-as-a-Service (IaaS/HaaS) solutions are the most popular and developed market segment of cloud computing. They deliver customizable infrastructure on demand. The available options within the IaaS offering umbrella range from single servers to entire infrastructures, including network devices, load balancers, and database and Web servers.

The main technology used to deliver and implement these solutions is hardware virtualization: one or more virtual machines opportunely configured and interconnected define the distributed system on top of which applications are installed and deployed. Virtual machines also constitute the atomic components that are deployed and priced according to the specific features of the virtual hardware: memory, number of processors, and disk storage. IaaS/HaaS solutions bring all the benefits of hardware virtualization: workload partitioning, application isolation, sandboxing, and hardware tuning. From the perspective of the service provider, IaaS/HaaS allows better exploiting the IT infrastructure and provides a more secure environment where executing third party applications. From the perspective of the customer it reduces the administration and maintenance cost as well as the capital costs allocated to purchase hardware. At the same time, users can take advantage of the full customization offered by virtualization to deploy their infrastructure in the cloud; in most cases virtual machines come with only the selected operating system installed and the system can be

Table 4.1 Cloud Computing Services Classification

Category	Characteristics	Product Type	Vendors and Products
SaaS	Customers are provided with applications that are accessible anytime and from anywhere.	Web applications and services (Web 2.0)	SalesForce.com (CRM) Clarizen.com (project management) Google Apps
PaaS	Customers are provided with a platform for developing applications hosted in the cloud.	Programming APIs and frameworks Deployment systems	Google AppEngine Microsoft Azure Manjrasoft Aneka Data Synapse
IaaS/HaaS	Customers are provided with virtualized hardware and storage on top of which they can build their infrastructure.	Virtual machine management infrastructure Storage management Network management	Amazon EC2 and S3 GoGrid Nirvanix

configured with all the required packages and applications. Other solutions provide prepackaged system images that already contain the software stack required for the most common uses: Web servers, database servers, or LAMP[1] stacks. Besides the basic virtual machine management capabilities, additional services can be provided, generally including the following: SLA resource-based allocation, workload management, support for infrastructure design through advanced Web interfaces, and the ability to integrate third-party IaaS solutions.

Figure 4.2 provides an overall view of the components forming an Infrastructure-as-a-Service solution. It is possible to distinguish three principal layers: the *physical infrastructure*, the *software management infrastructure*, and the *user interface*. At the top layer the user interface provides access to the services exposed by the software management infrastructure. Such an interface is

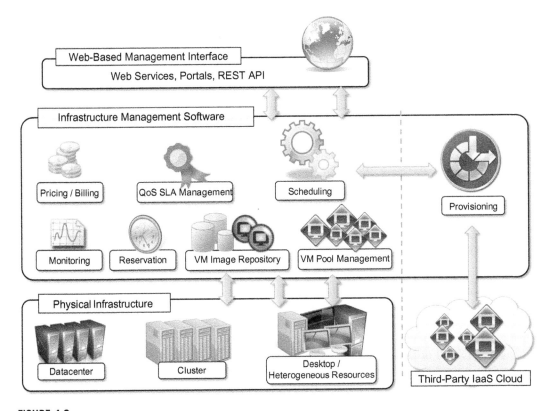

FIGURE 4.2

Infrastructure-as-a-Service reference implementation.

---

[1]*LAMP* is an acronym for *Linux Apache MySql and PHP* and identifies a specific server configuration running the Linux operating system, featuring Apache as Web server, MySQL as database server, and PHP: Hypertext Preprocessor (PHP) as server-side scripting technology for developing Web applications. LAMP stacks are the most common packaged solutions for quickly deploying Web applications.

generally based on Web 2.0 technologies: Web services, RESTful APIs, and mash-ups. These technologies allow either applications or final users to access the services exposed by the underlying infrastructure. Web 2.0 applications allow developing full-featured management consoles completely hosted in a browser or a Web page. Web services and RESTful APIs allow programs to interact with the service without human intervention, thus providing complete integration within a software system. The core features of an IaaS solution are implemented in the infrastructure management software layer. In particular, management of the virtual machines is the most important function performed by this layer. A central role is played by the scheduler, which is in charge of allocating the execution of virtual machine instances. The scheduler interacts with the other components that perform a variety of tasks:

- The *pricing and billing* component takes care of the cost of executing each virtual machine instance and maintains data that will be used to charge the user.
- The *monitoring* component tracks the execution of each virtual machine instance and maintains data required for reporting and analyzing the performance of the system.
- The *reservation* component stores the information of all the virtual machine instances that have been executed or that will be executed in the future.
- If support for QoS-based execution is provided, a *QoS/SLA management* component will maintain a repository of all the SLAs made with the users; together with the monitoring component, this component is used to ensure that a given virtual machine instance is executed with the desired quality of service.
- The *VM repository* component provides a catalog of virtual machine images that users can use to create virtual instances. Some implementations also allow users to upload their specific virtual machine images.
- A *VM pool manager* component is responsible for keeping track of all the live instances.
- Finally, if the system supports the integration of additional resources belonging to a third-party IaaS provider, a *provisioning* component interacts with the scheduler to provide a virtual machine instance that is external to the local physical infrastructure directly managed by the pool.

The bottom layer is composed of the physical infrastructure, on top of which the management layer operates. As previously discussed, the infrastructure can be of different types; the specific infrastructure used depends on the specific use of the cloud. A service provider will most likely use a massive datacenter containing hundreds or thousands of nodes. A cloud infrastructure developed in house, in a small or medium-sized enterprise or within a university department, will most likely rely on a cluster. At the bottom of the scale it is also possible to consider a heterogeneous environment where different types of resources—PCs, workstations, and clusters—can be aggregated. This case mostly represents an evolution of desktop grids where any available computing resource (such as PCs and workstations that are idle outside of working hours) is harnessed to provide a huge compute power. From an architectural point of view, the physical layer also includes the virtual resources that are rented from external IaaS providers.

In the case of complete IaaS solutions, all three levels are offered as service. This is generally the case with public clouds vendors such as Amazon, GoGrid, Joyent, Rightscale, Terremark, Rackspace, ElasticHosts, and Flexiscale, which own large datacenters and give access to their computing infrastructures using an IaaS approach. Other solutions instead cover only the user interface and the infrastructure software management layers. They need to provide credentials to access third-party IaaS providers or to own a private infrastructure in which the management software is installed. This is the case with Enomaly, Elastra, Eucalyptus, OpenNebula, and specific IaaS (M) solutions from VMware, IBM, and Microsoft.

The proposed architecture only represents a reference model for IaaS implementations. It has been used to provide general insight into the most common features of this approach for providing cloud computing services and the operations commonly implemented at this level. Different solutions can feature additional services or even not provide support for some of the features discussed here. Finally, the reference architecture applies to IaaS implementations that provide computing resources, especially for the scheduling component. If storage is the main service provided, it is still possible to distinguish these three layers. The role of infrastructure management software is not to keep track and manage the execution of virtual machines but to provide access to large infrastructures and implement storage virtualization solutions on top of the physical layer.

4.2.3 Platform as a service

Platform-as-a-Service (PaaS) solutions provide a development and deployment platform for running applications in the cloud. They constitute the middleware on top of which applications are built. A general overview of the features characterizing the PaaS approach is given in Figure 4.3.

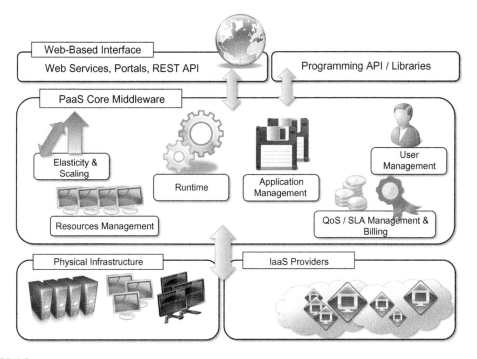

FIGURE 4.3

The Platform-as-a-Service reference model.

Application management is the core functionality of the middleware. PaaS implementations provide applications with a runtime environment and do not expose any service for managing the underlying infrastructure. They automate the process of deploying applications to the infrastructure, configuring application components, provisioning and configuring supporting technologies such as load balancers and databases, and managing system change based on policies set by the user. Developers design their systems in terms of applications and are not concerned with hardware (physical or virtual), operating systems, and other low-level services. The core middleware is in charge of managing the resources and scaling applications on demand or automatically, according to the commitments made with users. From a user point of view, the core middleware exposes interfaces that allow programming and deploying applications on the cloud. These can be in the form of a Web-based interface or in the form of programming APIs and libraries.

The specific development model decided for applications determines the interface exposed to the user. Some implementations provide a completely Web-based interface hosted in the cloud and offering a variety of services. It is possible to find integrated developed environments based on 4GL and visual programming concepts, or rapid prototyping environments where applications are built by assembling mash-ups and user-defined components and successively customized. Other implementations of the PaaS model provide a complete object model for representing an application and provide a programming language-based approach. This approach generally offers more flexibility and opportunities but incurs longer development cycles. Developers generally have the full power of programming languages such as Java, .NET, Python, or Ruby, with some restrictions to provide better scalability and security. In this case the traditional development environments can be used to design and develop applications, which are then deployed on the cloud by using the APIs exposed by the PaaS provider. Specific components can be offered together with the development libraries for better exploiting the services offered by the PaaS environment. Sometimes a local runtime environment that simulates the conditions of the cloud is given to users for testing their applications before deployment. This environment can be restricted in terms of features, and it is generally not optimized for scaling.

PaaS solutions can offer middleware for developing applications together with the infrastructure or simply provide users with the software that is installed on the user premises. In the first case, the PaaS provider also owns large datacenters where applications are executed; in the second case, referred to in this book as *Pure PaaS*, the middleware constitutes the core value of the offering. It is also possible to have vendors that deliver both middleware and infrastructure and ship only the middleware for private installations.

Table 4.2 provides a classification of the most popular PaaS implementations. It is possible to organize the various solutions into three wide categories: *PaaS-I*, *PaaS-II*, and *PaaS-III*. The first category identifies PaaS implementations that completely follow the cloud computing style for application development and deployment. They offer an integrated development environment hosted within the Web browser where applications are designed, developed, composed, and deployed. This is the case of Force.com and Longjump. Both deliver as platforms the combination of middleware and infrastructure. In the second class we can list all those solutions that are focused on providing a scalable infrastructure for Web application, mostly websites. In this case, developers generally use the providers' APIs, which are built on top of industrial runtimes, to develop

Table 4.2 Platform-as-a-Service Offering Classification

Category	Description	Product Type	Vendors and Products
PaaS-I	Runtime environment with Web-hosted application development platform. Rapid application prototyping.	Middleware + Infrastructure Middleware + Infrastructure	Force.com Longjump
PaaS-II	Runtime environment for scaling Web applications. The runtime could be enhanced by additional components that provide scaling capabilities.	Middleware + Infrastructure Middleware Middleware + Infrastructure Middleware + Infrastructure Middleware + Infrastructure Middleware	Google AppEngine AppScale Heroku Engine Yard Joyent Smart Platform GigaSpaces XAP
PaaS-III	Middleware and programming model for developing distributed applications in the cloud.	Middleware + Infrastructure Middleware Middleware Middleware Middleware Middleware	Microsoft Azure DataSynapse Cloud IQ Manjrasof Aneka Apprenda SaaSGrid GigaSpaces DataGrid

applications. Google AppEngine is the most popular product in this category. It provides a scalable runtime based on the Java and Python programming languages, which have been modified for providing a secure runtime environment and enriched with additional APIs and components to support scalability. AppScale, an open-source implementation of Google AppEngine, provides interface-compatible middleware that has to be installed on a physical infrastructure. Joyent Smart Platform provides a similar approach to Google AppEngine. A different approach is taken by Heroku and Engine Yard, which provide scalability support for Ruby- and Ruby on Rails-based Websites. In this case developers design and create their applications with the traditional methods and then deploy them by uploading to the provider's platform.

The third category consists of all those solutions that provide a cloud programming platform for any kind of application, not only Web applications. Among these, the most popular is Microsoft Windows Azure, which provides a comprehensive framework for building service-oriented cloud applications on top of the .NET technology, hosted on Microsoft's datacenters. Other solutions in the same category, such as Manjrasoft Aneka, Apprenda SaaSGrid, Appistry Cloud IQ Platform, DataSynapse, and GigaSpaces DataGrid, provide only middleware with different services. Table 4.2 shows only a few options available in the Platform-as-a-Service market segment.

The PaaS umbrella encompasses a variety of solutions for developing and hosting applications in the cloud. Despite this heterogeneity, it is possible to identify some criteria that are expected to be found in any implementation. As noted by Sam Charrington, product manager at Appistry.com,[2] there are some essential characteristics that identify a PaaS solution:

- *Runtime framework.* This framework represents the "software stack" of the PaaS model and the most intuitive aspect that comes to people's minds when they refer to PaaS solutions. The runtime framework executes end-user code according to the policies set by the user and the provider.
- *Abstraction.* PaaS solutions are distinguished by the higher level of abstraction that they provide. Whereas in the case of IaaS solutions the focus is on delivering "raw" access to virtual or physical infrastructure, in the case of PaaS the focus is on the applications the cloud must support. This means that PaaS solutions offer a way to deploy and manage applications on the cloud rather than a bunch of virtual machines on top of which the IT infrastructure is built and configured.
- *Automation.* PaaS environments automate the process of deploying applications to the infrastructure, scaling them by provisioning additional resources when needed. This process is performed automatically and according to the SLA made between the customers and the provider. This feature is normally not native in IaaS solutions, which only provide ways to provision more resources.
- *Cloud services.* PaaS offerings provide developers and architects with services and APIs, helping them to simplify the creation and delivery of elastic and highly available cloud applications. These services are the key differentiators among competing PaaS solutions and generally include specific components for developing applications, advanced services for application monitoring, management, and reporting.

Another essential component for a PaaS-based approach is the ability to integrate third-party cloud services offered from other vendors by leveraging service-oriented architecture. Such integration should happen through standard interfaces and protocols. This opportunity makes the development of applications more agile and able to evolve according to the needs of customers and users. Many of the PaaS offerings provide this facility, which is naturally built into the framework they leverage to provide a cloud computing solution.

One of the major concerns of leveraging PaaS solutions for implementing applications is *vendor lock-in.* Differently from IaaS solutions, which deliver bare virtual servers that can be fully customized in terms of the software stack installed, PaaS environments deliver a platform for developing applications, which exposes a well-defined set of APIs and, in most cases, binds the application to the specific runtime of the PaaS provider. Even though a platform-based approach strongly simplifies the development and deployment cycle of applications, it poses the risk of making these applications completely dependent on the provider. Such dependency can become a significant obstacle in retargeting the application to another environment and runtime if the commitments made with the provider cease. The impact of the vendor lock-in on applications obviously varies according to the various solutions. Some of them, such as Force.com, rely on a proprietary runtime framework, which makes the retargeting process very difficult. Others, such as Google AppEngine and Microsoft Azure, rely on industry-standard runtimes but utilize private data storage facilities and

---

[2]The full detail of this analysis can be found in the Cloud-pulse blog post available at the following address: http://Cloudpulseblog.com/2010/02/the-essential-characteristics-of-paas.

computing infrastructure. In this case it is possible to find alternatives based on PaaS solutions implementing the same interfaces, with perhaps different performance. Others, such as Appistry Cloud IQ Platform, Heroku, and Engine Yard, completely rely on open standards, thus making the migration of applications easier.

Finally, from a financial standpoint, although IaaS solutions allow shifting the capital cost into operational costs through outsourcing, PaaS solutions can cut the cost across development, deployment, and management of applications. It helps management reduce the risk of ever-changing technologies by offloading the cost of upgrading the technology to the PaaS provider. This happens transparently for the consumers of this model, who can concentrate their effort on the core value of their business. The PaaS approach, when bundled with underlying IaaS solutions, helps even small start-up companies quickly offer customers integrated solutions on a hosted platform at a very minimal cost. These opportunities make the PaaS offering a viable option that targets different market segments.

4.2.4 Software as a service

Software-as-a-Service (SaaS) is a software delivery model that provides access to applications through the Internet as a Web-based service. It provides a means to free users from complex hardware and software management by offloading such tasks to third parties, which build applications accessible to multiple users through a Web browser. In this scenario, customers neither need install anything on their premises nor have to pay considerable up-front costs to purchase the software and the required licenses. They simply access the application website, enter their credentials and billing details, and can instantly use the application, which, in most of the cases, can be further customized for their needs. On the provider side, the specific details and features of each customer's application are maintained in the infrastructure and made available on demand.

The SaaS model is appealing for applications serving a wide range of users and that can be adapted to specific needs with little further customization. This requirement characterizes SaaS as a "one-to-many" software delivery model, whereby an application is shared across multiple users. This is the case of CRM[3] and ERP[4] applications that constitute common needs for almost all enterprises, from small to medium-sized and large business. Every enterprise will have the same requirements for the basic features concerning CRM and ERP; different needs can be satisfied with further customization. This scenario facilitates the development of software platforms that provide a general set of features and support specialization and ease of integration of new components. Moreover, it constitutes the perfect candidate for hosted solutions, since the applications delivered to the user are the same, and the applications themselves provide users with the means to shape the

---

[3]CRM is an acronym for *customer relationship management* and identifies concerns related to interactions with customers and prospect sales. CRM solutions are software systems that simplify the process of managing customers and identifying sales strategies.

[4]ERP, an acronym for *enterprise resource planning*, generally refers to an integrated computer-based system used to manage internal and external resources, including tangible assets, materials, and financial and human resources. ERP software provides an integrated view of the enterprise and facilitates the management of the information flows between business functions and resources.

applications according to user needs. As a result, SaaS applications are naturally multitenant. *Multitenancy*, which is a feature of SaaS compared to traditional packaged software, allows providers to centralize and sustain the effort of managing large hardware infrastructures, maintaining and upgrading applications transparently to the users, and optimizing resources by sharing the costs among the large user base. On the customer side, such costs constitute a minimal fraction of the usage fee paid for the software.

As noted previously (see Section 1.2), the concept of software as a service preceded cloud computing, starting to circulate at the end of the 1990s, when it began to gain marketplace acceptance [31]. The acronym SaaS was then coined in 2001 by the *Software Information & Industry Association (SIIA)* [32] with the following connotation:

> In the software as a service model, the application, or service, is deployed from a centralized datacenter across a network—Internet, Intranet, LAN, or VPN—providing access and use on a recurring fee basis. Users "rent," "subscribe to," "are assigned," or "are granted access to" the applications from a central provider. Business models vary according to the level to which the software is streamlined, to lower price and increase efficiency, or value-added through customization to further improve digitized business processes.

The analysis carried out by SIIA was mainly oriented to cover application service providers (ASPs) and all their variations, which capture the concept of software applications consumed as a service in a broader sense. ASPs already had some of the core characteristics of SaaS:

- The product sold to customer is *application access*.
- The application is centrally managed.
- The service delivered is *one-to-many*.
- The service delivered is an integrated solution *delivered on the contract*, which means provided as promised.

Initially ASPs offered hosting solutions for packaged applications, which were served to multiple customers. Successively, other options, such as Web-based integration of third-party application services, started to gain interest and a new range of opportunities open up to independent software vendors and service providers. These opportunities eventually evolved into a more flexible model to deliver applications as a service: the SaaS model. ASPs provided access to packaged software solutions that addressed the needs of a variety of customers. Initially this approach was affordable for service providers, but it later became inconvenient when the cost of customizations and specializations increased. The SaaS approach introduces a more flexible way of delivering application services that are fully customizable by the user by integrating new services, injecting their own components, and designing the application and information workflows. Such a new approach has also been possible with the support of Web 2.0 technologies, which allowed turning the Web browser into a full-featured interface, able even to support application composition and development.

How is cloud computing related to SaaS? According to the classification of services shown in Figure 4.1, the SaaS approach lays on top of the cloud computing stack. It fits into the cloud computing vision expressed by the *XaaS* acronym, Everything-as-a-Service; and with SaaS, applications are delivered as a service. Initially the SaaS model was of interest only for lead users and early adopters. The benefits delivered at that stage were the following:

- Software cost reduction and total cost of ownership (TCO) were paramount
- Service-level improvements
- Rapid implementation
- Standalone and configurable applications
- Rudimentary application and data integration
- Subscription and pay-as-you-go (PAYG) pricing

With the advent of cloud computing there has been an increasing acceptance of SaaS as a viable software delivery model. This led to transition into SaaS 2.0 [40], which does not introduce a new technology but transforms the way in which SaaS is used.

In particular, SaaS 2.0 is focused on providing a more robust infrastructure and application platforms driven by SLAs. Rather than being characterized as a more rapid implementation and deployment environment, SaaS 2.0 will focus on the rapid achievement of business objectives. This is why such evolution does not introduce any new technology: The existing technologies are composed together in order to achieve business goals efficiently. Fundamental to this perspective is the ability to leverage existing solutions and integrate value-added business services. The existing SaaS infrastructures not only allow the development and customization of applications, but they also facilitate the integration of services that are exposed by other parties. SaaS applications are then the result of the interconnection and the synergy of different applications and components that together provide customers with added value. This approach dramatically changes the software ecosystem of the SaaS market, which is no longer monopolized by a few vendors but is now a fully interconnected network of service providers, clustered around some "big hubs" that deliver the application to the customer. In this scenario, each single component integrated into the SaaS application becomes responsible to the user for ensuring the attached SLA and at the same time could be priced differently. Customers can then choose how to specialize their applications by deciding which components and services they want to integrate.

Software-as-a-Service applications can serve different needs. CRM, ERP, and social networking applications are definitely the most popular ones. SalesForce.com is probably the most successful and popular example of a CRM service. It provides a wide range of services for applications: customer relationship and human resource management, enterprise resource planning, and many other features. SalesForce.com builds on top of the Force.com platform, which provides a fully featured environment for building applications. It offers either a programming language or a visual environment to arrange components together for building applications. In addition to the basic features provided, the integration with third-party-made applications enriches SalesForce.com's value. In particular, through AppExchange customers can publish, search, and integrate new services and features into their existing applications. This makes SalesForce.com applications completely extensible and customizable. Similar solutions are offered by NetSuite and RightNow. NetSuite is an integrated software business suite featuring financials, CRM, inventory, and ecommerce functionalities integrated all together. RightNow is customer experience-centered SaaS application that integrates together different features, from chat to Web communities, to support the common activity of an enterprise.

Another important class of popular SaaS applications comprises social networking applications such as Facebook and professional networking sites such as LinkedIn. Other than providing the basic features of networking, they allow incorporating and extending their capabilities by integrating third-party applications. These can be developed as plug-ins for the hosting platform, as happens for Facebook, and made available to users, who can select which applications they want to add to their profile. As a result, the integrated applications get full access to the network of contacts and users' profile data. The nature of these applications can be of different types: office automation components, games, or integration with other existing services.

Office automation applications are also an important representative for SaaS applications: Google Documents and Zoho Office are examples of Web-based applications that aim to address all user needs for documents, spreadsheets, and presentation management. They offer a Web-based interface for creating, managing, and modifying documents that can be easily shared among users and made accessible from anywhere.

It is important to note the role of SaaS solution enablers, which provide an environment in which to integrate third-party services and share information with others. A quite successful example is Box.net, an SaaS application providing users with a Web space and profile that can be enriched and extended with third-party applications such as office automation, integration with CRM-based solutions, social Websites, and photo editing.

4.3 Types of clouds

Clouds constitute the primary outcome of cloud computing. They are a type of parallel and distributed system harnessing physical and virtual computers presented as a unified computing resource. Clouds build the infrastructure on top of which services are implemented and delivered to customers. Such infrastructures can be of different types and provide useful information about the nature and the services offered by the cloud. A more useful classification is given according to the administrative domain of a cloud: It identifies the boundaries within which cloud computing services are implemented, provides hints on the underlying infrastructure adopted to support such services, and qualifies them. It is then possible to differentiate four different types of cloud:

- *Public clouds*. The cloud is open to the wider public.
- *Private clouds*. The cloud is implemented within the private premises of an institution and generally made accessible to the members of the institution or a subset of them.
- *Hybrid or heterogeneous clouds*. The cloud is a combination of the two previous solutions and most likely identifies a private cloud that has been augmented with resources or services hosted in a public cloud.
- *Community clouds*. The cloud is characterized by a multi-administrative domain involving different deployment models (public, private, and hybrid), and it is specifically designed to address the needs of a specific industry.

Almost all the implementations of clouds can be classified in this categorization. In the following sections, we provide brief characterizations of these clouds.

4.3.1 **Public clouds**

Public clouds constitute the first expression of cloud computing. They are a realization of the canonical view of cloud computing in which the services offered are made available to anyone, from anywhere, and at any time through the Internet. From a structural point of view they are a distributed system, most likely composed of one or more datacenters connected together, on top of which the specific services offered by the cloud are implemented. Any customer can easily sign in with the cloud provider, enter her credential and billing details, and use the services offered.

Historically, public clouds were the first class of cloud that were implemented and offered. They offer solutions for minimizing IT infrastructure costs and serve as a viable option for handling peak loads on the local infrastructure. They have become an interesting option for small enterprises, which are able to start their businesses without large up-front investments by completely relying on public infrastructure for their IT needs. What made attractive public clouds compared to the reshaping of the private premises and the purchase of hardware and software was the ability to grow or shrink according to the needs of the related business. By renting the infrastructure or subscribing to application services, customers were able to dynamically upsize or downsize their IT according to the demands of their business. Currently, public clouds are used both to completely replace the IT infrastructure of enterprises and to extend it when it is required.

A fundamental characteristic of public clouds is multitenancy. A public cloud is meant to serve a multitude of users, not a single customer. Any customer requires a virtual computing environment that is separated, and most likely isolated, from other users. This is a fundamental requirement to provide effective monitoring of user activities and guarantee the desired performance and the other QoS attributes negotiated with users. QoS management is a very important aspect of public clouds. Hence, a significant portion of the software infrastructure is devoted to monitoring the cloud resources, to bill them according to the contract made with the user, and to keep a complete history of cloud usage for each customer. These features are fundamental to public clouds because they help providers offer services to users with full accountability.

A public cloud can offer any kind of service: infrastructure, platform, or applications. For example, Amazon EC2 is a public cloud that provides infrastructure as a service; Google AppEngine is a public cloud that provides an application development platform as a service; and SalesForce.com is a public cloud that provides software as a service. What makes public clouds peculiar is the way they are consumed: They are available to everyone and are generally architected to support a large quantity of users. What characterizes them is their natural ability to scale on demand and sustain peak loads.

From an architectural point of view there is no restriction concerning the type of distributed system implemented to support public clouds. Most likely, one or more datacenters constitute the physical infrastructure on top of which the services are implemented and delivered. Public clouds can be composed of geographically dispersed datacenters to share the load of users and better serve them according to their locations. For example, Amazon Web Services has datacenters installed in the United States, Europe, Singapore, and Australia; they allow their customers to choose between three different regions: *us-west-1*, *us-east-1*, or *eu-west-1*. Such regions are priced differently and are further divided into availability zones, which map to specific datacenters. According to the specific class of services delivered by the cloud, a different software stack is installed to manage the infrastructure: virtual machine managers, distributed middleware, or distributed applications.

4.3.2 Private clouds

Public clouds are appealing and provide a viable option to cut IT costs and reduce capital expenses, but they are not applicable in all scenarios. For example, a very common critique to the use of cloud computing in its canonical implementation is the *loss of control*. In the case of public clouds, the provider is in control of the infrastructure and, eventually, of the customers' core logic and sensitive data. Even though there could be regulatory procedure in place that guarantees fair management and respect of the customer's privacy, this condition can still be perceived as a threat or as an unacceptable risk that some organizations are not willing to take. In particular, institutions such as government and military agencies will not consider public clouds as an option for processing or storing their sensitive data. The risk of a breach in the security infrastructure of the provider could expose such information to others; this could simply be considered unacceptable.

In other cases, the loss of control of where your virtual IT infrastructure resides could open the way to other problematic situations. More precisely, the geographical location of a datacenter generally determines the regulations that are applied to management of digital information. As a result, according to the specific location of data, some sensitive information can be made accessible to government agencies or even considered outside the law if processed with specific cryptographic techniques. For example, the USA PATRIOT Act[5] provides its government and other agencies with virtually limitless powers to access information, including that belonging to any company that stores information in the U.S. territory. Finally, existing enterprises that have large computing infrastructures or large installed bases of software do not simply want to switch to public clouds, but they use the existing IT resources and optimize their revenue. All these aspects make the use of a public computing infrastructure not always possible. Yet the general idea supported by the cloud computing vision can still be attractive. More specifically, having an infrastructure able to deliver IT services on demand can still be a winning solution, even when implemented within the private premises of an institution. This idea led to the diffusion of private clouds, which are similar to public clouds, but their resource-provisioning model is limited within the boundaries of an organization.

Private clouds are virtual distributed systems that rely on a private infrastructure and provide internal users with dynamic provisioning of computing resources. Instead of a pay-as-you-go model as in public clouds, there could be other schemes in place, taking into account the usage of the cloud and proportionally billing the different departments or sections of an enterprise. Private clouds have the advantage of keeping the core business operations in-house by relying on the existing IT infrastructure and reducing the burden of maintaining it once the cloud has been set up. In this scenario, security concerns are less critical, since sensitive information does not flow out of the private infrastructure. Moreover, existing IT resources can be better utilized because the private cloud can provide services to a different range of users. Another interesting opportunity that comes with private clouds is the possibility of testing applications and systems at a comparatively lower

---

[5]The USA PATRIOT Act is a statute enacted by the U.S. government that increases the ability of law enforcement agencies to search telephone, email, medical, financial, and other records and eases restrictions on foreign intelligence gathering within the United States. The full text of the act is available at the Website of the Library of the Congress at the following address: http://thomas.loc.gov/cgi-bin/bdquery/z?d107:hr03162: (accessed April 20, 2010).

price rather than public clouds before deploying them on the public virtual infrastructure. A Forrester report [34] on the benefits of delivering in-house cloud computing solutions for enterprises highlighted some of the key advantages of using a private cloud computing infrastructure:

- *Customer information protection.* Despite assurances by the public cloud leaders about security, few provide satisfactory disclosure or have long enough histories with their cloud offerings to provide warranties about the specific level of security put in place on their systems. In-house security is easier to maintain and rely on.
- *Infrastructure ensuring SLAs.* Quality of service implies specific operations such as appropriate clustering and failover, data replication, system monitoring and maintenance, and disaster recovery, and other uptime services can be commensurate to the application needs. Although public cloud vendors provide some of these features, not all of them are available as needed.
- *Compliance with standard procedures and operations.* If organizations are subject to third-party compliance standards, specific procedures have to be put in place when deploying and executing applications. This could be not possible in the case of the virtual public infrastructure.

All these aspects make the use of cloud-based infrastructures in private premises an interesting option.

From an architectural point of view, private clouds can be implemented on more heterogeneous hardware: They generally rely on the existing IT infrastructure already deployed on the private premises. This could be a datacenter, a cluster, an enterprise desktop grid, or a combination of them. The physical layer is complemented with infrastructure management software (i.e., IaaS (M); see Section 4.2.2) or a PaaS solution, according to the service delivered to the users of the cloud.

Different options can be adopted to implement private clouds. Figure 4.4 provides a comprehensive view of the solutions together with some reference to the most popular software used to deploy private clouds. At the bottom layer of the software stack, virtual machine technologies such as Xen [35], KVM [36], and VMware serve as the foundations of the cloud. Virtual machine management technologies such as VMware vCloud, Eucalyptus [37], and OpenNebula [38] can be used to control the virtual infrastructure and provide an IaaS solution. VMware vCloud is a proprietary solution, but Eucalyptus provides full compatibility with Amazon Web Services interfaces and supports different virtual machine technologies such as Xen, KVM, and VMware. Like Eucalyptus, OpenNebula is an open-source solution for virtual infrastructure management that supports KVM, Xen, and VMware, which has been designed to easily integrate third-party IaaS providers. Its modular architecture allows extending the software with additional features such as the capability of reserving virtual machine instances by using Haizea [39] as scheduler.

Solutions that rely on the previous virtual machine managers and provide added value are OpenPEX [40] and InterGrid [41]. OpenPEX is Web-based system that allows the reservation of virtual machine instances and is designed to support different back ends (at the moment only the support for Xen is implemented). InterGrid provides added value on top of OpenNebula and Amazon EC2 by allowing the reservation of virtual machine instances and managing multi-administrative domain clouds. PaaS solutions can provide an additional layer and deliver a high-level service for private clouds. Among the options available for private deployment of clouds we can consider DataSynapse, Zimory Pools, Elastra, and Aneka. DataSynapse is a global provider of application virtualization software. By relying on the VMware virtualization technology,

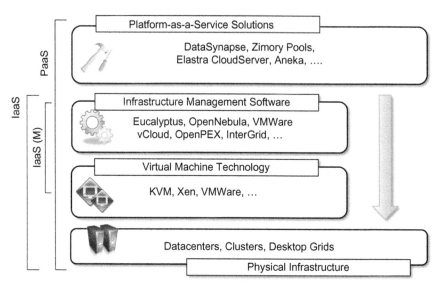

FIGURE 4.4

Private clouds hardware and software stack.

DataSynapse provides a flexible environment for building private clouds on top of datacenters. Elastra Cloud Server is a platform for easily configuring and deploying distributed application infrastructures on clouds. Zimory provides a software infrastructure layer that automates the use of resource pools based on Xen, KVM, and VMware virtualization technologies. It allows creating an internal cloud composed of sparse private and public resources and provides facilities for migrating applications within the existing infrastructure. Aneka is a software development platform that can be used to deploy a cloud infrastructure on top of heterogeneous hardware: datacenters, clusters, and desktop grids. It provides a pluggable service-oriented architecture that's mainly devoted to supporting the execution of distributed applications with different programming models: bag of tasks, MapReduce, and others.

Private clouds can provide in-house solutions for cloud computing, but if compared to public clouds they exhibit more limited capability to scale elastically on demand.

4.3.3 Hybrid clouds

Public clouds are large software and hardware infrastructures that have a capability that is huge enough to serve the needs of multiple users, but they suffer from security threats and administrative pitfalls. Although the option of completely relying on a public virtual infrastructure is appealing for companies that did not incur IT capital costs and have just started considering their IT needs (i.e., start-ups), in most cases the private cloud option prevails because of the existing IT infrastructure.

Private clouds are the perfect solution when it is necessary to keep the processing of information within an enterprise's premises or it is necessary to use the existing hardware and software infrastructure. One of the major drawbacks of private deployments is the inability to scale on demand and to efficiently address peak loads. In this case, it is important to leverage capabilities of public clouds as needed. Hence, a hybrid solution could be an interesting opportunity for taking advantage of the best of the private and public worlds. This led to the development and diffusion of hybrid clouds.

Hybrid clouds allow enterprises to exploit existing IT infrastructures, maintain sensitive information within the premises, and naturally grow and shrink by provisioning external resources and releasing them when they're no longer needed. Security concerns are then only limited to the public portion of the cloud that can be used to perform operations with less stringent constraints but that are still part of the system workload. Figure 4.5 provides a general overview of a hybrid cloud: It is a heterogeneous distributed system resulting from a private cloud that integrates additional services or resources from one or more public clouds. For this reason they are also called *heterogeneous clouds*. As depicted in the diagram, dynamic provisioning is a fundamental component in this scenario. Hybrid clouds address scalability issues by leveraging external resources for exceeding

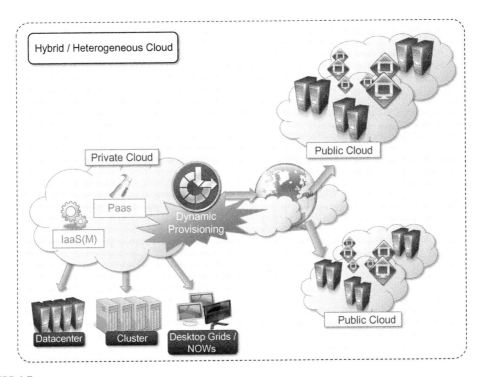

FIGURE 4.5

Hybrid/heterogeneous cloud overview.

capacity demand. These resources or services are temporarily leased for the time required and then released. This practice is also known as *cloudbursting*.[6]

Whereas the concept of hybrid cloud is general, it mostly applies to IT infrastructure rather than software services. Service-oriented computing already introduces the concept of integration of paid software services with existing application deployed in the private premises. In an IaaS scenario, *dynamic provisioning* refers to the ability to acquire on demand virtual machines in order to increase the capability of the resulting distributed system and then release them. Infrastructure management software and PaaS solutions are the building blocks for deploying and managing hybrid clouds. In particular, with respect to private clouds, dynamic provisioning introduces a more complex scheduling algorithm and policies, the goal of which is also to optimize the budget spent to rent public resources.

Infrastructure management software such as OpenNebula already exposes the capability of integrating resources from public clouds such as Amazon EC2. In this case the virtual machine obtained from the public infrastructure is managed as all the other virtual machine instances maintained locally. What is missing is then an advanced scheduling engine that's able to differentiate these resources and provide smart allocations by taking into account the budget available to extend the existing infrastructure. In the case of OpenNebula, advanced schedulers such as Haizea can be integrated to provide cost-based scheduling. A different approach is taken by InterGrid. This is essentially a distributed scheduling engine that manages the allocation of virtual machines in a collection of peer networks. Such networks can be represented by a local cluster, a gateway to a public cloud, or a combination of the two. Once a request is submitted to one of the InterGrid gateways, it is served by possibly allocating virtual instances in all the peered networks, and the allocation of requests is performed by taking into account the user budget and the peering arrangements between networks.

Dynamic provisioning is most commonly implemented in PaaS solutions that support hybrid clouds. As previously discussed, one of the fundamental components of PaaS middleware is the mapping of distributed applications onto the cloud infrastructure. In this scenario, the role of dynamic provisioning becomes fundamental to ensuring the execution of applications under the QoS agreed on with the user. For example, Aneka provides a provisioning service that leverages different IaaS providers for scaling the existing cloud infrastructure [42]. The provisioning service cooperates with the scheduler, which is in charge of guaranteeing a specific QoS for applications. In particular, each user application has a budget attached, and the scheduler uses that budget to optimize the execution of the application by renting virtual nodes if needed. Other PaaS implementations support the deployment of hybrid clouds and provide dynamic provisioning capabilities. Among those discussed for the implementation and management of private clouds we can cite Elastra CloudServer and Zimory Pools.

---

[6]According to the Cloud Computing Wiki, the term *cloudburst* has a double meaning; it also refers to the "failure of a cloud computing environment due to the inability to handle a spike in demand" (http://sites.google.com/site/Cloudcomputingwiki/Home/Cloud-computing-vocabulary). In this book, we always refer to the dynamic provisioning of resources from public clouds when mentioning this term.

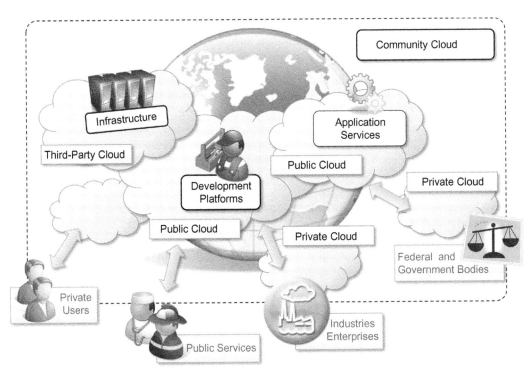

FIGURE 4.6

A community cloud.

4.3.4 **Community clouds**

Community clouds are distributed systems created by integrating the services of different clouds to address the specific needs of an industry, a community, or a business sector. The National Institute of Standards and Technologies (NIST) [43] characterizes community clouds as follows:

> *The infrastructure is shared by several organizations and supports a specific community that has shared concerns (e.g., mission, security requirements, policy, and compliance considerations). It may be managed by the organizations or a third party and may exist on premise or off premise.*

Figure 4.6 provides a general view of the usage scenario of community clouds, together with reference architecture. The users of a specific community cloud fall into a well-identified community, sharing the same concerns or needs; they can be government bodies, industries, or even simple users, but all of them focus on the same issues for their interaction with the cloud. This is a different scenario than public clouds, which serve a multitude of users with different needs. Community clouds are also different from private clouds, where the services are generally delivered within the institution that owns the cloud.

From an architectural point of view, a community cloud is most likely implemented over multiple administrative domains. This means that different organizations such as government bodies, private enterprises, research organizations, and even public virtual infrastructure providers contribute with their resources to build the cloud infrastructure.

Candidate sectors for community clouds are as follows:

- *Media industry.* In the media industry, companies are looking for low-cost, agile, and simple solutions to improve the efficiency of content production. Most media productions involve an extended ecosystem of partners. In particular, the creation of digital content is the outcome of a collaborative process that includes movement of large data, massive compute-intensive rendering tasks, and complex workflow executions. Community clouds can provide a shared environment where services can facilitate business-to-business collaboration and offer the horsepower in terms of aggregate bandwidth, CPU, and storage required to efficiently support media production.

- *Healthcare industry.* In the healthcare industry, there are different scenarios in which community clouds could be of use. In particular, community clouds can provide a global platform on which to share information and knowledge without revealing sensitive data maintained within the private infrastructure. The naturally hybrid deployment model of community clouds can easily support the storing of patient-related data in a private cloud while using the shared infrastructure for noncritical services and automating processes within hospitals.

- *Energy and other core industries.* In these sectors, community clouds can bundle the comprehensive set of solutions that together vertically address management, deployment, and orchestration of services and operations. Since these industries involve different providers, vendors, and organizations, a community cloud can provide the right type of infrastructure to create an open and fair market.

- *Public sector.* Legal and political restrictions in the public sector can limit the adoption of public cloud offerings. Moreover, governmental processes involve several institutions and agencies and are aimed at providing strategic solutions at local, national, and international administrative levels. They involve business-to-administration, citizen-to-administration, and possibly business-to-business processes. Some examples include invoice approval, infrastructure planning, and public hearings. A community cloud can constitute the optimal venue to provide a distributed environment in which to create a communication platform for performing such operations.

- *Scientific research.* Science clouds are an interesting example of community clouds. In this case, the common interest driving different organizations sharing a large distributed infrastructure is scientific computing.

The term *community cloud* can also identify a more specific type of cloud that arises from concern over the controls of vendors in cloud computing and that aspire to combine the principles of *digital ecosystems*[7] [44] with the case study of cloud computing. A community cloud is formed by harnessing the underutilized resources of user machines [45] and providing an infrastructure in

---

[7]*Digital ecosystems* are distributed, adaptive, and open sociotechnical systems with properties of self-organization, scalability, and sustainability inspired by natural ecosystems. The primary aim of digital ecosystems is to sustain the regional development of small and medium-sized enterprises (SMEs).

which each can be at the same time a consumer, a producer, or a coordinator of the services offered by the cloud. The benefits of these community clouds are the following:

- *Openness.* By removing the dependency on cloud vendors, community clouds are open systems in which fair competition between different solutions can happen.
- *Community.* Being based on a collective that provides resources and services, the infrastructure turns out to be more scalable because the system can grow simply by expanding its user base.
- *Graceful failures.* Since there is no single provider or vendor in control of the infrastructure, there is no single point of failure.
- *Convenience and control.* Within a community cloud there is no conflict between convenience and control because the cloud is shared and owned by the community, which makes all the decisions through a collective democratic process.
- *Environmental sustainability.* The community cloud is supposed to have a smaller carbon footprint because it harnesses underutilized resources. Moreover, these clouds tend to be more organic by growing and shrinking in a symbiotic relationship to support the demand of the community, which in turn sustains it.

This is an alternative vision of a community cloud, focusing more on the social aspect of the clouds that are formed as an aggregation of resources of community members. The idea of a heterogeneous infrastructure built to serve the needs of a community of people is also reflected in the previous definition, but in that case the attention is focused on the commonality of interests that aggregates the users of the cloud into a community. In both cases, the concept of community is fundamental.

4.4 Economics of the cloud

The main drivers of cloud computing are economy of scale and simplicity of software delivery and its operation. In fact, the biggest benefit of this phenomenon is financial: the *pay-as-you-go* model offered by cloud providers. In particular, cloud computing allows:

- Reducing the capital costs associated to the IT infrastructure
- Eliminating the depreciation or lifetime costs associated with IT capital assets
- Replacing software licensing with subscriptions
- Cutting the maintenance and administrative costs of IT resources

A *capital cost* is the cost occurred in purchasing an asset that is useful in the production of goods or the rendering of services. Capital costs are one-time expenses that are generally paid up front and that will contribute over the long term to generate profit. The IT infrastructure and the software are capital assets because enterprises require them to conduct their business. At present it does not matter whether the principal business of an enterprise is related to IT, because the business will definitely have an IT department that is used to automate many of the activities that are performed within the enterprise: payroll, customer relationship management, enterprise resource planning, tracking and inventory of products, and others. Hence, IT resources constitute a capital cost for any kind of enterprise. It is good practice to try to keep capital costs low because they introduce expenses that will generate profit over time; more than that, since they are associated with material things they are subject to *depreciation* over time, which in the end reduces the profit of the enterprise because such costs are directly subtracted from the enterprise revenues. In the case of IT capital costs, the depreciation costs are represented by the loss of value of the hardware over time and the aging of software products that need to be replaced because new features are required.

Before cloud computing diffused within the enterprise, the budget spent on IT infrastructure and software constituted a significant expense for medium-sized and large enterprises. Many enterprises own a small or medium-sized datacenter that introduces several operational costs in terms of maintenance, electricity, and cooling. Additional operational costs are occurred in maintaining an IT department and an IT support center. Moreover, other costs are triggered by the purchase of potentially expensive software. With cloud computing these costs are significantly reduced or simply disappear according to its penetration. One of the advantages introduced by the cloud computing model is that it shifts the capital costs previously allocated to the purchase of hardware and software into operational costs inducted by renting the infrastructure and paying subscriptions for the use of software. These costs can be better controlled according to the business needs and prosperity of the enterprise. Cloud computing also introduces reductions in administrative and maintenance costs. That is, there is no or limited need for having administrative staff take care of the management of the cloud infrastructure. At the same time, the cost of IT support staff is also reduced. When it comes to depreciation costs, they simply disappear for the enterprise, since in a scenario where all the IT needs are served by the cloud there are no IT capital assets that depreciate over time.

The amount of cost savings that cloud computing can introduce within an enterprise is related to the specific scenario in which cloud services are used and how they contribute to generate a profit for the enterprise. In the case of a small startup, it is possible to completely leverage the cloud for many aspects, such as:

- IT infrastructure
- Software development
- CRM and ERP

In this case it is possible to completely eliminate capital costs because there are no initial IT assets. The situation is completely different in the case of enterprises that already have a considerable amount of IT assets. In this case, cloud computing, especially IaaS-based solutions, can help manage unplanned capital costs that are generated by the needs of the enterprise in the short term. In this case, by leveraging cloud computing, these costs can be turned into operational costs that last as long as there is a need for them. For example, IT infrastructure leasing helps more efficiently manage peak loads without inducing capital expenses. As soon as the increased load does not justify the use of additional resources, these can be released and the costs associated with them disappear. This is the most adopted model of cloud computing because many enterprises already have IT facilities. Another option is to make a slow transition toward cloud-based solutions while the capital IT assets get depreciated and need to be replaced. Between these two cases there is a wide variety of scenarios in which cloud computing could be of help in generating profits for enterprises.

Another important aspect is the elimination of some indirect costs that are generated by IT assets, such as software licensing and support and carbon footprint emissions. With cloud computing, an enterprise uses software applications on a subscription basis, and there is no need for any licensing fee because the software providing the service remains the property of the provider. Leveraging IaaS solutions allows room for datacenter consolidation that in the end could result in a smaller carbon footprint. In some countries such as Australia, the carbon footprint emissions are taxable, so by reducing or completely eliminating such emissions, enterprises can pay less tax.

In terms of the pricing models introduced by cloud computing, we can distinguish three different strategies that are adopted by the providers:

- *Tiered pricing*. In this model, cloud services are offered in several tiers, each of which offers a fixed computing specification and SLA at a specific price per unit of time. This model is used by Amazon for pricing the EC2 service, which makes available different server configurations in terms of computing capacity (CPU type and speed, memory) that have different costs per hour.
- *Per-unit pricing*. This model is more suitable to cases where the principal source of revenue for the cloud provider is determined in terms of units of specific services, such as data transfer and memory allocation. In this scenario customers can configure their systems more efficiently according to the application needs. This model is used, for example, by GoGrid, which makes customers pay according to RAM/hour units for the servers deployed in the GoGrid cloud.
- *Subscription-based pricing*. This is the model used mostly by SaaS providers in which users pay a periodic subscription fee for use of the software or the specific component services that are integrated in their applications.

All of these costs are based on a pay-as-you-go model, which constitutes a more flexible solution for supporting the delivery on demand of IT services. This is what actually makes possible the conversion of IT capital costs into operational costs, since the cost of buying hardware turns into a cost for leasing it and the cost generated by the purchase of software turns into a subscription fee paid for using it.

4.5 Open challenges

Still in its infancy, cloud computing presents many challenges for industry and academia. There is a significant amount of work in academia focused on defining the challenges brought by this phenomenon [46−49]. In this section, we highlight the most important ones: the definition and the formalization of cloud computing, the interoperation between different clouds, the creation of standards, security, scalability, fault tolerance, and organizational aspects.

4.5.1 Cloud definition

As discussed earlier, there have been several attempts made to define cloud computing and to provide a classification of all the services and technologies identified as such. One of the most comprehensive formalizations is noted in the NIST working definition of cloud computing [43]. It **characterizes** cloud computing as on-demand self-service, broad network access, resource-pooling, rapid elasticity, and measured service; **classifies** services as SaaS, PaaS, and IaaS; and **categorizes** deployment models as public, private, community, and hybrid clouds. The view is in line with our discussion and shared by many IT practitioners and academics.

Despite the general agreement on the NIST definition, there are alternative taxonomies for cloud services. David Linthicum, founder of BlueMountains Labs, provides a more detailed classification,[8] which comprehends 10 different classes and better suits the vision of cloud computing within the enterprise. A different approach has been taken at the University of California, Santa Barbara (UCSB) [50], which departs from the XaaS concept and tries to define an ontology for cloud computing. In their work the concept of a cloud is dissected into five main layers: applications, software environments, software infrastructure, software kernel, and hardware. Each layer addresses the needs of a different class of users within the cloud computing community and most likely builds on the underlying layers. According to the authors, this work constitutes the first effort to provide a more robust interaction model between the different cloud entities on both the functional level and the semantic level.

These characterizations and taxonomies reflect what is meant by cloud computing at the present time, but being in its infancy the phenomenon is constantly evolving, and the same will happen to the attempts to capture the real nature of cloud computing. It is interesting to note that the principal characterization used in this book as a reference for introducing and explaining cloud computing is considered a working definition, which by nature identifies something that continuously changes over time by becoming refined.

4.5.2 Cloud interoperability and standards

Cloud computing is a service-based model for delivering IT infrastructure and applications like utilities such as power, water, and electricity. To fully realize this goal, introducing standards and allowing interoperability between solutions offered by different vendors are objectives of fundamental importance. Vendor lock-in constitutes one of the major strategic barriers against the seamless adoption of cloud computing at all stages. In particular there is major fear on the part of enterprises in which IT constitutes the significant part of their revenues. Vendor lock-in can prevent a customer from switching to another competitor's solution, or when this is possible, it happens at considerable conversion cost and requires significant amounts of time. This can occur either because the customer wants to find a more suitable solution for customer needs or because the vendor is no longer able to provide the required service. The presence of standards that are actually implemented and adopted in the cloud computing community could give room for interoperability and then lessen the risks resulting from vendor lock-in.

The current state of standards and interoperability in cloud computing resembles the early Internet era, when there was no common agreement on the protocols and technologies used and each organization had its own network. Yet the first steps toward a standardization process have been made, and a few organizations, such as the Cloud Computing Interoperability Forum (CCIF),[9]

---

[8]David Linthicum, Cloud Computing Ontology Framework; http://Cloudcomputing.sys-con.com/node/811519.
[9]www.Cloudforum.org.

the Open Cloud Consortium,[10] and the DMTF Cloud Standards Incubator,[11] are leading the path. Another interesting initiative is the Open Cloud Manifesto,[12] which embodies the point of view of various stakeholders on the benefits of open standards in the field.

The standardization efforts are mostly concerned with the lower level of the cloud computing architecture, which is the most popular and developed. In particular, in the IaaS market, the use of a proprietary virtual machine format constitutes the major reasons for the vendor lock-in, and efforts to provide virtual machine image compatibility between IaaS vendors can possibly improve the level of interoperability among them. The Open Virtualization Format (OVF) [51] is an attempt to provide a common format for storing the information and metadata describing a virtual machine image. Even though the OVF provides a full specification for packaging and distributing virtual machine images in completely platform-independent fashion, it is supported by few vendors that use it to import static virtual machine images. The challenge is providing standards for supporting the migration of running instances, thus allowing the real ability of switching from one infrastructure vendor to another in a completely transparent manner.

Another direction in which standards try to move is devising a general reference architecture for cloud computing systems and providing a standard interface through which one can interact with them. At the moment the compatibility between different solutions is quite restricted, and the lack of a common set of APIs make the interaction with cloud-based solutions vendor specific. In the IaaS market, Amazon Web Services plays a leading role, and other IaaS solutions, mostly open source, provide AWS-compatible APIs, thus constituting themselves as valid alternatives. Even in this case, there is no consistent trend in devising some common APIs for interfacing with IaaS (and, in general, XaaS), and this constitutes one of the areas in which a considerable improvement can be made in the future.

4.5.3 Scalability and fault tolerance

The ability to scale on demand constitutes one of the most attractive features of cloud computing. Clouds allow scaling beyond the limits of the existing in-house IT resources, whether they are infrastructure (compute and storage) or applications services. To implement such a capability, the cloud middleware has to be designed with the principle of scalability along different dimensions in mind—for example, performance, size, and load. The cloud middleware manages a huge number of resource and users, which rely on the cloud to obtain the horsepower that they cannot obtain within the premises without bearing considerable administrative and maintenance costs. These costs are a reality for whomever develops, manages, and maintains the cloud middleware and offers the service to customers. In this scenario, the ability to tolerate failure becomes fundamental, sometimes even more important than providing an extremely efficient and optimized system. Hence, the challenge in this case is designing highly scalable and fault-tolerant systems that are easy to manage and at the same time provide competitive performance.

---

[10]www.opencloudconsortium.org.
[11]www.dmtf.org/about/cloud-incubator.
[12]www.opencloudmanifesto.org.

4.5.4 **Security, trust, and privacy**

Security, trust, and privacy issues are major obstacles for massive adoption of cloud computing. The traditional cryptographic technologies are used to prevent data tampering and access to sensitive information. The massive use of virtualization technologies exposes the existing system to new threats, which previously were not considered applicable. For example, it might be possible that applications hosted in the cloud can process sensitive information; such information can be stored within a cloud storage facility using the most advanced technology in cryptography to protect data and then be considered safe from any attempt to access it without the required permissions. Although these data are processed in memory, they must necessarily be decrypted by the legitimate application, but since the application is hosted in a managed virtual environment it becomes accessible to the virtual machine manager that by program is designed to access the memory pages of such an application. In this case, what is experienced is a lack of control over the environment in which the application is executed, which is made possible by leveraging the cloud. It then happens that a new way of using existing technologies creates new opportunities for additional threats to the security of applications. The lack of control over their own data and processes also poses severe problems for the trust we give to the cloud service provider and the level of privacy we want to have for our data.

On one side we need to decide whether to trust the provider itself; on the other side, specific regulations can simply prevail over the agreement the provider is willing to establish with us concerning the privacy of the information managed on our behalf. Moreover, cloud services delivered to the end user can be the result of a complex stack of services that are obtained by third parties via the primary cloud service provider. In this case there is a chain of responsibilities in terms of service delivery that can introduce more vulnerability for the secure management of data, the enforcement of privacy rules, and the trust given to the service provider. In particular, when a violation of privacy or illegal access to sensitive information is detected, it could become difficult to identify who is liable for such violations. The challenges in this area are, then, mostly concerned with devising secure and trustable systems from different perspectives: technical, social, and legal.

4.5.5 **Organizational aspects**

Cloud computing introduces a significant change in the way IT services are consumed and managed. More precisely, storage, compute power, network infrastructure, and applications are delivered as metered services over the Internet. This introduces a billing model that is new within typical enterprise IT departments, which requires a certain level of cultural and organizational process maturity. In particular, a wide acceptance of cloud computing will require a significant change to business processes and organizational boundaries. Some interesting questions arise in considering the role of the IT department in this new scenario. In particular, the following questions have to be considered:

• What is the new role of the IT department in an enterprise that completely or significantly relies on the cloud?
• How will the compliance department perform its activity when there is a considerable lack of control over application workflows?

- What are the implications (political, legal, etc.) for organizations that lose control over some aspects of their services?
- What will be the perception of the end users of such services?

From an organizational point of view, the lack of control over the management of data and processes poses not only security threats but also new problems that previously did not exist. Traditionally, when there was a problem with computer systems, organizations developed strategies and solutions to cope with them, often by relying on local expertise and knowledge. One of the major advantages of moving IT infrastructure and services to the cloud is to reduce or completely remove the costs related to maintenance and support. As a result, users of such infrastructure and services lose a reference to deal with for IT troubleshooting. At the same time, the existing IT staff is required to have a different kind of competency and, in general, fewer skills, thus reducing their value. These are the challenges from an organizational point of view that must be faced and that will significantly change the relationships within the enterprise itself among the various groups of people working together.

SUMMARY

In this chapter we discussed the fundamental characteristics of cloud computing and introduced reference architecture for classifying and organizing cloud services. To best sum up the content of this chapter, we can recall the NIST working definition of cloud computing, which outlines the fundamental aspects of this phenomenon as follows:

- *Five essential characteristics.* In-demand self-service, broad network access, resource pooling, rapid elasticity, and measured service.
- *Three service models.* Software-as-a-Service (SaaS), Platform-as-a-Service (PaaS), and Infrastructure-as-a-Service (IaaS).
- *Four deployment models.* Public clouds, private clouds, community clouds, and hybrid clouds.

The major driving force for rapid adoption of cloud computing are the economics and the simplicity of software delivery and operation. Cloud computing presents considerable opportunity to increase the profits of enterprises by reducing capital costs of IT assets and transforming them into operational costs. For these reasons we have also discussed the economic and cost models introduced with cloud computing.

Although cloud computing has been rapidly adopted in industry, there are several open research challenges in areas such as management of cloud computing systems, their security, and social and organizational issues. There is significant room for advancement in software infrastructure and models supporting cloud computing.

Review questions

1. What does the acronym *XaaS* stand for?
2. What are the fundamental components introduced in the cloud reference model?

3. What does Infrastructure-as-a-Service refer to?

4. Which are the basic components of an IaaS-based solution for cloud computing?

5. Provide some examples of IaaS implementations.

6. What are the main characteristics of a Platform-as-a-Service solution?

7. Describe the different categories of options available in a PaaS market.

8. What does the acronym SaaS mean? How does it relate to cloud computing?

9. Give the name of some popular Software-as-a-Service solutions.

10. Classify the various types of clouds.

11. Give an example of the public cloud.

12. Which is the most common scenario for a private cloud?

13. What kinds of needs are addressed by heterogeneous clouds?

14. Describe the fundamental features of the economic and business model behind cloud computing.

15. How does cloud computing help to reduce the time to market for applications and to cut down capital expenses?

16. List some of the challenges in cloud computing.

Cloud Application Programming and the Aneka Platform

Aneka
Cloud Application Platform

Aneka is Manjrasoft Pty. Ltd.'s solution for developing, deploying, and managing cloud applications. Aneka consists of a scalable cloud middleware that can be deployed on top of heterogeneous computing resources. It offers an extensible collection of services coordinating the execution of applications, helping administrators monitor the status of the cloud, and providing integration with existing cloud technologies. One of Aneka's key advantages is its extensible set of application programming interfaces (APIs) associated with different types of programming models—such as Task, Thread, and MapReduce—used for developing distributed applications, integrating new capabilities into the cloud, and supporting different types of cloud deployment models: public, private, and hybrid (see Figure 5.1). These features differentiate Aneka from infrastructure management software and characterize it as a platform for developing, deploying, and managing execution of applications on various types of clouds.

This chapter provides a complete overview of the framework by first describing the architecture of the system. It introduces Aneka's components and the fundamental services that make up the Aneka Cloud and discusses some common deployment scenarios.

5.1 Framework overview

Aneka is a software platform for developing cloud computing applications. It allows harnessing of disparate computing resources and managing them into a unique virtual domain—the Aneka Cloud—in which applications are executed. According to the Cloud Computing Reference Model presented in Chapter 1, Aneka is a *pure PaaS* solution for cloud computing. Aneka is a cloud middleware product that can be deployed on a heterogeneous set of resources: a network of computers, a multicore server, datacenters, virtual cloud infrastructures, or a mixture of these. The framework provides both middleware for managing and scaling distributed applications and an extensible set of APIs for developing them.

Figure 5.2 provides a complete overview of the components of the Aneka framework. The core infrastructure of the system provides a uniform layer that allows the framework to be deployed over different platforms and operating systems. The physical and virtual resources representing the bare metal of the cloud are managed by the Aneka container, which is installed on each node and constitutes the basic building block of the middleware. A collection of interconnected containers constitute the Aneka Cloud: a single domain in which services are made available to users and

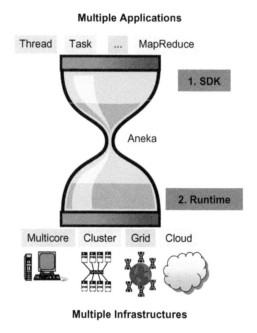

FIGURE 5.1

Aneka's capabilities at a glance.

developers. The container features three different classes of services: *Fabric Services*, *Foundation Services*, and *Execution Services*. These take care of infrastructure management, supporting services for the Aneka Cloud, and application management and execution, respectively. These services are made available to developers and administrators by means of the application management and development layer, which includes interfaces and APIs for developing cloud applications and the management tools and interfaces for controlling Aneka Clouds.

Aneka implements a service-oriented architecture (SOA), and services are the fundamental components of an Aneka Cloud. Services operate at container level and, except for the platform abstraction layer, they provide developers, users, and administrators with all features offered by the framework. Services also constitute the extension and customization point of Aneka Clouds: The infrastructure allows for the integration of new services or replacement of the existing ones with a different implementation. The framework includes the basic services for infrastructure and node management, application execution, accounting, and system monitoring; existing services can be extended and new features can be added to the cloud by dynamically plugging new ones into the container. Such extensible and flexible infrastructure enables Aneka Clouds to support different programming and execution models for applications. A programming model represents a collection of abstractions that developers can use to express distributed applications; the runtime support for a programming model is constituted by a collection of execution and foundation services interacting together to carry out application execution. Thus, the implementation of a new model requires the development of the specific programming abstractions used by application developers and the

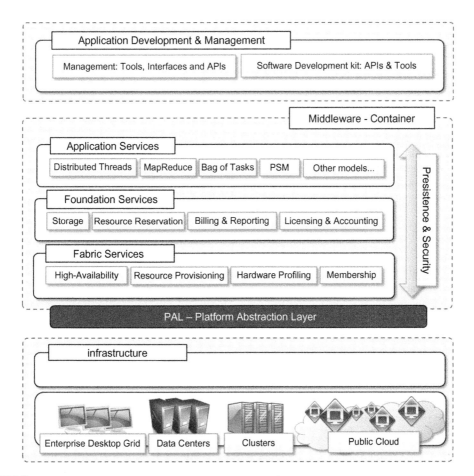

FIGURE 5.2

Aneka framework overview.

services, providing runtime support for them. Programming models are just one aspect of application management and execution. Within an Aneka Cloud environment, there are different aspects involved in providing a scalable and elastic infrastructure and distributed runtime for applications. These services involve:

- *Elasticity and scaling.* By means of the dynamic provisioning service, Aneka supports dynamically upsizing and downsizing of the infrastructure available for applications.
- *Runtime management.* The runtime machinery is responsible for keeping the infrastructure up and running and serves as a hosting environment for services. It is primarily represented by the container and a collection of services that manage service membership and lookup, infrastructure maintenance, and profiling.
- *Resource management.* Aneka is an elastic infrastructure in which resources are added and removed dynamically according to application needs and user requirements. To provide

QoS-based execution, the system not only allows dynamic provisioning but also provides capabilities for reserving nodes for exclusive use by specific applications.

- *Application management.* A specific subset of services is devoted to managing applications. These services include scheduling, execution, monitoring, and storage management.
- *User management.* Aneka is a multitenant distributed environment in which multiple applications, potentially belonging to different users, are executed. The framework provides an extensible user system via which it is possible to define users, groups, and permissions. The services devoted to user management build up the security infrastructure of the system and constitute a fundamental element for accounting management.
- *QoS/SLA management and billing.* Within a cloud environment, application execution is metered and billed. Aneka provides a collection of services that coordinate together to take into account the usage of resources by each application and to bill the owning user accordingly.

All these services are available to specific interfaces and APIs on top of which the software development kit (SDK) and management kit are built. The SDK mainly relates to application development and modeling; it provides developers with APIs to develop applications with the existing programming models and an object model for creating new models. The management kit is mostly focused on interacting with the runtime services for managing the infrastructure, users, and applications. The management kit gives a complete view of Aneka Clouds and allows monitoring Aneka's status, whereas the SDK is more focused on the single application and provides means to control its execution from a single user. Both components are meant to provide an easy-to-use interface via which to interact and manage containers that are the core component of the Aneka framework.

5.2 Anatomy of the Aneka container

The Aneka container constitutes the building blocks of Aneka Clouds and represents the runtime machinery available to services and applications. The container, the unit of deployment in Aneka Clouds, is a lightweight software layer designed to host services and interact with the underlying operating system and hardware. The main role of the container is to provide a lightweight environment in which to deploy services and some basic capabilities such as communication channels through which it interacts with other nodes in the Aneka Cloud. Almost all operations performed within Aneka are carried out by the services managed by the container. The services installed in the Aneka container can be classified into three major categories:

- Fabric Services
- Foundation Services
- Application Services

The services stack resides on top of the *Platform Abstraction Layer (PAL)*, representing the interface to the underlying operating system and hardware. It provides a uniform view of the software and hardware environment in which the container is running. Persistence and security traverse all the services stack to provide a secure and reliable infrastructure. In the following sections we discuss the components of these layers in more detail.

5.2.1 From the ground up: the platform abstraction layer

The core infrastructure of the system is based on the .NET technology and allows the Aneka container to be portable over different platforms and operating systems. Any platform featuring an ECMA-334 [52] and ECMA-335 [53] compatible environment can host and run an instance of the Aneka container.

The *Common Language Infrastructure (CLI)*, which is the specification introduced in the ECMA-334 standard, defines a common runtime environment and application model for executing programs but does not provide any interface to access the hardware or to collect performance data from the hosting operating system. Moreover, each operating system has a different file system organization and stores that information differently. The *Platform Abstraction Layer (PAL)* addresses this heterogeneity and provides the container with a uniform interface for accessing the relevant hardware and operating system information, thus allowing the rest of the container to run unmodified on any supported platform.

The PAL is responsible for detecting the supported hosting environment and providing the corresponding implementation to interact with it to support the activity of the container. The PAL provides the following features:

- Uniform and platform-independent implementation interface for accessing the hosting platform
- Uniform access to extended and additional properties of the hosting platform
- Uniform and platform-independent access to remote nodes
- Uniform and platform-independent management interfaces

The PAL is a small layer of software that comprises a detection engine, which automatically configures the container at boot time, with the platform-specific component to access the above information and an implementation of the abstraction layer for the Windows, Linux, and Mac OS X operating systems.

The collectible data that are exposed by the PAL are the following:

- Number of cores, frequency, and CPU usage
- Memory size and usage
- Aggregate available disk space
- Network addresses and devices attached to the node

Moreover, additional custom information can be retrieved by querying the properties of the hardware. The PAL interface provides means for custom implementations to pull additional information by using name-value pairs that can host any kind of information about the hosting platform. For example, these properties can contain additional information about the processor, such as the model and family, or additional data about the process running the container.

5.2.2 Fabric services

Fabric Services define the lowest level of the software stack representing the Aneka Container. They provide access to the resource-provisioning subsystem and to the monitoring facilities implemented in Aneka. Resource-provisioning services are in charge of dynamically providing new nodes on demand by relying on virtualization technologies, while monitoring services allow for hardware profiling and implement a basic monitoring infrastructure that can be used by all the services installed in the container.

5.2.2.1 Profiling and monitoring

Profiling and monitoring services are mostly exposed through the *Heartbeat, Monitoring*, and *Reporting Services*. The first makes available the information that is collected through the PAL; the other two implement a generic infrastructure for monitoring the activity of any service in the Aneka Cloud.

The Heartbeat Service periodically collects the dynamic performance information about the node and publishes this information to the membership service in the Aneka Cloud. These data are collected by the index node of the Cloud, which makes them available for services such as reservations and scheduling in order to optimize the use of a heterogeneous infrastructure. As already discussed, basic information about memory, disk space, CPU, and operating system is collected. Moreover, additional data are pulled into the "alive" message, such as information about the installed software in the system and any other useful information. More precisely, the infrastructure has been designed to carry over any type of data that can be expressed by means of text-valued properties. As previously noted, the information published by the Heartbeat Service is mostly concerned with the properties of the node. A specific component, called *Node Resolver*, is in charge of collecting these data and making them available to the Heartbeat Service. Aneka provides different implementations for such component in order to cover a wide variety of hosting environments. A variety of operating systems are supported with different implementations of the PAL, and different node resolvers allow Aneka to capture other types of data that do not strictly depend on the hosting operating system. For example, the retrieval of the public IP of the node is different in the case of physical machines or virtual instances hosted in the infrastructure of an IaaS provider such as EC2 or GoGrid. In virtual deployment, a different node resolver is used so that all other components of the system can work transparently.

The set of built-in services for monitoring and profiling is completed by a generic monitoring infrastructure, which allows any custom service to report its activity. This infrastructure is composed of the Reporting and Monitoring Services. The *Reporting Service* manages the store for monitored data and makes them accessible to other services or external applications for analysis purposes. On each node, an instance of the *Monitoring Service* acts as a gateway to the *Reporting Service* and forwards to it all the monitored data that has been collected on the node. Any service that wants to publish monitoring data can leverage the local monitoring service without knowing the details of the entire infrastructure. Currently several built-in services provide information through this channel:

- The *Membership Catalogue* tracks the performance information of nodes.
- The *Execution Service* monitors several time intervals for the execution of jobs.
- The *Scheduling Service* tracks the state transitions of jobs.
- The *Storage Service* monitors and makes available information about data transfer, such as upload and download times, filenames, and sizes.
- The *Resource Provisioning Service* tracks the provisioning and lifetime information of virtual nodes.

All this information can be stored on a relational database management system (RDBMS) or a flat file and can be further analyzed by specific applications. For example, the Management Console provides a view on such data for administrative purposes.

5.2.2.2 Resource management

Resource management is another fundamental feature of Aneka Clouds. It comprises several tasks: resource membership, resource reservation, and resource provisioning. Aneka provides a collection of services that are in charge of managing resources. These are the *Index Service* (or *Membership Catalogue*), *Reservation Service*, and *Resource Provisioning Service*.

The *Membership Catalogue* is Aneka's fundamental component for resource management; it keeps track of the basic node information for all the nodes that are connected or disconnected. The Membership Catalogue implements the basic services of a directory service, allowing the search for services using attributes such as names and nodes. During container startup, each instance publishes its information to the Membership Catalogue and updates it constantly during its lifetime. Services and external applications can query the membership catalogue to discover the available services and interact with them. To speed up and enhance the performance of queries, the membership catalogue is organized as a distributed database: All the queries that pertain to information maintained locally are resolved locally; otherwise the query is forwarded to the main index node, which has a global knowledge of the entire Cloud. The Membership Catalogue is also the collector of the dynamic performance data of each node, which are then sent to the local monitoring service to be persisted in the long term.

Indexing and categorizing resources are fundamental to resource management. On top of the basic indexing service, provisioning completes the set of features that are available for resource management within Aneka. Deployment of container instances and their configuration are performed by the infrastructure management layer and are not part of the Fabric Services.

Dynamic resource provisioning allows the integration and management of virtual resources leased from IaaS providers into the Aneka Cloud. This service changes the structure of the Aneka Cloud by allowing it to scale up and down according to different needs: handling node failures, ensuring the quality of service for applications, or maintaining a constant performance and throughput of the Cloud. Aneka defines a very flexible infrastructure for resource provisioning whereby it is possible to change the logic that triggers provisioning, support several back-ends, and change the runtime strategy with which a specific back-end is selected for provisioning. The resource-provisioning infrastructure built into Aneka is mainly concentrated in the *Resource Provisioning Service*, which includes all the operations that are needed for provisioning virtual instances. The implementation of the service is based on the idea of *resource pools*. A resource pool abstracts the interaction with a specific IaaS provider by exposing a common interface so that all the pools can be managed uniformly. A resource pool does not necessarily map to an IaaS provider but can be used to expose as dynamic resources a private cloud managed by a Xen Hypervisor or a collection of physical resources that are only used sporadically. The system uses an open protocol, allowing for the use of metadata to provide additional information for describing resource pools and to customize provisioning requests. This infrastructure simplifies the implementation of additional features and the support of different implementations that can be transparently integrated into the existing system.

Resource provisioning is a feature designed to support QoS requirements-driven execution of applications. Therefore, it mostly serves requests coming from the Reservation Service or the Scheduling Services. Despite this, external applications can directly leverage Aneka's resource-provisioning capabilities by dynamically retrieving a client to the service and interacting with the infrastructure to it. This extends the resource-provisioning scenarios that can be handled by Aneka, which can also be used as a virtual machine manager.

5.2.3 Foundation services

Fabric Services are fundamental services of the Aneka Cloud and define the basic infrastructure management features of the system. *Foundation Services* are related to the logical management of the distributed system built on top of the infrastructure and provide supporting services for the execution of distributed applications. All the supported programming models can integrate with and leverage these services to provide advanced and comprehensive application management. These services cover:

- Storage management for applications
- Accounting, billing, and resource pricing
- Resource reservation

Foundation Services provide a uniform approach to managing distributed applications and allow developers to concentrate only on the logic that distinguishes a specific programming model from the others. Together with the Fabric Services, Foundation Services constitute the core of the Aneka middleware. These services are mostly consumed by the execution services and Management Consoles. External applications can leverage the exposed capabilities for providing advanced application management.

5.2.3.1 Storage management

Data management is an important aspect of any distributed system, even in computing clouds. Applications operate on data, which are mostly persisted and moved in the format of files. Hence, any infrastructure that supports the execution of distributed applications needs to provide facilities for file/data transfer management and persistent storage. Aneka offers two different facilities for storage management: a centralized file storage, which is mostly used for the execution of compute-intensive applications, and a distributed file system, which is more suitable for the execution of data-intensive applications. The requirements for the two types of applications are rather different. Compute-intensive applications mostly require powerful processors and do not have high demands in terms of storage, which in many cases is used to store small files that are easily transferred from one node to another. In this scenario, a centralized storage node, or a pool of storage nodes, can constitute an appropriate solution. In contrast, data-intensive applications are characterized by large data files (gigabytes or terabytes), and the processing power required by tasks does not constitute a performance bottleneck. In this scenario, a distributed file system harnessing the storage space of all the nodes belonging to the cloud might be a better and more scalable solution.

Centralized storage is implemented through and managed by Aneka's *Storage Service*. The service constitutes Aneka's data-staging facilities. It provides distributed applications with the basic file transfer facility and abstracts the use of a specific protocol to end users and other components of the system, which are dynamically configured at runtime according to the facilities installed in the cloud. The option that is currently installed by default is normal File Transfer Protocol (FTP).

To support different protocols, the system introduces the concept of a *file channel* that identifies a pair of components: a file channel controller and a file channel handler. The *file channel controller* constitutes the server component of the channel, where files are stored and made available; the *file channel handler* represents the client component, which is used by user applications or other components of the system to upload, download, or browse files. The storage service uses the configured file channel factory to first create the server component that will manage the storage and then create the client component on demand. User applications that require support for file transfer are automatically configured with the appropriate file channel handler and transparently upload input files or download output files during application execution. In the same way, worker nodes are configured by the infrastructure to retrieve the required files for the execution of the jobs and to upload their results.

An interesting property of the file channel abstraction is the ability to chain two different channels to move files by using two different protocols. Each file in Aneka contains metadata that helps the infrastructure select the appropriate channel for moving the file. For example, an output file whose final location is an S3 bucket can be moved from the worker node to the Storage Service using the internal FTP protocol and then can be staged out on S3 by the FTP channel controller managed by the service. The Storage Service supports the execution of task-based programming such as the *Task* and the *Thread Model* as well as *Parameter Sweep*-based applications.

Storage support for data-intensive applications is provided by means of a distributed file system. The reference model for the distributed file system is the Google File System [54], which features a highly scalable infrastructure based on commodity hardware. The architecture of the file system is based on a master node, which contains a global map of the file system and keeps track of the status of all the storage nodes, and a pool of chunk servers, which provide distributed storage space in which to store files. Files are logically organized into a directory structure but are persisted on the file system using a flat namespace based on a unique ID. Each file is organized as a collection of *chunks* that are all of the same size. File chunks are assigned unique IDs and stored on different servers, eventually replicated to provide high availability and failure tolerance. The model proposed by the Google File System provides optimized support for a specific class of applications that expose the following characteristics:

- Files are huge by traditional standards (multi-gigabytes).
- Files are modified by appending new data rather than rewriting existing data.
- There are two kinds of major workloads: large streaming reads and small random reads.
- It is more important to have a sustained bandwidth than a low latency.

Moreover, given the huge number of commodity machines that the file system harnesses together, failure (process or hardware failure) is the norm rather than an exception. These characteristics strongly influenced the design of the storage, which provides the best performance for applications specifically designed to operate on data as described. Currently, the only programming model that makes use of the distributed file system is *MapReduce* [55], which has been the primary reason for the Google File System implementation. Aneka provides a simple distributed file system (DFS), which relies on the file system services of the Windows operating system.

5.2.3.2 Accounting, billing, and resource pricing

Accounting Services keep track of the status of applications in the Aneka Cloud. The collected information provides a detailed breakdown of the distributed infrastructure usage and is vital for the proper management of resources.

The information collected for accounting is primarily related to infrastructure usage and application execution. A complete history of application execution and storage as well as other resource utilization parameters is captured and minded by the Accounting Services. This information constitutes the foundation on which users are charged in Aneka.

Billing is another important feature of accounting. Aneka is a multitenant cloud programming platform in which the execution of applications can involve provisioning additional resources from commercial IaaS providers. Aneka Billing Service provides detailed information about each user's usage of resources, with the associated costs. Each resource can be priced differently according to the set of services that are available on the corresponding Aneka container or the installed software in the node. The accounting model provides an integrated view of budget spent for each application, a summary view of the costs associated to a specific user, and the detailed information about the execution cost of each job.

The accounting capabilities are concentrated within the *Accounting Service* and the *Reporting Service*. The former keeps track of the information that is related to application execution, such as the distribution of jobs among the available resources, the timing of each of job, and the associated cost. The latter makes available the information collected from the monitoring services for accounting purposes: storage utilization and CPU performance. This information is primarily consumed by the Management Console.

5.2.3.3 Resource reservation

Aneka's *Resource Reservation* supports the execution of distributed applications and allows for reserving resources for exclusive use by specific applications. Resource reservation is built out of two different kinds of services: Resource Reservation and the Allocation Service. Resource Reservation keeps track of all the reserved time slots in the Aneka Cloud and provides a unified view of the system. The *Allocation Service* is installed on each node that features execution services and manages the database of information regarding the allocated slots on the local node. Applications that need to complete within a given deadline can make a reservation request for a specific number of nodes in a given timeframe. If it is possible to satisfy the request, the Reservation Service will return a reservation identifier as proof of the resource booking. During application execution, such an identifier is used to select the nodes that have been reserved, and they will be used to execute the application. On each reserved node, the execution services will check with the Allocation Service that each job has valid permissions to occupy the execution timeline by verifying the reservation identifier. Even though this is the general reference model for the reservation infrastructure, Aneka allows for different implementations of the service, which mostly vary in the protocol that is used to reserve resources or the parameters that can be specified while making a reservation request. Different protocol and strategies are integrated in a completely transparent manner, and Aneka provides extensible APIs for supporting advanced services. At the moment, the framework supports three different implementations:

- *Basic Reservation.* Features the basic capability to reserve execution slots on nodes and implements the *alternate offers* protocol, which provides alternative options in case the initial reservation requests cannot be satisfied.
- *Libra Reservation.* Represents a variation of the previous implementation that features the ability to price nodes differently according to their hardware capabilities.
- *Relay Reservation.* Constitutes a very thin implementation that allows a resource broker to reserve nodes in Aneka Clouds and control the logic with which these nodes are reserved. This

implementation is useful in integration scenarios in which Aneka operates in an intercloud environment.

Resource reservation is fundamental to ensuring the quality of service that is negotiated for applications. It allows Aneka to have a predictable environment in which applications can complete within the deadline or not be executed at all. The assumptions made by the reservation service for accepting reservation requests are based on the static allocation of such requests to the existing physical (or virtual) infrastructure available at the time of the requests and by taking into account the current and future load. This solution is sensitive to node failures that could make Aneka unable to fulfill the service-level agreement (SLA) made with users. Specific implementations of the service tend to delay the allocation of nodes to reservation requests as late as possible in order to cope with temporary failures or limited outages, but in the case of serious outages in which the remaining available nodes are not able to cover the demand, this strategy is not enough. In this case, resource provisioning can provide an effective solution: Additional nodes can be provisioned from external resource providers in order to cover the outage and meet the SLA defined for applications. The current implementation of the resource reservation infrastructure leverages the provisioning capabilities of the fabric layer when the current availability in the system is not able to address the reservation requests already confirmed. Such behavior solves the problems of both insufficient resources and temporary failures.

5.2.4 Application services

Application Services manage the execution of applications and constitute a layer that differentiates according to the specific programming model used for developing distributed applications on top of Aneka. The types and the number of services that compose this layer for each of the programming models may vary according to the specific needs or features of the selected model. It is possible to identify two major types of activities that are common across all the supported models: scheduling and execution. Aneka defines a reference model for implementing the runtime support for programming models that abstracts these two activities in corresponding services: the *Scheduling Service* and the *Execution Service*. Moreover, it also defines base implementations that can be extended in order to integrate new models.

5.2.4.1 Scheduling

Scheduling Services are in charge of planning the execution of distributed applications on top of Aneka and governing the allocation of jobs composing an application to nodes. They also constitute the integration point with several other Foundation and Fabric Services, such as the Resource Provisioning Service, the Reservation Service, the Accounting Service, and the Reporting Service. Common tasks that are performed by the scheduling component are the following:

- Job to node mapping
- Rescheduling of failed jobs
- Job status monitoring
- Application status monitoring

Aneka does not provide a centralized scheduling engine, but each programming model features its own scheduling service that needs to work in synergy with the existing services of the middleware. As already mentioned, these services mostly belong to the fabric and the foundation layers of the architecture shown in Figure 5.2. The possibility of having different scheduling engines for different models gives great freedom in implementing scheduling and resource allocation strategies but, at the same time, requires a careful design of use of shared resources. In this scenario, common situations that have to be appropriately managed are the following: multiple jobs sent to the same node at the same time; jobs without reservations sent to reserved nodes; and jobs sent to nodes where the required services are not installed. Aneka's Foundation Services provide sufficient information to avoid these cases, but the runtime infrastructure does not feature specific policies to detect these conditions and provide corrective action. The current design philosophy in Aneka is to keep the scheduling engines completely separate from each other and to leverage existing services when needed. As a result, it is possible to enforce that only one job per programming model is run on each node at any given time, but the execution of applications is not mutually exclusive unless Resource Reservation is used.

5.2.4.2 Execution

Execution Services control the execution of single jobs that compose applications. They are in charge of setting up the runtime environment hosting the execution of jobs. As happens for the scheduling services, each programming model has its own requirements, but it is possible to identify some common operations that apply across all the range of supported models:

- Unpacking the jobs received from the scheduler
- Retrieval of input files required for job execution
- Sandboxed execution of jobs
- Submission of output files at the end of execution
- Execution failure management (i.e., capturing sufficient contextual information useful to identify the nature of the failure)
- Performance monitoring
- Packing jobs and sending them back to the scheduler

Execution Services constitute a more self-contained unit with respect to the corresponding scheduling services. They handle less information and are required to integrate themselves only with the Storage Service and the local Allocation and Monitoring Services. Aneka provides a reference implementation of execution services that has built-in integration with all these services, and currently two of the supported programming models specialize on the reference implementation.

Application Services constitute the runtime support of the programming model in the Aneka Cloud. Currently there are several supported models:

- *Task Model.* This model provides the support for the independent "bag of tasks" applications and many computing tasks. In this model, an application is modeled as a collection of tasks that are independent from each other and whose execution can be sequenced in any order.
- *Thread Model.* This model provides an extension to the classical multithreaded programming to a distributed infrastructure and uses the abstraction of *Thread* to wrap a method that is executed remotely.

- *MapReduce Model.* This is an implementation of MapReduce as proposed by Google on top of Aneka.
- *Parameter Sweep Model.* This model is a specialization of the Task Model for applications that can be described by a template task whose instances are created by generating different combinations of parameters, which identify a specific point into the domain of interest.

Other programming models have been developed for internal use and are at an experimental stage. These are the Dataflow Model [56], the Message-Passing Interface, and the Actor Model [57].

5.3 Building Aneka clouds

Aneka is primarily a platform for developing distributed applications for clouds. As a software platform it requires infrastructure on which to be deployed; this infrastructure needs to be managed. Infrastructure management tools are specifically designed for this task, and building clouds is one of the primary tasks of administrators. Aneka supports various deployment models for public, private, and hybrid clouds.

5.3.1 Infrastructure organization

Figure 5.3 provides an overview of Aneka Clouds from an infrastructure point of view. The scenario is a reference model for all the different deployments Aneka supports. A central role is played by the Administrative Console, which performs all the required management operations. A fundamental element for Aneka Cloud deployment is constituted by *repositories*. A repository provides storage for all the libraries required to lay out and install the basic Aneka platform. These libraries constitute the software image for the node manager and the container programs. Repositories can make libraries available through a variety of communication channels, such as HTTP, FTP, common file sharing, and so on. The Management Console can manage multiple repositories and select the one that best suits the specific deployment. The infrastructure is deployed by harnessing a collection of nodes and installing on them the Aneka node manager, also called the *Aneka daemon*. The daemon constitutes the remote management service used to deploy and control container instances. The collection of resulting containers identifies the Aneka Cloud.

From an infrastructure point of view, the management of physical or virtual nodes is performed uniformly as long as it is possible to have an Internet connection and remote administrative access to the node. A different scenario is constituted by the dynamic provisioning of virtual instances; these are generally created by prepackaged images already containing an installation of Aneka, which only need to be configured to join a specific Aneka Cloud. It is also possible to simply install the container or install the Aneka daemon, and the selection of the proper solution mostly depends on the lifetime of virtual resources.

5.3.2 Logical organization

The logical organization of Aneka Clouds can be very diverse, since it strongly depends on the configuration selected for each of the container instances belonging to the Cloud. The most common

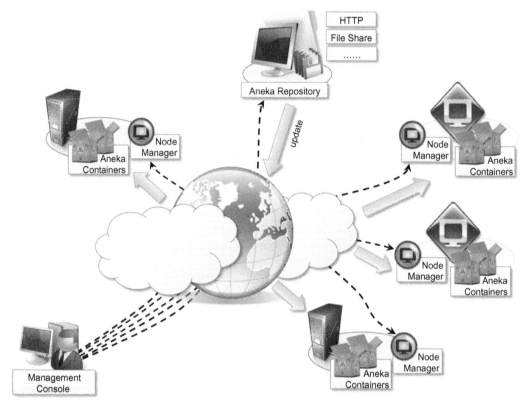

FIGURE 5.3

Aneka cloud infrastructure overview.

scenario is to use a master-worker configuration with separate nodes for storage, as shown in Figure 5.4.

The master node features all the services that are most likely to be present in one single copy and that provide the intelligence of the Aneka Cloud. What specifically characterizes a node as a master node is the presence of the *Index Service* (or Membership Catalogue) configured in master mode; all the other services, except for those that are mandatory, might be present or located in other nodes. A common configuration of the master node is as follows:

- Index Service (master copy)
- Heartbeat Service
- Logging Service
- Reservation Service
- Resource Provisioning Service
- Accounting Service
- Reporting and Monitoring Service
- Scheduling Services for the supported programming models

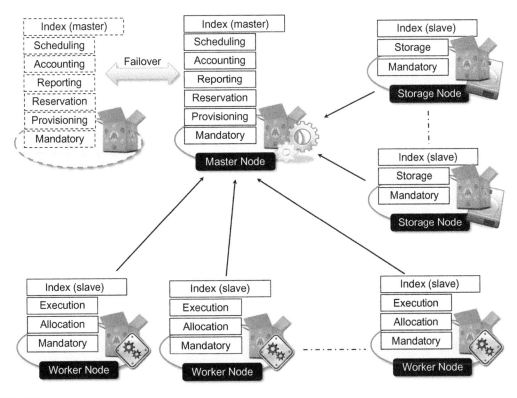

FIGURE 5.4

Logical organization of an Aneka cloud.

The master node also provides connection to an RDBMS facility where the state of several services is maintained. For the same reason, all the scheduling services are maintained in the master node. They share the application store that is normally persisted on the RDBMS in order to provide a fault-tolerant infrastructure. The master configuration can then be replicated in several nodes to provide a highly available infrastructure based on the failover mechanism.

The worker nodes constitute the workforce of the Aneka Cloud and are generally configured for the execution of applications. They feature the mandatory services and the specific execution services of each of the supported programming models in the Cloud. A very common configuration is the following:

- Index Service
- Heartbeat Service
- Logging Service
- Allocation Service
- Monitoring Service
- Execution Services for the supported programming models

A different option is to partition the pool of worker nodes with a different selection of execution services in order to balance the load between programming models and reserve some nodes for a specific class of applications.

Storage nodes are optimized to provide storage support to applications. They feature, among the mandatory and usual services, the presence of the Storage Service. The number of storage nodes strictly depends on the predicted workload and storage consumption of applications. Storage nodes mostly reside on machines that have considerable disk space to accommodate a large quantity of files. The common configuration of a storage node is the following:

- Index Service
- Heartbeat Service
- Logging Service
- Monitoring Service
- Storage Service

In specific cases, when the data transfer requirements are not demanding, there might be only one storage node. In some cases, for very small deployments, there is no need to have a separate storage node, and the Storage Service is installed and hosted on the master node.

All nodes are registered with the master node and transparently refer to any failover partner in the case of a high-availability configuration.

5.3.3 Private cloud deployment mode

A private deployment mode is mostly constituted by local physical resources and infrastructure management software providing access to a local pool of nodes, which might be virtualized. In this scenario Aneka Clouds are created by harnessing a heterogeneous pool of resources such has desktop machines, clusters, or workstations. These resources can be partitioned into different groups, and Aneka can be configured to leverage these resources according to application needs. Moreover, leveraging the Resource Provisioning Service, it is possible to integrate virtual nodes provisioned from a local resource pool managed by systems such as XenServer, Eucalyptus, and OpenStack.

Figure 5.5 shows a common deployment for a private Aneka Cloud. This deployment is acceptable for a scenario in which the workload of the system is predictable and a local virtual machine manager can easily address excess capacity demand. Most of the Aneka nodes are constituted of physical nodes with a long lifetime and a static configuration and generally do not need to be reconfigured often. The different nature of the machines harnessed in a private environment allows for specific policies on resource management and usage that can be accomplished by means of the Reservation Service. For example, desktop machines that are used during the day for office automation can be exploited outside the standard working hours to execute distributed applications. Workstation clusters might have some specific legacy software that is required for supporting the execution of applications and should be preferred for the execution of applications with special requirements.

5.3.4 Public cloud deployment mode

Public Cloud deployment mode features the installation of Aneka master and worker nodes over a completely virtualized infrastructure that is hosted on the infrastructure of one or more resource

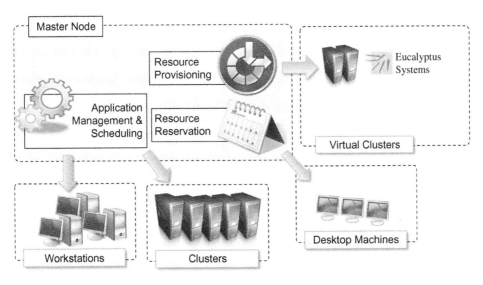

FIGURE 5.5

Private cloud deployment.

providers such as Amazon EC2 or GoGrid. In this case it is possible to have a static deployment where the nodes are provisioned beforehand and used as though they were real machines. This deployment merely replicates a classic Aneka installation on a physical infrastructure without any dynamic provisioning capability. More interesting is the use of the elastic features of IaaS providers and the creation of a Cloud that is completely dynamic. Figure 5.6 provides an overview of this scenario.

The deployment is generally contained within the infrastructure boundaries of a single IaaS provider. The reasons for this are to minimize the data transfer between different providers, which is generally priced at a higher cost, and to have better network performance. In this scenario it is possible to deploy an Aneka Cloud composed of only one node and to completely leverage dynamic provisioning to elastically scale the infrastructure on demand. A fundamental role is played by the Resource Provisioning Service, which can be configured with different images and templates to instantiate. Other important services that have to be included in the master node are the Accounting and Reporting Services. These provide details about resource utilization by users and applications and are fundamental in a multitenant Cloud where users are billed according to their consumption of Cloud capabilities.

Dynamic instances provisioned on demand will mostly be configured as worker nodes, and, in the specific case of Amazon EC2, different images featuring a different hardware setup can be made available to instantiate worker containers. Applications with specific requirements for computing capacity or memory can provide additional information to the scheduler that will trigger the appropriate provisioning request. Application execution is not the only use of dynamic instances; any service requiring elastic scaling can leverage dynamic provisioning. Another example is the Storage Service. In multitenant Clouds, multiple applications can leverage the support for storage; in this

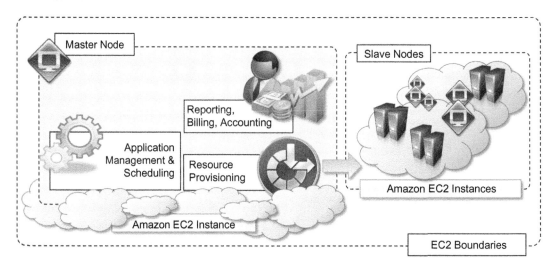

FIGURE 5.6

Public Aneka cloud deployment.

scenario it is then possible to introduce bottlenecks or simply reach the quota limits allocated for storage on the node. Dynamic provisioning can easily solve this issue as it does for increasing the computing capability of an Aneka Cloud.

Deployments using different providers are unlikely to happen because of the data transfer costs among providers, but they might be a possible scenario for federated Aneka Clouds [58]. In this scenario resources can be shared or leased among providers under specific agreements and more convenient prices. In this case the specific policies installed in the Resource Provisioning Service can discriminate among different resource providers, mapping different IaaS providers to provide the best solution to a provisioning request.

5.3.5 Hybrid cloud deployment mode

The hybrid deployment model constitutes the most common deployment of Aneka. In many cases, there is an existing computing infrastructure that can be leveraged to address the computing needs of applications. This infrastructure will constitute the static deployment of Aneka that can be elastically scaled on demand when additional resources are required. An overview of this deployment is presented in Figure 5.7.

This scenario constitutes the most complete deployment for Aneka that is able to leverage all the capabilities of the framework:

- Dynamic Resource Provisioning
- Resource Reservation
- Workload Partitioning
- Accounting, Monitoring, and Reporting

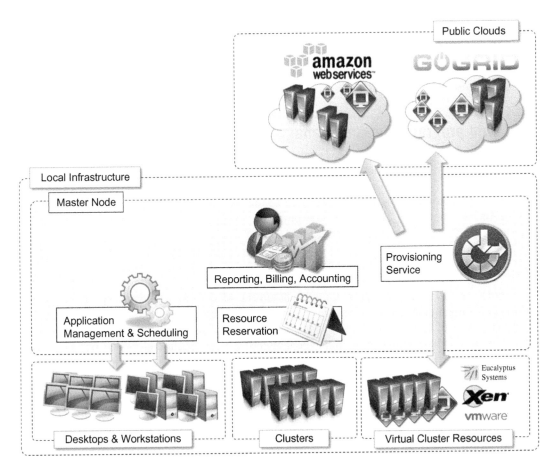

FIGURE 5.7

Hybrid cloud deployment.

Moreover, if the local premises offer some virtual machine management capabilities, it is possible to provide a very efficient use of resources, thus minimizing the expenditure for application execution.

In a hybrid scenario, heterogeneous resources can be used for different purposes. As we discussed in the case of a private cloud deployment, desktop machines can be reserved for low priority workload outside the common working hours. The majority of the applications will be executed on workstations and clusters, which are the nodes that are constantly connected to the Aneka Cloud. Any additional computing capability demand can be primarily addressed by the local virtualization facilities, and if more computing power is required, it is possible to leverage external IaaS providers.

Different from the Aneka Public Cloud deployment is the case in which it makes more sense to leverage a variety of resource providers to provision virtual resources. Since part of the infrastructure is local, a cost in data transfer to the external IaaS infrastructure cannot be avoided. It is then important to select the most suitable option to address application needs. The Resource Provisioning

Service implemented in Aneka exposes the capability of leveraging several resource pools at the same time and configuring specific policies to select the most appropriate pool for satisfying a provisioning request. These features simplify the development of custom policies that can better serve the needs of a specific hybrid deployment.

5.4 Cloud programming and management

Aneka's primary purpose is to provide a scalable middleware product in which to execute distributed applications. Application development and management constitute the two major features that are exposed to developers and system administrators. To simplify these activities, Aneka provides developers with a comprehensive and extensible set of APIs and administrators with powerful and intuitive management tools. The APIs for development are mostly concentrated in the Aneka SDK; management tools are exposed through the Management Console.

5.4.1 Aneka SDK

Aneka provides APIs for developing applications on top of existing programming models, implementing new programming models, and developing new services to integrate into the Aneka Cloud. The development of applications mostly focuses on the use of existing features and leveraging the services of the middleware, while the implementation of new programming models or new services enriches the features of Aneka. The SDK provides support for both programming models and services by means of the *Application Model* and the *Service Model*. The former covers the development of applications and new programming models; the latter defines the general infrastructure for service development.

5.4.1.1 Application model

Aneka provides support for distributed execution in the Cloud with the abstraction of programming models. A programming model identifies both the abstraction used by the developers and the runtime support for the execution of programs on top of Aneka. The *Application Model* represents the minimum set of APIs that is common to all the programming models for representing and programming distributed applications on top of Aneka. This model is further specialized according to the needs and the particular features of each of the programming models.

An overview of the components that define the Aneka Application Model is shown in Figure 5.8. Each distributed application running on top of Aneka is an instance of the *ApplicationBase* $<M>$ class, where M identifies the specific type of application manager used to control the application. Application classes constitute the developers' view of a distributed application on Aneka Clouds, whereas application managers are internal components that interact with Aneka Clouds in order to monitor and control the execution of the application. Application managers are also the first element of specialization of the model and vary according to the specific programming model used.

Whichever the specific model used, a distributed application can be conceived as a set of tasks for which the collective execution defines the execution of the application on the Cloud. Aneka further specializes applications into two main categories: (1) applications whose tasks are generated

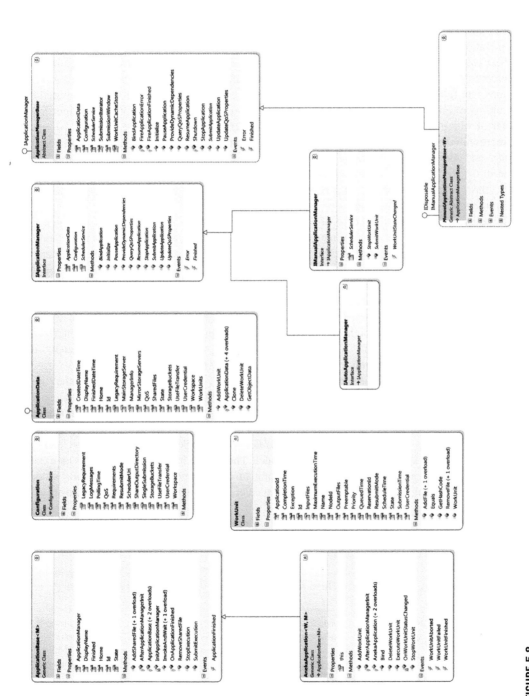

FIGURE 5.8

The Aneka application model.

by the user and (2) applications whose tasks are generated by the runtime infrastructure. These two categories generally correspond to different application base classes and different implementations of the application manager.

The first category is the most common and it is used as a reference for several programming models supported by Aneka: the *Task Model*, the *Thread Model*, and the *Parameter Sweep Model*. Applications that fall into this category are composed of a collection of units of work submitted by the user and represented by the *WorkUnit* class. Each unit of work can have input and output files, the transfer of which is transparently managed by the runtime. The specific type of *WorkUnit* class used to represent the unit of work depends on the programming model used (*AnekaTask* for the *Task Model* and *AnekaThread* for the *Thread Model*). All the applications that fall into this category inherit or are instances *of AnekaApplication* $<W,M>$, where W is the specific type of *WorkUnit* class used, and M is the type of application manager used to implement the *IManualApplicationManager* interface.

The second category covers the case of *MapReduce* and all those other scenarios in which the units of work are generated by the runtime infrastructure rather than the user. In this case there is no common unit-of-work class used, and the specific classes used by application developers strictly depend on the requirements of the programming model used. For example, in the case of the *MapReduce* programming model, developers express their distributed applications in terms of two functions, *map* and *reduce*; hence, the *MapReduceApplication* class provides an interface for specifying the *Mapper* $<K,V>$ and *Reducer* $<K,V>$ types and the input files required by the application. Other programming models might have different requirements and expose different interfaces. For this reason there are no common base types for this category except for *ApplicationBase* $<M>$, where M implements *IAutoApplicationManager*.

A set of additional classes completes the object model. Among these classes, the most notable are the *Configuration* class, which is used to specify the settings required to initialize the application and customize its behavior, and the *ApplicationData* class, which contains the runtime information of the application.

Table 5.1 summarizes the features that are available in the Aneka Application Model and the way they reflect into the supported programming model. The model has been designed to be extensible, and these classes can be used as a starting point to implement a new programming model. This can be done by augmenting the features (or specializing) an existing implementation of a

Table 5.1 Aneka's Application Model Features

Category	Description	Base Application Type	Work Units?	Programming Models
Manual	Units of work are generated by the user and submitted through the application.	*AnekaApplication* $<W,M>$ *IManualApplicationManager* $<W>$ *ManualApplicationManager* $<W>$	Yes	Task Model Thread Model Parameter Sweep Model
Auto	Units of work are generated by the runtime infrastructure and managed internally.	*ApplicationBase* $<M>$ *IAutoApplicationManager*	No	*MapReduce* Model

programming model or by using the base classes to define new models and abstractions. For example, the Parameter Sweep Model is a specialization of the Task Model, and it has been implemented in the context of management of applications on Aneka. It is achieved by providing a different interface to end users who just need to define a template task and the parameters that customize it.

5.4.1.2 Service model

The Aneka *Service Model* defines the basic requirements to implement a service that can be hosted in an Aneka Cloud. The container defines the runtime environment in which services are hosted. Each service that is hosted in the container must be compliant with the *IService* interface, which exposes the following methods and properties:

- Name and status
- Control operations such as *Start*, *Stop*, *Pause*, and *Continue* methods
- Message handling by means of the *HandleMessage* method

Specific services can also provide clients if they are meant to directly interact with end users. Examples of such services might be Resource Provisioning and Resource Reservation Services, which ship their own clients for allowing resource provisioning and reservation. Apart from control operations, which are used by the container to set up and shut down the service during the container life cycle, the core logic of a service resides in its message-processing functionalities that are contained in the *HandleMessage* method. Each operation that is requested to a service is triggered by a specific message, and results are communicated back to the caller by means of messages.

Figure 5.9 describes the reference life cycle of each service instance in the Aneka container. The shaded balloons indicate transient states; the white balloons indicate steady states. A service instance can initially be in the *Unknown* or *Initialized* state, a condition that refers to the creation of the service instance by invoking its constructor during the configuration of the container. Once the container is started, it will iteratively call the *Start* method on each service method. As a result the service instance is expected to be in a *Starting* state until the startup process is completed, after which it will exhibit the *Running* state. This is the condition in which the service will last as long as the container is active and running. This is the only state in which the service is able to process messages. If an exception occurs while starting the service, it is expected that the service will fall back to the *Unknown* state, thus signaling an error.

When a service is running it is possible to pause its activity by calling the *Pause* method and resume it by calling *Continue*. As described in the figure, the service moves first into the *Pausing* state, thus reaching the *Paused* state. From this state, it moves into the *Resuming* state while restoring its activity to return to the *Running* state. Not all the services need to support the pause/continue operations, and the current implementation of the framework does not feature any service with these capabilities.

When the container shuts down, the *Stop* method is iteratively called on each service running, and services move first into the transient *Stopping* state to reach the final *Stopped* state, where all resources that were initially allocated have been released.

Aneka provides a default base class for simplifying service implementation and a set of guidelines that service developers should follow to design and implement services that are compliant with Aneka. In particular, the guidelines define a *ServiceBase* class that can be further extended to

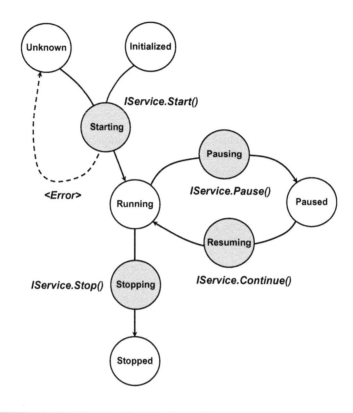

FIGURE 5.9

Service life cycle.

provide a proper implementation. This class is the base class of several services in the framework and provides some built-in features:

- Implementation of the basic properties exposed by *IService*
- Implementation of the control operations with logging capabilities and state control
- Built-in infrastructure for delivering a service specific client
- Support for service monitoring

Developers are provided with template methods for specializing the behavior of control operations, implementing their own message-processing logic, and providing a service-specific client.

Aneka uses a strongly typed message-passing communication model, whereby each service defines its own messages, which are in turn the only ones that the service is able to process. As a result, developers who implement new services in Aneka need also to define the type of messages that the services will use to communicate with services and clients. Each message type inherits from the base class *Message* defining common properties such as:

- Source node and target node
- Source service and target service
- Security credentials

Additional properties are added to carry the specific information for each type. Messages are generally used inside the Aneka infrastructure. In case the service exposes features directly used by applications, they may expose a service client that provides an object-oriented interface to the operations exposed by the service. Aneka features a ready-to-use infrastructure for dynamically injecting service clients into applications by querying the middleware. Services inheriting from the *ServiceBase* class already support such a feature and only need to define an interface and a specific implementation for the service client. Service clients are useful to integrate Aneka services into existing applications that do not necessarily need support for the execution of distributed applications or require access to additional services.

Aneka also provides advanced capabilities for service configuration. Developers can define editors and configuration classes that allow Aneka's management tools to integrate the configuration of services within the common workflow required by the container configuration.

5.4.2 Management tools

Aneka is a pure PaaS implementation and requires virtual or physical hardware to be deployed. Hence, infrastructure management, together with facilities for installing logical clouds on such infrastructure, is a fundamental feature of Aneka's management layer. This layer also includes capabilities for managing services and applications running in the Aneka Cloud.

5.4.2.1 Infrastructure management

Aneka leverages virtual and physical hardware in order to deploy Aneka Clouds. Virtual hardware is generally managed by means of the Resource Provisioning Service, which acquires resources on demand according to the need of applications, while physical hardware is directly managed by the Administrative Console by leveraging the Aneka management API of the PAL. The management features are mostly concerned with the provisioning of physical hardware and the remote installation of Aneka on the hardware.

5.4.2.2 Platform management

Infrastructure management provides the basic layer on top of which Aneka Clouds are deployed. The creation of Clouds is orchestrated by deploying a collection of services on the physical infrastructure that allows the installation and the management of containers. A collection of connected containers defines the platform on top of which applications are executed. The features available for platform management are mostly concerned with the logical organization and structure of Aneka Clouds. It is possible to partition the available hardware into several Clouds variably configured for different purposes. Services implement the core features of Aneka Clouds and the management layer exposes operations for some of them, such as Cloud monitoring, resource provisioning and reservation, user management, and application profiling.

5.4.2.3 Application management

Applications identify the user contribution to the Cloud. The management APIs provide administrators with monitoring and profiling features that help them track the usage of resources and relate them to users and applications. This is an important feature in a cloud computing scenario in which users are billed for their resource usage. Aneka exposes capabilities for giving summary and detailed information about application execution and resource utilization.

All these features are made accessible through the Aneka Cloud Management Studio, which constitutes the main Administrative Console for the Cloud.

SUMMARY

In this chapter we introduced Aneka, a platform for application programming in the cloud. Aneka is a pure PaaS implementation of the Cloud Computing Reference Model and constitutes a middleware product that enables the creation of computing clouds on top of heterogeneous hardware: desktop machines, clusters, and public virtual resources.

One of the key aspects of Aneka's framework is its configurable runtime environment, which allows for the creation of a service-based middleware where applications are executed. A fundamental element of the infrastructure is the container, which represents the deployment unit of Aneka Clouds. The container hosts a collection of services that define the capabilities of the middleware. Fundamental services in the Aneka middleware are:

- Fabric Services for monitoring, resource provisioning, hardware profiling, and membership
- Foundation Services for storage, resource reservation, billing, accounting, and reporting
- Application Services for scheduling and execution

From an application programming point of view, Aneka provides the capability of supporting different programming models, thus allowing developers to express distributed applications with different abstractions. The framework currently supports three different models: independent "bag of tasks" applications, multithreaded applications, and *MapReduce*.

The infrastructure is extensible, and Aneka provides both an application model and a service model that can be easily extended to integrate new services and programming models.

Review questions

1. Describe in a few words the main characteristics of Aneka.
2. What is the Aneka container and what is its use?
3. Which types of services are hosted inside the Aneka container?
4. Describe Aneka's resource-provisioning capabilities.
5. Describe the storage architecture implemented in Aneka.
6. What is a programming model?
7. List the programming models supported by Aneka.
8. Which are the components that compose the Aneka infrastructure?
9. Discuss the logical organization of an Aneka Cloud.
10. Which services are hosted in a worker node?
11. Discuss the private deployment of Aneka Clouds.
12. Discuss the public deployment of Aneka Clouds.

13. Discuss the role of dynamic provisioning in hybrid deployments.
14. Which facilities does Aneka provide for development?
15. Discuss the major features of the Aneka Application Model.
16. Discuss the major features of the Aneka Service Model.
17. Describe the features of the Aneka management tools in terms of infrastructure, platform, and applications.

Concurrent Computing
Thread Programming

6

Throughput computing focuses on delivering high volumes of computation in the form of transactions. Initially related to the field of transaction processing [60], throughput computing has since been extended beyond that domain. Advances in hardware technologies led to the creation of multicore systems, which have made possible the delivery of high-throughput computations, even in a single computer system. In this case, throughput computing is realized by means of multiprocessing and multithreading. *Multiprocessing* is the execution of multiple programs in a single machine, whereas *multithreading* relates to the possibility of multiple instruction streams within the same program.

This chapter presents the concept of multithreading and describes how it supports the development of high-throughput computing applications. It discusses how multithreaded programming, originally conceived to be contained within the boundaries of a single machine, can be extended to a distributed context and which limitations apply. The Aneka Thread Programming Model will be taken as a reference model to review a practical implementation of a multithreaded model for computing clouds.

6.1 Introducing parallelism for single-machine computation

Parallelism has been a technique for improving the performance of computers since the early 1960's, when Burroughs Corporation designed the D825, the first MIMD multiprocessor ever produced. From there on, a variety of parallel strategies have been developed. In particular, *multiprocessing*, which is the use of multiple processing units within a single machine, has gained a good deal of interest and gave birth to several parallel architectures.

One of the most important distinctions is made in terms of the symmetry of processing units. *Asymmetric multiprocessing* involves the concurrent use of different processing units that are specialized to perform different functions. *Symmetric multiprocessing* features the use of similar or identical processing units to share the computation load. Other examples are *nonuniform memory access (NUMA)* and *clustered multiprocessing*, which, respectively, define a specific architecture for accessing a shared memory between processors and the use of multiple computers joined together as a single virtual computer.

Symmetric and asymmetric multiprocessing are the techniques used to increase the performance of commodity computer hardware. The introduction of *graphical processing units (GPUs)*, which

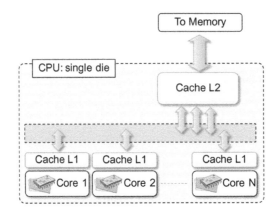

FIGURE 6.1

Multicore processor.

are *de facto* processors, is an application of asymmetric processing, whereas multicore technology is the latest evolution of symmetric multiprocessing. Multiprocessor and especially multicore technologies are now of fundamental importance because of the physical constraint imposed on frequency scaling,[1] which has been the common practice for performance gain in recent years. It became no longer possible to increase the frequency of the processor clock without paying in terms of power consumption and cooling, and this condition became unsustainable in May 2004, when Intel officially cancelled the development of two new microprocessors in favor of multicore development.[2] This date is generally considered the end of the frequency-scaling era and the beginning of multicore technology. Other issues also determined the end of frequency scaling, such as the continuously increasing gap between processor and memory speeds and the difficulty of increasing the instruction-level parallelism[3] in order to keep a single high-performance core busy.

Multicore systems are composed of a single processor that features multiple processing cores that share the memory. Each core has generally its own L1 cache, and the L2 cache is common to all the cores, which connect to it by means of a shared bus, as depicted in Figure 6.1. Dual- and quad-core configurations are quite popular nowadays and constitute the standard hardware configuration for commodity computers. Architectures with multiple cores are also available but are not designed for the commodity market. Multicore technology has been used not only as a support for processor design but also in other devices, such as GPUs and network devices, thus becoming a standard practice for improving performance.

---

[1]*Frequency scaling* refers to the practice of increasing the clock frequency of a processor to improve its performance. The increase of clock frequency leads to higher power consumption and a higher temperature on the die, which becomes unsustainable over certain values of the frequency clock. Also known as *frequency ramping*, this was the dominant technique for achieving performance gain from the mid-1980s to the end of 2004.

[2]www.nytimes.com/2004/05/08/business/08chip.html?ex = 1399348800&en = 98cc44ca97b1a562&ei = 5007.

[3]*Instruction-level parallelism* (ILP) is a measure of how many operations a computer program can perform at one time. There are several techniques that can be applied to increase the ILP at the microarchitectural level. One of these is *instruction pipelining*, which involves the division of instructions into stages so that a single processing unit can execute multiple instructions at the same time by carrying out different stages for each of them.

Multiprocessing is just one technique that can be used to achieve parallelism, and it does that by leveraging parallel hardware architectures. Parallel architectures are better exploited when programs are designed to take advantage of their features. In particular, an important role is played by the operating system, which defines the runtime structure of applications by means of the abstraction of *process* and *thread*. A process is the runtime image of an application, or better, a program that is running, while a thread identifies a single flow of the execution within a process. A system that allows the execution of multiple processes at the same time supports *multitasking*. It supports *multithreading* when it provides structures for explicitly defining multiple threads within a process.

Note that both multitasking and multithreading can be implemented on top of computer hardware that is constituted of a single processor and a single core, as was the common practice before the introduction of multicore technology. In this case, the operating system gives the illusion of concurrent execution by interleaving the execution of instructions of different processes and of different threads within the same process. This is also the case in multiprocessor/multicore systems, since the number of threads or processes is higher than the number of processors or cores. Nowadays, almost all the commonly used operating systems support multitasking and multithreading. Moreover, all the mainstream programming languages incorporate the abstractions of process and thread within their APIs, whereas direct support of multiple processors and cores for developers is very limited and often reduced and confined to specific libraries, which are available for a subset of the programming languages such as C/C++.

In this chapter, we concentrate our attention on multithreaded programming, which now has full support and constitutes the simplest way to achieve parallelism within a single process, despite the underlying hardware architecture.

6.2 Programming applications with threads

Modern applications perform multiple operations at the same time. Developers organize programs in terms of threads in order to express intraprocess concurrency. The use of threads might be implicit or explicit. *Implicit threading* happens when the underlying APIs use internal threads to perform specific tasks supporting the execution of applications such as graphical user interface (GUI) rendering, or garbage collection in the case of virtual machine-based languages. *Explicit threading* is characterized by the use of threads within a program by application developers, who use this abstraction to introduce parallelism. Common cases in which threads are explicitly used are I/O from devices and network connections, long computations, or the execution of background operations for which the outcome does not have specific time bounds. The use of threads was initially directed to allowing asynchronous operations—in particular, providing facilities for asynchronous I/O or long computations so that the user interface of applications did not block or became unresponsive. With the advent of parallel architectures the use of multithreading has become a useful technique to increase the throughput of the system and a viable option for throughput computing. To this purpose, the use of threads strongly impacts the design of algorithms that need to be refactored in order to leverage threads. In this section, we discuss the use of threading as a support for the design of parallel and distributed algorithms.

6.2.1 What is a thread?

A *thread* identifies a single control flow, which is a *logical sequence of instructions*, within a process. By logical sequence of instructions, we mean a sequence of instructions that have been designed to be executed one after the other one. More commonly, a thread identifies a kind of yarn that is used for sewing, and the feeling of continuity that is expressed by the interlocked fibers of that yarn is used to recall the concept that the instructions of thread express a logically continuous sequence of operations.

Operating systems that support multithreading identify threads as the minimal building blocks for expressing running code. This means that, despite their explicit use by developers, any sequence of instruction that is executed by the operating system is within the context of a thread. As a consequence, each process contains at least one thread but, in several cases, is composed of many threads having variable lifetimes. Threads within the same process share the memory space and the execution context; besides this, there is no substantial difference between threads belonging to different processes.

In a multitasking environment the operating system assigns different time slices to each process and interleaves their execution. The process of temporarily stopping the execution of one process, saving all the information in the registers (and in general the state of the CPU in order to restore it later), and replacing it with the information related to another process is known as a *context switch*. This operation is generally considered demanding, and the use of multithreading minimizes the latency imposed by context switches, thus allowing the execution of multiple tasks in a lighter fashion. The state representing the execution of a thread is minimal compared to the one describing a process. Therefore, switching between threads is a preferred practice over switching between processes. Obviously the use of multiple threads in place of multiple processes is justified if and only if the tasks implemented are logically related to each other and require sharing memory or other resources. If this is not the case, a better design is provided by separating them into different processes.

Figure 6.2 provides an overview of the relation between threads and processes and a simplified representation of the runtime execution of a multithreaded application. A running program is identified by a process, which contains at least one thread, also called the *main thread*. Such a thread is implicitly created by the compiler or the runtime environment executing the program. This thread is likely to last for the entire lifetime of the process and be the origin of other threads, which in general exhibit a shorter duration. As main threads, these threads can spawn other threads. There is no difference between the main thread and other threads created during the process lifetime. Each of them has its own local storage and a sequence of instructions to execute, and they all share the memory space allocated for the entire process. The execution of the process is considered terminated when all the threads are completed.

6.2.2 Thread APIs

Even though the support for multithreading varies according to the operating system and the specific programming languages that are used to develop applications, it is possible to identify a minimum set of features that are commonly available across all the implementations.

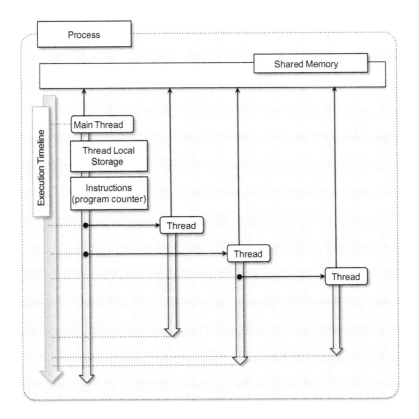

FIGURE 6.2

The relationship between processes and threads.

6.2.2.1 POSIX Threads

Portable Operating System Interface for Unix (POSIX) is a set of standards related to the application programming interfaces for a portable development of applications over the Unix operating system flavors. Standard POSIX 1.c (IEEE Std 1003.1c-1995) addresses the implementation of threads and the functionalities that should be available for application programmers to develop portable multithreaded applications. The standards address the Unix-based operating systems, but an implementation of the same specification has been provided for Windows-based systems.

The POSIX standard defines the following operations: creation of threads with attributes, termination of a thread, and waiting for thread completion (join operation). In addition to the logical structure of a thread, other abstractions, such as semaphores, conditions, reader-writer locks, and others, are introduced in order to support proper synchronization among threads.

The model proposed by POSIX has been taken as a reference for other implementations that might provide developers with a different interface but a similar behavior. What is important to remember from a programming point of view is the following:

- A thread identifies a logical sequence of instructions.
- A thread is mapped to a function that contains the sequence of instructions to execute.

- A thread can be created, terminated, or joined.
- A thread has a state that determines its current condition, whether it is executing, stopped, terminated, waiting for I/O, etc.
- The sequence of states that the thread undergoes is partly determined by the operating system scheduler and partly by the application developers.
- Threads share the memory of the process, and since they are executed concurrently, they need synchronization structures.
- Different synchronization abstractions are provided to solve different synchronization problems.

A default implementation of the POSIX 1.c specification has been provided for the C language. All the available functions and data structures are exposed in the *pthread.h* header file, which is part of the standard C implementations.

6.2.2.2 Threading support in java and .NET

Languages such as Java and C# provide a rich set of functionalities for multithreaded programming by using an object-oriented approach. Since both Java and .NET execute code on top of a virtual machine, the APIs exposed by the libraries refer to managed or logical threads. These are mapped to physical threads (i.e., those made available as abstractions by the underlying operating system) by the runtime environment in which programs developed with these languages execute. Despite such a mapping process, managed threads are considered, from a programming point of view, as physical threads and expose the same functionalities.

Both Java and .NET express the thread abstraction with the class *Thread* exposing the common operations performed on threads: *start*, *stop*, *suspend*, *resume*, *abort*, *sleep*, *join*, and *interrupt*. *Start* and *stop/abort* are used to control the lifetime of the thread instance, while *suspend* and *resume* are used to programmatically pause and then continue the execution of a thread. These two operations are generally deprecated in both of the two implementations that favor the use of appropriate techniques involving proper locks of the use of the *sleep* operation. This operation allows pausing the execution of a thread for a predefined period of time. This one is different from the *join* operation that makes one thread wait until another thread is completed. These waiting states can be interrupted by using the *interrupt* operation, which resumes the execution of the thread and generates an exception within the code of the thread to notify the abnormal resumption.

The two frameworks provide different support for implementing synchronization among threads. In general the basic features for implementing mutexes, critical regions, and reader-writer locks are completely covered by means of the basic class libraries or additional libraries. More advanced constructs than the thread abstraction are available in both languages. In the case of Java, most of them are contained in the *java.util.concurrent*[4] package, whereas the rich set of APIs for concurrent programming in .NET is further extended by the *.NET Parallel Extension* framework.[5]

---

[4]http://download.oracle.com/javase/6/docs/api/java/util/concurrent/package-summary.html.
[5]http://msdn.microsoft.com/en-us/concurrency/default.aspx.

6.2.3 **Techniques for parallel computation with threads**

Developing parallel applications requires an understanding of the problem and its logical structure. Understanding the dependencies and the correlation of tasks within an application is fundamental to designing the right program structure and to introducing parallelism where appropriate. *Decomposition* is a useful technique that aids in understanding whether a problem is divided into components (or tasks) that can be executed concurrently. If such decomposition is possible, it also provides a starting point for a parallel implementation, since it allows the breaking down into independent units of work that can be executed concurrently with the support provided by threads. The two main decomposition/partitioning techniques are *domain* and *functional* decompositions.

6.2.3.1 *Domain decomposition*

Domain decomposition is the process of identifying patterns of *functionally repetitive, but independent, computation on data*. This is the most common type of decomposition in the case of throughput computing, and it relates to the identification of repetitive calculations required for solving a problem.

When these calculations are identical, only differ from the data they operate on, and can be executed in any order, the problem is said to be *embarrassingly parallel* [59]. Embarrassingly parallel problems constitute the easiest case for parallelization because there is no need to synchronize different threads that do not share any data. Moreover, coordination and communication between threads are minimal; this strongly simplifies the code logic and allows a high computing throughput.

In many cases it is possible to devise a general structure for solving such problems and, in general, problems that can be parallelized through domain decomposition. The master-slave model is a quite common organization for these scenarios:

- The system is divided into two major code segments.
- One code segment contains the decomposition and coordination logic.
- Another code segment contains the repetitive computation to perform.
- A master thread executes the first code segment.
- As a result of the master thread execution, as many slave threads as needed are created to execute the repetitive computation.
- The collection of the results from each of the slave threads and an eventual composition of the final result are performed by the master thread.

Although the complexity of the repetitive computation strictly depends on the nature of the problem, the coordination and decomposition logic is often quite simple and involves identifying the appropriate number of units of work to create. In general, a *while* or a *for* loop is used to express the decomposition logic, and each iteration generates a new unit of work to be assigned to a slave thread. An optimization, of this process involves the use of thread pooling to limit the number of threads used to execute repetitive computations.

Several practical problems fall into this category; in the case of embarrassingly parallel problems, we can mention:

- Geometrical transformation of two (or higher) dimensional data sets
- Independent and repetitive computations over a domain such as Mandelbrot set and Monte Carlo computations

Even though embarrassingly parallel problems are quite common, they are based on the strong assumption that at each of the iterations of the decomposition method, it is possible to isolate an independent unit of work. This is what makes it possible to obtain a high computing throughput. Such a condition is not met if the values of all the iterations are dependent on some of the values obtained in the previous iterations. In this case, the problem is said to be *inherently sequential*, and it is not possible to directly apply the methodology described previously. Despite this, it can still be possible to break down the whole computation into a set of independent units of work, which might have a different granularity—for example, by grouping into single computation-dependent iterations. Figure 6.3 provides a schematic representation of the decomposition of embarrassingly parallel and inherently sequential problems.

To show how domain decomposition can be applied, it is possible to create a simple program that performs matrix multiplication using multiple threads.

Matrix multiplication is a binary operation that takes two matrices and produces another matrix as a result. This is obtained as a result of the composition of the linear transformation of the original matrices. There are several techniques for performing matrix multiplication; among them, the *matrix product* is the most popular. Figure 6.4 provides an overview of how a matrix product can be performed.

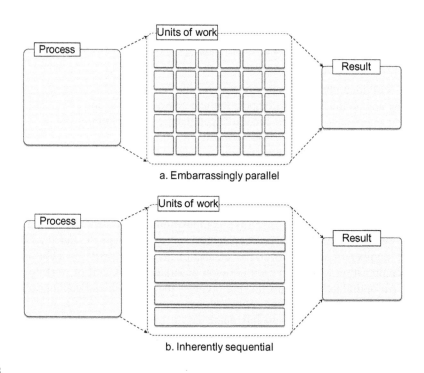

a. Embarrassingly parallel

b. Inherently sequential

FIGURE 6.3

Domain decomposition techniques.

The matrix product computes each element of the resulting matrix as a linear combination of the corresponding row and column of the first and second input matrices, respectively. The formula that applies for each of the resulting matrix elements is the following:

$$C_{ij} = \sum_{k=0}^{n-1} A_{ik}B_{kj}$$

Therefore, two conditions hold in order to perform a matrix product:

- Input matrices must contain values of a comparable nature for which the scalar product is defined.
- The number of columns in the first matrix must match the number of rows of the second matrix.

Given these conditions, the resulting matrix will have the number of rows of the first matrix and the number of columns of the second matrix, and each element will be computed as described by the preceding equation.

It is evident that the repetitive operation is the computation of each of the elements of the resulting matrix. These are subject to the same formula, and the computation does not depend on values that have been obtained by the computation of other elements of the resulting matrix. Hence, the problem is embarrassingly parallel, and we can logically organize the multithreaded program in the following steps:

- Define a function that performs the computation of the single element of the resulting matrix by implementing the previous equation.
- Create a double for loop (the first index iterates over the rows of the first matrix and the second over the columns of the second matrix) that spawns a thread to compute the elements of the resulting matrix.
- Join all the threads for completion, and compose the resulting matrix.

In order to give a practical example of the implementation of such a solution, we demonstrate the use of .NET threading. The .NET framework provides the *System.Threading.Thread* class that

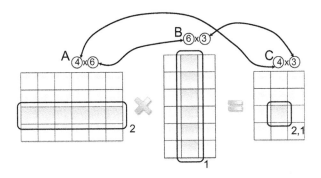

FIGURE 6.4

A matrix product.

can be configured with a function pointer, also known as a *delegate*, to execute asynchronously. Such a delegate must reference a defined method in some class. Hence, we can define a simple class that exposes as properties the row and the column to multiply and the result value. This class will also define the method for performing the actual computation. Listing 6.1 shows the class *ScalarProduct*.

The creation of the main thread of control is very simple. In this case, we skip the boilerplate code that is required to read the matrices from the standard input or from a file and concentrate our attention on the main control logic that decomposes the computation, creates threads, and waits for their completion in order to compose the resulting matrix.

To control the threads, we need to keep track of them so that we can query their status and obtain the result once they have completed the computation. We can create a simple program that reads the matrices, keeps track of all the threads in an appropriate data structure, and, once the threads have been completed, composes the final result. Listing 6.2 shows the content of the *MatrixProduct* class with some omissions.

Whereas the domain decomposition is quite simple, note that most of the complexity of the program resides in the management of threads. A few issues arise from the previous implementation:

- *Matrix layout.* Because of the way in which multidimensional arrays are stored, retrieving the column for the scalar product is not as straightforward as obtaining the row. This problem can be easily solved by memorizing the second matrix as *columns × rows* rather than *rows × columns*.
- *Result composition.* The composition of results is made on the master thread, and this requires keeping track of all the worker threads. Maintaining a reference to all the worker threads is in general a good programming practice, since it is necessary to terminate all of them before the application completes; but in this case it is possible to modify the application by using synchronization constructs that allow updating the resulting matrix from the worker threads. The new design implies storing the information about the indexes of rows and columns and a reference to the resulting matrix in the *ScalarProduct* class. As a result, there is no need to maintain a dictionary for threads, and we do not need the *ComposeResult* method in the master thread.

The example of a matrix product has been taken as a model to sketch the basic logic that is required to implement domain decomposition for an embarrassingly parallel problem and how to use threads in .NET to achieve throughput computing. This example can be taken as a reference to develop more sophisticated applications.

6.2.3.2 *Functional decomposition*

Functional decomposition is the process of identifying *functionally distinct but independent computations*. The focus here is on the type of computation rather than on the data manipulated by the computation. This kind of decomposition is less common and does not lead to the creation of a large number of threads, since the different computations that are performed by a single program are limited.

Functional decomposition leads to a natural decomposition of the problem in separate units of work because it does not involve partitioning the dataset, but the separation among them is clearly

```
///<summary>
/// Class ScalarProduct. Computes the scalar product between the row and the column
/// arrays.
///</summary>
public class ScalarProduct
{
   /// <summary>
   /// Scalar product.
   /// </summary>
   private double result;
   /// <summary>
   /// Gets the resulting scalar product.
   /// </summary>
   public double Result{ get { returnthis.result; } }

   /// <summary>
   /// Arrays containing the elements of the row and the column to multiply.
   /// </summary>
   private double[] row, column;

   /// <summary>
   /// Creates an instance of the ScalarProduct class and configures it with the given
   /// row and column arrays.
   /// </summary>
   /// <param name="row">Array with the elements of the row to be multiplied.</param>
   /// <param name="column">Array with the elements of the column to be multiplied.
   /// </param>
   public ScalarProduct(double[] row, double[] column)
   {
      this.row = row;
      this.colum = colum;
   }
   /// <summary>
   /// Executes the scalar product between the row and the colum.
   /// </summary>
   /// <param name="row">Array with the elements of the row to be multiplied.</param>
   /// <param name="column">Array with the elements of the column to be multiplied.
   /// </param>
   public void Multiply()
   {
      this.result = 0;
      for(int i=0; i<this.row.Length; i++)
      {
         this.result += this.row[i] * this.column[i];
      }
   }
}
```

LISTING 6.1

ScalarProduct Class.

```
using System;
using System.Threading;
using System.Collections.Generic;

///<summary>
/// Class MatrixProduct. Performs the matrix product of two matrices.
///</summary>
public class MatrixProduct
{
    ///<summary>
    /// First and second matrix of the produt.
    ///</summary>
    private static double[,]a, b;
    ///<summary>
    /// Result matrix.
    ///</summary>
    private static double[,] c;
    ///<summary>
    /// Dictionary mapping the thread instances to the corresponding ScalarProduct
    /// instances that are run inside.
    ///</summary>
    private static IDictionary<Thread, ScalarProduct>workers.

    ///<summary>
    /// Read the command line parameters and perform the scalar product.
    ///</summary>
    ///<param name="args">Array strings containing the command line parameters.</param>
    public static void Main(string[] args)
    {
        // reads the input matrices a and b.
        MatrixProduct.ReadMatrices();
        // executes the parallel matrix product.
        MatrixProduct.ExecuteProudct();
        // waits for all the threads to complete and
        // composes the final matrix.
        MatrixProduct.ComposeResult();
    }

    ///<summary>
    /// Executes the parallel matrix product by decomposing the problem in
    /// independent scalar product between rows and colums.
    ///</summary>
    private static void ExecuteThreads()
    {
        MatrixProduct.workers = newList<Thread>();
        int rows = MatrixProduct.a.Length;
        // in .NET matrices are arrays of arrays and the number of columns is
        // is represented by the length of the second array.
        int columns = MatrixProduct.b[0].Length;
        for(int i=0; i<rows; i++)
            for(int j=0; j<columns; j++)
            {
                double[] row = MatrixProduct.a[i];
                // because matrices are stored as arrays of arrays in order to
                // to get the columns we need to traverse the array and copy the
                // the data to another array.
```

LISTING 6.2

MatrixProduct Class (Main Program).

```
                    double[] column = new double[common];
                    for(int k=0; k<common; k++)
                    {
                        column[j] = MatrixProduct.b[j][i];
                    }
                    // creates a ScalarProduct instance with the previous rows and
                    // columns and starts a thread executing the Multiply method.
                    ScalarProduct scalar = newScalarProduct(row, column);
                    Thread worker = newThread(newThreadStart(scalar.Multiply));
                    worker.Name =string.Format("{0}.{1}",row,column);
                    worker.Start();
                    // adds the thread to the dictionary so that it can be
                    // further retrieved.
                    MatrixProduct.workers.Add(worker, scalar);
                }
            }


        ///<summary>
        /// Waits for the completion of all the threads and composes the final
        /// result matrix.
        ///</summary>
        private static void ComposeResult()
        {
            MatrixProduct.c = new double[rows,columns];
            foreach(KeyValuePair<Thread,ScalarProduct>pair in MatrixProduct.workers)
            {
                Thread worker = pair.Key;
                // we have saved the coordinates of each scalar product in the name
                // of the thread now we get them back by parsing the name .
                string[] indices = string.Split(worker.Name, new char[] {'.'});
                int i = int.Parse(indices[0]);
                int j = int.Parse(indices[1]);
                // we wait for the thread to complete
                worker.Join();
                // we set the result computed at the given coordinates.
                MatrixProduct.c[i,j] = pair.Value.Result;
            }
            MatrixProduct.PrintMatrix(MatrixProduct.c);
        }
        ///<summary>
        /// Reads the matrices.
        ///</summary>
        private static void ReadMatrices()
        {
            // code for reading the matrices a and b
        }
        ///<summary>
        /// Prints the given matrix.
        ///</summary>
        ///<param name="matrix">Matrix to print.</param>
        private static void PrintMatrices(double[,] matrix)
        {
            // code for printing the matrix.
        }
    }
```

LISTING 6.2

(Continued)

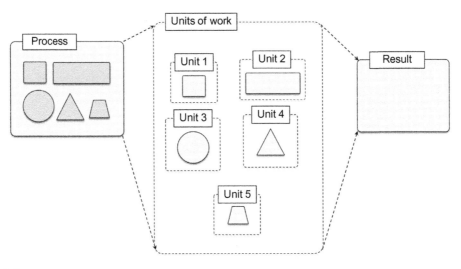

FIGURE 6.5

Functional decomposition.

defined by distinct logic operations. Figure 6.5 provides a pictorial view of how decomposition operates and allows parallelization.

As described by the schematic in Figure 6.5, problems that are subject to functional decomposition can also require a composition phase in which the outcomes of each of the independent units of work are composed together. In the case of domain decomposition, this phase often results in an aggregation process. The way in which results are composed in this case strongly depends on the type of operations that define the problem.

In the following, we show a very simple example of how a mathematical problem can be parallelized using functional decomposition. Suppose, for example, that we need to calculate the value of the following function for a given value of x:

$$f(x) = \sin(x) + \cos(x) + \tan(x)$$

It is apparent that, once the value of x has been set, the three different operations can be performed independently of each other. This is an example of functional decomposition because the entire problem can be separated into three distinct operations. A possible implementation of a parallel version of the computation is shown in Listing 6.3.

The program computes the *sine*, *cosine*, and *tangent* functions in three separate threads and then aggregates the results. The implementation provided constitutes an example of the alternative technique discussed in the previous sample program. Instead of using a data structure for keeping track of the worker threads that have been created, a function pointer is passed to each thread so that it can update the final result at the end of the computation. This technique introduces a synchronization problem that is properly handled with the *lock* statement in the method referenced by the function pointer. The *lock* statement creates a critical section that can only be accessed by one thread at time and guarantees that the final result is properly updated.

```
using System;
using System.Threading;
using System.Collections.Generic;

/// <summary>
/// Delegate UpdateResult. Function pointer that is used to update the final result
/// from the slave threads once the computation is completed.
/// </summary>
/// <param name="x">partial value to add.</param>
public delegate void UpdateResult(double x);

/// <summary>
/// Class Sine. Computes the sine of a given value.
/// </summary>
public class Sine
{
    /// <summary>
    /// Input value for which the sine function is computed.
    /// </summary>
    private double x;
    /// <summary>
    /// Gets the input value of the sine function.
    /// </summary>
    public double X { get { return this.x; } }
    /// <summary>
    /// Result value.
    /// </summary>
    private double y;
    /// <summary>
    /// Gets the result value of the sine function.
    /// </summary>
    public double Y { get { return this.y; } }
    /// <summary>
    /// Function pointer used to update the result.
    /// </summary>
    private UpdateResult updater;
    /// <summary>
    /// Creates an instance of the Sine and sets the input to the given angle.
    /// </summary>
    /// <param name="x">Angle in radiants.</param>
    /// <param name="updater">Function pointer used to update the result.</param>
    public Sine(double x, UpdateResultupdater)
    {
        this.x = x;
        this.updater = updater;
    }
    /// <summary>
    /// Executes the sine function.
    /// </summary>
    public void Apply()
    {
        this.y = Math.Sin(this.x);
        if (this.updater != null)
        {
            this.updater(this.y);
```

LISTING 6.3

Mathematical Function.

```
        }
      }
    }

    ///<summary>
    /// Class Cosine. Computes the cosine of a given value.
    ///</summary>
    public class Cosine
    {
        /// <summary>
        /// Input value for which the cosine function is computed.
        /// </summary>
        private double x;
        /// <summary>
        /// Gets the input value of the cosine function.
        /// </summary>
        public double X { get { return this.x; } }
        /// <summary>
        /// Result value.
        /// </summary>
        private double y;
        /// <summary>
        /// Gets the result value of the cosine function.
        /// </summary>
        public double Y { get { return this.y; } }
        /// <summary>
        /// Function pointer used to update the result.
        /// </summary>
        private UpdateResultupdater;
        /// <summary>
        /// Creates an instance of the Cosine and sets the input to the given angle.
        /// </summary>
        /// <param name="x">Angle in radiants.</param>
        /// <param name="updater">Function pointer used to update the result.</param>
        public Cosine(double x, UpdateResultupdater)
        {
            this.x = x;
            this.updater = updater;
        }
        /// <summary>
        /// Executes the cosine function.
        /// </summary>
        public void Apply()
        {
            this.y = Math.Cos(this.x);
            if (this.updater != null)
            {
                this.updater(this.y);
            }
        }
    }

    ///<summary>
    /// Class Tangent. Computes the tangent of a given value.
    ///</summary>
    public class Tangent
    {
```

LISTING 6.3

(Continued)

```
/// <summary>
/// Input value for which the tangent function is computed.
/// </summary>
private double x;
/// <summary>
/// Gets the input value of the tangent function.
/// </summary>
public double X { get { return this.x; } }
/// <summary>
/// Result value.
/// </summary>
private double y;
/// <summary>
/// Gets the result value of the tangent function.
/// </summary>
public double Y { get { return this.y; } }
/// <summary>
/// Function pointer used to update the result.
/// </summary>
private UpdateResultupdater;
/// <summary>
/// Creates an instance of the Tangent and sets the input to the given angle.
/// </summary>
/// <param name="x">Angle in radiants.</param>
/// <param name="updater">Function pointer used to update the result.</param>
public Tangent(double x, UpdateResultupdater)
{
   this.x = x;
   this.updater = updater;
}
/// <summary>
/// Executes the cosine function.
/// </summary>
public void Apply()
{
   this.y = Math.Tan(this.x);
   if (this.updater != null)
   {
       this.updater(this.y);
   }
}
}
/// <summary>
/// Class Program. Computes the function sin(x) + cos(x) + tan(x).
/// </summary>
public class Program
{
   /// <summary>
   /// Variable storing the coputed value for the function.
   /// </summary>
   private static double result;
   /// <summary>
   /// Synchronization instance used to avoid keeping track of the threads.
   /// </summary>
   private static object synchRoot = new object();
   /// <summary>
   /// Read the command line parameters and perform the scalar product.
```

LISTING 6.3

(Continued)

```csharp
        /// </summary>
        /// <param name="args">Array strings containing the command line parameters.</param>
        public static void Main(string[] args)
        {
            // gets a value for x
            double x = 3.4d;

            // creates the function pointer to the update method.
            UpdateResult updater = newUpdateResult(Program.Sum);

            // creates the sine thread.
            Sine sine = newSine(x, updater);
            Thread tSine =new Thread(new ThreadStart(sine.Apply);

            // creates the cosine thread.
            Cosine cosine = newCosine(x, updater);
            Thread tCosine =new Thread(new ThreadStart(cosine.Apply);

            // creates the tangent thread.
            Tangent tangent = newTangent(x, updater);
            Thread tTangent =new Thread(new ThreadStart(tangent.Apply);

            // shuffles the execution order.
            tTangent.Start();
            tSine.Start();
            tCosine.Start();

            // waits for the completion of the threads.
            tCosine.Join();
            tTangent.Join();
            tSine.Join();

            // the result is available, dumps it to console.
            Console.WriteLine("f({0}): {1}", x, Program.result);
        }
        /// <summary>
        /// Callback that is executed once the computation in the thread is completed
        /// and adds the partial value passed as a parameter to the result.
        /// </summary>
        /// <param name="partial">Partial value to add.</param>
        private static voidSum(double partial)
        {
            lock(Program.synchRoot)
            {
                Program.result += partial;
            }
        }
    }
```

LISTING 6.3

(Continued)

6.2.3.3 Computation vs. communication

In designing parallel and in general distributed applications, it is very important to carefully evaluate the communication patterns among the components that have been identified during problem decomposition. The two decomposition methods presented in this section and the corresponding sample applications are based on the assumption that the computations are *independent*. This means that:

- The input values required by one computation do not depend on the output values generated by another computation.
- The different units of work generated as a result of the decomposition do not need to interact (i.e., exchange data) with each other.

These two assumptions strongly simplify the implementation and allow achieving a high degree of parallelism and a high throughput. Having all the worker threads independent from each other gives the maximum freedom to the operating system (or the virtual runtime environment) scheduler in scheduling all the threads. The need to exchange data among different threads introduces dependencies among them and ultimately can result in introducing performance bottlenecks. For example, we did not introduce any queuing technique for threads; but queuing threads might potentially constitute a problem for the execution of the application if data need to be exchanged with some threads that are still in the queue. A more common disadvantage is the fact that while a thread exchanges data with another one, it uses some kind of synchronization strategy that might lead to blocking the execution of other threads. The more data that need to be exchanged, the more they block threads for synchronization, thus ultimately impacting the overall throughput.

As a general rule of thumb, it is important to minimize the amount of data that needs to be exchanged while implementing parallel and distributed applications. The lack of communication among different threads constitutes the condition leading to the highest throughput.

6.3 Multithreading with Aneka

As applications become increasingly complex, there is greater demand for computational power that can be delivered by a single multicore machine. Often this demand cannot be addressed with the computing capacity of a single machine. It is then necessary to leverage distributed infrastructures such as clouds. Decomposition techniques can be applied to partition a given application into several units of work that, rather than being executed as threads on a single node, can be submitted for execution by leveraging clouds.

Even though a distributed facility can dramatically increase the degree of parallelism of applications, its use comes with a cost in term of application design and performance. For example, since the different units of work are not executing within the same process space but on different nodes, both the code and the data need to be moved to a different execution context; the same happens for results that need to be collected remotely and brought back to the master process. Moreover, if there is any communication among the different workers, it is necessary to redesign the communication model eventually by leveraging the APIs, if any, provided by the middleware. In other words, the transition from a single-process multithreaded execution to a distributed execution is not transparent, and application redesign and reimplementation are often required.

The amount of effort required to convert an application often depends on the facilities offered by the middleware managing the distributed infrastructure. Aneka, as middleware for managing clusters, grids, and clouds, provides developers with advanced capabilities for implementing distributed applications. In particular, it takes traditional thread programming a step further. It lets you write multithreaded applications the traditional way, with the added twist that each of these threads can now be executed outside the parent process and on a separate machine. In reality, these "threads" are independent processes executing on different nodes and do not share memory or other resources, but they allow you to write applications using the same thread constructs for concurrency and synchronization as with traditional threads. Aneka threads, as they are called, let you easily port existing multithreaded compute-intensive applications to distributed versions that can run faster by utilizing multiple machines simultaneously, with minimum conversion effort.

6.3.1 Introducing the thread programming model

Aneka offers the capability of implementing multithreaded applications over the cloud by means of the *Thread Programming Model*. This model introduces the abstraction of distributed thread, also called *Aneka thread*, which mimics the behavior of local threads but executes over a distributed infrastructure. The Thread Programming Model has been designed to transparently port high-throughput multithreaded parallel applications over a distributed infrastructure and provides the best advantage in the case of embarrassingly parallel applications.

As described in Section 5.4.1, each application designed for Aneka is represented by a local object that interfaces to the middleware. According to the various programming models supported by the framework, such an interface exposes different capabilities, which are tailored to efficiently support the design and the implementation of applications by following a specific programming style. In the case of the Thread Programming Model, the application is designed as a collection of threads, the collective execution of which represents the application run. Threads are created and controlled by the application developer, while Aneka is in charge of scheduling their execution once they have been started. Threads are transparently moved and remotely executed while developers control them from local objects that act like proxies of the remote threads. This approach makes the transition from local multithreaded applications to distributed applications quite easy and seamless.

The Thread Programming Model exhibits APIs that mimic the ones exposed by .NET base class libraries for threading. In this way developers do not have to completely rewrite applications in order to leverage Aneka; the process of porting local multithreaded applications is as simple as replacing the *System.Threading.Thread* class and introducing the *AnekaApplication* class. There are three major elements that constitute the object model of applications based on the Thread Programming Model:

- *Application.* This class represents the interface to the Aneka middleware and constitutes a local view of a distributed application. In the Thread Programming Model the single units of work are created by the programmer. Therefore, the specific class used will be *Aneka.Entity. AnekaApplication* $<T,M>$, with T and M properly selected.
- *Threads.* Threads represent the main abstractions of the model and constitute the building blocks of the distributed application. Aneka provides the *Aneka.Threading.AnekaThread* class, which represents a distributed thread. This class exposes a subset of the methods exposed by the

System.Threading.Thread class, which has been reduced to those operations and properties that make sense or can be efficiently implemented in a distributed context.

- *Thread Manager.* This is an internal component that is used to keep track of the execution of distributed threads and provide feedback to the application. Aneka provides a specific version of the manager for this model, which is implemented in the *Aneka.Threading.ThreadManager* class.

As a result, porting local multithreaded applications to Aneka involves defining an instance of the *AnekaApplication < AnekaThread, ThreadManager >* class and replacing any occurrence of *System.Threading.Thread* with *Aneka.Threading.AnekaThread*. Developers can start creating threads, control their life cycles, and coordinate their execution similarly to local threads.

Aneka applications expose additional other properties, such as events that notify the completion of threads, their failure, the completion of the entire application, and thread state transitions. These operations are also available for the Thread Programming Model and constitute additional features that can be leveraged while porting local multithreaded applications, where this support needs to be explicitly programmed. Also, the *AnekaApplication* class provides support for files, which are automatically and transparently moved in the distributed environment.

6.3.2 Aneka thread vs. common threads

To efficiently run on a distributed infrastructure, Aneka threads have certain limitations compared to local threads. These limitations relate to the communication and synchronization strategies that are normally used in multithreaded applications.

6.3.2.1 Interface compatibility

The *Aneka.Threading.AnekaThread* class exposes almost the same interface as the *System.Threading.Thread* class with the exception of a few operations that are not supported. Table 6.1 compares the operations that are exposed by the two classes. The reference namespace that defines all the types referring to the support for threading is *Aneka.Threading* rather than *System.Threading*.

The basic control operations for local threads such as *Start* and *Abort* have a direct mapping, whereas operations that involve the temporary interruption of the thread execution have not been supported. The reasons for such a design decision are twofold. First, the use of the *Suspend/Resume* operations is generally a deprecated practice, even for local threads, since *Suspend* abruptly interrupts the execution state of the thread. Second, thread suspension in a distributed environment leads to an ineffective use of the infrastructure, where resources are shared among different tenants and applications. This is also the reason that the *Sleep* operation is not supported. Therefore, there is no need to support the *Interrupt* operation, which forcibly resumes the thread from a waiting or a sleeping state. To support synchronization among threads, a corresponding implementation of the *Join* operation has been provided.

Besides the basic thread control operations, the most relevant properties have been implemented, such as name, unique identifier, and state. Whereas the name can be freely assigned, the identifier is generated by Aneka, and it represents a globally unique identifier (GUID) in its string form rather than an integer. Properties such as *IsBackground*, *Priority*, and *IsThreadPoolThread* have been provided for interface compatibility but actually do not have any effect on thread scheduling and always expose the values reported in the table. Other properties concerning the state of the

Table 6.1 Thread API Comparison

.Net Threading API	Aneka Threading API
System.Threading	Aneka.Threading
Thread	AnekaThread
Thread.ManagedThreadId (int)	AnekaThread.Id (string)
Thread.Name	AnekaThread.Name
Thread.ThreadState (ThreadState)	AnekaThread.State
Thread.IsAlive	AnekaThread.IsAlive
Thread.IsRunning	AnekaThread.IsRunning
Thread.IsBackground	AnekaThread.IsBackground[false]
Thread.Priority	AnekaThread.Priority[ThreadPriority.Normal]
Thread.IsThreadPoolThread	AnekaThread.IsThreadPoolThread [false]
Thread.Start	AnekaThread.Start
Thread.Abort	AnekaThread.Abort
Thread.Sleep	[Not provided]
Thread.Interrupt	[Not provided]
Thread.Suspend	[Not provided]
Thread.Resume	[Not provided]
Thread.Join	AnekaThread.Join

thread, such as *IsAlive* and *IsRunning*, exhibit the expected behavior, whereas a slightly different behavior has been implemented for the *ThreadState* property that is mapped to the *State* property. The remaining methods of the *System.Threading.Thread* class (.NET 2.0) are not supported.

Finally, it is important to note differences in thread creation. Local threads implicitly belong to the hosting process and their range of action is limited by the process boundaries. To create local threads it is only necessary to provide a pointer to a method to execute in the form of the *ThreadStart* or *ParameterizedThreadStart* delegates. Aneka threads live in the context of a distributed application, and multiple distributed applications can be managed within a single process; for this reason, thread creation also requires the specification of the reference to the application to which the thread belongs.

Interface compatibility between Aneka threading APIs and the base class library allow quick porting of most of the local multithreaded applications to Aneka by simply replacing the class names and modifying the thread constructors.

6.3.2.2 Thread life cycle

Since Aneka threads live and execute in a distributed environment, their life cycle is necessarily different from the life cycle of local threads. For this reason, it is not possible to directly map the state values of a local thread to those exposed by Aneka threads. Figure 6.6 provides a comparative view of the two life cycles.

The white balloons in the figure indicate states that do not have a corresponding mapping on the other life cycle; the shaded balloons indicate the common states. Moreover, in local threads most of the state transitions are controlled by the developer, who actually triggers the state transition by invoking methods on the thread instance, whereas in Aneka threads, many of the state transitions are controlled

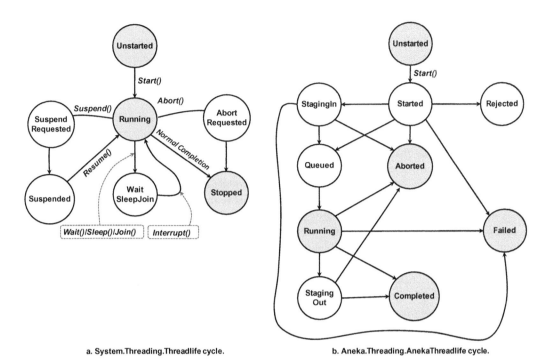

a. System.Threading.Threadlife cycle.   b. Aneka.Threading.AnekaThreadlife cycle.

FIGURE 6.6

Thread life-cycle comparison.

by the middleware. As depicted in Figure 6.6, Aneka threads exhibit more states than local threads because Aneka threads support file staging and they are scheduled by the middleware, which can queue them for a considerable amount of time. As Aneka supports the reservation of nodes for execution of thread related to a specific application, an explicit state indicating execution failure due to missing reservation credential has been introduced. This occurs when a thread is sent to an execution node in a time window where only nodes with specific reservation credentials can be executed.

An Aneka thread is initially found in the *Unstarted* state. Once the *Start()* method is called, the thread transits to the *Started* state, from which it is possible to move to the *StagingIn* state if there are files to upload for its execution or directly to the *Queued* state. If there is any error while uploading files, the thread fails and it ends its execution with the *Failed* state, which can also be reached for any exception that occurred while invoking *Start()*.

Another outcome might be the *Rejected* state that occurs if the thread is started with an invalid reservation token. This is a final state and implies execution failure due to lack of rights. Once the thread is in the queue, if there is a free node where to execute it, the middleware moves all the object data and depending files to the remote node and starts its execution, thus changing the state into *Running*. If the thread generates an exception or does not produce the expected output files, the execution is considered failed and the final state of the thread is set to *Failed*. If the execution is successful, the final state is set to *Completed*. If there are output files to retrieve, the thread state is set to *StagingOut* while files are collected and sent to their final destination, and then it transits to *Completed*. At any point, if the developer stops the execution of the application or directly calls the *Abort()* method, the thread is aborted and its final state is set to *Aborted*.

In most cases, the normal state transition will resemble the one occurring for local threads: *Unstarted* → *[Started]* → *[Queued]* → *Running* → *Completed/Aborted/Failed*.

6.3.2.3 Thread synchronization

The .NET base class libraries provide advanced facilities to support thread synchronization by the means of monitors, semaphores, reader-writer locks, and basic synchronization constructs at the language level. Aneka provides minimal support for thread synchronization that is limited to the implementation of the *join* operation for thread abstraction. Most of the constructs and classes that are provided by the .NET framework are used to provide controlled access to shared data from different threads in order to preserve their integrity. This requirement is less stringent in a distributed environment, where there is no shared memory among the thread instances and therefore it is not necessary. Moreover, the reason for porting a local multithread application to Aneka threads implicitly involves the need for a distributed facility in which to execute a large number of threads, which might not be executing all at the same time. Providing coordination facilities that introduce a locking strategy in such an environment might lead to distributed deadlocks that are hard to detect. Therefore, by design Aneka threads do not feature any synchronization facility that goes beyond the simple *join* operation between executing threads.

6.3.2.4 Thread priorities

The *System.Threading.Thread* class supports thread priorities, where the scheduling priority can be one selected from one of the values of the *ThreadPriority* enumeration: *Highest*, *AboveNormal*, *Normal*, *BelowNormal*, or *Lowest*. However, operating systems are not required to honor the priority of a thread, and the current version of Aneka does not support thread priorities. For interface compatibility purposes the *Aneka.Threading.Thread* class exhibits a *Priority* property whose type is *ThreadPriority*, but its value is always set to *Normal*, and changes to it do not produce any effect on thread scheduling by the Aneka middleware.

6.3.2.5 Type serialization

Aneka threads execute in a distributed environment in which the object code in the form of libraries and live instances information are moved over the network. This condition imposes some limitations that are mostly concerned with the serialization of types in the .NET framework.

Local threads execute all within the same address space and share memory; therefore, they do not need objects to be copied or transferred into a different address space. Aneka threads are distributed and execute on remote computing nodes, and this implies that the object code related to the method to be executed within a thread needs to be transferred over the network. Since delegates can point to instance methods, the state of the enclosing instance needs to be transferred and reconstructed on the remote execution environment. This is a particular feature at the class level and goes by the term *type serialization*.

A .NET type is considered *serializable* if it is possible to convert an instance of the type into a binary array containing all the information required to revert it to its original form or into a possibly different execution context. This property is generally given for several types defined in the .NET framework by simply tagging the class definition with the *Serializable* attribute. If the class exposes a specific set of characteristics, the framework will automatically provide facilities to serialize and deserialize instances of that type. Alternatively, custom serialization can be implemented for any user-defined type.

Aneka threads execute methods defined in serializable types, since it is necessary to move the enclosing instance to remote execution method. In most cases, providing serialization is as easy as tagging the class definition with the *Serializable* attribute; in other cases it might be necessary to implement the *ISerializable* interface and provide appropriate constructors for the type. This is not a strong limitation, since there are very few cases in which types cannot be defined as serializable. For example, local threads, network connections, and streams are not serializable since they directly access local resources that cannot be implicitly moved onto a different node.

6.4 Programming applications with Aneka threads

To show how it is possible to quickly port multithreaded application to Aneka threads, we provide a distributed implementation of the previously discussed examples for local threads.

6.4.1 Aneka threads application model

The *Thread Programming Model* is a programming model in which the programmer creates the units of work as Aneka threads. Therefore, it is necessary to utilize the *AnekaApplication < W,M >* class, which is the application reference class for all the programming models falling into this category. The Aneka APIs make strong use of generics and characterize the support given to different programming models through template specialization. Hence, to develop distributed applications with Aneka threads, it is necessary to specialize the template type as follows:

AnekaApplication < AnekaThread, ThreadManager >

This will be the class type for all the distributed applications that use the Thread Programming Model. These two types are defined in the *Aneka.Threading* namespace noted in the *Aneka. Threading.dll* library of the Aneka SDK.

Another important component of the application model is the *Configuration* class, which is defined in the *Aneka.Entity* namespace (*Aneka.dll*). This class contains a set of properties that allow the application class to configure its interaction with the middleware, such as the address of the Aneka index service, which constitutes the main entry point of Aneka Clouds; the user credentials required to authenticate the application with the middleware; some additional tuning parameters; and an extended set of properties that might be used to convey additional information to the middleware. The code excerpt presented in Listing 6.4 demonstrates how to create a simple application instance and configure it to connect to an Aneka Cloud whose index service is local.

Once the application has been created, it is possible to create threads by specifying the reference to the application and the method to execute in each thread, and the management of the application execution is mostly concerned with controlling the execution of each thread instance. Listing 6.5 provides a very simple example of how to create Aneka threads.

The rest of the operations relate to the common management of thread instances, similar to local multithreaded applications discussed earlier.

```
// namespaces containing types of common use
using System;
using System.Collections.Generic;
// common Aneka namespaces.
using Aneka;
using Aneka.Util;
using Aneka.Entity;
// Aneka Thread Programming Model user classes
using Aneka.Threading;

// ..........

///<summary>
///Creates an instance of the Aneka Application configured to use the
/// Thread Programming Model.
/// </summary>
/// <returns>Application instance.</returns>
private AnekaApplication<AnekaThread,ThreadManager> CreateApplication();
{
   Configuration conf =new Configuration();
   // this is the common address and port of a local installation
   // of the Aneka Cloud.
   conf.SchedulerUri = newUri("tcp://localhost:9090/Aneka");
   conf.Credentials =newUserCredentials("Administrator", string.Empty);
   // we will not need support for file transfer, hence we optimize the
   // application in order to not require any file transfer service.
   conf.UseFileTransfer = false;
   // we do not need any other configuration setting

   // we create the application instance and configure it.
   AnekaApplication<AnekaThread,ThreadManager> app =
               new AnekaApplication<AnekaThread,ThreadManager>(conf);
   return app;
}
```

LISTING 6.4

Application Creation and Configuration.

6.4.2 Domain decomposition: matrix multiplication

To port to Aneka threads the multithreaded matrix multiplication, we need to apply the considerations made in the previous section. Hence, we start reviewing the code by first making the proper changes to the *ScalarProduct* class. Listing 6.6 shows the modified version of *ScalarProduct*.

The class has been tagged with the *Serializable* attribute and extended with the methods required to implement custom serialization. Supporting custom serialization implies the following:

- Including the *System.Runtime.Serialization* namespace.
- Implementing the *ISerializable* interface. This interface has only one method that is void *GetObjectData(SerializationInfo, StreamingContext)*, and it is called when the runtime needs to serialize the instance.
- Providing a constructor with the following signature: *ScalarProduct(SerializationInfo, StreamingContext)*. This constructor is invoked when the instance is deserialized.

```
// ........... continues from the previous listing
///<summary>
///Thread worker method (implementation skipped).
///</summary>
private void WorkerMethod()
{
    // ...........
}
///<summary>
///Creates a collection of threads that are executed in the context of the
/// the given application.
///</summary>
/// <param name="app">>Application instance.</param>
private void CreateThreads(AnekaApplication<AnekaThread,ThreadManager> app);
{
    // creates a delegate to the method to execute inside the threads.
    ThreadStart worker = newThreadStart(this.WorkerMethod);
    // iterates over a loop and creates ten threads.
    for(int i=0; i<10; i++)
    {
        AnekaThread thread = new AnekaThread(worker, app);
        thread.Start();
    }
}
```

LISTING 6.5

Thread Creation and Execution.

The *SerializationInfo* class has a central role of providing a repository where all the properties defining the serialized format of a class can be stored and referenced by name. With minimum changes to the class layout, it would be possible to rely on the default serialization provided by the framework. To leverage such capability, it is necessary that all the properties defining the state of an instance are accessible through both *get* and *set* methods. In that case, it would be possible to simply tag the class as serialization, since all the fields constituting the state of the instance are also serializable. It can be noted that, apart from serialization, there is no need to make any change to the way the class operates.

The second step is to change the *MatrixProduct* class to leverage Aneka threads. We need to first create a properly configured application and then substitute the occurrences of the *System. Threading.Thread* class with *Aneka.Threading.Thread* (see Listing 6.7).

As shown in Listing 6.7, the changes that need to be applied to the logic of the program are minimal, and most of the modifications are related to exception management and the proper use of Aneka logging facilities. The *MatrixProduct* class integrates the method discussed in the previous section for application creation and setup and introduces a *try...catch...finally* block to handle exceptions that occurred while the application was executing. The rest of the code, except for renaming the occurrences of the *Thread* class, is unchanged.

There is only one important change to note: Once the Aneka thread instance is completed, the updated reference to the object containing the remotely executed method is exposed by the

```
using System.Runtime.Serialization;

///<summary>
/// Class ScalarProduct. Computes the scalar product between the row and the column
/// arrays. The class uses custom serialization. In order to do so it implements the
/// the ISerializable interface.
///</summary>
[Serializable]
public class ScalarProduct : ISerializable
{
    /// <summary>
    /// Scalar product.
    /// </summary>
    private double result;
    /// <summary>
    /// Gets the resulting scalar product.
    /// </summary>
    public double Result{get { returnthis.result; }}

    /// <summary>
    /// Arrays containing the elements of the row and the column to multiply.
    /// </summary>
    private double[] row, column;

    /// <summary>
    /// Creates an instance of the ScalarProduct class and configures it with the given
    /// row and column arrays.
    /// </summary>
    /// <param name="row">Array with the elements of the row to be multiplied.</param>
    /// <param name="column">Array with the elements of the column to be multiplied.
    /// </param>
    public ScalarProduct(double[] row, double[] column)
    {
        this.row = row;
        this.colum = colum;
    }
    /// <summary>
    /// Deserialization constructor used by the .NET runtime to recreate instances of
    /// of types implementing custom serialization.
    /// </summary>
    /// <param name="info">Bag containing the serialized data instance.</param>
    /// <param name="context">Serialization context (not used).</param>
    public ScalarProduct(SerializationInfo info, StreamingContext context)
    {
        this.result = info.GetDouble("result");
        this.row = info.GetValue("row", typeof(double[])) as double[];
        this.column = info.GetValue("column", typeof(double[])) as double[];
    }
}
```

LISTING 6.6

ScalarProduct Class (Modified Version).

```
/// <summary>
/// Executes the scalar product between the row and the colum.
/// </summary>
/// <param name="row">Array with the elements of the row to be multiplied.</param>
/// <param name="column">Array with the elements of the column to be multiplied.
/// </param>
public void Multiply()
{
    this.result = 0;
    for(int i=0; i<this.row.Length; i++)
    {
        this.result += this.row[i] * this.column[i];
    }
}
/// <summary>
/// Serialization method used by the .NET runtime to serialize instances of
/// of types implementing custom serialization.
/// </summary>
/// <param name="info">Bag containing the serialized data instance.</param>
/// <param name="context">Serialization context (not used).</param>
public ScalarProduct(SerializationInfo info, StreamingContext context)
{
    this.result = info.GetDouble("result");
    this.row = info.GetValue("row", typeof(double[])) as double[];
    this.column = info.GetValue("column", typeof(double[])) as double[];
}
/// <summary>
/// Executes the scalar product between the row and the colum.
/// </summary>
/// <param name="row">Array with the elements of the row to be multiplied.</param>
/// <param name="column">Array with the elements of the column to be multiplied.
/// </param>
public void Multiply()
{
    this.result = 0;
    for(int i=0; i<this.row.Length; i++)
    {
        this.result += this.row[i] * this.column[i];
    }
}
/// <summary>
/// Serialization method used by the .NET runtime to serialize instances of
/// of types implementing custom serialization.
/// </summary>
/// <param name="info">Bag containing the serialized data instance.</param>
/// <param name="context">Serialization context (not used).</param>
public void GetObjectData(SerializationInfo info, StreamingContext context)
{
    info.AddValue("result",this.result);
    info.AddValue("row", this.row,typeof(double[]));
    info.AddValue("column", this.column,typeof(double[]));
}
}
```

LISTING 6.6

(Continued)

```
using System;
// we do not anymore need the reference to the threading namespace.
// using System.Threading;
using System.Collections.Generic;

// reference to the Aneka namespaces of interest.
// common Aneka namespaces.
using Aneka;
using Aneka.Util;
using Aneka.Entity;
// Aneka Thread Programming Model user classes
using Aneka.Threading;

/// <summary>
/// Class MatrixProduct. Performs the matrix product of two matrices.
/// </summary>
public class MatrixProduct
{
    /// <summary>
    /// First and second matrix of the produt.
    /// </summary>
    private static double[,]a, b;
    /// <summary>
    /// Result matrix.
    /// </summary>
    private static double[,] c;
    ///<summary>
    /// Dictionary mapping the thread instances to the corresponding ScalarProduct
    ///instances that are run inside.The occurrence of the Thread class has been
    ///substituted with AnekaThread.
    ///</summary>
    private static IDictionary<AnekaThread, ScalarProduct> workers.
    /// <summary>
    /// Reference to the distributed application the threads belong to.
    /// </summary>
    private static AnekaApplication<AnekaThread, ThreadManager> app;

    /// <summary>
    /// Read the command line parameters and perform the scalar product.
    /// </summary>
    /// <param name="args">Array strings containing the command line parameters.</param>
    public static void Main(string[] args)
    {
        try
        {
            // activates the logging facility.
            Logger.Start();

            // creates the Aneka application instance.
            MatrixProduct.app =Program.CreateApplication();

            // reads the input matrices a and b.
            MatrixProduct.ReadMatrices();
            // executes the parallel matrix product.
            MatrixProduct.ExecuteProudct();
            // waits for all the threads to complete and
            // composes the final matrix.
```

LISTING 6.7

MatrixProduct Class (Modified Version).

```
        MatrixProduct.ComposeResult();
    }
    catch(Exception ex)
    {
        IOUtil.DumpErrorReport(ex, "Matrix Multiplication - Error executing " +
                                   "the application");
    }
    finally
    {
        try
        {
            // checks whether the application instance has been created
            // stops it.
            if (MatrixProduct.app != null)
            {
                MatrixProduct.app.Stop();
            }
        }
        catch(Exception ex)
        {
            IOUtil.DumpErrorReport(ex, "Matrix Multiplication - Error stopping " +
                                       "the application");
        }
        // stops the logging thread.
        Logger.Stop();
    }
}

/// <summary>
/// Executes the parallel matrix product by decomposing the problem in
/// independent scalar product between rows and colums.
/// </summary>
private static void ExecuteThreads()
{
    // we replace the Thread class with AnekaThread.
    MatrixProduct.workers = new Dictionary<AnekaThread, ScalarProduct>();
    int rows = MatrixProduct.a.Length;
    // in .NET matrices are arrays of arrays and the number of columns is
    // is represented by the length of the second array.
    int columns = MatrixProduct.b[0].Length;

    for(int i=0; i<rows; i++)
    for(int j=0; j<columns; j++)
    {
        double[] row = MatrixProduct.a[i];
        // beacause matrices are stored as arrays of arrays in order to
        // to get the columns we need to traverse the array and copy the
        // the data to another array.
        double[] column = new double[common];
        for(int k=0; k<common; k++)
        {
            column[j] = MatrixProduct.b[j][i];
        }
        // creates a ScalarProduct instance with the previous rows and
        // columns and starts a thread executing the Multiply method.
        ScalarProduct scalar = newScalarProduct(row, column);
        // we change the System.Threading.Thread class with the corresponding
```

LISTING 6.7

(Continued)

```
        // Aneka.Threading.AnekaThread class and reference the application instance.
        AnekaThread worker = newAnekaThread(newThreadStart(scalar.Multiply), app);
        worker.Name =string.Format("{0}.{1}",row,column);
        worker.Start();
        // adds the thread to the dictionary so that it can be
        // further retrieved.
        MatrixProduct.workers.Add(worker, scalar);
    }
}
/// <summary>
/// Waits for the completion of all the threads and composes the final
/// result matrix.
/// </summary>
private static void ComposeResult()
{
    MatrixProduct.c = new double[rows,columns];
    // we replace the Thread class with AnekaThread.
    foreach(KeyValuePair<AnekaThread,ScalarProduct>pair in MatrixProduct.workers)
    {
        AnekaThread worker = pair.Key;
        // we have saved the coordinates of each scalar product in the name
        // of the thread now we get them back by parsing the name.
        string[] indices = string.Split(worker.Name, new char[] {'.'});
        int i = int.Parse(indices[0]);
        int j = int.Parse(indices[1]);
        // we wait for the thread to complete
        worker.Join();
        // instead of using the local value of the ScalarProduct instance
        // we use the one that has is stored in the Target property.
        // MatrixProduct.c[i,j] = pair.Value.Result;
        MatrixProduct.c[i,j] = ((ScalarProduct) worker.Target).Result;
    }
    MatrixProduct.PrintMatrix(MatrixProduct.c);
}
/// <summary>
/// Reads the matrices.
/// </summary>
private static void ReadMatrices()
{
    // code for reading the matrices a and b
}
/// <summary>
/// Prints the given matrix.
/// </summary>
/// <param name="matrix">Matrix to print.</param>
private static voidPrintMatrices(double[,] matrix)
{
    // code for printing the matrix.
}
/// <summary>
/// Creates an instance of the Aneka Application configured to use the
/// Thread Programming Model.
/// </summary>
/// <returns>Application instance.</returns>
private AnekaApplication<AnekaThread,ThreadManager> CreateApplication();
{
```

LISTING 6.7

(Continued)

```
    Configuration conf =new Configuration();
    // this is the common address and port of a local installation
    // of the Aneka Cloud.
    conf.SchedulerUri = newUri("tcp://localhost:9090/Aneka");
    conf.Credentials =newUserCredentials("Administrator", string.Empty);
    // we will not need support for file transfer, hence we optimize the
    // application in order to not require any file transfer service.
    conf.UseFileTransfer = false;
    // we do not need any other configuration setting

    // we create the application instance and configure it.
    AnekaApplication<AnekaThread,ThreadManager> app =
                new AnekaApplication<AnekaThread,ThreadManager>(conf);
    return app;
  }
 }
```

LISTING 6.7

(Continued)

AnekaThread.Target property and not the local variable referencing the object that was initially used to create the delegate.

6.4.3 Functional decomposition: *Sine, Cosine,* and *Tangent*

The modifications required to port this sample to Aneka threads are basically the same as those discussed in the previous example. There is only one significant difference in this case: Each of the threads has a reference to a delegate that is used to update the global sum at the end of the computation. Since we are operating in a distributed environment, the instance on which the object will operate is not shared among the threads, but each thread instance has its own local copy. This prevents the global sum from being updated in the master thread and requires a change in the update strategy utilized.

This example also illustrates how to modify the classes *Sine, Cosine,* and *Tangent* so that they can leverage the default serialization capabilities of the framework (see Listing 6.8).

This example demonstrated how to change the logic of the application in case the worker methods executed in the threads have a reference to a local object that is updated as a consequence of the execution. To allow the execution of such applications with Aneka threads, it is necessary to extrapolate the update logic from the worker method of the threads and perform it into the master thread.

SUMMARY

This chapter provided a brief overview of multithreaded programming and the technologies used for multiprocessing on a single machine. We introduced the basics of multicore technology, which is the latest technological advancement for achieving parallelism on a single computer, and discussed how such parallelism can be leveraged to speed up applications by using multithreaded programming. A thread defines a single control flow within a process, which is the logical unit for

```
using System;
// we do not anymore need the reference to the threading namespace.
// using System.Threading;
using System.Collections.Generic;

// reference to the Aneka namespaces of interest.
// common Aneka namespaces.
using Aneka;
using Aneka.Util;
using Aneka.Entity;
// Aneka Thread Programming Model user classes
using Aneka.Threading;


// this is not needed anymore.
// /// <summary>
// /// Delegate UpdateResult. Function pointer that is used to update the final result
// /// from the slave threads once the computation is completed.
// /// </summary>
// /// <param name="x">partial value to add.</param>
// public delegate void UpdateResult(double x);


/// <summary>
/// Class Sine. Computes the sine of a given value.
/// </summary>
[Serializable]
public class Sine
{
    /// <summary>
    /// Input value for which the sine function is computed.
    /// </summary>
    private double x;
    /// <summary>
    /// Gets or sets the input value of the sine function.
    /// </summary>
    public double X { get { return this.x; } set { this.x = value; } }
    /// <summary>
    /// Result value.
    /// </summary>
    private double y;
    /// <summary>
    /// Gets or sets the result value of the sine function.
    /// </summary>
    public double Y { get { return this.y; } set { this.y = value; } }
    // we can't use this anymore.
    // /// <summary>
    // /// Function pointer used to update the result.
    // /// </summary>
    // private UpdateResult updater;

    // we need a default constructor, which is automatically provided by the compiler
    // if we do not specify any constructor.
    // /// <summary>
    // /// Creates an instance of the Sine and sets the input to the given angle.
    // /// </summary>
    // /// <param name="x">Angle in radiants.</param>
    // /// <param name="updater">Function pointer used to update the result.</param>
```

LISTING 6.8

Mathematical Function (Modified Version).

```
// public Sine(double x, UpdateResult updater)
// {
//     this.x = x;
//      this.updater = updater;
// }
/// <summary>
/// Executes the sine function.
/// </summary>
public void Apply()
{
    this.y = Math.Sin(this.x);
    // we cannot use this anymore because there is no
    // shared memory space.
    // if (this.updater != null)
    // {
    //      this.updater(this.y);
    // }
}
}

///<summary>
/// Class Cosine. Computes the cosine of a given value. The same changes have been
/// applied by removing the code not needed anymore rather than commenting it out.
///</summary>
[Serializable]
public class Cosine
{
    /// <summary>
    /// Input value for which the cosine function is computed.
    /// </summary>
    private double x;
    /// <summary>
    /// Gets or sets the input value of the cosine function.
    /// </summary>
    public double X { get { return this.x; } set { this.x = value; } }
    /// <summary>
    /// Result value.
    /// </summary>
    private double y;
    /// <summary>
    /// Gets or sets the result value of the cosine function.
    /// </summary>
    public double Y { get { return this.y; } set { this.y = value; } }
    /// <summary>
    /// Executes the cosine function.
    /// </summary>
    public voidApply()
    {
        this.y = Math.Cos(this.x);
    }
}

///<summary>
/// Class Cosine. Computes the cosine of a given value. The same changes have been
/// applied by removing the code not needed anymore rather than commenting it out.
///</summary>
[Serializable]
```

LISTING 6.8

(Continued)

```
public class Tangent
{
    /// <summary>
    /// Input value for which the tangent function is computed.
    /// </summary>
    private double x;
    /// <summary>
    /// Gets or sets the input value of the tangent function.
    /// </summary>
    public double X { get { return this.x; } set { this.x = value; } }
    /// <summary>
    /// Result value.
    /// </summary>
    private double y;
    /// <summary>
    /// Gets or sets the result value of the tangent function.
    /// </summary>
    public double Y { get { return this.y; } set { this.y = value; } }
    /// <summary>
    /// Executes the tangent function.
    /// </summary>
    public voidApply()
    {
        this.y = Math.Cos(this.x);
    }
}


///<summary>
/// Class Cosine. Computes the cosine of a given value. The same changes have been
/// applied by removing the code not needed anymore rather than commenting it out.
///</summary>
[Serializable]
public class Tangent
{
    /// <summary>
    /// Input value for which the tangent function is computed.
    /// </summary>
    private double x;
    /// <summary>
    /// Gets or sets the input value of the tangent function.
    /// </summary>
    public double X { get { return this.x; } set { this.x = value; } }
    /// <summary>
    /// Result value.
    /// </summary>
    private double y;
    /// <summary>
    /// Gets or sets the result value of the tangent function.
    /// </summary>
    public double Y { get { return this.y; } set { this.y = value; } }
    /// <summary>
    /// Executes the tangent function.
    /// </summary>
    public voidApply()
    {
        this.y = Math.Tan(this.x);
    }
}
```

LISTING 6.8

(Continued)

```
        }

/// <summary>
/// Class Program. Computes the function sin(x) + cos(x) + tan(x).
/// </summary>
public class Program
{
    /// <summary>
    /// Variable storing the coputed value for the function.
    /// </summary>
    private static double result;

    // we do not need synchronization anymore, because the update of the global
    // sum is done sequentially.
    // /// <summary>
    // /// Synchronization instance used to avoid keeping track of the threads.
    // /// </summary>
    // private static object synchRoot = new object();

    /// <summary>
    /// Reference to the distributed application the threads belong to .
    /// </summary>
    private static AnekaApplication<AnekaThread, ThreadManager> app;

    /// <summary>
    /// Read the command line parameters and perform the scalar product.
    /// </summary>
    /// <param name="args">Array strings containing the command line parameters. </param>
    public static voidMain(string[] args)
    {
        try
        {
            // activates the logging facility.
            Logger.Start();
            // creates the Aneka application instance.
            app = Program.CreateApplication();

            // gets a value for x
            double x = 3.4d;

            // creates the function pointer to the update method.
            UpdateResult updater = newUpdateResult(Program.Sum);

            // creates the sine thread.
            Sine sine = newSine(x, updater);
            AnekaThread tSine =newAnekaThread(new ThreadStart(sine.Apply), app);

            // creates the cosine thread.
            Cosine cosine = newCosine(x, updater);
            AnekaThread tCosine =newAnekaThread(new ThreadStart(cosine.Apply), app);

            // creates the tangent thread.
            Tangent tangent = newTangent(x, updater);
            AnekaThread tTangent =newAnekaThread(new ThreadStart(tangent.Apply), app);

            // shuffles the execution order.
            tTangent.Start();
```

LISTING 6.8

(Continued)

```
        tSine.Start();
        tCosine.Start();

        // waits for the completion of the threads.
        tCosine.Join();
        tTangent.Join();
        tSine.Join();

        // once we have joined all the threads the values have been collected back
        // and we use the Target property in order to obtain the object with the
        // updated values.
        sine = (Sine) tSine.Target;
        cosine = (Cosine) tSine.Target;
        tangent = (Tangent) tSine.Target;

        Program.result = sine.Target.Y + cosine.Y + tangent.Y;

        // the result is available, dumps it to console.
        Console.WriteLine("f({0}): {1}", x, Program.result);
    }
    catch(Exception ex)
    {
        IOUtil.DumpErrorReport(ex, "Math Functions - Error executing " +
                                    "the application");

    }
    finally
    {
        try
        {
            // checks whether the application instance has been created
            // stops it.
            if (app != null)
            {
                app.Stop();
            }
        }
        catch(Exception ex)
        {
            IOUtil.DumpErrorReport(ex, "Math Functions - Error stopping " +
                                        "the application");
        }
        // stops the logging thread.
        Logger.Stop();
    }
}
// we do not need this anymore.
// /// <summary>
// /// Callback that is executed once the computation in the thread is completed
// /// and adds the partial value passed as a parameter to the result.
// /// </summary>
// /// <param name="partial">Partial value to add.</param>
// private static void Sum(double partial)
// {
//     lock(Program.synchRoot)
//     {
//         Program.result += partial;
//     }
```

LISTING 6.8

(Continued)

```
// }
/// <summary>
/// Creates an instance of the Aneka Application configured to use the
/// Thread Programming Model.
/// </summary>
/// <returns>Application instance.</returns>
private AnekaApplication<AnekaThread,ThreadManager> CreateApplication();
{
    Configuration conf =new Configuration();
    // this is the common address and port of a local installation
    // of the Aneka Cloud.
    conf.SchedulerUri = newUri("tcp://localhost:9090/Aneka");
    conf.Credentials =newUserCredentials("Administrator", string.Empty);
    // we will not need support for file transfer, hence we optimize the
    // application in order to not require any file transfer service.
    conf.UseFileTransfer = false;
    // we do not need any other configuration setting

    // we create the application instance and configure it.
    AnekaApplication<AnekaThread,ThreadManager> app =
                    new AnekaApplication<AnekaThread,ThreadManager>(conf);

    return app;
}
}
```

LISTING 6.8

(Continued)

representing a running program in modern operating systems. Currently, all the most popular operating systems support multithreading, irrespective of whether the underlying hardware explicitly supports real parallelism or not. Real parallelism is supported by the use of multiple processors or cores at the same time, if they are available; otherwise, multithreading is obtained by interleaving the execution of multiple threads on the same processing unit.

To support multithreaded programming, programming languages define the abstraction of process and thread in their class libraries. A popular standard for operations on threads and thread synchronization is POSIX, which is supported by all the Linux/UNIX operating systems and is available as an additional library for the Windows operating systems family. A common implementation of POSIX is given in C/C++ as a library of functions. New-generation languages such as Java and C# (.NET) provide a set of abstractions for thread management and synchronization that is compliant and that most closely follows the object-oriented design that characterizes these languages. These implementations are portable over any operating system that provides an implementation for the runtime environment required by these languages.

Multithreaded programming is a practice that allows achieving parallelism within the boundaries of a single machine. Applications requiring a high degree of parallelism cannot be supported by normal multithreaded programming and must rely on distributed infrastructures such as clusters, grids, or, most recently, clouds. The use of these facilities imposes application redesign and the use of specific APIs, which might require significant changes to the existing applications. To address this issue, Aneka provides the Thread Programming Model, which extends the philosophy behind multithreaded programming beyond the boundaries of a single node and allows leveraging heterogeneous distributed infrastructure for execution. To minimize application reconversion, the Thread Programming Model mimics the API of the *System.Threading* namespace, with some limitations that are imposed by the fact that threads are executed on a distributed infrastructure. High-throughput applications can be easily ported to Aneka threads with minimal or no changes at all to their logic. Examples of such features and the basic steps of converting a local multithreaded application to Aneka threads were given in the chapter by discussing simple applications demonstrating the methodology of domain and functional decomposition for parallel problems.

As a framework for distributed programming, Aneka provides many built-in features that are not generally of use while architecting an application in terms of concurrent threads. These are, for example, event notification and support for file transfer. These capabilities are available as core features of the Aneka application model but have not been demonstrated in the case of the Thread Programming Model, which is concerned with providing support for partitioning the execution of algorithms to speed up execution. However, they are indeed of great use in the case of "bag of tasks" applications, discussed in the next chapter.

Review questions

1. What is throughput computing and what does it aim to achieve?
2. What is multiprocessing? Describe the different techniques for implementing multiprocessing.
3. What is multicore technology and how does it relate to multiprocessing?
4. Briefly describe the architecture of a multicore system.
5. What is multitasking?
6. What is multithreading and how does it relate to multitasking?
7. Describe the relationship between a process and a thread.
8. Does parallelism of applications depend on parallel hardware architectures?
9. Describe the principal characteristics of a thread from a programming point of view and the uses of threads for parallelizing application execution.
10. What is POSIX?
11. Describe the support given for programming with threads in new-generation languages such as Java or C#.
12. What do the terms *logical thread* and *physical thread* refer to?
13. What are the common operations implemented for a thread?
14. Describe the two major techniques used to define a parallel implementation of computer algorithms.
15. What is an *embarrassingly parallel* problem?
16. Describe how to implement a parallel matrix scalar product by using domain decomposition.
17. How does communication impact design and the implementation of parallel or distributed algorithms?
18. Which kind of support does Aneka provide for multithreading?
19. Describe the major differences between Aneka threads and local threads.
20. What are the limitations of the Thread Programming Model?
21. Design a parallel implementation for the tabulation of the Gaussian function by using simple threads and then convert it to Aneka threads.

High-Throughput Computing

Task Programming

7

Task computing is a wide area of distributed system programming encompassing several different models of architecting distributed applications, which, eventually, are based on the same fundamental abstraction: the *task*. A task generally represents a program, which might require input files and produce output files as a result of its execution. Applications are then constituted of a collection of tasks. These are submitted for execution and their output data are collected at the end of their execution. The way tasks are generated, the order in which they are executed, or whether they need to exchange data differentiate the application models that fall under the umbrella of task programming.

This chapter characterizes the abstraction of a task and provides a brief overview of the distributed application models that are based on the task abstraction. The Aneka Task Programming Model is taken as a reference implementation to illustrate the execution of *bag-of-tasks (BoT)* applications on a distributed infrastructure.

7.1 Task computing

Organizing an application in terms of tasks is the most intuitive and common practice for developing parallel and distributed computing applications. A task identifies one or more operations that produce a distinct output and that can be isolated as a single logical unit. In practice, a task is represented as a distinct unit of code, or a *program*, that can be separated and executed in a remote runtime environment. Programs are the most common option for representing tasks, especially in the field of scientific computing, which has leveraged distributed computing for its computational needs.

Multithreaded programming is mainly concerned with providing a support for parallelism within a single machine. Task computing provides distribution by harnessing the compute power of several computing nodes. Hence, the presence of a distributed infrastructure is explicit in this model. Historically, the infrastructures that have been leveraged to execute tasks are clusters, supercomputers, and computing grids. Now clouds have emerged as an attractive solution to obtain a huge computing power on demand for the execution of distributed applications. To achieve it, suitable middleware is needed. A reference scenario for task computing is depicted in Figure 7.1.

The *middleware* is a software layer that enables the coordinated use of multiple resources, which are drawn from a datacenter or geographically distributed networked computers. A user

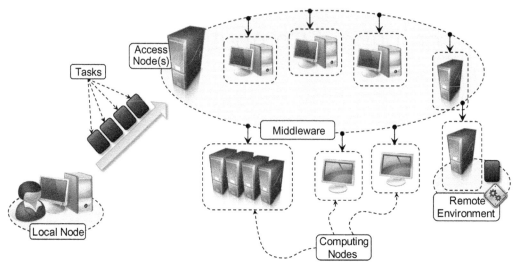

FIGURE 7.1

Task computing scenario.

submits the collection of tasks to the access point(s) of the middleware, which will take care of scheduling and monitoring the execution of tasks. Each computing resource provides an appropriate runtime environment, which may vary from implementation to implementation (a simple shell, a sandboxed environment, or a virtual machine). Task submission is normally done using the APIs provided by the middleware, whether a Web or programming language interface. Appropriate APIs are also provided to monitor task status and collect their results upon completion.

Because task abstraction is general, there exist different models of distributed applications falling under the umbrella of task computing. Despite this variety, it is possible to identify a set of common operations that the middleware needs to support the creation and execution of task-based applications. These operations are:

- Coordinating and scheduling tasks for execution on a set of remote nodes
- Moving programs to remote nodes and managing their dependencies
- Creating an environment for execution of tasks on the remote nodes
- Monitoring each task's execution and informing the user about its status
- Access to the output produced by the task

Models for task computing may differ in the way tasks are scheduled, which in turn depends on whether tasks are interrelated or they need to communicate among themselves.

7.1.1 Characterizing a task

A *task* is a general abstraction that identifies a program or a combination of programs that constitute a computing unit of a distributed application with a tangible output. A task represents a component of an application that can be logically isolated and executed separately. Distributed applications are composed of tasks, the collective execution and interrelations of which define the nature of the applications. A task can be represented by different elements:

- A shell script composing together the execution of several applications
- A single program
- A unit of code (a Java/C++/.NET class) that executes within the context of a specific runtime environment

A task is generally characterized by input files, executable code (programs, shell scripts, etc.), and output files. In many cases the common runtime environment in which tasks execute is represented by the operating system or an equivalent sandboxed environment. A task may also need specific software appliances on the remote execution nodes in addition to the library dependencies that can be transferred to the node.

Some distributed applications may have additional constraints. For example, distributed computing frameworks that present the abstraction of tasks at programming level, by means of a class to inherit or an interface to implement, might require additional constraints (i.e., compliance to the inheritance rules) but also a richer set of features that can be exploited by developers. Based on the specific model of application, tasks might have dependencies.

7.1.2 Computing categories

According to the specific nature of the problem, a variety of categories for task computing have been proposed over time. These categories do not enforce any specific application model but provide an overall view of the characteristics of the problems. They implicitly impose requirements on the infrastructure and the middleware. Applications falling into this category are *high-performance computing (HPC)*, *high-throughput computing (HTC)*, and *many-task computing (MTC)*.

7.1.2.1 High-performance computing
High-performance computing (HPC) is the use of distributed computing facilities for solving problems that need large computing power. Historically, supercomputers and clusters are specifically designed to support HPC applications that are developed to solve "Grand Challenge" problems in science and engineering. The general profile of HPC applications is constituted by a large collection of compute-intensive tasks that need to be processed in a short period of time. It is common to have parallel and tightly coupled tasks, which require low-latency interconnection networks to minimize the data exchange time. The metrics to evaluate HPC systems are *floating-point operations per second (FLOPS)*, now tera-FLOPS or even peta-FLOPS, which identify the number of floating-point operations per second that a computing system can perform.

7.1.2.2 High-throughput computing
High-throughput computing (HTC) is the use of distributed computing facilities for applications requiring large computing power over a long period of time. HTC systems need to be robust and to reliably operate over a long time scale. Traditionally, computing grids composed of heterogeneous resources (clusters, workstations, and volunteer desktop machines) have been used to support HTC. The general profile of HTC applications is that they are made up of a large number of tasks of which the execution can last for a considerable amount of time (i.e., weeks or months). Classical

examples of such applications are scientific simulations or statistical analyses. It is quite common to have independent tasks that can be scheduled in distributed resources because they do not need to communicate. HTC systems measure their performance in terms of jobs completed per month.

7.1.2.3 Many-task computing

The *many-task computing (MTC)* [61] model started receiving attention recently and covers a wide variety of applications. It aims to bridge the gap between HPC and HTC. MTC is similar to HTC, but it concentrates on the use of many computing resources over a short period of time to accomplish many computational tasks. In brief, MTC denotes high-performance computations comprising multiple distinct activities coupled via file system operations. What characterizes MTC is the heterogeneity of tasks that might be of considerably different nature: Tasks may be small or large, single-processor or multiprocessor, compute-intensive or data-intensive, static or dynamic, homogeneous or heterogeneous. The general profile of MTC applications includes loosely coupled applications that are generally communication-intensive but not naturally expressed using the message-passing interface commonly found in HPC, drawing attention to the many computations that are heterogeneous but not embarrassingly parallel. Given the large number of tasks commonly composing MTC applications, any distributed facility with a large availability of computing elements is able to support MTC. Such facilities include supercomputers, large clusters, and emerging cloud infrastructures.

7.1.3 Frameworks for task computing

There are several frameworks that can be used to support the execution of task-based applications on distributed computing resources, including clouds. Some popular software systems that support the task-computing framework are *Condor* [5], *Globus Toolkit* [12], *Sun Grid Engine (SGE)* [13], *BOINC* [14], *Nimrod/G* [164], and *Aneka*.

Architecture of all these systems is similar to the general reference architecture depicted in Figure 7.1. They consist of two main components: a scheduling node (one or more) and worker nodes. The organization of the system components may vary. For example, multiple scheduling nodes can be organized in hierarchical structures. This configuration is quite common in the middleware for computing grids, which harness a variety of distributed resources from one or more organizations or sites. Each of these sites may have their own scheduling engine, especially if the system contributes to the grid but also serves local users.

A classic example is the cluster setup where the system might feature an installation of Condor or SGE for batch job submission; these services are generally used locally to the site, but the cluster can be integrated into a larger grid where meta-schedulers such as *GRAM (Globus Resource Allocation Manager)*[1] can dispatch a collection of jobs to the cluster. Other options include the presence of gateway nodes that do not have any scheduling capabilities and simply constitute the access point to the system. These nodes have indexing services that allow users to identify the available resources in the system, its current status, and the available schedulers. For worker nodes, they generally provide a sandboxed environment where tasks are executed on behalf of a specific

---

[1]Globus Resource Allocation Manager, or GRAM, is a software component of the Globus Toolkit that is in charge of locating, submitting, monitoring, and canceling jobs in grid computing systems.

user or within a given security context, limiting the operations that can be performed by programs such as file system access. File staging is also a fundamental feature supported by these systems. Clusters are normally equipped with shared file systems and parallel I/O facilities. Grids provide users with various staging facilities, such as credential access to remote worker nodes or automated staging services that transparently move files from user local machine to remote nodes.

Condor is probably the most widely used and long-lived middleware for managing clusters, idle workstations, and a collection of clusters. Condor-G is a version of Condor that supports integration with grid computing resources, such as those managed by Globus. Condor supports common features of batch-queuing systems along with the capability to checkpoint jobs and manage overload nodes. It provides a powerful job resource-matching mechanism, which schedules jobs only on resources that have the appropriate runtime environment. Condor can handle both serial and parallel jobs on a wide variety of resources. It is used by hundreds of organizations in industry, government, and academia to manage infrastructures ranging from a handful to well over thousands of workstations.

Sun Grid Engine (SGE), now Oracle Grid Engine, is middleware for workload and distributed resource management. Initially developed to support the execution of jobs on clusters, SGE integrated additional capabilities and now is able to manage heterogeneous resources and constitutes middleware for grid computing. It supports the execution of parallel, serial, interactive, and parametric jobs and features advanced scheduling capabilities such as budget-based and group-based scheduling, scheduling applications that have deadlines, custom policies, and advance reservation.

The Globus Toolkit is a collection of technologies that enable grid computing. It provides a comprehensive set of tools for sharing computing power, databases, and other services across corporate, institutional, and geographic boundaries without sacrificing local autonomy. The toolkit features software services, libraries, and tools for resource monitoring, discovery, and management as well as security and file management. The Globus Toolkit addresses core issues of grid computing: the management of a distributed environment composed of heterogeneous resources spanning different organizations, with all this condition implies in terms of security and interoperation. To provide valid support for grid computing in such scenarios, the toolkit defines a collection of interfaces and protocol for interoperation that enable different systems to integrate with each other and expose resources outside their boundaries.

Nimrod/G [164] is a tool for automated modeling and execution of parameter sweep applications (parameter studies) over global computational grids. It provides a simple declarative parametric modeling language for expressing parametric experiments. A domain expert can easily create a plan for a parametric experiment and use the Nimrod/G system to deploy jobs on distributed resources for execution. It has been used for a very wide range of applications over the years, ranging from quantum chemistry to policy and environmental impact. Moreover, it uses novel resource management and scheduling algorithms based on economic principles. Specifically, it supports deadline- and budget-constrained scheduling of applications on distributed grid resources to minimize the execution cost and at the same deliver results in a timely manner.

Berkeley Open Infrastructure for Network Computing (BOINC) is framework for volunteer and grid computing. It allows us to turn desktop machines into volunteer computing nodes that are leveraged to run jobs when such machines become inactive. BOINC is composed of two main components: the *BOINC server* and the *BOINC client*. The former is the central node that keeps track of all the available resources and scheduling jobs; the latter is the software component that is deployed on desktop machines and that creates the BOINC execution environment for job submission. Given the volatility of BOINC clients, BOINC supports job checkpointing and duplication. Even if mostly focused on volunteer computing, BOINC systems can be easily set up to provide more stable support for job execution by creating computing grids with dedicated machines. To leverage BOINC, it is necessary to create an application project. When installing BOINC clients, users can decide the application project to which they want to donate the CPU cycles of their computer. Currently several projects, ranging from medicine to astronomy and cryptography, are running on the BOINC infrastructure.

7.2 Task-based application models

There are several models based on the concept of the task as the fundamental unit for composing distributed applications. What makes these models different from one another is the way in which tasks are generated, the relationships they have with each other, and the presence of dependencies or other conditions—for example, a specific set of services in the runtime environment—that have to be met. In this section, we quickly review the most common and popular models based on the concept of the task.

7.2.1 Embarrassingly parallel applications

Embarrassingly parallel applications constitute the most simple and intuitive category of distributed applications. As we discussed in Chapter 6, embarrassingly parallel applications constitute a collection of tasks that are independent from each other and that can be executed in any order. The tasks might be of the same type or of different types, and they do not need to communicate among themselves.

This category of applications is supported by the majority of the frameworks for distributed computing. Since tasks do not need to communicate, there is a lot of freedom regarding the way they are scheduled. Tasks can be executed in any order, and there is no specific requirement for tasks to be executed at the same time. Therefore, scheduling these applications is simplified and mostly concerned with the optimal mapping of tasks to available resources. Frameworks and tools supporting embarrassingly parallel applications are the Globus Toolkit, BOINC, and Aneka.

There are several problems that can be modeled as embarrassingly parallel. These include image and video rendering, evolutionary optimization, and model forecasting. In image and video rendering the task is represented by the rendering of a pixel (more likely a portion of the image) or a frame, respectively. For evolutionary optimization metaheuristics, a task is identified by a single run of the algorithm with a given parameter set. The same applies to model forecasting applications. In general, scientific applications constitute a considerable source of embarrassingly parallel applications, even though they mostly fall into the more specific category of parameter sweep applications.

7.2.2 Parameter sweep applications

Parameter sweep applications are a specific class of embarrassingly parallel applications for which the tasks are identical in their nature and differ only by the specific parameters used to execute them. Parameter sweep applications are identified by a template task and a set of parameters. The *template task* defines the operations that will be performed on the remote node for the execution of tasks. The template task is parametric, and the parameter set identifies the combination of variables whose assignments specialize the template task into a specific instance. The combination of parameters, together with their range of admissible values, identifies the multidimensional domain of the application, and each point in this domain identifies a task instance.

Any distributed computing framework that provides support for embarrassingly parallel applications can also support the execution of parameter sweep applications, since the tasks composing the application can be executed independently of each other. The only difference is that the tasks that will be executed are generated by iterating over all the possible and admissible combinations of parameters. This operation can be performed by frameworks natively or tools that are part of the distributed computing middleware. For example, Nimrod/G is natively designed to support the execution of parameter sweep applications, and Aneka provides client-based tools for visually composing a template task, defining parameters, and iterating over all the possible combinations of such parameters.

A plethora of applications fall into this category. Mostly they come from the scientific computing domain: evolutionary optimization algorithms, weather-forecasting models, computational fluid dynamics applications, Monte Carlo methods, and many others. For example, in the case of evolutionary algorithms it is possible to identify the domain of the applications as a combination of the relevant parameters of the algorithm. For genetic algorithms these might be the number of individuals of the population used by the optimizer and the number of generations for which to run the optimizer. The following example in pseudo-code demonstrates how to use parameter sweeping for the execution of a generic evolutionary algorithm which can be configured with different population sizes and generations.

```
individuals = {100, 200, 300, 500, 1000}
generations = {50, 100, 200, 400}
foreach indiv in individuals do
foreach generation in generations do

  task = generate_task(indiv, generation)
  submit_task(task)
```

The algorithm sketched in the example defines a bidimensional domain composed of discrete variables and then iterated over each combination of individuals and generations to generate all the tasks composing the application. In this case 20 tasks are generated. The function *generate_task* is specific to the application and creates the task instance by substituting the values of *indiv* and *generation* to the corresponding variables in the template definition. The function *submit_task* is specific to the middleware used and performs the actual task submission.

A template task is in general a composition of operations concerning the execution of legacy applications with the appropriate parameters and set of file system operations for moving data. Therefore, frameworks that natively support the execution of parameter sweep applications often provide a set of useful commands for manipulating or operating on files. Also, the template task is often expressed as single file that composes together the commands provided. The commonly available commands are:

- *Execute*. Executes a program on the remote node.
- *Copy*. Copies a file to/from the remote node.
- *Substitute*. Substitutes the parameter values with their placeholders inside a file.
- *Delete*. Deletes a file.

All these commands can operate with parameters that are substituted with their actual values for each task instance.

Figures 7.2 and 7.3 provide examples of two possible task templates, the former as defined according to the notation used by Nimrod/G, and the latter as required by Aneka.

The template file has two sections: a header for the definition of the parameters, and a task definition section that includes shell commands mixed with Nimrod/G commands. The prefix *node:* identifies the remote location where the task is executed. Parameters are identified with the $*{...}* notation. The example shown remotely executes the *echo* command and copies to the local user directory the output of the command by saving it into a file named according to the values of the parameters *x* and *y*.

The Aneka Parameter Sweep file defines the template task for executing the BLAST application. The file is an XML document containing several sections, the most important of which are *sharedFiles*, *parameters*, and *task*. *parameters* contains the definition of the parameters that will customize the template task. Two different types of parameters are defined: a single value and a range parameter. The *sharedFiles* section contains the files that are required to execute the task; *task* specifies the operations that characterize the template task. The task has a collection of input and output files for which local and remote paths are defined, as well as a collection of commands. In the case presented, a simple *execute* command is shown. With respect to the previous example there is no need to explicitly move the files to the remote destination, but this operation is automatically performed by Aneka.

7.2.3 MPI applications

Message Passing Interface (MPI) is a specification for developing parallel programs that communicate by exchanging messages. Compared to earlier models, MPI introduces the constraint of communication that involves MPI tasks that need to run at the same time. MPI has originated as an attempt to create common ground from the several distributed shared memory and message-passing

```
parameter x float range from 1 to 10 step 1;
parameter y float range from -4 to 5 step 1;

task main
  node:execute /bin/echo X:${x} Y:${y} > output
  copy node:output output.`expr ${y}\*10+${x}`
endtask
```

FIGURE 7.2

Nimrod/G task template definition.

```
<psm>
  <name>Aneka Blast</name>
  <description>BLAST simulation</description>
  <workspace>C:\Projects\Explorer\blast</workspace>
  <parameters>
    <single name="p" type="String" comment="The name of the program" value="blastn"/>
    <single name="d" type="String" comment="The database file" value="ecoli.nt"/>
    <range name="s" type="String" comment="The sequence file" from="0" to="2" interval="1"/>
  </parameters>
  <sharedFiles>
    <file path="blastall.exe" vpath="blastall.exe"/>
    <file path="ecoli.nt.nhr" vpath="ecoli.nt.nhr"/>
    <file path="ecoli.nt.nin" vpath="ecoli.nt.nin"/>
    <file path="ecoli.nt.nnd" vpath="ecoli.nt.nnd"/>
    <file path="ecoli.nt.nni" vpath="ecoli.nt.nni"/>
    <file path="ecoli.nt.nsd" vpath="ecoli.nt.nsd"/>
    <file path="ecoli.nt.nsi" vpath="ecoli.nt.nsi"/>
    <file path="ecoli.nt.nsq" vpath="ecoli.nt.nsq"/>
  </sharedFiles>
  <task>
    <inputs>
      <file path="seq($s).txt" vpath="seq($s).txt"/>
    </inputs>
    <outputs>
      <file path="output($s).txt" vpath="output($s).txt"/>
    </outputs>
    <commands>
      <execute cmd="blastall.exe" args="-p ($p) -d ($d) -i seq($s).txt -o output($s).txt"/>
    </commands>
  </task>
</psm>
```

FIGURE 7.3

Aneka parameter sweep file.

infrastructures available for distributed computing. Nowadays, MPI has become a *de facto* standard for developing portable and efficient message-passing HPC applications. Interface specifications have been defined and implemented for C/C++ and Fortran.

MPI provides developers with a set of routines that:

- Manage the distributed environment where MPI programs are executed

- Provide facilities for point-to-point communication
- Provide facilities for group communication
- Provide support for data structure definition and memory allocation
- Provide basic support for synchronization with blocking calls

The general reference architecture is depicted in Figure 7.4. A distributed application in MPI is composed of a collection of MPI processes that are executed in parallel in a distributed infrastructure that supports MPI (most likely a cluster or nodes leased from clouds).

MPI applications that share the same MPI runtime are by default as part of a global group called *MPI_COMM_WORLD*. Within this group, all the distributed processes have a unique identifier that allows the MPI runtime to localize and address them. It is possible to create specific groups as subsets of this global group—for example, for isolating all the MPI processes that belong to the same application. Each MPI process is assigned a rank within the group to which it belongs. The rank is a unique identifier that allows processes to communicate with each other within a group. Communication is made possible by means of a communicator component that can be defined for each group.

To create an MPI application it is necessary to define the code for the MPI process that will be executed in parallel. This program has, in general, the structure described in Figure 7.5. The section of code that is executed in parallel is clearly identified by two operations that set up the MPI environment and shut it down, respectively. In the code section defined within these two operations, it is possible to use all the MPI functions to send or receive messages in either asynchronous or synchronous mode.

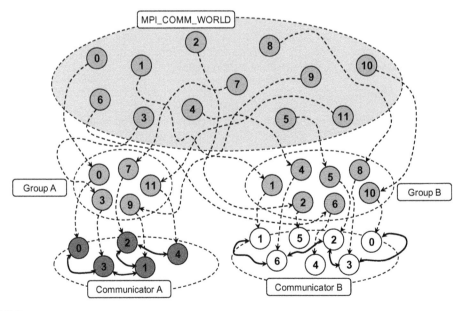

FIGURE 7.4

MPI reference scenario.

The diagram in Figure 7.5 might suggest that the MPI might allow the definition of completely symmetrical applications, since the portion of code executed in each node is the same. In reality, it is possible to implement distributed applications based on complex communication patterns by differentiating the operations performed by each node according to the rank of the program, which is known at runtime. A common model used in MPI is the *master-worker model*, whereby one MPI process (usually the one with rank 0) coordinates the execution of others that perform the same task.

Once the program has been defined in one of the available MPI implementations, it is compiled with a modified version of the compiler for the language. This compiler introduces additional code in order to properly manage the MPI runtime. The output of the compilation process can be run as a distributed application by using a specific tool provided with the MPI implementation.

A general installation that supports the execution of the MPI application is composed of a cluster. In this scenario MPI is normally installed in the shared file system and an MPI daemon is started on each node of the cluster in order to coordinate the parallel execution of MPI applications. Once the environment is set up, it is possible to run parallel applications by using the tools provided with the MPI implementation and to specify several options, such as the number of nodes to use to run the application.

At present there are several MPI implementations that can be leveraged to develop distributed applications, and the MPI specifications have currently reached version 2. One of the most popular MPI software environments (www.mcs.anl.gov/mpi/) is developed by the Argonne National Laboratory in the United States. MPI has gained a good deal of success as a parallel and distributed

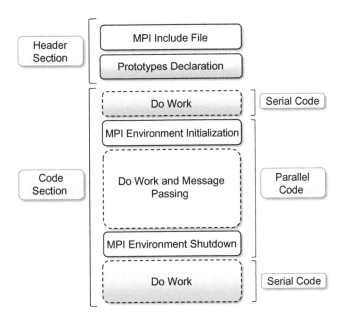

FIGURE 7.5

MPI program structure.

programming model for CPU-intensive mathematical computations such as linear systems solvers, matrix computations, finite element computations, linear algebra, and numerical simulations.

7.2.4 Workflow applications with task dependencies

Workflow applications are characterized by a collection of tasks that exhibit dependencies among them. Such dependencies, which are mostly data dependencies (i.e., the output of one task is a prerequisite of another task), determine the way in which the applications are scheduled as well as where they are scheduled. Concerns in this case are related to providing a feasible sequencing of tasks and to optimizing the placement of tasks so that the movement of data is minimized.

7.2.4.1 What is a workflow?

The term *workflow* has a long tradition in the business community, where the term is used to describe a composition of services that all together accomplish a business process. As defined by the Workflow Management Coalition, a workflow is *the automation of a business process, in whole or part, during which documents, information, or tasks are passed from one participant (a resource; human or machine) to another for action, according to a set of procedural rules* [64]. The concept of workflow as a structured execution of tasks that have dependencies on each other has demonstrated itself to be useful for expressing many scientific experiments and gave birth to the idea of *scientific workflow*. Many scientific experiments are a combination of problem-solving components, which, connected in a particular order, define the specific nature of the experiment. When such experiments exhibit a natural parallelism and need to execute a large number of operations or deal with huge quantities of data, it makes sense to execute them on a distributed infrastructure. In the case of scientific workflows, the process is identified by an application to run, the elements that are passed among participants are mostly tasks and data, and the participants are mostly computing or storage nodes. The set of procedural rules is defined by a workflow definition scheme that guides the scheduling of the application. A scientific workflow generally involves data management, analysis, simulation, and middleware supporting the execution of the workflow.

A scientific workflow is generally expressed by a *directed acyclic graph (DAG)*, which defines the dependencies among tasks or operations. The nodes on the DAG represent the tasks to be executed in a workflow application; the arcs connecting the nodes identify the dependencies among tasks and the data paths that connect the tasks. The most common dependency that is realized through a DAG is *data dependency*, which means that the output files of a task (or some of them) constitute the input files of another task. This dependency is represented as an arc originating from the node that identifies the first task and terminating in the node that identifies the second task.

The DAG in Figure 7.6 describes a sample Montage workflow.[2] *Montage* is a toolkit for assembling images into mosaics; it has been specially designed to support astronomers in composing the images taken from different telescopes or points of view into a coherent image. The toolkit provides several applications for manipulating images and composing them together; some of the applications perform background reprojection, perspective transformation, and brightness and color

---

[2]Montage workflow: http://vgrads.rice.edu/research/applications/images/montage-workflow/view.

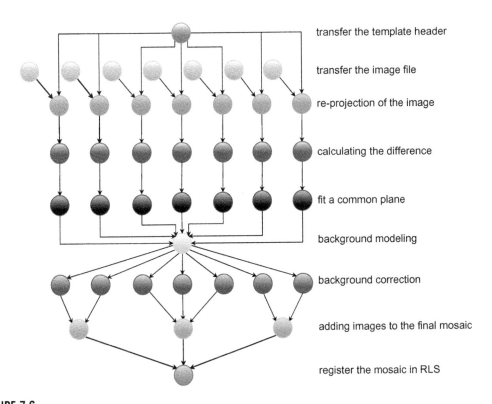

transfer the template header

transfer the image file

re-projection of the image

calculating the difference

fit a common plane

background modeling

background correction

adding images to the final mosaic

register the mosaic in RLS

FIGURE 7.6

Sample Montage workflow.

correction. The workflow depicted in Figure 7.6 describes the general process for composing a mosaic; the labels on the right describe the different tasks that have to be performed to compose a mosaic. In the case presented in the diagram, a mosaic is composed of seven images. The entire process can take advantage of a distributed infrastructure for its execution, since there are several operations that can be performed in parallel. For each of the image files, the following process has to be performed: image file transfer, reprojection, calculation of the difference, and common plane placement. Therefore, each of the images can be processed in parallel for these tasks. Here is where a distributed infrastructure helps in executing workflows.

There might be another reason for executing workflows on a distributed infrastructure: It might be convenient to move the computation on a specific node because of data locality issues. For example, if an operation needs to access specific resources that are only available on a specific node, that operation cannot be performed elsewhere, whereas the rest of the operations might not have the same requirements. A scientific experiment might involve the use of several problem-solving components that might require the use of specific instrumentation; in this case all the tasks that have these constraints need to be executed where the instrumentation is available, thus creating a distributed execution of a process that is not parallel in principle.

7.2.4.2 Workflow technologies

Business-oriented computing workflows are defined as compositions of services, and there are specific languages and standards for the definition of workflows, such as *Business Process Execution Language (BPEL)* [65]. In the case of scientific computing there is no common ground for defining workflows, but several solutions and workflow languages coexist [66]. Despite such differences, it is possible to identify an abstract reference model for a workflow management system [67], as depicted in Figure 7.7. Design tools allow users to visually compose a workflow application. This specification is normally stored in the form of an XML document based on a specific workflow language and constitutes the input of the workflow engine, which controls the execution of the workflow by leveraging a distributed infrastructure. In most cases, the workflow engine is a client-side component that might interact directly with resources or with one or several middleware components for executing the workflow. Some frameworks can natively support the execution of workflow applications by providing a scheduler capable of directly processing the workflow specification.

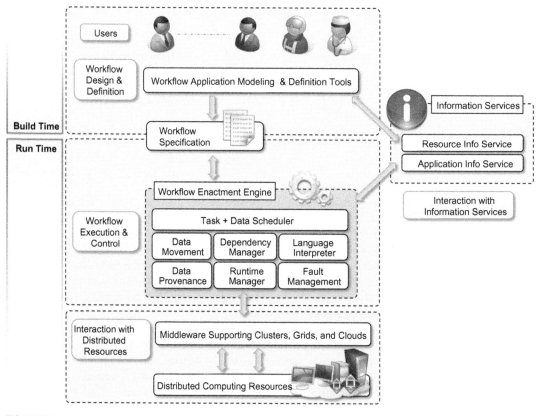

FIGURE 7.7

Abstract model of a workflow system.

Some of the most relevant technologies for designing and executing workflow-based applications are *Kepler, DAGMan, Cloudbus Workflow Management System,* and *Offspring.*

Kepler [68] is an open-source scientific workflow engine built from the collaboration of several research projects. The system is based on the *Ptolemy II* system [72], which provides a solid platform for developing dataflow-oriented workflows. Kepler provides a design environment based on the concept of actors, which are reusable and independent blocks of computation such as Web services, database calls, and the like. The connection between actors is made with ports. An actor consumes data from the input ports and writes data/results to the output ports. The novelty of Kepler is in its ability to separate the flow of data among components from the coordination logic that is used to execute workflow. Thus, for the same workflow, Kepler supports different models, such as synchronous and asynchronous models. The workflow specification is expressed using a proprietary XML language.

DAGMan (Directed Acyclic Graph Manager) [69], part of the Condor [5] project, constitutes an extension to the Condor scheduler to handle job interdependencies. Condor finds machines for the execution of programs but does not support the scheduling of jobs in a specific sequence. Therefore, DAGMan acts as a metascheduler for Condor by submitting the jobs to the scheduler in the appropriate order. The input of DAGMan is a simple text file that contains the information about the jobs, pointers to their job submission files, and the dependencies among jobs.

Cloudbus Workflow Management System (WfMS) [70] is a middleware platform built for managing large application workflows on distributed computing platforms such as grids and clouds. It comprises software tools that help end users compose, schedule, execute, and monitor workflow applications through a Web-based portal. The portal provides the capability of uploading workflows or defining new ones with a graphical editor. To execute workflows, WfMS relies on the Gridbus Broker, a grid/cloud resource broker that supports the execution of applications with quality-of-service (QoS) attributes over a heterogeneous distributed computing infrastructure, including Linux-based clusters, Globus, and Amazon EC2. WfMS uses a proprietary XML language for the specification of workflows.

A different perspective is taken by *Offspring* [71], which offers a programming-based approach to developing workflows. Users can develop strategies and plug them into the environment, which will execute them by leveraging a specific distribution engine. The advantage provided by Offspring over other solutions is the ability to define dynamic workflows. This strategy represents a semistructured workflow that can change its behavior at runtime according to the execution of specific tasks. This allows developers to dynamically control the dependencies of tasks at runtime rather than statically defining them. Offspring supports integration with any distributed computing middleware that can manage a simple bag-of-tasks application. It provides a native integration with Aneka and supports a simulated distribution engine for testing strategies during development. Because Offspring allows the definition of workflows in the form of plug-ins, it does not use any XML specification.

7.3 Aneka task-based programming

Aneka provides support for all the flavors of task-based programming by means of the *Task Programming Model*, which constitutes the basic support given by the framework for supporting the execution of bag-of-tasks applications. Task programming is realized through the abstraction of the *Aneka.Tasks.ITask*. By using this abstraction as a basis support for execution of legacy applications, parameter sweep applications and workflows have been integrated into the framework. In this section, we introduce the fundamental concepts of the model and provide examples of how to develop applications for all the previously discussed application models.

7.3.1 Task programming model

The *Task Programming Model* provides a very intuitive abstraction for quickly developing distributed applications on top of Aneka. It provides a minimum set of APIs that are mostly centered on the *Aneka.Tasks.ITask* interface. This interface, together with the services supporting the execution of tasks in the middleware, constitutes the core feature of the model. Figure 7.8 provides an overall view of the components of the Task Programming Model and their roles during application execution.

Developers create distributed applications in terms of *ITask* instances, the collective execution of which describes a running application. These tasks, together with all the required dependencies (data files and libraries), are grouped and managed through the *AnekaApplication* class, which is specialized to support the execution of tasks. Two other components, *AnekaTask* and *TaskManager*, constitute the client-side view of a task-based application. The former constitutes the runtime wrapper Aneka uses to represent a task within the middleware; the latter is the underlying component that interacts with Aneka, submits the tasks, monitors their execution, and collects the results. In the middleware, four services coordinate their activities in order to execute task-based applications. These are *MembershipCatalogue*, *TaskScheduler*, *ExecutionService*, and *StorageService*.

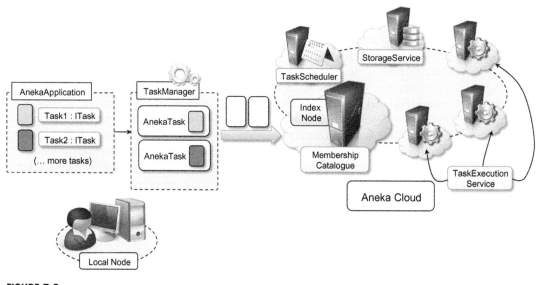

FIGURE 7.8

Task programming model scenario.

MembershipCatalogue constitutes the main access point of the cloud and acts as a service directory to locate the *TaskScheduler* service that is in charge of managing the execution of task-based applications. Its main responsibility is to allocate task instances to resources featuring the *ExecutionService* for task execution and for monitoring task state. If the application requires the data transfer support in the form of data files, input files, or output files, an available *StorageService* will be used as a staging facility for the application.

The features provided by the task model are completed by a Web service that allows any client to submit the execution of tasks to Aneka. The procedure for submitting tasks through the Web services is the same as that done by using the framework APIs. The user creates an application on Aneka and submits tasks within the context of this application. The Web service limits the type of tasks that can be submitted. Only a limited collection of tasks is available for submission; despite that, these tasks cover the functionality commonly found in other distributed computing systems.

7.3.2 Developing applications with the task model

Execution of task-based applications involves several components. The development of such applications is limited to the following operations:

- Defining classes implementing the *ITask* interface
- Creating a properly configured *AnekaApplication* instance
- Creating *ITask* instances and wrapping them into *AnekaTask* instances
- Executing the application and waiting for its completion

Moreover, from a design point of view, the process of defining a task application ultimately reduces to the definition of the classes that implement *ITask*, which will be those that contribute to form the workload generated by the application.

7.3.2.1 ITask and AnekaTask

Almost all the client-side features for developing task-based applications with Aneka are contained in the *Aneka.Tasks* namespace (*Aneka.Tasks.dll*). The most important component for designing tasks is the *ITask* interface, which is defined in Listing 7.1. This interface exposes only one method: *Execute*. The method is invoked in order to execute the task on the remote node.

The *ITask* interface provides a programming approach for developing native tasks, which means tasks implemented in any of the supported programming languages of the .NET framework. The restrictions on implementing task classes are minimal; other than implementing the *ITask* interface, they need to be serializable, since task instances are created and moved over the network. Listing 7.2 describes a simple implementation of a task class that computes the Gaussian distribution for a given point *x*.

ITask provides minimum restrictions on how to implement a task class and decouples the specific operation of the task from the runtime wrapper classes. It is required for managing tasks within Aneka. This role is performed by the *AnekaTask* class that represents the task instance in accordance with the Aneka application model APIs. This class extends the *Aneka.Entity.WorkUnit* class and provides the feature for embedding *ITask* instances. *AnekaTask* is mostly used internally, and for end users it provides facilities for specifying input and output files for the task.

```
namespace Aneka.Tasks
{
    ///<summary>
    ///Interface ITask. Defines the interface for implementing a task.
    ///</summary>
    public interface ITask
    {
        ///<summary>
        ///Executes the sine function.
        ///</summary>
        public void Execute();
    }
}
```

LISTING 7.1

ITask interface.

Listing 7.3 describes how to wrap an *ITask* instance into an *AnekaTask*. It also shows how to add input and output files specific to a given task. The Task Programming Model leverages the basic capabilities for file management that belong to the *WorkUnit* class, from which the *AnekaTask* class inherits. As discussed when we presented the Aneka Application Model (see Chapter 5). *WorkUnit* has two collections of files, *InputFiles* and *OutputFiles*; developers can add files to these collections and the runtime environment will automatically move these files where it is necessary. Input files will be staged into the Aneka Cloud and moved to the remote node where the task is executed. Output files will be collected from the execution node and moved to the local machine or a remote FTP server.

7.3.2.2 Controlling task execution

Task classes and *AnekaTask* define the computation logic of a task-based application, whereas the *AnekaApplication* class provides the basic feature for implementing the coordination logic of the application.

AnekaApplication is a generic class that can be specialized to support different programming models. In task programming, it assumes the form of *AnekaApplication < AnekaTask, TaskManager >*. The operations provided for the task model as well as for other programming models are:

- Static and dynamic task submission
- Application state and task state monitoring
- Event-based notification of task completion or failure

By composing these features all together, it is possible to define the logic that is required to implement a specific task application. Static submission is a very common pattern in the case of task-based applications, and it involves the creation of all the tasks that need to be executed in one loop and their submission as a single bag. More complex task submission strategies are then required for implementing workflow-based applications, where the execution of tasks is determined by dependencies among them. In this case a dynamic submission of tasks is a more efficient

```
// File: GaussTask.cs
using System;
using Aneka.Tasks;

namespace GaussSample
{
    /// <summary>
    /// Class GaussTask. Implements the ITask interface for computing the Gauss function.
    /// </summary>
    [Serializable]
    public class GaussTask : ITask
    {
        /// <summary>
        /// Input value.
        /// </summary>
        private double x;
        /// <summary>
        /// Gets the input value of the Gauss function.
        /// </summary>
        public double X { get { return this.x; } set { this.x = value; } }
        /// <summary>
        /// Result value.
        /// </summary>
        private double y;
        /// <summary>
        /// Gets the result value of the Gauss function.
        /// </summary>
        public double Y { get { return this.y; } set { this.y = value; } }

        /// <summary>
        /// Executes the Gauss function.
        /// </summary>
        public void Execute()
        {
            this.y = Math.Exp(-this.x*this.x);
        }
    }
}
```

LISTING 7.2

ITask interface implementation.

technique and involves the submission of tasks as a result of the event-based notification mechanism implemented in the *AnekaApplication* class.

Listing 7.4 shows how to create and submit 400 Gauss tasks as a bag by using the static submission approach. The *AnekaApplication* class has a collection of tasks containing all the tasks that have been submitted for execution. Each task can be referenced using its unique identifier (*WorkUnit.Id*) by the indexer operator [] applied to the application class. In the case of static submission, the tasks are added to the application, and the method *SubmitExecution()* is called.

```
// create a Gauss task and wraps it into an AnekaTaskinstance
GaussTaskgauss = new GaussTask();
AnekaTask task = newAnekaTask(gauss);
// add one input and one output files
task.AddFile("input.txt", FileDataType.Input, FileAttributes.Local);
task.AddFile("result.txt", FileDataType.Output, FileAttributes.Local);
```

LISTING 7.3

Wrapping an *ITask* into an *AnekaTask* Instance.

```
// get an instance of the Configuration class from file
Configuration conf = Configuration.GetConfiguration("conf.xml");
// specify that the submission of task is static (all at once)
conf.SingleSubmission = true;
AnekaApplication<AnekaTask, TaskManager> app =
new AnekaApplication<Task,TaskManager>(conf);
for(int i=0; i<400; i++)
{
    GaussTaskgauss = new GaussTask();
    gauss.X = i;
    AnekaTask task = new AnekaTask(gauss);
    // add the task to the bag of work units to submit
    app.AddWorkunit(task);
}
// submit the entire bag
app.SubmitExecution();
```

LISTING 7.4

Static task submission.

A different scenario is constituted by dynamic submission, where tasks are submitted as a result of other events that occur during the execution—for example, the completion or the failure of previously submitted tasks or other conditions that are not related to the interaction of Aneka. In this case, developers have more freedom in selecting the most appropriate task submission strategy. For example, it is possible that an initial bag of tasks is submitted as described in Listing 7.4, and subsequently, as a result of the completion of some tasks, other tasks are generated and submitted. To implement this scenario it is necessary to rely on the event-based notification system provided by the *AnekaApplication* class and trigger the submission of tasks according to the firing of specific events. In particular, we are interested in the *WorkUnitFailed* and *WorkUnitCompleted* events.

Listing 7.5 extends the previous example and implements a dynamic task submission strategy for refining the computation of Gaussian distribution. Both static and dynamic task submissions are used: An initial bag of 400 Gauss tasks is submitted to Aneka, and as soon as these tasks are completed, a new task for the computation of an intermediate value of the distribution is submitted. To capture the failure and the completion of tasks, it is necessary to listen to the events

```
///<summary>
///Main method for submitting tasks.
///</summary>
public void SubmitApplication()
{
    // get an instance of the Configuration class from file
    Configuration conf = Configuration.GetConfiguration("conf.xml");
    // specify that the submission of task is dynamic
    conf.SingleSubmission = false;
    AnekaApplication<AnekaTask, TaskManager> app =
                    new AnekaApplication<Task,TaskManager>(conf);
    // attach methods to the event handler that notify the client code
    // when tasks are completed or failed
    app.WorkUnitFailed +=
                    new EventHandler<WorkUnitEventArgs<AnekaTask>>(this.OnWorkUnitFailed);
    app.WorkUnitFinished +=
                    new EventHandler<WorkUnitEventArgs<AnekaTask>>(this.OnWorkUnitFinished);
    for(int i=0; i<400; i++)
    {
        GaussTask gauss = new GaussTask();
        gauss.X = i;
        AnekaTask task = newAnekaTask(gauss);
        // add the task to the bag of work units to submit
        app.AddWorkunit(task);
    }
    // submit the entire bag
    app.SubmitExecution();
}
/// <summary>
/// Event handler for task failure.
/// </summary>
/// <param name="sender">Event source: the application instance.</param>
/// <param name="args">Event arguments.</param>
private void OnWorkUnitFailed(object sender, WorkUnitEventArgs<AnekaTask>args)
{
    // do nothing, we are not interested in task failure at the moment
    // just dump to console the failure.
    if (args.WorkUnit != null)
    {
        Exception error = args.WorkUnit.Exception;
        Console.WriteLine("Task {0} failed - Exception: {1}",
        args.WorkUnit.Name, (error == null ? "[Not given]" : error.Message);
    }
}
```

LISTING 7.5

Dynamic task submission.

WorkUnitFailed and *WorkUnitFinished.* The event signature requires the methods to have an object parameter (as for all the event handlers), which will contain the application instance, and a *WorkUnitEventArgs* < *AnekaTask* > argument containing the information about the *WorkUnit* that triggered the event. This class exposes a *WorkUnit* property that, if not null, gives access to the

```
/// <summary>
/// Event handler for task completion.
/// </summary>
/// <param name="sender">Event source: the application instance.</param>
/// <param name="args">Event arguments.</param>
private void OnWorkUnitFinished(object sender, WorkUnitEventArgs<AnekaTask> args)
{
    // if the task is completed for sure we have a WorkUnit instance
    // and we do not need to check as we did before.
    GaussTask gauss = (GaussTask) args.WorkUnit.Task;
    // we check whether it is an initially submitted task or a task
    // that we submitted as a reaction to the completion of another task
    if (task.X - Math.Abs(task.X) == 0)
    {
        // ok it was an original task, then we increment of 0.5 the
        // value of X and submit another task

        GaussTask fraq = GaussTask();
        fraq.X = gauss.X + 0.5;
        AnekaTask task =new AnekaTask(fraq);

        // we call the ExecuteWorkUnit method that is used
        // for dynamic submission
        app.ExecuteWorkUnit(task);
    }
    Console.WriteLine("Task {0} completed - [X:{1},Y:{2}]",
    args.WorkUnit.Name, gauss.X, gauss.Y);
}
```

LISTING 7.5

Dynamic task submission.

task instance. The event handler for the task failure simply dumps the information that the task is failed to the console, with, if possible, additional information about the error that occurred. The event handler for task completion checks whether the task completed was submitted within the original bag, and in this case submits another task by using the *ExecuteWorkUnit(AnekaTask task)* method. To discriminate tasks submitted within the initial bag and other tasks, the value of *GaussTask.X* is used. If *X* contains a value with no fractional digits, it is an initial task; otherwise, it is not.

Static and dynamic submission influence the way the application termination condition is determined. In static submission the determination of this condition is automatic: Once all the initially submitted tasks are failed or completed, the application is terminated. It is important in this case to activate, in the configuration of the application, the *SingleSubmission* flag by setting it to *true*. This will tell the runtime to automatically determine the completion of the application. In dynamic submission, it is impossible for the runtime to determine the termination of the application, since it is always to possible to submit new tasks. In this case it is the responsibility of the developer to signal to the application class the termination of the application by invoking the *StopExecution* method when appropriate.

In designing the coordination logic of the application, it is important to note that the task submission identifies an asynchronous execution pattern, which means that the method *SubmitExecution*, as well as the method *ExecuteWorkUnit*, returns when the submission of tasks is completed, but not the actual completion of tasks. This requires the developer to put in place the proper synchronization logic to let the main thread of the application wait until all the tasks are terminated and the application is completed. This behavior can be implemented using the synchronization APIs provided by the *System.Threading* namespace: *System.Threading.AutoResetEvent* or *System.Threading.ManualResetEvent*. These two APIs, together with a minimal logic, count all the tasks to be collected and signal the main thread (put in waiting state by calling the method *WaitHandle.Wait()*) once all tasks are terminated. It can also provide the required infrastructure for properly managing the execution flow of the application. Listing 7.6 provides a complete implementation of the task submission program, implementing dynamic submission and the appropriate synchronization logic.

The listing provides a complete definition of the *GaussApp* class, which also contains the main entry point of the application. A very simple logic for controlling the execution of the application has been implemented. The *GaussApp* application keeps track of the number of currently running tasks by using the *taskCount* field. When this value reaches zero, there are no more tasks to wait for and the application is stopped by calling *StopExecution*. This method fires the *ApplicationFinished* event whose event handler (*OnApplicationFinished*) unblocks the main thread by signalling the semaphore. The value of *taskCount* is initially set to 400, which is the size of the initial bag of tasks. Every time a task fails or completes, this field is decremented by one unit; if there is a new task submission, the field is incremented by one unit. At the end of the two event handlers (*OnWorkUnitFailed* and *OnWorkUnitFinished*), the value of *taskCount* is checked to see whether it is equal to zero and it is necessary to stop the application. We can observe that, besides the use of the *ManualResetEvent*, there is no need for other synchronization structures. Because the code that manipulates the value of *taskCount* is executed in one single thread, there will not be any races while incrementing or decrementing the value.

A final aspect that can be considered for controlling the execution of the task application is the resubmission strategy that is used. By default the configuration of the application sets the resubmission strategy as manual; this means that if a task fails because of an exception that occurred during its execution, the task instance is sent back to the client application, and it is the developer's responsibility to resubmit the task if necessary. In automatic resubmission, Aneka will keep resubmitting the task until a maximum number of attempts is reached. If the task keeps failing, the task failure event will eventually be fired. This property can be controlled by setting the configuration value *Configuration.ResubmitMode* to *ResubmitMode.Manual* or *ResubmitMode.Auto*. As previously stated, this property is set to *ResubmitMode.Manual* by default.

7.3.2.3 File management

Task-based applications normally deal with files to perform their operations. As we've discussed, files may constitute input data for tasks, may contain the result of a computation, or may represent executable code or library dependencies. Therefore, providing support for file transfers for task-based applications is essential. Aneka provides built-in capabilities for file management in a distributed infrastructure, and the Task Programming Model transparently leverages these capabilities. Any model based on the *WorkUnit* and *ApplicationBase* classes has built-in support for file

```csharp
// File: GaussApp.cs
using System;
using System.Threading;

using Aneka.Entity;
using Aneka.Tasks;

namespace GaussSample
{
    /// <summary>
    /// Class GaussApp. Defines the coordination logic of the
    /// distributed application for computing the gaussian distribution.
    /// </summary>
    public class GaussApp
    {
        /// <summary>
        /// Semaphore used to make the main thread wait while
        /// all the tasks are terminated.
        /// </summary>
        private ManualResetEvent semaphore;
        /// <summary>
        /// Counter of the running tasks.
        /// </summary>
        private int taskCount = 0;
        /// <summary>
        /// Aneka application instance.
        /// </summary>
        private AnekaApplication<AnekaTask, TaskManager> app;

        /// <summary>
        /// Main entry point for the application.
        /// </summary>
        /// <param name="args">An array of strings containing the command line.</param>
        public static void Main(string[] args)
        {
            try
            {
                // initialize the logging system
                Logger.Start();

                string confFile = "conf.xml";
                if (args.Length > 0)
                {
                    confFile = args[0];
                }
                // get an instance of the Configuration class from file
                Configuration conf = Configuration.GetConfiguration(confFile);
                // create an instance of the GaussApp and starts its execution
                // with the given configuration instance
                GaussApp application = new GaussApp();
                application.SubmitApplication(conf);
            }
```

LISTING 7.6

GaussApplication.

```
catch(Exception ex)
{
   IOUtil.DumpErrorReport(ex, "Fatal error while executing application.");
}
finally
{
   // terminate the logging thread
   Logger.Stop();

   }
}


/// <summary>
/// Application submission method.
/// </summary>
/// <param name="conf">Application configuration.</param>
public void SubmitApplication(Configuration conf)
{
   // initialize the semaphore and the number of
   // task initially submitted
   this.semaphore = new ManualResetEvent(false);
   this.taskCount = 400;

   // specify that the submission of task is dynamic
   conf.SingleSubmission = false;
   this.app = new AnekaApplication<Task,TaskManager>(conf);
   // attach methods to the event handler that notify the client code
   // when tasks are completed or failed
   this.app.WorkUnitFailed +=
         new EventHandler<WorkUnitEventArgs<AnekaTask>>(this.OnWorkUnitFailed);
   this.app.WorkUnitFinished +=
         new EventHandler<WorkUnitEventArgs<AnekaTask>>(this.OnWorkUnitFinished);

   // attach the method OnAppFinished to the Finished event so we can capture
   // the application termination condition, this event will be fired in case of
   // both static application submission or dynamic application submission
   app.Finished += new EventHandler<ApplicationEventArgs>(this.OnAppFinished);

   for(int i=0; i<400; i++)
   {
      GaussTask gauss = new GaussTask();
      gauss.X = i;
      AnekaTask task = newAnekaTask(gauss);
      // add the task to the bag of work units to submit
      app.AddWorkunit(task);
   }
   // submit the entire bag
   app.SubmitExecution();

   // wait until signaled, once the thread is signaled the application is completed
   this.semaphore.Wait();
}
```

LISTING 7.6

(Continued)

```
/// <summary>
/// Event handler for task failure.
/// </summary>
/// <param name="sender">Event source: the application instance.</param>
/// <param name="args">Event arguments.</param>
private void OnWorkUnitFailed(object sender, WorkUnitEventArgs<AnekaTask> args)
{
   // do nothing, we are not interested in task failure at the moment
   // just dump to console the failure.
   if (args.WorkUnit != null)
   {
      Exception error = args.WorkUnit.Exception;
      Console.WriteLine("Task {0} failed - Exception: {1}",
      args.WorkUnit.Name,
      (error == null ? "[Not given]" : error.Message);
   }
   // we do not have to synchronize this operation because
   // events handlers are run all in the same thread, and there
   // will not be other threads updating this variable

   this.taskCount--;
   if (this.taskCount == 0)
   {
      this.app.StopExecution();
   }
}
/// <summary>
/// Event handler for task completion.
/// </summary>
/// <param name="sender">Event source: the application instance.</param>
/// <param name="args">Event arguments.</param>
private void OnWorkUnitFinished(object sender, WorkUnitEventArgs<AnekaTask> args)
{
   // we do not have to synchronize this operation because
   // events handlers are run all in the same thread, and there
   // will not be other threads updating this variable
   this.taskCount--;

   // if the task is completed for sure we have a WorkUnit instance
   // and we do not need to check as we did before.
   GaussTask gauss = (GaussTask) args.WorkUnit.Task;
   // we check whether it is an initially submitted task or a task
   // that we submitted as a reaction to the completion of another task
   if (task.X - Math.Abs(task.X) == 0)
   {
      // ok it was an original task, then we increment of 0.5 the
      // value of X and submit another task
      GaussTask fraq = GaussTask();
      fraq.X = gauss.X + 0.5;
      AnekaTask task =new AnekaTask(fraq);
```

LISTING 7.6

(Continued)

```
            this.taskCount++;
            // we call the ExecuteWorkUnit method that is used
            // for dynamic submission
            app.ExecuteWorkUnit(task);
        }
        Console.WriteLine("Task {0} completed - [X:{1},Y:{2}]",
                        args.WorkUnit.Name, gauss.X, gauss.Y);
        if (this.taskCount == 0)
        {
            this.app.StopExecution();
        }
    }
    /// <summary>
    /// Event handler for the application termination.
    /// </summary>
    /// <param name="sender">Event source: the application instance.</param>
    /// <param name="args">Event arguments.</param>
    private void OnWorkUnitFinished(object sender, ApplicationEventArgs args)
    {
        // unblock the main thread, because we have identified the termination
        // of the application
        this.semaphore.Set();
    }
}
}
```

LISTING 7.6

(Continued)

management. It is possible to provide input files that are common to all the *WorkUnit* instances, through the *ApplicationBase.SharedFiles* collection, and instance-specific input and output files by leveraging the *WorkUnit.InputFiles* and *WorkUnit.OutputFiles* collections.

A fundamental component for the management of files is the *FileData* class, which constitutes the logic representation of physical files, as defined in the *Aneka.Data.Entity* namespace (*Aneka.Data.dll*). A *FileData* instance provides information about a file:

- Its nature: whether it is a shared file, an input file, or an output file
- Its path both in the local and in the remote file system, including a different name
- A collection of attributes that provides other information (such as the final destination of the file or whether the file is transient or not, etc.)

Using the *FileData* class, the user specifies the file dependencies of tasks and the application, and the Aneka APIs will automatically transfer them to and from the Aneka Cloud when needed. Aneka allows specifying of both local and remote files stored on FTP servers or Amazon S3. A *FileData* instance is identified by three elements: an owner, a name, and a type. By means of the corresponding ID, the owner identifies which is the computing element that needs the file: application instance or work unit. The type specifies whether the file is shared or an input or output file. The name represents the name of the corresponding physical file.

Listing 7.7 demonstrates how to add file dependencies to the application and to tasks. It is possible to add both *FileData* instances, thus having more control of the information attached to the file, or to use more intuitive approaches that simply require the name and the type of the file.

The general interaction flow for file management is as follows:

- Once the application is submitted, the shared files are staged into the Aneka Cloud.
- If the file is local it will be searched into the directory location identified by the property *Configuration.Workspace*; if the file is remote, the specific configuration settings mapped by the *FileData.StorageBucketId* property will be used to access the remote server and stage in the file.
- If there is any failure in staging input files, the application will be terminated with an error.
- For each of the tasks belonging to the application, the corresponding input files are staged into the Aneka Cloud, as is done for shared files.
- Once the task is dispatched for execution to a remote node, the runtime will transfer all the shared files of the application and the input files of the task into the working directory of the task and eventually get renamed if the *FileData.VirtualPath* property is not null.
- After the execution of the task, the runtime will look for all the files that have been added into the *WorkUnit.OutputFiles* collection. If not null, the value of the *FileData.VirtualPath* property will be used to locate the files; otherwise, the *FileData.FileName* property will be the reference. All the files that do not contain the *FileAttributes.Optional* attribute need to be present; otherwise, the execution of the task is classified as a failure.
- Despite the successful execution or the failure of a task, the runtime tries to collect and move to their respective destinations all the files that are found. Files that contain the *FileAttributes. Local* attribute are moved to the local machine from where the application is saved and stored in the directory location identified by the property *Configuration.Workspace*. Files that have a *StorageBucketId* property set will be staged out to the corresponding remote server.

The infrastructure for file management provides a transparent and extensible service for the movement of data. The architecture for file management is based on the concept of factories and storage buckets. A *factory*, namely *IFileTransferFactory*, is a component that is used to abstract the creation of client and server components for file transfer so that the entire architecture can work with interfaces rather than specific implementations. *Storage buckets* are collections of string properties that are used to specialize these components through configuration files. Storage buckets are specified by the user, either by the configuration file or by programmatically adding this information to the configuration object, before submitting the application. Factories are used by the *StorageService* to pull in remote input and shared files and to pull out remote output files.

Listing 7.8 shows a sample configuration file containing the settings required to access the remote files through the FTP and S3 protocols. Within the *< Groups >* tag, there is a specific group named *StorageBuckets*; this group maintains the configuration settings for each storage bucket that needs to be used in for file transfer. Each *< Group >* tag represents a storage bucket and the *name* property contains the values referenced in the *FileData.StorageBucketId* property. The content of each of these groups is specific to the type of storage bucket used, which is identified by the *Scheme* property. These values are used by the specific implementations for the FTP and S3 protocols to access the remote servers and transfer the files.

```
// get an instance of the Configuration class from file
Configuration conf = Configuration.GetConfiguration("conf.xml");
AnekaApplication<Task,TaskManager>app =new AnekaApplication<Task,TaskManager>(conf);

// attach shared files with different methods by using the FileData class and directly
// using the API provided by the AnekaApplication class

// create a local shared file whose local and remote name is "pi.tab"
FileDatapiTab = newFileData("pi.tab",FileDataType.Shared);
app.AddSharedFile(piTab);
// once the file is added to the collection of shared files, its OwnerId property
// references app.Id

// create a remote shared file by specifying the attributes whose name is "pi.dat"
FileDatapiDat = newFileData("pi.dat",FileDataType.Shared, FileAttributes.None);
// the StorageBucketId property points a specific configuration section that is
// used to store the information for retrieving the file from the remote server
piDat.StorageBucketId = "FTPStore";
app.AddSharedFile(piDat);
// once the file is added to the collection of shared files, its OwnerId property
// references app.Id

// adds a local shared file
app.AddSharedFile("pi.xml");

for(int i=0; i<400; i++)
{
    GaussTask gauss = new GaussTask();
    gauss.X = i;
    AnekaTask task = newAnekaTask(gauss);

    // adds a local input file for the current task whose name is "<i>.txt"
    // where <i> is the value of the loop variable
    FileData input = new FileData(string.Format("{0}.txt", i);
    FileDataType.Input, FileAttributes.Local);
    // once transferred to the remote node, the file will have the name
    // "input.txt". Since tasks are executed in separate directories there
    // will be no name clashing
    input.VirtualPath ="input.txt";
    task.AddFile(input);
    // once the file is added to the task, it will be stored in the InputFiles
    // collection and its OwnerId property will referenced task.Id

    // adds anoutput file for the current task whose name is "out.txt" that will
    // be stored on S3
```

LISTING 7.7

File dependencies management.

```
    FileData output =new FileData("out.txt", FileDataType.Input, FileAttributes.None);
    // once transferred to the remote server, the file will have the name
    // "<i>.out"where <i> is the value of the loop variable. In this way we
    // easily avoid name clashing while storing output files into a single
    // directory
    output.VirtualPath =string.Format("{0}.out", i);
    output.StorageBucketId = "S3Store";
    task.AddFile(output);
    // once the file is added to the task, it will be stored in the InputFiles
    // collection and its OwnerId property will referenced task.Id

    // adds a localoutput file for the current task whose name is "trace.log".
    // The file is optional, this means that if after the execution of the task the file

    // is not present no exception or task failure will be risen.
    FileData trace =new FileData("trace.log", FileDataType.Input,
    FileAttributes.Local | FileAttributes.Optional);
    // once transferred to the local machine, the file will have the name
    // "<i>.log"where <i> is the value of the loop variable. In this way we
    // easily avoid name clashing while storing output files into a single
    // directory
    trace.VirtualPath =string.Format("{0}.log", i);
    task.AddFile(trace);
    // once the file is added to the task, it will be stored in the InputFiles
    // collection and its OwnerId property will referenced task.Id

    // add the task to the bag of work units to submit
    app.AddWorkunit(task);
}

// submit the entire bag, files will be moved automatically by the Aneka APIs
app.SubmitExecution();
```

LISTING 7.7

(Continued)

7.3.2.4 Task libraries

Aneka provides a set of ready-to-use tasks for performing the most basic operations for remote file management. These tasks are part of the *Aneka.Tasks.BaseTasks* namespace, which is part of the *Aneka.Tasks.dll* library. The following operations are implemented:

- *File copy.* The *LocalCopyTask* performs the copy of a file on the remote node; it takes a file as input and produces a copy of it under a different name or path.
- *Legacy application execution.* The *ExecuteTask* allows executing external and legacy applications by using the *System.Diagnostics.Process* class. It requires the location of the executable file to run, and it is also possible to specify command-line parameters. *ExecuteTask* also collects the standard error and standard output produced by the execution of the application.

```
<?xmlversion="1.0"encoding="utf-8"?>
<Aneka>
  <UseFileTransfer value="true" />
  <Workspace value="." />
  <SingleSubmission value="false" />
  <ResubmitMode value="Manual" />
  <PollingTime value="1000" />
  <LogMessages value="true" />
  <SchedulerUri value="tcp://localhost:9090/Aneka"/>
  <UserCredential type="Aneka.Security.UserCredentials" assembly="Aneka.dll">
    <UserCredentials username="Administrator" password=""/>
  </UserCredential>
  <Groups>
    <Group name="StorageBuckets">
      <Groups>
        <Group name="FTPStore">
          <Property name="Scheme" value="ftp"/>
          <Property name="Host" value="www.remoteftp.org"/>
          <Property name="Port" value="21"/>
          <Property name="Username" value="anonymous"/>
          <Property name="Password" value="nil"/>
        </Group>
        <Group name="S3Store">
          <Propertyname="Scheme" value="S3"/>
          <Propertyname="Host"value="www.remoteftp.org"/>
          <Propertyname="Port"value="21"/>
          <Propertyname="Username"value="anonymous"/>
          <Propertyname="Password"value="nil"/>
        </Group>
      </Groups>
    </Group>
  </Groups>
</Aneka>
```

LISTING 7.8

Aneka application configuration file.

- *Substitute operation.* The *SubstituteTask* performs a search-and-replace operation within a given file by saving the resulting file under a different name. It is possible to specify a collection of string-based name-value pairs representing the strings to search together with their corresponding replacements.
- *File deletion.* The *DeleteTask* deletes a file that is accessible through the file system on the remote node.
- *Timed delay.* The *WaitTask* introduces a timed delay. This task can be used in several scenarios; for example, it can be used for profiling or simply for simulation of the execution. In addition, it can also be used to introduce a pause between the execution of two applications if needed.

- *Task composition.* The *CompositeTask* implements the composite pattern[3] and allows expressing a task as a composition of multiple tasks that are executed in sequence. This task is very useful to perform complex tasks involving the combination of operations implemented in other tasks.

The base task library does not provide any support for data transfer since this operation is automatically performed by the infrastructure when needed. Besides these simple tasks, the Aneka API allows for the creation of any user-defined task by simply implementing the *ITask* interface and supporting object serialization.

7.3.2.5 Web services integration

Aneka provides integration with other technologies and applications by means of Web services, which allow some of the services hosted in the Aneka Cloud to be accessible in platform-independent fashion. Among these, the task submission Web service allows third-party applications to submit tasks as they happen in traditional computing grids.

The task submission Web service is an additional component that can be deployed in any ASP.NET Web server and that exposes a simple interface for job submission, which is compliant with the Aneka Application Model. The task Web service provides an interface that is more compliant with the traditional way fostered by grid computing. Therefore, the new concept of the term *job*, which is a collection of predefined tasks, is introduced. The reference scenario for Web-based submission is depicted in Figure 7.9. Users create a distributed application instance on the cloud and, within the context of this application, they can submit jobs querying the status of the application or a single job. It is up to the users to then terminate the application when all the jobs are completed or to abort it if there is no need to complete job execution.

Jobs can be created by putting together the tasks defined in the basic task library. Operations supported through the Web service interface are the following:

- Local file copy on the remote node
- File deletion
- Legacy application execution through the common shell services
- Parameter substitution

It is also possible specify input and output files for each job. The only restriction in this case is that both input and output files need to reside in remote FTP servers. This enables Aneka to automatically stage the files from these servers without user intervention. Figure 7.10 gives detailed information about the object model exposed through the Web service for job submission.

Traditional grid technologies such as the Gridbus Broker [15] and the Workflow Engine [70] can make use of a task Web service to submit their tasks for execution on Cloud nodes managed by Aneka.

---

[3]In software engineering, the composite pattern is a software design pattern that allows expressing a combination of components as a single component. The advantage of using such a pattern resides in creating a software infrastructure that allows forwarding the execution of an operation to a group of objects by treating it as single unit and in a completely transparent manner. Reference: E. Gamma, R. Helm, R. Johnson, and J. M. Vlissides, *Design Patterns: Elements of Reusable Software Design*, Addison-Wesley, 1995, ISBN: 0201633612.

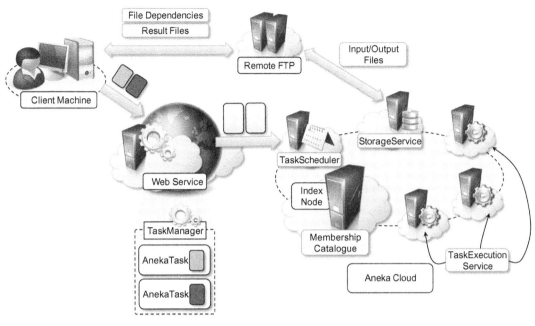

FIGURE 7.9

Web service submission scenario.

7.3.3 Developing a parameter sweep application

Aneka integrates support for parameter-sweeping applications on top of the task model by means of a collection of client components that allow developers to quickly prototype applications through either programming APIs or graphical user interfaces (GUIs). The set of abstractions and tools supporting the development of parameter sweep applications constitutes the *Parameter Sweep Model (PSM)*.

The PSM is organized into several namespaces under the common root *Aneka.PSM*. More precisely:

- *Aneka.PSM.Core (Aneka.PSM.Core.dll)* contains the base classes for defining a template task and the client components managing the generation of tasks, given the set of parameters.
- *Aneka.PSM.Workbench (Aneka.PSM.Workbench.exe)* and *Aneka.PSM.Wizard (Aneka.PSM. Wizard.dll)* contain the user interface support for designing and monitoring parameter sweep applications. Mostly they contain the classes and components required by the *Design Explorer*, which is the main GUI for developing parameter sweep applications.
- *Aneka.PSM.Console (Aneka.PSM.Console.exe)* contains the components and classes supporting the execution of parameter sweep applications in console mode.

These namespaces define the support for developing and controlling parameter sweep applications on top of Aneka.

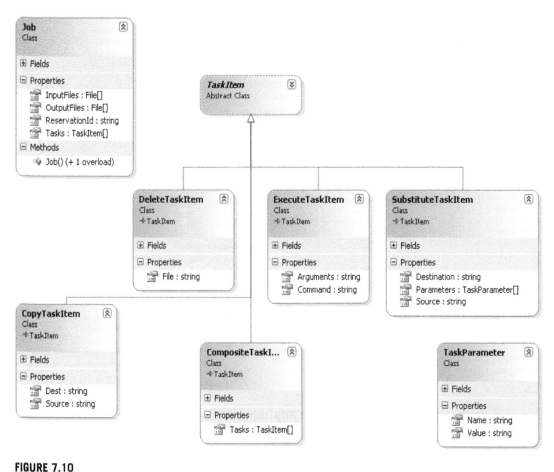

FIGURE 7.10

Job object model.

7.3.3.1 Object model

The fundamental elements of the Parameter Sweep Model are defined in the *Aneka.PSM.Core* namespace. This model introduces the concept of *job (Aneka.PSM.Core.PSMJobInfo)*, which identifies a parameter sweep application. A job comprises file dependencies and parameter definitions, together with their admissible domains, and the definition of the template task. Figure 7.11 shows the most relevant components of the object model.

The root component for application design is the *PSMJobInfo* class, which contains information about shared files and input and output files (*PSMFileInfo*). In accordance with the Aneka Application Model, shared files are common to all the instances of the template task, whereas input

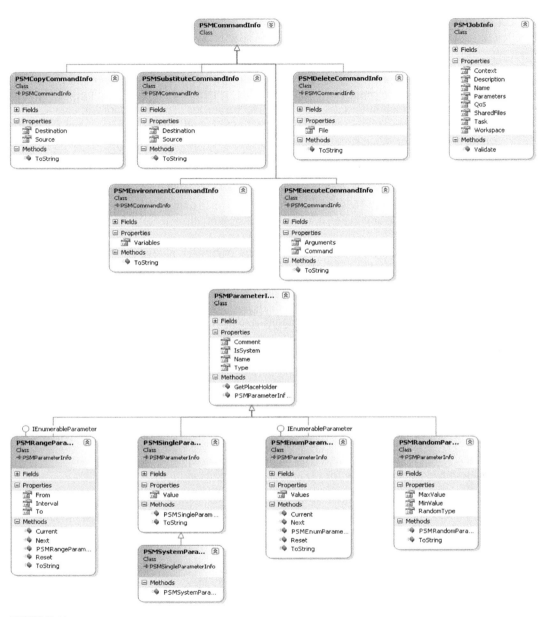

FIGURE 7.11

PSM object model (relevant classes).

and output files are specific to a given task instance. Therefore, these files can be expressed as a function of the parameters. Currently, it is possible to specify five different types of parameters:

- *Constant parameter (PSMSingleParameterInfo)*. This parameter identifies a specific value that is set at design time and will not change during the execution of the application.
- *Range parameter (PSMRangeParameterInfo)*. This parameter allows defining a range of allowed values, which might be integer or real. The parameter identifies a domain composed of discrete values and requires the specification of a lower bound, an upper bound, and a step for the generation of all the admissible values.
- *Random parameter (PSMRandomParameterInfo)*. This parameter allows the generation of a random value in between a given range defined by a lower and an upper bound. The value generated is real.
- *Enumeration parameter (PSMEnumParameterInfo)*. This parameter allows for specifying a discrete set of values of any type. It is useful to specify discrete sets that are not based on numeric values.
- *System parameter (PSMSystemParameterInfo)*. This parameter allows for mapping a specific value that will be substituted at runtime while the task instance is executed on the remote node.

Other than these parameters, the object model reserves special parameters that are used to identify specific values of the PSM object model, such as the task identifier and other data. Parameters have access to the execution environment by means of an execution context (*PSMContext*) that is responsible for providing default and runtime values. The task template is defined as a collection of commands (*PSMCommandInfo*), which replicate and extend the features available in the base task library. The available commands for composing the task template perform the following operations:

- Local file copy on the remote node (*PSMCopyCommandInfo*)
- Remote file deletion (*PSMDeleteCommandInfo*)
- Execution of programs through the shell (*PSMExecuteCommandInfo*)
- Environment variable setting on the remote node (*PSMEnvironmentCommandInfo*)
- String pattern replacement within files (*PSMSubstituteCommandInfo*)

By following the same approach described for the creation of tasks, it is possible to define the task template by composing these basic blocks. All the properties exposed by these commands can include the previously defined parameters, the values of which will be provided during the generation of the task instances.

A parameter sweep application is executed by means of a job manager (*IJobManager*), which interfaces the developer with the underlying APIs of the task model. Figure 7.12 shows the relationships among the PSM APIs, with a specific reference to the job manager, and the task model APIs.

Through the *IJobManager* interface it is possible to specify user credentials and configuration for interacting with the Aneka middleware. The implementation of *IJobManager* will then create a corresponding Aneka application instance and leverage the task model API to submit all the task instances generated from the template task. The interface also exposes facilities for controlling and monitoring the execution of the parameter sweep application as well as support for registering the statistics about the application.

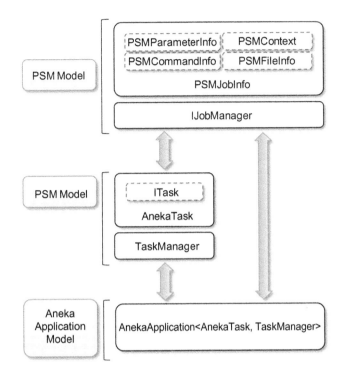

FIGURE 7.12

Parameter sweep model APIs.

7.3.3.2 Development and monitoring tools

The core libraries allow developers to directly program parameter sweep applications and embed them into other applications. Additional tools simplify design and development of parameter sweep applications by providing support for visual design of the applications and interactive and noninteractive application execution. These tools are the *Aneka Design Explorer* and the *Aneka PSM Console*.

The *Aneka Design Explorer* is an integrated visual environment for quickly prototyping parameter sweep applications, executing them, and monitoring their status. It provides a simple wizard that helps the user visually define any aspect of parameter sweep applications, such as file dependencies and result files, parameters, and template tasks. The environment also provides a collection of components that help users monitor application execution, aggregate statistics about application execution, gain detailed task transition monitoring, and gain extensive access to application logs.

The *Aneka PSM Console* is a command-line utility designed to run parameter sweep applications in noninteractive mode. The console offers a simplified interface for running applications with essential features for monitoring their execution. With respect to the Design Explorer, the console offers less support for keeping and visualizing aggregate statistics, but it exposes the same data in a more simplified textual form.

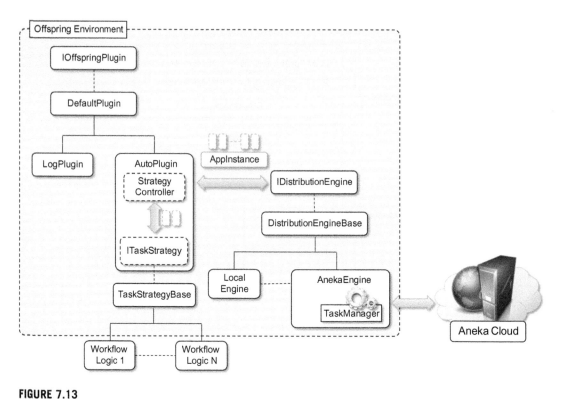

FIGURE 7.13

Offspring architecture.

7.3.4 Managing workflows

Support for workflow in Aneka is not native but is obtained with plug-ins that allow client-based workflow managers to submit tasks to Aneka. Currently, two different workflow managers can leverage Aneka for task execution: the *Workflow Engine* [70] and *Offspring* [71]. The former leverages the task submission Web service exposed by Aneka; the latter directly interacts with the Aneka programming APIs. The Workflow Engine plug-in for Aneka constitutes an example of the integration capabilities offered by the framework, which allows client applications developed with any technology and language to leverage Aneka for task execution. The integration developed for Offspring constitutes another example of how it is possible to construct another programming model on top of the existing APIs available in the framework. Therefore, we discuss this solution in more detail.

Figure 7.13 describes the Offspring architecture. The system is composed of two types of components: plug-ins and a distribution engine. Plug-ins are used to enrich the environment of features; the distribution engine represents access to the distributed computing infrastructure leveraged for task execution. Among the available plug-ins, *AutoPlugin* provides facilities for the definition of workflows in terms of strategies. A *strategy* generates the tasks that are submitted for execution and defines the logic, in terms of sequencing, coordination, and dependencies, used to submit the task through the engine. A specific component, the *StrategyController*, decouples the strategies

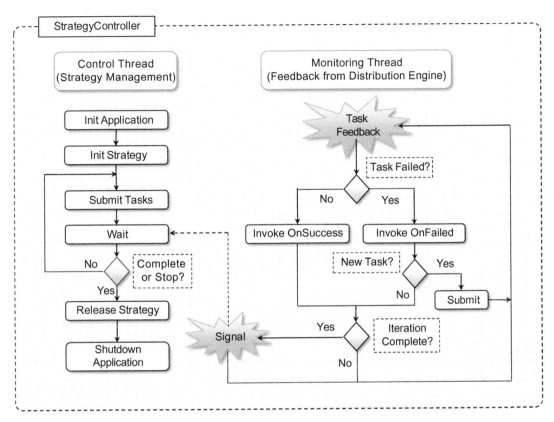

FIGURE 7.14

Workflow coordination.

from the distribution engine; therefore, strategies can be defined independently of the specific middleware used. The connection with Aneka is realized through the *AnekaEngine*, which implements the operations of *IDistributionEngine* for the Aneka middleware and relies on the services exposed by the task model programming APIs.

The system allows for the execution of a dynamic workflow, the structure of which is defined as the workflow executes. Two different types of tasks can be defined: native tasks and legacy tasks. *Native tasks* are completely implemented in managed code. *Legacy tasks* manage file dependencies and wrap all the data necessary for the execution of legacy programs on a remote node. Furthermore, a strategy may define shared file dependencies that are necessary to all the tasks generated by the workflow. The dependencies among tasks are implicitly defined by the execution of the strategy by the *StrategyController* and the events fired by the distributed engine.

Figure 7.14 describes the interactions among these components. Two main execution threads control the execution of a strategy. A *control thread* manages the execution of the strategy, whereas a *monitoring thread* collects the feedback from the distribution engine and allows for the dynamic reaction of the strategy to the execution of previously submitted tasks. From the workflow developer's point of view, the logic is quite simple. The execution of a strategy is composed of three macro steps: setup, execution, and finalization. The first step involves the setup of the strategy and the application mapping it. Correspondingly, the finalization step is in charge of releasing all the internal resources allocated by the strategy and shutting down the application. The core of the workflow execution resides in the execution step, which is broken down into a set of iterations. During each of the iterations a collection of tasks is submitted; these tasks do not have dependencies from each other and can be executed in parallel. As soon as a task completes or fails, the strategy is queried to see whether a new set of tasks needs to be executed. In this way, dependencies among tasks are implemented. If there are more tasks to be executed, they are submitted and the controller waits for feedback from the engine; otherwise, an iteration of the strategy is completed. At the end of each iteration, the controller checks to see whether the strategy has completed the execution, and in this case, the finalization step is performed.

The *AnekaEngine* creates an instance of the *AnekaApplication* class for each execution of a strategy and configures the template class with a specific implementation of the *TaskManager*, which overrides the behavior implemented for file management and optimizes the staging of output files. To support the implementation of workflows without any dependency from the distribution engine, the application configuration settings are controlled by the distribution engine and shared among all the strategies executed through the engine.

SUMMARY

This chapter introduced the concept of task-based programming and provided an overview of the technologies supporting the development of distributed applications based on the concept of tasks. Task-based programming constitutes the most intuitive approach to distributing the computation of an application over a set of nodes. The main abstraction of task-based programming is the concept of a *task*, which represents a group of operations that can be isolated and executed as a single unit. A task can be a simple program that is executed through the shell or a more complex piece of code requiring a specific runtime environment to execute. Quite often, tasks require input files for their execution and produce output files as a result. According to this model, an application is expressed as a collection of tasks; the way these tasks are interrelated and their specific nature and characteristics differentiate the various models that are an expression of task-based programming.

Traditionally, the task-based programming model has been successfully used in the development of distributed applications in many areas. We identified three major computing categories in which the task model can be utilized. *High-performance computing (HPC)* refers to the use of distributed computing facilities for solving problems that need large computing power. Common HPC applications feature a large collection of compute-intensive tasks, the duration of which is relatively short. *High-throughput computing (HTC)* identifies scenarios in which distributed computing facilities are used to support the execution of applications that need large computing power for a long period of time. Tasks may not be numerous, but they have a long duration, and infrastructure reliability becomes fundamental. *Many-task computing (MTC)* is the latest emergent trend and identifies a heterogeneous set of applications and requirements for applications, which fills the gap between HPC and HTC.

We have briefly reviewed common models related to task programming. *Embarrassingly parallel* applications are composed of a collection of tasks that do not relate to each other, can be executed in any order, and do not require co-allocation. *Parameter sweep* applications are a special instance of the embarrassingly parallel model. They are characterized by a collection of independent tasks that are automatically generated from a template task by varying the combination of parameter values. In this case, the executed task is the same in terms of computation logic, but it operates on different data. Therefore, a parameter sweep application can also be considered an expression of the *single program, multiple data (SPMD)* model. *MPI* applications are characterized by a collection of tasks that need to be executed all together and that exchange data by message passing. Even though the program executed by an MPI application tasks might be the same, it is quite common to provide an implementation logic that differentiates the behavior of each task according to its rank. *Workflow* applications are characterized by a collection of tasks for which the dependencies can be expressed in terms of a directed acyclic graph. Dependencies are mostly represented by files, which are produced as output of a specific task, and are required for the computation of the dependent tasks. The nature of the tasks and the kind of computation performed by each task differ generally.

We introduced the task model and the services implemented in Aneka that support task-based programming as a practical example of a framework that enables the development and execution of distributed applications based on tasks. The task model comprises a set of services (directory, scheduling, execution, and storage) of which the coordination constitutes runtime support for the execution of embarrassingly parallel applications. The fundamental features of the task model in terms of task definition, submission, execution, and file dependencies management was demonstrated with a practical example. On top of this infrastructure, client-side components and integration with other technologies allow providers to support parameter sweep and workflow applications. Parameter sweep applications are realized through the Parameter Sweep Model (PSM), which is characterized by a collection of client-side components that provide different, and more suitable, interfaces for this kind of application. Workflow applications are not natively supported by Aneka, but integration with other technologies allows us to leverage Aneka for workflow execution. For example, a plug-in using the Aneka task submission Web service allows the Workflow Engine to use Aneka as a back-end for workflow execution. The Aneka distribution engine implemented in Offspring provides another example of how it is possible to quickly prototype another programming model (in this case, a workflow-based model) by leveraging the base APIs of the task model.

Review questions

1. What is a task? How does task computing relate to distributed computing?
2. List and explain the computing categories that relate to task computing.
3. What are the main functionalities of a framework that supports task computing?
4. List some of the most popular frameworks for task computing.
5. What does the term *bag of tasks* mean?
6. Give an example of a parameter sweep application.
7. What is MPI? What are its main characteristics?

8. What is a workflow? What are the additional properties of this application model with respect to an embarrassingly parallel application?
9. Describe the reference model of a workflow management system.
10. How does Aneka support task computing?
11. What are the main components of the Task Programming Model?
12. Discuss the differences between ITask and AnekaTask.
13. Discuss the differences between static and dynamic task submission.
14. Discuss the facilities and the general architecture provided by Aneka for movement of data for task-based applications.
15. How it is possible to run a legacy application using the Task Programming Model?
16. Does Aneka provide any feature for leveraging the Task Programming Model from other technologies and platforms?
17. Using the Task Programming Model, design and implement a simple application that performs the discrete computation of the integral according to the method proposed by Riemann[4] of a given function over a specified interval.
18. What are the features provided by Aneka for the execution of parameter sweep applications?
19. Does Aneka provide native support for the execution of workflows?
20. By taking as a reference the Montage workflow described in Figure 7.6, design a sketch of the control flow of an Offspring strategy that can be used to execute a workflow on Aneka.

---

[4]http://en.wikipedia.org/wiki/Riemann_inegral.

Data-Intensive Computing

MapReduce Programming

8

Data-intensive computing focuses on aa class of applications that deal with a large amount of data. Several application fields, ranging from computational science to social networking, produce large volumes of data that need to be efficiently stored, made accessible, indexed, and analyzed. These tasks become challenging as the quantity of information accumulates and increases over time at higher rates. Distributed computing is definitely of help in addressing these challenges by providing more scalable and efficient storage architectures and a better performance in terms of data computation and processing. Despite this fact, the use of parallel and distributed techniques as a support of data-intensive computing is not straightforward, but several challenges in the form of data representation, efficient algorithms, and scalable infrastructures need to be faced.

This chapter characterizes the nature of data-intensive computing and presents an overview of the challenges introduced by production of large volumes of data and how they are handled by storage systems and computing models. It describes *MapReduce*, which is a popular programming model for creating data-intensive applications and their deployment on clouds. Practical examples of MapReduce applications for data-intensive computing are demonstrated using the Aneka MapReduce Programming Model.

8.1 What is data-intensive computing?

Data-intensive computing is concerned with production, manipulation, and analysis of large-scale data in the range of hundreds of megabytes (MB) to petabytes (PB) and beyond [73]. The term *dataset* is commonly used to identify a collection of information elements that is relevant to one or more applications. Datasets are often maintained in *repositories*, which are infrastructures supporting the storage, retrieval, and indexing of large amounts of information. To facilitate the classification and search, relevant bits of information, called *metadata*, are attached to datasets.

Data-intensive computations occur in many application domains. Computational science is one of the most popular ones. People conducting scientific simulations and experiments are often keen to produce, analyze, and process huge volumes of data. Hundreds of gigabytes of data are produced every second by telescopes mapping the sky; the collection of images of the sky easily reaches the scale of petabytes over a year. Bioinformatics applications mine databases that may end up containing terabytes of data. Earthquake simulators process a massive amount of data, which is produced as a result of recording the vibrations of the Earth across the entire globe.

Besides scientific computing, several IT industry sectors require support for data-intensive computations. Customer data for any telecom company would easily be in the range of 10−100 terabytes. This volume of information is not only processed to generate billing statements, but it is also mined to identify scenarios, trends, and patterns that help these companies provide better service. Moreover, it is reported that U.S. handset mobile traffic has reached 8 petabytes per month and it is expected to grow up to 327 petabytes per month by 2015.[1] The scale of petabytes is even more common when we consider IT giants such as Google, which is reported to process about 24 petabytes of information per day [55] and to sort petabytes of data in hours.[2] Social networking and gaming are two other sectors in which data-intensive computing is now a reality. Facebook inbox search operations involve crawling about 150 terabytes of data, and the whole uncompressed data stored by the distributed infrastructure reach to 36 petabytes.[3] Zynga, *a* social gaming platform, moves 1 petabyte of data daily and it has been reported to add 1,000 servers every week to store the data generated by games like Farmville and Frontierville.[4]

8.1.1 Characterizing data-intensive computations

Data-intensive applications not only deal with huge volumes of data but, very often, also exhibit compute-intensive properties [74]. Figure 8.1 identifies the domain of data-intensive computing in the two upper quadrants of the graph.

Data-intensive applications handle datasets on the scale of multiple terabytes and petabytes. Datasets are commonly persisted in several formats and distributed across different locations. Such applications process data in multistep analytical pipelines, including transformation and fusion stages. The processing requirements scale almost linearly with the data size, and they can be easily processed in parallel. They also need efficient mechanisms for data management, filtering and fusion, and efficient querying and distribution [74].

8.1.2 Challenges ahead

The huge amount of data produced, analyzed, or stored imposes requirements on the supporting infrastructures and middleware that are hardly found in the traditional solutions for distributed computing. For example, the location of data is crucial as the need for moving terabytes of data becomes an obstacle for high-performing computations. Data partitioning as well as content replication and scalable algorithms help in improving the performance of data-intensive applications. Open challenges in data-intensive computing given by Ian Gorton et al. [74] are:

- Scalable algorithms that can search and process massive datasets
- New metadata management technologies that can scale to handle complex, heterogeneous, and distributed data sources

---

[1]Coda Research Consultancy, www.codaresearch.co.uk/usmobileinternet/index.htm.
[2]Google's Blog, http://googleblog.blogspot.com/2008/11/sorting-1pb-with-mapreduce.html.
[3]OSCON 2010, David Recordon (Senior Open Programs Manager, Facebook): Today's LAMP Stack, Keynote Speech. Available at www.oscon.com/oscon2010/public/schedule/speaker/2442.
[4]http://techcrunch.com/2010/09/22/zynga-moves-1-petabyte-of-data-daily-adds-1000-servers-a-week/.

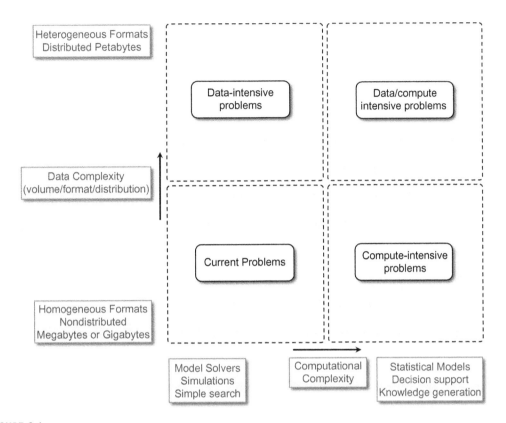

FIGURE 8.1

Data-intensive research issues.

- Advances in high-performance computing platforms aimed at providing a better support for accessing in-memory multiterabyte data structures
- High-performance, highly reliable, petascale distributed file systems
- Data signature-generation techniques for data reduction and rapid processing
- New approaches to software mobility for delivering algorithms that are able to move the computation to where the data are located
- Specialized hybrid interconnection architectures that provide better support for filtering multigigabyte datastreams coming from high-speed networks and scientific instruments
- Flexible and high-performance software integration techniques that facilitate the combination of software modules running on different platforms to quickly form analytical pipelines

8.1.3 Historical perspective

Data-intensive computing involves the production, management, and analysis of large volumes of data. Support for data-intensive computations is provided by harnessing storage, networking technologies, algorithms, and infrastructure software all together. We track the evolution of this phenomenon by highlighting the most relevant contributions in the area of storage and networking and infrastructure software.

8.1.3.1 The early age: high-speed wide-area networking

The evolution of technologies, protocols, and algorithms for data transmission and streaming has been an enabler of data-intensive computations [75]. In 1989, the first experiments in high-speed networking as a support for remote visualization of scientific data led the way. Two years later, the potential of using high-speed wide area networks for enabling high-speed, TCP/IP-based distributed applications was demonstrated at Supercomputing 1991 (SC91). On that occasion, the remote visualization of large and complex scientific datasets (a high-resolution magnetic resonance image, or MRI, scan of the human brain) was set up between the Pittsburgh Supercomputing Center (PSC) and Albuquerque, New Mexico, the location of the conference.

A further step was made by the Kaiser project [76], which made available as remote data sources high data rate and online instrument systems. The project leveraged the Wide Area Large Data Object (WALDO) system [77], which was used to provide the following capabilities: automatic generation of metadata; automatic cataloguing of data and metadata while processing the data in real time; facilitation of cooperative research by providing local and remote users access to data; and mechanisms to incorporate data into databases and other documents.

The first data-intensive environment is reported to be the MAGIC project, a DARPA-funded collaboration working on distributed applications in large-scale, high-speed networks. Within this context, the *Distributed Parallel Storage System (DPSS)* was developed, later used to support *TerraVision* [78], a terrain visualization application that lets users explore and navigate a tridimensional real landscape.

Another important milestone was set with the Clipper project,[5] a collaborative effort of several scientific research laboratories, with the goal of designing and implementing a collection of independent but architecturally consistent service components to support data-intensive computing. The challenges addressed by the Clipper project included management of substantial computing resources, generation or consumption of high-rate and high-volume data flows, human interaction management, and aggregation of disperse resources (multiple data archives, distributed computing capacity, distributed cache capacity, and guaranteed network capacity). Clipper's main focus was to develop a coordinated collection of services that can be used by a variety of applications to build on-demand, large-scale, high-performance, wide-area problem-solving environments.

8.1.3.2 Data grids

With the advent of grid computing [8], huge computational power and storage facilities could be obtained by harnessing heterogeneous resources across different administrative domains. Within this context, *data grids* [79] emerge as infrastructures that support data-intensive computing. A data grid provides services that help users discover, transfer, and manipulate large datasets stored in distributed repositories as well as create and manage copies of them. Data grids offer two main functionalities: high-performance and reliable file transfer for moving large amounts of data, and scalable replica

---

[5]www.nersc.gov/news/annual_reports/annrep98/16clipper.html.

discovery and management mechanisms for easy access to distributed datasets [80]. Because data grids span different administration boundaries, access control and security are important concerns.

Data grids mostly provide storage and dataset management facilities as support for scientific experiments that produce huge volumes of data. The reference scenario might be one depicted in Figure 8.2. Huge amounts of data are produced by scientific instruments (telescopes, particle accelerators, etc.). The information, which can be locally processed, is then stored in repositories and made available for experiments and analysis to scientists, who can be local or, most likely, remote. Scientists can leverage specific discovery and information services, which help in determining the locations of the closest datasets of interest for their experiments. Datasets are replicated by the infrastructure to provide better availability. Since processing of this information also requires a large computational power, specific computing sites can be accessed to perform analysis and experiments.

Like any other grid infrastructure, heterogeneity of resources and different administrative domains constitute a fundamental aspect that needs to be properly addressed with security measures and the use of *virtual organizations (VO)*. Besides heterogeneity and security, data grids have their own characteristics and introduce new challenges [79]:

- *Massive datasets.* The size of datasets can easily be on the scale of gigabytes, terabytes, and beyond. It is therefore necessary to minimize latencies during bulk transfers, replicate content with appropriate strategies, and manage storage resources.
- *Shared data collections.* Resource sharing includes distributed collections of data. For example, repositories can be used to both store and read data.
- *Unified namespace.* Data grids impose a unified logical namespace where to locate data collections and resources. Every data element has a single logical name, which is eventually mapped to different physical filenames for the purpose of replication and accessibility.
- *Access restrictions.* Even though one of the purposes of data grids is to facilitate sharing of results and data for experiments, some users might want to ensure confidentiality for their data and restrict access to them to their collaborators. Authentication and authorization in data grids involve both coarse-grained and fine-grained access control over shared data collections.

With respect to the combination of several computing facilities through high-speed networking, data grids constitute a more structured and integrated approach to data-intensive computing. As a result, several scientific research fields, including high-energy physics, biology, and astronomy, leverage data grids, as briefly discussed here:

- *The LHC Grid.* A project funded by the European Union to develop a worldwide grid computing environment for use by high-energy physics researchers around the world who are collaborating on the Large Hadron Collider (LHC) experiment. It supports storage and analysis of large-scale datasets, from hundreds of terabytes to petabytes, generated by the LHC experiment (http://lhc.web.cern.ch/lhc/).
- *BioInformatics Research Network (BIRN).* BIRN is a national initiative to advance biomedical research through data sharing and online collaboration. Funded by the National Center for Research Resources (NCRR), a component of the U.S. National Institutes of Health (NIH), BIRN provides a data-sharing infrastructure, software tools, and strategies and advisory services (www.birncommunity.org).

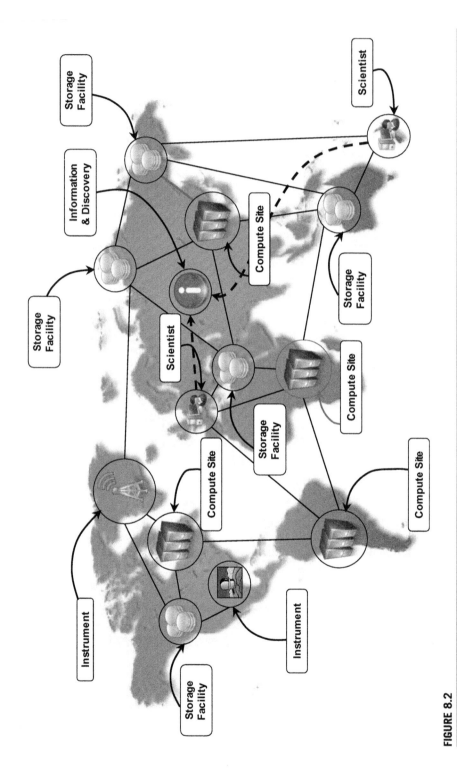

FIGURE 8.2

Data grid reference scenario.

- *International Virtual Observatory Alliance (IVOA).* IVOA is an organization that aims to provide improved access to the ever-expanding astronomical data resources available online. It does so by promoting standards for *virtual observatories*, which are a collection of interoperating data archives and software tools that use the Internet to form a scientific research environment in which astronomical research programs can be conducted. This allows scientists to discover, access, analyze, and combine lab data from heterogeneous data collections (www. ivoa.net).

A complete taxonomy of Data Grids can be found in Venugopal et al. [79].

8.1.3.3 Data clouds and "Big Data"

Large datasets have mostly been the domain of scientific computing. This scenario has recently started to change as massive amounts of data are being produced, mined, and crunched by companies that provide Internet services such as searching, online advertising, and social media. It is critical for such companies to efficiently analyze these huge datasets because they constitute a precious source of information about their customers. *Log analysis* is an example of a data-intensive operation that is commonly performed in this context; companies such as Google have a massive amount of data in the form of logs that are daily processed using their distributed infrastructure. As a result, they settled upon an analytic infrastructure, which differs from the grid-based infrastructure used by the scientific community.

Together with the diffusion of cloud computing technologies that support data-intensive computations, the term *Big Data* [82] has become popular. This term characterizes the nature of data-intensive computations today and currently identifies datasets that grow so large that they become complex to work with using on-hand database management tools. Relational databases and desktop statistics/visualization packages become ineffective for that amount of information, instead requiring "massively parallel software running on tens, hundreds, or even thousands of servers" [82].

Big Data problems are found in nonscientific application domains such as weblogs, radio frequency identification (RFID), sensor networks, social networks, Internet text and documents, Internet search indexing, call detail records, military surveillance, medical records, photography archives, video archives, and large scale ecommerce. Other than the massive size, what characterizes all these examples is that new data are accumulated with time rather than replacing the old data. In general, the term *Big Data* applies to datasets of which the size is beyond the ability of commonly used software tools to capture, manage, and process within a tolerable elapsed time. Therefore, Big Data sizes are a constantly moving target, currently ranging from a few dozen terabytes to many petabytes of data in a single dataset [82].

Cloud technologies support data-intensive computing in several ways:

- By providing a large amount of compute instances on demand, which can be used to process and analyze large datasets in parallel.
- By providing a storage system optimized for keeping large blobs of data and other distributed data store architectures.
- By providing frameworks and programming APIs optimized for the processing and management of large amounts of data. These APIs are mostly coupled with a specific storage infrastructure to optimize the overall performance of the system.

A *data cloud* is a combination of these components. An example is the *MapReduce* framework [55], which provides the best performance for leveraging the Google File System [54] on top of Google's large computing infrastructure. Another example is the *Hadoop* system [83], the most mature, large, and open-source data cloud. It consists of the Hadoop Distributed File System (HDFS) and Hadoop's implementation of MapReduce. A similar approach is proposed by *Sector* [84], which consists of the Sector Distributed File System (SDFS) and a compute service called *Sphere* [84] that allows users to execute arbitrary user-defined functions (UDFs) over the data managed by SDFS. *Greenplum* uses a shared-nothing massively parallel processing (MPP) architecture based on commodity hardware. The architecture also integrates MapReduce-like functionality into its platform. A similar architecture has been deployed by *Aster*, which uses an MPP-based data-warehousing appliance that supports MapReduce and targets 1 PB of data.

8.1.3.4 Databases and data-intensive computing

Traditionally, distributed databases [85] have been considered the natural evolution of database management systems as the scale of the datasets becomes unmanageable with a single system. Distributed databases are a collection of data stored at different sites of a computer network. Each site might expose a degree of autonomy, providing services for the execution of local applications, but also participating in the execution of a global application. A distributed database can be created by splitting and scattering the data of an existing database over different sites or by federating together multiple existing databases. These systems are very robust and provide distributed transaction processing, distributed query optimization, and efficient management of resources. However, they are mostly concerned with datasets that can be expressed using the relational model [86], and the need to enforce ACID properties on data limits their abilities to scale as data clouds and grids do.

8.2 Technologies for data-intensive computing

Data-intensive computing concerns the development of applications that are mainly focused on processing large quantities of data. Therefore, storage systems and programming models constitute a natural classification of the technologies supporting data-intensive computing.

8.2.1 Storage systems

Traditionally, database management systems constituted the *de facto* storage support for several types of applications. Due to the explosion of unstructured data in the form of blogs, Web pages, software logs, and sensor readings, the relational model in its original formulation does not seem to be the preferred solution for supporting data analytics on a large scale [88]. Research on databases and the data management industry are indeed at a turning point, and new opportunities arise. Some factors contributing to this change are:

* *Growing of popularity of Big Data.* The management of large quantities of data is no longer a rare case but instead has become common in several fields: scientific computing, enterprise applications, media entertainment, natural language processing, and social network analysis. The large volume of data imposes new and more efficient techniques for data management.

- *Growing importance of data analytics in the business chain.* The management of data is no longer considered a cost but a key element of business profit. This situation arises in popular social networks such as Facebook, which concentrate their focus on the management of user profiles, interests, and connections among people. This massive amount of data, which is constantly mined, requires new technologies and strategies to support data analytics.
- *Presence of data in several forms, not only structured.* As previously mentioned, what constitutes relevant information today exhibits a heterogeneous nature and appears in several forms and formats. Structured data are constantly growing as a result of the continuous use of traditional enterprise applications and system, but at the same time the advances in technology and the democratization of the Internet as a platform where everyone can pull information has created a massive amount of information that is unstructured and does not naturally fit into the relational model.
- *New approaches and technologies for computing.* Cloud computing promises access to a massive amount of computing capacity on demand. This allows engineers to design software systems that incrementally scale to arbitrary degrees of parallelism. It is no longer rare to build software applications and services that are dynamically deployed on hundreds or thousands of nodes, which might belong to the system for a few hours or days. Classical database infrastructures are not designed to provide support to such a volatile environment.

All these factors identify the need for new data management technologies. This not only implies a new research agenda in database technologies and a more holistic approach to the management of information but also leaves room for alternatives (or complements) to the relational model. In particular, advances in distributed file systems for the management of raw data in the form of files, distributed object stores, and the spread of the NoSQL movement constitute the major directions toward support for data-intensive computing.

8.2.1.1 High-performance distributed file systems and storage clouds

Distributed file systems constitute the primary support for data management. They provide an interface whereby to store information in the form of files and later access them for read and write operations. Among the several implementations of file systems, few of them specifically address the management of huge quantities of data on a large number of nodes. Mostly these file systems constitute the data storage support for large computing clusters, supercomputers, massively parallel architectures, and lately, storage/computing clouds.

Lustre. The Lustre file system is a massively parallel distributed file system that covers the needs of a small workgroup of clusters to a large-scale computing cluster. The file system is used by several of the Top 500 supercomputing systems, including the one rated the most powerful supercomputer in the June 2012 list.[6] Lustre is designed to provide access to petabytes (PBs) of storage to serve thousands of clients with an I/O throughput of hundreds of gigabytes per second (GB/s). The system is composed of a metadata server that contains the metadata about the file system and a collection of object storage servers that are in charge of providing storage. Users access the file system via a POSIX-compliant client, which can be either mounted as a module in the

---

[6]Top 500 supercomputers list: www.top500.org (accessed in June 2012).

kernel or through a library. The file system implements a robust failover strategy and recovery mechanism, making server failures and recoveries transparent to clients.

IBM General Parallel File System (GPFS). GPFS [88] is the high-performance distributed file system developed by IBM that provides support for the RS/6000 supercomputer and Linux computing clusters. GPFS is a multiplatform distributed file system built over several years of academic research and provides advanced recovery mechanisms. GPFS is built on the concept of shared disks, in which a collection of disks is attached to the file system nodes by means of some switching fabric. The file system makes this infrastructure transparent to users and stripes large files over the disk array by replicating portions of the file to ensure high availability. By means of this infrastructure, the system is able to support petabytes of storage, which is accessed at a high throughput and without losing consistency of data. Compared to other implementations, GPFS distributes the metadata of the entire file system and provides transparent access to it, thus eliminating a single point of failure.

Google File System (GFS). GFS [54] is the storage infrastructure that supports the execution of distributed applications in Google's computing cloud. The system has been designed to be a fault-tolerant, highly available, distributed file system built on commodity hardware and standard Linux operating systems. Rather than a generic implementation of a distributed file system, GFS specifically addresses Google's needs in terms of distributed storage for applications, and it has been designed with the following assumptions:

- The system is built on top of commodity hardware that often fails.
- The system stores a modest number of large files; multi-GB files are common and should be treated efficiently, and small files must be supported, but there is no need to optimize for that.
- The workloads primarily consist of two kinds of reads: large streaming reads and small random reads.
- The workloads also have many large, sequential writes that append data to files.
- High-sustained bandwidth is more important than low latency.

The architecture of the file system is organized into a single master, which contains the metadata of the entire file system, and a collection of chunk servers, which provide storage space. From a logical point of view the system is composed of a collection of software daemons, which implement either the master server or the chunk server. A file is a collection of chunks for which the size can be configured at file system level. Chunks are replicated on multiple nodes in order to tolerate failures. Clients look up the master server and identify the specific chunk of a file they want to access. Once the chunk is identified, the interaction happens between the client and the chunk server. Applications interact through the file system with a specific interface supporting the usual operations for file creation, deletion, read, and write. The interface also supports *snapshots* and *record append* operations that are frequently performed by applications. GFS has been conceived by considering that failures in a large distributed infrastructure are common rather than a rarity; therefore, specific attention has been given to implementing a highly available, lightweight, and fault-tolerant infrastructure. The potential single point of failure of the single-master architecture has been addressed by giving the possibility of replicating the master node on any other node belonging to the infrastructure. Moreover, a stateless daemon and extensive logging capabilities facilitate the system's recovery from failures.

Sector. Sector [84] is the storage cloud that supports the execution of data-intensive applications defined according to the Sphere framework. It is a user space file system that can be deployed on commodity hardware across a wide-area network. Compared to other file systems, Sector does not partition a file into blocks but replicates the entire files on multiple nodes, allowing users to customize the replication strategy for better performance. The system's architecture is composed of four nodes: a security server, one or more master nodes, slave nodes, and client machines. The security server maintains all the information about access control policies for user and files, whereas master servers coordinate and serve the I/O requests of clients, which ultimately interact with slave nodes to access files. The protocol used to exchange data with slave nodes is UDT [89], which is a lightweight connection-oriented protocol optimized for wide-area networks.

Amazon Simple Storage Service (S3). Amazon S3 is the online storage service provided by Amazon. Even though its internal details are not revealed, the system is claimed to support high availability, reliability, scalability, infinite storage, and low latency at commodity cost. The system offers a flat storage space organized into buckets, which are attached to an Amazon Web Services (AWS) account. Each bucket can store multiple objects, each identified by a unique key. Objects are identified by unique URLs and exposed through HTTP, thus allowing very simple *get-put* semantics. Because of the use of HTTP, there is no need for any specific library for accessing the storage system, the objects of which can also be retrieved through the Bit Torrent protocol.[7] Despite its simple semantics, a POSIX-like client library has been developed to mount S3 buckets as part of the local file system. Besides the minimal semantics, security is another limitation of S3. The visibility and accessibility of objects are linked to AWS accounts, and the owner of a bucket can decide to make it visible to other accounts or the public. It is also possible to define authenticated URLs, which provide public access to anyone for a limited (and configurable) period of time.

Besides these examples of storage systems, there exist other implementations of distributed file systems and storage clouds that have architecture that is similar to the models discussed here. Except for the S3 service, it is possible to sketch a general reference architecture in all the systems presented that identifies two major roles into which all the nodes can be classified. Metadata or master nodes contain the information about the location of files or file chunks, whereas slave nodes are used to provide direct access to the storage space. The architecture is completed by client libraries, which provide a simple interface for accessing the file system, which is to some extent or completely compliant to the POSIX specification. Variations of the reference architecture can include the ability to support multiple masters, to distribute the metadata over multiple nodes, or to easily interchange the role of nodes. The most important aspect common to all these different implementations is the ability to provide fault-tolerant and highly available storage systems.

8.2.1.2 NoSQL systems

The term *Not Only SQL (NoSQL)* was originally coined in 1998 to identify a relational database that did not expose a SQL interface to manipulate and query data but relied on a set of UNIX shell scripts and commands to operate on text files containing the actual data. In a very strict sense, NoSQL cannot be considered a relational database since it is not a monolithic piece of software organizing information according to the relational model, but rather is a collection of scripts that

---

[7]Bit Torrent is a P2P file-sharing protocol used to distribute large amounts of data. The key characteristic of the protocol is the ability to allow users to download a file in parallel from multiple hosts.

allow users to manage most of the simplest and more common database tasks by using text files as information stores. Later, in 2009, the term *NoSQL* was reintroduced with the intent of labeling all those database management systems that did not use a relational model but provided simpler and faster alternatives for data manipulation. Nowadays, the term *NoSQL* is a big umbrella encompassing all the storage and database management systems that differ in some way from the relational model. Their general philosophy is to overcome the restrictions imposed by the relational model and to provide more efficient systems. This often implies the use of tables without fixed schemas to accommodate a larger range of data types or avoid joins to increase the performance and scale horizontally.

Two main factors have determined the growth of the NoSQL movement: in many cases simple data models are enough to represent the information used by applications, and the quantity of information contained in unstructured formats has grown considerably in the last decade. These two factors made software engineers look to alternatives that were more suitable to specific application domains they were working on. As a result, several different initiatives explored the use of nonrelational storage systems, which considerably differ from each other. A broad classification is reported by Wikipedia,[8] which distinguishes NoSQL implementations into:

- *Document stores* (Apache Jackrabbit, Apache CouchDB, SimpleDB, Terrastore).
- *Graphs* (AllegroGraph, Neo4j, FlockDB, Cerebrum).
- *Key-value stores*. This is a macro classification that is further categorized into key-value stores on disk, key-value caches in RAM, hierarchically key-value stores, eventually consistent key-value stores, and ordered key-value store.
- *Multivalue databases* (OpenQM, Rocket U2, OpenInsight).
- *Object databases* (ObjectStore, JADE, ZODB).
- *Tabular stores* (Google BigTable, Hadoop HBase, Hypertable).
- *Tuple stores* (Apache River).

Let us now examine some prominent implementations that support data-intensive applications.

Apache CouchDB and MongoDB. Apache CouchDB [91] and MongoDB [90] are two examples of document stores. Both provide a schema-less store whereby the primary objects are documents organized into a collection of key-value fields. The value of each field can be of type string, integer, float, date, or an array of values. The databases expose a RESTful interface and represent data in JSON format. Both allow querying and indexing data by using the MapReduce programming model, expose JavaScript as a base language for data querying and manipulation rather than SQL, and support large files as documents. From an infrastructure point of view, the two systems support data replication and high availability. CouchDB ensures ACID properties on data. MongoDB supports *sharding*, which is the ability to distribute the content of a collection among different nodes.

Amazon Dynamo. Dynamo [92] is the distributed key-value store that supports the management of information of several of the business services offered by Amazon Inc. The main goal of Dynamo is to provide an incrementally scalable and highly available storage system. This goal helps in achieving reliability at a massive scale, where thousands of servers and network components build an infrastructure serving 10 million requests per day. Dynamo provides a simplified

---

[8]http://en.wikipedia.com/wiki/NoSQL.

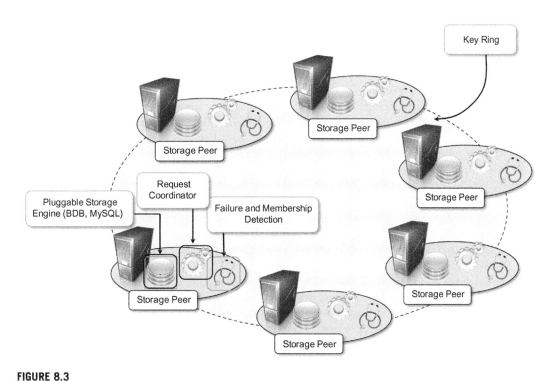

FIGURE 8.3

Amazon Dynamo architecture.

interface based on *get/put* semantics, where objects are stored and retrieved with a unique identifier (key). The main goal of achieving an extremely reliable infrastructure has imposed some constraints on the properties of these systems. For example, ACID properties on data have been sacrificed in favor of a more reliable and efficient infrastructure. This creates what it is called an *eventually consistent* model, which means that in the long term all the users will see the same data.

The architecture of the Dynamo system, shown in Figure 8.3, is composed of a collection of storage peers organized in a ring that shares the key space for a given application. The key space is partitioned among the storage peers, and the keys are replicated across the ring, avoiding adjacent peers. Each peer is configured with access to a local storage facility where original objects and replicas are stored. Furthermore, each node provides facilities for distributing the updates among the rings and to detect failures and unreachable nodes. With some relaxation of the consistency model applied to replicas and the use of object versioning, Dynamo implements the capability of being an *always-writable store*, where consistency of data is resolved in the background. The downside of such an approach is the simplicity of the storage model, which requires applications to build their own data models on top of the simple building blocks provided by the store. For example, there are no referential integrity constraints, relationships are not embedded in the storage model, and therefore join operations are not supported. These restrictions are not prohibitive in the case of Amazon services for which the single key-value model is acceptable.

Google Bigtable. Bigtable [93] is the distributed storage system designed to scale up to petabytes of data across thousands of servers. Bigtable provides storage support for several Google applications that expose different types of workload: from throughput-oriented batch-processing jobs to latency-sensitive serving of data to end users. Bigtable's key design goals are wide applicability, scalability, high performance, and high availability. To achieve these goals, Bigtable organizes the data storage in tables of which the rows are distributed over the distributed file system supporting the middleware, which is the Google File System. From a logical point of view, a table is a multidimensional sorted map indexed by a key that is represented by a string of arbitrary length. A table is organized into rows and columns; columns can be grouped in column family, which allow for specific optimization for better access control, the storage and the indexing of data. A simple data access model constitutes the interface for client applications that can address data at the granularity level of the single column of a row. Moreover, each column value is stored in multiple versions that can be automatically time-stamped by Bigtable or by the client applications.

Besides the basic data access, Bigtable APIs also allow more complex operations such as single row transactions and advanced data manipulation by means of the Sazwall[9] [95] scripting language or the MapReduce APIs.

Figure 8.4 gives an overview of the infrastructure that enables Bigtable. The service is the result of a collection of processes that coexist with other processes in a cluster-based environment. Bigtable identifies two kinds of processes: master processes and tablet server processes. A tablet server is responsible for serving the requests for a given tablet that is a contiguous partition of rows of a table. Each server can manage multiple tablets (commonly from 10 to 1,000). The master server is responsible for keeping track of the status of the tablet servers and of the allocation of tablets to tablet servers. The server constantly monitors the tablet servers to check whether they are alive, and in case they are not reachable, the allocated tablets are reassigned and eventually partitioned to other servers.

Chubby [96]—a distributed, highly available, and persistent lock service—supports the activity of the master and tablet servers. System monitoring and data access are filtered through Chubby, which is also responsible for managing replicas and providing consistency among them. At the very bottom layer, the data are stored in the Google File System in the form of files, and all the update operations are logged into the file for the easy recovery of data in case of failures or when tablets need to be reassigned to other servers. Bigtable uses a specific file format for storing the data of a tablet, which can be compressed for optimizing the access and storage of data.

Bigtable is the result of a study of the requirements of several distributed applications in Google. It serves as a storage back-end for 60 applications (such as Google Personalized Search, Google Anlytics, Google Finance, and Google Earth) and manages petabytes of data.

Apache Cassandra. Cassandra [94] is a distributed object store for managing large amounts of structured data spread across many commodity servers. The system is designed to avoid a single point of failure and offer a highly reliable service. Cassandra was initially developed by Facebook; now it is part of the Apache incubator initiative. Currently, it provides storage support for several very large Web applications such as Facebook itself, Digg, and Twitter. Cassandra is defined as a

---

[9]*Sazwall* is an interpreted procedural programming language developed at Google for the manipulation of large quantities of tabular data. It includes specific capabilities for supporting statistical aggregation of values read or computed from the input and other features that simplify the parallel processing of petabytes of data.

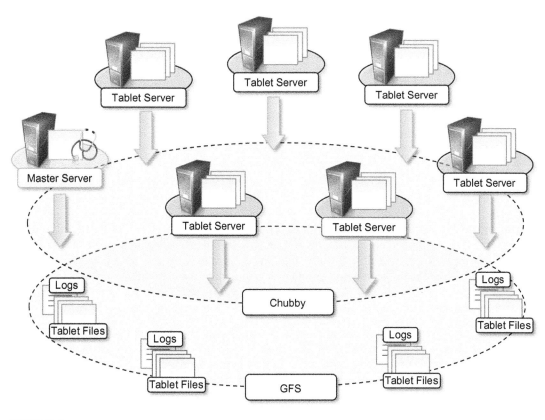

FIGURE 8.4

Bigtable architecture.

second-generation distributed database that builds on the concept of Amazon Dynamo, which follows a fully distributed design, and Google Bigtable, from which it inherits the "column family" concept. The data model exposed by Cassandra is based on the concept of a table that is implemented as a distributed multidimensional map indexed by a key. The value corresponding to a key is a highly structured object and constitutes the row of a table. Cassandra organizes the row of a table into columns, and sets of columns can be grouped into column families. The APIs provided by the system to access and manipulate the data are very simple: insertion, retrieval, and deletion. The insertion is performed at the row level; retrieval and deletion can operate at the column level.

In terms of the infrastructure, Cassandra is very similar to Dynamo. It has been designed for incremental scaling, and it organizes the collection of nodes sharing a key space into a ring. Each node manages multiple and discontinuous portions of the key space and replicates its data up to N other nodes. Replication uses different strategies; it can be *rack aware*, *data center aware*, or *rack unaware*, meaning that the policies can take into account whether the replication needs to be made within the same cluster or datacenter or not to consider the geo-location of nodes. As in Dynamo, node membership information is based on gossip protocols.[10] Cassandra makes also use of this information diffusion mode for other tasks, such as disseminating the system control state. The local file system of each node is used for data persistence, and Cassandra makes extensive use of commit logs, which makes the system able to recover from transient failures. Each write operation is applied in memory only after it has been logged on disk so that it can be easily reproduced in case of failures. When the data in memory trespasses a specified size, it is dumped to disk. Read operations are performed in-memory first and then on disk. To speed up the process, each file includes a summary of the keys it contains so that it is possible to avoid unnecessary file scanning to search for a key.

As noted earlier, Cassandra builds on the concepts designed in Dynamo and Bigtable and puts them together to achieve a completely distributed and highly reliable storage system. The largest Cassandra deployment to our knowledge manages 100 TB of data distributed over a cluster of 150 machines.

Hadoop HBase. HBase is the distributed database that supports the storage needs of the Hadoop distributed programming platform. HBase is designed by taking inspiration from Google Bigtable; its main goal is to offer real-time read/write operations for tables with billions of rows and millions of columns by leveraging clusters of commodity hardware. The internal architecture and logic model of HBase is very similar to Google Bigtable, and the entire system is backed by the Hadoop Distributed File System (HDFS), which mimics the structure and services of GFS.

In this section, we discussed the storage solutions that support the management of data-intensive applications, especially those referred as *Big Data*. Traditionally, database systems, most likely based on the relational model, have been the primary solution for handling large quantities of data. As we discussed, when it comes to extremely huge quantities of unstructured data, relational databases become impractical and provide poor performance. Alternative and more effective solutions have significantly reviewed the fundamental concepts at the base of distributed file systems and storage systems. The next level comprises providing programming platforms that, by leveraging the discussed storage systems, can capitalize on developers' efforts to handle massive amounts of data. Among them, MapReduce and all its variations play a fundamental role.

8.2.2 Programming platforms

Platforms for programming data-intensive applications provide abstractions that help express the computation over a large quantity of information and runtime systems able to efficiently manage huge volumes of data. Traditionally, database management systems based on the relational model have been used to express the structure and connections between the entities of a data model. This approach has proven unsuccessful in the case of Big Data, where information is mostly found unstructured or semistructured and where data are most likely to be organized in files of large size or a huge number of medium-sized files rather than rows in a database. Distributed workflows have often been used to analyze and process large amounts of data [66,67]. This approach introduced a plethora of frameworks for workflow management systems, as discussed in Section 7.2.4, which

---

[10]A *gossip protocol* is a style of communication protocol inspired by the form of gossip seen in social networks. Gossip protocols are used in distributed systems as an alternative to distributed and propagate information that is efficient compared to flooding or other kinds of algorithms.

eventually incorporated capabilities to leverage the elastic features offered by cloud computing [70]. These systems are fundamentally based on the abstraction of a *task*, which puts a big burden on the developer, who needs to deal with data management and, often, data transfer issues.

Programming platforms for data-intensive computing provide higher-level abstractions, which focus on the processing of data and move into the runtime system the management of transfers, thus making the data always available where needed. This is the approach followed by the MapReduce [55] programming platform, which expresses the computation in the form of two simple functions—map and reduce—and hides the complexities of managing large and numerous data files into the distributed file system supporting the platform. In this section, we discuss the characteristics of MapReduce and present some variations of it, which extend its capabilities for wider purposes.

8.2.2.1 The MapReduce programming model

MapReduce [55] is a programming platform Google introduced for processing large quantities of data. It expresses the computational logic of an application in two simple functions: *map* and *reduce*. Data transfer and management are completely handled by the distributed storage infrastructure (i.e., the Google File System), which is in charge of providing access to data, replicating files, and eventually moving them where needed. Therefore, developers no longer have to handle these issues and are provided with an interface that presents data at a higher level: as a collection of key-value pairs. The computation of MapReduce applications is then organized into a workflow of *map* and *reduce* operations that is entirely controlled by the runtime system; developers need only specify how the *map* and *reduce* functions operate on the key-value pairs.

More precisely, the MapReduce model is expressed in the form of the two functions, which are defined as follows:

$$map\ (k1, v1) \rightarrow list(k2, v2)$$
$$reduce(k2, list(v2)) \rightarrow list(v2)$$

The *map* function reads a key-value pair and produces a list of key-value pairs of different types. The *reduce* function reads a pair composed of a key and a list of values and produces a list of values of the same type. The types (*k1,v1,k2,v2*) used in the expression of the two functions provide hints as to how these two functions are connected and are executed to carry out the computation of a MapReduce job: The output of map tasks is aggregated together by grouping the values according to their corresponding keys and constitutes the input of *reduce* tasks that, for each of the keys found, reduces the list of attached values to a single value. Therefore, the input of a MapReduce computation is expressed as a collection of key-value pairs $<k1,v1>$, and the final output is represented by a list of values: *list(v2)*.

Figure 8.5 depicts a reference workflow characterizing MapReduce computations. As shown, the user submits a collection of files that are expressed in the form of a list of $<k1,v1>$ pairs and specifies the *map* and *reduce* functions. These files are entered into the distributed file system that supports MapReduce and, if necessary, partitioned in order to be the input of map tasks. Map tasks generate intermediate files that store collections of $<k2,\ list(v2)>$ pairs, and these files are saved into the distributed file system. The MapReduce runtime might eventually aggregate the values corresponding to the same keys. These files constitute the input of reduce tasks, which finally produce output files in the form of *list(v2)*. The operation performed by reduce tasks is generally expressed

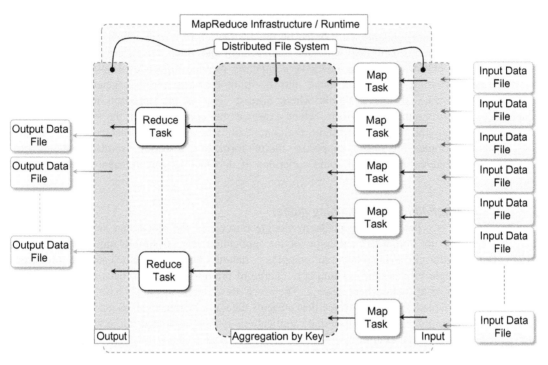

FIGURE 8.5

MapReduce computation workflow.

as an aggregation of all the values that are mapped by a specific key. The number of map and reduce tasks to create, the way files are partitioned with respect to these tasks, and the number of map tasks connected to a single reduce task are the responsibilities of the MapReduce runtime. In addition, the way files are stored and moved is the responsibility of the distributed file system that supports MapReduce.

The computation model expressed by MapReduce is very straightforward and allows greater productivity for people who have to code the algorithms for processing huge quantities of data. This model has proven successful in the case of Google, where the majority of the information that needs to be processed is stored in textual form and is represented by Web pages or log files. Some of the examples that show the flexibility of MapReduce are the following [55]:

- *Distributed grep.* The *grep* operation, which performs the recognition of patterns within text streams, is performed across a wide set of files. MapReduce is leveraged to provide a parallel and faster execution of this operation. In this case, the input file is a plain text file, and the *map* function emits a line into the output each time it recognizes the given pattern. The reduce task aggregates all the lines emitted by the map tasks into a single file.
- *Count of URL-access frequency.* MapReduce is used to distribute the execution of Web server log parsing. In this case, the *map* function takes as input the log of a Web server and emits into the output file a key-value pair $<URL,1>$ for each page access recorded in the log. The

reduce function aggregates all these lines by the corresponding URL, thus summing the single accesses, and outputs a < *URL, total-count* > pair.

- *Reverse Web-link graph.* The Reverse Web-link graph keeps track of all the possible Web pages that might lead to a given link. In this case input files are simple HTML pages that are scanned by map tasks emitting < *target, source* > pairs for each of the links found in the Web page *source*. The reduce task will collate all the pairs that have the same target into a < *target, list (source)* > pair. The final result is given one or more files containing these mappings.

- *Term vector per host.* A term vector recaps the most important words occurring in a set of documents in the form of *list(< word, frequency >)*, where the number of occurrences of a word is taken as a measure of its importance. MapReduce is used to provide a mapping between the origin of a set of document, obtained as the host component of the URL of a document, and the corresponding term vector. In this case, the map task creates a pair < *host, term-vector* > for each text document retrieved, and the reduce task aggregates the term vectors corresponding to documents retrieved from the same host.

- *Inverted index.* The inverted index contains information about the presence of words in documents. This information is useful to allow fast full-text searches compared to direct document scans. In this case, the map task takes as input a document, and for each document it emits a collection of < *word, document-id* > . The *reduce* function aggregates the occurrences of the same word, producing a pair < *word, list(document-id)* > .

- *Distributed sort.* In this case, MapReduce is used to parallelize the execution of a *sort* operation over a large number of records. This application mostly relies on the properties of the MapReduce runtime, which sorts and creates partitions of the intermediate files, rather than in the operations performed in the map and reduce tasks. Indeed, these are very simple: The map task extracts the key from a record and emits a < *key, record* > pair for each record; the reduce task will simply copy through all the pairs. The actual sorting process is performed by the MapReduce runtime, which will emit and partition the key-value pair by ordering them according to the key.

The reported example are mostly concerned with text-based processing. MapReduce can also be used, with some adaptation, to solve a wider range of problems. An interesting example is its application in the field of machine learning [97], where statistical algorithms such as *Support Vector Machines (SVM), Linear Regression (LR), Naïve Bayes (NB)*, and *Neural Network (NN)*, are expressed in the form of *map* and *reduce* functions. Other interesting applications can be found in the field of compute-intensive applications, such as the computation of Pi with a high degree of precision. It has been reported that the Yahoo! Hadoop cluster has been used to compute the $10^{15} + 1$ bit of Pi.[11] Hadoop is an open-source implementation of the MapReduce platform.

In general, any computation that can be expressed in the form of two major stages can be represented in the terms of MapReduce computation. These stages are:

- *Analysis.* This phase operates directly on the data input file and corresponds to the operation performed by the map task. Moreover, the computation at this stage is expected to be embarrassingly parallel, since map tasks are executed without any sequencing or ordering.

---

[11]The full details of this computation can be found in the Yahoo! Developer Network blog in the following blog post: http://developer.yahoo.com/blogs/hadoop/posts/2009/05/hadoop_computes_the_10151st_bi/.

- *Aggregation.* This phase operates on the intermediate results and is characterized by operations that are aimed at aggregating, summing, and/or elaborating the data obtained at the previous stage to present the data in their final form. This is the task performed by the *reduce* function.

Adaptations to this model are mostly concerned with identifying the appropriate keys, creating reasonable keys when the original problem does not have such a model, and finding ways to partition the computation between *map* and *reduce* functions. Moreover, more complex algorithms can be decomposed into multiple MapReduce programs, where the output of one program constitutes the input of the following program.

The abstraction proposed by MapReduce provides developers with a very minimal interface that is strongly focused on the algorithm to implement rather than the infrastructure on which it is executed. This is a very effective approach, but at the same time it demands a lot of common tasks, which are of concern in the management of a distributed application to the MapReduce runtime, allowing the user to specify only configuration parameters to control the behavior of applications. These tasks are managing data transfer and scheduling map and reduce tasks over a distributed infrastructure. Figure 8.6 gives a more complete overview of a MapReduce infrastructure, according to the implementation proposed by Google [55].

As depicted, the user submits the execution of MapReduce jobs by using the client libraries that are in charge of submitting the input data files, registering the *map* and *reduce* functions, and returning control to the user once the job is completed. A generic distributed infrastructure (i.e., a cluster) equipped with job-scheduling capabilities and distributed storage can be used to run MapReduce applications. Two different kinds of processes are run on the distributed infrastructure: a master process and a worker process.

The master process is in charge of controlling the execution of map and reduce tasks, partitioning, and reorganizing the intermediate output produced by the map task in order to feed the reduce tasks. The worker processes are used to host the execution of map and reduce tasks and provide basic I/O facilities that are used to interface the map and reduce tasks with input and output files. In a MapReduce computation, input files are initially divided into splits (generally 16 to 64 MB) and stored in the distributed file system. The master process generates the map tasks and assigns input splits to each of them by balancing the load.

Worker processes have input and output buffers that are used to optimize the performance of map and reduce tasks. In particular, output buffers for map tasks are periodically dumped to disk to create intermediate files. Intermediate files are partitioned using a user-defined function to evenly split the output of map tasks. The locations of these pairs are then notified to the master process, which forwards this information to the reduce tasks, which are able to collect the required input via a remote procedure call in order to read from the map tasks' local storage. The key range is then sorted and all the same keys are grouped together. Finally, the reduce task is executed to produce the final output, which is stored in the global file system. This process is completely automatic; users may control it through configuration parameters that allow specifying (besides the *map* and *reduce* functions) the number of map tasks, the number of partitions into which to separate the final output, and the *partition* function for the intermediate key range.

Besides orchestrating the execution of map and reduce tasks as previously described, the MapReduce runtime ensures a reliable execution of applications by providing a fault-tolerant

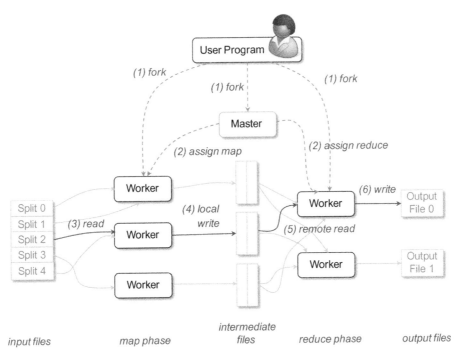

FIGURE 8.6

Google MapReduce infrastructure overview.

infrastructure. Failures of both master and worker processes are handled, as are machine failures that make intermediate outputs inaccessible. Worker failures are handled by rescheduling map tasks somewhere else. This is also the technique that is used to address machine failures since the valid intermediate output of map tasks has become inaccessible. Master process failure is instead addressed using checkpointing, which allows restarting the MapReduce job with a minimum loss of data and computation.

8.2.2.2 Variations and extensions of MapReduce

MapReduce constitutes a simplified model for processing large quantities of data and imposes constraints on the way distributed algorithms should be organized to run over a MapReduce infrastructure. Although the model can be applied to several different problem scenarios, it still exhibits limitations, mostly due to the fact that the abstractions provided to process data are very simple, and complex problems might require considerable effort to be represented in terms of *map* and *reduce* functions only. Therefore, a series of extensions to and variations of the original MapReduce model have been proposed. They aim at extending the MapReduce application space and providing developers with an easier interface for designing distributed algorithms. In this section, we briefly present a collection of MapReduce-like frameworks and discuss how they differ from the original MapReduce model.

Hadoop. Apache Hadoop [83] is a collection of software projects for reliable and scalable distributed computing. Taken together, the entire collection is an open-source implementation of the MapReduce framework supported by a GFS-like distributed file system. The initiative consists of mostly two projects: Hadoop Distributed File System (HDFS) and Hadoop MapReduce. The former is an implementation of the Google File System [54]; the latter provides the same features and abstractions as Google MapReduce. Initially developed and supported by Yahoo!, Hadoop now constitutes the most mature and large data cloud application and has a very robust community of developers and users supporting it. Yahoo! now runs the world's largest Hadoop cluster, composed of 40,000 machines and more than 300,000 cores, made available to academic institutions all over the world. Besides the core projects of Hadoop, a collection of other projects related to it provides services for distributed computing.

Pig. Pig[12] is a platform that allows the analysis of large datasets. Developed as an Apache project, Pig consists of a high-level language for expressing data analysis programs, coupled with infrastructure for evaluating these programs. The Pig infrastructure's layer consists of a compiler for a high-level language that produces a sequence of MapReduce jobs that can be run on top of distributed infrastructures such as Hadoop. Developers can express their data analysis programs in a textual language called *Pig Latin*, which exposes a SQL-like interface and is characterized by major expressiveness, reduced programming effort, and a familiar interface with respect to MapReduce.

Hive. Hive[13] is another Apache initiative that provides a data warehouse infrastructure on top of Hadoop MapReduce. It provides tools for easy data summarization, *ad hoc* queries, and analysis of large datasets stored in Hadoop MapReduce files. Whereas the framework provides the same capabilities as a classical data warehouse, it does not exhibit the same performance, especially in terms of query latency, and for this reason does not constitute a valid solution for online transaction processing. Hive's major advantages reside in the ability to scale out, since it is based on the Hadoop framework, and in the ability to provide a data warehouse infrastructure in environments where there is already a Hadoop system running.

Map-Reduce-Merge. Map-Reduce-Merge [98] is an extension of the MapReduce model, introducing a third phase to the standard MapReduce pipeline—the Merge phase—that allows efficiently merging data already partitioned and sorted (or hashed) by map and reduce modules. The Map-Reduce-Merge framework simplifies the management of heterogeneous related datasets and provides an abstraction able to express the common relational algebra operators as well as several join algorithms.

Twister. Twister [99] is an extension of the MapReduce model that allows the creation of iterative executions of MapReduce jobs. With respect to the normal MapReduce pipeline, the model proposed by Twister proposes the following extensions:

1. Configure Map
2. Configure Reduce

---

[12]http://pig.apache.org/.
[13]http://hive.apache.org/.

3. While Condition Holds True Do
   a. Run MapReduce
   b. Apply Combine Operation to Result
   c. Update Condition
4. Close

Besides the iterative MapReduce computation, Twister provides additional features such as the ability for *map* and *reduce* tasks to refer to static and in-memory data; the introduction of an additional phase called *combine*, run at the end of the MapReduce job, that aggregates the output together; and other tools for management of data.

8.2.2.3 *Alternatives to MapReduce*

MapReduce, other abstractions provide support for processing large datasets and execute data-intensive workloads. To different extents, these alternatives exhibit some similarities to the MapReduce approach.

Sphere. Sphere [84] is the distributed processing engine that leverages the Sector Distributed File System (SDFS). Rather than being a variation of MapReduce, Sphere implements the stream processing model (*Single Program, Multiple Data*) and allows developers to express the computation in terms of *user-defined functions (UDFs)*, which are run against the distributed infrastructure. A specific combination of UDFs allows Sphere to express MapReduce computations. Sphere strongly leverages the Sector distributed file systems, and it is built on top of Sector's API for data access. UDFs are expressed in terms of programs that read and write streams. A *stream* is a data structure that provides access to a collection of data segments mapping one or more files in the SDFS. The collective execution of UDFs is achieved through the distributed execution of *Sphere Process Engines (SPEs)*, which are assigned with a given stream segment. The execution model is a master-slave model that is client controlled; a Sphere client sends a request for processing to the master node, which returns the list of available slaves, and the client will choose the slaves on which to execute Sphere processes and orchestrate the entire distributed execution.

All-Pairs. All-Pairs [100] is an abstraction and a runtime environment for the optimized execution of data-intensive workloads. It provides a simple abstraction—in terms of the *All-pairs* function—that is common in many scientific computing domains:

$$All\text{-}pairs(A\text{:}set, B\text{:}set, F\text{:}function) \rightarrow M\text{:}matrix$$

Examples of problems that can be represented in this model can be found in the field of biometrics, where similarity matrices are composed as a result of the comparison of several images that contain subject pictures. Another example is several applications and algorithms in data mining. The model expressed by the *All-pairs* function can be easily solved by the following algorithm:

1. For each $i in A
2. For each $j in B
3. Submit job F $i $j

This implementation is quite naïve and produces poor performance in general. Moreover, other problems, such as data distribution, dispatch latency, number of available compute nodes, and probability of failure, are not handled specifically. The All-Pairs model tries to address these issues by introducing a specification for the nature of the problem and an engine that, according to this specification, optimizes the distribution of tasks over a conventional cluster or grid infrastructure. The execution of a distributed application is controlled by the engine and develops in four stages: (1) model the system; (2) distribute the data; (3) dispatch batch jobs; and (4) clean up the system. The interesting aspect of this model is mostly concentrated on the first two phases, where the performance model of the system is built and the data are opportunistically distributed in order to create the optimal number of tasks to assign to each node and optimize the utilization of the infrastructure.

DryadLINQ. Dryad [101] is a Microsoft Research project that investigates programming models for writing parallel and distributed programs to scale from a small cluster to a large datacenter. Dryad's aim is to provide an infrastructure for automatically parallelizing the execution of applications without requiring the developer to know about distributed and parallel programming.

In Dryad, developers can express distributed applications as a set of sequential programs that are connected by means of channels. More precisely, a Dryad computation can be expressed in terms of a directed acyclic graph in which nodes are the sequential programs and vertices represent the channels connecting such programs. Because of this structure, Dryad is considered a superset of the MapReduce model, since its general application model allows expressing graphs representing MapReduce computation as well. An interesting feature exposed by Dryad is the capability of supporting dynamic modification of the graph (to some extent) and of partitioning, if possible, the execution of the graph into stages. This infrastructure is used to serve different applications and tools for parallel programming. Among them, DryadLINQ [102] is a programming environment that produces Dryad computations from the Language Integrated Query (LINQ) extensions to C# [103]. The resulting framework provides a solution that is completely integrated into the .NET framework and able to express several distributed computing models, including MapReduce.

8.3 Aneka MapReduce programming

Aneka provides an implementation of the MapReduce abstractions by following the reference model introduced by Google and implemented by Hadoop. MapReduce is supported as one of the available programming models that can be used to develop distributed applications.

8.3.1 Introducing the MapReduce programming model

The *MapReduce Programming Model* defines the abstractions and runtime support for developing MapReduce applications on top of Aneka. Figure 8.7 provides an overview of the infrastructure supporting MapReduce in Aneka. A MapReduce job in Google MapReduce or Hadoop corresponds to the execution of a MapReduce application in Aneka. The application instance is specialized, with components that identify the *map* and *reduce* functions to use. These functions are expressed in terms of *Mapper* and *Reducer* classes that are extended from the Aneka MapReduce APIs. The runtime support is composed of three main elements:

- *MapReduce Scheduling Service*, which plays the role of the master process in the Google and Hadoop implementation
- *MapReduce Execution Service*, which plays the role of the worker process in the Google and Hadoop implementation
- A specialized distributed file system that is used to move data files

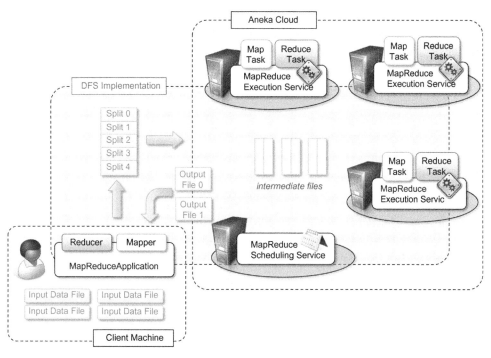

FIGURE 8.7

Aneka MapReduce infrastructure.

Client components, namely the *MapReduceApplication*, are used to submit the execution of a MapReduce job, upload data files, and monitor it. The management of data files is transparent: local data files are automatically uploaded to Aneka, and output files are automatically downloaded to the client machine if requested.

In the following sections, we introduce these major components and describe how they collaborate to execute MapReduce jobs.

8.3.1.1 Programming abstractions

Aneka executes any piece of user code within the context of a distributed application. This approach is maintained even in the MapReduce programming model, where there is a natural mapping between the concept of a MapReduce job—used in Google MapReduce and Hadoop—and the Aneka application concept. Unlike other programming models, the task creation is not the responsibility of the user but of the infrastructure once the user has defined the *map* and *reduce* functions. Therefore, the Aneka MapReduce APIs provide developers with base classes for developing *Mapper* and *Reducer* types and use a specialized type of application class—*MapReduceApplication*—that better supports the needs of this programming model.

Figure 8.8 provides an overview of the client components defining the MapReduce programming model. Three classes are of interest for application development: *Mapper<K,V>*, *Reducer<K,V>*, and *MapReduceApplication<M,R>*. The other classes are internally used to implement all the functionalities required by the model and expose simple interfaces that require minimum amounts of coding for implementing the *map* and *reduce* functions and controlling the job submission. *Mapper<K,V>* and *Reducer<K,V>* constitute the starting point of the application design and implementation. Template specialization is used to keep track of keys and values types on which these two functions operate. Generics provide a more natural approach in terms of object manipulation from within the *map* and *reduce* methods and simplify the programming by removing the necessity of casting and other type check operations. The submission and execution of a MapReduce job is performed through the class *MapReduceApplication<M,R>*, which provides the interface to the Aneka Cloud to support the MapReduce programming model. This class exposes two generic types: *M* and *R*. These two placeholders identify the specific types of *Mapper<K,V>* and *Reducer<K,V>* that will be used by the application.

Listing 8.1 shows in detail the definition of the *Mapper<K,V>* class and of the related types that developers should be aware of for implementing the *map* function. To implement a specific mapper, it is necessary to inherit this class and provide actual types for key *K* and the value *V*. The *map* operation is implemented by overriding the abstract method *void Map(IMapInput<K,V> input)*, while the other methods are internally used by the framework. *IMapInput<K,V>* provides access to the input key-value pair on which the *map* operation is performed.

Listing 8.2 shows the implementation of the *Mapper<K,V>* component for the Word Counter sample. This sample counts the frequency of words in a set of large text files. The text files are divided into lines, each of which will become the value component of a key-value pair, whereas the key will be represented by the offset in the file where the line begins. Therefore, the mapper is specialized by using a *long integer* as the key type and a *string* for the value. To count the frequency of words, the *map* function will emit a new key-value pair for each word contained in the line by using the word as the key and the number 1 as the value. This implementation will emit two pairs for the same word if the word occurs twice in the line. It will be the responsibility of the reducer to appropriately sum all these occurrences.

Listing 8.3 shows the definition of the *Reducer<K,V>* class. The implementation of a specific reducer requires specializing the generic class and overriding the abstract method: *Reduce (IReduceInputEnumerator<V> input)*. Since the *reduce* operation is applied to a collection of values that are mapped to the same key, the *IReduceInputEnumerator<V>* allows developers to iterate over such collections. Listing 8.4 shows how to implement the reducer function for the word-counter example.

In this case the *Reducer<K,V>* class is specialized using a *string* as a key type and an *integer* as a value. The reducer simply iterates over all the values that are accessible through the enumerator and sums them. Once the iteration is completed, the sum is dumped to file.

It is important to note that there is a link between the types used to specialize the mapper and those used to specialize the reducer. The key and value types used in the reducer are those defining the key-value pair emitted by the mapper. In this case the mapper generates a key-value pair *(string,int)*; hence the reducer is of type *Reducer< string,int >*.

The *Mapper<K,V>* and *Reducer<K,V>* classes provide facilities for defining the computation performed by a MapReduce job. To submit, execute, and monitor its progress, Aneka provides

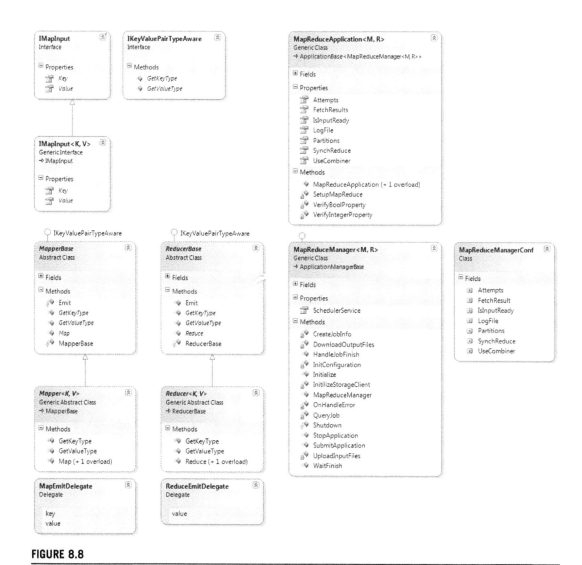

FIGURE 8.8

MapReduce Abstractions Object Model.

the *MapReduceApplication* < *M,R* > class. As happens for the other programming models introduced in this book, this class represents the local view of distributed applications on top of Aneka. Due to the simplicity of the MapReduce model, such class provides limited facilities that are mostly concerned with starting the MapReduce job and waiting for its completion. Listing 8.5 shows the interface of *MapReduceApplication* < *M,R* > .

The interface of the class exhibits only the MapReduce-specific settings, whereas the control logic is encapsulated in the *ApplicationBase* < *M* > class. From this class it is possible set the

```
using Aneka.MapReduce.Internal;

namespaceAneka.MapReduce
{
    /// <summary>
    /// Interface IMapInput<K,V>. Extends IMapInput and provides a strongly-
    /// typed version of the extended interface.
    /// </summary>
    public interface IMapInput<K,V>: IMapInput
    {
        /// <summary>
        /// Property <i>Key</i> returns the key of key/value pair.
        /// </summary>
        K Key { get; }
        /// <summary>
        /// Property <i>Value</i> returns the value of key/value pair.
        /// </summary>
        V Value { get; }
    }

    /// <summary>
    /// Delegate MapEmitDelegate. Defines the signature of a method
    /// that is used to doEmit intermediate results generated by the mapper.
    /// </summary>
    /// <param name="key">The <i>key</i> of the <i>key-value</i> pair.</param>
    /// <param name="value">The <i>value</i> of the <i>key-value</i> pair.</param>
    public delegate void MapEmitDelegate(object key, object value);

    /// <summary>
    /// Class Mapper. Extends MapperBase and provides a reference implementation that
    /// can be further extended in order to define the specific mapper for a given
    /// application. The definition of a specific mapper class only implies the
    /// implementation of the Mapper<K,V>.Map(IMapInput<K,V>) method.
    /// </summary>
    public abstract class Mapper<K,V> : MapperBase
    {
        /// <summary>
        /// Emits the intermediate result source by using doEmit.
        /// </summary>
        /// <param name="source">An instance implementing IMapInput containing the
        /// <i>key-value</i> pair representing the intermediate result.</param>
        /// <param name="doEmit">A MapEmitDelegate instance that is used to write to the
        /// output stream the information about the output of the Map operation.</param>
        public void Map(IMapInput input, MapEmitDelegate emit) { … }
        /// <summary>
        /// Gets the type of the <i>key</i> component of a <i>key-value</i> pair.
        /// </summary>
        /// <returns>A Type instance containing the metadata about the type of the
        /// <i>key</i>.</returns>
        public override Type GetKeyType(){ return typeof(K); }
```

LISTING 8.1

Map Function APIs.

```
    /// <summary>
    /// Gets the type of the <i>value</i> component of a <i>key-value</i> pair.
    /// </summary>
    /// <returns>A Type instance containing the metadata about the type of the
    /// <i>value</i>.</returns>
    public overrideType GetValueType(){ return typeof(V); }

    #region Template Methods
    /// <summary>
    /// Function Map is overrided by users to define a map function.
    /// </summary>
    /// <param name="source">The source of Map function is IMapInput, which contains
    /// a key/value pair.</param>
    protected abstract void Map(IMapInput<K, V> input);
    #endregion
    }
}
```

LISTING 8.1
_____

(Continued)

behavior of MapReduce for the current execution. The parameters that can be controlled are the following:

- *Partitions.* This property stores an integer number containing the number of partitions into which to divide the final results. This value also determines the number of reducer tasks that will be created by the runtime infrastructure. The default value is 10.
- *Attempts.* This property contains the number of times that the runtime will retry to execute a task before declaring it failed. The default value is 3.
- *UseCombiner.* This property stores a Boolean value that indicates whether the MapReduce runtime should add a combiner phase to the map task execution in order to reduce the number of intermediate files that are passed to the reduce task. The default value is set to *true.*
- *SynchReduce.* This property stores a Boolean value that indicates whether to synchronize the reducers or not. The default value is set to *true* and currently is not used to determine the behavior of MapReduce.
- *IsInputReady.* This is a Boolean property that indicates whether the input files are already stored in the distributed file system or must be uploaded by the client manager before the job can be executed. The default value is set to *false.*
- *FetchResults.* This is a Boolean property that indicates whether the client manager needs to download to the local computer the result files produced by the execution of the job. The default value is set to *true.*
- *LogFile.* This property contains a string defining the name of the log file used to store the performance statistics recorded during the execution of the MapReduce job. The default value is *mapreduce.log.*

The core control logic governing the execution of a MapReduce job resides within the *MapReduceApplicationManager* < *M,R* >, which interacts with the MapReduce runtime.

```
using Aneka.MapReduce;

namespace Aneka.MapReduce.Examples.WordCounter
{
    /// <summary>
    /// Class WordCounterMapper. Extends Mapper<K,V> and provides an
    /// implementation of the map function for the Word Counter sample. This mapper
    /// emits a key-value pair (word,1) for each word encountered in the input line.
    /// </summary>
    public class WordCounterMapper: Mapper<long,string>
    {
        /// <summary>
        /// Reads the source and splits into words. For each of the words found
        /// emits the word as a key with a vaue of 1.
        /// </summary>
        /// <param name="source">map source</param>
        protected override void Map(IMapInput<long,string> input)
        {
            // we don't care about the key, because we are only interested on
            // counting the word of each line.
            string value = input.Value;

            string[] words = value.Split(" \t\n\r\f\"\'!!-=()[]<>:{}.#".ToCharArray(),
                                          StringSplitOptions.RemoveEmptyEntries);

            // we emit each word without checking for repetitions. The word becomes
            // the key and the value is set to 1, the reduce operation will take care
            // of merging occurrences of the same word and summing them.
            foreach(string word in words)
            {
                this.Emit(word, 1);
            }
        }
    }
}
```

LISTING 8.2

Simple *Mapper< K,V>* Implementation.

Developers can control the application by using the methods and the properties exposed by the *ApplicationBase < M >* class. Listing 8.6 displays the collection of methods that are of interest in this class for the execution of MapReduce jobs.

Besides the constructors and the common properties that are of interest for all the applications, the two methods in bold in Listing 8.6 are those that are most commonly used to execute MapReduce jobs. These are two different overloads of the *InvokeAndWait* method: the first one simply starts the execution of the MapReduce job and returns upon its completion; the second one executes a client-supplied callback at the end of the execution. The use of *InvokeAndWait* is blocking; therefore, it is not possible to stop the application by calling *StopExecution* within the same thread. If it is necessary to implement a more sophisticated management of the MapReduce job, it

```
using Aneka.MapReduce.Internal;
namespace Aneka.MapReduce
{
    /// <summary>
    /// Delegate ReduceEmitDelegate. Defines the signature of a method
    /// that is used to emit aggregated value of a collection of values matching the
    /// same key and that is generated by a reducer.
    /// </summary>
    /// <param name="value">The <i>value</i> of the <i>key-value</i> pair.</param>
    public delegate void ReduceEmitDelegate(object value);

    /// <summary>
    /// Class <i>Reducer</i>. Extends the ReducerBase class and provides an

    /// implementation of the common operations that are expected from a <i>Reducer</i>.
    /// In order to define reducer for specific applications developers have to extend
    /// implementation of the Reduce(IReduceInputEnumerator<V>) method that reduces a
    /// this class and provide an collection of <i>key-value</i> pairs as described by
    /// the <i>map-reduce</i> model.
    /// </summary>
    public abstract class Reducer<K,V> : ReducerBase
    {
        /// <summary>
        /// Performs the <i>reduce</i> phase of the <i>map-reduce</i> model.
        /// </summary>
        /// <param name="source">An instance of IReduceInputEnumerator allowing to
        /// iterate over the collection of values that have the same key and will be
        /// aggregated.</param>
        /// <param name="emit">An instance of the ReduceEmitDelegate that is used to
        /// write to the output stream the aggregated value.</param>
        public void Reduce(IReduceInputEnumerator input, ReduceEmitDelegate emit) { … }
        /// <summary>
        /// Gets the type of the <i>key</i> component of a <i>key-value</i> pair.
        /// </summary>
        /// <returns>A Type instance containing the metadata about the type of the
        /// <i>key</i>.</returns>
        public override Type GetKeyType(){return typeof(K);}
        /// <summary>
        /// Gets the type of the <i>value</i> component of a <i>key-value</i> pair.
        /// </summary>
        /// <returns>A Type instance containing the metadata about the type of the
        /// <i>value</i>.</returns>
        public override Type GetValueType(){return typeof(V);}

        #region Template Methods
        /// <summary>
        /// Recuces the collection of values that are exposed by
        /// <paramref name="source"/> into a single value. This method implements the
        /// <i>aggregation</i> phase of the <i>map-reduce</i> model, where multiple
        /// values matching the same key are composed together to generate a single
        /// value.
        /// </summary>
        /// <param name="source">AnIReduceInputEnumerator<V> instancethat allows to
        /// iterate over all the values associated with same key.</param>
        protected abstract void Reduce(IReduceInputEnumerator<V> input);
        #endregion
    }
}
```

LISTING 8.3

Reduce Function APIs.

```
using Aneka.MapReduce;

namespace Aneka.MapReduce.Examples.WordCounter
{
    /// <summary>
    /// Class <b><i>WordCounterReducer</i></b>. Reducer implementation for the Word
    /// Counter application. The Reduce method iterates all over values of the
    /// enumerator and sums the values before emitting the sum to the output file.
    /// </summary>
    public class WordCounterReducer: Reducer<string,int>
    {
        /// <summary>
        /// Iterates all over the values of the enumerator and sums up
        /// all the values before emitting the sum to the output file.
        /// </summary>
        /// <param name="source">reduce source</param>
        protected override void Reduce(IReduceInputEnumerator<int>input)
        {
            int sum = 0;

            while(input.MoveNext())
            {
                int value = input.Current;
                sum += value;
            }
            this.Emit(sum);
        }
    }
}
```

LISTING 8.4

Simple *Reducer< K,V >* Implementation.

is possible to use the *SubmitExecution* method, which submits the execution of the application and returns without waiting for its completion.

In terms of management of files, the MapReduce implementation will automatically upload all the files that are found in the *Configuration.Workspace* directory and will ignore the files added by the *AddSharedFile* methods.

Listing 8.7 shows how to create a MapReduce application for running the word-counter example defined by the previous *WordCounterMapper* and *WordCounterReducer* classes.

The lines of interest are those put in evidence in the *try { ... } catch { ... } finally { ...}* block. As shown, the execution of a MapReduce job requires only three lines of code, where the user reads the configuration file, creates a *MapReduceApplication< M,R >* instance and configures it, and then starts the execution. All the rest of the code is mostly concerned with setting up the logging and handling exceptions.

8.3.1.2 Runtime support

The runtime support for the execution of MapReduce jobs comprises the collection of services that deal with scheduling and executing MapReduce tasks. These are the *MapReduce Scheduling*

```
using Aneka.MapReduce.Internal;

namespace Aneka.MapReduce
{
    /// <summary>
    /// Class <b><i>MapReduceApplication</i></b>. Defines a distributed application
    /// based on the MapReduce Model. It extends the ApplicationBase<M> and specializes
    /// it with the MapReduceManager<M,R> application manager. A MapReduceApplication is
    /// a generic type that is parameterized with a specific type of MapperBase and a
    /// specific type of ReducerBase. It controls the execution of the application and
    /// it is in charge of collecting the results or resubmitting the failed tasks.
    /// </summary>
    /// <typeparam name="M">Placeholder for the mapper type.</typeparam>
    /// <typeparam name="R">Placeholder for the reducer type.</typeparam>
    public class MapReduceApplication<M, R> : ApplicationBase<MapReduceManager<M, R>>
          where M: MapReduce.Internal.MapperBase
          where R: MapReduce.Internal.ReducerBase
    {
        /// <summary>
        /// Default value for the Attempts property.
        /// </summary>
        public const intDefaultRetry = 3;
        /// <summary>
        /// Default value for the Partitions property.
        /// </summary>
        public const intDefaultPartitions = 10;
        /// <summary>
        /// Default value for the LogFile property.
        /// </summary>
        public const stringDefaultLogFile = "mapreduce.log";

        /// <summary>
        /// List containing the result files identifiers.
        /// </summary>
        private List<string>resultFiles = new List<string>();
        /// <summary>
        /// Property group containing the settings for the MapReduce application.
        /// </summary>
        private PropertyGroupmapReduceSetup;

        /// <summary>
        /// Gets, sets an integer representing the number of partions for the key space.
        /// </summary>
        public int Partitions { get { … } set { … } }
        /// <summary>
        /// Gets, sets an boolean value indicating in whether to combine the result
        /// after the map phase in order to decrease the number of reducers used in the
        /// reduce phase.
        /// </summary>
        public bool UseCombiner { get { … } set { … } }
        /// <summary>
        /// Gets, sets an boolean indicating whether to synchronize the reduce phase.
        /// </summary>
        public bool SynchReduce { get { … } set { … } }
```

LISTING 8.5

MapReduceApplication < M,R>.

```
/// <summary>
/// Gets or sets a boolean indicating whether the source files required by the
/// required by the application is already uploaded in the storage or not.
/// </summary>
public bool IsInputReady { get { … } set { … } }
/// <summary>
/// Gets, sets the number of attempts that to run failed tasks.
/// </summary>
public int Attempts { get { … } set { … } }
/// <summary>
/// Gets or sets a string value containing the path for the log file.
/// </summary>
public string LogFile { get { … } set { … } }
/// <summary>
/// Gets or sets a boolean indicating whether application should download the
/// result files on the local client machine at the end of the execution or not.
/// </summary>
public bool FetchResults { get { … } set { … } }

/// <summary>
/// Creates a MapReduceApplication<M,R> instance and configures it with
    /// the given configuration.
/// </summary>
/// <param name="configuration">A Configuration instance containing the
/// information that customizes the execution of the application.</param>
public MapReduceApplication(Configurationconfiguration) :
                    base("MapReduceApplication", configuration){ … }
/// <summary>
/// Creates MapReduceApplication<M,R> instance and configures it with
/// the given configuration.
/// </summary>
/// <param name="displayName">A string containing the friendly name of the
/// application.</param>
/// <param name="configuration">A Configuration instance containing the
/// information that customizes the execution of the application.</param>
public MapReduceApplication(string displayName, Configuration configuration) :
                    base(displayName, configuration) { … }

// here follows the private implementation…
    }
  }
```

LISTING 8.5

(Continued)

Service and the *MapReduce Execution Service*. These two services integrate with the existing services of the framework in order to provide persistence, application accounting, and the features available for the applications developed with other programming models.

Job and Task Scheduling. The scheduling of jobs and tasks is the responsibility of the *MapReduce Scheduling Service*, which covers the same role as the master process in the Google MapReduce implementation. The architecture of the Scheduling Service is organized into two major components: the *MapReduceSchedulerService* and the *MapReduceScheduler*. The former is a wrapper around the scheduler, implementing the interfaces Aneka requires to expose a software

```
Namespace Aneka.Entity
{
    /// <summary>
    /// Class <b><i>ApplicationBase<M></i></b>. Defines the base class for the
    /// application instances for all the programming model supported by Aneka.
    /// </summary>
    public class ApplicationBase<M> where M : IApplicationManager, new()
    {
        /// <summary>
        /// Gets the application unique identifier attached to this instance. The
        /// application unique identifier is the textual representation of a System.Guid
        /// instance, therefore is a globally unique identfier. This identifier is
        /// automatically created when a new instance of an application is created.
        /// </summary>
        public string Id { get { … } }
        /// <summary>
        /// Gets the unique home directory for the AnekaApplication<W,M>.
        /// </summary>
        public string Home { get { … } }
        /// <summary>
        /// Gets the current state of the application.
        /// </summary>
        public ApplicationState State{get{ … }}
        /// <summary>
        /// Gets a boolean value indicating whether the application is terminated.
        /// </summary>
        public bool Finished { get { … } }

        /// <summary>
        /// Gets the underlying IApplicationManager that ismanaging the execution of the
        /// application instanceon the client side.
        /// </summary>
        public M ApplicationManager { get { … } }

        /// <summary>
        /// Gets, sets the application display name. This is a friendly name which is
        ///    /// to identify an application by means of a textual and human intelligible
        ///    /// sequence of characters, but it is NOT a unique identifier and no check about
        ///    /// uniqueness of the value of this property is done. For a unique indentifier
        ///    /// please check the Id property.
        /// </summary>
        public string DisplayName { get { … } set { … } }

        /// <summary>
        /// Occurs when the application instance terminates its execution.
        /// </summary>
        public event EventHandler<ApplicationEventArgs> ApplicationFinished;

        /// <summary>
        /// Creates an application instance with the given settings and sets the
        ///    /// application display name to null.
        /// </summary>
        /// <param name="configuration">Configuration instance specifying the
        ///    /// application settings.</param>
        public ApplicationBase(Configuration configuration): this(null, configuration)
```

LISTING 8.6

ApplicationBase < M>.

```
{ … }
/// <summary>
/// Creates an application instance withthe given settings and display name. As
      /// a result of the invocation, a new application unique identifier is created
      /// and the underlying application manager is initialized.
/// </summary>
/// <param name="configuration">Configurationinstance specifying the application
      /// settings.</param>
/// <param name="displayName">Application friendly name.</param>
public ApplicationBase(string displayName, Configuration configuration){ … }
/// <summary>
/// Starts the execution of the application instanceon Aneka.
/// </summary>
public void SubmitExecution() { … }
/// <summary>
/// Stops the execution of the entire application instance.
/// </summary>
public void StopExecution() { … }
/// <summary>
/// Invoke the application and wait until the application finishes.
/// </summary>
public void InvokeAndWait() { this.InvokeAndWait(null); }
/// <summary>
/// Invoke the application and wait until the application finishes, then invokes
      /// the given callback.
/// </summary>
/// <param name="handler">A pointer to a method that is executed at the end of
/// the application.</param>
public void InvokeAndWait(EventHandler<ApplicationEventArgs> handler) { … }


/// <summary>
      /// Adds a shared file to the application.
/// </summary>
/// <param name="file">A string containing the path to the file to add.</param>
public virtual void AddSharedFile(string file) { … }
/// <summary>
      /// Adds a shared file to the application.
/// </summary>
/// <param name="file">A FileData instance containing the information about the
/// file to add.</param>
public virtual void AddSharedFile(FileData fileData) { … }
/// <summary>
      /// Removes a file from the list of the shared files of the application.
      /// </summary>
      /// <param name="file"> A string containing the path to the file to
/// remove.</param>
public virtual void RemoveSharedFile(string filePath) { … }

      // here come the private implementation.

   }

}
```

LISTING 8.6

(Continued)

```
using System.IO;
using Aneka.Entity;
using Aneka.MapReduce;

namespace Aneka.MapReduce.Examples.WordCounter
{
    /// <summary>
    /// Class <b><i>Program<M></i></b>. Application driver for the Word Counter sample.
    /// </summary>
    public class Program
    {
        /// <summary>
        /// Reference to the configuration object.
        /// </summary>
        private static Configuration configuration = null;
    /// <summary>
    /// Location of the configuration file.
    /// </summary>
    private static string confPath = "conf.xml";

    /// <summary>
    /// Processes the arguments given to the application and according
    /// to the parameters read runs the application or shows the help.
    /// </summary>
    /// <param name="args">program arguments</param>
    private static void Main(string[] args)
    {
        try
        {
            Logger.Start();

            // get the configuration
            configuration = Configuration.GetConfiguration(confPath);

            // configure MapReduceApplication
            MapReduceApplication<WordCountMapper, WordCountReducer> application =
                new MapReduceApplication<WordCountMapper, WordCountReducer>
                    ("WordCounter",  configuration);
            // invoke and wait for result
            application.InvokeAndWait(new
                                        EventHandler<ApplicationEventArgs>(OnDone));

                // alternatively we can use the following call
                // application.InvokeAndWait();
        }
        catch(Exception ex)
        {
            Usage();
            IOUtil.DumpErrorReport(ex, "Aneka WordCounter Demo - Error Log");
        }
        finally
        {
            Logger.Stop();
        }
```

LISTING 8.7

WordCounter Job.

```
        }
        /// <summary>
        /// Hooks the ApplicationFinished events and Process the results
        /// if the application has been successful.
        /// </summary>
        /// <param name="sender">event source</param>
        /// <param name="e">event information</param>
        private static void OnDone(object sender, ApplicationEventArgs e) { ... }
        /// <summary>
        /// Displays a simple informative message explaining the usage of the
        /// application.
        /// </summary>
        private static void Usage() { ... }
    }
}
```

LISTING 8.7

(Continued)

component as a service; the latter controls the execution of jobs and schedules tasks. Therefore, the main role of the service wrapper is to translate messages coming from the Aneka runtime or the client applications into calls or events directed to the scheduler component, and vice versa. The relationship of the two components is depicted in Figure 8.9.

The core functionalities for job and task scheduling are implemented in the *MapReduceScheduler* class. The scheduler manages multiple queues for several operations, such as uploading input files into the distributed file system; initializing jobs before scheduling; scheduling map and reduce tasks; keeping track of unreachable nodes; resubmitting failed tasks; and reporting execution statistics. All these operations are performed asynchronously and triggered by events happening in the Aneka middleware.

Task Execution. The execution of tasks is controlled by the *MapReduce Execution Service*. This component plays the role of the worker process in the Google MapReduce implementation. The service manages the execution of map and reduce tasks and performs other operations, such as sorting and merging intermediate files. The service is internally organized, as described in Figure 8.10.

There are three major components that coordinate together for executing tasks: *MapReduce-SchedulerService*, *ExecutorManager*, and *MapReduceExecutor*. The *MapReduceSchedulerService* interfaces the *ExecutorManager* with the Aneka middleware; the *ExecutorManager* is in charge of keeping track of the tasks being executed by demanding the specific execution of a task to the *MapReduceExecutor* and of sending the statistics about the execution back to the Scheduler Service. It is possible to configure more than one *MapReduceExecutor* instance, and this is helpful in the case of multicore nodes, where more than one task can be executed at the same time.

8.3.1.3 Distributed file system support

Unlike the other programming models Aneka supports, the MapReduce model does not leverage the default Storage Service for storage and data transfer but uses a distributed file system implementation. The reason for this is because the requirements in terms of file management are significantly different with respect to the other models. In particular, MapReduce has been designed to

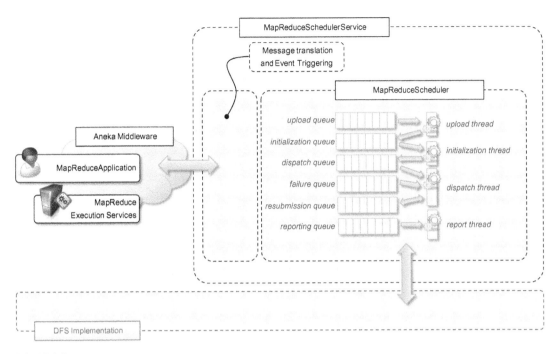

FIGURE 8.9

MapReduce Scheduling Service architecture.

process large quantities of data stored in files of large dimensions. Therefore, the support provided by a distributed file system, which can leverage multiple nodes for storing data, is more appropriate. Distributed file system implementations guarantee high availability and better efficiency by means of replication and distribution. Moreover, the original MapReduce implementation assumes the existence of a distributed and reliable storage; hence, the use of a distributed file system for implementing the storage layer is natural.

Aneka provides the capability of interfacing with different storage implementations, as described in Chapter 5 (Section 5.2.3), and it maintains the same flexibility for the integration of a distributed file system. The level of integration required by MapReduce requires the ability to perform the following tasks:

- Retrieving the location of files and file chunks
- Accessing a file by means of a stream

The first operation is useful to the scheduler for optimizing the scheduling of *map* and *reduce* tasks according to the location of data; the second operation is required for the usual I/O operations to and from data files. In a distributed file system, the stream might also access the network if the file chunk is not stored on the local node. Aneka provides interfaces that allow performing such operations and the capability to plug different file systems behind them by providing the appropriate implementation. The current implementation provides bindings to HDFS.

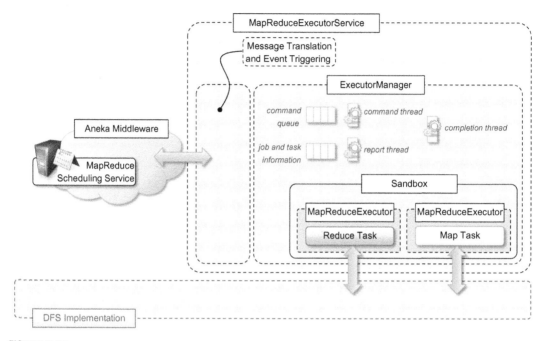

FIGURE 8.10

MapReduce Execution Service architecture.

On top of these low-level interfaces, the MapReduce programming model offers classes to read from and write to files in a sequential manner. These are the classes *SeqReader* and *SeqWriter*. They provide sequential access for reading and writing key-value pairs, and they expect a specific file format, which is described in Figure 8.11.

An Aneka MapReduce file is composed of a header, used to identify the file, and a sequence of record blocks, each storing a key-value pair. The header is composed of 4 bytes: the first 3 bytes represent the character sequence *SEQ* and the fourth byte identifies the version of the file. The record block is composed as follows: the first 8 bytes are used to store two integers representing the length of the rest of the block and the length of the key section, which is immediately following. The remaining part of the block stores the data of the value component of the pair. The *SeqReader* and *SeqWriter* classes are designed to read and write files in this format by transparently handling the file format information and translating key and value instances to and from their binary representation. All the .NET built-in types are supported. Since MapReduce jobs operate very often with data represented in common text files, a specific version of the *SeqReader* and *SeqWriter* classes have been designed to read and write text files as a sequence of key-value pairs. In the case of the read operation, each value of the pair is represented by a line in the text file, whereas the key is automatically generated and assigned to the position in bytes where the line starts in the file. In the write operation, the writing of the key is skipped and the values are saved as single lines.

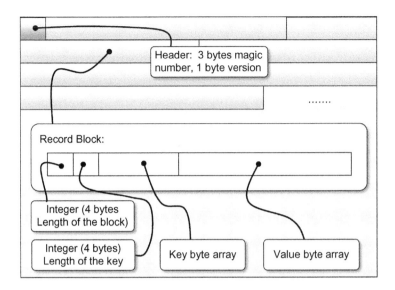

FIGURE 8.11

Aneka MapReduce data file format.

Listing 8.8 shows the interface of the *SeqReader* and *SeqWriter* classes. The *SeqReader* class provides an enumerator-based approach through which it is possible to access the key and the value sequentially by calling the *NextKey()* and the *NextValue()* methods, respectively. It is also possible to access the raw byte data of keys and values by using the *NextRawKey()* and *NextRawValue()*. *HasNext()* returns a Boolean, indicating whether there are more pairs to read or not. The *SeqWriter* class exposes different versions of the *Append* method.

Listing 8.9 shows a practical use of the *SeqReader* class by implementing the callback used in the word-counter example. To visualize the results of the application, we use the *SeqReader* class to read the content of the output files and dump it into a proper textual form that can be visualized with any text editor, such as the Notepad application.

The *OnDone* callback checks to see whether the application has terminated successfully. If there are no errors, it iterates over the result files downloaded in the workspace output directory. By default, the files are saved in the *output* subdirectory of the workspace directory. For each of the result files, it opens a *SeqReader* instance on it and dumps the content of the key-value pair into a text file, which can be opened by any text editor.

8.3.2 Example application

MapReduce is a very useful model for processing large quantities of data, which in many cases are maintained in a semistructured form, such as logs or Web pages. To demonstrate how to program real applications with Aneka MapReduce, we consider a very common task: log parsing. We design a MapReduce application that processes the logs produced by the Aneka container in order to extract some summary information about the behavior of the Cloud. In this section, we describe in

```
using Aneka.MapReduce.Common;

namespace Aneka.MapReduce.DiskIO
{
    /// <summary>
    /// Class <b><i>SeqReader</i></b>. This class implements a file reader for the sequence
    /// file, which isa standard file split used by MapReduce.NET to store a partition of a
    ///    /// fixed size of a data file. This classprovides an interface for exposing the content
    /// of a file split as an enumeration of key-value pairs and offersfacilities for both
     /// accessing keys and values as objects and their corresponding binary values.
    /// </summary>
    public class SeqReader
    {
        /// <summary>
        /// Creates a SeqReader instance and attaches it to the given file. This constructor
        /// initializes the instance with the default value for the internal buffers and does
        /// not set any information about the types of the keys and values read from the
        /// file.
        /// </summary>
        public SeqReader(string file) : this(file, null, null) { … }
        /// <summary>
        /// Creates a SeqReader instance, attaches it to the given file, and sets the
        /// internal buffer size to bufferSize. This constructor does not provide any
        /// information about the types of the keys and values read from the file.
        /// </summary>
        public SeqReader(string file, int bufferSize) : this(file,null,null,bufferSize) { … }
        /// <summary>
        /// Creates a SeqReader instance, attaches it to the given file, and provides
        /// metadata information about the content of the file in the form of keyType and
        /// valueType. The internal buffers are initialized with the default dimension.
        /// </summary>
        public SeqReader(string file, Type keyType, Type valueType)
            : this(file, keyType, valueType, SequenceFile.DefaultBufferSize) { … }
        /// <summary>
        /// Creates a SeqReader instance, attaches it to the given file, and provides
        /// metadata information about the content of the file in the form of keyType and
        /// valueType. The internal buffers are initialized with the bufferSize dimension.
        /// </summary>
        public SeqReader(string file, Type keyType, Type valueType, int bufferSize){ … }
        /// <summary>
        /// Sets the metadata information about the keys and the values contained in the data
        /// file.
        /// </summary>
        public void SetType(Type keyType, Type valueType) { … }
        /// <summary>
        /// Checks whether there is another record in the data file and moves the current
        /// file pointer to its beginning.
        /// </summary>
        public bool HaxNext() { … }
        /// <summary>
        /// Gets the object instance corresponding to the next key in the data file.
        /// in the data file.
        /// </summary>
        public object NextKey() { … }
```

LISTING 8.8

SeqReader and *SeqWriter* Classes.

```
        /// <summary>
        /// Gets the object instance corresponding to the next value in the data file.
        /// in the data file.
        /// </summary>
        public object NextValue() { … }
        /// <summary>
        /// Gets the raw bytes that contain the value of the serializedinstance of the
        /// current key.
        /// </summary>
        public BufferInMemory NextRawKey() { … }
        /// <summary>
        /// Gets the raw bytes that contain the value of the serialized instance of the
        /// current value.
        /// </summary>
        public BufferInMemory NextRawValue() { … }

        /// <summary>
        /// Gets the position of the file pointer as an offset from its beginning.
        /// </summary>
        public long CurrentPosition() { … }
        /// <summary>
        /// Gets the size of the file attached to this instance of SeqReader.
        /// </summary>
        public long StreamLength() { … }
        /// <summary>
        /// Moves the file pointer to position. If the value of position is 0 or negative,
        /// returns the current position of the file pointer.
        /// </summary>
        public long Seek(long position) { … }
        /// <summary>
        /// Closes the SeqReader instanceand releases all the resources that have been
        /// allocated to read fromthe file.
        /// </summary>
        public void Close() { … }

        // private implementation follows
    }

/// <summary>
/// Class SeqWriter. This class implements a file writer for the sequence
/// sequence file, which is a standard file split used by MapReduce.NET to store a
/// partition of a fixed size of a data file. This classprovides an interface to add a
/// sequence of key-value pair incrementally.
/// </summary>
public class SeqWriter
{

        /// <summary>
        /// Creates a SeqWriter instance for writing to file. This constructor initializes
        /// the instance with the default value for the internal buffers.
        /// </summary>
        public SeqWriter(string file) : this(file, SequenceFile.DefaultBufferSize){ … }
        /// <summary>
        /// Creates a SeqWriter instance, attachesit to the given file, and sets the
        /// internal buffer size to bufferSize.
        /// </summary>
        public SeqWriter(string file, int bufferSize) { … }
```

LISTING 8.8

(Continued)

```
/// <summary>
/// Appends a key-value pair to the data file split.
/// </summary>
public void Append(object key, object value) { … }
/// <summary>
/// Appends a key-value pair to the data file split.
/// </summary>
public void AppendRaw(byte[] key, byte[] value) { … }
/// <summary>
/// Appends a key-value pair to the data file split.
/// </summary>
public void AppendRaw(byte[] key, int keyPos, int keyLen,
                      byte[] value, int valuePos, int valueLen) { … }


/// <summary>
/// Gets the length of the internal buffer or 0 if no buffer has been allocated.
/// </summary>
public longLength() { … }
/// <summary>
/// Gets the length of data file split on disk so far.
/// </summary>
public long FileLength() { … }
/// <summary>
/// Closes the SeqReader instance and releases all the resources that have been
/// allocated to write to the file.
/// </summary>
public void Close() { … }

// private implementation follows
    }
}
```

LISTING 8.8

(Continued)

detail the problem to be addressed and design the *Mapper* and *Reducer* classes that are used to execute log-parsing and data extraction operations.

8.3.2.1 Parsing Aneka logs

Aneka components (daemons, container instances, and services) produce a lot of information that is stored in the form of log files. The most relevant information is stored in the container instances logs, which store the information about the applications that are executed on the Cloud. In this example, we parse these logs to extract useful information about the execution of applications and the usage of services in the Cloud.

The entire framework leverages the *log4net* library for collecting and storing the log information. In Aneka containers, the system is configured to produce a log file that is partitioned into chunks every time the container instance restarts. Moreover, the information contained in the log file can be customized in its appearance. Currently the default layout is the following:

DD MMM YY hh:mm:ss level − message

```
using System.IO;
using Aneka.Entity;
using Aneka.MapReduce;

namespace Aneka.MapReduce.Examples.WordCounter
{
    /// <summary>
    /// Class Program. Application driver for the Word Counter sample.
    /// </summary>
    public class Program
    {
        /// <summary>
        /// Reference to the configuration object.
        /// </summary>
        private static Configuration configuration = null;
        /// <summary>
        /// Location of the configuration file.
        /// </summary>
        private static string confPath = "conf.xml";

        /// <summary>
        /// Processes the arguments given to the application and according
        /// to the parameters read runs the application or shows the help.
        /// </summary>
        /// <param name="args">program arguments</param>
        private static void Main(string[] args)
        {
            try
            {
                Logger.Start();

                // get the configuration
                Program.configuration = Configuration.GetConfiguration(confPath);

                // configure MapReduceApplication
                MapReduceApplication<WordCountMapper, WordCountReducer> application =
                    new MapReduceApplication<WordCountMapper, WordCountReducer>("WordCounter",
configuration);
                // invoke and wait for result
                application.InvokeAndWait(newEventHandler<ApplicationEventArgs>(OnDone));

                    // alternatively we can use the following call
                    // application.InvokeAndWait();
            }
            catch(Exception ex)
            {
                Program.Usage();
                IOUtil.DumpErrorReport(ex, "Aneka WordCounter Demo - Error Log");
            }
            finally
            {
                Logger.Stop();
            }
        }
    }
```

LISTING 8.9

WordCounter Job.

```
/// <summary>
/// Hooks the ApplicationFinished events and process the results
/// if the application has been successful.
/// </summary>
/// <param name="sender">event source</param>
/// <param name="e">event information</param>
private static void OnDone(object sender, ApplicationEventArgs e)
{
    if (e.Exception != null)
    {
        IOUtil.DumpErrorReport(e.Exception, "Aneka WordCounter Demo - Error");
    }
    else
    {
        string outputDir = Path.Combine(configuration.Workspace, "output");
        try
        {
            FileStream resultFile = new FileStream("WordResult.txt",FileMode.Create,
                                                        FileAccess.Write);
            Stream WritertextWriter = new StreamWriter(resultFile);

            DirectoryInfo sources = new DirectoryInfo(outputDir);
            FileInfo[] results = sources.GetFiles();
            foreach(FileInfo result in results)
            {
                SeqReader seqReader = newSeqReader(result.FullName);
                seqReader.SetType(typeof(string), typeof(int));

                while(seqReader.HaxNext() == true)
                {
                    object key = seqReader.NextKey();
                    object value = seqReader.NextValue();

                    textWriter.WriteLine("{0}\t{1}", key, value);
                }

                seqReader.Close();
            }
            textWriter.Close();
            resultFile.Close();

            // clear the output directory
            sources.Delete(true);

            Program.StartNotePad("WordResult.txt");
        }
        catch(Exception ex)
        {
            IOUtil.DumpErrorReport(e.Exception, "Aneka WordCounter Demo - Error");
        }
    }
}
```

LISTING 8.9

(Continued)

```
/// <summary>
/// Starts the notepad process and displays the given file.
/// </summary>
private static voidStartNotepad(string file) { … }
/// <summary>
/// Displays a simple informative message explaining the usage of the
/// application.
/// </summary>
private static void Usage() { … }
    }
}
```

LISTING 8.9

(Continued)

Some examples of formatted log messages are:

15 Mar 2011 10:30:07 DEBUG—SchedulerService: …
HandleSubmitApplication—SchedulerService: …
15 Mar 2011 10:30:07 INFO—SchedulerService: Scanning candidate storage …
15 Mar 2011 10:30:10 INFO—Added [WU: 51d55819-b211-490f-b185-8a25734ba705,
4e86fd02…
15 Mar 2011 10:30:10 DEBUG—StorageService:NotifyScheduler—Sending
FileTransferMessage…
15 Mar 2011 10:30:10 DEBUG—IndependentSchedulingService:QueueWorkUnit—Queueing…
15 Mar 2011 10:30:10 INFO—AlgorithmBase::AddTasks[64] Adding 1 Tasks
15 Mar 2011 10:30:10 DEBUG—AlgorithmBase:FireProvisionResources—Provision
Resource: 1

In the content of the sample log lines, we observe that the message parts of almost all the log lines exhibit a similar structure, and they start with the information about the component that enters the log line. This information can be easily extracted by looking at the first occurrence of the : character following a sequence of characters that do not contain spaces.

Possible information that we might want to extract from such logs is the following:

- The distribution of log messages according to the level
- The distribution of log messages according to the components

This information can be easily extracted and composed into a single view by creating *Mapper* tasks that count the occurrences of log levels and component names and emit one simple key-value pair in the form *(level-name, 1)* or *(component-name, 1)* for each of the occurrences. The *Reducer* task will simply sum up all the key-value pairs that have the same key. For both problems, the structure of the *map* and *reduce* functions will be the following:

$$map: (long, \ string) = > (string, \ long)$$
$$reduce: (string, \ long) = > (string, long)$$

The *Mapper* class will then receive a key-value pair containing the position of the line inside the file as a key and the log message as the value component. It will produce a key-value pair containing a string representing the name of the log level or the component name and 1 as value. The *Reducer* class will sum up all the key-value pairs that have the same name. By modifying the canonical structure we discussed, we can perform both analyses at the same time instead of developing two different MapReduce jobs. Note that the operation performed by the *Reducer* class is the same in both cases, whereas the operation of the *Mapper* class changes, but the type of the key-value pair that is generated is the same for the two jobs. Therefore, it is possible to combine the two tasks performed by the *map* function into one single *Mapper* class that will produce two key-value pairs for each input line. Moreover, we can differentiate the name of Aneka components from the log-level names by using an initial underscore character it will be very easy to post-process the output of the *reduce* function in order to present and organize data.

8.3.2.2 Mapper design and implementation

The operation performed by the *map* function is a very simple text extraction that identifies the level of the logging and the name of the component entering the information in the log. Once this information is extracted, a key-value pair *(string, long)* is emitted by the function. Since we decided to combine the two MapReduce jobs into one single job, each *map* task will at most emit two key-value pairs. This is because some of the log lines do not record the name of the component that entered the line; for these lines, only the key-value pair corresponding to the log level will be emitted.

Listing 8.10 shows the implementation of the *Mapper* class for the log parsing task. The *Map* method simply locates the position of the log-level label into the line, extracts it, and emits a corresponding key-value pair *(label, 1)*. It then tries to locate the position of the name of the Aneka component that entered the log line by looking for a sequence of characters that is limited by a colon. If such a sequence does not contain spaces, it then represents the name of the Aneka component. In this case, another key-value pair *(component-name, 1)* is emitted. As already discussed, to differentiate the log-level labels from component names, an underscore is prefixed to the name of the key in this second case.

8.3.2.3 Reducer design and implementation

The implementation of the *reduce* function is even more straightforward; the only operation that needs to be performed is to add all the values that are associated to the same key and emit a key-value pair with the total sum. The infrastructure will already aggregate all the values that have been emitted for a given key; therefore, we simply need to iterate over the collection of values and sum them up.

As we see in Listing 8.11, the operation to perform is very simple and actually is the same for both of the two different key-value pairs extracted from the log lines. It will be the responsibility of the driver program to differentiate among the different types of information assembled in the output files.

8.3.2.4 Driver program

LogParsingMapper and *LogParsingReducer* constitute the core functionality of the *MapReduce* job, which only requires to be properly configured in the main program in order to process and produce text tiles. Moreover, since we have designed the mapper component to extract two different types of information, another task that is performed in the driver application is the separation of these two statistics into two different files for further analysis.

```
using Aneka.MapReduce;

namespace Aneka.MapReduce.Examples.LogParsing
{
    /// <summary>
    /// Class LogParsingMapper. Extends Mapper<K,V> and provides an
    /// implementation of the map function for parsing the Aneka container log files.
    /// This mapper emits a key-value (log-level, 1) and potentially another key-value
    /// (_aneka-component-name,1) if it is able to extract such information from the
    /// input.
    /// </summary>
    public class LogParsingMapper: Mapper<long,string>
    {
        /// <summary>
        /// Reads the input and extracts the information about the log level and if
        /// found the name of the aneka component that entered the log line.
        /// </summary>
        /// <param name="input">map input</param>
        protected override void Map(IMapInput<long,string>input)
        {
            // we don't care about the key, because we are only interested on
            // counting the word of each line.
            string value = input.Value;
            long quantity = 1;

            // first we extract the log level name information. Since the date is reported
            // in the standard format DD MMM YYYY mm:hh:ss it is possible to skip the first
            // 20 characters (plus one space) and then extract the next following characters
            // until the next position of the space character.
            int start = 21;
            int stop = value.IndexOf(' ', start);
            string key = value.Substring(start, stop - start);

            this.Emit(key, quantity);

            // now we are looking for the Aneka component name that entered the log line
            // if this is inside the log line it is just right after the log level preceeded
            // by the character sequence <space><dash><space> and terminated by the <c olon>
            // character.

            start = stop + 3; // we skip the <space><dash><space> sequence.
            stop = value.IndexOf(':', start);

            key = value.Substring(start, stop - start);

            // we now check whether the key contains any space, if not then it is the name
            // of an Aneka component and the line does not need to be skipped.
            if (key.IndexOf(' ') == -1)
            {
                this.Emit("_" + key, quantity);
            }
        }
    }
}
```

LISTING 8.10

Log-Parsing Mapper Implementation.

```
using Aneka.MapReduce;

namespace Aneka.MapReduce.Examples.LogParsing
{
    /// <summary>
    /// Class <b><i>LogParsingReducer</i></b>. Extends Reducer<K,V> and provides an
    /// implementation of the redcuce function for parsing the Aneka container log files .
    /// The Reduce method iterates all over values of the enumerator and sums the values
    /// before emitting the sum to the output file.
    /// </summary>
    public class LogParsingReducer : Reducer<string,long>
    {
        /// <summary>
        /// Iterates all over the values of the enumerator and sums up
        /// all the values before emitting the sum to the output file.
        /// </summary>
        /// <param name="input">reduce source</param>
        protected override void Reduce(IReduceInputEnumerator<long>input)
        {
            long sum = 0;

            while(input.MoveNext())
            {
                long value = input.Current;
                sum += value;
            }
            this.Emit(sum);
        }
    }
}
```

LISTING 8.11

Aneka Log-Parsing Reducer Implementation.

Listing 8.12 shows the implementation of the driver program. With respect to the previous examples, there are three things to be noted:

- The configuration of the *MapReduce* job
- The post-processing of the result files
- The management of errors

The configuration of the job is performed in the *Initialize* method. This method reads the configuration file from the local file system and ensures that the input and output formats of files are set to *text*. MapReduce jobs can be configured using a specific section of the configuration file named *MapReduce*. Within this section, two subsections control the properties of input and output files and are named *Input* and *Output*, respectively. The input and output sections may contain the following properties:

- *Format (string)* defines the format of the input file. If this property is set, the only supported value is *text*.

- *Filter (string)* defines the search pattern to be used to filter the input files to process in the workspace directory. This property only applies for the Output properties group.
- *NewLine (string)* defines the sequence of characters that is used to detect (or write) a new line in the text stream. This value is meaningful when the input/output format is set to *text* and the default value is selected from the execution environment if not set.
- *Separator (character)* property is only present in the *Output* section and defines the character that needs to be used to separate the key from the value in the output file. As with the previous property, this value is meaningful when the input/output format is set to *text*.

Besides the specific setting for input and output files, it is possible to control other parameters of a *MapReduce* job. These parameters are defined in the main *MapReduce* configuration section; their meaning was discussed in Section 8.3.1.

Instead of a programming approach for the initialization of the configuration, it is also possible to embed these settings into the standard Aneka configuration file, as demonstrated in Listing 8.13.

As demonstrated, it is possible to open a *< Group name = "MapReduce" > ... </Group>* tag and enter all the properties that are required for the execution. The Aneka configuration file is based on a flexible framework that allows simply entering groups of name-value properties. The *Aneka.Property* and *Aneka.PropertyGroup* classes also provide facilities for converting the strings representing the value of a property into a corresponding built-in type if possible. This simplifies the task of reading from and writing to configuration objects.

The second element shown in Listing 8.12 is represented by the post-processing of the output files. This operation is performed in the *OnDone* method, whose invocation is triggered either if an error occurs during the execution of the MapReduce job or if it completes successfully. This method separates the occurrences of log-level labels from the occurrences of Aneka component names by saving them into two different files, *loglevels.txt* and *components.txt*, under the workspace directory, and then deletes the output directory where the output files of the reduce phase have been downloaded. These two files contain the aggregated result of the analysis and can be used to extract statistic information about the content of the log files and display in a graphical manner, as shown in the next section.

A final aspect that can be considered is the management of errors. Aneka provides a collection of APIs that are contained in the *Aneka.Util* library and represent utility classes for automating tedious tasks such as the appropriate collection of stack trace information associated with an exception or information about the types of the exception thrown. In our example, the reporting features, which are triggered in case of exceptions, are implemented in the *ReportError* method. This method utilizes the facilities offered by the *IOUtil* class to dump a simple error report to both the console and a log file that is named using the following pattern: *error.YYYY-MM-DD_hh-mm-ss.log*.

8.3.2.5 Running the application

Aneka produces a considerable amount of logging information. The default configuration of the logging infrastructure creates a new log file for each activation of the Container process or as soon as the dimension of the log file goes beyond 10 MB. Therefore, by simply continuing to run an Aneka Cloud for a few days, it is quite easy to collect enough data to mine for our sample application. Moreover, this

```csharp
using System.IO;
using Aneka.Entity;
using Aneka.MapReduce;

namespace Aneka.MapReduce.Examples.LogParsing
{
    /// <summary>
    /// Class Program. Application driver. This class sets up the MapReduce
    /// job and configures it with the <i>LogParsingMapper</i> and <i>LogParsingReducer</i>
    /// classes. It also configures the MapReduce runtime in order sets the appropriate
    /// format for input and output files.
    /// </summary>
    public class Program
    {
        /// <summary>
        /// Reference to the configuration object.
        /// </summary>
        private static Configuration configuration = null;
        /// <summary>
        /// Location of the configuration file.
        /// </summary>
        private static string confPath = "conf.xml";

        /// <summary>
        /// Processes the arguments given to the application and according
        /// to the parameters read runs the application or shows the help.
        /// </summary>
        /// <param name="args">program arguments</param>
        private static void Main(string[] args)
        {
            try
            {
                Logger.Start();

                // get the configuration
                Program.configuration = Program.Initialize(confPath);
                // configure MapReduceApplication
                MapReduceApplication<LogParsingMapper, LogParsingReducer> application =
                 new MapReduceApplication<LogParsingMapper, LogParsingReducer>("LogParsing",
configuration);
                // invoke and wait for result
                application.InvokeAndWait(newEventHandler<ApplicationEventArgs>(OnDone));

                    // alternatively we can use the following call
                    // application.InvokeAndWait();
            }
            catch(Exception ex)
            {
                Program.ReportError(ex);
            }
            finally
            {
                Logger.Stop();
            }
```

LISTING 8.12

Driver Program Implementation.

```
        Console.Readline();
    }
/// <summary>
/// Initializes the configuration and ensures that the appropriate input
/// and output formats.are set
/// </summary>
/// <param name="configFile">A string containing the path to the config file.</param>
/// <returns>An instance of the configuration class.</returns>
private static Configuration Initialize(stringconfigFile)
{
    Configuration conf = Configuration.GetConfiguration(confPath);
    // we ensure that the input and the output formats are simple
    // text files.
    PropertyGroup mapReduce = conf["MapReduce"];
    if (mapReduce == null)
    {
        mapReduce = newPropertyGroup("MapReduce");
        conf.Add("MapReduce") = mapReduce;
    }
    // handling input properties
    PropertyGroup group = mapReduce.GetGroup("Input");
    if (group == null)
    {
        group = newPropertyGroup("Input");
        mapReduce.Add(group);
    }
    string val = group["Format"];
    if (string.IsNullOrEmpty(val) == true)
    {
        group.Add("Format","text");
    }
    val = group["Filter"];
    if (string.IsNullOrEmpty(val) == true)
    {
        group.Add("Filter","*.log");
    }
    // handling output properties
    group = mapReduce.GetGroup("Output");
    if (group == null)
    {
        group = newPropertyGroup("Output");
        mapReduce.Add(group);
    }
    val = group["Format"];
    if (string.IsNullOrEmpty(val) == true)
    {
        group.Add("Format","text");
    }
    return conf;
}

/// <summary>
/// Hooks the ApplicationFinished events and process the results
/// if the application has been successful.
```

LISTING 8.12

(Continued)

```
        /// </summary>
        /// <param name="sender">event source</param>
        /// <param name="e">event information</param>
        private static void OnDone(object sender, ApplicationEventArgs e)
        {
            if (e.Exception != null)
            {
                Program.ReportError(ex);
            }
            else
            {
                Console.Write("Aneka Log Parsing-Job Terminated: SUCCESS");

                FileStream logLevelStats = null;
                FileStream componentStats = null;
                string workspace = Program.configuration.Workspace;
                string outputDir = Path.Combine(workspace, "output");
                DirectoryInfo sources = new DirectoryInfo(outputDir);
                FileInfo[] results = sources.GetFiles();

                try
                {
                    logLevelStats = new FileStream(Path.Combine(workspace,"loglevels.txt"),

    FileMode.Create,FileAccess.Write));

                    componentStats = new FileStream(Path.Combine(workspace,"components.txt"),
                                                    FileMode.Create,
FileAccess.Write));
                    using(StreamWriter logWriter = new StreamWriter(logLevelStats))
                    {
                        using(StreamWritercompWriter = newStreamWriter(componentStats))
                        {
                            foreach(FileInfo result in results)
                            {
                                using(StreamReader reader =
                                    new StreamReader(result.OpenRead()))
                                {
                                    while(reader.EndOfStream == false)
                                    {
                                        string line = reader.ReadLine();
                                        if (line != null)
                                        {
                                            if (line.StartsWith("_") == true)
                                            {
                                                compWriter.WriteLine(line.Substring(1));
                                            }
                                            else
                                            {
                                                logWriter.WriteLine(line);
                                            }
                                        }
                                    }
                                }
                            }
                        }
                    }
```

LISTING 8.12

(Continued)

```
                // clear the output directory
                sources.Delete(true);

                Console.WriteLine("Statistics saved to:[loglevels.txt, components.txt]");

                    Environment.ExitCode = 0;
            }
            catch(Exception ex)
            {
                Program.ReportError(ex);
            }
            Console.WriteLine("<Press Return>");
        }
    }
    /// <summary>
    /// Displays a simple informative message explaining the usage of the


    /// application.
    /// </summary>
    private static void Usage()
    {
        Console.WriteLine("Aneka Log Parsing - Usage Log.Parsing.Demo.Console.exe"
        + " [conf.xml]");
    }
    /// <summary>
    /// Dumps the error to the console, sets the exit code of the application to -1
    /// and saves the error dump into a file.
    /// </summary>
    /// <param name="ex">runtime exception</param>
    private static void ReportError(Exception ex)
    {
        IOUtil.DumpErrorReport(Console.Out, ex,"Aneka Log Parsing-Job Terminated: "
                + "ERROR");
        IOUtil.DumpErrorReport(ex, "Aneka Log Parsing-Job Terminated: ERROR");
        Program.Usage();j
        Environment.ExitCode = -1;
    }
}
}
```

LISTING 8.12

(Continued)

scenario also constitutes a real case study for MapReduce, since one of its most common practical applications is extracting semistructured information from logs and traces of execution.

In the execution of the test, we used a distributed infrastructure consisting of seven worker nodes and one master node interconnected through a LAN. We processed 18 log files of several sizes for a total aggregate size of 122 MB. The execution of the MapReduce job over the collected data produced the results that are stored in the *loglevels.txt* and *components.txt* files and represented graphically in Figures 8.12 and 8.13, respectively.

```xml
<?xml version="1.0" encoding="utf-8" ?>
<Aneka>
  <UseFileTransfervalue="false" />
  <Workspacevalue="Workspace" />
  <SingleSubmissionvalue="AUTO" />
  <PollingTimevalue="1000"/>
  <LogMessagesvalue="false" />
  <SchedulerUrivalue="tcp://localhost:9090/Aneka" />
  <UserCredential type="Aneka.Security.UserCredentials" assembly="Aneka.dll">
    <UserCredentials username="Administrator" password=""/>
  </UserCredentials>
  <Groups>
    <Group name="MapReduce">
      <Groups>
        <Group name="Input">
        <Property name="Format" value="text" />
        <Property name="Filter" value="*.log" />
      </Group>
        <Group name="Output">
          <Property name="Format" value="text" />
        </Group>
      </Groups>
      <Property name="LogFile" value="Execution.log"/>
      <Property name="FetchResult" value="true" />
      <Property name="UseCombiner" value="true" />
      <Property name="SynchReduce" value="false" />
      <Property name="Partitions" value="1" />
      <Property name="Attempts" value="3" />
    </Group>
      </Groups>
  </Aneka>
```

LISTING 8.13

Driver Program Configuration File (conf.xml).

The two graphs show that there is a considerable amount of unstructured information in the log files produced by the Container processes. In particular, about 60% of the log content is skipped during the classification. This content is more likely due to the result of stack trace dumps into the log file, which produces—as a result of ERROR and WARN entries—a sequence of lines that are not recognized. Figure 8.13 shows the distribution among the components that use the logging APIs. This distribution is computed over the data recognized as a valid log entry, and the graph shows that just about 20% of these entries have not been recognized by the parser implemented in the *map* function. We can then infer that the meaningful information extracted from the log analysis constitutes about 32% (80% of 40% of the total lines parsed) of the entire log data.

Despite the simplicity of the parsing function implemented in the *map* task, this practical example shows how the Aneka MapReduce programming model can be used to easily perform massive data analysis tasks. The purpose of the case study was not to create a very refined parsing function but to demonstrate how to logically and programmatically approach a realistic data analysis case study with MapReduce and how to implement it on top of the Aneka APIs.

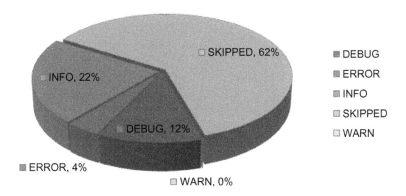

FIGURE 8.12

Log-level entries distribution.

SUMMARY

This chapter introduced the main characteristics of *data-intensive computing*. Data-intensive applications process or produce high volumes of data and may also exhibit compute-intensive properties. The amounts of data that have triggered the definition of data-intensive computation has changed over time, together with the technologies and the programming and storage models used for data-intensive computing. Data-intensive computing is a field that was originally prominent in high-speed WAN applications. It is now the domain of storage clouds, where the dimensions of data reach the size of terabytes, if not petabytes, and are referred to as *Big Data*. This term identifies the massive amount of information that is produced, processed, and mined, not only by scientific applications but also by companies providing Internet services, such as search, online advertising, social media, and social networking.

One of the interesting characteristics of our Big Data world is that the data are represented in a semistructured or unstructured form. Therefore, traditional approaches based on relational databases are not capable of efficiently supporting data-intensive applications. New approaches and storage models have been investigated to address these challenges. In the context of storage systems, the most significant efforts have been directed toward the implementation of high-performance distributed file systems, storage clouds, and NoSQL-based systems. For the support of programming data-intensive applications, the most relevant innovation has been the introduction of MapReduce, together with all its variations aiming at extending the applicability of the proposed approach to a wider range of scenarios.

MapReduce was proposed by Google and provides a simple approach to processing large quantities of data based on the definition of two functions, *map* and *reduce*, that are applied to the data in a two-phase process. First, the *map* phase extracts the valuable information from the data and stores it in key-value pairs, which are eventually aggregated together in the *reduce* phase. This model, even though constraining, proves successful in several application scenarios.

We discussed the reference model of MapReduce as proposed by Google and provided pointers to relevant variations. We described the implementation of MapReduce in Aneka. Similar to thread

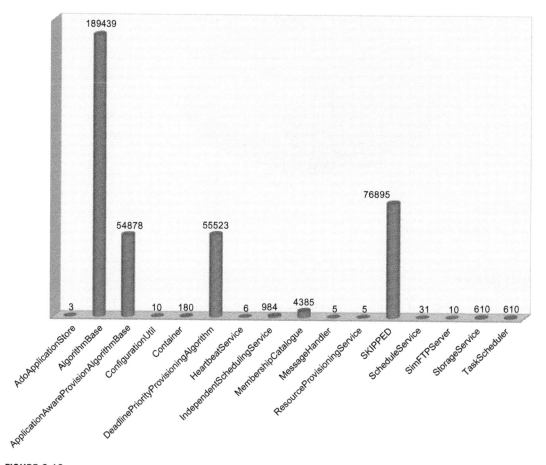

FIGURE 8.13

Component entries distribution.

and task programming models in Aneka, we discussed the programming abstractions supporting the design and implementation of MapReduce applications. We presented the structure and organization of Aneka's runtime services for the execution of MapReduce jobs. Finally, we included step-by-step examples of how to design and implement applications using Aneka MapReduce APIs.

Review questions

1. What is a data-intensive computing? Describe the characteristics that define this term.
2. Provide an historical perspective on the most important technologies that support data-intensive computing.

3. What are the characterizing features of so-called Big Data?

4. List some of the important storage technologies that support data-intensive computing and describe one of them.

5. Describe the architecture of the Google File System.

6. What does the term NoSQL mean?

7. Describe the characteristics of Amazon Simple Storage Service (S3).

8. What is Google Bigtable?

9. What are the requirements of a programming platform that supports data-intensive computations?

10. What is MapReduce?

11. Describe the kinds of problems MapReduce can solve and give some real examples.

12. List some of the variations on or extensions to MapReduce.

13. What are the major components of the Aneka MapReduce Programming Model?

14. How does the MapReduce model differ from the other models supported by Aneka and discussed in this book?

15. Describe the components of the Scheduling and Execution Services that constitute the runtime infrastructure supporting MapReduce.

16. Describe the architecture of the data storage layer designed for Aneka MapReduce and the I/O APIs for handling MapReduce files.

17. Design and implement a simple program that uses MapReduce for the computation of Pi.

Industrial Platforms and New Developments

Cloud Platforms in Industry

Cloud computing allows end users and developers to leverage large distributed computing infrastructures. This is made possible thanks to infrastructure management software and distributed computing platforms offering on-demand compute, storage, and, on top of these, more advanced services. There are several different options for building enterprise cloud computing applications or for using cloud computing technologies to integrate and extend existing industrial applications. An overview of a few prominent cloud computing platforms and a brief description of the types of service they offer are shown in Table 9.1. A cloud computing system can be developed using either a single technology and vendor or a combination of them.

This chapter presents some of the representative cloud computing solutions offered as Infrastructure-as-a-Service (IaaS) and Platform-as-a-Service (PaaS) services in the market. It provides some insights into and practical issues surrounding the architecture of the major cloud computing technologies and their service offerings.

9.1 Amazon web services

Amazon Web Services (AWS) is a platform that allows the development of flexible applications by providing solutions for elastic infrastructure scalability, messaging, and data storage. The platform is accessible through SOAP or RESTful Web service interfaces and provides a Web-based console where users can handle administration and monitoring of the resources required, as well as their expenses computed on a pay-as-you-go basis.

Figure 9.1 shows all the services available in the AWS ecosystem. At the base of the solution stack are services that provide raw compute and raw storage: *Amazon Elastic Compute (EC2)* and *Amazon Simple Storage Service (S3)*. These are the two most popular services, which are generally complemented with other offerings for building a complete system. At the higher level, *Elastic MapReduce* and *AutoScaling* provide additional capabilities for building smarter and more elastic computing systems. On the data side, *Elastic Block Store (EBS)*, *Amazon SimpleDB*, *Amazon RDS*, and *Amazon ElastiCache* provide solutions for reliable data snapshots and the management of structured and semistructured data. Communication needs are covered at the networking level by *Amazon Virtual Private Cloud (VPC)*, *Elastic Load Balancing*, *Amazon Route 53*, and *Amazon Direct Connect*. More advanced services for connecting applications are *Amazon Simple Queue*

Table 9.1 Some Example Cloud Computing Offerings

Vendor/Product	Service Type	Description
Amazon Web Services	IaaS, PaaS, SaaS	Amazon Web Services (AWS) is a collection of Web services that provides developers with compute, storage, and more advanced services. AWS is mostly popular for IaaS services and primarily for its elastic compute service EC2.
Google AppEngine	PaaS	Google AppEngine is a distributed and scalable runtime for developing scalable Web applications based on Java and Python runtime environments. These are enriched with access to services that simplify the development of applications in a scalable manner.
Microsoft Azure	PaaS	Microsoft Azure is a cloud operating system that provides services for developing scalable applications based on the proprietary Hyper-V virtualization technology and the .NET framework.
SalesForce.com and Force.com	SaaS, PaaS	SalesForce.com is a Software-as-a-Service solution that allows prototyping of CRM applications. It leverages the Force.com platform, which is made available for developing new components and capabilities for CRM applications.
Heroku	PaaS	Heroku is a scalable runtime environment for building applications based on Ruby.
RightScale	IaaS	Rightscale is a cloud management platform with a single dashboard to manage public and hybrid clouds.

Service (SQS), *Amazon Simple Notification Service (SNS)*, and *Amazon Simple E-mail Service (SES)*. Other services include:

- *Amazon CloudFront* content delivery network solution
- *Amazon CloudWatch* monitoring solution for several Amazon services
- *Amazon Elastic BeanStalk* and *CloudFormation* flexible application packaging and deployment

As shown, AWS comprise a wide set of services. We discuss the most important services by examining the solutions proposed by AWS regarding compute, storage, communication, and complementary services.

9.1.1 Compute services

Compute services constitute the fundamental element of cloud computing systems. The fundamental service in this space is Amazon EC2, which delivers an IaaS solution that has served as a reference model for several offerings from other vendors in the same market segment. Amazon EC2 allows deploying servers in the form of virtual machines created as instances of a specific image. Images come with a preinstalled operating system and a software stack, and instances can be configured for memory, number of processors, and storage. Users are provided with credentials to remotely access the instance and further configure or install software if needed.

9.1.1.1 Amazon machine images

Amazon Machine Images (AMIs) are templates from which it is possible to create a virtual machine. They are stored in Amazon S3 and identified by a unique identifier in the form of *ami-xxxxxx* and

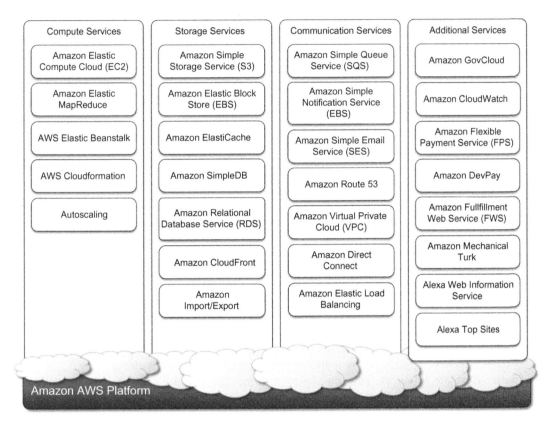

FIGURE 9.1

Amazon Web Services ecosystem.

a manifest XML file. An AMI contains a physical file system layout with a predefined operating system installed. These are specified by the *Amazon Ramdisk Image* (*ARI*, id: *ari-yyyyyy*) and the *Amazon Kernel Image* (*AKI*, id: *aki-zzzzzz*), which are part of the configuration of the template. AMIs are either created from scratch or "bundled" from existing EC2 instances. A common practice is to prepare new AMIs to create an instance from a preexisting AMI, log into it once it is booted and running, and install all the software needed. Using the tools provided by Amazon, we can convert the instance into a new image. Once an AMI is created, it is stored in an S3 bucket and the user can decide whether to make it available to other users or keep it for personal use. Finally, it is also possible to associate a product code with a given AMI, thus allowing the owner of the AMI to get revenue every time this AMI is used to create EC2 instances.

9.1.1.2 EC2 instances

EC2 instances represent virtual machines. They are created using AMI as templates, which are specialized by selecting the number of cores, their computing power, and the installed memory. The processing power is expressed in terms of virtual cores and EC2 Compute Units (ECUs). The ECU is a measure of the computing power of a virtual core; it is used to express a predictable quantity of real CPU power that is allocated to an instance. By using compute units instead of real frequency values, Amazon can change over time the mapping of such units to the underlying real amount of computing power allocated, thus keeping the performance of EC2 instances consistent with standards set by the times. Over time, the hardware supporting the underlying infrastructure will be replaced by more powerful hardware, and the use of ECUs helps give users a consistent view of the performance offered by EC2 instances. Since users rent computing capacity rather than buying hardware, this approach is reasonable. One ECU is defined as giving the same performance as a 1.0−1.2 GHz 2007 Opteron or 2007 Xeon processor.[1]

Table 9.2 shows all the currently available configurations for EC2 instances. We can identify six major categories:

- *Standard instances.* This class offers a set of configurations that are suitable for most applications. EC2 provides three different categories of increasing computing power, storage, and memory.
- *Micro instances.* This class is suitable for those applications that consume a limited amount of computing power and memory and occasionally need bursts in CPU cycles to process surges in the workload. Micro instances can be used for small Web applications with limited traffic.
- *High-memory instances.* This class targets applications that need to process huge workloads and require large amounts of memory. Three-tier Web applications characterized by high traffic are the target profile. Three categories of increasing memory and CPU are available, with memory proportionally larger than computing power.
- *High-CPU instances.* This class targets compute-intensive applications. Two configurations are available where computing power proportionally increases more than memory.
- *Cluster Compute instances.* This class is used to provide virtual cluster services. Instances in this category are characterized by high CPU compute power and large memory and an extremely high I/O and network performance, which makes it suitable for HPC applications.
- *Cluster GPU instances.* This class provides instances featuring graphic processing units (GPUs) and high compute power, large memory, and extremely high I/O and network performance. This class is particularly suited for cluster applications that perform heavy graphic computations, such as rendering clusters. Since GPU can be used for general-purpose computing, users of such instances can benefit from additional computing power, which makes this class suitable for HPC applications.

EC2 instances are priced hourly according to the category they belong to. At the beginning of every hour of usage, the user will be charged the cost of the entire hour. The hourly expense charged for one instance is constant. Instance owners are responsible for providing their own backup strategies, since there is no guarantee that the instance will run for the entire hour. Another alternative is represented by *spot instances.* These instances are much more dynamic in terms of pricing and lifetime since they are made available to the user according to the load of EC2 and the availability of resources. Users define an upper bound for a price they want to pay for these instances; as long as the current price (the spot price) remains under the given bound, the instance is kept running. The price is sampled at the beginning of each hour. Spot instances are more volatile than normal instances; whereas for normal instances EC2 will try as much as possible to keep

---

[1]http://aws.amazon.com/ec2/faqs/#What_is_an_EC2_Compute_Unit_and_why_did_you_introduce_it.

Table 9.2 Amazon EC2 (On-Demand) Instances Characteristics

Instance Type	ECU	Platform	Memory	Disk Storage	Price (U.S. East) (USD/hour)
Standard instances					
Small	1(1 × 1)	32 bit	1.7 GB	160 GB	$0.085 Linux $0.12 Windows
Large	4(2 × 2)	64 bit	7.5 GB	850 GB	$0.340 Linux $0.48 Windows
Extra Large	8(4 × 2)	64 bit	15 GB	1,690 GB	$0.680 Linux $0.96 Windows
Micro instances					
Micro	< = 2	32/64 bit	613 MB	EBS Only	$0.020 Linux $0.03 Windows
High-Memory instances					
Extra Large	6.5(2 × 3.25)	64 bit	17.1 GB	420 GB	$0.500 Linux $0.62 Windows
Double Extra Large	13(4 × 3.25)	64 bit	34.2 GB	850 GB	$1.000 Linux $1.24 Windows
Quadruple Extra Large	26(8 × 3.25)	64 bit	68.4 GB	1,690 GB	$2.000 Linux $2.48 Windows
High-CPU instances					
Medium	5(2 × 2.5)	32 bit	1.7 GB	350 GB	$0.170 Linux $0.29 Windows
Extra Large	20(8 × 2.5)	64 bit	7 GB	1,690 GB	$0.680 Linux $1.16 Windows
Cluster instances					
Quadruple Extra Large	33.5	64 bit	23 GB	1,690 GB	$1.600 Linux $1.98 Windows
Cluster GPU instances					
Quadruple Extra Large	33.5	64 bit	22 GB	1,690 GB	$2.100 Linux $2.60 Windows

them active, there is no such guarantee for spot instances. Therefore, implementing backup and checkpointing strategies is inevitable.

EC2 instances can be run either by using the command-line tools provided by Amazon, which connects the Amazon Web Service that provides remote access to the EC2 infrastructure, or via the AWS console, which allows the management of other services, such as S3. By default an EC2 instance is created with the kernel and the disk associated to the AMI. These define the architecture (32 bit or 64 bit) and the space of disk available to the instance. This is an ephemeral disk; once the instance is shut down, the content of the disk will be lost. Alternatively, it is possible to attach an EBS volume to the instance, the content of which will be stored in S3. If the default AKI and ARI are not suitable, EC2 provides capabilities to run EC2 instances by specifying a different AKI and ARI, thus giving flexibility in the creation of instances.

9.1.1.3 EC2 environment

EC2 instances are executed within a virtual environment, which provides them with the services they require to host applications. The EC2 environment is in charge of allocating addresses, attaching storage volumes, and configuring security in terms of access control and network connectivity.

By default, instances are created with an internal IP address, which makes them capable of communicating within the EC2 network and accessing the Internet as clients. It is possible to associate an *Elastic IP* to each instance, which can then be remapped to a different instance over time. Elastic IPs allow instances running in EC2 to act as servers reachable from the Internet and, since they are not strictly bound to specific instances, to implement failover capabilities. Together with an external IP, EC2 instances are also given a domain name that generally is in the form *ec2-xxx-xxx-xxx.compute-x.amazonaws.com*, where *xxx-xxx-xxx* normally represents the four parts of the external IP address separated by a dash, and *compute-x* gives information about the availability zone where instances are deployed. Currently, there are five availability zones that are priced differently: two in the United States (Virginia and Northern California), one in Europe (Ireland), and two in Asia Pacific (Singapore and Tokyo).

Instance owners can partially control where to deploy instances. Instead, they have a finer control over the security of the instances as well as their network accessibility. Instance owners can associate a key pair to one or more instances when these instances are created. A key pair allows the owner to remotely connect to the instance once this is running and gain root access to it. Amazon EC2 controls the accessibility of a virtual instance with basic firewall configuration, allowing the specification of source address, port, and protocols (TCP, UDP, ICMP). Rules can also be attached to security groups, and instances can be made part of one or more groups before their deployment. Security groups and firewall rules constitute a flexible way of providing basic security for EC2 instances, which has to be complemented by appropriate security configuration within the instance itself.

9.1.1.4 Advanced compute services

EC2 instances and AMIs constitute the basic blocks for building an IaaS computing cloud. On top of these, Amazon Web Services provide more sophisticated services that allow the easy packaging and deploying of applications and a computing platform that supports the execution of MapReduce-based applications.

AWS CloudFormation

AWS CloudFormation constitutes an extension of the simple deployment model that characterizes EC2 instances. CloudFormation introduces the concepts of *templates*, which are JSON formatted text files that describe the resources needed to run an application or a service in EC2 together with the relations between them. CloudFormation allows easily and explicitly linking EC2 instances together and introducing dependencies among them. Templates provide a simple and declarative way to build complex systems and integrate EC2 instances with other AWS services such as S3, SimpleDB, SQS, SNS, Route 53, Elastic Beanstalk, and others.

AWS elastic beanstalk

AWS Elastic Beanstalk constitutes a simple and easy way to package applications and deploy them on the AWS Cloud. This service simplifies the process of provisioning instances and deploying application code and provides appropriate access to them. Currently, this service is available only for Web applications developed with the Java/Tomcat technology stack. Developers can conveniently package their Web application into a WAR file and use Beanstalk to automate its deployment on the AWS Cloud.

With respect to other solutions that automate cloud deployment, Beanstalk simplifies tedious tasks without removing the user's capability of accessing—and taking over control of—the underlying EC2 instances that make up the virtual infrastructure on top of which the application is running. With respect to AWS CloudFormation, AWS Elastic Beanstalk provides a higher-level approach for application deployment on the cloud, which does not require the user to specify the infrastructure in terms of EC2 instances and their dependencies.

Amazon elastic MapReduce
Amazon Elastic MapReduce provides AWS users with a cloud computing platform for MapReduce applications. It utilizes Hadoop as the MapReduce engine, deployed on a virtual infrastructure composed of EC2 instances, and uses Amazon S3 for storage needs.

Apart from supporting all the application stack connected to Hadoop (Pig, Hive, etc.), Elastic MapReduce introduces elasticity and allows users to dynamically size the Hadoop cluster according to their needs, as well as select the appropriate configuration of EC2 instances to compose the cluster (Small, High-Memory, High-CPU, Cluster Compute, and Cluster GPU). On top of these services, basic Web applications allowing users to quickly run data-intensive applications without writing code are offered.

9.1.2 Storage services

AWS provides a collection of services for data storage and information management. The core service in this area is represented by Amazon *Simple Storage Service (S3)*. This is a distributed object store that allows users to store information in different formats. The core components of S3 are two: *buckets* and *objects*. Buckets represent virtual containers in which to store objects; objects represent the content that is actually stored. Objects can also be enriched with metadata that can be used to tag the stored content with additional information.

9.1.2.1 S3 key concepts
As the name suggests, S3 has been designed to provide a simple storage service that's accessible through a Representational State Transfer (REST) interface, which is quite similar to a distributed file system but which presents some important differences that allow the infrastructure to be highly efficient:

- *The storage is organized in a two-level hierarchy*. S3 organizes its storage space into buckets that cannot be further partitioned. This means that it is not possible to create directories or other kinds of physical groupings for objects stored in a bucket. Despite this fact, there are few limitations in naming objects, and this allows users to simulate directories and create logical groupings.
- *Stored objects cannot be manipulated like standard files*. S3 has been designed to essentially provide storage for objects that will not change over time. Therefore, it does not allow renaming, modifying, or relocating an object. Once an object has been added to a bucket, its

content and position is immutable, and the only way to change it is to remove the object from the store and add it again.

- *Content is not immediately available to users.* The main design goal of S3 is to provide an eventually consistent data store. As a result, because it is a large distributed storage facility, changes are not immediately reflected. For instance, S3 uses replication to provide redundancy and efficiently serve objects across the globe; this practice introduces latencies when adding objects to the store—especially large ones—which are not available instantly across the entire globe.
- *Requests will occasionally fail.* Due to the large distributed infrastructure being managed, requests for object may occasionally fail. Under certain conditions, S3 can decide to drop a request by returning an internal server error. Therefore, it is expected to have a small failure rate during day-to-day operations, which is generally not identified as a persistent failure.

Access to S3 is provided with RESTful Web services. These express all the operations that can be performed on the storage in the form of HTTP requests (*GET, PUT, DELETE, HEAD,* and *POST*), which operate differently according to the element they address. As a rule of thumb *PUT/ POST* requests add new content to the store, *GET/HEAD* requests are used to retrieve content and information, and *DELETE* requests are used to remove elements or information attached to them.

Resource naming

Buckets, objects, and attached metadata are made accessible through a REST interface. Therefore, they are represented by *uniform resource identifiers (URIs)* under the *s3.amazonaws.com* domain. All the operations are then performed by expressing the entity they are directed to in the form of a request for a URI.

Amazon offers three different ways of addressing a bucket:

- *Canonical form: http://s3.amazonaws.com/bukect_name/.* The bucket name is expressed as a path component of the domain name s3.amazonaws.com. This is the naming convention that has less restriction in terms of allowed characters, since all the characters that are allowed for a path component can be used.
- *Subdomain form: http://bucketname.s3.amazon.com/.* Alternatively, it is also possible to reference a bucket as a subdomain of s3.amazonaws.com. To express a bucket name in this form, the name has to do all of the following:
  - Be between 3 and 63 characters long
  - Contain only letters, numbers, periods, and dashes
  - Start with a letter or a number
  - Contain at least one letter
  - Have no fragments between periods that start with a dash or end with a dash or that are empty strings

  This form is equivalent to the previous one when it can be used, but it is the one to be preferred since it works more effectively for all the geographical locations serving resources stored in S3.
- *Virtual hosting form: http://bucket-name.com/.* Amazon also allows referencing of its resources with custom URLs. This is accomplished by entering a CNAME record into the DNS that points to the subdomain form of the bucket URI.

Since S3 is logically organized as a flat data store, all the buckets are managed under the s3. amazonaws.com domain. Therefore, the names of buckets must be unique across all the users.

Objects are always referred as resources local to a given bucket. Therefore, they always appear as a part of the resource component of a URI. Since a bucket can be expressed in three different ways, objects indirectly inherit this flexibility:

- Canonical form: http://s3.amazonaws.com/bukect_name/object_name
- Subdomain form: http://bucket-name/s3.amzonaws.com/object_name
- Virtual hosting form: http://bucket-name.com/object_name

Except for the *?*, which separates the resource path of a URI from the set of parameters passed with the request, all the characters that follow the / after the bucket reference constitute the name of the object. For instance, path separator characters expressed as part of the object name do not have corresponding physical layout within the bucket store. Despite this fact, they can still be used to create logical groupings that look like directories.

Finally, specific information about a given object, such as its access control policy or the server logging settings defined for a bucket, can be referenced using a specific parameter. More precisely:

- Object ACL: http://s3.amazonaws.com/bukect_name/object_name?acl
- Bucket server logging: http://s3.amzonaws.com/bucket_name?logging

Object metadata are not directly accessible through a specific URI, but they are manipulated by adding attributes in the request of the URL and are not part of the identifier.

Buckets

A *bucket* is a container of objects. It can be thought of as a virtual drive hosted on the S3 distributed storage, which provides users with a flat store to which they can add objects. Buckets are top-level elements of the S3 storage architecture and do not support nesting. That is, it is not possible to create "subbuckets" or other kinds of physical divisions.

A bucket is located in a specific geographic location and eventually replicated for fault tolerance and better content distribution. Users can select the location at which to create buckets, which by default are created in Amazon's U.S. datacenters. Once a bucket is created, all the objects that belong to the bucket will be stored in the same availability zone of the bucket. Users create a bucket by sending a *PUT* request to http://s3.amazonaws.com/ with the name of the bucket and, if they want to specify the availability zone, additional information about the preferred location. The content of a bucket can be listed by sending a *GET* request specifying the name of the bucket. Once created, the bucket cannot be renamed or relocated. If it is necessary to do so, the bucket needs to be deleted and recreated. The deletion of a bucket is performed by a *DELETE* request, which can be successful if and only if the bucket is empty.

Objects and metadata

Objects constitute the content elements stored in S3. Users either store files or push to the S3 text stream representing the object's content. An object is identified by a name that needs to be unique within the bucket in which the content is stored. The name cannot be longer than 1,024 bytes when encoded in UTF-8, and it allows almost any character. Since buckets do not support nesting, even characters normally used as path separators are allowed. This actually compensates for the lack of a structured file system, since directories can be emulated by properly naming objects.

Users create an object via a *PUT* request that specifies the name of the object together with the bucket name, its contents, and additional properties. The maximum size of an object is 5 GB. Once an object is created, it cannot be modified, renamed, or moved into another bucket. It is possible to retrieve an object via a *GET* request; deleting an object is performed via a *DELETE* request.

Objects can be tagged with metadata, which are passed as properties of the *PUT* request. Such properties are retrieved either with a *GET* request or with a *HEAD* request, which only returns the object's metadata without the content. Metadata are both system and user defined: the first ones are used by S3 to control the interaction with the object, whereas the second ones are meaningful to the user, who can store up to 2 KB per metadata property represented by a key-value pair of strings.

Access control and security

Amazon S3 allows controlling the access to buckets and objects by means of *Access Control Policies (ACPs)*. An ACP is a set of *grant permissions* that are attached to a resource expressed by means of an XML configuration file. A policy allows defining up to 100 access rules, each of them granting one of the available permissions to a grantee. Currently, five different permissions can be used:

- *READ* allows the grantee to retrieve an object and its metadata and to list the content of a bucket as well as getting its metadata.
- *WRITE* allows the grantee to add an object to a bucket as well as modify and remove it.
- *READ_ACP* allows the grantee to read the ACP of a resource.
- *WRITE_ACP* allows the grantee to modify the ACP of a resource.
- *FULL_CONTROL* grants all of the preceding permissions.

Grantees can be either single users or groups. Users can be identified by their canonical IDs or the email addresses they provided when they signed up for S3. For groups, only three options are available: all users, authenticated users, and log delivery users.[2]

Once a resource is created, S3 attaches a default ACP granting full control permissions to its owner only. Changes to the ACP can be made by using the request to the resource URI followed by *?acl*. A *GET* method allows retrieval of the ACP; a *PUT* method allows uploading of a new ACP to replace the existing one. Alternatively, it is possible to use a predefined set of permissions called *canned policies* to set the ACP at the time a resource is created. These policies represent the most common access patterns for S3 resources.

ACPs provide a set of powerful rules to control S3 users' access to resources, but they do not exhibit fine grain in the case of nonauthenticated users, who cannot be differentiated and are considered as a group. To provide a finer grain in this scenario, S3 allows defining *signed URIs*, which grant access to a resource for a limited amount of time to all the requests that can provide a temporary access token.

---

[2]This group identifies a specific group of accounts that automated processes use to perform bucket access logging.

Advanced features

Besides the management of buckets, objects, and ACPs, S3 offers other additional features that can be helpful. These features are server access logging and integration with the *BitTorrent* file-sharing network.

Server access logging allows bucket owners to obtain detailed information about the request made for the bucket and all the objects it contains. By default, this feature is turned off; it can be activated by issuing a *PUT* request to the bucket URI followed by *?logging*. The request should include an XML file specifying the target bucket in which to save the logging files and the file name prefix. A *GET* request to the same URI allows the user to retrieve the existing logging configuration for the bucket.

The second feature of interest is represented by the capability of exposing S3 objects to the *BitTorrent* network, thus allowing files stored in S3 to be downloaded using the *BitTorrent* protocol. This is done by appending *?torrent* to the URI of the S3 object. To actually download the object, its ACP must grant read permission to everyone.

9.1.2.2 Amazon elastic block store

The Amazon Elastic Block Store (EBS) allows AWS users to provide EC2 instances with persistent storage in the form of volumes that can be mounted at instance startup. They accommodate up to 1 TB of space and are accessed through a block device interface, thus allowing users to format them according to the needs of the instance they are connected to (raw storage, file system, or other). The content of an EBS volume survives the instance life cycle and is persisted into S3. EBS volumes can be cloned, used as boot partitions, and constitute durable storage since they rely on S3 and it is possible to take incremental snapshots of their content.

EBS volumes normally reside within the same availability zone of the EC2 instances that will use them to maximize the I/O performance. It is also possible to connect volumes located in different availability zones. Once mounted as volumes, their content is lazily loaded in the background and according to the request made by the operating system. This reduces the number of I/O requests that go to the network. Volume images cannot be shared among instances, but multiple (separate) active volumes can be created from them. In addition, it is possible to attach multiple volumes to a single instance or create a volume from a given snapshot and modify its size, if the formatted file system allows such an operation.

The expense related to a volume comprises the cost generated by the amount of storage occupied in S3 and by the number of I/O requests performed against the volume. Currently, Amazon charges $0.10/GB/month of allocated storage and $0.10 per 1 million requests made to the volume.

9.1.2.3 Amazon ElastiCache

ElastiCache is an implementation of an elastic in-memory cache based on a cluster of EC2 instances. It provides fast data access from other EC2 instances through a Memcached-compatible protocol so that existing applications based on such technology do not need to be modified and can transparently migrate to ElastiCache.

ElastiCache is based on a cluster of EC2 instances running the caching software, which is made available through Web services. An ElastiCache cluster can be dynamically resized according to the demand of the client applications. Furthermore, automatic patch management and failure detection and recovery of cache nodes allow the cache cluster to keep running without administrative intervention from AWS users, who have only to elastically size the cluster when needed.

ElastiCache nodes are priced according to the EC2 costing model, with a small price difference due to the use of the caching service installed on such instances. It is possible to choose between different types of instances; Table 9.3 provides an overview of the pricing options.

The prices indicated in Table 9.3 are related to the Amazon offerings during 2011–2012, and the amount of memory specified represents the memory available after taking system software overhead into account.

9.1.2.4 Structured storage solutions

Enterprise applications quite often rely on databases to store data in a structured form, index, and perform analytics against it. Traditionally, RDBMS have been the common data back-end for a wide range of applications, even though recently more scalable and lightweight solutions have been proposed. Amazon provides applications with structured storage services in three different forms: preconfigured EC2 AMIs, *Amazon Relational Data Storage (RDS)*, and *Amazon SimpleDB*.

Preconfigured EC2 AMIs

Preconfigured EC2 AMIs are predefined templates featuring an installation of a given database management system. EC2 instances created from these AMIs can be completed with an EBS volume for storage persistence. Available AMIs include installations of IBM DB2, Microsoft SQL Server, MySQL, Oracle, PostgreSQL, Sybase, and Vertica. Instances are priced hourly according to the EC2 cost model. This solution poses most of the administrative burden on the EC2 user, who has to configure, maintain, and manage the relational database, but offers the greatest variety of products to choose from.

Amazon RDS

RDS is relational database service that relies on the EC2 infrastructure and is managed by Amazon. Developers do not have to worry about configuring the storage for high availability, designing

Table 9.3 Amazon EC2 (On-Demand) Cache Instances Characteristics, 2011–2012

Instance Type	ECU	Platform	Memory	I/O Capacity	Price (U.S. East) (USD/hour)
Standard instances					
Small	1(1 × 1)	64 bit	1.3 GB	Moderate	$0.095
Large	4(2 × 2)	64 bit	7.1 GB	High	$0.380
Extra Large	8(4 × 2)	64 bit	14.6 GB	High	$0.760
High-Memory instances					
Extra Large	6.5(2 × 3.25)	64 bit	16.7 GB	High	$0.560
Double Extra Large	13(4 × 3.25)	64 bit	33.8 GB	High	$1.120
Quadruple Extra Large	26(8 × 3.25)	64 bit	68 GB	High	$2.240
High-CPU instances					
Extra Large	26(8 × 3.25)	64 bit	6.6 GB	High	$0.760

failover strategies, or keeping the servers up-to-date with patches. Moreover, the service provides users with automatic backups, snapshots, point-in-time recoveries, and facilities for implementing replications. These and the common database management services are available through the AWS console or a specific Web service. Two relational engines are available: MySQL and Oracle.

Two key advanced features of RDS are *multi-AZ deployment* and *read replicas*. The first option provides users with a failover infrastructure for their RDBMS solutions. The high-availability solution is implemented by keeping in standby synchronized copies of the services in different availability zones that are activated if the primary service goes down. The second option provides users with increased performance for applications that are heavily based on database reads. In this case, Amazon deploys copies of the primary service that are only available for database reads, thus cutting down the response time of the service.

The available options and the relative pricing of the service during 2011−2012 are shown in Table 9.4. The table shows the costing details of the on-demand instances. There is also the possibility of using reserved instances for long terms (one to three years) by paying up-front at discounted hourly rates.

With respect to the previous solution, users are not responsible for managing, configuring, and patching the database management software, but these operations are performed by the AWS. In addition, support for elastic management of servers is simplified. Therefore, this solution is optimal for applications based on the Oracle and MySQL engines, which are migrated on the AWS infrastructure and require a scalable database solution.

Amazon SimpleDB

Amazon SimpleDB is a lightweight, highly scalable, and flexible data storage solution for applications that do not require a fully relational model for their data. SimpleDB provides support for semistructured data, the model for which is based on the concept of *domains*, *items*, and *attributes*. With respect to the relational model, this model provides fewer constraints on the structure of data entries, thus obtaining improved performance in querying large quantities of data. As happens for Amazon RDS, this service frees AWS users from performing configuration, management, and high-availability design for their data stores.

Table 9.4 Amazon RDS (On-Demand) Instances Characteristics, 2011−2012

Instance Type	ECU	Platform	Memory	I/O Capacity	Price (U.S. East) (USD/hour)
Standard instances					
Small	1(1 × 1)	64 bit	1.7 GB	Moderate	$0.11
Large	4(2 × 2)	64 bit	7.5 GB	High	$0.44
Extra Large	8(4 × 2)	64 bit	15 GB	High	$0.88
High-Memory instances					
Extra Large	6.5(2 × 3.25)	64 bit	17.1 GB	High	$0.65
Double Extra Large	13(4 × 3.25)	64 bit	34 GB	High	$1.30
Quadruple Extra Large	26(8 × 3.25)	64 bit	68 GB	High	$2.60

SimpleDB uses *domains* as top-level elements to organize a data store. These domains are roughly comparable to tables in the relational model. Unlike tables, they allow items not to have all the same column structure; each item is therefore represented as a collection of attributes expressed in the form of a key-value pair. Each domain can grow up to 10 GB of data, and by default a single user can allocate a maximum of 250 domains. Clients can create, delete, modify, and make snapshots of domains. They can insert, modify, delete, and query items and attributes. Batch insertion and deletion are also supported. The capability of querying data is one of the most relevant functions of the model, and the *select* clause supports the following test operators: $=$, $!=$, $<$, $>$, $<=$, $>=$, *like, not like, between, is null, is not null,* and *every()*. Here is a simple example on how to query data:

select * from domain_name where every(attribute_name) = 'value'

Moreover, the *select* operator can extend its query beyond the boundaries of a single domain, thus allowing users to query effectively a large amount of data.

To efficiently provide AWS users with a scalable and fault-tolerant service, SimpleDB implements a relaxed constraint model, which leads to *eventually consistent* data. The adverb *eventually* denotes the fact that multiple accesses on the same data might not read the same value in the very short term, but they will eventually converge over time. This is because SimpleDB does not lock all the copies of the data during an update, which is propagated in the background. Therefore, there is a transient period of time in which different clients can access different copies of the same data that have different values. This approach is very scalable with minor drawbacks, and it is also reasonable, since the application scenario for SimpleDB is mostly characterized by querying and indexing operations on data. Alternatively, it is possible to change the default behavior and ensure that all the readers are blocked during an update.

Even though SimpleDB is not a transactional model, it allows clients to express conditional insertions or deletions, which are useful to prevent lost updates in multiple-writer scenarios. In this case, the operation is executed if and only if the condition is verified. This condition can be used to check preexisting values of attributes for an item.

Table 9.5 provides an overview of the pricing options for the SimpleDB service for data transfer during 2011−2012. The service charges either for data transfer or stored data. Data transfer within the AWS network is not charged. In addition, SimpleDB also charges users for machine usage. The first 25 SimpleDB instances per month are free; after this threshold there is an hourly charge ($0.140 hour in the U.S. East region).

If we compare this cost model with the one characterizing S3, it becomes evident that S3 is a cheaper option for storing large objects. This is useful information for clarifying the different nature of SimpleDB with respect to S3: The former has been designed to provide fast access to semistructured collections of small objects and not for being a long-term storage option for large objects.

9.1.2.5 Amazon CloudFront

CloudFront is an implementation of a content delivery network on top of the Amazon distributed storage infrastructure. It leverages a collection of edge servers strategically located around the globe to better serve requests for static and streaming Web content so that the transfer time is reduced as much as possible.

Table 9.5 Amazon SimpleDB Data Transfer Charges, 2011−2012

Instance Type	Price (U.S. East) (USD)
Data Transfer In	
All data transfer in	$0.000
Data Transfer Out	
1st GB/month	$0.000
Up to 10 TB/month	$0.120
Next 40 TB/month	$0.090
Next 100 TB/month	$0.070
Next 350 TB/month	$0.050
Next 524 TB/month	Special arrangements
Next 4 PB/month	Special arrangements
Greater than 5 PB/month	Special arrangements

AWS provides users with simple Web service APIs to manage CloudFront. To make available content through CloudFront, it is necessary to create a distribution. This identifies an origin server, which contains the original version of the content being distributed, and it is referenced by a DNS domain under the *Cloudfront.net* domain name (i.e., my-distribution.Cloudfront.net). It is also possible to map a given domain name to a distribution. Once the distribution is created, it is sufficient to reference the distribution name, and the CloudFront engine will redirect the request to the closest replica and eventually download the original version from the origin server if the content is not found or expired on the selected edge server.

The content that can be delivered through CloudFront is static (HTTP and HTTPS) or streaming (Real Time Messaging Protocol, or RMTP). The origin server hosting the original copy of the distributed content can be an S3 bucket, an EC2 instance, or a server external to the Amazon network. Users can restrict access to the distribution to only one or a few of the available protocols, or they can set up access rules for finer control. It is also possible to invalidate content to remove it from the distribution or force its update before expiration.

Table 9.6 provides a breakdown of the pricing during 2011−2012. Note that CloudFront is cheaper than S3. This reflects its different purpose: CloudFront is designed to optimize the distribution of very popular content that is frequently downloaded, potentially from the entire globe and not only the Amazon network.

9.1.3 Communication services

Amazon provides facilities to structure and facilitate the communication among existing applications and services residing within the AWS infrastructure. These facilities can be organized into two major categories: *virtual networking* and *messaging*.

9.1.3.1 Virtual networking

Virtual networking comprises a collection of services that allow AWS users to control the connectivity to and between compute and storage services. *Amazon Virtual Private Cloud (VPC)* and

Table 9.6 Amazon CloudFront On-Demand Pricing, 2011–2012

Pricing Item	United States	Europe	Hong Kong and Singapore	Japan	South America
Requests					
Per 10,000 HTTP requests	$0.0075	$0.0090	$0.0090	$0.0095	$0.0160
Per 10,000 HTTPS requests	$0.0100	$0.0120	$0.0120	$0.0130	$0.0220
Regional Data Transfer Out					
First 10 TB/month	$0.120/GB	$0.120/GB	$0.190/GB	$0.201/GB	$0.250/GB
Next 40 TB/month	$0.080/GB	$0.080/GB	$0.140/GB	$0.148/GB	$0.200/GB
Next 100 TB/month	$0.060/GB	$0.060/GB	$0.120/GB	$0.127/GB	$0.180/GB
Next 350 TB/month	$0.040/GB	$0.040/GB	$0.100/GB	$0.106/GB	$0.160/GB
Next 524 TB/month	$0.030/GB	$0.030/GB	$0.080/GB	$0.085/GB	$0.140/GB
Next 4 PB/month	$0.025/GB	$0.025/GB	$0.070/GB	$0.075/GB	$0.130/GB
Greater than 5 PB/month	$0.020/GB	$0.020/GB	$0.060/GB	$0.065/GB	$0.125/GB

Amazon Direct Connect provide connectivity solutions in terms of infrastructure; *Route 53* facilitates connectivity in terms of naming.

Amazon VPC provides a great degree of flexibility in creating virtual private networks within the Amazon infrastructure and beyond. The service providers prepare either templates covering most of the usual scenarios or a fully customizable network service for advanced configurations. Prepared templates include public subnets, isolated networks, private networks accessing Internet through network address translation (NAT), and hybrid networks including AWS resources and private resources. Also, it is possible to control connectivity between different services (EC2 instances and S3 buckets) by using the *Identity Access Management (IAM)* service. During 2011, the cost of Amazon VPC was $0.50 per connection hour.

Amazon Direct Connect allows AWS users to create dedicated networks between the user private network and Amazon Direct Connect locations, called *ports*. This connection can be further partitioned in multiple logical connections and give access to the public resources hosted on the Amazon infrastructure. The advantage of using Direct Connect versus other solutions is the consistent performance of the connection between the users' premises and the Direct Connect locations. This service is compatible with other services such as EC2, S3, and Amazon VPC and can be used in scenarios requiring high bandwidth between the Amazon network and the outside world. There are only two available ports located in the United States, but users can leverage external providers that offer guaranteed high bandwidth to these ports. Two different bandwidths can be chosen: 1 Gbps, priced at $0.30 per hour, and 10 Gbps, priced at $2.25 per hour. Inbound traffic is free; outbound traffic is priced at $0.02 per GB.

Amazon Route 53 implements dynamic DNS services that allow AWS resources to be reached through domain names different from the amazon.com domain. By leveraging the large and globally distributed network of Amazon DNS servers, AWS users can expose EC2 instances or S3 buckets as resources under a domain of their property, for which Amazon DNS servers become authoritative.[3] EC2 instances are likely to be more dynamic than the physical machines, and S3 buckets might also exist for a limited time. To cope with such a volatile nature, the service provides AWS users with the capability of dynamically mapping names to resources as instances are launched on EC2 or as new buckets are created in S3. By interacting with the Route 53 Web service, users can manage a set of *hosted zones*, which represent the user domains controlled by the service, and edit the resources made available through it. Currently, a single user can have up to 100 zones. The costing model includes a fixed amount ($1 per zone per month) and a dynamic component that depends on the number of queries resolved by the service for the hosted zones ($0.50 per million queries for the first billion of queries a month, $0.25 per million queries over 1 billion of queries a month).

9.1.3.2 Messaging

Messaging services constitute the next step in connecting applications by leveraging AWS capabilities. The three different types of messaging services offered are *Amazon Simple Queue Service (SQS)*, *Amazon Simple Notification Service (SNS)*, and *Amazon Simple Email Service (SES)*.

Amazon SQS constitutes disconnected model for exchanging messages between applications by means of message queues, hosted within the AWS infrastructure. Using the AWS console or directly the underlying Web service AWS, users can create an unlimited number of message queues and configure them to control their access. Applications can send messages to any queue they have access to. These messages are securely and redundantly stored within the AWS infrastructure for a limited period of time, and they can be accessed by other (authorized) applications. While a message is being read, it is kept locked to avoid spurious processing from other applications. Such a lock will expire after a given period.

Amazon SNS provides a publish-subscribe method for connecting heterogeneous applications. With respect to Amazon SQS, where it is necessary to continuously poll a given queue for a new message to process, Amazon SNS allows applications to be notified when new content of interest is available. This feature is accessible through a Web service whereby AWS users can create a topic, which other applications can subscribe to. At any time, applications can publish content on a given topic and subscribers can be automatically notified. The service provides subscribers with different notification models (HTTP/HTTPS, email/email JSON, and SQS).

Amazon SES provides AWS users with a scalable email service that leverages the AWS infrastructure. Once users are signed up for the service, they have to provide an email that SES will use to send emails on their behalf. To activate the service, SES will send an email to verify the given address and provide the users with the necessary information for the activation. Upon verification, the user is given an SES sandbox to test the service, and he can request access to the production version. Using SES, it is possible to send either SMTP-compliant emails or raw emails by specifying email headers and Multipurpose Internet Mail Extension (MIME) types. Emails are queued for

---

[3]A DNS server is responsible for resolving a name to a corresponding IP address. Since DNS servers implement a distributed database without a single global control, a single DNS server does not have the complete knowledge of all the mappings between names and IP addresses, but it has direct knowledge only of a small subset of them. Such a DNS server is therefore authoritative for these names because it can directly resolve the names. For resolving the other names, the nearest authoritative DNS is contacted.

delivery, and the users are notified of any failed delivery. SES also provides a wide range of statistics that help users to improve their email campaigns for effective communication with customers.

With regard to the costing, all three services do not require a minimum commitment but are based on a pay-as-you go model. Currently, users are not charged until they reach a minimum threshold. In addition, data transfer-in is not charged, but data transfer-out is charged by ranges.

9.1.4 Additional services

Besides compute, storage, and communication services, AWS provides a collection of services that allow users to utilize services in aggregation. The two relevant services are *Amazon CloudWatch* and *Amazon Flexible Payment Service (FPS)*.

Amazon CloudWatch is a service that provides a comprehensive set of statistics that help developers understand and optimize the behavior of their application hosted on AWS. CloudWatch collects information from several other AWS services: EC2, S3, SimpleDB, CloudFront, and others. Using CloudWatch, developers can see a detailed breakdown of their usage of the service they are renting on AWS and can devise more efficient and cost-saving applications. Earlier services of CloudWatch were offered only through subscription, but now it is made available for free to all the AWS users.

Amazon FPS infrastructure allows AWS users to leverage Amazon's billing infrastructure to sell goods and services to other AWS users. Using Amazon FPS, developers do not have to set up alternative payment methods, and they can charge users via a billing service. The payment models available through FPS include one-time payments and delayed and periodic payments, required by subscriptions and usage-based services, transactions, and aggregate multiple payments.

9.1.5 Summary

Amazon provides a complete set of services for developing, deploying, and managing cloud computing systems by leveraging the large and distributed AWS infrastructure. Developers can use EC2 to control and configure the computing infrastructure hosted in the cloud. They can leverage other services, such as AWS CloudFormation, Elastic Beanstalk, or Elastic MapReduce, if they do not need complete control over the computing stack. Applications hosted in the AWS Cloud can leverage S3, SimpleDB, or other storage services to manage structured and unstructured data. These services are primarily meant for storage, but other options, such as Amazon SQS, SNS, and SES, provide solutions for dynamically connecting applications from both inside and outside the AWS Cloud. Network connectivity to AWS applications is addressed by Amazon VPC and Amazon Direct Connect.

9.2 Google AppEngine

Google AppEngine is a PaaS implementation that provides services for developing and hosting scalable Web applications. AppEngine is essentially a distributed and scalable runtime environment that leverages Google's distributed infrastructure to scale out applications facing a large number of requests by allocating more computing resources to them and balancing the load among them. The runtime is completed by a collection of services that allow developers to design and implement applications that naturally scale on AppEngine. Developers can develop applications in Java, Python, and Go, a new programming language developed by Google to simplify the development of Web applications. Application usage of Google resources and services is metered by AppEngine, which bills users when their applications finish their free quotas.

9.2.1 Architecture and core concepts

AppEngine is a platform for developing scalable applications accessible through the Web (see Figure 9.2). The platform is logically divided into four major components: infrastructure, the runtime environment, the underlying storage, and the set of scalable services that can be used to develop applications.

9.2.1.1 Infrastructure

AppEngine hosts Web applications, and its primary function is to serve users requests efficiently. To do so, AppEngine's infrastructure takes advantage of many servers available within Google datacenters. For each HTTP request, AppEngine locates the servers hosting the application that processes the request, evaluates their load, and, if necessary, allocates additional resources (i.e., servers) or redirects the request to an existing server. The particular design of applications, which does not expect any state information to be implicitly maintained between requests to the same application, simplifies the work of the infrastructure, which can redirect each of the requests to any of the servers hosting the target application or even allocate a new one.

The infrastructure is also responsible for monitoring application performance and collecting statistics on which the billing is calculated.

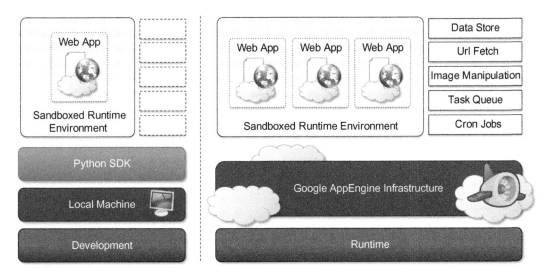

FIGURE 9.2

Google AppEngine platform architecture.

9.2.1.2 Runtime environment

The runtime environment represents the execution context of applications hosted on AppEngine. With reference to the AppEngine infrastructure code, which is always active and running, the runtime comes into existence when the request handler starts executing and terminates once the handler has completed.

Sandboxing

One of the major responsibilities of the runtime environment is to provide the application environment with an isolated and protected context in which it can execute without causing a threat to the server and without being influenced by other applications. In other words, it provides applications with a *sandbox*.

Currently, AppEngine supports applications that are developed only with managed or interpreted languages, which by design require a runtime for translating their code into executable instructions. Therefore, sandboxing is achieved by means of modified runtimes for applications that disable some of the common features normally available with their default implementations. If an application tries to perform any operation that is considered potentially harmful, an exception is thrown and the execution is interrupted. Some of the operations that are not allowed in the sandbox include writing to the server's file system; accessing computer through network besides using *Mail*, *UrlFetch*, and *XMPP*; executing code outside the scope of a request, a queued task, and a cron job; and processing a request for more than 30 seconds.

Supported runtimes

Currently, it is possible to develop AppEngine applications using three different languages and related technologies: *Java*, *Python*, and *Go*.

AppEngine currently supports Java 6, and developers can use the common tools for Web application development in Java, such as the *Java Server Pages (JSP)*, and the applications interact with the environment by using the *Java Servlet* standard. Furthermore, access to AppEngine services is provided by means of Java libraries that expose specific interfaces of provider-specific implementations of a given abstraction layer. Developers can create applications with the AppEngine Java SDK, which allows developing applications with either Java 5 or Java 6 and by using any Java library that does not exceed the restrictions imposed by the sandbox.

Support for Python is provided by an optimized Python 2.5.2 interpreter. As with Java, the runtime environment supports the Python standard library, but some of the modules that implement potentially harmful operations have been removed, and attempts to import such modules or to call specific methods generate exceptions. To support application development, AppEngine offers a rich set of libraries connecting applications to AppEngine services. In addition, developers can use a specific Python Web application framework, called *webapp*, simplifying the development of Web applications.

The Go runtime environment allows applications developed with the Go programming language to be hosted and executed in AppEngine. Currently the release of Go that is supported by AppEngine is r58.1. The SDK includes the compiler and the standard libraries for developing applications in Go and interfacing it with AppEngine services. As with the Python environment, some of the functionalities have been removed or generate a runtime exception. In addition, developers can include third-party libraries in their applications as long as they are implemented in pure Go.

9.2.1.3 Storage

AppEngine provides various types of storage, which operate differently depending on the volatility of the data. There are three different levels of storage: in memory-cache, storage for semistructured data, and long-term storage for static data. In this section, we describe *DataStore* and the use of static file servers. We cover *MemCache* in the application services section.

Static file servers

Web applications are composed of dynamic and static data. Dynamic data are a result of the logic of the application and the interaction with the user. Static data often are mostly constituted of the components that define the graphical layout of the application (CSS files, plain HTML files, JavaScript files, images, icons, and sound files) or data files. These files can be hosted on static file servers, since they are not frequently modified. Such servers are optimized for serving static content, and users can specify how dynamic content should be served when uploading their applications to AppEngine.

DataStore

DataStore is a service that allows developers to store semistructured data. The service is designed to scale and optimized to quickly access data. DataStore can be considered as a large object database in which to store objects that can be retrieved by a specified key. Both the type of the key and the structure of the object can vary.

With respect to the traditional Web applications backed by a relational database, DataStore imposes less constraint on the regularity of the data but, at the same time, does not implement some of the features of the relational model (such as reference constraints and join operations). These design decisions originated from a careful analysis of data usage patterns for Web applications and were taken in order to obtain a more scalable and efficient data store. The underlying infrastructure of *DataStore* is based on *Bigtable* [93], a redundant, distributed, and semistructured data store that organizes data in the form of tables (see Section 8.2.1).

DataStore provides high-level abstractions that simplify interaction with Bigtable. Developers define their data in terms of *entity* and *properties*, and these are persisted and maintained by the service into tables in *Bigtable*. An entity constitutes the level of granularity for the storage, and it identifies a collection of properties that define the data it stores. Properties are defined according to one of the several primitive types supported by the service. Each entity is associated with a key, which is either provided by the user or created automatically by AppEngine. An entity is associated with a *named kind* that AppEngine uses to optimize its retrieval from Bigtable. Although entities and properties seem to be similar to rows and tables in SQL, there are a few differences that have to be taken into account. Entities of the same kind might not have the same properties, and properties of the same name might contain values of different types. Moreover, properties can store different versions of the same values. Finally, keys are immutable elements and, once created, they cannot be changed.

DataStore also provides facilities for creating indexes on data and to update data within the context of a transaction. Indexes are used to support and speed up queries. A query can return zero or more objects of the same kind or simply the corresponding keys. It is possible to query the data store by specifying either the key or conditions on the values of the properties. Returned result sets can be sorted by key value or properties value. Even though the queries are quite similar to SQL queries, their implementation is substantially different. DataStore has been designed to be extremely fast in returning result sets; to do so it needs to know in advance all the possible queries that can be done for a given kind, because it stores for each of them a separate index. The indexes are provided by the user while uploading the application to AppEngine and can be automatically defined by the development server. When the developer tests the application, the server monitors all the different types of queries made against the simulated data store and creates an index for them. The structure of the indexes is saved in a configuration file and can be further changed by the developer before uploading the application. The use of precomputed indexes makes the query execution time-independent from the size of the stored data but only influenced by the size of the result set.

The implementation of transaction is limited in order to keep the store scalable and fast. AppEngine ensures that the update of a single entity is performed atomically. Multiple operations on the same entity can be performed within the context of a transaction. It is also possible to update multiple entities atomically. This is only possible if these entities belong to the same *entity group*. The entity group to which an entity belongs is specified at the time of entity creation and cannot be changed later. With regard to concurrency, AppEngine uses an *optimistic concurrency control*: If one user tries to update an entity that is already being updated, the control returns and the operation fails. Retrieving an entity never incurs into exceptions.

9.2.1.4 Application services

Applications hosted on AppEngine take the most from the services made available through the run-time environment. These services simplify most of the common operations that are performed in Web applications: access to data, account management, integration of external resources, messaging and communication, image manipulation, and asynchronous computation.

UrlFetch

Web 2.0 has introduced the concept of composite Web applications. Different resources are put together and organized as meshes within a single Web page. Meshes are fragments of HTML generated in different ways. They can be directly obtained from a remote server or rendered from an XML document retrieved from a Web service, or they can be rendered by the browser as the result of an embedded and remote component. A common characteristic of all these examples is the fact that the resource is not local to the server and often not even in the same administrative domain. Therefore, it is fundamental for Web applications to be able to retrieve remote resources.

The sandbox environment does not allow applications to open arbitrary connections through sockets, but it does provide developers with the capability of retrieving a remote resource through HTTP/HTTPS by means of the *UrlFetch* service. Applications can make synchronous and asynchronous Web requests and integrate the resources obtained in this way into the normal request-handling cycle of the application. One of the interesting features of UrlFetch is the ability to set deadlines for requests so that they can be completed (or aborted) within a given time. Moreover, the ability to perform such requests asynchronously allows the applications to continue with their logic while the resource is retrieved in the background. UrlFetch is not only used to integrate meshes into a Web page but also to leverage remote Web services in accordance with the SOA reference model for distributed applications.

MemCache

AppEngine provides developers with access to fast and reliable storage, which is DataStore. Despite this, the main objective of the service is to serve as a scalable and long-term storage, where data are persisted to disk redundantly in order to ensure reliability and availability of data against failures. This design poses a limit on how much faster the store can be compared to other solutions, especially for objects that are frequently accessed—for example, at each Web request.

AppEngine provides caching services by means of *MemCache*. This is a distributed in-memory cache that is optimized for fast access and provides developers with a volatile store for the objects that are frequently accessed. The caching algorithm implemented by MemCache will automatically remove the objects that are rarely accessed. The use of MemCache can significantly reduce the access time to data; developers can structure their applications so that each object is first looked up into MemCache and if there is a miss, it will be retrieved from DataStore and put into the cache for future lookups.

Mail and instant messaging

Communication is another important aspect of Web applications. It is common to use email for following up with users about operations performed by the application. Email can also be used to trigger activities in Web applications. To facilitate the implementation of such tasks, AppEngine provides developers with the ability to send and receive mails through *Mail*. The service allows sending email on behalf of the application to specific user accounts. It is also possible to include several types of attachments and to target multiple recipients. Mail operates asynchronously, and in case of failed delivery the sending address is notified through an email detailing the error.

AppEngine provides also another way to communicate with the external world: the Extensible Messaging and Presence Protocol (XMPP). Any chat service that supports XMPP, such as Google Talk, can send and receive chat messages to and from the Web application, which is identified by its own address. Even though the chat is a communication medium mostly used for human interactions, XMPP can be conveniently used to connect the Web application with chat bots or to implement a small administrative console.

Account management

Web applications often keep various data that customize their interaction with users. These data normally go under the user profile and are attached to an account. AppEngine simplifies account management by allowing developers to leverage Google account management by means of *Google Accounts*. The integration with the service also allows Web applications to offload the implementation of authentication capabilities to Google's authentication system.

Using Google Accounts, Web applications can conveniently store profile settings in the form of key-value pairs, attach them to a given Google account, and quickly retrieve them once the user authenticates. With respect to a custom solution, the use of Google Accounts requires users to have a Google account, but it does not require any further implementation. The use of Google Accounts is particularly advantageous for developing Web applications within a corporate environment using Google Apps. In this case, the applications can be easily integrated with all the other services (and profile settings) included in Google Apps.

Image manipulation

Web applications render pages with graphics. Often simple operations, such as adding watermarks or applying simple filters, are required. AppEngine allows applications to perform image resizing, rotation, mirroring, and enhancement by means of *Image Manipulation*, a service that is also used in other Google products. Image Manipulation is mostly designed for lightweight image processing and is optimized for speed.

9.2.1.5 Compute services

Web applications are mostly designed to interface applications with users by means of a ubiquitous channel, that is, the Web. Most of the interaction is performed synchronously: Users navigate the Web pages and get instantaneous feedback in response to their actions. This feedback is often the result of some computation happening on the Web application, which implements the intended logic to serve the user request. Sometimes this approach is not applicable—for example, in long computations or when some operations need to be triggered at a given point in time. A good design for these scenarios provides the user with immediate feedback and a notification once the required operation is completed. AppEngine offers additional services such as *Task Queues* and *Cron Jobs* that simplify the execution of computations that are off-bandwidth or those that cannot be performed within the timeframe of the Web request.

Task queues

Task Queues allow applications to submit a task for a later execution. This service is particularly useful for long computations that cannot be completed within the maximum response time of a request handler. The service allows users to have up to 10 queues that can execute tasks at a configurable rate.

In fact, a task is defined by a Web request to a given URL, and the queue invokes the request handler by passing the payload as part of the Web request to the handler. It is the responsibility of the request handler to perform the "task execution," which is seen from the queue as a simple Web request. The queue is designed to reexecute the task in case of failure in order to avoid transient failures preventing the task from a successful completion.

Cron jobs

Sometimes the length of computation might not be the primary reason that an operation is not performed within the scope of the Web request. It might be possible that the required operation needs to be performed at a specific time of the day, which does not coincide with the time of the Web request. In this case, it is possible to schedule the required operation at the desired time by using the *Cron Jobs* service. This service operates similarly to Task Queues but invokes the request handler specified in the task at a given time and does not reexecute the task in case of failure. This behavior can be useful to implement maintenance operations or send periodic notifications.

9.2.2 Application life cycle

AppEngine provides support for almost all the phases characterizing the life cycle of an application: testing and development, deployment, and monitoring. The SDKs released by Google provide developers with most of the functionalities required by these tasks. Currently there are two SDKs available for development: Java SDK and Python SDK.

9.2.2.1 Application development and testing

Developers can start building their Web applications on a local development server. This is a self-contained environment that helps developers tune applications without uploading them to AppEngine. The development server simulates the AppEngine runtime environment by providing a mock implementation of DataStore, MemCache, UrlFetch, and the other services leveraged by Web applications. Besides hosting Web applications, the development server contains a complete set of monitoring features that are helpful to profile the behavior of applications, especially regarding access to the DataStore service and the queries performed against it. This is a particularly important feature that will be of relevance in deploying the application to AppEngine. As discussed earlier, AppEngine builds indexes for each of the queries performed by a given application in order to speed up access to the relevant data. This capability is enabled by *a priori* knowledge about all the possible queries made by the application; such knowledge is made available to AppEngine by the developer while uploading the application. The development server analyzes application behavior while running and traces all the queries made during testing and development, thus providing the required information about the indexes to be built.

Java SDK

The Java SDK provides developers with the facility for building applications with the Java 5 and Java 6 runtime environments. Alternatively, it is possible to develop applications within the Eclipse development environment by using the Google AppEngine plug-in, which integrates the features of the SDK within the powerful Eclipse environment. Using the Eclipse software installer, it is possible to download and install Java SDK, Google Web Toolkit, and Google AppEngine plug-ins into Eclipse. These three components allow developers to program powerful and rich Java applications for AppEngine.

The SDK supports the development of applications by using the *servlet* abstraction, which is a common development model. Together with servlets, many other features are available to build applications. Moreover, developers can easily create Web applications by using the *Eclipse Web Platform*, which provides a set of tools and components.

The plug-in allows developing, testing, and deploying applications on AppEngine. Other tasks, such as retrieving the log of applications, are available by means of command-line tools that are part of the SDK.

Python SDK

The Python SDK allows developing Web applications for AppEngine with Python 2.5. It provides a standalone tool, called *GoogleAppEngineLauncher*, for managing Web applications locally and deploying them to AppEngine. The tool provides a convenient user interface that lists all the available Web applications, controls their execution, and integrates them with the default code editor for editing application files. In addition, the launcher provides access to some important services for application monitoring and analysis, such as the logs, the SDK console, and the dashboard. The log console captures all the information that is logged by the application while it is running. The console SDK provides developers with a Web interface via which they can see the application profile in terms of utilized resource. This feature is particularly useful because it allows developers to preview the behavior of the applications once they are deployed on AppEngine, and it can be used to tune applications made available through the runtime.

The Python implementation of the SDK also comes with an integrated Web application framework called *webapp* that includes a set of models, components, and tools that simplify the development of Web applications and enforce a set of coherent practices. This is not the only Web framework that can be used to develop Web applications. There are dozens of available Python Web frameworks that can be used. However, due to the restrictions enforced by the sandboxed environment, all of them cannot be used seamlessly. The *webapp* framework has been reimplemented and made available in the Python SDK so that it can be used with AppEngine. Another Web framework that is known to work well is *Django*.[4]

The SDK is completed by a set of command-line tools that allows developers to perform all the operations available through the launcher and more from the command shell.

9.2.2.2 *Application deployment and management*
Once the application has been developed and tested, it can be deployed on AppEngine with a simple click or command-line tool. Before performing such task, it is necessary to create an application identifier, which will be used to locate the application from the Web browser by typing the address *http://<application-id>.appspot.com*. Alternatively, it is also possible to map the application with a registered DNS domain name. This is particularly useful for commercial development, where users want to make the application available through a more appropriate name.

An application identifier is mandatory because it allows unique identification of the application while it's interacting with AppEngine. Developers use an app identifier to upload and update applications. Besides being unique, it also needs to be compliant to the rules that are enforced for domain names. It is possible to register an application identifier by logging into AppEngine and selecting the "Create application" option. It is also possible to provide an application title that is descriptive of the application; the title can be changed over time.

Once an application identifier has been created, it is possible to deploy an application on AppEngine. This task can be done using either the respective development environment (*GoogleAppEngineLauncher* and *Google AppEngine* plug-in) or the command-line tools. Once the application is uploaded, nothing else needs to be done to make it available. AppEngine will take care of everything. Developers can then manage the application by using the administrative console. This is the primary tool used for application monitoring and provides users with insight into resource usage (CPU, bandwidth) and services and other useful counters. It is also possible to manage multiple versions of a single application, select the one available for the release, and manage its billing-related issues.

9.2.3 **Cost model**
AppEngine provides a free service with limited quotas that get reset every 24 hours. Once the application has been tested and tuned for AppEngine, it is possible to set up a billing account and obtain more allowance and be charged on a pay-per-use basis. This allows developers to identify the appropriate daily budget that they want to allocate for a given application.

---

[4]www.djangoproject.com.

An application is measured against *billable quotas*, *fixed quotas*, and *per-minute quotas*. Google AppEngine uses these quotas to ensure that users do not spend more than the allocated budget and that applications run without being influenced by each other from a performance point of view. Billable quotas identify the daily quotas that are set by the application administrator and are defined by the daily budget allocated for the application. AppEngine will ensure that the application does not exceed these quotas. Free quotas are part of the billable quota and identify the portion of the quota for which users are not charged. Fixed quotas are internal quotas set by AppEngine that identify the infrastructure boundaries and define operations that the application can carry out on the infrastructure (services and runtime). These quotas are generally bigger than billable quotas and are set by AppEngine to avoid applications impacting each other's performance or overloading the infrastructure. The costing model also includes per-minute quotas, which are defined in order to avoid applications consuming all their credit in a very limited period of time, monopolizing a resource, and creating service interruption for other applications.

Once an application reaches the quota for a given resource, the resource is depleted and will not be available to the application until the quota is replenished. Once a resource is depleted, subsequent requests to that resource will generate an error or an exception. Resources such as CPU time and incoming or outgoing bandwidth will return an "HTTP 403" error page to users; all the other resources and services will generate an exception that can be trapped in code to provide more useful feedback to users.

Resources and services quotas are organized into free default quotas and billing-enabled default quotas. For these two categories, a daily limit and a maximum rate are defined. A detailed explanation of how quotas work, their limits, and the amount that is charged to the user can be found on the AppEngine Website at the following Internet address: http://code.google.com/appengine/docs/quotas.html.

9.2.4 Observations

AppEngine, a framework for developing scalable Web applications, leverages Google's infrastructure. The core components of the service are a scalable and sandboxed runtime environment for executing applications and a collection of services that implement most of the common features required for Web development and that help developers build applications that are easy to scale. One of the characteristic elements of AppEngine is the use of simple interfaces that allow applications to perform specific operations that are optimized and designed to scale. Building on top of these blocks, developers can build applications and let AppEngine scale them out when needed.

With respect to the traditional approach to Web development, the implementation of rich and powerful applications requires a change of perspective and more effort. Developers have to become familiar with the capabilities of AppEngine and implement the required features in a way that conforms with the AppEngine application model.

9.3 Microsoft Azure

Microsoft Windows Azure is a cloud operating system built on top of Microsoft datacenters' infrastructure and provides developers with a collection of services for building applications with cloud technology. Services range from compute, storage, and networking to application connectivity, access control, and business intelligence. Any application that is built on the Microsoft technology can be scaled using the Azure platform, which integrates the scalability features into the common Microsoft technologies such as Microsoft Windows Server 2008, SQL Server, and ASP.NET.

Figure 9.3 provides an overview of services provided by Azure. These services can be managed and controlled through the *Windows Azure Management Portal*, which acts as an administrative console for all the services offered by the Azure platform. In this section, we present the core features of the major services available with Azure.

9.3.1 Azure core concepts

The Windows Azure platform is made up of a foundation layer and a set of developer services that can be used to build scalable applications. These services cover compute, storage, networking, and identity management, which are tied together by middleware called *AppFabric*. This scalable computing environment is hosted within Microsoft datacenters and accessible through the Windows Azure Management Portal. Alternatively, developers can recreate a Windows Azure environment (with limited capabilities) on their own machines for development and testing purposes. In this section, we provide an overview of the Azure middleware and its services.

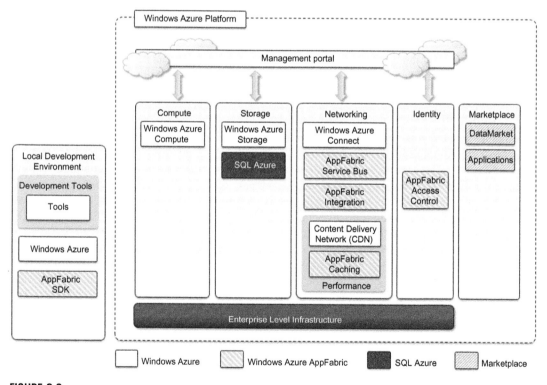

FIGURE 9.3

Microsoft Windows Azure Platform Architecture.

9.3.1.1 Compute services

Compute services are the core components of Microsoft Windows Azure, and they are delivered by means of the abstraction of *roles*. A role is a runtime environment that is customized for a specific compute task. Roles are managed by the Azure operating system and instantiated on demand in order to address surges in application demand. Currently, there are three different roles: *Web role*, *Worker role*, and *Virtual Machine (VM) role*.

Web role

The *Web role* is designed to implement scalable Web applications. Web roles represent the units of deployment of Web applications within the Azure infrastructure. They are hosted on the IIS 7 Web Server, which is a component of the infrastructure that supports Azure. When Azure detects peak loads in the request made to a given application, it instantiates multiple Web roles for that application and distributes the load among them by means of a load balancer.

Since version 3.5, the .NET technology natively supports Web roles; developers can directly develop their applications in Visual Studio, test them locally, and upload to Azure. It is possible to develop ASP.NET (*ASP.NET Web Role* and *ASP.NET MVC 2 Web Role*) and WCF (*WCF Service Web Role*) applications. Since IIS 7 also supports the PHP runtime environment by means of the FastCGI module, Web roles can be used to run and scale PHP Web applications on Azure (*CGI Web Role*). Other Web technologies that are not integrated with IIS can still be hosted on Azure (i.e., Java Server Pages on Apache Tomcat), but there is no advantage to using a Web role over a Worker role.

Worker role

Worker roles are designed to host general compute services on Azure. They can be used to quickly provide compute power or to host services that do not communicate with the external world through HTTP. A common practice for Worker roles is to use them to provide background processing for Web applications developed with Web roles.

Developing a worker role is like a developing a service. Compared to a Web role whose computation is triggered by the interaction with an HTTP client (i.e., a browser), a Worker role runs continuously from the creation of its instance until it is shut down. The Azure SDK provides developers with convenient APIs and libraries that allow connecting the role with the service provided by the runtime and easily controlling its startup as well as being notified of changes in the hosting environment. As with Web roles, the .NET technology provides complete support for Worker roles, but any technology that runs on a Windows Server stack can be used to implement its core logic. For example, Worker roles can be used to host Tomcat and serve JSP-based applications.

Virtual machine role

The *Virtual Machine role* allows developers to fully control the computing stack of their compute service by defining a custom image of the Windows Server 2008 R2 operating system and all the service stack required by their applications. The Virtual Machine role is based on the Windows Hyper-V virtualization technology (see Section 3.6.3), which is natively integrated in the Windows server technology at the base of Azure. Developers can image a Windows server installation complete with all the required applications and components, save it into a Virtual Hard Disk (VHD)

Table 9.7 Windows Azure Compute Instances Characteristics, 2011−2012

Compute Instance Type	CPU	Memory	Instance Storage	I/O Performance	Hourly Cost (USD)
Extra Small	1.0 GHz	768 MB	20 GB	Low	$0.04
Small	1.6 GHz	1.75 GB	225 GB	Moderate	$0.12
Medium	2 × 1.6 GHz	3.5 GB	490 GB	High	$0.24
Large	4 × 1.6 GHz	7 GB	1,000 GB	High	$0.48
Extra Large	8 × 1.6 GHz	14 GB	2,040 GB	High	$0.96

file, and upload it to Windows Azure to create compute instances on demand. Different types of instances are available, and Table 9.7 provides an overview of the options offered during 2011−2012.

Compared to the Worker and Web roles, the VM role provides finer control of the compute service and resource that are deployed on the Azure Cloud. An additional administrative effort is required for configuration, installation, and management of services.

9.3.1.2 Storage services

Compute resources are equipped with local storage in the form of a directory on the local file system that can be used to temporarily store information that is useful for the current execution cycle of a role. If the role is restarted and activated on a different physical machine, this information is lost.

Windows Azure provides different types of storage solutions that complement compute services with a more durable and redundant option compared to local storage. Compared to local storage, these services can be accessed by multiple clients at the same time and from everywhere, thus becoming a general solution for storage.

Blobs

Azure allows storing large amount of data in the form of binary large objects (BLOBs) by means of the *blobs* service. This service is optimal to store large text or binary files. Two types of blobs are available:

- *Block blobs.* Block blobs are composed of blocks and are optimized for sequential access; therefore they are appropriate for media streaming. Currently, blocks are of 4 MB, and a single block blob can reach 200 GB in dimension.
- *Page blobs.* Page blobs are made of pages that are identified by an offset from the beginning of the blob. A page blob can be split into multiple pages or constituted of a single page. This type of blob is optimized for random access and can be used to host data different from streaming. Currently, the maximum dimension of a page blob can be 1 TB.

Blobs storage provides users with the ability to describe the data by adding metadata. It is also possible to take snapshots of a blob for backup purposes. Moreover, to optimize its distribution, blobs storage can leverage the Windows Azure CDN so that blobs are kept close to users requesting them and can be served efficiently.

Azure drive

Page blobs can be used to store an entire file system in the form of a single *Virtual Hard Drive (VHD)* file. This can then be mounted as a part of the NTFS file system by Azure compute resources, thus providing persistent and durable storage. A page blob mounted as part of an NTFS tree is called an *Azure Drive*.

Tables

Tables constitute a semistructured storage solution, allowing users to store information in the form of entities with a collection of properties. Entities are stored as rows in the table and are identified by a key, which also constitutes the unique index built for the table. Users can insert, update, delete, and select a subset of the rows stored in the table. Unlike SQL tables, there are no schema enforcing constraints on the properties of entities and there is no facility for representing relationships among entities. For this reason, tables are more similar to spreadsheets rather than SQL tables.

The service is designed to handle large amounts of data and queries returning huge result sets. This capability is supported by partial result sets and table partitions. A partial result set is returned together with a continuation token, allowing the client to resume the query for large result sets. Table partitions allow tables to be divided among several servers for load-balancing purposes. A partition is identified by a key, which is represented by three of the columns of the table.

Currently, a table can contain up to 100 TB of data, and rows can have up to 255 properties, with a maximum of 1 MB for each row. The maximum dimension of a row key and partition keys is 1 KB.

Queues

Queue storage allows applications to communicate by exchanging messages through durable queues, thus avoiding lost or unprocessed messages. Applications enter messages into a queue, and other applications can read them in a first-in, first-out (FIFO) style.

To ensure that messages get processed, when an application reads a message it is marked as invisible; hence it will not be available to other clients. Once the application has completed processing the message, it needs to explicitly delete the message from the queue. This two-phase process ensures that messages get processed before they are removed from the queue, and the client failures do not prevent messages from being processed. At the same time, this is also a reason that the queue does not enforce a strict FIFO model: Messages that are read by applications that crash during processing are made available again after a timeout, during which other messages can be read by other clients. An alternative to reading a message is *peeking*, which allows retrieving the message but letting it stay visible in the queue. Messages that are peeked are not considered processed.

All the services described are geo-replicated three times to ensure their availability in case of major disasters. *Geo-replication* involves the copying of data into a different datacenter that is hundreds or thousands of miles away from the original datacenter.

9.3.1.3 Core infrastructure: AppFabric

AppFabric is a comprehensive middleware for developing, deploying, and managing applications on the cloud or for integrating existing applications with cloud services. AppFabric implements an optimized infrastructure supporting scaling out and high availability; sandboxing and multitenancy; state management; and dynamic address resolution and routing. On top of this infrastructure, the middleware offers a collection of services that simplify many of the common tasks in a distributed application, such as communication, authentication and authorization, and data access. These services are available through language-agnostic interfaces, thus allowing developers to build heterogeneous applications.

Access control

AppFabric provides the capability of encoding access control to resources in Web applications and services into a set of rules that are expressed outside the application code base. These rules give a great degree of flexibility in terms of the ability to secure components of the application and define access control policies for users and groups.

Access control services also integrate several authentication providers into a single coherent identity management framework. Applications can leverage Active Directory, Windows Live, Google, Facebook, and other services to authenticate users. This feature also allows easy building of hybrid systems, with some parts existing in the private premises and others deployed in the public cloud.

Service bus

Service Bus constitutes the messaging and connectivity infrastructure provided with AppFabric for building distributed and disconnected applications in the Azure Cloud and between the private premises and the Azure Cloud. Service Bus allows applications to interact with different protocols and patterns over a reliable communication channel that guarantees delivery.

The service is designed to allow transparent network traversal and to simplify the development of loosely coupled applications, without renouncing security and reliability and letting developers focus on the logic of the interaction rather than the details of its implementation. Service Bus allows services to be available by simple URLs, which are untied from their deployment location. It is possible to support publish-subscribe models, full-duplex communications point to point as well as in a peer-to-peer environment, unicast and multicast message delivery in one-way communications, and asynchronous messaging to decouple application components.

In order to leverage these features, applications need to be connected to the bus, which provides these services. A connection is the Service Bus element that is priced by Azure on a pay-as-you-go basis. Users are billed on a connections-per-month basis, and they can buy advance "connection packs," which have a discounted price, if they can estimate their needs in advance.

Azure cache

Windows Azure provides a set of durable storage solutions that allow applications to persist their data. These solutions are based on disk storage, which might constitute a bottleneck for the applications that need to gracefully scale along the clients' requests and dataset size dimensions.

Azure Cache is a service that allows developers to quickly access data persisted on Windows Azure storage or in SQL Azure. The service implements a distributed in-memory cache of which the size can be dynamically adjusted by applications according to their needs. It is possible to store any .NET managed object as well as many common data formats (table rows, XML, and binary data) and control its access by applications. Azure Cache is delivered as a service, and it can be easily integrated with applications. This is a particularly true for ASP.NET applications, which already integrate providers for session state and page output caching based on Azure Cache.

The service is priced according the size of cache allocated by applications per month, despite their effective use of the cache. Currently, several cache sizes are available, ranging from 128 MB ($45/month) to 4 GB ($325/month).

9.3.1.4 Other services

Compute, storage, and middleware services constitute the core components of the Windows Azure platform. Besides these, other services and components simplify the development and integration of applications with the Azure Cloud. An important area for these services is applications connectivity, including virtual networking and content delivery.

Windows Azure virtual network

Networking services for applications are offered under the name *Windows Azure Virtual Network*, which includes *Windows Azure Connect* and *Windows Azure Traffic Manager.*

Windows Azure Connect allows easy setup of IP-based network connectivity among machines hosted on the private premises and the roles deployed on the Azure Cloud. This service is particularly useful in the case of VM roles, where machines hosted in the Azure Cloud become part of the private network of the enterprise and can be managed with the same tools used in the private premises.

Windows Azure Traffic Manager provides load-balancing features for services listening to the HTTP or HTTPS ports and hosted on multiple roles. It allows developers to choose from three different load-balancing strategies: Performance, Round-Robin, and Failover.

Currently, the two services are still in beta phase and are available for free only by invitation.

Windows Azure content delivery network

Windows Azure Content Delivery Network (CDN) is the content delivery network solution that improves the content delivery capabilities of Windows Azure Storage and several other Microsoft services, such as *Microsoft Windows Update* and *Bing* maps. The service allows serving of Web objects (images, static HTML, CSS, and scripts) as well as streaming content by using a network of 24 locations distributed across the world.

9.3.2 **SQL Azure**

SQL Azure is a relational database service hosted on Windows Azure and built on the SQL Server technologies. The service extends the capabilities of SQL Server to the cloud and provides developers with a scalable, highly available, and fault-tolerant relational database. SQL Azure is accessible from either the Windows Azure Cloud or any other location that has access to the Azure Cloud. It is fully compatible with the interface exposed by SQL Server, so applications built for SQL Server can transparently migrate to SQL Azure. Moreover, the service is fully manageable using REST APIs, allowing developers to control databases deployed in the Azure Cloud as well as the firewall rules set up for their accessibility.

Figure 9.4 shows the architecture of SQL Azure. Access to SQL Azure is based on the Tabular Data Stream (TDS) protocol, which is the communication protocol underlying all the different

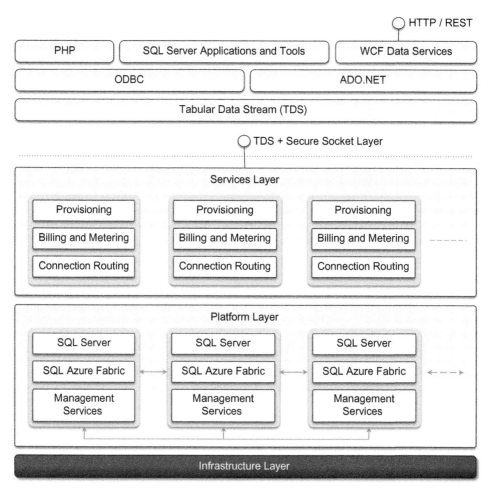

FIGURE 9.4

SQL Azure architecture.

interfaces used by applications to connect to a SQL Server-based installation such as ODBC and ADO.NET. On the SQL Azure side, access to data is mediated by the service layer, which provides provisioning, billing, and connection-routing services. These services are logically part of server instances, which are managed by SQL Azure Fabric. This is the distributed database middleware that constitutes the infrastructure of SQL Azure and that is deployed on Microsoft datacenters.

Developers have to sign up for a Windows Azure account in order to use SQL Azure. Once the account is activated, they can either use the Windows Azure Management Portal or the REST APIs to create servers and logins and to configure access to servers. SQL Azure servers are abstractions that closely resemble physical SQL Servers: They have a fully qualified domain name under the *database.windows.net* (i.e., *server-name.database.windows.net*) domain name. This simplifies the management tasks and the interaction with SQL Azure from client applications. SQL Azure ensures that multiple copies of each server are maintained within the Azure Cloud and that these copies are kept synchronized when client applications insert, update, and delete data on them.

Currently, the SQL Azure service is billed according to space usage and the type of edition. Currently, two different editions are available: Web Edition and Business Edition. The former is suited for small Web applications and supports databases with a maximum size of 1 GB or 5 GB. The latter is suited for independent software vendors, line-of-business applications, and enterprise applications and supports databases with a maximum size from 10 GB to 50 GB, in increments of 10 GB. Moreover, a bandwidth fee applies for any data transfer trespassing the Windows Azure Cloud or the region where the database is located. A monthly fee per user/database is also charged and is based on the peak size the database reaches during the month.

9.3.3 Windows Azure platform appliance

The Windows Azure platform can also be deployed as an appliance on third-party data centers and constitutes the cloud infrastructure governing the physical servers of the datacenter. The Windows Azure Platform Appliance includes Windows Azure, SQL Azure, and Microsoft-specified configuration of network, storage, and server hardware. The appliance is a solution that targets governments and service providers who want to have their own cloud computing infrastructure.

As introduced earlier, Azure already provides a development environment that allows building applications for Azure in their own premises. The local development environment is not intended to be production middleware, but it is designed for developing and testing the functionalities of applications that will eventually be deployed on Azure. The Azure appliance is instead a full-featured implementation of Windows Azure. Its goal is to replicate Azure on a third-party infrastructure and make available its services beyond the boundaries of the Microsoft Cloud. The appliance addresses two major scenarios: institutions that have very large computing needs (such as government agencies) and institutions that cannot afford to transfer their data outside their premises.

9.3.4 Observations

Windows Azure is Microsoft's solution for developing cloud computing applications. Azure is an implementation of the PaaS layer and provides the developer with a collection of services and scalable middleware hosted on Microsoft datacenters that address compute, storage, networking, and identity management needs of applications. The services Azure offers can be used either individually or all together for building both applications that integrate cloud features and elastic computing systems completely hosted in the cloud.

The core components of the platform are composed of compute services, storage services, and middleware. Compute services are based on the abstraction of roles, which identify a sandboxed environment where developers can build their distributed and scalable components. These roles are useful for Web applications, back-end processing, and virtual computing. Storage services include solutions for static and dynamic content, which is organized in the form of tables with fewer constraints than those imposed by the relational model. These and other services are implemented and made available through AppFabric, which constitutes the distributed and scalable middleware of Azure.

SQL Azure is another important element of Windows Azure and provides support for relational data in the cloud. SQL Azure is an extension of the capabilities of SQL Server adapted for the cloud environment and designed for dynamic scaling.

The platform is mostly based on the .NET technology and Windows systems, even though other technologies and systems can be supported. For this reason, Azure constitutes the solution of choice for migrating to the cloud applications that are already based on the .NET technology.

SUMMARY

This chapter introduced some cloud platforms that are widely used in industry for building real commercial applications: Amazon Web Services, Google AppEngine, and Microsoft Windows Azure.

Amazon Web Services (AWS) provides solutions for building infrastructure in the Amazon Cloud. Amazon EC2 and Amazon S3 represent AWS's core value offering. The former allows developers to create virtual servers and customize their computing stack as required. The latter is a storage solution that allows users to store documents of any size. These core services are then complemented by a wide collection of services, covering networking, data management, content distribution, computing middleware, and communication, which make AWS a complete solution for developing entire cloud computing systems on top of the Amazon infrastructure.

Google AppEngine is a distributed and scalable platform for building Web applications in the Cloud. AppEngine is a scalable runtime that offers developers a collection of services for simplifying the development of Web applications. These services are designed with scalability in mind and constitute functional blocks that can be reused to define applications. Developers can build their applications in either Java or Python, first locally using the AppEngine SDK. Once the applications have been completed and fully tested, they can deploy the application on AppEngine.

Windows Azure is the cloud operating system deployed on Microsoft datacenters for building dynamically scalable applications. Azure's core components are represented by compute services expressed in terms of roles, storage services, and the AppFabric, the middleware that ties together all these services and constitutes the infrastructure of Azure. A role is a sandboxed runtime environment specialized for a specific development scenario: Web applications, background processing, and virtual computing. Developers define their Azure applications in terms of roles and then deploy these roles on Azure. Storage services represent a natural complement to roles. Besides storage for static data and semistructured data, Windows Azure also provides storage for relational data by means of the SQL Azure service.

AppEngine and Windows Azure are PaaS solutions. AWS extends its services across all three layers of the Cloud Computing Reference Model, although it is well known for its IaaS offerings, represented by EC2 and S3.

Review questions

1. What is AWS? What types of services does it provide?
2. Describe Amazon EC2 and its basic features.
3. What is a bucket? What type of storage does it provide?
4. What are the differences between Amazon SimpleDB and Amazon RDS?
5. What type of problems does the Amazon Virtual Private Cloud address?
6. Introduce and present the services provided by AWS to support connectivity among applications.
7. What is the Amazon CloudWatch?
8. What type of service is AppEngine?
9. Describe the core components of AppEngine.
10. What are the development technologies currently supported by AppEngine?
11. What is DataStore? What type of data can be stored in it?
12. Discuss the compute services offered by AppEngine.
13. What is Windows Azure?
14. Describe the architecture of Windows Azure.
15. What is a role? What types of roles can be used?
16. What is AppFabric, and which services does it provide?
17. Discuss the storage services provided by Windows Azure.
18. What is SQL Azure?
19. Illustrate the architecture of SQL Azure.
20. What is the Windows Azure Platform Appliance? For which kinds of scenarios was this appliance designed?

Cloud Applications

Cloud computing has gained huge popularity in industry due to its ability to host applications for which the services can be delivered to consumers rapidly at minimal cost. This chapter discusses some application case studies, detailing their architecture and how they leveraged various cloud technologies. Applications from a range of domains, from scientific to engineering, gaming, and social networking, are considered.

10.1 Scientific applications

Scientific applications are a sector that is increasingly using cloud computing systems and technologies. The immediate benefit seen by researchers and academics is the potentially infinite availability of computing resources and storage at sustainable prices compared to a complete in-house deployment. Cloud computing systems meet the needs of different types of applications in the scientific domain: high-performance computing (HPC) applications, high-throughput computing (HTC) applications, and data-intensive applications. The opportunity to use cloud resources is even more appealing because minimal changes need to be made to existing applications in order to leverage cloud resources.

The most relevant option is IaaS solutions, which offer the optimal environment for running bag-of-tasks applications and workflows. Virtual machine instances are opportunely customized to host the required software stack for running such applications and coordinated together with distributed computing middleware capable of interacting with cloud-based infrastructures. PaaS solutions have been considered as well. They allow scientists to explore new programming models for tackling computationally challenging problems. Applications have been redesigned and implemented on top of cloud programming application models and platforms to leverage their unique capabilities. For instance, the MapReduce programming model provides scientists with a very simple and effective model for building applications that need to process large datasets. Therefore it has been widely used to develop data-intensive scientific applications. Problems that require a higher degree of flexibility in terms of structuring of their computation model can leverage platforms such as Aneka, which supports MapReduce and other programming models. We now discuss some interesting case studies in which Aneka has been used.

10.1.1 Healthcare: ECG analysis in the cloud

Healthcare is a domain in which computer technology has found several and diverse applications: from supporting the business functions to assisting scientists in developing solutions to cure diseases.

353

An important application is the use of cloud technologies to support doctors in providing more effective diagnostic processes. In particular, here we discuss electrocardiogram (ECG) data analysis on the cloud [160].

The capillary development of Internet connectivity and its accessibility from any device at any time has made cloud technologies an attractive option for developing health-monitoring systems. ECG data analysis and monitoring constitute a case that naturally fits into this scenario. ECG is the electrical manifestation of the contractile activity of the heart's myocardium. This activity produces a specific waveform that is repeated over time and that represents the heartbeat. The analysis of the shape of the ECG waveform is used to identify arrhythmias and is the most common way to detect heart disease. Cloud computing technologies allow the remote monitoring of a patient's heartbeat data, data analysis in minimal time, and the notification of first-aid personnel and doctors should these data reveal potentially dangerous conditions. This way a patient at risk can be constantly monitored without going to a hospital for ECG analysis. At the same time, doctors and first-aid personnel can instantly be notified of cases that require their attention.

An illustration of the infrastructure and model for supporting remote ECG monitoring is shown in Figure 10.1. Wearable computing devices equipped with ECG sensors constantly monitor the patient's heartbeat. Such information is transmitted to the patient's mobile device, which will eventually forward it to the cloud-hosted Web service for analysis. The Web service forms the front-end of a platform that is entirely hosted in the cloud and that leverages the three layers of the cloud computing stack: SaaS, PaaS, and IaaS. The Web service constitute the SaaS application that will store ECG data in the Amazon S3 service and issue a processing request to the scalable cloud platform. The runtime platform is composed of a dynamically sizable number of instances running the workflow engine and Aneka. The number of workflow engine instances is controlled according to the number of requests in the queue of each instance, while Aneka controls the number of EC2 instances used to execute the single tasks defined by the workflow engine for a single ECG processing job. Each of these jobs consists of a set of operations involving the extraction of the waveform from the heartbeat data and the comparison of the waveform with a reference waveform to detect anomalies. If anomalies are found, doctors and first-aid personnel can be notified to act on a specific patient.

Even though remote ECG monitoring does not necessarily require cloud technologies, cloud computing introduces opportunities that would be otherwise hardly achievable. The first advantage is the elasticity of the cloud infrastructure that can grow and shrink according to the requests served. As a result, doctors and hospitals do not have to invest in large computing infrastructures designed after capacity planning, thus making more effective use of budgets. The second advantage is ubiquity. Cloud computing technologies have now become easily accessible and promise to deliver systems with minimum or no downtime. Computing systems hosted in the cloud are accessible from any Internet device through simple interfaces (such as SOAP and REST-based Web services). This makes these systems not only ubiquitous, but they can also be easily integrated with other systems maintained on the hospital's premises. Finally, cost savings constitute another reason for the use of cloud technology in healthcare. Cloud services are priced on a pay-per-use basis and with volume prices for large numbers of service requests. These two models provide a set of flexible options that can be used to price the service, thus actually charging costs based on effective use rather than capital costs.

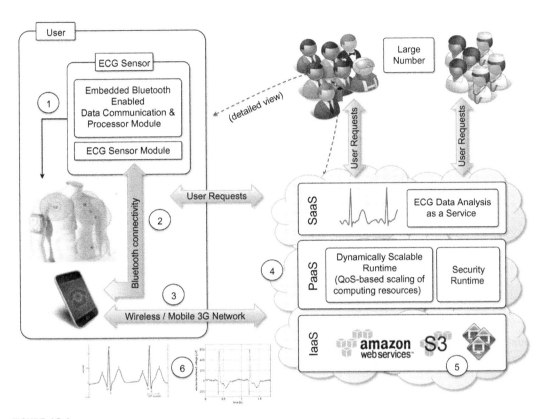

FIGURE 10.1

An online health monitoring system hosted in the cloud.

10.1.2 Biology: protein structure prediction

Applications in biology often require high computing capabilities and often operate on large data-sets that cause extensive I/O operations. Because of these requirements, biology applications have often made extensive use of supercomputing and cluster computing infrastructures. Similar capabilities can be leveraged on demand using cloud computing technologies in a more dynamic fashion, thus opening new opportunities for bioinformatics applications.

Protein structure prediction is a computationally intensive task that is fundamental to different types of research in the life sciences. Among these is the design of new drugs for the treatment of diseases. The geometric structure of a protein cannot be directly inferred from the sequence of genes that compose its structure, but it is the result of complex computations aimed at identifying the structure that minimizes the required energy. This task requires the investigation of a space with a massive number of states, consequently creating a large number of computations for each of these states. The computational power required for protein structure prediction can now be acquired on demand, without owning a cluster or navigating the bureaucracy to get access to

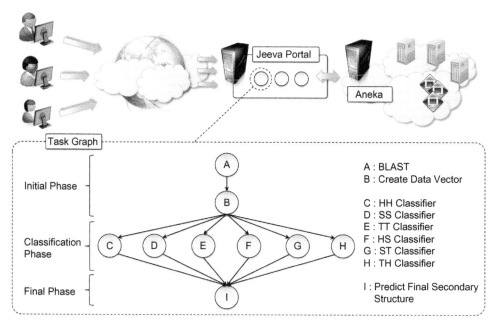

FIGURE 10.2

Architecture and overview of the Jeeva Portal.

parallel and distributed computing facilities. Cloud computing grants access to such capacity on a pay-per-use basis.

One project that investigates the use of cloud technologies for protein structure prediction is *Jeeva* [161]—an integrated Web portal that enables scientists to offload the prediction task to a computing cloud based on Aneka (see Figure 10.2). The prediction task uses machine learning techniques (support vector machines) for determining the secondary structure of proteins. These techniques translate the problem into one of pattern recognition, where a sequence has to be classified into one of three possible classes (E, H, and C). A popular implementation based on support vector machines divides the pattern recognition problem into three phases: *initialization, classification,* and a *final phase*. Even though these three phases have to be executed in sequence, it is possible to take advantage of parallel execution in the classification phase, where multiple classifiers are executed concurrently. This creates the opportunity to sensibly reduce the computational time of the prediction. The prediction algorithm is then translated into a task graph that is submitted to Aneka. Once the task is completed, the middleware makes the results available for visualization through the portal.

The advantage of using cloud technologies (i.e., Aneka as scalable cloud middleware) versus conventional grid infrastructures is the capability to leverage a scalable computing infrastructure that can be grown and shrunk on demand. This concept is distinctive of cloud technologies and constitutes a strategic advantage when applications are offered and delivered as a service.

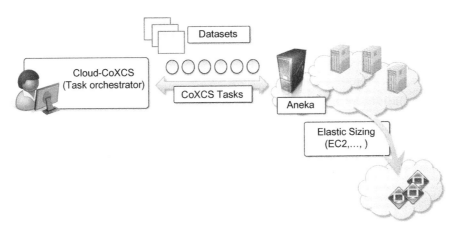

FIGURE 10.3

Cloud-CoXCS: An environment for microarray data processing on the cloud.

10.1.3 Biology: gene expression data analysis for cancer diagnosis

Gene expression profiling is the measurement of the expression levels of thousands of genes at once. It is used to understand the biological processes that are triggered by medical treatment at a cellular level. Together with protein structure prediction, this activity is a fundamental component of drug design, since it allows scientists to identify the effects of a specific treatment.

Another important application of gene expression profiling is cancer diagnosis and treatment. Cancer is a disease characterized by uncontrolled cell growth and proliferation. This behavior occurs because genes regulating the cell growth mutate. This means that all the cancerous cells contain mutated genes. In this context, gene expression profiling is utilized to provide a more accurate classification of tumors. The classification of gene expression data samples into distinct classes is a challenging task. The dimensionality of typical gene expression datasets ranges from several thousands to over tens of thousands of genes. However, only small sample sizes are typically available for analysis.

This problem is often approached with learning classifiers, which generate a population of condition-action rules that guide the classification process. Among these, the *eXtended Classifier System (XCS)* has been successfully utilized for classifying large datasets in the bioinformatics and computer science domains. However, the effectiveness of XCS, when confronted with high dimensional datasets (such as microarray gene expression data sets), has not been explored in detail. A variation of this algorithm, CoXCS [162], has proven to be effective in these conditions. CoXCS divides the entire search space into subdomains and employs the standard XCS algorithm in each of these subdomains. Such a process is computationally intensive but can be easily parallelized because the classifications problems on the subdomains can be solved concurrently. Cloud-CoXCS (see Figure 10.3) is a cloud-based implementation of CoXCS that leverages Aneka to solve the classification problems in parallel and compose their outcomes. The algorithm is controlled by strategies, which define the way the outcomes are composed together and whether the process needs to be iterated.

Because of the dynamic nature of XCS, the number of required compute resources to execute it can vary over time. Therefore, the use of scalable middleware such as Aneka offers a distinctive advantage.

10.1.4 Geoscience: satellite image processing

Geoscience applications collect, produce, and analyze massive amounts of geospatial and nonspatial data. As the technology progresses and our planet becomes more instrumented (i.e., through the deployment of sensors and satellites for monitoring), the volume of data that needs to be processed increases significantly. In particular, the geographic information system (GIS) is a major element of geoscience applications. GIS applications capture, store, manipulate, analyze, manage, and present all types of geographically referenced data. This type of information is now becoming increasingly relevant to a wide variety of application domains: from advanced farming to civil security and natural resources management. As a result, a considerable amount of geo-referenced data is ingested into computer systems for further processing and analysis. Cloud computing is an attractive option for executing these demanding tasks and extracting meaningful information to support decision makers.

Satellite remote sensing generates hundreds of gigabytes of raw images that need to be further processed to become the basis of several different GIS products. This process requires both I/O and compute-intensive tasks. Large images need to be moved from a ground station's local storage to compute facilities, where several transformations and corrections are applied. Cloud computing provides the appropriate infrastructure to support such application scenarios. A cloud-based implementation of such a workflow has been developed by the Department of Space, Government of India [163]. The system shown in Figure 10.4 integrates several technologies across the entire computing stack. A SaaS application provides a collection of services for such tasks as geocode generation and data visualization. At the PaaS level, Aneka controls the importing of data into the virtualized infrastructure and the execution of image-processing tasks that produce the desired outcome from raw satellite images. The platform leverages a Xen private cloud and the Aneka technology to dynamically provision the required resources (i.e., grow or shrink) on demand.

The project demonstrates how cloud computing technologies can be effectively employed to offload local computing facilities from excessive workloads and leverage more elastic computing infrastructures.

10.2 Business and consumer applications

The business and consumer sector is the one that probably benefits the most from cloud computing technologies. On one hand, the opportunity to transform capital costs into operational costs makes clouds an attractive option for all enterprises that are IT-centric. On the other hand, the sense of ubiquity that the cloud offers for accessing data and services makes it interesting for end users as well. Moreover, the elastic nature of cloud technologies does not require huge up-front investments, thus allowing new ideas to be quickly translated into products and services that can comfortably grow with the demand. The combination of all these elements has made cloud computing the

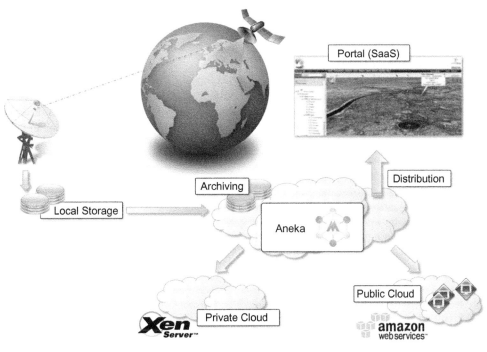

FIGURE 10.4

A cloud environment for satellite data processing.

preferred technology for a wide range of applications, from CRM and ERP systems to productivity and social-networking applications.

10.2.1 CRM and ERP

Customer relationship management (CRM) and *enterprise resource planning (ERP)* applications are market segments that are flourishing in the cloud, with CRM applications the more mature of the two. Cloud CRM applications constitute a great opportunity for small enterprises and start-ups to have fully functional CRM software without large up-front costs and by paying subscriptions. Moreover, CRM is not an activity that requires specific needs, and it can be easily moved to the cloud. Such a characteristic, together with the possibility of having access to your business and customer data from everywhere and from any device, has fostered the spread of cloud CRM applications. ERP solutions on the cloud are less mature and have to compete with well-established in-house solutions. ERP systems integrate several aspects of an enterprise: finance and accounting, human resources, manufacturing, supply chain management, project management, and CRM. Their goal is to provide a uniform view and access to all operations that need to be performed to sustain a complex organization. Because of the organizations that they target, the transition to cloud-based models is more difficult: he cost advantage over the long term might not be clear, and the switch to the cloud could be difficult if organizations already have large ERP installations. For this reason cloud ERP solutions are less popular than CRM solutions at this time.

10.2.1.1 Salesforce.com

Salesforce.com is probably the most popular and developed CRM solution available today. As of today more than 100,000 customers have chosen Safesforce.com to implement their CRM solutions. The application provides customizable CRM solutions that can be integrated with additional features developed by third parties. Salesforce.com is based on the Force.com cloud development platform. This represents scalable and high-performance middleware executing all the operations of all Salesforce.com applications.

The architecture of the Force.com platform is shown in Figure 10.5. Initially designed to support scalable CRM applications, the platform has evolved to support the entire life cycle of a wider range of cloud applications by implementing a flexible and scalable infrastructure. At the core of the platform resides its metadata architecture, which provides the system with flexibility and scalability. Rather than being built on top of specific components and tables, application core logic and business rules are saved as metadata into the Force.com store. Both application structure and

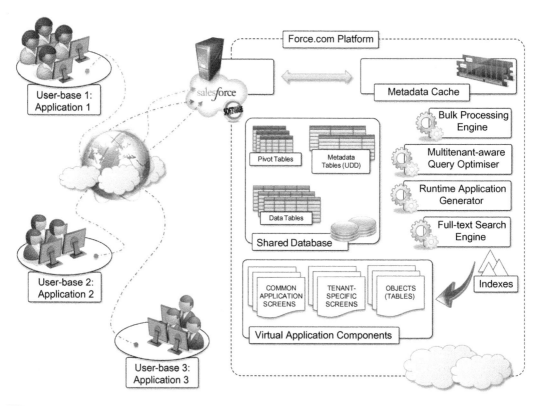

FIGURE 10.5

Salesforce.com and Force.com architecture.

application data are stored in the store. A runtime engine executes application logic by retrieving its metadata and then performing the operations on the data. Although running in isolated containers, different applications logically share the same database structure, and the runtime engine executes all of them uniformly. A full-text search engine supports the runtime engine. This allows application users to have an effective user experience despite the large amounts of data that need to be crawled. The search engine maintains its indexing data in a separate store and is constantly updated by background processes triggered by user interaction.

Users can customize their application by leveraging the "native" Force.com application framework or by using programmatic APIs in the most popular programming languages. The application framework allows users to visually define either the data or the core structure of a Force.com application, while the programmatic APIs provide them with a more conventional way for developing applications that relies on Web services to interact with the platform. Customization of application processes and logic can also be implemented by developing scripts in APEX. This is a Java-like language that provides object-oriented and procedural capabilities for defining either scripts executed on demand or triggers. APEX also offers the capability of expressing searches and queries to have complete access to the data managed by the Force.com platform.

10.2.1.2 Microsoft dynamics CRM

Microsoft Dynamics CRM is the solution implemented by Microsoft for customer relationship management. Dynamics CRM is available either for installation on the enterprise's premises or as an online solution priced as a monthly per-user subscription.

The system is completely hosted in Microsoft's datacenters across the world and offers to customers a 99.9% SLA, with bonus credits if the system does not fulfill the agreement. Each CRM instance is deployed on a separate database, and the application provides users with facilities for marketing, sales, and advanced customer relationship management. Dynamics CRM Online features can be accessed either through a Web browser interface or programmatically by means of SOAP and RESTful Web services. This allows Dynamics CRM to be easily integrated with both other Microsoft products and line-of-business applications. Dynamics CRM can be extended by developing plug-ins that allow implementing specific behaviors triggered on the occurrence of given events. Dynamics CRM can also leverage the capability of Windows Azure for the development and integration of new features.

10.2.1.3 NetSuite

NetSuite provides a collection of applications that help customers manage every aspect of the business enterprise. Its offering is divided into three major products: *NetSuite Global ERP*, *NetSuite Global CRM+*, and *NetSuite Global Ecommerce*. Moreover, an all-in-one solution: *NetSuite One World*, integrates all three products together.

The services NetSuite delivers are powered by two large datacenters on the East and West coasts of the United States, connected by redundant links. This allows NetSuite to guarantee 99.5% uptime to its customers. Besides the prepackaged solutions, NetSuite also provides an infrastructure and a development environment for implementing customized applications. The *NetSuite Business Operating System (NS-BOS)* is a complete stack of technologies for building SaaS business applications that leverage the capabilities of NetSuite products. On top of the SaaS infrastructure, the NetSuite Business Suite components offer accounting, ERP, CRM, and ecommerce capabilities.

An online development environment, *SuiteFlex*, allows integrating such capabilities into new Web applications, which are then packaged for distribution by *SuiteBundler*. The entire infrastructure is hosted in the NetSuite datacenters, which provide warranties regarding application uptime and availability.

10.2.2 Productivity

Productivity applications replicate in the cloud some of the most common tasks that we are used to performing on our desktop: from document storage to office automation and complete desktop environments hosted in the cloud.

10.2.2.1 Dropbox and iCloud

One of the core features of cloud computing is availability anywhere, at any time, and from any Internet-connected device. Therefore, document storage constitutes a natural application for such technology. Online storage solutions preceded cloud computing, but they never became popular. With the development of cloud technologies, online storage solutions have turned into SaaS applications and become more usable as well as more advanced and accessible.

Perhaps the most popular solution for online document storage is *Dropbox*, an online application that allows users to synchronize any file across any platform and any device in a seamless manner (see Figure 10.6). Dropbox provides users with a free amount of storage that is accessible through the abstraction of a folder. Users can either access their Dropbox folder through a browser or by downloading and installing a Dropbox client, which provides access to the online storage by means of a special folder. All the modifications into this folder are silently synched so that changes are notified to all the local instances of the Dropbox folder across all the devices. The key

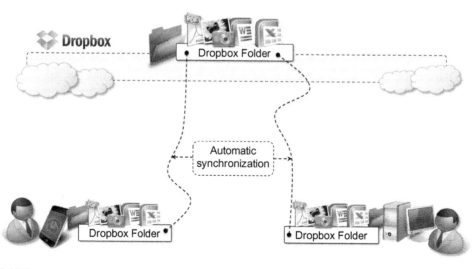

FIGURE 10.6

Dropbox usage scenario.

advantage of Dropbox is its availability on different platforms (Windows, Mac, Linux, and mobile) and the capability to work seamlessly and transparently across all of them.

Another interesting application in this area is *iCloud*, a cloud-based document-sharing application provided by Apple to synchronize iOS-based devices in a completely transparent manner. Unlike Dropbox, which provides synchronization through the abstraction of a local folder, iCloud has been designed to be completely transparent once it has been set up. Documents, photos, and videos are automatically synched as changes are made, without any explicit operation. This allows the system to efficiently automate common operations without any human intervention: taking a picture with your iPhone and having it automatically available in iPhoto on your Mac at home; editing a document on the iMac at home and having the changes updated in your iPad. Unfortunately, this capability is limited to iOS devices, and currently there are no plans to provide iCloud with a Web-based interface that would make user content accessible from even unsupported platforms.

There are other solutions for online document sharing, such as *Windows Live*, *Amazon Cloud Drive*, and *CloudMe*, that are popular and that we did not cover. These solutions offer more or less the same capabilities of those we've discussed, with different levels of integration between platform and devices.

10.2.2.2 Google docs

Google Docs is a SaaS application that delivers the basic office automation capabilities with support for collaborative editing over the Web. The application is executed on top of the Google distributed computing infrastructure, which allows the system to dynamically scale according to the number of users using the service.

Google Docs allows users to create and edit text documents, spreadsheets, presentations, forms, and drawings. It aims to replace desktop products such as Microsoft Office and OpenOffice and provide similar interface and functionality as a cloud service. It supports collaborative editing over the Web for most of the applications included in the suite. This eliminates tedious emailing and synchronization tasks when documents need to be edited by multiple users. By being stored in the Google infrastructure, these documents are always available from anywhere and from any device that is connected to the Internet. Moreover, the suite allows users to work offline if Internet connectivity is not available. Support for various formats such as those that are produced by the most popular desktop office solutions allows users to easily import and move documents in and out of Google Docs, thus eliminating barriers to the use of this application.

Google Docs is a good example of what cloud computing can deliver to end users: ubiquitous access to resources, elasticity, absence of installation and maintenance costs, and delivery of core functionalities as a service.

10.2.2.3 Cloud desktops: EyeOS and XIOS/3

Asynchronous JavaScript and XML (AJAX) technologies have considerably augmented the capabilities that can be implemented in Web applications. This is a fundamental aspect for cloud computing, which delivers a considerable amount of its services through the Web browser. Together with the opportunity to leverage large-scale storage and computation, this technology has made possible the replication of complex desktop environments in the cloud and made them available through the Web browser. These applications, called *cloud desktops*, are rapidly gaining in popularity.

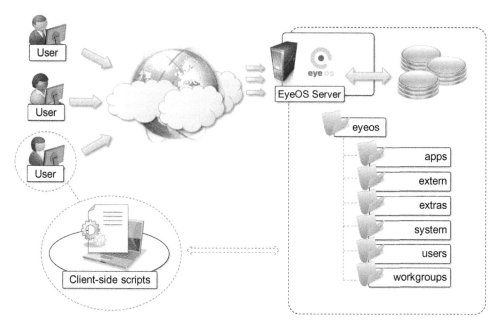

FIGURE 10.7

EyeOS architecture.

EyeOS[1] is one of the most popular Web desktop solutions based on cloud technologies. It replicates the functionalities of a classic desktop environment and comes with pre-installed applications for the most common file and document management tasks (see Figure 10.7). Single users can access the EyeOS desktop environment from anywhere and through any Internet-connected device, whereas organizations can create a private EyeOS Cloud on their premises to virtualize the desktop environment of their employees and centralize their management.

The EyeOS architecture is quite simple: On the server side, the EyeOS application maintains the information about user profiles and their data, and the client side constitutes the access point for users and administrators to interact with the system. EyeOS stores the data about users and applications on the server file system. Once the user has logged in by providing credentials, the desktop environment is rendered in the client's browser by downloading all the JavaScript libraries required to build the user interface and implement the core functionalities of EyeOS. Each application loaded in the environment communicates with the server by using AJAX; this communication model is used to access user data as well as to perform application operations: editing documents, visualizing images, copying and saving files, sending emails, and chatting.

EyeOS also provides APIs for developing new applications and integrating new capabilities into the system. EyeOS applications are server-side components that are defined by at least two files (stored in the *eyeos/apps/appname* directory): *appname.php* and *appname.js*. The first file defines

---

[1]www.eyeos.org.

and implements all the operations that the application exposes; the JavaScript file contains the code that needs to be loaded in the browser in order to provide user interaction with the application.

Xcerion XML Internet OS/3 (XIOS/3) is another example of a Web desktop environment. The service is delivered as part of the CloudMe application, which is a solution for cloud document storage. The key differentiator of XIOS/3 is its strong leverage of XML, used to implement many of the tasks of the OS: rendering user interfaces, defining application business logics, structuring file system organization, and even application development.The architecture of the OS concentrates most of the functionalities on the client side while implementing server-based functionalities by means of XML Web services. The client side renders the user interface, orchestrates processes, and provides data-binding capabilities on XML data that is exchanged with Web services. The server is responsible for implementing core functions such as transaction management for documents edited in a collaborative mode and core logic of installed applications into the environment. XIOS/3 also provides an environment for developing applications (XIDE), which allows users to quickly develop complex applications by visual tools for the user interface and XML documents for business logic.

XIOS/3 is released as open-source software and implements a marketplace where third parties can easily deploy applications that can be installed on top of the virtual desktop environment. It is possible to develop any type of application and feed it with data accessible through XML Web services: developers have to define the user interface, bind UI components to service calls and operations, and provide the logic on how to process the data. XIDE will package this information into a proper set of XML documents, and the rest will be performed by an XML virtual machine implemented in XIOS.

XIOS/3 is an advanced Web desktop environment that focuses on the integration of services into the environment by means of XML-based services and that simplifies collaboration with peers.

10.2.3 Social networking

Social networking applications have grown considerably in the last few years to become the most active sites on the Web. To sustain their traffic and serve millions of users seamlessly, services such as Twitter and Facebook have leveraged cloud computing technologies. The possibility of continuously adding capacity while systems are running is the most attractive feature for social networks, which constantly increase their user base.

10.2.3.1 Facebook

Facebook is probably the most evident and interesting environment in social networking. With more than 800 million users, it has become one of the largest Websites in the world. To sustain this incredible growth, it has been fundamental that Facebook be capable of continuously adding capacity and developing new scalable technologies and software systems while maintaining high performance to ensure a smooth user experience.

Currently, the social network is backed by two data centers that have been built and optimized to reduce costs and impact on the environment. On top of this highly efficient infrastructure, built and designed out of inexpensive hardware, a completely customized stack of opportunely modified and refined open-source technologies constitutes the back-end of the largest social network. Taken all together, these technologies constitute a powerful platform for developing cloud applications.

This platform primarily supports Facebook itself and offers APIs to integrate third-party applications with Facebook's core infrastructure to deliver additional services such as social games and quizzes created by others.

The reference stack serving Facebook is based on *LAMP* (*Linux, Apache, MySQL,* and *PHP*). This collection of technologies is accompanied by a collection of other services developed in-house. These services are developed in a variety of languages and implement specific functionalities such as search, news feeds, notifications, and others. While serving page requests, the *social graph* of the user is composed. The social graph identifies a collection of interlinked information that is of relevance for a given user. Most of the user data are served by querying a distributed cluster of MySQL instances, which mostly contain key-value pairs. These data are then cached for faster retrieval. The rest of the relevant information is then composed together using the services mentioned before. These services are located closer to the data and developed in languages that provide better performance than PHP.

The development of services is facilitated by a set of internally developed tools. One of the core elements is *Thrift*. This is a collection of abstractions (and language bindings) that allow cross-language development. Thrift allows services developed in different languages to communicate and exchange data. Bindings for Thrift in different languages take care of data serialization and deserialization, communication, and client and server boilerplate code. This simplifies the work of the developers, who can quickly prototype services and leverage existing ones. Other relevant services and tools are *Scribe*, which aggregates streaming log feeds, and applications for alerting and monitoring.

10.2.4 Media applications

Media applications are a niche that has taken a considerable advantage from leveraging cloud computing technologies. In particular, video-processing operations, such as encoding, transcoding, composition, and rendering, are good candidates for a cloud-based environment. These are computationally intensive tasks that can be easily offloaded to cloud computing infrastructures.

10.2.4.1 Animoto

Animoto[2] is perhaps the most popular example of media applications on the cloud. The Website provides users with a very straightforward interface for quickly creating videos out of images, music, and video fragments submitted by users. Users select a specific theme for a video, upload the photos and videos and order them in the sequence they want to appear, select the song for the music, and render the video. The process is executed in the background and the user is notified via email once the video is rendered.

The core value of Animoto is the ability to quickly create videos with stunning effects without user intervention. A proprietary artificial intelligence (AI) engine, which selects the animation and transition effects according to pictures and music, drives the rendering operation. Users only have to define the storyboard by organizing pictures and videos into the desired sequence. If users don't like the result, the video can be rendered again and the engine will select a different composition, thus producing a different outcome every time. The service allows users to create 30-second videos

---

[2]www.animoto.com.

for free. By paying a monthly or a yearly subscription it is possible to produce videos of any length and to choose among a wider range of templates.

The infrastructure supporting Animoto is complex and is composed of different systems that all need to scale (see Figure 10.8). The core function is implemented on top of the Amazon Web Services infrastructure. In particular, it uses Amazon EC2 for the Web front-end and the worker nodes; Amazon S3 for the storage of pictures, music, and videos; and Amazon SQS for connecting all the components. The system's auto-scaling capabilities are managed by Rightscale, which monitors the load and controls the creation of new worker instances as well as their reclaim. Front-end nodes collect the components required to make the video and store them in S3. Once the storyboard of the video is completed, a video-rendering request is entered into a SQS queue. Worker nodes pick up rendering requests and perform the rendering. When the process is completed, another message is entered into a different SQS queue and another request is served. This last queue is cleared routinely and users are notified about the completion. The life of EC2 instances is controlled by Rightscale, which constantly monitors the load and the performance of the system and decides whether it is necessary to grow or shrink.

The architecture of the system has proven to be very scalable and reliable by using up to 4,000 servers on EC2 in peak times without dropping requests but simply causing acceptable temporary delays for the rendering process.

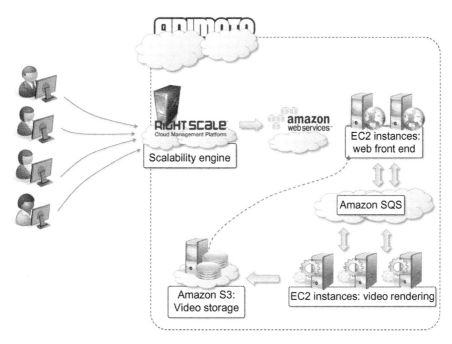

FIGURE 10.8

Animoto reference architecture.

10.2.4.2 Maya rendering with Aneka

Interesting applications of media processing are found in the engineering disciplines and the movie production industry. Operations such as rendering of models are now an integral part of the design workflow, which has become computationally demanding. The visualization of mechanical models is not only used at the end of the design process, it is iteratively used to improve the design. It is then fundamental to perform such tasks as fast as possible. Cloud computing provides engineers with the necessary computing power to make this happen.

A private cloud solution for rendering train designs has been implemented by the engineering department of GoFront group, a division of China Southern Railway (see Figure 10.9). The department is responsible for designing models of high-speed electric locomotives, metro cars, urban transportation vehicles, and motor trains. The design process for prototypes requires high-quality, three-dimensional (3D) images. The analysis of these images can help engineers identify problems and correct their design. Three-dimensional rendering tasks take considerable amounts of time, especially in the case of huge numbers of frames, but it is critical for the department to reduce the time spent in these iterations. This goal has been achieved by leveraging cloud computing technologies, which turned the network of desktops in the department into a desktop cloud managed by Aneka.

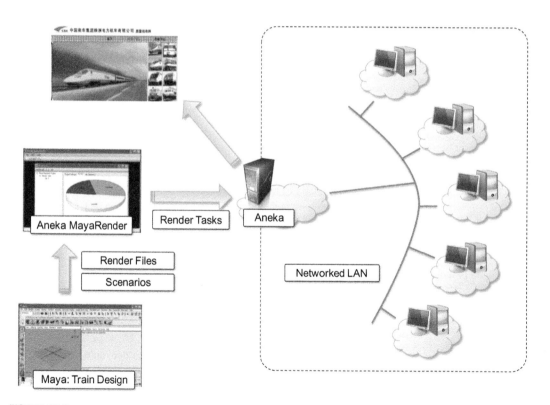

FIGURE 10.9

3D rendering on private clouds.

The implemented system includes a specialized client interface that can be used by GoFront engineers to enter all the details of the rendering process (the number of frames, the number of cameras, and other parameters). The application is used to submit the rendering tasks to the Aneka Cloud, which distributes the load across all the available machines. Every rendering task triggers the execution of the local Maya batch renderer and collects the result of the execution. The renders are then retrieved and put all together for visualization.

By turning the local network into a private cloud, the resources of which can be used off-peak (i.e., at night, when desktops are not utilized), it has been possible for GoFront to sensibly reduce the time spent in the rendering process from days to hours.

10.2.4.3 Video encoding on the cloud: Encoding.com

Video encoding and transcoding are operations that can greatly benefit from using cloud technologies: They are computationally intensive and potentially require considerable amounts of storage. Moreover, with the continuous improvement of mobile devices as well as the diffusion of the Internet, requests for video content have significantly increased. The variety of devices with video playback capabilities has led to an explosion of formats through which a video can be delivered. Software and hardware for video encoding and transcoding often have prohibitive costs or are not flexible enough to support conversion from any format to any format. Cloud technologies present an opportunity for turning these tedious and often demanding tasks into services that can be easily integrated into a variety of workflows or made available to everyone according to their needs.

Encoding.com is a software solution that offers video-transcoding services on demand and leverages cloud technology to provide both the horsepower required for video conversion and the storage for staging videos. The service integrates with both Amazon Web Services technologies (*EC2, S3,* and *CloudFront*) and Rackspace (*Cloud Servers, Cloud Files,* and *Limelight CDN* access). Users can access the services through a variety of interfaces: the Encoding.com Website, Web service XML APIs, desktop applications, and watched folders. To use the service, users have to specify the location of the video to transcode, the destination format, and the target location of the video. Encoding.com also offers other video-editing operations such as the insertion of thumbnails, watermarks, or logos. Moreover, it extends its capabilities to audio and image conversion.

The service provides various pricing options: monthly fee, pay-as-you-go (by batches), and special prices for high volumes. Encoding.com now has more than 2,000 customers and has already processed more than 10 million videos.

10.2.5 Multiplayer online gaming

Online multiplayer gaming attracts millions of gamers around the world who share a common experience by playing together in a virtual environment that extends beyond the boundaries of a normal LAN. Online games support hundreds of players in the same session, made possible by the specific architecture used to forward interactions, which is based on game log processing. Players update the game server hosting the game session, and the server integrates all the updates into a log that is made available to all the players through a TCP port. The client software used for the game connects to the log port and, by reading the log, updates the local user interface with the actions of other players.

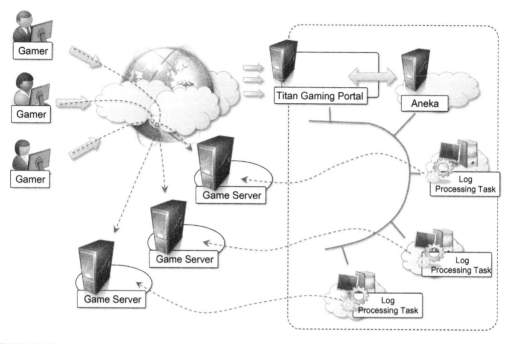

FIGURE 10.10

Scalable processing of logs for network games.

Game log processing is also utilized to build statistics on players and rank them. These features constitute the additional value of online gaming portals that attract more and more gamers. The processing of game logs is a potentially compute-intensive operation that strongly depends on the number of players online and the number of games monitored. Moreover, gaming portals are Web applications and therefore might suffer from the spiky behavior of users that can randomly generate large amounts of volatile workloads that do not justify capacity planning.

The use of cloud computing technologies can provide the required elasticity for seamlessly processing these workloads and scale as required when the number of users increases. A prototypal implementation of cloud-based game log processing has been implemented by Titan Inc. (now Xfire), a company based in California that extended its gaming portal for offload game log processing to an Aneka Cloud. The prototype (shown in Figure 10.10) uses a private cloud deployment that allowed Titan Inc. to process concurrently multiple logs and sustain a larger number of users.

SUMMARY

This chapter presented a brief overview of applications developed for the cloud or that leverage cloud technologies in some form. Different application domains, from scientific to business and consumer applications, can take advantage of cloud computing.

Scientific applications take great benefit from the elastic scalability of cloud environments, which also provide the required degree of customization to allow the deployment and execution of scientific experiments. Business and consumer applications can leverage several other characteristics: CRM and ERP applications in the cloud can reduce or even eliminate maintenance costs due to hardware management, system administration, and software upgrades. Moreover, they can also become ubiquitous and accessible from any device and anywhere. Productivity applications, such as office automation products, can make your document not only accessible but also modifiable from anywhere. This eliminates, for instance, the need to copy documents between devices. Media applications such as video encoding can offload lengthy and compute-intensive encoding tasks onto the cloud. Social networks can leverage the capability of continuously adding capacity without major service disruptions and by maintaining expected performance levels.

All these new opportunities have transformed the way we use these applications on a daily basis, but they also introduced new challenges for developers, who have to rethink their designs to better benefit from elastic scalability, on-demand resource provisioning, and ubiquity. These are key features of cloud technology that make it an attractive solution in several domains.

Review questions

1. What are the types of applications that can benefit from cloud computing?
2. What fundamental advantages does cloud technology bring to scientific applications?
3. Describe how cloud computing technology can be applied to support remote ECG monitoring.
4. Describe an application of cloud computing technology in the field of biology.
5. What are the advantages cloud computing brings to the field of geoscience? Explain with an example.
6. Describe some examples of CRM and ERP implementations based on cloud computing technologies.
7. What is Salesforce.com?
8. What are Dropbox and iCloud? Which kinds of problems do they solve by using cloud technologies?
9. Describe the key features of Google Apps.
10. What are Web desktops? What is their relationship to cloud computing?
11. What is the most important advantage of cloud technologies for social networking applications?
12. Provide some examples of media applications that use cloud technologies.
13. Describe an application of cloud technologies for online gaming.

Advanced Topics in Cloud Computing

Cloud computing is a rapidly moving target. New technological advances and application services are regularly introduced. There are many open challenges, especially in the context of energy-efficient management of datacenters and the marketplace for cloud computing.

This chapter presents an overview of various open issues in cloud computing that need long-term investigation. It discusses issues involved in energy-efficient cloud computing and presents a "green" cloud computing architecture. It discusses market models needed for realizing an open market for cloud computing systems from the perspective of federations of clouds and agreements between clouds. A general overview of some of the existing standards that enable interoperation between clouds and a brief look at third-party cloud services are presented.

11.1 Energy efficiency in clouds

Modern datacenters that operate under the cloud computing model are hosting a variety of applications ranging from those that run for a few seconds (e.g., serving requests of Web applications such as ecommerce and social network portals) to those that run for longer periods of time (e.g., simulations or large dataset processing) on shared hardware platforms. The need to manage multiple applications in a datacenter creates the challenge of on-demand resource provisioning and allocation in response to time-varying workloads. Normally, datacenter resources are statically allocated to applications based on peak load characteristics in order to maintain isolation and provide performance guarantees. Until recently, high performance has been the sole concern in datacenter deployments, and this demand has been fulfilled without paying much attention to energy consumption. According to the McKinsey report on "Revolutionizing Data Center Energy Efficiency" [118], a typical datacenter consumes as much energy as 25,000 households. Energy costs of powering a typical data center doubles every five years. Because energy costs are increasing while availability dwindles, there is a need to shift focus from optimizing datacenter resource management for pure performance alone to optimizing for energy efficiency while maintaining high service-level performance (see Figure 11.1).

Datacenters are not only expensive to maintain, they are also unfriendly to the environment. Carbon emissions due to datacenters worldwide are now more than the emissions of both Argentina and the Netherlands [118]. High energy costs and huge carbon footprints are incurred due to the massive amount of electricity needed to power and cool the numerous servers hosted in these

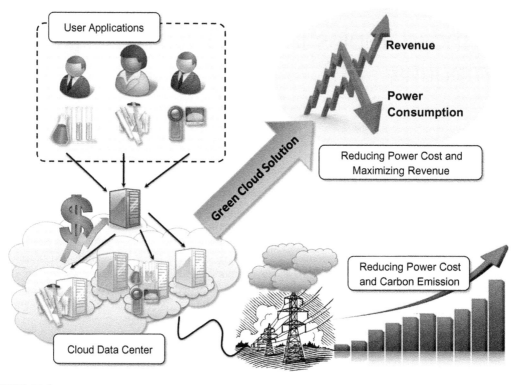

FIGURE 11.1

A "green" cloud computing scenario.

datacenters. Cloud service providers need to adopt measures to ensure that their profit margins are not dramatically reduced due to high energy costs. According to Amazon's estimate, the energy-related costs of its datacenters amount to 42% of the total budget, which includes both direct power consumption and the cooling infrastructure amortized over a 15-year period. As a result, companies such as Google, Microsoft, and Yahoo! are building large datacenters in barren desert land surrounding the Columbia River in the United States to exploit cheap hydroelectric power. There is also increasing pressure from governments worldwide to reduce carbon footprints, which have a significant impact on climate change. To address these concerns, leading IT vendors have recently formed a global consortium, called The Green Grid, to promote energy efficiency for datacenters and minimize their impact on the environment. Pike Research forecasts that datacenter energy expenditures worldwide will reduce from $23.3 billion in 2010 to $16.0 billion in 2020, as well as causing a 28% reduction in greenhouse gas (GHG) emissions from 2010 levels as a result of the adoption of the cloud computing model for delivering IT services.

Lowering the energy usage of datacenters is a challenging and complex issue because computing applications and data are growing so quickly that larger servers and disks are needed to process them fast enough within the required time period. *Green cloud computing* is envisioned to achieve

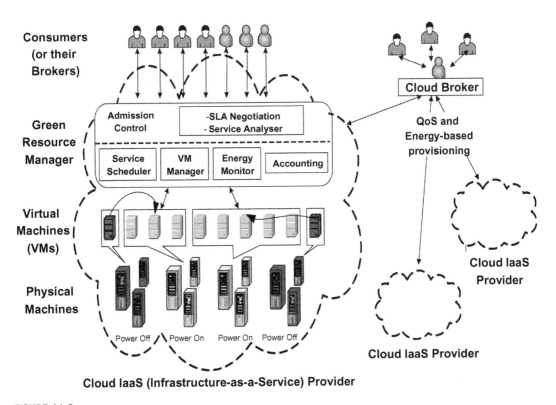

FIGURE 11.2

High-level system architectural framework for green cloud computing.

not only efficient processing and utilization of computing infrastructure but also minimize energy consumption. This is essential for ensuring that the future growth of cloud computing is sustainable. Cloud computing, with increasingly pervasive front-end client devices such as iPhones interacting with back-end datacenters, will cause an enormous escalation in energy usage. To address this problem, datacenter resources need to be managed in an energy-efficient manner to drive green cloud computing. In particular, cloud resources need to be allocated not only to satisfy QoS requirements specified by users via service-level agreements (SLAs) but also to reduce energy usage. This can be achieved by applying market-based utility models to accept user requests that can be fulfilled to enhance revenue along with energy-efficient utilization of cloud infrastructure.

11.1.1 Energy-efficient and green cloud computing architecture

A high-level architecture for supporting energy-efficient resource allocation in a green cloud computing infrastructure is shown in Figure 11.2. It consists of four main components:

- *Consumers/brokers.* Cloud consumers or their brokers submit service requests from anywhere in the world to the cloud. It is important to note that there can be a difference between cloud consumers and users of deployed services. For instance, a consumer can be a company deploying a Web application, which presents varying workloads according to the number of "users" accessing it.

- *Green Resource Allocator.* Acts as the interface between the cloud infrastructure and consumers. It requires the interaction of the following components to support energy-efficient resource management:
  - *Green Negotiator.* Negotiates with the consumers/brokers to finalize the SLAs with specified prices and penalties (for violations of SLAs) between the cloud provider and the consumer, depending on the consumer's QoS requirements and energy-saving schemes. In Web applications, for instance, the QoS metric can be 95% of requests being served in less than 3 seconds.
  - *Service Analyzer.* Interprets and analyzes the service requirements of a submitted request before deciding whether to accept or reject it. Hence, it needs the latest load and energy information from VM Manager and Energy Monitor, respectively.
  - *Consumer Profiler.* Gathers specific characteristics of consumers so that important consumers can be granted special privileges and prioritized over other consumers.
  - *Pricing.* Decides how service requests are charged to manage the supply and demand of computing resources and facilitate prioritizing service allocations effectively.
  - *Energy Monitor.* Observes and determines which physical machines to power on or off.
  - *Service Scheduler.* Assigns requests to VMs and determines resource entitlements for allocated VMs. It also decides when VMs are to be added or removed to meet demand.
  - *VM Manager.* Keeps track of the availability of VMs and their resource entitlements. It is also in charge of migrating VMs across physical machines.
  - *Accounting.* Maintains the actual usage of resources by requests to compute usage costs. Historical usage information can also be used to improve service allocation decisions.
- *VMs.* Multiple VMs can be dynamically started and stopped on a single physical machine to meet accepted requests, hence providing maximum flexibility to configure various partitions of resources on the same physical machine to different specific requirements of service requests. Multiple VMs can also run concurrently applications based on different operating system environments on a single physical machine. In addition, by dynamically migrating VMs across physical machines, workloads can be consolidated and unused resources can be put on a low-power state, turned off, or configured to operate at low performance levels (e.g., using *Dynamic Voltage and Frequency Scaling*, or DVFS) to save energy.
- *Physical machines.* The underlying physical computing servers provide hardware infrastructure for creating virtualized resources to meet service demands.

11.1.1.1 Energy-aware dynamic resource allocation

Recent developments in virtualization have resulted in its use across datacenters. Virtualization enables dynamic migration of VMs across physical nodes according to QoS requirements. Unused VMs can be logically resized and consolidated on a minimal number of physical nodes, while idle nodes can be turned off (or hibernated). Through consolidation of VMs, large numbers of users can share a single physical server, which increases utilization and in turn reduces the total number of servers required. Moreover, VM consolidation can be applied dynamically by capturing the workload variability and adapting the VM placement at runtime using migration.

Currently, resource allocation in a cloud datacenter aims at providing high performance while meeting SLAs, with limited or no consideration for energy consumption during VM allocations. However, to explore both performance and energy efficiency, two crucial issues must be addressed. First, turning off resources in a dynamic environment puts QoS at risk; aggressive consolidation may cause some VMs to obtain insufficient resources to serve a spike in load. Second, agreed SLAs bring challenges to application performance management in virtualized environments. These issues require effective consolidation policies that can minimize energy use without compromising user QoS requirements. The current approaches to dynamic VM consolidation are weak in terms of providing performance guarantees. One of the ways to prove performance bounds is to divide the problem of energy-efficient dynamic VM consolidation into a few subproblems that can be analyzed individually. It is important to analytically model the problem and derive optimal and near-optimal approximation algorithms that provide provable efficiency. To achieve this goal, clouds need novel analytical models and QoS-based resource allocation algorithms that optimize VM placements with the objective of minimizing energy consumption under performance constraints.

11.1.1.2 InterClouds and integrated allocation of resources

Cloud providers have been deploying datacenters in multiple locations throughout the globe. For example, Amazon EC2 Cloud services are available via Amazon datacenters located in the United States, Europe, and Singapore. This disbursement is leading to the emergence of a notion, called the *InterCloud*, supporting scalable delivery of application services by harnessing multiple datacenters from one or more providers. In addition to enhancing performance and reliability, these InterClouds provide a powerful means of reducing energy-related costs. One reason is that the local demand for electricity varies with time of day and weather. This causes time-varying differences in the price of electricity at each location.Moreover, each site has a different source of energy (such as coal, hydroelectric, or wind), with different environmental costs.This gives scope to adjust the load sent to each location, and the number of servers powered on at each location, to improve efficiency.

In such environments, algorithms that make routing decisions by considering the location of the user, the energy-efficiency of the hardware at each site, the energy mix, and the number of servers currently on at each location are needed. A particularly promising approach is to use this routing to make work "follow the renewables."A major problem with renewable energy is that most sources are intermittent and uncontrollable.Dynamically routing requests to locations with available renewable energy can greatly reduce the nonrenewable energy used and facilitate the widespread use of clean energy.

Sending loads to remote datacenters incurs both delay costs and energy costs due to the increased amounts of data that are transferred over the Internet. Improvements in energy-efficient transport technology should lead to significant reductions in the power consumption of the cloud software services [120].

11.2 Market-based management of clouds

Cloud computing is still in its infancy, and its prominent use is twofold: (1) complete replacement of in-house IT infrastructure and services with the same capabilities rented by service providers;

and (2) elastic scaling of existing computing systems in order to address peak workloads. The efforts in research and industry have been mostly oriented to design and implement systems that actually enable business vendors and enterprises to achieve these goals. The real potential of cloud computing resides in the fact that it actually facilitates the establishment of a market for trading IT utilities. This opportunity until now has been mildly explored and falls in the domain of what it is called *market-oriented cloud computing* [30].

11.2.1 Market-oriented cloud computing

Cloud computing already embodies the concept of providing IT assets as utilities. Then, what makes cloud computing different from *market-oriented* cloud computing? First, it is important to understand what we intend by the term *market*. The *Oxford English Dictionary* (OED)[1] defines a *market* as a "place where a trade is conducted" (Def. I). More precisely, *market* refers to a meeting or a gathering together of people for the purchase and sale of goods. A broader characterization defines the term *market* as the action of buying and selling, a commercial transaction, a purchase, or a bargain. Therefore, essentially the word *market* is the act of trading mostly performed in an environment—either physical or virtual—that is specifically dedicated to such activity.

If we consider the way IT assets and services are consumed as utilities, it is evident that there is a trade-off between the service provider and the consumer; this enables the use of the service by the user under a given SLA. Therefore, cloud computing already expresses the concept of trade, even though the interaction between consumer and provider is not as sophisticated as happens in real markets: Users generally select one cloud computing vendor from among a group of competing providers and leverage its services as long as they need them. Moreover, at present, most service providers have *inflexible pricing*, generally limited to flat rates or tariffs based on usage thresholds. In addition, many providers have proprietary interfaces to their services, thus restricting the ability of consumers to quickly move—and with minimal conversion costs—from one vendor to another. This rigidity, known as *vendor lock-in*, undermines the potential of cloud computing to be an open market where services are freely traded. Therefore, to remove such restrictions, it is required that vendors expose services through standard interfaces. This enables full commoditization and thus would pave the way for the creation of a market infrastructure for trading services.

What differentiates *market-oriented cloud computing (MOCC)* from cloud computing is the presence of a virtual marketplace where IT services are traded and brokered dynamically. This is something that still has to be achieved and that will significantly evolve the way cloud computing services are eventually delivered to the consumer. More precisely, what is missing is the availability of a market where desired services are published and then automatically bid on by matching the requirements of customers and providers. At present, some cloud computing vendors are already moving in this direction[2]; this phenomenon is happening in the IaaS domain—which is the market

---

[1]The definition of *market* according to the OED can be found at www.oed.com/view/Entry/114178?rskey =13s2aI&result=1#eid (retrieved July 5, 2011).
[2]Amazon introduced the concept of *spot instances* that are dynamically offered by the provider according to their availability and bid on by customers. Their effective usage and consumption is then determined by the spot price established by Amazon and the maximum price provided by the customers.

sector that is more consolidated and mature for cloud computing—but it has not taken off broadly yet. We can clearly characterize the relationship between cloud computing and MOCC as follows:

Market Oriented Computing has the same characteristics as Cloud Computing; therefore it is a dynamically provisioned unified computing resource allowing you to manage software and data storage as on aggregate capacity resulting in "real-time" infrastructure across public and private infrastructures. Market Oriented Cloud Computing goes one step further by allowing spread into multiple public and hybrid environments dynamically composed by trading service. [122]

The realization of this vision is technically possible today but is not probable, given the lack of standards and overall immaturity of the market. Nonetheless, it is expected that in the near future, with the introduction of standards, concerns about security and trust will begin to disappear and enterprises will feel more comfortable leveraging a market-oriented model for integrating IT infrastructure and services from the cloud. Moreover, the presence of a demand-based marketplace represents an opportunity for enterprises to shape their infrastructure for dynamically reacting to workload spikes and for cutting maintenance costs. It also allows the possibility to temporarily lease some in-house capacity during low usage periods, thus giving a better return on investment. These developments will lead to the complete realization of market-oriented cloud computing.

11.2.2 A reference model for MOCC

Market-oriented cloud computing originated from the coordination of several components: service consumers, service providers, and other entities that make trading between these two groups possible. Market orientation not only influences the organization on the global scale of the cloud computing market. It also shapes the internal architecture of cloud computing providers that need to support a more flexible allocation of their resources, which is driven by additional parameters such as those defining the quality of service.

11.2.2.1 A global view of market-oriented cloud computing

A reference scenario that realizes MOCC at a global scale is given in Figure 11.3. It provides guidance on how MOCC can be implemented in practice.

Several components and entities contribute to the definition of a global market-oriented architecture. The fundamental component is the virtual marketplace—represented by the *Cloud Exchange (CEx)*—which acts as a market maker, bringing service producers and consumers together. The principal players in the virtual marketplace are the *cloud coordinators* and the *cloud brokers*. The cloud coordinators represent the cloud vendors and publish the services that vendors offer. The cloud brokers operate on behalf of the consumers and identify the subset of services that match customers' requirements in terms of service profiles and quality of service. Brokers perform the same function as they would in the real world: They mediate between coordinators and consumers by acquiring services from the first and subleasing them to the latter. Brokers can accept requests from many users. At the same time, users can leverage different brokers. A similar relationship can be considered between coordinators and cloud computing services vendors. Coordinators take responsibility for publishing and advertising services on behalf of vendors and can gain benefits from reselling services to brokers. Every single participant has its own utility function, that they all want to optimize rewards. Negotiations and trades are carried out in a secure

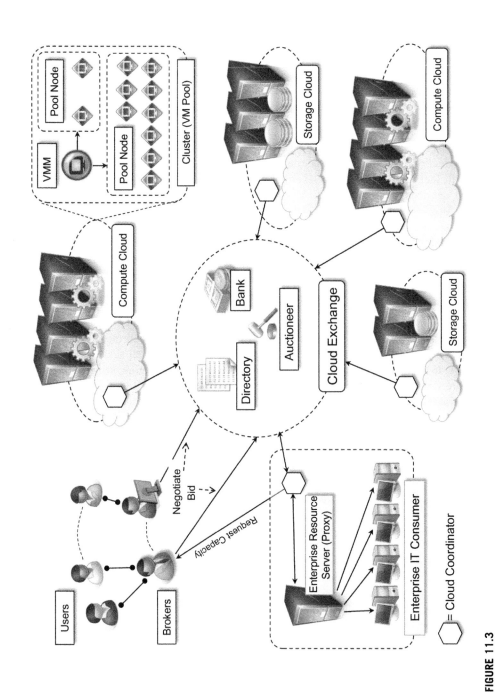

FIGURE 11.3

Market-oriented cloud computing scenario.

and dependable environment and are mostly driven by SLAs, which each party has to fulfill. There might be different models for negotiation among entities, even though the auction model seems to be the more appropriate in the current scenario. The same consideration can be made for the pricing models: Prices can be fixed, but it is expected that they will most likely change according to market conditions.

Several components contribute to the realization of the Cloud Exchange and implement its features. In the reference model depicted in Figure 11.3, it is possible to identify three major components:

- *Directory.* The market directory contains a listing of all the published services that are available in the cloud marketplace. The directory not only contains a simple mapping between service names and the corresponding vendor (or cloud coordinators) offering them. It also provides additional metadata that can help the brokers or the end users in filtering from among the services of interest those that can really meet the expected quality of service. Moreover, several indexing methods can be provided to optimize the discovery of services according to various criteria. This component is modified in its content by service providers and queried by service consumers.
- *Auctioneer.* The auctioneer is in charge of keeping track of the running auctions in the marketplace and of verifying that the auctions for services are properly conducted and that malicious market players are prevented from performing illegal activities.
- *Bank.* The bank is the component that takes care of the financial aspect of all the operations happening in the virtual marketplace. It also ensures that all the financial transactions are carried out in a secure and dependable environment. Consumers and providers may register with the bank and have one or multiple accounts that can be used to perform the transactions in the virtual marketplace.

This organization, as described, constitutes only a reference model that is used to guide system architects and designers in laying out the foundations of a Cloud Exchange system. In reality, the architecture of such a system is more complex and articulated since other elements have to be taken into account. For instance, since the cloud marketplace supports trading, which ultimately involves financial transactions between different parties, security becomes of fundamental importance. It is then important to put in place all the mechanisms that enable secure electronic transactions. These and other aspects are not unique to the design and implementation of MOCC systems but are of concern for any distributed computing system; therefore, they have been only mentioned here.

11.2.2.2 Market-oriented architecture for datacenters

Datacenters are the building blocks of the computing infrastructure that backs the services offered by a cloud computing vendor, no matter its specific category (IaaS, PaaS, or SaaS). In this section, we present these systems by taking into account the elements that are fundamental for realizing computing infrastructures that support MOCC. These criteria govern the logical organization of these systems—rather than their physical layout and hardware characteristics—and provide guidance for designing architectures that are market oriented. In other words, we describe a reference architecture for MOCC datacenters.

Figure 11.4 provides an overall view of the components that can support a cloud computing provider in making available its services on a market-oriented basis [123]. More specifically, the

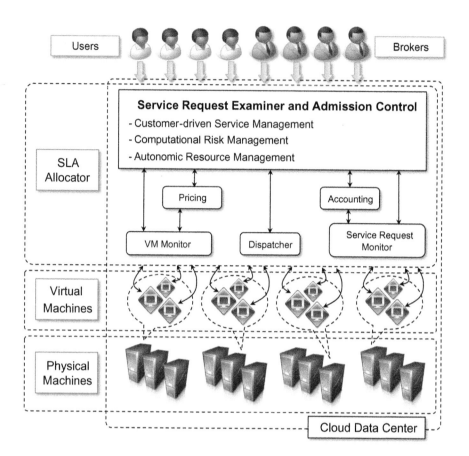

FIGURE 11.4

Reference architecture for a cloud datacenter.

model applies to PaaS and IaaS providers that explicitly leverage virtualization technologies to serve customers' needs. There are four major components of the architecture:

- *Users and brokers.* They originate the workload that is managed in the cloud datacenter. Users either require virtual machine instances to which to deploy their systems (IaaS scenario) or deploy applications in the virtual environment made available to them by the provider (PaaS scenario). These service requests are issued by service brokers that act on behalf of users and look for the best deal for them.
- *SLA resource allocator.* The allocator represents the interface between the datacenter and the cloud service provider and the external world. Its main responsibility is ensuring that service requests are satisfied according to the SLA agreed to with the user. Several components coordinate allocator activities in order to realize this goal:
  - *Service Request Examiner and Admission Control Module.* This module operates in the front-end and filters user and broker requests in order to accept those that are feasible given

the current status of the system and the workload that is already processing. Accepted requests are allocated and scheduled for execution. IaaS service providers allocate one or more virtual machine instances and make them available to users. PaaS providers identify a suitable collection of computing nodes to which to deploy the users' applications.

- *Pricing Module.* This module is responsible for charging users according to the SLA they signed. Different parameters can be considered in charging users; for instance, the most common case for IaaS providers is to charge according to the characteristics of the virtual machines requested in terms of memory, disk size, computing capacity, and the time they are used. It is very common to calculate the usage in time blocks of one hour, but several other pricing schemes exist. PaaS providers can charge users based on the number of requests served by their application or the usage of internal services made available by the development platform to the application while running.

- *Accounting Module.* This module maintains the actual information on usage of resources and stores the billing information for each user. These data are made available to the Service Request Examiner and Admission Control module when assessing users' requests. In addition, they constitute a rich source of information that can be mined to identify usage trends and improve the vendor's service offering.

- *Dispatcher.* This component is responsible for the low-level operations that are required to realize admitted service requests. In an IaaS scenario, this module instructs the infrastructure to deploy as many virtual machines as are needed to satisfy a user's request. In a PaaS scenario, this module activates and deploys the user's application on a selected set of nodes; deployment can happen either within a virtual machine instance or within an appropriate sandboxed environment.

- *Resource Monitor.* This component monitors the status of the computing resources, either physical or virtual. IaaS providers mostly focus on keeping track of the availability of VMs and their resource entitlements. PaaS providers monitor the status of the distributed middleware, enabling the elastic execution of applications and loading of each node.

- *Service Request Monitor.* This component keeps track of the execution progress of service requests. The information collected through the Service Request Monitor is helpful for analyzing system performance and for providing quality feedback about the provider's capability to satisfy requests. For instance, elements of interest are the number of requests satisfied versus the number of incoming requests, the average processing time of a request, or its time to execution. These data are important sources of information for tuning the system.

 The SLA allocator executes the main logic that governs the operations of a single datacenter or a collection of datacenters. Features such as failure management are most likely to be addressed by other software modules, which can either be a separate layer or can be integrated within the SLA resource allocator.

- *Virtual machines (VMs).* Virtual machines constitute the basic building blocks of a cloud computing infrastructure, especially for IaaS providers. VMs represent the unit of deployment for addressing users' requests. Infrastructure management software is in charge of keeping operational the computing infrastructure backing the provider's commercial service offering. As we discussed, VMs play a fundamental role in providing an appropriate hosting environment for users' applications and, at the same time, isolate application execution from the infrastructure, thus preventing applications from harming the hosting environment. Moreover,

VMs are among the most important components influencing the QoS with which a user request is served. VMs can be tuned in terms of their emulated hardware characteristics so that the amount of computing resource of the physical hardware allocated to a user can be finely controlled. PaaS providers do not directly expose VMs to the final user, but they may internally leverage virtualization technology in order to fully and securely utilize their own infrastructure. As previously discussed, PaaS providers often leverage given middleware for executing user applications and might use different QoS parameters to charge application execution rather than the emulated hardware profile.

- *Physical machines.* At the lowest level of the reference architecture resides the physical infrastructure that can comprise one or more datacenters. This is the layer that provides the resources to meet service demands.

This architecture provides cloud services vendors with a reference model suitable to enabling their infrastructure for MOC. As mentioned, these observations mostly apply to PaaS and IaaS providers, whereas SaaS vendors operate at a higher abstraction level. Still, it is possible to identify some of the elements of the SLA resource allocator, which will be modified to deal with the services offered by the provider. For instance, rather than linking user requests to virtual machine instances and platform nodes, the allocator will be mostly concerned with scheduling the execution of requests within the provider's SaaS framework, and lower layers in the technology stack will be in charge of controlling the computing infrastructure. Accounting, pricing, and service request monitoring will still perform their roles.

Regardless of the specific service offering category, the reference architecture discussed here aims to support cloud computing vendors in delivering commercial solutions that are able to [123]:

- Support customer-driven service management based on customer profiles and requested service requirements
- Define computational risk management tactics to identify, assess, and manage risks involved in the execution of applications with regard to service requirements and customer needs
- Derive appropriate market-based resource management strategies encompassing both customer-driven service management and computational risk management in order to sustain SLA-oriented resource allocation
- Incorporate autonomic resource management models that effectively self-manage changes in service requirements to satisfy both new service demands and existing service obligations
- Leverage—when appropriate—VM technology to dynamically assign resource shares according to service requirements

These capabilities are of fundamental importance for competitiveness in the cloud computing market and for addressing a scenario characterized by dynamic SLA negotiations as envisioned by MOCC. Currently, there is no or limited support for such a dynamic negotiation model, which constitutes the next step toward the full realization of cloud computing.

11.2.3 Technologies and initiatives supporting MOCC

Existing cloud computing solutions have very limited support for market-oriented strategies to deliver services to customers. Most current solutions mainly focused on enabling cloud computing concern the delivery of infrastructure, distributed runtime environments, and services. Since cloud computing has been recently adopted, the consolidation of the technology constitutes the first step toward the full realization of its promise. Until now, a good deal of interest has been directed toward IaaS solutions, which represent a well-consolidated sector in the cloud computing market, with several different players and competitive offers. New PaaS solutions are gaining momentum, but it is harder for them to penetrate the market dominated by giants such as Google, Microsoft, and Force.com.

11.2.3.1 Framework for trading computing utilities

From an academic point of view, a considerable amount of research has been carried out in defining models that enable the trading of computing utilities, with a specific focus on the design of market-oriented schedulers for grid computing systems. As discussed in the introduction, computing grids aggregate a heterogeneous set of resources that are geographically distributed and might belong to different organizations. Such resources are often leased for long-term use by means of agreements among these organizations. Within this context, market-oriented schedulers, which are aware of the price of a given computing resource and schedule user's applications according to their budgets, have been investigated and implemented. The research in this area is of relevance to MOCC, since cloud computing leverages preexisting distributed computing technologies, including grid computing.

Garg and Buyya [124] have provided a complete taxonomy and analysis of such schedulers, which is reported in Figure 11.5. A major classification categorizes these schedulers according to *allocation decision, objective, market model, application model,* and *participant focus.* Of particular interest is the classification according to the market model, which is the mechanism used for trading between users and providers. Along this dimension, it is possible to classify the schedulers into the following categories:

- *Game theory.* In market models that are based on game theory, participants interact in the form of an allocation game, with different payoffs as a result of specific actions that employ various strategies.
- *Proportional share.* This market model originates from proportional share scheduling, which aims to allocate jobs fairly over a set of resources. This original concept has been contextualized within a market-oriented scenario in which the shares of the cluster are directly proportional to the user's bid.
- *Commodity market.* In this model the resource provider specifies the price of resources and charges users according to the amount of resources they consume. The provider's determination of the price is the result of a decision process involving investment and management costs, current demand, and supply. Moreover, prices might be subject to vary over time.
- *Posted price.* This model is similar to the commodity market, but the provider may make special offers and discounts to new clients. Furthermore, with respect to the commodity market, prices are fixed over time.
- *Contract-Net.* In market models based on the Contract-Net [125] protocol, users advertise their demand and invite resource owners to submit bids. Resource owners check these advertisements with respect to their requirements. If the advertisement is favorable to them, the providers will respond with a bid. The user will then consolidate all the bids and compare them to select those

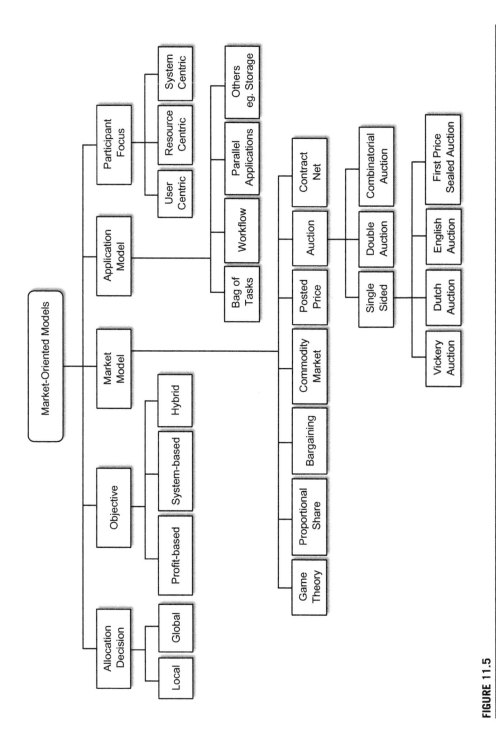

FIGURE 11.5

Market-oriented scheduler taxonomy.

most favorable to him. The providers are then informed about the outcome of their bids, which can be acceptance or rejection.

- *Bargaining.* In market models based on bargaining, the negotiation among resource consumers and providers is carried out until a mutual agreement is reached or it is stopped when either of the parties is no longer interested.
- *Auction.* In market models based on auctions, the price of resources is unknown, and competitive bids regulated by a third party—the auctioneer—contribute to determining the final price of a resource. The bid that ultimately sets the price of a resource is the winning bid, and the corresponding user gains access to the resource.

The most popular and interesting market models for trading computing utilities are the *commodity market*, *posted price*, and *auction* models. Commodity market and posted price models, or variations/combinations of them, are driving the majority of cloud computing services offerings today. Auction-based models can instead potentially constitute the reference market-models for MOCC, since they are able to seamlessly support dynamic negotiations.

Academic research has led to the development of a considerable number of software projects that implement either user resource brokers or resource management systems able to trade computing utilities according to one, or some, of the market models described previously. Some of them—namely *SHARP* [126], *Tycoon* [127], *Bellagio* [128], and *Shirako* [129]—have focused on trading VM-based resource slices and are more likely to be applicable within the MOCC scenario. In addition, it is worth noting some relevant research projects focusing on resource brokering, such as *Nimrod-G* [164] and *Gridbus Broker* [15], which have evolved to integrate capabilities for leasing cloud computing resources.

11.2.3.2 Industrial implementations

Even though market-oriented models have been mostly developed in the academic domain, industrial implementations of some aspects of MOCC are becoming available and gaining popularity. In particular, some interesting initiatives show how different aspects of MOCC, such as flexible pricing models, virtual market place, and market directories, have been made available to the wider public.

Flexible pricing models: amazon spot instances

Amazon Web Services (AWS), one of the biggest players in the IaaS market, recently introduced the concept of spot instances,[3] which allows EC2 customers to bid on unused Amazon EC2 capacity and run those instances for as long as their bid exceeds the current spot price. The spot price varies periodically according to the supply of and demand for EC2 instances and is kept constant within a single hour block. Spot instances can be terminated at any time, and they are usually priced at a lower price with respect to the traditional (on-demand and reserved) instances, since they rely on exceeding capacity available in the EC2 infrastructure. Therefore, it is the responsibility of the user to periodically persist the state of applications executing within spot instances. Spot instances represent an interesting opportunity for both Amazon and EC2 users to benefit from the current condition of the market: The provider can make revenue from a capacity that would have

---

[3]Full details about the spot instances service offering can be found in Amazon Web Services at the following link: http://aws.amazon.com/ec2/spot-instances/ (retrieved May 9, 2011).

been wasted if priced at the normal level, and the consumer has the opportunity to pay less by taking major risks.

Despite their volatile nature, spot instances have been demonstrated to be reasonably reliable and usable for performing tasks that have a lower priority and are not critical. In other words, they are suitable for applications that can tolerate QoS limitations. Moreover, they are profitably used to extend the capacity of an existing infrastructure at lower costs [130].

Virtual market place: SpotCloud

SpotCloud[4] is an online portal that implements a virtual marketplace, where sellers and buyers can register and trade cloud computing services. The platform is a market place operating in the IaaS sector. Buyers are looking for compute capacity that can meet the requirements of their applications, while sellers can make available their infrastructure to serve buyers' needs and earn revenue. *SpotCloud* provides a comprehensive set of features that are expected for a virtual marketplace. Some of them include:

- Detailed logging of all the buyers' transactions
- Full metering, billing for any capacity
- Full control over pricing and availability of capacity in the market
- Management of quotas and utilization levels for providers
- Federation management (many providers, many customers, but one platform)
- Hybrid cloud support (internal and external resource management)
- Full market administration and reporting
- Applications and pre-build appliances directories

Besides being an online portal, the virtual market realized by SpotCloud can also be replicated in the private premises. Transactions are carried out with real money and based on credit that buyers and sellers must top up once they create an account.

SpotCloud is the most representative implementation of a platform that enables MOCC, even though with some limitations. SpotCloud's working principle is a common and unique platform that sellers need to share in order to join the portal and make available computing capacity. SpotCloud currently supports Enomaly ECP[5] and OpenStack.[6]

Market directories: AppSpot, the cloud market

SpotCloud is implemented as an application hosted on *AppSpot*. This is a huge portal serving applications built on top of the Google *AppEngine* infrastructure: *appspot.com* is a namespace under which all the scalable Web applications developed with the Google AppEngine technology are made available to the community of Internet users. A solution that is more oriented toward listing available cloud building blocks is *The Cloud Market*,[7] which features a comprehensive listing of Amazon EC2 images. Even though these solutions do not provide a complete implementation of a

---

[4]www.spotCloud.com.
[5]www.enomaly.com.
[6]www.openstack.org.
[7]www.theCloudmarket.com.

market directory, they constitute a step toward the realization of MOCC, since they provide a means to easily locate components useful in building cloud computing systems.

11.2.3.3 A case study: the cloudbus toolkit

An interesting case study coming from research is the *Cloudbus* toolkit [131]. This is a collection of technologies and components that comprehensively try to address the challenges involved in realizing the vision of market-oriented cloud computing.

Figure 11.6 provides a comprehensive view of the Cloudbus components and how they interact together to provide a platform for MOCC. Real-life applications belonging to various scenarios, such as finance, science, education, engineering, multimedia, and others, require cloud computing facilities for processing their workloads and storing data.

The Cloudbus toolkit can act as a general front-end by providing mediated access to cloud computing services that best serve applications' needs. It does so by making available tools and technologies to implement a service-brokering infrastructure and middleware for deploying applications in the cloud. Brokering services are implemented by the Market Maker, which allows users to take full advantage of the cloud marketplace. It relies on different middleware implementations to fulfill the requests of users; these can be either Cloudbus technologies or third-party implementations. Technologies such as Aneka or Workflow Engine provide services for executing applications in the cloud. These can be public clouds, private intranets, or datacenters that can all be uniformly managed within an *InterCloud* [114] realm, which federates computing clouds that belong to different organizations into a unique domain characterizing agreements among parties.

Table 11.1 provides an overview of all the components that constitute the *Cloudbus* Toolkit, together with a brief description of their function. The toolkit also includes facilities for developing algorithms and deployments in a simulated environment by means of *CloudSim* [132]. This is a toolkit that enables users to simulate many aspects of cloud computing environments, from the basic building blocks of a cloud (datacenters, computing nodes, cores, network, and virtual machines) to the resource allocation algorithms and policies. As an example of its versatility, the toolkit has been used to simulate power-aware scheduling policies [133] for reducing energy consumption in large datacenters.

11.2.4 Observations

In this section we have briefly reviewed the fundamental concepts of market-oriented cloud computing. As with any technology, there exists a consolidation phase during which the concepts laying out its foundations are investigated, experimented, absorbed, and leveraged. Cloud computing is a relative evolution of distributed computing and has provided new ways to deliver IT infrastructure and services in a more efficient way to both enterprise and single users. Initially, considerable development interest and effort have been oriented toward the consolidation of the IaaS sector and its integration within the existing computing systems and workflow processes. Currently, PaaS solutions are gaining popularity and being used more consistently to deliver commercial and mainstream software applications and systems. This is the appropriate context where technologies and systems supporting MOCC can be implemented and made available. Most of the work done in this sense still belongs to the domain of academic research, even though the first commercial and industrial implementations are reaching the wider audience.

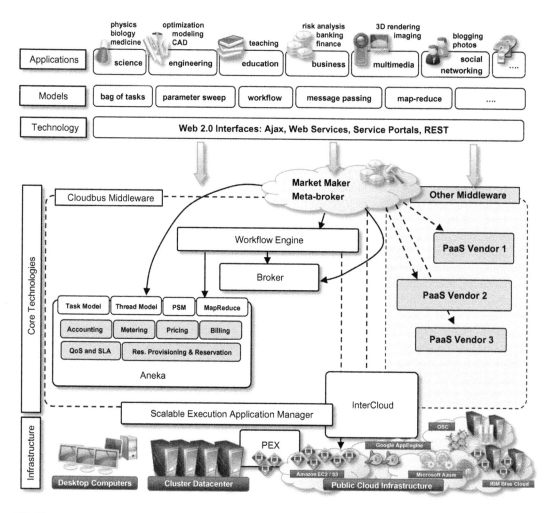

FIGURE 11.6

Cloudbus Toolkit.

11.3 Federated clouds/InterCloud

In the previous section we discussed how to define models and systems for trading computing resources as utilities and how cloud computing systems can interact with each other to make this trading happen. In this section, we address the same problem from the administrative and organizational points of view and introduce the concept of *cloud federation* and the *InterCloud*. These are enablers for MOCC since they provide means for interoperation among different cloud providers.

Cloud computing strongly implies the presence of financial agreements between parties, since services are available on demand on a pay-per-use basis. Nonetheless, the concepts characterizing

Table 11.1 Cloudbus Toolkit Components and Technologies	
Technology	**Description**
Aneka	Middleware for cloud applications development and deployment.
Broker	Middleware for scheduling distributed applications across heterogeneous systems based on the bag-of-tasks model.
Workflow management system	Middleware for the execution, composition, management, and monitoring of workflows across heterogeneous systems.
Market Maker/Meta-Broker	A matchmaker that matches the user's requirements with service providers' capabilities within the context of a marketplace.
InterCloud	A framework for the federation of independent computing clouds.
MetaCDN	Middleware that leverages storage clouds for intelligently delivering users' content based on their QoS and budget preferences.
Energy-efficient computing	Ongoing research on developing techniques and technologies for addressing scalability and energy efficiency.

cloud federation and the InterCloud are applicable, with some limitations, to building aggregations of clouds that belong to different administrative domains.

11.3.1 **Characterization and definition**

The terms *cloud federation* and *InterCloud*, often used interchangeably, convey the general meaning of an aggregation of cloud computing providers that have separate administrative domains. It is important to clarify what these two terms mean and how they apply to cloud computing.

The term *federation* implies the creation of an organization that supersedes the decisional and administrative power of the single entities and that acts as a whole.[8] Within a cloud computing context, the word *federation* does not have such a strong connotation but implies that there are agreements between the various cloud providers, allowing them to leverage each other's services in a privileged manner. A definition of the term *cloud federation* was given by Reuven Cohen, founder and CTO of Enomaly Inc.[9] :

> *Cloud federation manages consistency and access controls when two or more independent geographically distinct Clouds share either authentication, files, computing resources, command and control or access to storage resources.*

This definition is broad enough to include all the different expressions of cloud services aggregations that are governed by agreements between cloud providers, rather than composed by the user.

InterCloud is a term that is often used interchangeably to express the concept of Cloud federation. It was introduced by Cisco for expressing a composition of clouds that are interconnected by

---

[8]This is the definition given by the Merriam-Webster online dictionary: www.merriam-webster.com/dictionary/federation (retrieved May 10, 2011).
[9]www.elasticvapor.com/2008/08/standardized-Cloud.html (retrieved May 10, 2011).

means of open standards to provide a universal environment that leverages cloud computing services. By mimicking the Internet term, often referred as the "network of networks," InterCloud represents a "Cloud of Clouds"[10] and therefore expresses the same concept of federating together clouds that belong to different administrative organizations. Whereas this is in many cases acceptable, some practitioners and experts—like Ellen Rubin, founder and VP of Products at CloudSwitch[11] —prefer to give different connotations to the two terms:

> *The primary difference between the InterCloud and federation is that the InterCloud is based on future standards and open interfaces, while federation uses a vendor version of the control plane. With the InterCloud vision, all Clouds will have a common understanding of how applications should be deployed. Eventually workloads submitted to a Cloud will include enough of a definition (resources, security, service level, geo-location, etc.) that the Cloud is able to process the request and deploy the application. This will create the true utility model, where all the requirements are met by the definition and the application can execute "as is" in any Cloud with the resources to support it.*

Therefore, the term *InterCloud* refers mostly to a global vision in which interoperability among different cloud providers is governed by standards, thus creating an open platform where applications can shift workloads and freely compose services from different sources. On the other hand, the concept of a *cloud federation* is more general and includes *ad hoc* aggregations between cloud providers on the basis of private agreements and proprietary interfaces.

11.3.2 Cloud federation stack

Creating a cloud federation involves research and development at different levels: conceptual, logical and operational, and infrastructural. Figure 11.7 provides a comprehensive view of the challenges faced in designing and implementing an organizational structure that coordinates together cloud services that belong to different administrative domains and makes them operate within a context of a single unified service middleware.

Each cloud federation level presents different challenges and operates at a different layer of the IT stack. It then requires the use of different approaches and technologies. Taken together, the solutions to the challenges faced at each of these levels constitute a reference model for a cloud federation.

11.3.2.1 Conceptual level

The conceptual level addresses the challenges in presenting a cloud federation as a favorable solution with respect to the use of services leased by single cloud providers. In this level it is important to clearly identify the advantages for either service providers or service consumers in joining a federation and to delineate the new opportunities that a federated environment creates with respect to the single-provider solution. Elements of concern at this level are:

• Motivations for cloud providers to join a federation

---

[10]http://www.samj.net/2009/06/interCloud-is-global-Cloud-of-Clouds.html.
[11]CloudSwitch is a Cloud company that focuses on delivering an enterprise gateway to several cloud computing systems; www.Cloudswitch.com/page/Cloud-federation-and-the-interCloud (retrieved May 10, 2011).

- Motivations for service consumers to leverage a federation
- Advantages for providers in leasing their services to other providers
- Obligations of providers once they have joined the federation
- Trust agreements between providers
- Transparency versus consumers

Among these aspects, the most relevant are the motivations of both service providers and consumers in joining a federation.

From the perspective of cloud service providers, being part of federation is favorable if it helps increase their revenue and if it provides new opportunities to increase their business. Moreover, the option of joining a federation can also be considered convenient if it helps sustain the QoS ensured to customers in periods of peak load, which put extreme demand on the infrastructure of the single provider. More precisely, it is possible to identify functional and nonfunctional requirements that cloud service providers have behind these motivations. The functional requirements include:

- *Supplying low-latency access to customers, regardless of their location.* It is very unlikely that single cloud providers have a capillary distribution of their datacenters. Therefore, services that require low latency might provide poor performance because of unfortunate geo-location. Within this scenario the federation might help the single providers deliver the same service and meet the expected QoS.

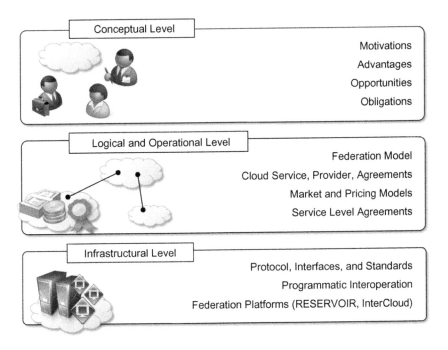

FIGURE 11.7

Cloud federation reference stack.

- *Handling bursts in demand.* Even though cloud computing gives the illusion of infinite capacity and continuous availability, service providers rely on a finite IT infrastructure that eventually will be fully utilized. A natural solution to this problem is increasing the infrastructure by adding more capacity. For example, to keep up with the increasing demand for storage and computation, Google has increased its number of servers from 8,000 to more than 450,000 in five years and moved from four server farms to more than 60 datacenters; Facebook has recently doubled its datacenter capacity. Such huge provisions are affordable for large IT companies that can make appropriate forecasts about increasing demand. Irregular demand can be better addressed by renting capacity from other providers, since not every cloud provider is in the position of being an IT giant. Cloud federation facilitates such activity by providing a context within which the lease of resources or services is encouraged.

- *Scaling existing applications and services beyond the capabilities of the owned infrastructure.* The need for additional capacity can also originate from the growth in scale of existing applications that are temporarily hosted and do not constitute a vital part of the service provider core business. Again, the opportunities for leasing additional services from a federated provider can constitute a potential advantage for a cloud federation.

- *Make revenue from unused capacity.* To provide the illusion of continuous availability and infinite capacity, cloud service providers generally own large computing systems, which generate costs in terms of maintenance and power consumption despite their real use. Energy-efficient computing solutions can help reduce costs and the impact of IT on the environment. A different opportunity is given by the cloud federation, whereby providers can lease their services to other providers for a limited period of time and thus make revenue, even without direct customers.

The motivations for joining a cloud federation also include nonfunctional requirements. The most relevant are the following:

- *Meeting compulsory regulations about the location of data.* Geo-location might become an in issue that limits a provider's capability to serve consumers. In this particular scenario it is not lack of capacity on the provider side that is the reason for leveraging the federation but, instead, the opportunity for identifying a provider that is in a position to deliver the service to the customer because of the location of its datacenter. Geo-location of data becomes an important matter when cloud services deal with confidential data that require specific levels of secrecy. Different countries have different regulations with respect to, for instance, the level of access to confidential data that government institutions may have.

- *Containing transient spikes in operational costs.* Operational costs can experience temporary spikes when there is a sudden change in electrical power due to natural disasters. This situation makes it inconvenient to fully exploit a given datacenter and provides an opportunity for leveraging federation resources to deliver services a cheaper price.

- *Disaster recovery.* Natural disasters happen, and if datacenters are co-located a disaster can put an entire datacenter or more out of service for an undefined period of time. In this scenario agreements between providers to handle disaster conditions are more likely to be settled in a federated context than in a competitive market.

For all these cases, cloud federation helps provide not only conceptual solutions but also practical means to realize these goals.

Cloud federation is an overlay that mostly benefits cloud service providers and that is supposed to be transparent to service consumers. Besides the indirect benefits to end users, there are indeed some potential direct benefits originating specifically from the concept of federation. Indirect benefits are mostly related to the QoS perceived by the end users. Real QoS is possible by enforcing admission control, which ensures that if a request is accepted, it will be served in compliance with the QoS profile defined in the SLA signed with the customer. Currently, the major cloud service providers engage QoS agreements that are mostly based on availability rather than other quality factors. For instance, in an IaaS scenario the published hardware features of a VM instance might not mirror its real performance. Since there is no SLA enforcement of such features, the provider will always try to serve requests, even when risking delivery of poor performance. In a federated scenario, requests may be served by leveraging other providers, thus ensuring that the expected performance profile is met. Therefore, as indirect benefit for users, cloud federation can help increase the overall QoS the user experiences when requesting a service. Direct benefits instead constitute something that is an advantage to end users, and they are perceivable because of the existence of federated clouds.

Cloud providers that offer different services can support each other since they are not competitors. A good example can be taken from the cooperation between the airline and accommodation market segments. Airline companies provide you with selected options for accommodation to be paired with a flight booking. This is generally the result of an agreement between the hotel and airline companies that might support each other, thus providing better service to the customer. Since companies operating in the two sectors are not competing with each other, they can both gain advantage if they provide customers with a complete solution. It is possible to replicate this type of collaboration in a federated cloud computing environment. For instance, providers that reside in different market segments (IaaS, PaaS, SaaS) might advertise each other to provide better service to the user. Enterprises that have legacy systems will be primarily looking at IaaS solutions to deploy and scale their systems. IaaS vendors can complement their offerings with advantageous access to some PaaS services by selecting those that might be complementary, of interest to the user, and offered by federated providers.

In the future, Amazon AWS might provide discounted access to AppEngine or simply provide a better interaction with the services exposed by Google in terms of data transfer, network connection, and bandwidth. How does this help the customer? The same company that is already hosting its Web application on Amazon EC2 might in the future want to integrate new features and develop them with a scalable technology. Due to performance advantages gained in leveraging AppEngine from an EC2 deployment, this could be the solution of choice. This is more likely to be possible within the context of a cloud federation. Moreover, federated clouds can provide better service to users, even when they reside in the same market segment but provide different services. For instance, in an IaaS scenario a specific provider might not be able to serve VM templates for hosting a specific operating system, but it can suggest or point the customer to another provider that's able to supply that capability. This scenario is applicable if the two providers have mutual agreements that are facilitated by belonging to a federation.

Being part of a federation also implies providers' obligations to avoid parasitic behaviors. For instance, each provider is expected to be an active member of the federation by contributing its resources. This makes an organization such as the federation dependable and increases the trust that each provider puts in it. Obligations, such as always making available a fraction of resources and services to the federation, might be considered disadvantages, but they may also constitute potential benefits. For instance, large companies such as Google are charged for energy usage according to the peak requests rather than detailed actual usage over a month [135]. This means that if in one month a datacenter reaches 90% of peak capacity and on average works at 60%, it will pay power bills for the cost of operating at 90% capacity for the entire month. This has led companies to put a lot of effort into optimizing the utilization of datacenters. A cloud federation might be an alternative to frenetic optimization, since it might make internal resources available for usage by other member of the federation. The revenue obtained from leasing these resources is an opportunity to compensate the energy costs for peak request.

All these aspects provide a rationale for the existence of federated clouds. Obstacles at the conceptual level are the implications for security and trust. For instance, in a federated context a provider might offload a portion of the service consumers' requests to another provider with which it has agreements. This is done transparently to the user, who might not desire such behavior. These are challenges that have to be properly addressed in order to make the concept of cloud federation a viable way to efficiently exploit cloud computing as a technology.

11.3.2.2 Logical and operational level

The logical and operational level of a federated cloud identifies and addresses the challenges in devising a framework that enables the aggregation of providers that belong to different administrative domains within a context of a single overlay infrastructure, which is the cloud federation. At this level, policies and rules for interoperation are defined. Moreover, this is the layer at which decisions are made as to how and when to lease a service to—or to leverage a service from—another provider. The logical component defines a context in which agreements among providers are settled and services are negotiated, whereas the operational component characterizes and shapes the dynamic behavior of the federation as a result of the single providers' choices. This is the level where MOCC is implemented and realized.

It is important at this level to address the following challenges:

- How should a federation be represented?
- How should we model and represent a cloud service, a cloud provider, or an agreement?
- How should we define the rules and policies that allow providers to join a federation?
- What are the mechanisms in place for settling agreements among providers?
- What are providers responsibilities with respect to each other?
- When should providers and consumers take advantage of the federation?
- Which kinds of services are more likely to be leased or bought?
- How should we price resources that are leased, and which fraction of resources should we lease?

The logical and operational level provides opportunities for both academia and industry. Whereas the need for a federation—or more generally, some sort of interoperation—has now been assessed, there is no common and clear guideline for defining a model for cloud federation and addressing these challenges. Indeed, several initiatives are developing. On the research side, several works are investigating organizational models for cloud interoperability and studying economical models for describing the behavior of cloud service providers and service consumers in a federated environment. Within industry, the major IT giants are working on promoting standards and drafting proposals for interoperable clouds.

Particular attention on this level has been put on the necessity for SLAs and their definition [150]. The need for SLAs is an accepted fact in both academy and industry, since SLAs define more clearly what is leased or bought between different providers. Moreover, SLAs allow us to assess whether the services traded are delivered according to the expected quality profile. It is then possible to specify policies that regulate the transactions among providers and establish penalties in case of degraded service delivery. This is particularly important because it increases the level of trust that each party puts in cloud federation.

SLAs have been in use since 1980 and originated in the telecommunications domain [152] to define the QoS attached to a contract between a consumer and a network provider. From there on, they have been used in several fields, including Web services, grid computing, and cloud computing. The specific nature of SLA varies from domain to domain, but it can be generally defined as "an explicit statement of expectations and obligations that exist in a business relationship between two organizations: the service provider and the service consumer.[12]" SLAs define the provider's performance delivery ability, the consumer's performance profile, and the means to monitor and measure the delivered performance. An implementation of an SLA should specify [153]:

- *Purpose*. Objectives to achieve by using a SLA.
- *Restrictions*. Necessary steps or actions that need to be taken to ensure that the requested level of service is delivered.
- *Validity period*. Period of time during which the SLA is valid.
- *Scope*. Services that will be delivered to the consumer and services that are outside the SLA.
- *Parties*. Any involved organizations or individual and their roles (e.g. provider, consumer).
- *Service-level objectives (SLOs)*. Levels of services on which both parties agree. These are expressed by means of service-level indicators such as availability, performance, and reliability.
- *Penalties*. The penalties that will occur if the delivered service does not achieve the defined SLOs.
- *Optional services*. Services that are not mandatory but might be required.
- *Administration*. Processes that are used to guarantee that SLOs are achieved and the related organization responsibilities for controlling these processes.

Parties that are willing to operate under an SLA engage a multistep process that generally involves the discovery or creation of the SLA, its operational phase, and its termination once its validity is over or there has been a violation of the contract [154]. A more articulated process has been detailed by the Sun Internet Data Center Group, which includes six steps for the SLA life cycle:

1. Discover service provider.
2. Define SLA.
3. Establish agreement.
4. Monitor SLA violation.
5. Terminate SLA.
6. Enforce penalties for SLA violation.

---

[12]Dinesh V, Supporting Service Level Agreements on IP Networks, Proceedings of IEEE/IFIP Network Operations and Management Symposium, 92(9):1382−1388, NY, USA, 2004.

Currently, a very rudimentary level of SLA management is present and the interoperability among different cloud providers is mostly characterized by *ad hoc* aggregation. The proposed process constitutes a reference model that still needs to be realized rather than a common implementation. Considerable work has been done in the academic domain regarding each of the steps defined here [150], but within industry, SLAs are still unilateral arrangements that are imposed by service providers and that the user can only accept rather than negotiate.

11.3.2.3 Infrastructural level

The infrastructural level addresses the technical challenges involved in enabling heterogeneous cloud computing systems to interoperate seamlessly. It deals with the technology barriers that keep separate cloud computing systems belonging to different administrative domains. By having standardized protocols and interfaces, these barriers can be overcome. In other words, this level for the federation is what the TCP/IP stack is for the Internet: a model and a reference implementation of the technologies enabling the interoperation of systems.

The infrastructural level lays its foundations in the IaaS and PaaS layers of the Cloud Computing Reference Model (discussed in Section 4.2). Services for interoperation and interface may also find implementation at the SaaS level, especially for the realization of negotiations and of federated clouds. At this level it is important to address the following issues:

- What kind of standards should be used?
- How should design interfaces and protocols be designed for interoperation?
- Which are the technologies to use for interoperation?
- How can we realize a software system, design platform components, and services enabling interoperability?

Interoperation and composition among different cloud computing vendors is possible only by means of open standards and interfaces. Moreover, interfaces and protocols change considerably at each layer of the Cloud Computing Reference Model. As the more mature layer, the IaaS layer has evolved more in this sense. Almost every IaaS provider exposes Web interfaces for packaging virtual machine templates, launching, monitoring, and terminating virtual instances. Even though not standardized, these interfaces leverage the Web services and are quite similar to each other. The use of a common technology simplifies the interoperation among vendors, since a minimum amount of code is required to enable such interoperation. These APIs allow for defining an abstraction layer that uniformly accesses the services of several IaaS vendors. There are already tools—both open-source and commercial—and specifications that provide interoperability by implementing such a layer.

To fully support the vision of a cloud federation, more sophisticated capabilities need to be implemented. For instance, the possibility of dynamically moving virtual machine instances among different providers is essential to supporting dynamic load balancing among different IaaS vendors. In this direction, the *Open Virtualization Format (OVF)* [51] aims to be a solution for this problem and may eventually be successful, since it has been endorsed by several cloud computing vendors. If we consider the PaaS layer, the interoperations become even harder since each cloud computing vendor provides its own runtime environment, which might differ from others in terms of implementation language, abstractions used to develop applications, and purpose. Currently, there is no sign of interoperation at this level and no proposed standards simplifying the interoperation among vendors. Regarding the SaaS layer, the variety of services offered makes the operation less crucial.

An interesting case for interoperability at the SaaS layer is provided by online office automation solutions such as Google Documents, Zoho Office, and others; several of them provide the capability to export and import documents to and from different formats, thus simplifying the exchange of data. Alternatively, composition seems to be a more attractive opportunity; different SaaS services can be glued together to provide users with more complex applications. Composition is also important in considering interoperability across cloud computing platforms operating at different layers. Even in this case it is important to note that, currently, cloud computing providers operating at one layer often implement on their own infrastructure any lower layer that is required to provide the service to the end user, and they are not willing to open their stack of technologies to support interoperation.

The vision proposed by a federated environment of cloud service vendors still poses a lot of challenges at each level, especially the logical and infrastructural level, where appropriate system organizations need to be designed and effective technologies need to be deployed. Considerable research effort has been carried out on the logical and operational level, and initial implementations and drafts of interoperable technologies are now developed especially for the IaaS market segment.

11.3.3 Aspects of interest

Several aspects contribute to the successful realization of a cloud federation. Besides motivation and technical enablers, other elements should be considered. In particular, standards for interoperability, security, and legal issues have to been taken into consideration while defining a platform for interoperability among cloud vendors.

11.3.3.1 Standards

Standards play a fundamental role in building a federation. Their main role is to organize a platform for interoperation that goes beyond *ad hoc* aggregations and private settlements between providers. Standardized interfaces and protocols facilitate the realization of an open organization where providers can easily join. The advantages are primarily technical; standards facilitate the development of software and services that interconnect systems. Furthermore, they help in defining clear paths for new providers to join, thus contributing to the realization of open systems.

Interoperation between vendors has always been an element of concern for enterprises and one of the reasons that initially prevented them from fully embracing the cloud computing model. More specifically, the absence of common standards for developing applications and systems in a portable way initially developed the fear of *vendor lock-in*. Applications and systems developed to be deployed on a specific cloud computing vendor's infrastructure could not be easily moved to another vendor. IaaS solutions still leverage proprietary formats for virtual machine instances and templates. This prevents instances from being moved from one vendor's platform to another. The technical barriers are even more considerable in the case of PaaS solutions, where even the development technology might differ. These technical barriers led to the development of solutions that tried to overcome these obstacles, at least for a limited number of providers. *Rightscale*,[13] for instance, is a

---

[13]www.rightscale.com.

solution that provides customers with a development platform that can be transparently deployed over different IaaS vendors. On the PaaS segment, *Aneka* provides middleware that can harness heterogeneous hardware and support cross-platform deployment across IaaS vendors. The *jClouds* project[14] defines a set of libraries and components that allows uniform use of different IaaS providers to develop applications on the cloud in Java.

These initiatives constitute technical improvements that help system designers and developers develop systems that are less subject to the vendor lock-in problem. They are far from providing the appropriate support that is required for building a federation, which can only be achieved by means of standards, protocols, and formats designed for interoperation. The efforts to create standards are carried out within the contexts of open organizations and consortia of major industry partners. Some minor efforts can be found in the academic world.

Open cloud manifesto

The Open Cloud Manifesto[15] constitutes the first step toward the realization of a cloud interoperability platform. The manifesto was drafted in 2009 as a result of the coordinated activity of different cloud vendors and currently lists more than 400 cloud computing services providers that support the vision it embodies. More than proposing standards, the manifesto is a declaration of intent, endorsed by commercial players in the field of cloud computing, to realize an interoperable and open cloud computing platform. The document is intended to be of guidance to the CIOs, governments, IT users, and business leaders who want to use cloud computing and to establish a set of core principles for cloud computing.

The document enumerates the advantages of cloud computing and discusses the challenges and barriers to its adoption. It introduces the goals of an open cloud platform, which can be summarized as follows:

- *Choice*. With the use of open technology it will be possible for IT consumers to select the best provider, architecture, or usage model as the business environment changes. Furthermore, the use of open technologies simplifies the integration of cloud computing solutions provided by different vendors or with the existing infrastructure, thus facilitating its adoption.
- *Flexibility*. The change between one provider and another becomes easier if the different vendors do not use a closed proprietary technology, which implies considerable conversion costs.
- *Speed* and *Agility*. As noted before, open technologies facilitate the integration of cloud computing solutions within existing software systems, thus realizing the promise of scaling demand with speed and agility.
- *Skills*. Open technologies simplify the learning process and contribute to developing a common knowledge that can be used to design, develop, and deploy systems across multiple providers. This simplifies the chances for organizations to find someone with the appropriate skills for their needs.

The manifesto ends with a set of recommendations for cloud computing vendors to pursue an open collaboration and an appropriate use of standards. Existing standards rather than proprietary

---

[14]http://code.google.com/p/jClouds/.
[15]www.opencloudmanifesto.org.

solutions are encouraged to be leveraged and, where appropriate, new standards should be drafted as a result of a community-based effort.

By evidencing the advantages of an open cloud platform, the manifesto lays the conceptual foundations for a cloud federation scenario. In fact, the use of open technologies will create a more flexible environment where IT consumers will more comfortably choose cloud computing technologies, without feeling the menace of vendor lock-in. The concept of cloud federation constitutes an evolution of this initial vision, which implies a more structured and explicit collaboration.

Distributed management task force

The *Distributed Management Task Force (DMTF)* is an organization involving more than 4,000 active members, 44 countries, and nearly 200 organizations. It is the industry organization leading the development, adoption, and promotion of interoperable management standards and initiatives. With specific reference to cloud computing, the DMTF introduced the *Open Virtualization Format (OVF)* and supported several initiatives for interoperable cloud technologies, such as the *Open Cloud Standards Incubator*, the *Cloud Management Working Group (CMWG)*, and the *Cloud Audit Data Federation Working Group (CADFWG)*.

The *Open Virtualization Format (OVF)* [51] is a vendor-independent format for packaging standards designed to facilitate the portability and deployment of virtual appliances across different virtualization platforms. OVF can be used by independent software vendors (ISVs) to package and securely distribute applications, and system images can be imported and deployed on multiple platforms, thus enabling cross-platform portability. The specification is the result of the collaborative effort of Dell, HP, IBM, Microsoft, VMWare, and XenSource in defining a platform-independent virtualization format for packaging software appliances. An initial draft was submitted to the DMTF in 2008, and currently the DMTF has released version 1.1.0 of the specification, which has also been ratified as American National Standards Institute (ANSI) standard INCITS 469-2010. The main purpose of the specification is to provide a platform-neutral format for distributing packaged software systems. Therefore, the key features of the format are the following:

- *Optimized for distribution.* The format supports verification and integrity checks based on industry-standard public key infrastructure and provides a basic license management scheme.
- *Optimized for a simple, automated user experience.* Supports validation of the entire package as well as each virtual machine or metadata component.
- *Supports both single VM and multi-VM configurations.* Provides the ability to package either single-image applications or complex multitier systems.
- *Portable vendor- and platform-independent VM packaging.* OVF is platform-neutral by design but also allows the embedding of platform-specific enhancements.
- *Extensible.* Even though the current specification is already capable of capturing all the required data for packaging a virtual appliance, it provides ways to extend and define new features for future needs.
- *Localizable.* The format allows embedding user-visible descriptions in multiple locales, thus being immediately ready to be processed over a wide range of systems and markets.
- *Open standard.* The format has arisen from the collaboration of key vendors in the industry and its evolution will be driven in an accepted industry forum in order to guarantee its future diffusion and use.

From a technical point of view, the OVF defines a transport mechanism for virtual machine templates. One single OVF package can contain one or more virtual machine images, and once deployed to the host system, it adds a self-containing, self-consistent software solution for achieving a particular goal. Examples are a Linux, Apache, MySQL, and PHP (LAMP) stack or any other combination of components divided into one or more virtual images. OVF's focus is to deliver a packaged, portable, ready-to-use, and verifiable software appliance. To achieve this goal, it allows the packaging of multiple virtual instances together with all the necessary descriptors for their deployment on virtual hardware. Currently, it is quite common to implement a software application or system by using a multitier architecture, which may spread across several computing nodes the components of the system, each of them requiring different operating systems and hardware characteristics. By supporting multiple virtual images within a single package, ISVs can package and certify entire systems as a whole and distribute them as a single component.

Portability is a fundamental property of the OVF. To fully address the potential issues arising in deploying a software appliance over a wide range of virtual hardware, different levels of portability are identified:

- *Level 1*. The packaged appliance runs on a particular product and/or CPU architecture and/or virtual hardware selection.
- *Level 2*. The packaged appliance runs on a specific family of virtual hardware.
- *Level 3*. The packaged appliance runs on multiple families of virtual hardware.

What determines the level of portability of an OVF package is the information that is packaged in the appliance and its specific requirements. Level 1 portability is mostly due to virtual hardware-specific information preventing the OVF's deployment even on a similar family of hypervisors. This information might be, for instance, a virtual machine suspended state or snapshot. Level 2 portability is acceptable within a single administrative domain where the decisions about the virtualization technology to adopt are most likely to be centralized. Level 3 portability is the one expected and desired by ISVs that want to package appliances capable of deployment on any virtual platform. In the context of a cloud federation, this is the expected level of portability for a seamless collaboration among different vendors. The OVF specification has been accepted quite positively since its inception, and several open-source initiatives and commercial products can import software appliances distributed as OVF packages.

The *Open Cloud Standards Incubator* is another important initiative that is driven by the DMTF to promote interoperability among cloud technologies. The focus of the incubator was the standardization of the interactions between cloud computing environments by developing cloud management use cases, architectures, and defining interactions. The activity of the incubator ended in July 2010 and produced a collection of white papers ([137, [138], and [139]) that are of guidance for developing interoperable cloud systems. These white papers were the starting point of the *Cloud Management Working Group (CMWG)*, the aim of which is to deliver a set of prescriptive specifications that confer architectural semantics and define implementation details to achieve interoperable management of clouds between service requestors/developers and providers. Another relevant initiative of the DMTF is the *Cloud Audit Data Federation (CADF)* working group, which will focus its interests on defining interoperable APIs for producing and sharing specific audit events, log information, and reports on a per-tenant basis, thus simplifying monitoring heterogeneous cloud computing environments.

The DMTF has made a significant contribution toward the realization of an interoperable cloud environment. The only concrete activity has been the release of the OVF specification. However, activities of the working groups and associated documents pave the way for realization of open cloud federation.

Open cloud computing interface

The *Open Cloud Computing Interface (OCCI)*[16] is an open organization that comprises a set of specifications driven by the community and delivered through the Open Grid Forum. These specifications define protocols and APIs for several kinds of management tasks. Initially conceived to create a remote management API for IaaS-type services, the OCCI has evolved into a wider set of APIs focusing on integration, portability, and interoperability. The current set of specifications covers all three market segments of cloud computing: IaaS, PaaS, and SaaS. OCCI has currently delivered three documents that define:

- The formal definition of the OCCI core model
- The definition of the OCCI infrastructure extensions for the IaaS domain
- The OCCI rendering model, which defines how to interact with the OCCI core model through REST over HTTP

Besides these, the OCCI is also working on other specifications that cover the following topics: billing, monitoring, advanced reservation, negotiation, and agreement features.

Figure 11.8 provides a reference scenario for the Open Cloud Computing Interface, which defines a single access point to the resources managed by a given cloud resource provider.

The most relevant specification for defining an interoperable platform is the OCCI Core Model (*GFD.183—OCCI Core*). This document defines the boundary protocol and API that acts as a service front-end to the provider's internal management framework. This interface was designed to serve both service consumers and other systems. This specification is not focused on defining any particular domain, but its main scope is to provide a built-in type classification system allowing for safe extensions toward domain-specific usage. Therefore, it provides a reference model for building a type system that is as flexible as possible and that supports extensibility. This allows clients to dynamically discover the resource model of any provider supporting this specification. *Resources*, which are the fundamental element of the model, can be of any type and vary according to the context in which the resource provider operates: a virtual machine or a template in case of IaaS providers, a job or a task in the case of a job management system, and so on. These resources are connected through *links*, which allow the clients to see how they are connected together. Resources and links are *entities* that can be used to define a specific type. Besides the entities, a type (also called a *kind*) is defined by *actions*, which represent the operations that can be done on instances of that type. To support flexibility and extensions, *mixins* are used to aggregate preexisting types and augment their capabilities.

This reference model is then specialized by the OCCI Infrastructure document (*GFD.184—OCCI Infrastructure*) that defines how an OCCI implementation can model and implement an IaaS API according to the previous reference model. Common resources in this scenario are *Compute*, *Storage*, and *Network*. Links might be of type *NetworkInterface* and *StorageLink*.

---

[16]http://occi-wg.org/.

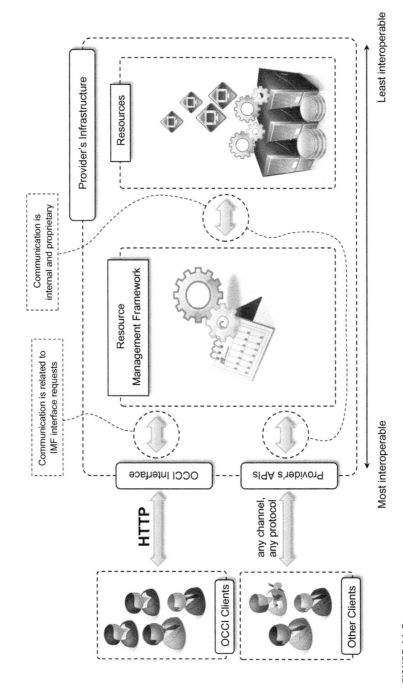

FIGURE 11.8

OCCI reference scenario.

These components can be used to represent any services offered by any IaaS provider and can describe their behavior and properties.

A practical implementation of an OCCI model is then made accessible through RESTful interfaces over HTTP. The OCCI rendering model specification (*GFD.185−OCCI HTTP Rendering*[17]) defines how the model can be transmitted and serialized through HTTP. Therefore, a cloud resource provider has to implement the following two steps in order to be OCCI compliant:

1. Define the services and resources it offers, according to the OCCI core model.
2. Provide a RESTful interface that allows clients to discover the set of resources it exposes according to the OCCI HTTP rendering model.

If the cloud vendor is an IaaS provider, the OCCI Infrastructure document constitutes a starting point from which the vendor develops its own representation.

Currently, the Open Cloud Computing Interface provides linking with several technologies for building cloud computing services, principally within the IaaS market segment. Various opensource initiatives (jCloud, libvirt, OpenNebula, and OpenStack), research projects (RESERVOIR, Big Grid, Morfeo Claudia, Emotive), and consortia (SLA@SOI) are offering OCCI interfaces to their services. Initially developed as a joint effort of Sun Microsystems, Rabbit MQ, and the Univesidad Complutense de Madrid, now OCCI involves more than 250 organizations in both academia and industry, such as Rackspace, Oracle, GoGrid, and Flexiscale. Because of such strong support, OCCI is a promising step toward the definition of cloud interoperability standards for a cloud federation scenario.

Cloud data management interface

The *Cloud Data Management Interface (CDMI)* [136] is a specification for a functional interface that applications will use to create, retrieve, update, and delete data elements from the cloud. This interface also provides facilities for discovering the properties of a given cloud storage offering. CDMI has been proposed by the *Cloud Storage Technical Working Group* of the *Storage Network Industry Association (SNIA)*, an association promoting standards in the management of IT information with a particular focus on data storage. SNIA has also produced a reference implementation of the CDMI, thus facilitating the process of quickly producing a working standard by means of feedback from the community.

The specification introduces and defines the concept of cloud storage as a "delivery of virtualized storage on demand," also known as *Data storage-as-a-Service (DaaS)*. The main concept of DaaS is to abstract data storage behind a set of interfaces and to make it available on demand. This definition encloses a considerably wide range of storage architectures. Figure 11.9 provides the overall context in which cloud storage interfaces will operate. A cloud data management service provides a CDMI made available to clients through RESTful interfaces. Such an interface provides access to information, data, and storage services that can be leveraged to access storage clouds. These can eventually rely on several different technologies to implement data and storage services.

---

[17]The document is reported to be published but was not available at the time of writing.

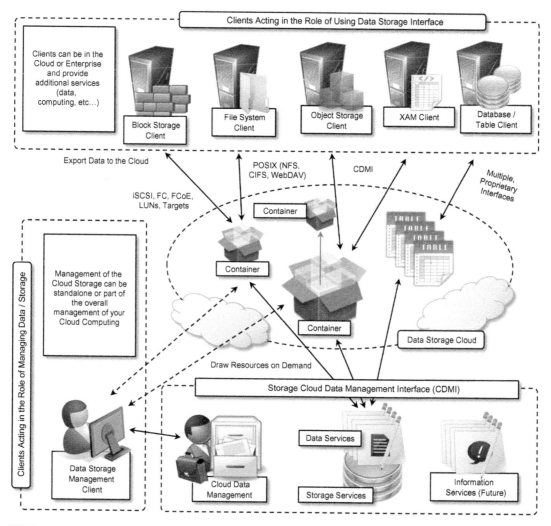

FIGURE 11.9

Cloud storage reference model.

The interface exposes an object model that allows clients to manipulate and discover data components. The object model contains the following components:

- *Data objects*. These are the fundamental storage component in CDMI and are analogous to file in a file system. Data objects can have a set of well-defined single-value fields. In addition, they can support metadata used to describe the object, which can be provided by either the storage system or the client.

- *Container objects*. Container objects are the fundamental abstraction used to group stored data. A container may have zero or more child objects and a set of well-defined fields. As happens for data objects, containers support metadata as well. Containers support nesting, and a child container inherits all the data system metadata from its parent.

- *Domain objects.* Domain objects are quite similar to container objects and they are used to represent administrative ownership stored within a CDMI storage system. As containers, they support nesting and facilitate the flow of information upward since an aggregate view of data is useful for administrative purposes.
- *Queue objects.* Queues are a special class of containers that are used to provide first-in, first-out (FIFO) access when storing and retrieving data. Queues are useful to support writer-reader and producer-consumer patterns for storage data management. A queue always has a parent object from which it inherits the system metadata.
- *Capability objects.* Capability objects are a special class of container object that allow a CDMI client to discover what subset of the CDMI standard is implemented by a CDMI provider. Capabilities are descriptors of the set of interactions that the system is capable of performing against the URI to which they are attached. Each entity defined in the object model is expected to have a field that represents the URI from which the capabilities for that object can be retrieved. Every CDMI-compliant interface must be able to list the capabilities for each given object, but support for all the capabilities listed in the standard is optional.

Using the simple operation defined by REST, clients can discover and manipulate these objects by creating, retrieving, updating, and deleting objects (*CRUD: Create, Retrieve, Update, and Delete*). The set of operations that are supported is defined by the capabilities attached to each entity. Besides the fundamental operations allowed by REST, the CDMI also provides support for snapshots, serialization and deserialization, logging, and interoperation compared to other protocols and standards.

The CDMI was initially proposed in 2010 and collected consensus from several other bodies involved in the standardization of cloud computing technologies and was included in roadmaps and studies. Currently, SNIA is moving toward transforming CDMI into a *de jure* standard by interoperating with the major standardization organizations, such as ISO/IEC and INCITS.[18]

Cloud security alliance

The *Cloud Security Alliance (CSA)* is nonprofit organization with the mission of promoting the use of best practices for providing security assurance in cloud computing and education on the use of cloud computing to help secure all other forms of computing. Rather than acting as a standardizing body, CSA offers a context in which to discuss security practices and provide guidance for developing reliable and secure cloud computing systems.

The most relevant initiative of the CSA has been the *Cloud Controls Matrix (CCM)*. The matrix is specifically designed to provide fundamental security principles for guiding cloud vendors and for assisting prospective cloud service consumers in assessing the overall risks implied in leveraging a cloud service provider. This document was prepared by taking into account the most important security standards, regulations, and control frameworks, such as ISO 27001/27002, ISACA COBIT, PCI, and NIST. The CCM strengthens existing information security control environments

---

[18]*InterNational Committee for Information Technology Standards (INCITS)* is the primary U.S. focus of standardization in the field of information and telecommunication technologies (ICT).

within a cloud computing context and provides a way to align the security practices that should be adopted in the cloud with those that already exist in other domains.

The CCM's relevance in a cloud federation scenario is quite evident. It provides a standardized way to assess the security measures put in place by each cloud service provider and helps define a minimum-security profile within a cloud federated scenario, thus increasing the trust in the concept of federation.

Other initiatives

Besides the major standardization efforts, many initiatives have obtained minor popularity, are endorsed by specific organizations, or are related to the use of cloud computing in a very specific context. Among the most relevant are these:

- *National Institute of Standards and Technologies (NIST).* As discussed in Chapter 4, NIST proposed a working definition of cloud computing that is now widely accepted. Another important initiative is the *Standards Acceleration to Jumpstart Adoption of Cloud Computing (SAJACC).* This initiative's activities are mostly related to the assessment of existing standards in cloud computing, to actively contributing to the creation of open standards, and to the identification of gaps within existing standards.
- *Cloud Computing Interoperability Forum (CCIF).* This industry forum was initially supported by several players in the field of cloud computing and was formed to enable a global cloud computing ecosystem whereby organizations can seamlessly operate together to foster wider adoption of the technology. The activity of the forum is limited to one single event in 2009 and led to the proposal of the *Unified Cloud Interface (UCI),*[19] which is an attempt to provide a unified interface to the various APIs exposed by different vendors. Functional implementations exist for Amazon EC2 and Enomaly ECP.
- *Open Cloud Consortium (OCC).* This not-for-profit organization manages cloud computing infrastructures to support scientific research. It also develops reference implementations, benchmarks, and standards for cloud technologies.
- *Global Inter-Cloud Technology Forum (GICTF).* The GICTF is a Japanese organization whose aim is to bring together the knowledge developed by industry, academia, and government and to support research and development feasibility tests on the technologies related to cloud interoperability. More precisely, the forum focuses on the standardization of the network protocols that enable interoperation among clouds and of the interfaces through which this interoperation happens.
- *Cloud Work Group.* This initiative of the Open Group is aimed at creating a common understanding between buyers and suppliers as to how enterprises of all sizes and scales can leverage cloud computing technologies. The group has established several activities to enhance business understanding, analysis, and uptake of cloud computing technologies.

Several other initiatives exist. They cover the creation of standards and specifications for areas of cloud computing, which are not strictly related to supporting the interoperation among different cloud service providers but still constitute a step toward the development of supporting

---

[19]Available at http://code.google.com/p/unifiedCloud/ (retrieved May 17, 2011).

technologies for a cloud federation scenario that is based on the definition of the rules, policies, and a model for a cloud federation.

11.3.3.2 Security

Cloud computing supports the development of elastically scalable systems by leveraging large computing infrastructures that eventually host applications, services, and data. In this scenario, security arrangements constitute a fundamental requirement that cannot be overlooked. Security management becomes even more complex in the case of a cloud federation, where confidential information is dynamically moved across several cloud computing vendors.

One of the first questions that should be asked is whether the cloud vendors offer enough transparency to implement the security management process required to protect your data and applications. Implementing and deploying the required security infrastructure is important to understanding the responsibilities of those who offer cloud computing services and of those who use them. Cloud computing is a new territory for security; compared to managed services providers, where the management of security infrastructure is completely handled by the service provider, in a cloud deployment security management is divided between the provider and the customer. The responsibilities of the two parties change according to the type of service offering. IaaS vendors are required to provide basic security in terms of auditing and logging of access to virtual machine instances or cloud storage. PaaS vendors are expected to offer a secure development platform and a runtime environment for applications. SaaS vendors have the major responsibilities in terms of security, since they have to build a secure computing stack (infrastructure, platform, and applications) that users customize for their needs.

Despite the novelty introduced by cloud computing, it is possible to consider existing security frameworks and practices as a starting point for securely running applications and systems. In particular, the standard *ISO/IEC 27001/27002* and the *Information Technology Infrastructure Library (ITIL)* service management framework are industry standards that provide guidance in terms of security management processes and practices. ITIL is a set of guidelines that define a security framework in terms of *policies, processes, procedures*, and *work instructions*. ITIL is not a standard, and therefore organizations and management systems cannot be certified "ITIL-compliant." Despite this fact, these guidelines constitute a reference model for implementing security measures. ISO/IEC 27001/27002 formally define the mandatory requirements for an information security management system and provide guidelines for the security controls to implement within a security system. In short, these standards help organizations ensure that the current security levels are appropriate to their needs and to implement security.

Key elements in management of security in a cloud scenario have been identified as the following [156]:

- Availability management (ITIL)
- Access control (ISO/IEC 27002, ITIL)
- Vulnerability management (ISO/IEC 27002)
- Patch management (ITIL)
- Configuration management (ITIL)
- Incident response (ISO/IEC 27002)
- System use and access monitoring (ISO/IEC 27002)

Put together, these elements can compose a reference security framework for cloud computing systems. They invest all the layers of the cloud computing reference model and are differently supported across the market segments characterizing cloud computing.

Table 11.2 Customer Responsibilities for Security Management in the Cloud [156]

Activities	IaaS	PaaS	SaaS
Availability management	Manage VM availability with fault-tolerant architecture	Manage this activity for applications deployed in the PaaS platform (the provider is responsible for runtime engine and services)	Provider responsibility
Patch and configuration management	Manage VM image hardening Harden your VMs, applications, and database using your established security hardening process Manage activities for your VMs, database, and applications using your established security management process	Manage this activity for applications deployed in the PaaS platform Test your applications for OWASP Top 10 vulnerabilities[20]	Provider responsibility
Vulnerability management Access control management	Manage OS, applications, and database vulnerabilities leveraging your established vulnerability management process Manage network and user access control to VMs, secure privileged access to management consoles, install host Intrusion Detection System (IDS), and manage host firewall policies	Manage this activity for applications deployed in the PaaS platform (the provider is responsible for their runtime engine and service) Manage developer access to provisioning Restrict access using authentication methods (user- and network-based controls) Federate identity and enable SSO if SAML[21] is supported	Provider responsibility Manage user provisioning Restrict user access using authentication methods (user- and network-based controls) Federate identity and enable SSO if SAML is supported

An overall view of the security aspects and how they are addressed by cloud vendors at three different levels (IaaS, PaaS, and SaaS) is shown in Table 11.2. A good starting point in identifying a customer's security responsibilities and planning the appropriate measures is the service contract made with the provider. This contract clearly defines the scope of action of the provider and the warranties given to the customers. Moreover, cloud providers' APIs and services help in managing security and accountability. Cloud providers offer service dashboards that could be usefully integrated into the organization's internal management processes and tools. Currently, the missing bit

---

[20]The *Open Web Application Security Project (OWASP)* is an open community dedicated to enabling organizations to conceive, develop, maintain, acquire, and operate applications that can be trusted. In 2010 the organization published the OWASP Top Ten Project, which lists the top 10 vulnerabilities for applications; www.owasp.org/index.php/CategoryOWASP_Top_Ten_Project.

[21]*SSO*, an acronym that stands for *single sign-on*, identifies the capability offered by a collection of services that allows users to authenticate only once rather than explicitly providing each of the services with their credentials. SAML, an acronym that stands for *Security Assertion Markup Language*, is an XML dialect that is used to provide a portable framework to define security in a federated environment.

from a security point of view is the lack of enterprise-grade access for managing the security of cloud computing systems where system administrators can have a holistic view of the security defined for cloud computing applications.

Cloud federation security

Cloud federation introduces additional issues that have to be addressed in order to provide a secure environment in which to move applications and services among a collection of federated providers. Baseline security needs to be guaranteed across all cloud vendors that are part of the federation.

An interesting aspect is represented by the management of the digital identity across diverse organizations, security domains, and application platforms. In particular, the term *federated identity management* refers to standards-based approaches for handling authentication, single sign-on (SSO), role-based access control, and session management in a federated environment [157]. This enables users to utilize services more effectively in a federated context by providing their authentication details only once to log into a network composed of several entities involved in a transaction. This capability is realized by either relying on open industry standards or openly published specifications (*Liberty Alliance Identity Federation*, *OASIS Security Assertion Markup Language*, and *WS-Federation*) such that interoperation can be achieved. No matter the specific protocol and framework, two main approaches can be considered:

- *Centralized federation model.* This is the approach taken by several identity federation standards. It distinguishes two operational roles in an SSO transaction: the identity provider and the service provider.
- *Claim-based model.* This approach addresses the problem of user authentication from a different perspective and requires users to provide claims answering who they are and what they can do in order to access content or complete a transaction.

The first model is currently used today; the second constitutes a future vision for identity management in the cloud.

Digital identity management constitutes a fundamental aspect of security management in a cloud federation. To transparently perform operations across different administrative domains, it is of mandatory importance to have a robust framework for authentication and authorization, and federated identity management addresses this issue. Our previous considerations of security contribute to design and implement a secure system comprising the cloud vendor stack and the user application; federated identity management allows us to tie together the computing stacks of different vendors and present them as a single environment to users from a security point of view.

11.3.3.3 Legal issues

Besides the technical complexities required to make cloud computing happen, legal issues related to access rights, privacy, and control are peculiar to cloud computing. This section provides an overview of this topic and discusses the potential legal implications of a cloud federation scenario.

Enterprises and end users leveraging cloud computing relegate the control of systems, applications, or personal data to third parties. This is not much different from normal outsourcing practices, which have been widely in precedence. Also, a considerable similarity to application service providers (ASPs) can be found. If we compare cloud computing with traditional outsourcing and ASP service delivery, we can observe that [140]:

- Outsourcing arrangements generally cover an entire business or IT process of a business organization, and they are geared toward running the business for the benefit of the customer. The software generally belongs to the customer, and it is deployed and managed on the customer's equipment. Moreover, arrangements are highly negotiable and defined by long and complex contracts.
- The ASP model constitutes an early implementation of the SaaS delivery model, which does not imply any sort of scalability on demand. In this scenario the provider owns the software and the hardware, which might be located in several locations but are statically known *a priori*. Arrangements are negotiable but not as complex as those regulating outsourcing.
- Cloud computing covers multiple service models: software, infrastructure, and runtime platforms. Arrangements between consumers and providers are quite limited and mostly based on a pay-per-use model, which is metered according to appropriate units (time, bandwidth, storage size, or transactions). Economics of performance drive the activity of the provider, which may choose to locate, or relocate, applications and systems in order to minimize costs and improve efficiency. Moreover, providers may have multiple datacenters located sparsely, either to better serve a wide variety of customers or to exploit advantageous environment conditions.

What makes cloud computing different from traditional approaches is the global scale at which providers operate and deliver services. The need to serve a potentially massive number of customers makes providers look for solutions that guarantee optimal service delivery and low operational costs. Therefore, having a sparse infrastructure, normally spanning several countries, is quite common. Second, because cloud computing delivers IT services as utilities, the dynamics of service lease and consumption make the common arrangements unsuitable for commercial use. As a result, multiple service-contracting models have been introduced: licensing, service agreements, and online agreements.

This new scenario makes more complicated the legal management of existing issues and introduces new ones. For instance, a disperse geography of datacenters makes it harder to guarantee confidentiality and privacy of data, especially when data are located in different countries with different jurisdictions. There already are laws and regulations for management of sensitive information, but the heterogeneous context in which cloud computing services are delivered requires a different approach from a legal perspective. Moreover, the dynamics of contracts between service consumers and providers introduce new challenges; arrangements need to be more flexible and cannot be defined by lengthy contracts obtained by complex negotiations. As we have seen, vendor lock-in is a sensitive issue in cloud computing; what will then happen when a provider files for bankruptcy or gets acquired by another provider? Will the previous SLAs still be honored? What are the warranties for customers with respect to this situation? Furthermore, service providers might stipulate agreements between themselves, which leads to a definitely more complex management of customers' sensitive data. For instance, customers do not generally have control over where the service they are leasing operates; in a federated scenario, a service might offered by a different provider from the one the customer has stipulated in the SLA. In such a case, what are the warranties offered by the other provider in terms of confidentiality, secrecy, integrity, and data retention?

We can categorize the wide range of legal issues that are connected with cloud computing in the following three major areas: *privacy, security, and intellectual property*; *business and commercial*; and *legislation and jurisdiction*. As happens for any disruptive technology, there is always a lag between the regulations that govern the interaction within parties and the new opportunities and approaches that such technology brings. In the case of cloud computing, the law lags behind the technology innovation, even though several initiatives are now taking place.

Privacy, security, and intellectual property related issues

This category includes all the legal issues arising from the management of data, applications, and services by the cloud service provider on behalf of the customer as part of its service offering. As previously noted, cloud computing implies the relegation of control over data and applications to third parties. To provide customers with a reliable and commercially viable service, cloud computing providers are expected to implement appropriate procedures to protect the integrity of data, data secrecy, and the privacy of users. In this scenario, different pieces of legislation apply, which sometimes may also be conflicting.

The legislation concerning privacy and security of data is perhaps the most developed. This is because it does not only apply to cloud computing-based systems. Again, different countries, and different states within the same country, have different approaches and advancement stages. The United States has a considerable amount of legislation regulating privacy and security measures; these laws also apply to cloud computing. An important U.S. player is the *Federal Trade Commission (FTC)*, which is in charge of conducting investigations to assess the liability of any organization that provides financial services or that engages in a commercial activity aimed at selling products if that organization breaks security and privacy regulations. In particular, *data breach*, *protection*, and *accessibility* are objects of current legislation:

- *Data breach*, or loss of unencrypted electronically stored information, is a very sensitive matter. Avoiding data breach is important for both cloud services consumers and providers. The former have a direct loss caused by the potential misuse of sensitive information from third parties (stolen Social Security numbers, misuse of credit cards, and access to personal medical data or financial statements). The latter are damaged because of financial harm, potential lawsuits, damage to reputation, FTC investigations, and loss of customers. Therefore there is interest on both sides to embrace measures that prevent data breach. This is also supported by the legislation: Almost all 50 U.S. states require the affected person to be notified upon the occurrence of data breach. Therefore, cloud providers that have their systems compromised are required to notify the affected persons and coordinate with those who provided such data. Relevant legislation for data breach includes the *Health Insurance Portability and Accountability Act (HIPAA)* [145] and the *Health Information Technology for Economic and Clinical Health (HITECH) Act* [144].
- *Data protection*. Other interesting considerations can be made regarding the measures that should be put in place to ensure the confidentiality of personal information. The *Gramm-Leach-Bliley (GLB) Act* [141] requires that financial institutions implement appropriate procedures to protect personal information and prevent unauthorized access to data. Cloud providers managing sensitive information will then be required to (1) demonstrate that they have deployed appropriate measures for the protection of sensitive data; (2) contractually agree to prevent

unauthorized access; or (3) both. Under the GLB Act, the FTC requires that all businesses significantly involved in the provision of financial services and product have a written security plan to protect information related to customers (*Safeguards Rules* [142]). Another important protection measure is represented by the *Red Flag Rules* [143], which force financial institutions to monitor and block suspicious activities that potentially might represent evidence of identity theft. Organizations need to have documented policies describing the measures they take to prevent identity theft.

- *Data access.* Legal issues also arise when it comes to determining who, besides their respective owners, can have access to sensitive data. The U.S. legislation has a considerably aggressive approach with respect to this issue. The USA PATRIOT Act [146] confers the right to any organization operating on behalf of the U.S. government to gain access to personal financial information and student information stored in electronic systems without any suspicion of wrongdoing of the person whose information it seeks. The act requires the organization to prevent a government's certification that the information accessed can be relevant to an ongoing criminal investigation. The institution holding the financial information might be prevented from informing their clients about governmental access to their data. The power conferred by this act puts a cloud provider in the difficult position of being required to provide sensitive information without giving notice to the respective user.

Other countries and interstate organizations have different approaches. The European Union (EU) in 1995 passed the *European Union Directive on the Protection of Individuals with Regard to the Processing of Personal Data and Movement of Such Data Privacy Directive*. The directive states that countries belonging to the EU must pass a data protection law covering both government and private entities that process business and consumer data. Furthermore, the directive mandates that any geography to which EU personal data are sent must have a level of data protection as measured by EU standards. This directly impacts on the possibility for many cloud providers entering and operating lawfully in the EU. Therefore, the possibility of conducting business in the European Union must be carefully studied.

Besides the EU, many other countries have passed legislation protecting privacy and security of data. Argentina has an approach similar to that of the EU. Hong Kong has a *Personal Data Ordinance* [148] that covers both public and private data processors of either electronic or non-electronic documents. Other countries, like Brazil, express the constitutional right to privacy but do not have a comprehensive law on the subject. A different approach is taken by Canada, which has an organization-to-organization approach. The *Personal Information Protection and Electronic Document Act (PIPEDA)* [149] regulates the level of protection for personal data whenever interacting with a Canadian-based company, regardless of its geographical location. In brief, Canadian organizations are held accountable for the protection of personal information they transfer to third parties, whether such parties are inside or outside Canada. All these different regulations are not only a source of international conflicts of law but also identify the immature state of legal support with regard to the globalization of computing utilities trading.

Another element of concern that directly relates to the way sensitive information is handled in the cloud is the management of intellectual property (IP) rights. It is important in this case not to protect the data from entities external to the cloud service provider but to ensure the IP attached to the data, or generated by applications, that is hosted in the cloud still belongs to the user of the cloud. This is generally the rule of thumb that applies for the protection of IP rights, which needs to be enforced by appropriate contractual terms between the service consumer and the service provider. This is particularly important in case cloud service providers file for bankruptcy and the hosted IP is used to augment the value of the company, thus facilitating the provider's exit from bankruptcy.

Business and commerce-related issues

Legal issues can also arise as a result of specific contractual terms and arrangements between the cloud provider and the user. Contractual terms need to be able to deal with issues such as:

- What is defined as a service that is agreed between the two parties?
- What is the liability of each of the parties?
- What risk are users running while relying on a given provider?
- What are measures that are put in place to guarantee users access to their data?

The first types of legal issues we can consider are contractual ones. These relate to the specific nature of the agreement between the cloud provider and the consumer. Licensing agreements, the most used form of contractual agreement for software before the spread of SOA, are no longer applicable. Service agreements are a more appropriate form for settling arrangements in a cloud computing scenario, since there is no real transmission of a software artifact from the contracting entities and since IT services are offered and priced as utilities. In any market segment of cloud computing (Iaas, Paas, or SaaS), the control and access points are offered by the cloud provider and the agreement covers all the basic terms and conditions of use of the service, with clear specification of provider liabilities in case of service interruption. Generally, users have very limited options and the contractual terms are in the form of online agreements that the user cannot negotiate. Since this is the only documents that binds the two entities, it is really important to have a clear specification of the privacy policy adopted by the provider and the compliance of such policies with the current laws on the subject. It is also important to verify what will be the provider's liability in case of data breach. In most cases, providers have a very limited liability and compensate users with service credit in the best cases. Since these terms are not negotiable, the service agreement is of use to the consumer in carefully evaluating whether to sign an agreement with the provider. As more enterprises and mission-critical applications move to the cloud, a more robust and balanced contractual form is needed.

Some business and commercial considerations may also influence the contractual arrangements between providers and consumers. For instance, measures aimed at minimizing the consumer's, considerations about the provider's viability, and the future availability of the data stored in the cloud are all element of concern. These issues must be referenced in the agreement. Elements that contribute to minimizing the risk are measures aimed at protecting the integrity of data, specific SLAs indicating the guaranteed percentage of availability of the service outside scheduled outages, and disaster-recovery measures. The provider's viability is another aspect that contributes to the final decision to enter an agreement with a given provider. Since vendor lock-in is still a reality, the ability of the provider's business to survive is fundamental also because source-code escrow[22] does not help in this scenario. The risk of bankruptcy is not the only menace that could prevent

---

[22]*Source-code escrow* is the deposit of software source code with a third-party escrow agent to ensure the maintenance of the software in case the party licensing the software files for bankruptcy.

durable and continuous access to data and applications in the future. Other conditions include termination of the provider's business activity or provider acquisition by another company. In these cases, the SLA with the customer should clearly specify which policies are in place to guarantee durable access to customer data.

Jurisdictional and procedural issues

Jurisdictional and procedural legal issues arise from two major aspects of cloud computing: the geo-location of data and applications served by cloud providers and the laws and regulations that are applied in case of litigation.

Jurisdictional issues are mostly related to location of data and the specific laws that apply in that location. Cloud service providers locate their datacenters in order to reduce their operational costs. The placement of datacenters is influenced by the desire to optimally serve customers on a global scale. For this reason it is quite common to distribute the infrastructure of a single cloud provider over the globe. Specific issues arise from the different laws that are applied for the protection of data. For instance, the EU directive states that any personal data generated within the European Union are subject to European law as well as concerning the export of these data to a third-party country. This limits the mobility of data among datacenters located in different countries, if an appropriate level of data protection is not guaranteed. Furthermore, SLAs are agreed to within a context defined by a specific governing law, but due to the mobility of data, such laws might not be effective and could fail in their purpose of protecting customer rights. The condition is even worse when there is no specific statement indicating the governing law under which the agreement was signed.

Jurisdictional issues may also arise in the case of subcontracting. This is a quite common scenario in the case of cloud federation: A cloud provider leverages other providers' services and facilities to provide services to customers. This is mostly done transparently to the user. In case of failure in service delivery, it will be difficult for the cloud user to identity the real causes. In this case, the scenario is complicated by the fact that, besides different geographies, different organizations are involved in delivering the service to the end user.

Different jurisdictions lead to what is also called the *conflict of laws*, which acknowledges the fact that laws of different countries may operate in opposition to each other, even if they relate to the same subject matter. The general rule of thumb is that, since each nation is sovereign within its own territory, the laws of a country will affect all the people and property within it, including contracts made and actions carried out within its borders. As already observed, the SLA should clearly specify the governing law as well as the other potential jurisdictions that may be involved in delivering the service to the end user.

Besides jurisdictional issues, there are other important aspects concerning the application of the law in case of *litigation*, which is the process of bringing a legal dispute to a court. In this context, one party might require the other party to provide evidence of data in terms of electronic documents (emails, reports, financial records, etc.). This process is also known as *ediscovery* and poses an interesting challenge in the case of cloud computing, where control over data and systems is relegated to third parties. Failing to comply with an ediscovery process because of lack electronically stored information is not an option and in most cases will result in several charges.

Traditionally, enterprises organized staff and internal procedures to respond to an ediscovery process with the required information. In a scenario where an enterprise leverages cloud providers, there is no infrastructure nor staff that directly manages such activities; instead, the maintenance of data and its accessibility are all offloaded to the cloud provider. Therefore, the challenges concern the storage and retrieval of sensitive data over the long term. Since storage is normally billed and has an operational cost in the cloud, this may pose an additional burden to enterprises that want to leverage the cloud. Second, access to data despite the survival of the provider's business activity is another element of concern with regard to ediscovery.

Implications in a cloud federation scenario

In this section we have mostly discussed the nature of the legal issues that may arise in leveraging cloud computing solutions, from the perspective of the interaction between cloud service consumers and providers. How do these issues impact a cloud federation scenario? And are there other elements to consider from a legal perspective?

We can observe that interactions among different cloud providers can occur in the form of subcontracting, which has been discussed, or as a normal interaction between a consumer and a provider, where the role of the consumer is played by another cloud provider. Therefore, all the legal issues introduced previously apply. As noted, the case in which services offered by different providers are composed together to deliver the final service to the cloud user poses additional complications. This is because the contractual interaction may spawn over heterogeneous geographies and necessarily involve different organizations. Hopefully, the creation of a federation will help define a better body of laws that are compliant with all the legislation of the countries involved in possible transactions among cloud providers and users and uniform across all the federation.

11.3.4 Technologies for cloud federations

Even though the concept of cloud federation or the InterCloud is still immature, there are some supporting technologies that enable the deployment of interoperable clouds, at least from an operational point of view. These initiatives mostly originated within academia and principally focus on supporting interoperability among different IaaS implementations, with a limited implementation of the capabilities defined at the logical level.

11.3.4.1 Reservoir

Resources and Services Virtualization Without Barriers, or *RESERVOIR* [155], is a European research project focused on developing an architecture that supports providers of cloud infrastructures to dynamically partner with each other to extend their capabilities while preserving their administrative autonomy. RESERVOIR defines a software stack enabling interoperation at the IaaS layer and providing support for SLA-based execution of applications on top of the infrastructure overlay that results from the federation of infrastructure providers.

RESERVOIR is based on the concept of dynamic federation: Each infrastructure provider is an autonomous business with its own business goals and that might decide to partner with other businesses when needed. The federation is obtained by means of the RESERVOIR middleware that needs to be deployed at each site. The IT management at a specific site is fully autonomous and dictated to by policies that depend on the site's business goals. When needed, internal IT resources are leased to other providers within the context of a negotiated SLA. The role of RESERVOIR is to orchestrate this process and to minimize the barriers obstructing interoperation among different administrative domains.

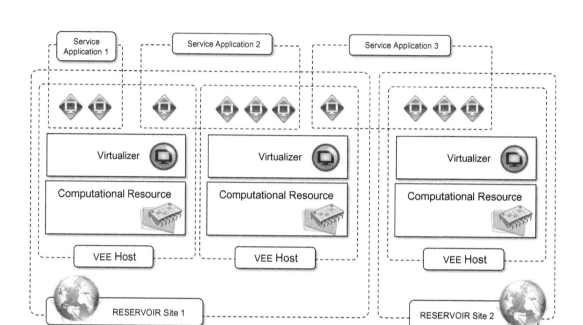

FIGURE 11.10

RESERVOIR cloud deployment.

Figure 11.10 provides a general overview of a RESERVOIR cloud. The framework defines an infrastructure overlay that spans multiple administrative domains and different geographic locations. Each site runs the RESERVOIR software stack and provides an on-demand execution environment in which components of a service application can be deployed and executed. The model introduces a clear separation between service providers and infrastructure providers. Service providers are the entities that understand the needs of a particular business and offer service applications to address those needs; they do not own infrastructure but rather lease it from infrastructure providers. Infrastructure providers operate RESERVOIR sites and offer a virtually infinite pool of computational, network, and storage resources. Service providers define service applications that are modeled as a collection of components that can be deployed over a distributed virtual infrastructure, which can be either explicitly or implicitly provisioned. In the first case, the service provider conducts sizing and capacity-planning studies to identify the appropriate number of components to be required for a given workload condition. The specification is obtained by means of minimal service configuration and a set of elasticity rules that are used by RESERVOIR to dynamically provision resources under varying workload conditions. In the second case, the service provider provides neither a minimal service configuration nor elasticity rules. The sizing is automatically made by the RESERVOIR middleware, which tries to minimize overprovisioning. Service providers are billed on a pay-as-you-go model and can ask for usage reports to verify the billing.

Service application components are represented as virtual packages, which also specify execution environment requirements. Infrastructure providers can leverage any virtualization technology

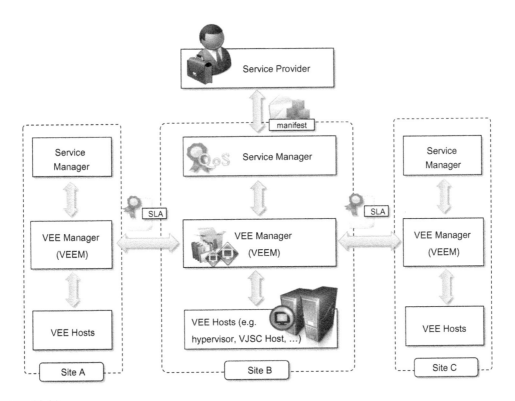

FIGURE 11.11

RESERVOIR architecture.

of choice and are in charge of providing the required environment for such applications. An important element for determining the virtual environment for service applications is the *service manifest*. This is one of the key elements of the **RESERVOIR** model and specifies the structure of the service applications in terms of component types that are to be deployed as *virtual execution environments (VEEs)*. The service manifest contains a reference to a master image, which is a self-contained software stack (OS, middleware, applications, data, and configuration) that fully captures the functionality of the component type. Additional information and rules specify how many instances to deploy and how to dynamically grow and shrink their number. Moreover, the manifest also specifies the grouping of components into virtual networks and/or tiers that form the service applications. The manifest is expressed by extending the Open Virtualization Format to simplify interoperability and leverage an already existing popular standard.

Figure 11.11 describes the internal architecture of a RESERVOIR site that enables the federated and SLA-based execution of applications. The RESERVOIR stack consists of three major components:

- *Service Manager.* The Service Manager is the highest level of abstraction and constitutes the front-end used by service providers to submit service manifests, negotiate pricing, and monitor applications. This component deploys and provisions VEEs according to the service manifest and monitors and enforces SLA compliance by controlling the capacity of a service application.

- *Virtual Execution Environment (VEE) Manager.* This component is the core of the RESERVOIR middleware and is responsible for the optimal placement of VEEs into VEE hosts according to the constraints expressed by the Service Manager. Moreover, the VEE Manager also interacts with VEE Managers in other sites to provision additional instances for the execution of service applications or move VEEs to other sites in case of overload. This component realizes the cloud federation.
- *VEE Host (VEEH).* This is the lowest level of abstraction and interacts with the VEE Manager to put into practice the IT management decisions regarding heterogeneous sets of virtualization platforms. This level is also in charge of ensuring appropriate and isolated networking among VEEs that belong to the same application. The VEEH encapsulates all platform-specific management that is required to expose the used virtualization technology through a standardized interface to the VEE Manager.

Each of these components adopts a standardized interface and protocol to interoperate with the adjacent layer. This design decision was made to promote a variety of innovative approaches at each layer. It offers infrastructure providers the freedom to integrate the RESERVOIR middleware with their own existing technology.

11.3.4.2 InterCloud

InterCloud is a service-oriented architectural framework for cloud federation that supports utility-driven interconnection of clouds. It is composed of a set of decoupled elements that interact via a market-oriented system to enable trading of cloud assets such as computing power, storage, and execution of applications. As depicted in Figure 11.12, the InterCloud model comprises two main elements: CloudExchange and CloudCoordinator:

- *CloudExchange.* This is the market-making component of the architecture. It offers services that allow providers to find each other in order to directly trade cloud assets, as well as allowing parties to register and run auctions. In the former case, CloudExchange acts as a directory service for the federation. In the latter case, it runs the auction. For offering such services to the federation, CloudExchange implements a Web service-based interface that allows datacenters to join and leave the federation; to publish resources they want to sell; to register their resource requirements so that parties interested in selling providers are able to locate potential buyers for their resources; to query resource offers that match specific requirements; to query requirements that match available resources from a party; to withdraw offers and requests from the coordinator; to offer resources in auctions; to register bids; and to consult the status of a running auction.
- *CloudCoordinator.* This component manages domain-specific issues related to the federation. This component is present on each party that wants join the federation. CloudCoordinator has front-end components (i.e., elements that interact with the federation) as well as back-end components (i.e., components that interact with the associated datacenter). Front-end components interact with the CloudExchange and with other coordinators. The former allows datacenters to announce their offers and requirements, whereas the latter allows the Coordinator to learn about the current state of the datacenter to decide whether actions from the federation

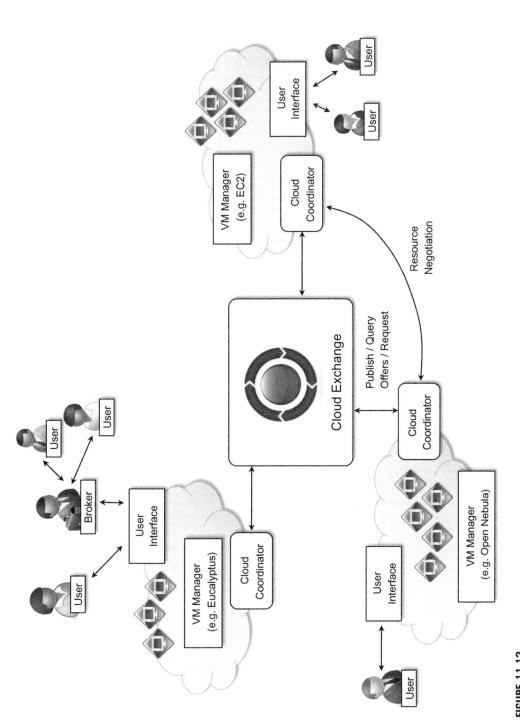

FIGURE 11.12

InterCloud architecture.

are required or not. Therefore, wherever the Coordinator detects that extra resources are required by the datacenter, it triggers the process of discovery of potential providers (by interacting with the cloud federation). Once potential providers are discovered and the preferred one is selected, the Coordinator contacts the remote Coordinator and negotiates. Similarly, when the Coordinator detects that local resources are underutilized, they can publish an offer for resources in the CloudExchange or they can look for matches among requirements registered in the Exchange service.

Negotiation between parties follows the Alternate Offers protocol. The value that each Coordinator is willing to pay for a resource, as well as the value for which each Coordinator wants to sell resources, is not defined by the federation; instead, each Coordinator is free to value resources according to utilization and profit estimation (or any other criteria that a federation member wants to consider), and they are also free to reject offers that are not attractive for them. This flexibility of providers in deciding how and when to buy or sell resources, how many of them, when, and for what price is a big motivator for providers to join an InterCloud federation. Providers are free to refuse to buy or sell resources if they disagree with the price; similarly, they may opt for using the method that seems more profitable to them (e.g., auction or fixed price).

Moreover, InterCloud acts primarily in the operational layer. That means that issues related to security, VM images, and networking are not handled by the framework. Similarly, providers' obligations and expectations for joining the federation are also not addressed by the framework. Therefore, existing approaches for these layers, or even new solutions for them, can be applied in the InterCloud without changes to its architecture.

11.3.5 Observations

Cloud service providers, which may be competing with each other, need to have clear objectives and incentives for establishing a federation. One primary reason can be to improve the overall QoS perceived by their customers. The second step toward the creation of a federated scenario is the definition of a reference model for the cloud federation, together with a set of rules and policies. This is the level where market-oriented models are adopted and opportunities for renting and leasing resources develop. The development and maturity at this stage are still very limited. At a very low level the federation of different cloud vendors is realized through interoperable technologies. This is an area that has seen considerable development, especially concerning the drafting and adoption of standards that support interoperability. We have discussed the most relevant initiatives in this direction and analyzed some reference and prototypal implementations of systems enabling cloud federation at the IaaS level.

11.4 Third-party cloud services

One of the key elements of cloud computing is the possibility of composing services that belong to different vendors or integrating them into existing software systems. The service-oriented model, which is the basis of cloud computing, facilitates such an approach and provides the opportunity for developing a new class of services that can be called *third-party cloud services*. These are the result of adding value to preexisting cloud computing services, thus providing customers with a different and more sophisticated service. Added value can be either created by smartly coordinating existing services or implementing additional features on top of an existing basic service.

Besides this general definition, there is no specific feature that characterizes this class of service. Therefore, in this section, we describe some examples of third-party services.

11.4.1 MetaCDN

MetaCDN [158] provides users with a Content Delivery Network (CDN) [159] [service by leveraging and harnessing together heterogeneous storage clouds. It implements a software overlay that coordinates the service offerings of different cloud storage vendors and uses them as distributed elastic storage on which the user content is stored. MetaCDN provides users with the high-level services of a CDN for content distribution and interacts with the low-level interfaces of storage clouds to optimally place the user content in accordance with the expected geography of its demand. By leveraging the cloud as a storage back-end it makes a complex—and generally expensive—content delivery service available to small enterprises.

The architecture of MetaCDN is shown in Figure 11.13. The MetaCDN interface exposes its services through users and applications through the Web; users interact with a portal, while applications take advantage of the programmatic access provided by means of Web services. The main operations of MetaCDN are the creation of deployments over storage clouds and their management. The portal constitutes a more intuitive interface for users with basic requirements, while the Web service provides access to the full capabilities of MetaCDN and allows for more complex and sophisticated deployment.

In particular, four different deployment options can be selected:

- *Coverage and performance-optimized deployment.* In this case MetaCDN will deploy as many replicas as possible to all available locations.
- *Direct deployment.* In this case MetaCDN allows the selection of the deployment regions for the content and will match the selected regions with the supported providers serving those areas.
- *Cost-optimized deployment.* In this case MetaCDN deploys as many replicas in the locations identified by the deployment request. The available storage transfer allowance and budget will be used to deploy the replicas and keep them active for as long as possible.
- *QoS optimized deployment.* In this case MetaCDN selects the providers that can better match the QoS requirements attached to the deployment, such as average response time and throughput from a particular location.

A collection of components coordinate their activities in order to offer the services we described. These constitute the additional value that MetaCDN brings on top of the direct use of storage clouds by the users. Of particular importance are three components: the *MetaCDN Manager*, the *MetaCDN QoS Monitor*, and the *Load Redirector*. The Manager is responsible for ensuring that all the content deployments are meeting the expected QoS. It is supported in this activity by the Monitor, which constantly probes storage providers and monitors data transfers to assess the performance of each provider. Content serving is controlled by the Load Redirector, which is in charge of redirecting user content requests to the most suitable replica given the condition of the systems and the options specified during the deployment. Interactions with storage

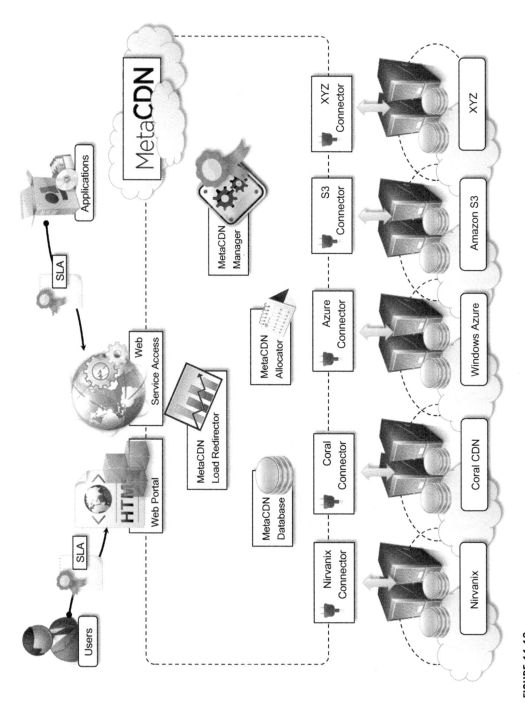

FIGURE 11.13

MetaCDN architecture.

clouds are managed by means of connectors, which abstract away the different interfaces exposed by the providers and present a uniform interface within the MetaCDN system.

As discussed, the core value of MetaCDN resides in the software overlay that enables the uniform use of heterogeneous storage clouds as a single, large, distributed content delivery network. The advantage is not only given by providing a CDN service at accessible costs but also in enriching the original service offering of existing cloud services with additional functionalities, thus creating a new and more sophisticated service that is of interest to a new market sector.

11.4.2 SpotCloud

SpotCloud has already been introduced as an example of a virtual marketplace. By acting as an intermediary for trading compute and storage between consumers and service providers, it provides the two parties with added value. For service consumers, it acts as a market directory where they can browse and compare different IaaS service offerings and select the most appropriate solution for them. For service providers it constitutes an opportunity for advertising their offerings. In addition, it allows users with available computing capacity to easily turn themselves into service providers by deploying the runtime environment required by SpotCloud on their infrastructure (see Figure 11.14).

SpotCloud is not only an enabler for IaaS providers and resellers, but its intermediary role also includes a complete bookkeeping of the transactions associated with the use of resources. Users deposit credit on their SpotCloud account and capacity sellers are paid following the usual pay-per-use model. SpotCloud retains a percentage of the amount billed to the user. Moreover, by leveraging a uniform runtime environment and virtual machine management layer, it provides users with a vendor lock-in-free solution, which might be strategic for specific applications.

The two previously presented examples give an idea of how different in nature third-party services can be: MetaCDN provides end users with a different service from the simple cloud storage offerings; SpotCloud does not change the type of service that is finally offered to end users, but it enriches it with additional features that result in more effective use of it. These are just two examples of the market segment that is now developing as a result of the consolidation of cloud computing as an approach to a more intelligent use of IT resources.

SUMMARY

This chapter introduced some advanced topics that will characterize and drive research and development in cloud computing. These topics become particularly important as cloud computing technologies become increasingly consolidated.

Given the huge size of the computing facilities backing the service offerings of cloud providers, energy-efficient solutions play a fundamental role. These involve smarter and greener datacenter designs, efficient placement of virtual machines, and energy-driven server management. Energy-efficient solutions not only help cut power bills, they also reduce the impact of computing facilities on the environment. Although the advantage cloud computing brings to this issue is still controversial, it has the potential to deliver greener technology.

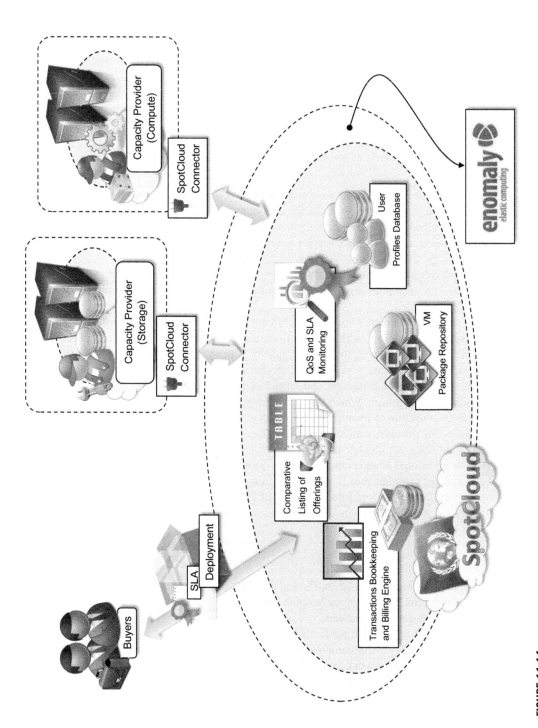

FIGURE 11.14

SpotCloud market architecture.

Besides energy efficiency, market-oriented cloud computing (MOCC) and InterCloud arrangements for optimal service delivery constitute important advancements. MOCC is the natural evolution of cloud computing once the technology enabling it is consolidated and commoditized. Maturity in the IaaS market segment facilitates the creation of more sophisticated market models. Recent advances have shown that cloud service brokering- and auction-based models are useful strategies for better resource management. MOCC's ultimate goal is to create a global virtual marketplace that facilitates computing utilities trading.

Moreover, cloud federations support the implementation of MOCC by deploying infrastructure and defining organizational models enabling interoperability among cloud providers. Currently, customers rely on a single provider or compose services from different cloud vendors by themselves. With the advent of cloud federation, users will be able to leverage multiple clouds.

Finally, we discussed third party services such as MetaCDN and SpotCloud, which are built by leveraging services offered by multiple cloud vendors.Several SaaS solutions might be classified as third-party services, which are essentially value-added resellers. This means that they compose and use other cloud services, adding value to and selling them.

Review questions

1. What is energy-efficient computing, and why it is fundamental to cloud computing?
2. What is the basic principle behind all the power management techniques?
3. What does DVFS stand for, and how will it help in cloud computing?
4. Compare hardware and software power management techniques.
5. What is server consolidation? How it can be considered a power management strategy?
6. What is market-oriented cloud computing?
7. What are the main components that implement a MOCC-based system?
8. What is a virtual marketplace?
9. What is a cloud federation?
10. What are the three different levels that express the concept of the InterCloud and cloud federation?
11. What are the motivations leading to the creation of a federation?
12. What kind of challenges must be addressed at the operational and logical level?
13. What is the domain of the infrastructural level, and which layers of the Cloud Computing Reference Model represent this level?
14. What kind of standards and protocols can be used to achieve interoperability in a cloud federation?
15. What is the InterCloud?
16. Describe the major characteristics of the RESERVOIR project.
17. Describe the role of standards in a federated environment.
18. What are the security implications in a federated environment?
19. What are the possible legal issues arising in the context of a cloud federation?
20. What is a third-party cloud service?
21. Give some examples of a third-party cloud service.

References

[1] Tanenbaum AS, Van Steen M. Distributed systems: principles and paradigm. Upper Saddle River, NJ, USA: Prentice Hall PTR; 2001.

[2] Coulouris G, Dellimore J, Kindberg T. Distributed systems: concepts and design. 4th ed. Boston, MA, USA: Addison Wesley; 2005.

[3] Pfister G. In search of clusters. 2nd ed. Upper Saddle River, NJ, USA: Prentice Hall PTR; 1998.

[4] Buyya R. High-performance cluster computing: architecture and systems. Upper Saddle River, NJ, USA: Prentice Hall PTR; 1999.

[5] Thain D, Tannenbaum T, Livny M. Distributed computing in practice: the condor experience. Concurrency Comput Pract Exper 2005;17(2−4):323−56.

[6] Sunderam VS. PVM: a framework for parallel distributed computing. Concurrency: Pract Exper 1990;2(4):315−39.

[7] Gropp W, Lusk E, Doss N, Skjellum A. A high-performance, portable implementation of the MPI message passing interface. Parallel Comput 1996;22(6):789−828.

[8] Foster I, Kesselman C. The grid: blueprint for a new computing infrastructure. San Francisco, CA, USA: Morgan Kaufmann Publishing; 1999.

[9] Foster I, Kesselman C, Tuecke S. The anatomy of the grid: enabling scalable virtual organizations. Int J High Perform Comput Appl 2001;15(3).

[10] Broberg J, Venugopal S, Buyya R. Market oriented grids and utility computing: the state of the art and future directions. J Grid Comput 2008;6(3):255−76 [Springer Netherlands].

[11] Buyya R, Bubendorfer K. Market-oriented grid computing and utility computing. Hoboken, NJ, USA: Wiley; 2009.

[12] Foster I. Globus toolkit version 4: software for service-oriented systems. IFIP International conference on network and parallel computing. Lecture notes in computer science (LNCS) 3779. Springer-Verlag; 2005. pp. 2−13.

[13] Gentzsch W. Sun grid engine: towards creating a compute power grid. Proceedings of the first IEEE/ACM international symposium on cluster computing and the grid (CCGrid 2001). Brisbane, Australia: IEEE Computer Society; 2001. pp. 35−36.

[14] Anderson DP. BOINC: a system for public-resource computing and storage, Proceedings of the fifth IEEE/ACM international workshop on grid computing. Pittsburgh, PA, USA: 2004.

[15] Buyya R, Venugopal S. The gridbus toolkit for service oriented grid and utility computing: an overview and status report. Proceedings of the first IEEE international workshop on grid economics and business models (GECON 2004). NJ, USA: IEEE Press; 2004.

[16] Popek GJ, Goldberg RP. Formal requirements for virtualizable third generation architectures. Commun ACM 1974;17(7):412−21.

[17] Whitaker A, Shaw M, Gribble D. Denali: a scalable isolation kernel. Proceedings of the tenth ACM SIGOPS European workshop. France: Saint-Emilion; 2002.

[18] Chaudhury A, Kuilboer JP. e-Business and e-Commerce infrastructure. NY, USA: McGraw Hill; 2002.

[19] Papazoglou MP, Traverso P, Dustdar S, Leymann. F. Service-oriented computing: state of the art and research challenges. IEEE Comput 2007;40(11):38−45 [IEEE Computing Society]

[20] Papazoglou MP, van den Heuvel. W-J. Service-Oriented Architecture: Approaches, Technologies, and Research Issues. Very Large Data Bases (VLDB) J 2007;16(3):389−415 VLDB Endowment Inc.

[21] Papazoglou MP. Web services: principles and technology. Hoboken, NJ, USA: Prentice Hall; 2007.

[22] W3C. Web service definition language (WSDL) 1.1. [Online Document] Available at <www.w3.org/TR/wsdl/>.

[23] W3C. Simple object access protocol (SOAP) specifications. [Online Document]. Available at <www.w3.org/TR/soap/>.

[24] Liberty J, Hurwitz D. Programming ASP.NET. 3rd ed. Sebastopol, CA, USA: O'Reilly Media; 2005.

[25] Ka lok Tong K. Developing web services with apache axis2. Birmingham, UK: TipTec Development; 2008.

[26] DiNucci D. Fragmented future. Design & New Media; 1999 [Online Document]. Available at <www.cdinucci.com/Darcy2/articles/Print/Printarticle7.html>

[27] O'Reilly T. What is web 2.0? Design patterns and business model for the next generation of software. O'Reilly Media; 2005 [Online Document]. Available at <http://oreilly.com/pub/a/web2/archive/what-is-web-20.html>

[28] Armbrust M, Fox A, Griffith R, Joseph A, Katz R, Konwinski A, et al. Technical Report No. UCB/EECS-2009-28 Above the clouds: a berkeley view of cloud computing. USA: University of California at Berkeley; 2009

[29] Reese G. Cloud application architectures: building applications and infrastructure in the cloud. Sebastopol, CA, USA: O'Reilly Media Inc.; 2009.

[30] Buyya R, Yeo CS, Venugopal S. Market oriented cloud computing: vision, hype, and reality for delivering IT services as computing utilities. Proceedings of the tenth conference on high performance computing and communications (HPCC 2008, IEEE Press, Los Alamitos, CA). Dalian, China: 2008.

[31] Bennett KH, Layzell PJ, Budgen D, Brereton P, Macaulay LA, Munro M. Service-based software: the future for flexible software, Proceedings of the seventh Asia-Pacific software engineering conference (ASPEC 2000). Singapore: IEEE Computer Society; December 2000.

[32] Strategic backgrounder: software as a service. Software & Information Industry Association; February 2001. [Online Document] Available at <www.siia.net/estore/pubs/SSB-01.pdf>.

[33] Koenig M, Guptill B, McNee B, Cassell J. SaaS 2.0: Software-as-a-Service as next gen business platform. Saugatuck Technologies; 2006. Available at <www.saugatech.com/239order.htm>

[34] Staten J, Yates S, Ryme J, Gillett F, Nelson LE. Deliver cloud benefits inside your walls: economic and self-service gains are within reach. Forrester Research Inc.; 2009.

[35] Barham P, Dragovic B, Fraser K, Hand S, Harris T, Ho A, et al. Xen and the art of virtualization. Proceedings of the 19th ACM symposium on operating systems principles (SOSP). Lake George, NY, USA: October 2003.

[36] Warnke R, Ritzau T. ISBN: 978-3-8370-0876-0 qemu-kvm& libvirt. 4th ed. Norderstedt: Books on Demand GmbH; 2010

[37] Nurmi D, Wolski R, Grzegorczyk C, Obertelli G, Soman S, Youseff L, et al. The eucalyptus opensource cloud computing system. In: Proceedings ninth IEEE/ACM international symposium on cluster computing and the grid (CCGrid 2009). Shanghai, China: May 2009.

[38] Llorente I, Moreno-Vozmediano R, Montero. R. Cloud computing for on-demand grid resource provisioning. Advances in parallel computing, 18. IOS Press; 2009.

[39] Sotomayor B, Keahey K, Foster I. Combining batch execution and leasing using virtual machines. HPDC '08: Proceedings of the 17th international symposium on high performance distributed computing. ACM; 2008. pp. 87–96.

[40] Venugopal S, Broberg J, Buyya R. OpenPEX: an open provisioning and execution system for virtual machines. Proceedings of the 17th international conference on advanced computing and communications (ADCOM 2009). Bengaluru, India: December. 14–18, 2009.

[41] Costanzo A, Assunção M, Buyya R. Harnessing cloud technologies for a virtualized distributed computing infrastructure. IEEE Internet Comput 2009;13(5):14–22.

[42] Vecchiola C, Chu X, Mattess M, Buyya R. Aneka: integration of public and private clouds. Cloud computing: principles and paradigms. Hoboken, NJ, USA: Wiley; 2011.

[43] Mell P, Grance T. NIST working definition on cloud computing. National Institute of Standard and Technology (NIST); [Online Document] Available at <http://csrc.nist.gov/publications/nistpubs/800-145/SP800-145.pdf>.

[44] Briscoe G, De Wilde P. Digital ecosystems: evolving service oriented architectures. Proceedings of the first international conference of bio inspired models of network Information and Computing Systems (BIONETICS). Cavalese, Italy: IEEE Press; December 2006.

[45] G. Briscoe and M. Alexandros. Digital ecosystems in the clouds: towards community cloud computing. Proceedings of the third IEEE international conference on digital ecosystems and technologies (DEST 2009). New York, USA: IEEE; 2009. pp. 103–108.

[46]. Sriram I, Khajeh-Hosseini A. Research agenda in cloud technologies Technical Report. UK: University of Bristol; 2010. [Online Document] Available at <http://arxiv.org/ftp/arxiv/papers/1001/1001.3259.pdf>.

[47] Khajeh-Hosseini A, Sriram I, Sommerville I. Research challenges for enterprise cloud computing. UK: University of Bristol; 2010 [Online Document] Available at <http://arxiv.org/ftp/arxiv/papers/1001/1001.3257.pdf>.

[48] Vouk AM. Cloud computing issues, research, and implementations, Proceedings of the 30th international conference of information technologies and interfaces (ITI 2008). Cavtat/Dubrovnick, Croatia: June 2008. pp. 31–40.

[49] Birman K, Chockler G, van Renesse R. Toward a cloud computing research agenda. SIGACT News 2009;40(2):68–80.

[50] Youssef L, Butrico M, Da Silva D. Towards a unified ontology of cloud computing. Grid computing environments workshop (GCE08). Austin, Texas, USA: IEEE; November 2008.

[51] Open virtualization format specification. Distributed Management Task Force; February 2009. [Online Document] Available at <www.dmtf.org/standards/published_documents/DSP0243_1.0.pdf>.

[52] Standard ECMA-334. C# Language specification. Available at <www.ecma-international.org/publications/standards/Ecma-334.htm>.

[53] Standard ECMA-335. Common language infrastructure (CLI). Available at <www.ecma-international.org/publications/standards/Ecma-335.htm>.

[54] Ghemawat S, Gobioff H, Leung S-T. The google file system. Proceedings of the 19th ACM symposium of operating systems principles (SOSP'03). Lake George, NY, USA: ACM; October 2003. pp. 29–43.

[55] Dean J. Ghemawat S. MapReduce: simplified data processing on large clusters. Proceedings of the 6th symposium on operating system design and implementation (OSDI'04) USENIX. San Francisco, CA, USA: December 2004.

[56] Jin C, Buyya. R. Dataflow computations on enterprise grids. ISBN: 978-981-283-943-5. In: Misra S, Misra SC, Woungang I, editors. Selected topics in communication networks and distributed systems. Singapore: World Scientific; 2010.

[57] Agha. G. ISBN: 0-262-01092-5 Actors: a model of concurrent computation in distributed systems. Cambridge, MA, USA: MIT Press; 1986

[58] Buyya R, Ranjan R, Calheiros RN. InterCloud: utility-oriented federation of cloud computing environments for scaling of application services. Proceedings of the tenth international conference on algorithms and architectures for parallel processing (ICA3PP'10), LNCS 6081. Springer; 2010. pp. 13–31.

[59] Fox GC, Williams RD, Messina PC. Parallel computing works. San Francisco, CA, USA: Morgan Kaufmann; 1994.

[60] Gray J, Reuter A. Transaction processing: concepts and techniques. San Mateo, CA, USA: Morgan Kaufmann; 1992.

[61] Raicu I. Many-task computing: bridging the gap between high throughput computing and high perfor-mance computing. Saarbrücken, Germany: VDM Verlag; 2009.

[62] Wilde M, Foster I, Iskra K, Beckman P, Zhang Z, Espinosa A, et al. Parallel scripting for applications at the petascale and beyond. IEEE Comp 2009;42(11):50−60 IEEE Computing Society.

[63] Raicu I, Zhang Z, Wilde M, Foster I, Beckman P, Iskra K, Clifford B. Toward loosely coupled program-ming on petascale systems. Proceedings of the 2008 ACM/IEEE conference on supercomputing (SC08). Austin, TX, USA: November 15−21, 2008.

[64] Hollingsworth D. The workflow reference model. Workflow Management Coalition, Document nr. tc00-1003. 1993. [Online Document] Available at <www.wfmc.org/standards/docs/tc003v11.pdf>.

[65] The OASIS Committee. Web services business process execution language (WS-BPEL) Version 2.0. 2007. [Online Document] Available at http://docs.oasis-open.org/wsbpel/2.0/wsbpel-v2.0.pdf.

[66] Barker A, van Hemert J. Scientific workflow: a survey and research directions. Proceedings of the sev-enth international conference parallel processing and applied mathematics (PPAM 2007). September 9−12, 2007.

[67] Yu J, Buyya. R. A taxonomy of scientific workflow systems for grid computing. SIGMOD Rec 2005;34 (3):44−9.

[68] Ludäscher B, Altintas I, Berkley C, Higgins D, Jaeger E, Jones M, et al. Scientific workflow manage-ment and the kepler system. Concurrency Comput Pract Exper 2005;18(10):1039−45.

[69] Couvares P, Kosar T, Roy A, Weber J, Wenger K. Workflow management in condor, Workflow for e-Science. London: Springer; 2007. pp. 357−375.

[70] Pandey S, Karunamoorthy D, Buyya R. Workflow engine for clouds ISBN-13: 978-0470887998 In: Buyya R, Broberg J, Goscinski A, editors. Cloud computing: principles and paradigms. New York, USA: Wiley Press; 2010.

[71] Vecchiola C, Kirley M, Buyya R. Multi-objective problem solving with offspring on enterprise clouds. Proceedings of the tenth international conference on high-performance computing in asia-pacific region (HPC Asia 2009). Kaoshiung, Taiwan: 2009.

[72] Buck JT, Ha S, Lee EA, Masserschmitt DG. Ptolemy: a framework for simulating and prototyping heterogeneous systems. J Comput Simul 2004;4:155−82.

[73] Moore R, Prince TA, Ellisman M. Data-intensive computing and digital libraries. Commun ACM 1998;41(11):56−62.

[74] Gorton I, Greenfield P, Szalay A, Williams. R. Data-intensive computing in the 21st century. IEEE Comput 2010.

[75] Johnston W. High-speed, Wide area, data-intensive computing: a ten years retrospective. Proceedings of the seventh symposium high-performance distributed computing. IEEE Press; 1998. pp. 280−291.

[76] Thompson M, Johnston W, Guojun J, Lee J, Tierney B, Terdiman JF. Distributed healthcare imaging information systems, PACS Design and Evaluation: Engineering and Clinical Issues. SPIE Medical Imaging; 1997.

[77] Johnston W, Jin G, Larsen C, Lee J, Hoo G, Thompson M, et al. Real-time generation and cataloguing of large object in widely distributed environments. Int J Digit Libr Spec Issue Digit Libr Med 1997; November.

[78] Lau S, Leclerc Y. Technical Note 540 TerraVision: a terrain visualization system. Menlo Park, CA: SRI International; 1994.

[79] Venugopal S, Buyya R, Kotagiri. R. A taxonomy of data grids for distributed data sharing, management, and processing. ACM Comput Surv 2006;38(1):1−53.

[80] Chervenak A, Foster I, Kesselman C, Salisbury C, Tuecke S. The data grid: towards an architecture for the distributed management and analysis of large scientific datasets. J Netw Comput Appl 2000;23(3):187−200.

[81] Stark C, Breitkreutz BJ, Chatr-Aryamontri A, Boucher L, Oughtred R, Livstone MS, et al. The BioGRID Interaction Database: 2011 Update. Nucleic Acids Res 2010.

[82] Jacobs. A. The pathologies of big data. NY, USA: ACMQueue, ACM Press; 2009.

[83] White T. Hadoop: the definitive guide. Sebastopol, CA, USA: O'Reilly & Associates, Inc.; 2009.

[84] Gu Y, Grossman RL. Sector and sphere: the design and implementation of a high performance data cloud. Phil Trans R Soc 2009;367(1897):2429–45 A 28.

[85] Ceri S, Pelagatti G. Distributed databases: principles and systems. New York, USA: McGraw-Hill; 1984.

[86] Codd. EF. A relational model for large shared data banks. Commun ACM 1970;13(6):377–87.

[87] Oram A. Peer-to-peer: harnessing the power of disruptive technologies. Sebastopol, CA, USA: O'Reilly & Associates, Inc.; 2001.

[88] Schmuck F Haskin R. GPFS: a shared-disk file system for large computing clusters. Proceedings of file and storage technologies 2002 (FAST 2002). Monterey, CA, USA: January 2002.

[89] Gu Y, Grossman RL. UDT: UDP-based data transfer for high-speed wide area networks. Comput Netw 2007;51(7) (Elsevier)

[90] Chodorow K, Dirolf M. ISBN: 978-1449381561 MongoDB: the definitive guide. Sebastopol, CA, USA: O'Reilly Media; 2010.

[91] Anderson JC, Lehnardt J, Slater. N. ISBN: 978-0596155896. CouchDB: the definitive guide: time to relax. Sebastopol, CA, USA: O'Reilly Media; 2010.

[92] DeCandia G, Hastorum D, Jampani M, Kakulapati G, Lakshman A, Pilchin A, et al. Dynamo: amazon's highly available key-value store. Proceedings of the 21st symposium on operating system principles. Stevenson, WA, USA: October 14–17, 2007.

[93] Chang F, Dean J, Ghemawat S, Hsieh WC, Wallach DA, Burrows M, et al. Bigtable: a distributed storage system for structured data. Proceedings of the seventh USENIX symposium on operating system design and implementation. Seattle, USA: November 2006.

[94] Lakshman A Malik P. Cassandra: a decentralized structured storage system. Proceedings of the third ACM SIGOPS international workshop on large scale distributed systems and middleware (LADIS 2009). Big Sky, MT, USA: October 2009.

[95] Pike R, Dorward S, Griesemer R, Quinland S. Interpreting the data: parallel analysis with sawzall. Sci Program J 2005;13(4):227–98.

[96] M. Burrows. The chubby lock service for loosely coupled distributed systems. Proceedings of the seventh USENIX symposium on operating system design and implementation (OSDI '06). Seattle, WA, USA: November 2006.

[97] Chu CT, Kim SK, Lin YA, Yu YY, Bradski G, Ng AY, et al. Map-reduce for machine learning on multicore. In: Schölkopf B, Platt J, Hoffman T editors. Advances of neural information processing systems. 19, 2007.

[98] Yang HC, Dasdan A, Hsiao RL, Stott Parker D. Map-Reduce-Merge: simplified relational data processing on large clusters. Proceedings of the 2007 ACM SIGMOD international conference on management of data. Beijing, China: June 2007.

[99] Ekanayake J, Li H, Zhang B, Gunarathne T, Bae S-H, Qiu J, et al. Twister: a runtime for iterative MapReduce. The first international workshop on MapReduce and its applications (MAPREDUCE'10), HPDC2010. Chicago, Illinois, USA: June 2010.

[100] Moretti C, Bui H, Hollingsworth K, Rich B, Flynn P, Thain D. All-pairs: an abstraction for data-intensive computing on campus grids. IEEE T Parall Distr Syst 2010;21(1):33–46.

[101] Isard M, Budiu M, Yu Y, Birrell A, Fetterly D. Dryad: distributed data-parallel programs from sequential building blocks. European conference on computer systems (EuroSys). Lisbon, Portugal: March 21–23, 2007.

[102] Yu Y, Isard M, Fetterly D, Budiu M, Erlingsson U, Gunda PK, et al. DryadLINQ: a system for general-purpose distributed data-parallel computing using a high-level language. Symposium on operating system design and implementation (OSDI). San Diego, CA: December 8–10, 2008.

[103] Calvert C, Kulkarni D. Essential LINQ. Boston, MA, USA: Addison-Wesley Professional; 2009.

[104] Perry DE, Wolf AL. Foundations for the study of software architecture. ACM SIGSOFT Softw Eng Notes 1992;17(4):40–52 ACM Press.

[105] Garlan D, Shaw M. Software architecture: perspectives on an emerging discipline. Upper Saddle River, NJ: Prentice-Hall; 1996.

[106] Gamma E, Helm R, Johnson R, Vlissides JM. ISBN: 0201633612 Design patterns: elements of reusable software design. Boston, MA, USA: Addison-Wesley; 1995.

[107] Box D. A guide to developing and running connected systems with indigo, MSDN magazine. January 2004. Available at: <http://msdn.microsoft.com/en-us/magazine/cc135505.aspx>.

[108] Erl T. Service-oriented architecture: concepts, technology, and design. Upper Saddle River, NJ, USA: Prentice Hall PTR; 2009.

[109] Bell M. Introduction to service-oriented modeling. In: Service-oriented modeling: service analysis, design, and architecture. ISBN: 978-0-470-14111-3, Hoboken, NJ, USA: Wiley & Sons, 2008.

[110] OASIS. Reference architecture foundation for service oriented architecture, version 1.0, October 2009. [Online Document] Available at <http://docs.oasis-open.org/soa-rm/soa-ra/v1.0/soa-ra-cd-02.pdf>.

[111] Nelson BJ. PARC CSL-81-9 Remote procedure call. Palo Alto, CA: Xerox Palo Alto Resource Center; 1981.

[112] Birrell AD, Nelson BJ. Implementing remote procedure calls. ACM T Comput Syst 1984;2(1).

[113] Slee M, Agarwal A, Kwiatkowski M. Thrift: scalable cross-language service implementation. [Online Document] Available at <http://incubator.apache.org/thrift/static/thrift-20070401.pdf>.

[114] Buyya R, Ranjan R, Calheiros RN. InterCloud: utility-oriented federation of cloud computing environments for scaling of application services. Proceedings of the tenth international conference on algorithms and architectures for parallel processing (ICA3PP 2010, LNCS 6081, Springer, Germany). Busan, South Korea: May 21–23, 2010. pp. 13–31.

[115] Beloglazov A, Buyya R, Lee YC, Zomaya A. A taxonomy and survey of energy-efficient data centers and cloud computing systems. In: Zelkowitz M, editor. Advances in computers, 82. Amsterdam, The Netherlands: Elsevier; 2011.

[116] Buyya R, Beloglazov A, Abawajy J. Energy-efficient management of data center resources for cloud computing: a vision, architectural elements, and open challenges. Proceedings of the 2010 international conference on parallel and distributed processing techniques and applications (PDPTA 2010). Las Vegas, NV, USA: July 12–15, 2010.

[117] Garg S, Buyya. R. In: Murugesan S, Gangadharan G, editors. Green cloud computing and environmental sustainability, harnessing green it: principles and practices. West Sussex, UK: Wiley Press; 2011.

[118] Kaplan J, Forrest W, Kindler N. Revolutionizing data center energy efficiency. San Francisco, CA, USA: McKinsey; 2008.

[119] Oppenheimer D, Ganapathi A, Patterson DA. Why do internet services fail, and what can be done about it? Proceedings of the fourth conference on USENIX symposium on internet technologies and systems. vol. 4, Seattle, WA: March 26–28, 2003.

[120] Baliga J, Ayre RWA, Hinton K, Tucker RS. Green cloud computing: balancing energy in processing, storage and transport. Proc IEEE 2011;99(1):149–67.

[121] Kleinrock L. A vision for the Internet. ST J Res 2005;.

[122] Vecchiola C, Duncan D, Buyya R. The structure of new IT Frontier: market oriented cloud computing–part II. Strateg Facil Mag 2010;(Issue 10):59–66 [Pacific & Strategic Holdings Pte Ltd, Singapore]

[123] Buyya R, Yeo CS, Venugopal S, Broberg J, Brandic. I. Cloud computing and emerging it platforms: vision, hype, and reality for delivering computing as the 5th utility. Future Gener Comp Syst 2009;25 (6):599–616.

[124] Garg SK, Buyya R. Cooperative Networking Market-oriented resource management and scheduling: a taxonomy and survey. New York, USA: Wiley Press; 2011.

[125] Smith. R. The contract-net protocol: high-level communication and control in a distributed problem solver. IEEE Trans Comput 1980;4:1104–13.

[126] Fu Y, Chase J, Chun B, Schwab S, Vahdat. A. SHARP: an architecture for secure resource peering. ACM SIGOPS Oper Syst Rev 2003;37(5):133–48.

[127] Lai K, Rasmusson L, Adar E, Zhang L, Huberman BA. Tycoon: an implementation of a distributed, market-based resource allocation system. Multiagent Grid Syst 2005;1(3):169–82.

[128] AuYoung A, Chun B, Snoeren A, Vahdat A. Resource allocation in federated distributed computing infrastructures. In: Proceedings first workshop on operating system and architectural support for the on-demand IT infrastructure. Boston, MA, USA: October 2004.

[129] Irwin DE, Chase JS, Grit LE, Yumerefendi AR, Becker D, Yocum K. Sharing networked resources with brokered leases. Proceedings of 2006 USENIX annual technical conference, USENIX 2006. Boston, MA, USA: June 2006.

[130] Mattess M, Vecchiola C, Buyya R. Managing peak loads by leasing cloud infrastructure services from a spot market. 12th IEEE international conference on high performance computing and communications (HPCC 2010). Melbourne, Australia: 2010.

[131] Buyya R, Pandey S, Vecchiola C. Cloudbus toolkit for market oriented cloud computing. Proceeding of the first international conference on cloud computing (CloudCom 2009, Springer, Germany). Beijing, China: December 1–4, 2009.

[132] Calheiros R, Ranjan R, Beloglazov A, De Rose C, Buyya R. CloudSim: a toolkit for modeling and simulation of cloud computing environments and evaluation of resource provisioning algorithms. Softw Prac Exper 2011;41(1):23–50 Wiley Press, New York, NY, USA.

[133] Beloglazov A, Buyya R. Optimal Online Deterministic Algorithms and Adaptive Heuristics for Energy and Performance Efficient Dynamic Consolidation of Virtual Machines in Cloud Data Centers. Concurrency Comput Prac Exper 2012;24(13):1397–420 Wiley Press, New York, NY, USA.

[134] Brown R, Masanet E, Nordman B, Tschudi B, Shehabi A, Stanley J, et al. Report to congress on server and data center energy efficiency: Public law 109–431. Berkeley, CA, USA: Lawrence Berkeley National Laboratory; 2008.

[135] Barroso LA Fan X. Power provisioning of warehouse-sized computer. Proceedings of the 34th annual symposium on computer architecture.San Diego, CA, USA: 2007. pp. 13–23.

[136] Cloud Storage Technical Working Group. Cloud data management interface (CDMI) v1.0. Storage Network Industry Association (SNIA); 2010. [Online Document]. Available at <www.snia.org/tech_activities/standards/curr_standards/cdmi/CDMI_SNIA_Architecture_v1.0.pdf>.

[137] Open Cloud Standard Incubator. Interoperable clouds: a white paper from the open cloud standards incubator, DSP-IS0101. Distributed Management Task Force (DMTF); November 2009. [Online Document] Available at <www.dmtf.org/sites/default/files/standards/documents/DSP-IS0101_1.0.0.pdf>.

[138] Open Cloud Standard Incubator. Architecture for managing clouds: a white paper from the open cloud standards incubator, DSP-IS0102. Distributed Management Task Force (DMTF); June 2010. [Online Document] Available at <www.dmtf.org/sites/default/files/standards/documents/DSP-IS0102_1.0.0.pdf>.

[139] Open Cloud Standard Incubator. Use cases and interactions for managing clouds: a white paper from the open cloud standards incubator, DSP-IS0103. Distributed Management Task Force (DMTF); June 2010. [Online Document] Available at <www.dmtf.org/sites/default/files/standards/documents/DSP-IS0103_1.0.0.pdf>.

[140] Bowen JA. Legal issues in cloud computing. Cloud computing: principles and paradigms. New York, NY, USA: Wiley Press; 2011.

[141] Gramm-Leach-Bliley Financial Services Modernization Act (GLB Act), Title V of the Financial Services Modernization Act of 1999, Pub. L. No. 106-102, 113 Stat. 1338, U.S. Government. November 1999.

[142] Federal Trade Commission on Business Compliance with Safeguards Rule, U.S. Government, 2009. [Online Document] Available at www.ftc.gov/bcp/edu/pubs/business/idtheft/bus54.shtm.

[143] Identity theft red flags and address discrepancies under the fair and accurate credit transactions act of 2003; final rule, Federal Trade Commission, U.S. Government, November 2007. Available at www.ftc.gov/os/fedreg/2007/november/071109redflags.pdf.

[144] Health Insurance Technology for Economic and Clinical Health (HITECH) Act, Title III of Division A and Title IV of Division B of the American Recovery and Reinvestment Act (ARRA), Pub. L. 111-5, 123 Stat. 115, U.S. Government, February 2009.

[145] Health Insurance Portability and Accountability Act (HIPAA), Pub. L. No. 104-191, 110 Stat. 1936, U. S. Government, August 1996.

[146] Uniting and Strengthening America by Providing Appropriate Tools Required to Intercept and Obstruct Terrorism Act (USA PATRIOT Act), Pub. L. No. 107-56, 115 Stat. 272, U.S. Government, 2001.

[147] EU Directive 95/46/EC of the European Parliament and of the Council of 24 October 1995 on the Protection of Individuals with Regard to the Processing of Personal Data and on the Free Movement of Such Data, European Commission, October 1995. Available at <http://eur-lex.europa.eu/LexUriServ/LexUriServ.do?uri = CELEX:31995L0046:en:NOT>.

[148] Personal Data (Privacy) Ordinance, Office of the Privacy Commissioner for Personal Data, Hong Kong, 2009. Available at <www.pcpd.org.hk/english/ordinance/ordfull.html>.

[149] Personal Information Protection and Electronics Document Act, Minister of Justice, Canada, Feburary 2012. Available at <http://laws-lois.justice.gc.ca/PDF/P-8.6.pdf>.

[150] Wu L, Buyya R. Service level agreement (SLA) in utility computing systems. Performance and dependability in service computing: concepts, techniques and research directions. Hershey, PA, USA: IGI Global; 2011.

[151] Bouillet E, Mitra D, Ramakrishnan K. The structure and management of service level agreement in networks. IEEE J Sel Area Comm 2002;20(4):691−9.

[152] Dinesh V, Supporting service level agreements on IP networks. Proceedings of IEEE/IFIP network operations and management symposium, 92(2), New York, USA, 2004.

[153] Jin LJ, Machiraju VA. Technical Report HPL-2002-180 Analysis on service level agreement of web services. Software Technologies Laboratory, HP Laboratory; 2002

[154] Ron S Aliko P. Service level agreements, Internet NG, Internet NG Project. 2001. [Online Document] Available at <http://ing.ctit.utwente.nl/WU2/>.

[155] Rochwerger B, Caceres J, Montero R, Breitgand D, Elmroth E, Galis A, et al. The RESERVOIR model and architecture for open federated cloud computing. IBM Syst J 2009;53(4):1−11.

[156] Mather T, Kumaraswarmy S, Lathif S. Cloud security and privacy: an enterprise perspective on risks and compliance. O'Reilly Media Inc; 2009.

[157] Rittinghouse JW, Ransome JF. Cloud computing implementation, management, and security. CRC Press; 2010.

[158] Broberg J, Buyya R, Tari Z. MetaCDN: harnessing 'storage clouds' for high performance content delivery. J Netw Comp Appl 2009;32(5):1012−22 Elsevier, Amsterdam, The Netherlands.

[159] Buyya R, Pathan M, Vakali A, editors. Content delivery networks. Berlin, Germany: Springer; 2008.

[160] Pandey S, Voorsluys W, Niu S, Khandoker A, Buyya R. An autonomic cloud environment for hosting ECG data analysis services. Future Generation Comput Syst 2012;28(1):147−54 Elsevier Science, Amsterdam, The Netherlands.

[161] Jin C, Gubbi J, Buyya R, Palaniswami M, Jeeva: enterprise grid-enabled web portal for protein secondary structure prediction. Proceedings of the 16th international conference on advanced computing and communication (ADCOM 2008). Chennai, India: December 14—17, 2008.

[162] Vecchiola C, Abedini M, Kirley M, Chu X, Buyya R. Gene expression classification with a novel coevolutionary based learning classifier system on public clouds. Proceedings of the 2010 sixth IEEE international conference on e-Science workshops (IEEE CS Press, USA). Brisbane, Australia: December 7, 2010. pp. 92—97.

[163] Raghavendra K, Akilan A, Ravi N, Kumar KP, Varadan G. Satellite data product generation using aneka cloud. Research demo at the 10th IEEE international symposium on cluster, Cloud, and Grid Computing (CCGrid 2010). Melbourne, Australia: 2010.

[164] Buyya R, Abramson D. The Nimrod/G grid resource broker for economic-based scheduling ISBN: 978-0470287682 In: Buyya R, Bubendorfer K, editors. Market oriented grid and utility computing. Hoboken, NJ, USA: Wiley Press; 2009.

[165] Buyya R, Venugopal S, Chu X, Nadiminti K. System and method for grid and cloud computing, Patent No: 8,230,070. United States Patent and Trademark Office; July 24, 2012. Available at <www.uspto .gov/web/patents/patog/week30/OG/html/1380-4/US08230070-20120724.html>.

Index

Note: Page numbers followed by "*f*", "*t*" and "*b*" refer to figures, tables and boxes, respectively.